D0851993

MAINSTREAMS OF MODERN ART

Ingres: *The Bather of Valpinçon*

On the principle that anyone beginning a trip should have a general idea of the route he is to take, the following fifteen paintings are offered as an introduction to this book. They are waystops, and they reappear in the body of the text.

As the nineteenth century opened, painting was dominated by France (as it continued to be), and French painting was dominated by the classicists. As an adjunct to the political idealism of the French Revolution in its first days, classicism in painting was dedicated to a revival of the intellectual purity and the moral force of ancient Greece and Rome as they were currently imagined by philosophers and aestheticians. But before long, classicism degenerated into a fettering code of arbitrary rules and standards. By the middle of the century the demigod of the school was a pedantic tyrant and a great artist named Jean Auguste Dominique Ingres, who mercilessly dictated these sterile recipes, yet rose above them in his own art. His *The Bather of Valpinçon* observes the rules in its precision, its enamellike surface, its carefully controlled drawing, its limitation of color within sharply defined boundaries. But in spirit the picture is sensuous beneath its careful surface. Ingres was a classicist by habitual conviction, but by the evidence of his work he had more in common than he realized with the warmth and sentiment of the men who were in revolt against his dogma — the romantics. (Louvre, Paris. Reproduction courtesy Phaidon Press, Ltd.)

Delacroix: *The Abduction of Rebecca*

The romantics believed in the expression of emotion at whatever violation of convention, believed in originality rather than in rule, in complication rather than in purity, and preferred risk to safety. Romanticism was a way of life as well as a revolt in the arts, and its triumph was inevitable in times when the world's disorder gave little support to the classical ideal of ultimate order and serenity. Romanticism was international, with a strong early impulse in Germany, but found its leader and spokesman, as far as painting was concerned, in Eugène Delacroix, another Frenchman. His *Abduction of Rebecca* contrasts in every way with Ingres's *The Bather of Valpinçon;* it is a turbulent subject turbulently painted in rich colors that shatter and explode across swarming and fluttering masses, expressing everywhere the agony and excitement of the human spirit. Yet for all this emotionalized effect, Delacroix as much as Ingres, or even more than Ingres, achieved his ends by intellectualized use of his means. He regarded himself as a true classicist and the nominal classicists as false ones, since his goal was the total expression of human emotion on the grand scale, in images of universal significance. (Metropolitan Museum of Art, New York, Wolfe Fund.)

Eakins: *Miss Van Buren*

In spite of their differences, the classicists and the romantics shared a mutual characteristic: they were idealists who ignored the world around them to explore imagined ones. As the century began to coalesce into the great age of the common man, dominated not by theoretical ideals but by bourgeois practicality, a new school triumphed over the two earlier ones and put an end to their war with one another. The Ingres and the Delacroix of realism was Gustave Courbet, who said, "Show me an angel and I will paint one." In one form or another, realism dominated painting until near the end of the century, and in America it found a great man in Thomas Eakins, for whom Ingres's serene bathers and Delacroix's abducted maidens were less interesting than the people he saw going about their daily affairs in his native Philadelphia. Eakins's portrait of Miss Van Buren is one of the most impressive of his revelations of personality and his creations of poetic mood achieved through what seems to be nothing more than the objective recreation of the natural appearance of an everyday subject. (Phillips Collection, Washington, D. C.)

Manet: *Boating*

In France, realism found its most delightful expression in its variation, impressionism. The impressionists are the best loved painters today. Everyone knows Renoir, Degas, and Monet. But the early struggles of these men were without precedent. Some of them were frequently without money to buy paints while established hacks, now forgotten, sold pictures for high prices as fast as they could paint them.

The impressionists' first martyr was a man a little older than they, who paved the way for them — Édouard Manet. He fortunately had private means of support while he was attacked and vilified for the revolutionary character of an art that now seems conventional enough. Impressionism was an art of suggestion, an art of intimate charm, of commonplace subjects informally presented but elevated above the commonplace by unusual perceptions and a vibrant love of the good but simple things of life. Manet's *Boating* was painted late in his career when he adopted some of the impressionists' cursory technique and shared briefly their fascination with subjects in open air impregnated with shimmering light. This detail, at approximately the size of the original, may show why impressionism offended a public that had become accustomed to the idea of painting as the approximation of the appearance of objects in photographic detail. (Metropolitan Museum of Art, New York, H. O. Havemeyer Collection.)

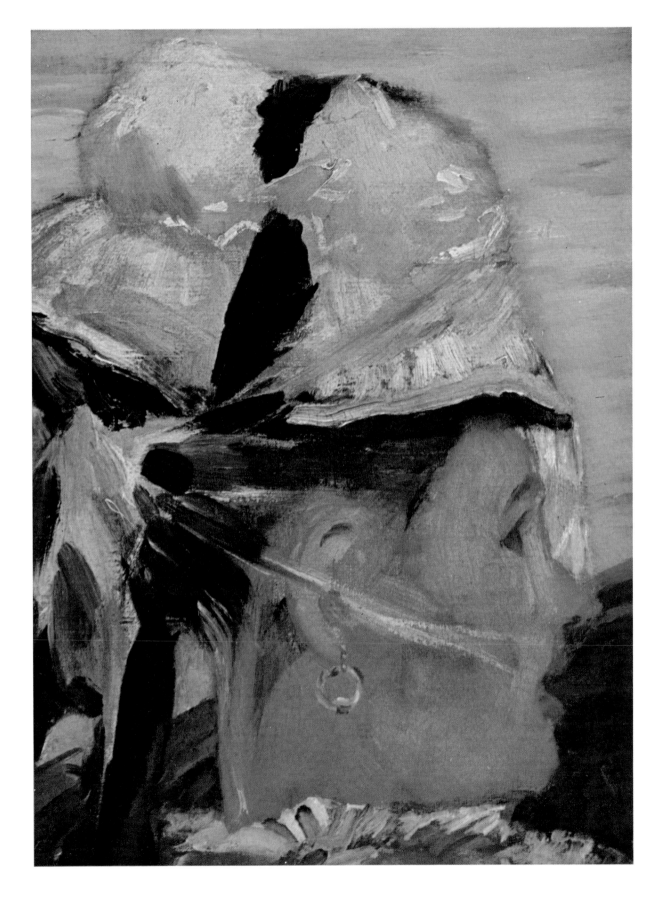

Seurat: *The Bridge at Courbevoie*

By the time the century entered its last decade, the impressionists had won their battle, but impressionism had also revealed its limitations. The several men who departed from impressionism to open the way to what we call "modern" art are grouped under the not very descriptive title of post-impressionists, which means nothing more than that they found their individual solutions to problems with which impressionism was not concerned.

Georges Seurat based his art on impressionism's bright, broken color, but he disciplined it relentlessly into myriads and myriads of tiny dots applied with scientific calculation. Impressionism's limitation was a loss of form, a suggestion of transience and hence of triviality. Seurat returned to the classical ideal of rule and regulation, of precision and exquisitely adjusted balance. But he retained the impressionist love of sparkling light and communion with the world of everyday experience. He died just as he entered his thirties, but not before he had demonstrated that formal discipline need not imply sterile repetition. (Home House Society, Courtauld Institute of Art, London.)

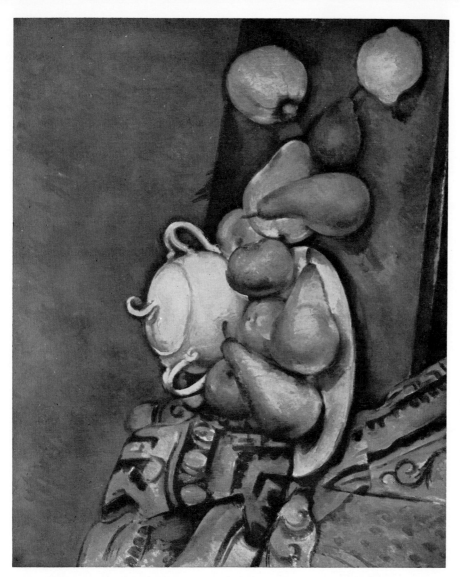

Cézanne: *The White Sugar Bowl*

The problem of reconciling impressionism and formal discipline was attacked in a different way, and a more revolutionary one, by the giant of modern painting — Paul Cézanne.

To try to say much about Cézanne's theories in a paragraph is utterly pointless. We can say that they were based on the conviction that impressionist intimacy and love of the visible world could be combined with the classical ideal of universal statement, that common objects and people could be as majestic as mountains and gods. Cézanne's overwhelming importance in modern painting is that in solving his problems he never hesitated to violate such conventions as perspective and "normal" appearance, to tilt or warp a form into balance with another, itself tilted or warped, until his picture was brought into a state of balance that represented the inherent order of the universe and the dignity of man within it. Cézanne's distortions are acceptable now even to the uninitiated, because in comparison with the much more violent distortions of contemporary art, of which they were a source, they seem mild. But through these distortions and through the theories that led to them, Cézanne changed the direction that art had been following for nearly seven hundred years. (Collection Henry P. Mc-Ilhenny, Philadelphia.)

Van Gogh: *Self-portrait*

Seurat and Cézanne reinterpreted and revitalized the classical ideal. Two other men, in the meanwhile, continued and extended the romantic tradition of revolt and personal emotionalism. They were Vincent van Gogh and Paul Gauguin, whose tragic and disastrous lives were interlocked.

Van Gogh, who was not mad, has become the symbol of the mad genius cherished by everyone who believes that emotionalized painting is a spontaneous gushing-out of the soul onto the canvas. Van Gogh's art seems to support such an idea, in its rush, its vehemence, even in the physical character of his pigment, which may twist and swirl or be thrust upon the canvas as if the artist were impelled to create by forces beyond his control. But everything that van Gogh wrote about his way of work, and all the studies he made for his paintings, show that his intensity is relayed to us through means that he developed painfully and studiously. Poverty, loneliness, and ill health drove him to suicide in his thirties. During his lifetime he had sold exactly one picture, unless we count those that he traded for paints and brushes.

(Courtesy of the Fogg Art Museum, Harvard University. Bequest of Maurice Wertheim.)

Gauguin: *The Vision after the Sermon – Jacob Wrestling
with the Angel*

Gauguin also died in poverty, alone, and miserably, and his life was at least as disordered as van Gogh's. The difference is that Gauguin chose his way of life, while van Gogh's was imposed upon him. A successful businessman, Gauguin first painted as a hobby, then as a passion that bankrupted him, cost him his family, and led him finally to a life in the South Seas that was idyllic enough in theory but sordid and violent in fact.

Gauguin was led to the South Seas by an appetite for primitive and exotic subjects that had preoccupied him from his earliest days as an artist. He painted *The Vision after the Sermon*, showing Breton peasants witnessing their literal conception of the struggle between Jacob and the Angel, in much the same spirit in which, later, he painted the natives of the South Seas haunted by the spirits they believed in. In returning to forms of primitive inspiration and expressing his primitive subjects in nonnaturalistic color, Gauguin along with Cézanne and van Gogh gave impetus to the modern idea of painting as the invention of forms and colors rather than as the imitation of nature. (National Gallery of Scotland, Edinburgh.)

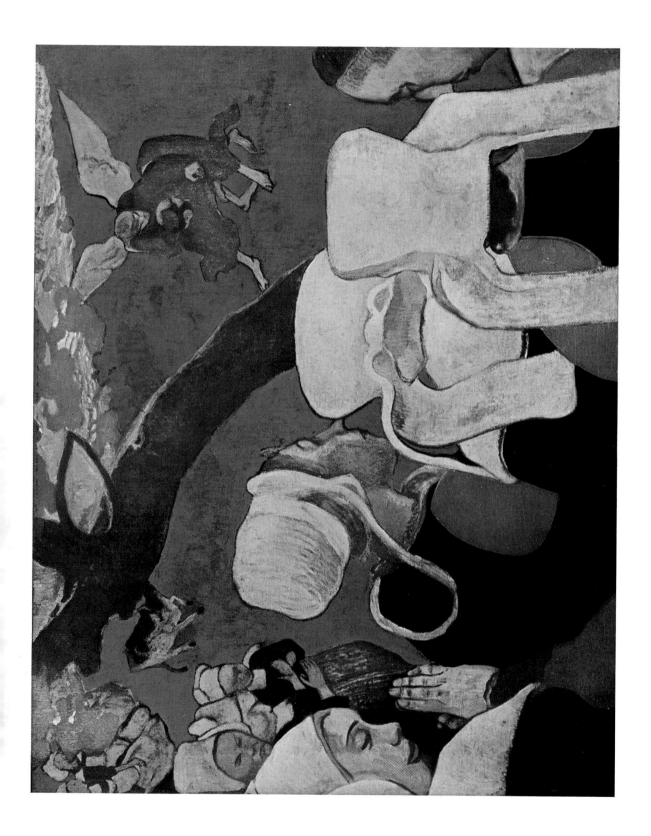

Nolde: *Life of Maria Aegyptiaca*, First Episode:
"Early Sinful Life"

From these men and others who struck out in new directions, the complicated and contradictory revolutions, assaults, and forays of twentieth-century art developed. The most direct followers of van Gogh and Gauguin were the German expressionists, who painted vigorously from the first decade of the new century until the time of Hitler with his art "reforms." Religion, sex, and the compassionate observation of human misery were among the major obsessions of the expressionists, always with the most intense personal reference, in pictures dedicated as were van Gogh's to the release of some inner anguish. As all the new isms were to be, expressionism was greeted with furor, diatribes, and laughter by the general public but was supported by an increasing number of dealers, collectors, and advanced critics. Emil Nolde's *Life of Maria Aegyptiaca* with its intentional ugliness, its therapeutic coarseness, its exaggerated violence of color, was offensive to a public that had only recently come around to accepting as "modern" the gentle, lyrical world created by the impressionists. The expressionist movement spread beyond Germany but was basically northern in its brooding emotionalism, just as van Gogh, the Dutchman painting in France, was northern in his similar introspection. (Kunsthalle, Hamburg. Reproduction courtesy Frederick A. Praeger, Inc.)

Matisse: *Madame Matisse (The Green Line)*

The pathos, melancholy, and brutality of expressionism as it developed in Germany were foreign to the temperament and tradition of France. The parallel movement there was fauvism, also based on color, as German expressionism so largely was, but more closely related to the decorative color compositions of Gauguin than to the emotionalized color of van Gogh. The use of color for its own sake as much as for its expressive power marks Henri Matisse's fauvist portrait of his wife (usually called *The Green Line*) as an intellectual and theoretical exercise in spite of its undeniable expressive force. Balancing color against color, Matisse reduces his background to arbitrary areas, and in the face he introduces the unnaturalistic green line down the center for the reason that it is needed there as part of a scheme that falls to pieces without it.

Fauvism was a brief and loosely organized movement, the result of the largely coincidental appearance of a group of young Frenchmen experimenting with color as an abstract structural device. In a matter of a few years each member of the group had branched off into further experiments in different directions. More than any of them, Matisse remained first of all a colorist in a long lifetime during which, with Picasso, he became a most potent force in the transformation of the art of painting in the twentieth century. (*Statens Museum for Kunst,* Copenhagen, Rump Collection. Permission courtesy Mme. Marguerite Duthuit.)

Gris: *The Violin*

Even more than fauvism, cubism was an affront to a startled public and the majority of painters and critics. The two movements appeared at the same time; of the two, cubism was the more fertile one and the more disruptive.

Cézanne had established the idea that the form of natural objects might be subjected to whatever dislocations best served the painter in his effort to build pictorial structures. The cubists went further, extending this aspect of Cézanne's theories and combining them with others, until the visible world was only a point of departure for the creation of complicated geometrical structures in which objects finally became totally undecipherable. Juan Gris's *The Violin* was painted at a time when cubism had passed through its most extreme phase, and the objects that had been disintegrated in a theoretical demonstration had been partially reassembled. *The Violin* is a pattern in which discipline, harmony, and even poetic mood should be apparent to anyone willing to accept the legitimacy of other standards in painting than purely representational ones. But even today not everyone can do so, in spite of the fact that cubism as an independent movement has been absorbed by later ones, and the public has had half a century to absorb its shock. (*Kunstmuseum*, Basel.)

Picasso: *Girl before a Mirror*

Cubism released the genius of the most prolific, the most inventive, and the most eruptive painter of the century, the Spaniard Pablo Picasso. In spirit Picasso's work ranges from the tender melancholy of certain pre-cubist pictures to the titanic wrath of his *Guernica,* from sheer playful legerdemain to philosophical speculation to a kind of willful and grotesque brutality. Since cubism, of which of course he was an originator, Picasso has sallied away from and back to and around and about cubism's theories, adapting and transforming them in a hundred ways. Like so much of his work, his *Girl before a Mirror* is many things to many men — an analytical challenge to psychiatrists, a stunning pattern ready for filching to decorators, a landmark to historians of Picasso's development, a symbol of the twentieth century to sociologically minded aestheticians, and still, after so long a time, a gargantuan piece of charlatanry to people who refuse to accept its premises as honest ones. (Collection, The Museum of Modern Art, New York. Gift of Mrs. Simon Guggenheim.)

Léger: *The City*

Cubism produced variants at every hand. Conspicuous among them was the mechanistic art of Fernand Léger, one of several painters and groups of painters who held the theory that since the twentieth century is the age of the machine, twentieth-century painting must "bear comparison with any manufactured object" in sleekness, and reflect at the same time the driving, pistonlike energies of the age, and the clamorous, dehumanized, strident rhythms of the modern metropolis. Léger attempted a synthesis of these ideas in *The City* with its clashing forms, its raucous color, but at the same time its painstaking pseudomechanical conventionalizations of such forms as telephone poles, billboards, girders, factories, robotlike human beings, and less readily identifiable elements suggesting parts of motors. But in the end, *The City* is an abstract painting rather than a subject picture – that is, pure form and pure color must be enjoyed more for themselves than for anything they "say." (Philadelphia Museum of Art, A. E. Gallatin Collection.)

Rivera: *Sugar Cane*

The most frequent and the most legitimate objection to abstract art is that the artist may sacrifice more through loss of meaning to a large audience than he gains in interest to a small one. The most forthright rejection of abstraction was made on the American continent, first in Mexico and then in the United States, by artists who had experimented with it and found it wanting. In Mexico the rejection was most dramatic when a group of painters undertook to decorate public buildings with frescoes directed not toward the intellectual pleasure of aesthetes but to the consciousness of the mass of the people, telling them the story of their national history and propagandizing for the government. In unabashedly propagandistic terms, Diego Rivera's *Sugar Cane* shows a foreign landlord prostituting the resources and the people of Mexico under a semifeudal system that the government intended to abolish.

In the United States the reaction against abstraction took a somewhat different form, glorifying the homely and provincial aspects of life in the part of the country least sympathetic to the cosmopolitanism of abstract art, or sometimes mildly satirizing the mores of the self-righteous. (Philadelphia Museum of Art, Gift of Mr. and Mrs. Herbert C. Morris.)

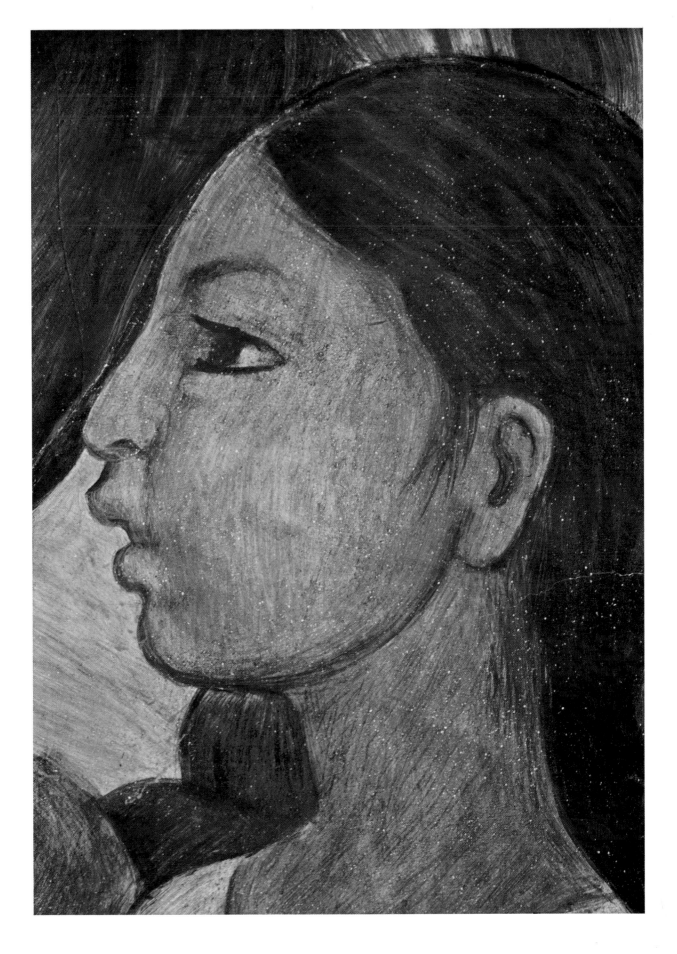

Chirico: *Melancholy and Mystery of a Street*

In Europe also there was a reaction against the often frigid and impersonally logical nature of abstraction. Surrealism, the cult of the mysterious, the irrational, and the bizarre, was an art of poetry and dream, distinguished from other painting of this general kind by its preoccupation with contemporary investigations of morbid psychology, and particularly with the theories of Sigmund Freud. In order to present their fantasies at maximum shock strength, the surrealists abandoned abstraction for the most acutely detailed representation of objects, although these objects were combined in irrational and usually nightmarish ways.

The great surrealist was Giorgio de Chirico, a man who had no formal connection with the movement but anticipated it in his vistas of deserted city squares illuminated by vivid but inexplicable light and spotted here and there with inexplicably sinister objects or figures. As a manifestation of the romantic spirit, surrealism, now dead as an organized movement, has been absorbed, with the other schools and movements we have seen here, into the mainstream of contemporary painting as it continues to flow, to meander, to divide, and to rejoin itself on its course into the future. (Collection Mr. and Mrs. Stanley Resor, New Canaan, Conn.)

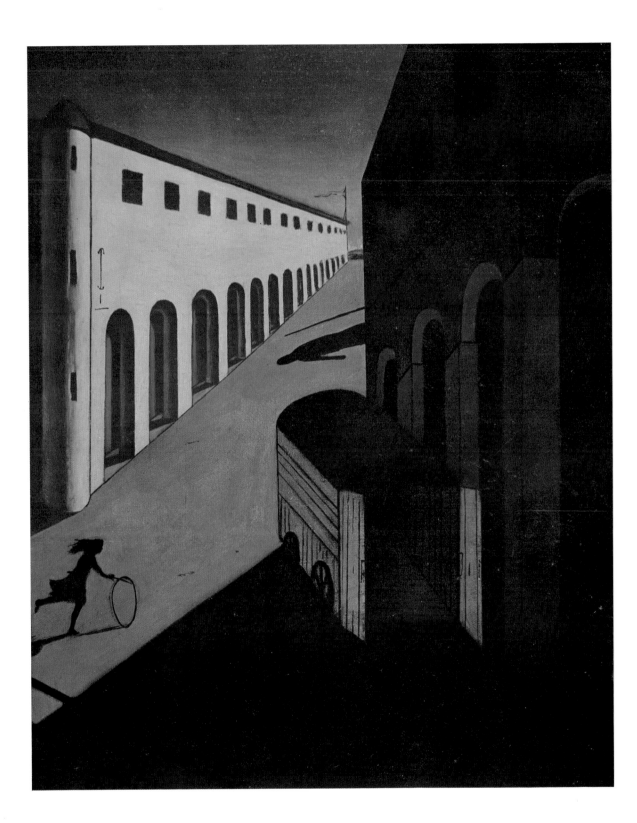

MAINSTREAMS OF MODERN ART

John Canaday

ART CRITIC, THE
NEW YORK TIMES

MAINSTREAMS OF MODERN ART

HOLT, RINEHART AND WINSTON · NEW YORK

456789 038 1918

COPYRIGHT © 1959 BY JOHN CANADAY
LIBRARY OF CONGRESS CATALOG CARD NUMBER: 59–8693

ISBN 0-03-005030-8

RAMAC 2050300

PRINTED IN THE UNITED STATES OF AMERICA
TRADE EDITION DISTRIBUTED BY SIMON AND SCHUSTER, INC.

A BOOK OF THIS KIND INVOLVES SO MANY PEOPLE IN ITS PREPARATION THAT WHEN it is completed the author feels that it is only partly his own. The museums and the collectors who have made possible the illustrations are acknowledged in the captions, but there are so many other individuals who have been helpful to the author, or merely patient with him, that only a few of them can be thanked here.

The first must be Marshall B. Davidson of the Metropolitan Museum of Art; to him I owe the opportunity to write this book, which I hope will not disappoint him.

Among readers of the manuscript in various stages, Thomas M. Folds of Northwestern University managed to point out flaws and suggest corrections without damaging an old friendship. William C. Kortlander of the University of Texas offered numerous specific comments to the benefit of the text while it was in progress, and David M. Robb of the University of Pennsylvania read the final draft with infinite charity.

Without the assistance of Mrs. Alice H. Fincke of the Carl Schurz Memorial Foundation, in Philadelphia, there would have been no illustrations for many of the nineteenth-century German paintings discussed in one section of the book. Bruce St. John of the Wilmington Society of the Fine Arts supplied some interesting material on Burne-Jones, in connection with the Samuel and Mary R. Bancroft collection of Pre-Raphaelite painting under his care. Mrs. Henry W. Howell, Jr., of the Frick Art Reference Library, and members of her staff, ferreted out several bits of obscure information. Pearl L. Moeller of The Museum of Modern Art went out of her way to solve several problems that arose in connection with color plates. And everybody at the Philadelphia Museum of Art was considerate, with Marjorie E. Lyons, the Museum's librarian, and Alfred H. Wyatt, its photographer, doing more than their share in responding to daily cries for assistance.

To all these people I am grateful. But to one other I am more than grateful and more than indebted for practical help, for encouragement, and for a sharing of ideas about painting. The best parts of this book belong

To Katherine

J. C.
Philadelphia Museum of Art
April 29, 1959

CONTENTS

ILLUSTRATIONS

PART I

The Nineteenth Century in France

CHAPTER 1

Revolution

Modern Art, Tradition, and David

Where does modern art begin? And why does this version of its story begin with a man named Jacques Louis David, born more than 200 years ago?

Modern art begins nowhere because it begins everywhere. It is fed by a thousand roots, from cave paintings 30,000 years old to the spectacular novelties in last week's exhibitions. We are pressed upon by bewildering accumulations of every art from every period; a painter may live in South Dakota and find his major stimulation in the sculpture of ancient China. His art may be a compound of his reactions to objects and ideas as diverse as the structure of the internal combustion engine, the theories of Sigmund Freud, and the painting of Rembrandt. The public museum is something new; we think of it as having always existed, but it is a modern institution, and what the old masters knew of the art of the past was only a fraction of what any casual student can see today in museums—and cannot avoid seeing in floods of reproductions that have added their special complication by taking the Sistine Ceiling, for instance, and transforming it into a miniature painting the size of an ordinary envelope.

For the artist, the past used to be a stream; now it is an ocean. It used to be a road, now it is a forest. Tradition in art used to mean a steady sequence of change within boundaries. Today the boundaries are vague, if they exist at all. Horizons are infinite; the artist is tempted to explore in a hundred directions at once.

As an example more obvious than most, the art of the modern Italian painter Amedeo Modigliani (1884–1920) reflects in

1. BELGIAN CONGO: *Head.* Wood, 13¾″ high. University Museum, Philadelphia.

2. BOTTICELLI: Detail from *Birth of Venus, c.* 1485. Uffizi, Florence. (Photo Anderson.)

about equal parts the wonderful linear contours of his compatriot of nearly 500 years before, Botticelli, and the stylizations of African tribal sculpture. African sculpture [1] is part of the savage ritual of magic and incantation. Botticelli's Venus [2] is a Renaissance intellectual's revery upon classical antiquity. Yet these two arts, so wildly separated, are harmoniously unified in another that is concerned with the Parisian bohemia of the early twentieth century [3]. Half a dozen other influences contributed to Modigliani's painting, quite aside from the infinite number that are bound into it in secondary ways. They would include the French classical master, Ingres; Modigliani's contemporaries, the expressionists; probably the late medieval religious paint-

ings of the Sienese school; the revolutionary art of Cézanne; the *fin-de-siècle* art of Toulouse-Lautrec. But the most important factor in the compound of Modigliani's art is not Botticelli or African sculpture. Nor is it Ingres or the expressionists or the Sienese or Cézanne or Toulouse-Lautrec. It is Modigliani, an artist of creative talent, sensitive intelligence, and aesthetic discretion, who imitates none of these men or schools but fuses whatever he takes from them with his own perception of the world into an expressive art of great individuality.

We talk about "traditional" painting today, meaning the opposite of "modern" painting. Yet if tradition means the transmission of ideas or ways of doing things from ancestors to posterity—as the diction-

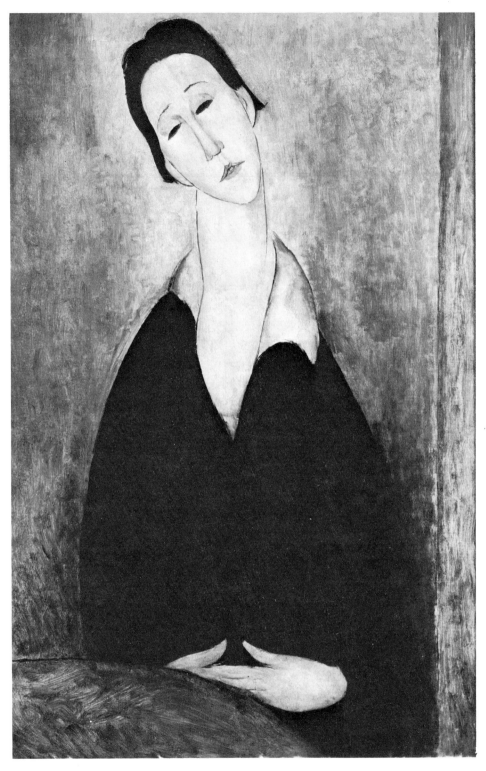

3. MODIGLIANI: *Female Portrait*, 1918. 39½ x 25½". Collection Louis E. Stern, New York.

ary says it does—then Modigliani must be one of the most traditional painters who ever lived. But, like other modern artists, he has found his ancestors in the most diverse and unexpected combinations. The orderly sequence from one generation of painters to the next has given way to a series of abrupt dislocations to such an extent that, if we have a tradition, it is the contradictory one that each new generation is under some kind of obligation to refute and violate the ideas of the preceding one.

For this reason Jacques Louis David offers a starting point for this story of modern art. He cut off from a long tradition to begin a new one, and he cut off so suddenly, with such violence even, that the course of painting ever since has been a history of revolutions and counterrevolutions, developing so rapidly that one is hardly established before it is being shouldered aside by the next. As successive groups of painters seek to establish a norm within this infinitely rich chaos, other groups arise, determined to upset whatever norm is temporarily achieved. The history of modern painting begins with David's break from tradition just as the history of modern Europe begins with the French Revolution, in which David was a conspicuous figure.

David's Life

As often as not, a knowledge of the events of a painter's life is unnecessary to understanding his art, but David's is one of those cases where some acquaintance is imperative. Early disappointments, an attempted suicide, a Roman experience, and thereafter his participation in the turbulent political events of his time not only determined the character of his own art but redirected the course of European painting. During twenty years of roaring success, David painted a series of sensational pictures that annihilated not only every living competitor of the old school but the tradition of the most eminent painters for several generations back as well. He established himself as art dictator of France, where his paintings influenced everything from philo-

sophical morality to interior decoration. Political theorists used his paintings to support their arguments, and every woman in Europe with any pretensions to chic discarded her wardrobe and changed her hair-do to make herself over in the pattern of the female type he invented to enact his pictorial dramas. It was the most drastic "new look" in the history of fashion, but it was only a footnote to David's career.

As a student David was a protegé of the Royal Academy of Painting and Sculpture, an institution that he would later cut down, then make over in his own image. He attempted suicide after four consecutive failures to win its *Prix de Rome*. This "Rome Prize" was (and still is) the most coveted official student award in France. It took the winner to the Academy's branch in Rome for three years; during this time his only obligation was to produce one work annually to send back to Paris. A *Prix de Rome* man was also assured of very considerable advantages upon his return to France, since his career was sponsored by established academicians in a position to throw commissions and attention his way. The whole situation, of course, was based on the premise that a *Prix de Rome* winner was dedicated to the perpetuation of the academic tradition.

David failed in his suicide when fellow students broke into his studio in the Louvre, suspicious because it had been locked for days. (The Louvre was not then a museum; the buildings included, among many other things, quarters for the talented young men who, like David, received stipends from the king to follow their studies.) He had intended to starve himself to death and probably would have done so. The choice of method says a great deal about David's temperament, at once intense and dogged, sensitive yet Spartan. These characteristics appear in his art, where emotion is held in check by icy control.

In 1774 David competed once again for the *Prix de Rome* and won it. He was twenty-six years old, unusually mature for a *Prix de Rome* winner and—which was even more unusual—full of hidden resentment against the Academy and suspicious of its standards.

4. DAVID: *Marie Antoinette on the Way to Execution,*
1793. Pen and ink, 5¾ x 4″. Louvre, Paris.

By a unique extension of artistic success
into the field of government, possible only
in the one country in the world where art
is debated as fervently as politics, the pictures David painted during the next fifteen
years lifted him from the position of a near-
failure to the eminence of the Revolution's
prophet and then made him one of its leading participants. (Just how this happened
we will see when we look at the pictures
themselves.) He served among other capacities as a member of the legislative body
voting life or death for his former patron,
Louis XVI. David's vote was among those
that sent this ineffectual, confused, and
incompetent young man to the guillotine.
David also guillotined the Royal Academy
in which he had been nurtured, crying out
for its abolition "in the name of humanity,

in the name of justice, for the love of art,
and above all for the love of youth." He
called the Academy's schools *funeste,* an
adjective that pales in translation as *fatal*
or *deadly.* Fatal or deadly they may have
been, but a few years after David abolished
them they rose from their own ashes, more
funeste than ever, dominated this time by
the theories of David himself.

The Revolution was followed by the period of violence and confusion so appropriately called the Terror, when no man's
neck was safe from the knife. During these
days David, still among the powerful, abandoned personal friends to the executioner
with an expedient callousness for which he
has never been forgiven. Some of his actions at this time make it difficult not to
see him as a fanatic. Mrs. Siddons, the English actress, reported to a friend that she
was present when David, told that eighty
people had been beheaded that morning,
answered, "Not more?" He used to sit outside the *Café de la Régence* sketching the
prisoners on their way to the scaffold. When
Marie Antoinette was beheaded, he did a
heartrending sketch of her [4], bound hand
and foot as he saw her from a window on
the way to execution, bedraggled, emaci-
ated, prematurely aged by her frightful imprisonment, with no suggestion of beauty
left, yet with a dignity she had never managed to achieve as queen of France.

This man David was a curious personality, given to passionate loyalties and passionate grudges, a man of fervent temperament who imposed upon himself a frigid
manner, of sensitive perceptions which he
rejected as unworthy. Because his career
and his art are full of contradictions, his
biographers have taken sides according to
their own convictions. Some see in him a
bloodthirsty despot never forgiving the men
who for so long had denied him the *Prix
de Rome,* using his power vengefully to destroy the tradition they represented. Others
find him devoted to high principles, even
if a little prone to inflict them on others as
severely as he imposed them upon himself.
Frequently the same facts support either
judgment, since they must be evaluated in
the unnatural lights of the Revolution and
the Terror.

Despot or idealist, David himself narrowly escaped the guillotine. He fell from power with his Jacobin partner Robespierre, whose terrorist excesses had become intolerable. Robespierre was beheaded. But there was a delay before David came to trial; when he did, his defense was that he had never been sympathetic to Robespierre's policies, that he had strung along with him only to give what service and protection he could to the arts of France. It is recorded that he "sweated enormously" on the witness stand, that he was pale and trembling, mumbling and stammering pitifully in his own defense against the murderous oratory of the prosecutor, one of the finest speakers of the day. It is not surprising that a man in danger of his life, with no reason to expect clemency, should sweat, nor is it damning that, in the circumstances, one should mumble whose upper lip was disfigured, as David's was, with a tumor that impeded his speech even in the happiest situations. In any case, David escaped execution. Instead, he was imprisoned.

But for this extraordinary man even the circumstances of prison were exceptional and rebounded ultimately to his advantage. His cell was a room in the Luxembourg Palace overlooking a corner of some of the loveliest gardens in the world. The family governess made daily trips to the palace gardens where David's children played as he watched from his window. Former students kept him supplied with painting materials, and he began work on sketches for one of his most ambitious pictures, *The Battle of the Romans and Sabines* [11], a work that was to re-establish him more firmly than ever in a career which seemed lost. When he was released in a general amnesty, he had been in prison only a few months.

David completed *The Sabines* in a studio where women of fashion begged to pose for him as if they already knew the picture was to be one of the most famous in the world. In the meanwhile France had come under the leadership of the young general Napoleon Bonaparte. He visited David's studio to see *The Sabines* and recognized the potential of this man's art as propaganda that could be as effective for the empire he

planned as it had been for the Revolution. Napoleon conceived an image of himself as a modern version of a conquering Roman emperor, partly because of his personal conviction that he was just that and partly as a matter of what would now be called public relations. Official architecture had been a recombination of classical elements under the dictates of the Royal Academy, but now Napoleon demanded an architecture that would be true archaeologically. Paris was to become a second Rome—but larger—as a setting for the new conqueror. For his church, La Madeleine, Napoleon demanded of his architects the most perfect classical temple since antiquity. The Arc de Triomphe is a handsomely inflated version of ancient Roman models, so large that the originals would look like guard stalls alongside it. David's painting was the perfect accessory to these conceptions, and Napoleon took the artist under his wing.

Thus the young man who had begun his career under the patronage of the king of France, who had continued it as spokesman for the Revolution and the Terror, finally became First Painter to the Emperor and art dictator of the country that has set the course of Western painting ever since.

Napoleon once said, "David, I salute you." He was commenting on a painting, recognizing its success without risking a critical judgment. But the same comment, with the same reservation, could refer in all appropriateness to David's life.

David's Painting

David won his *Prix de Rome* with a respectful exercise giving no indication—except by hindsight—of the Davidian revolution to come. *Antiochus and Stratonice* [5] is full of derivative references flattering to the leading academicians of the day. Like any other student involved in a school competition, David produced a demonstration of how well he had learned his lessons. The picture includes a nude torso to prove that he knew muscular anatomy and could draw and paint the human body accurately with conventional heroic modifications; his skill with drapery is demonstrated to the point

5. DAVID: *Antiochus and Stratonice*, 1774 (*Prix de Rome*). 47¼ x 61″. *École des Beaux Arts*, Paris. (Photo Giraudon.)

of excess in great billowing areas wherever he needs filler; the male figure leaning forward just to the right of the picture's center, reduced almost to silhouette in the head and shoulders and emerging into brilliant illumination in the hand and the spread of cloak just below, is a sort of final examination passed with honors in chiaroscuro, which means the revelation of forms in strong light and dark shadow. The elaborated architectural background shows that the candidate had mastered perspective, and also supplies the air of pomp and circumstance necessary to a picture obliged to take itself so seriously. Compositionally—that is, in the way the objects and figures are arranged in the picture space—these various exercises are nicely, if conventionally, pieced together.

The story, for whatever bearing it has, tells of the young prince Antiochus (supine upon the couch) who languished to the point of death from an unidentifiable malady until the doctor Erasistratus (seated beside him, at the left) diagnosed it for what it was: Antiochus was lovesick for his father's wife, the beautiful Stratonice (standing at the right). Such a tale of repressed passion offers material for tense and personal expression—and received it, later on, in a painting by one of David's own pupils [67]—but David uses it only as a framework for a charade posed by models in appropriate attitudes. But hindsight shows us that, if most of the picture is blowzy and pointlessly complicated, the figure of Erasistratus has an aggressive force in which we can imagine the germ of the style of the picture that redirected the course of French painting and began the history of modern art—David's *The Oath of the Horatii.*

"The Oath of the Horatii"

With *The Oath of the Horatii* [6], which he completed in 1785, David came fully into his own as an original creative painter. It is a superb picture. It is called stiff and cold; such adjectives as *harsh* and *wiry* are habitually applied to its color and drawing, with only partial justice, as if they were entirely derogatory. Actually these qualities are in themselves remarkable, and they have an expressive reason for being.

The Oath of the Horatii contrasts on every hand with *Antiochus and Stratonice*. Its surface is as hard as enamel, the edges of its forms are mercilessly uncompromising, revealed in a flat, uniform illumination instead of theatrical spotlights. In drapery passages the windy profligacy of the earlier picture has been chastened into order and definition. Everywhere the antithesis continues. Compositionally, *Antiochus and Stratonice* is extravagant; *The Oath of the Horatii* is spare, organized almost mathematically into unit variations of the number 3. Against three simple arches the participants are divided into three groups of generally triangular shapes—the three sons, the father holding their three swords, and the group of women. In this last group the triangular severity is appropriately relaxed (but not abandoned), and the linear patterns are appropriately more graceful. The three groups, considered as a unit, are united in a final triangle binding the picture into a decisive whole. The subterfuge of the "academic machine," which means a picture organized on standard formulas with all their complicated trappings, has been rejected for a rigid structure where economy, precision, and force must reveal any weak or extraneous element. *The Oath of the Horatii* offers the artist no refuge behind the facile piling-up of incidentals; he must be revealed as the master of his expression or be exposed as inadequate to its demands.

That David invented a new style of painting need not have had any importance in itself; the important thing is that he had to invent it in order to express what amounted to a moral and philosophical revolution in art, which also explains his choice of subject. The three stalwart young Romans are vowing to their father that they will return victorious or give their lives in a duel with three warrior brothers of the city of Alba, a duel to be fought in the presence of the armies of both cities to determine which city will rule the other. The special complication in this situation is that one of the grieving women to the right is not only the wife of one of the Roman warriors but the sister of one of the Albans as well. In addition, the youngest of the women is a sister of the Romans but the fiancée of one of the Albans.

Thus the subject of *The Oath of the Horatii* is dedication and sacrifice. Instead of the lovesick Antiochus we have vigorous young males pledging their lives to the defense of their honor, their family, and their country. The chaste matron and the swooning girl express their grief with admirable reserve, submissive to the will of the dominant men. Their dignity is a rebuke to Stratonice's simpering grace, just as the virility of the young Horatii is contemptuous of Antiochus's amorous languor. Service to a moral and social ideal is glorified as a virtue opposed to its parallel vice, the indulgence of personal yearnings. Just so, severity and masculine force replace elegance and feminine sensitivity in David's new style. Rich complications have given way to austerity; fashionable invention has been rejected for philosophical order.

Composition of this kind is not achieved in a single step; the rule in picture-making is that simplicity is reached by reduction from complexity. When he first began work, David chose another incident from the story of the Horatii as dramatized by Corneille, the god of French classical drama. In this tragedy the three Albans and two of the Roman brothers are killed; the remaining son returns covered with the blood of his sister's fiancé, and she denounces him and Rome. As a patriot, he runs his sister through with his sword.

An early sketch for the picture represents this final scene, where the elder Horatius pleads for his son while the body of his daughter lies on the steps of the platform where they stand. The composition was to have been even more elaborate than

6. DAVID: *The Oath of the Horatii*, small version, after 1784. 50 x 65″. Toledo Museum of Art, Gift of Edward Drummond Libbey.

Antiochus and Stratonice. The old father, swathed in a toga, gestures grandiloquently in one direction while two male figures rush past him in another. The son stands in elaborate theatrical battle gear, including a voluminous cape. The background was to have been a palatial architectural invention on several levels, rising above masses of incidental figures in the foreground and supporting other agitated groups on a balcony. For good measure, there was to have been a full landscape in the distance, including a large temple.

Such a fulsome arrangement was out of key with the ideal of sincerity and moral strength, and David abandoned it (perhaps upon the advice of friends) for the scene showing the sons taking their oath before departure. The palace in the background was reduced to a stark enclosure; the landscape was eliminated as having nothing to do with the action; costumes were simplified. The new composition was less obviously dramatic but more forceful, and with the narrative reduced to a minimum its symbolism was emphasized.

The Oath of the Horatii was a sensation when David exhibited it in his studio in Rome. He completed it there during a second sojourn made possible by his father-in-law, who supplied him with funds to support himself, his wife and family, and an

7. DAVID: *The Death of Socrates*, 1787. 51 x 77¼". Metropolitan Museum of Art, New York, Wolfe Fund.

entourage of servants and assistants. The investment was a good one. The picture was brought back to Paris for the Salon (the annual official exhibition dominated by the Academy) and although badly placed, it caused such riotous excitement that it was rehung in a better position. A few pedants criticized the composition as oversimplified and on a single plane—that is, stretching across the picture surface rather than, so to speak, "puncturing" the canvas and going back into space. But these objections were lost in the general enthusiasm, which was increased by a factor that was to affect the reception of David's work from this time on: *The Oath of the Horatii* was interpreted as an allegory of contemporary events.

To adherents of the burgeoning Revolution, the picture seemed to proclaim the virility of new republican ideals in opposition to the degeneracy of the old regime. It is impossible to know how specifically David meant to reflect political convictions or theories, but it is certain enough that his own temperament was sympathetic to the new ideas—or at least unsympathetic to the

established order, of which the Academy was a manifestation. With the explosive success of *The Horatii* David became identified with antiroyalist thought. Ironically, the picture had been commissioned by the king. And it was so admired by one high-living member of the court, the Comte de Vaudreuil, an intimate of Marie Antoinette, that he commissioned David to do a copy in a smaller size. (He had to sell it later to pay gambling debts.) The smaller version is illustrated here. It differs from the larger one in the Louvre by the addition of the spindle lying on the floor by the grieving women.

David followed *The Horatii* with an even icier painting reflecting again the theme of self-sacrifice with moral and philosophical associations translatable into terms of revolutionary political ideas, *The Death of Socrates* [7]. The philosopher whose thought was based on the idea of studying man instead of inventing systems of false rhetoric, who sought the moral bases for human conduct, who did his teaching where crowds of the people gathered instead of within a

8. DAVID: *Lictors Bringing Back to Brutus the Bodies of His Sons*, 1789. 128 x 166½".
Louvre, Paris.

closed circle of sophisticates, and who died
for the defense of his ideas, was even more
directly identifiable with the principles of
the Revolution than *The Horatii* had been.
David shows Socrates about to carry out
the sentence of death by drinking hemlock,
while his disciples do their best to conceal
the weakness of emotionalism.

These "stoic" pictures with political overtones reached their climax—not aesthetically, but politically—in a picture of Brutus,
First Consul of Rome, sternly repressing his
grief as the bodies of his two sons, whom he
had condemned to death for conspiring
against Roman liberty, are carried home for
burial. *Lictors Bringing Back to Brutus the
Bodies of His Sons* [8] was completed and
exhibited the very year of the Revolution.
Even more than *The Horatii* it was a sensation as a political allegory. Just as Brutus
had sacrificed his own sons to the cause of
Roman liberty, so must the French people

purify their country at no matter what costs.
Brutus's strength was openly compared
with the weakness of Louis XVI, who had
allowed members of his family to emigrate
and take up arms for other countries against
France. Again the pedants objected, this
time because the figure of Brutus, the main
character, was thrown into deep shadow.
The dramatic and psychological effectiveness of this device is obvious, of course, but
it went against the rules. No one else cared;
the picture was a fantastic success, talked
of everywhere, and in the theater where
Voltaire's drama on the same subject was
being performed, the actors assumed the
attitudes painted by David. *Brutus*, too,
was purchased by Louis XVI. David's
apologists point out that later on, when he
voted for the death of the King, David
could not have done otherwise without
giving the lie to the moral themes of *The
Horatii* and *Brutus*.

David and the Revolution

With the Revolution achieved, David found himself its spokesman and propagandist, the pictorial historian of its great events. One of the most important of these events was the Oath of the Tennis Court, when on the 28th of June, 1789, the deputies of the Third Estate swore not to disband until they had given France a constitution. Louis had refused them their usual room for assembly and they had met instead in the indoor tennis court from which the event, and David's picture of it, are named. But the picture was never finished. Before it was nearly done too many of the men represented in it had become suspect.

For a few years after the Revolution David turned his hand to any professional chore for the new government. He was the official supervisor of state ceremonies and designed celebrations on such a scale that virtually the entire population of Paris was directed to take part in them. The citizens grumbled somewhat at this; it seemed a little out of line with the new freedom. David designed playing cards eliminating the king, queen, and knave, now too suggestive of royalty. He designed a new costume for the citizens' everyday dress; it failed to catch on. He was involved with the seizure of the royal collections and others, which were declared the property of the people and have been so ever since as the core of the Louvre Museum. And he produced a painting that may be his masterpiece: *Marat* [9].

David is always a contradictory figure. No sooner is he identified in one character than he reveals himself in another. In *Marat*, painted four years after the *Brutus*, he abandons the harshness of his stoic conceptions for a compassionate nobility all the more surprising in a subject that in essence was both violent and grotesque.

Marat, a leading figure in the Reign of Terror and a close friend of David's, was assassinated in his bathtub by a woman named Charlotte Corday. Although she was a Revolutionary sympathizer, Corday was outraged by the excesses of the Terror and appointed herself judge and executioner of at least one of the guilty, Marat, and was

9. David: *Marat*, 1793. 65 x 50⅝". *Musée Royal des Beaux Arts, Brussels.*

herself guillotined for his assassination. All this occurred, and David's picture was painted, in 1793.

The idea of a dedicated lady in full visiting regalia attacking a naked man in his tub has inevitable associations with the ludicrous along with the terrible, even after we know that the bath was a medicinal one in which Marat spent his days because he was afflicted with an eczema. Lining the tub with sheets and wrapping his head in a turban, no doubt also medicated, he received callers and carried on business as usual—or as best he could in the circumstances. Corday gained an audience by sending a note saying she had information of vital importance to France. Marat's tub was rigged with a cover to serve as a desk;

10. Berthault, engraved after Swebach: *Assassination of Marat*, from *Collection Complète des Tableaux Historiques de la Révolution Française*, Paris, 1802. Philadelphia Museum of Art, Gift of Mr. and Mrs. Adrian Siegel.

only his head and shoulders emerged above it and thus imprisoned he had no defense against Corday's dagger.

From this situation, which would seem impossibly guignolesque, David extracted a great picture. How he went about it may be revealed by a feeble treatment of the same subject [10] included in a pictorial history of the Revolution published in Paris in 1802. Here various people, attracted by the victim's cries, have rushed into the room and seized Corday (hat either knocked askew or set at a modish angle; it is impossible to tell which). But in spite of all that is supposed to be going on, no feeling of excitement is relayed to the observer. The story is not even clearly told, although presumably it is faithful to factual circumstance. Included in the general clutter of incidental figures is each detail selected by

David: the tub, the cloth hanging over its side, Marat in his turban, some writing materials on a stand by the tub's side, Corday's letter requesting an audience. But where one picture remains an ill-told anecdote at best, the other, by selection, modification, and arrangement of a few meager elements, distills from the event its essence as David felt it.

Bathed in a gentle fall of light with quiet modulations of shadow, each ugly, ordinary, or utilitarian object is invested with dignity, and all are unified with one another in quiet harmony. From a particularized subject full of sordid and commonplace details, David developed a generalized statement in noble and ideal terms. Here he approaches a classicism truer than that of his classical subjects with their trappings imitated from ancient Rome.

11. DAVID: *The Battle of the Romans and Sabines,* 1799. 152 x 204¾". Louvre, Paris.

David: The Triumph of Classicism

David's preoccupation with the ancient classical world, while not specifically mentioned, has been implied in the early series of "stoic" pictures: *The Horatii, Socrates,* and *Brutus.* Classicism in one form or another is a constant in French art, and David's art was the climax of a vogue for classical decoration that had already been stimulated by the first excavations of the buried Roman cities of Pompeii and Herculaneum. One of David's masters was Joseph Marie Vien (1716–1809), who made considerable but quite superficial use of classical motifs in his painting and who was appointed director of the Academy's school in Rome the same year David won the *Prix.*

Student and master left Paris together, with David declaring that he would not be "seduced by the antique" because it lacked vivacity and life—which it certainly did in Vien's hands. But when David saw the remains of Pompeii he said it was as if "cataracts had been removed from his eyes."

Neo-classicism* usually manifested itself in superficial borrowing from the forms of ancient art, capitalizing on their grace and novelty with no concern for their corresponding philosophical ideas. But David's

---

* *Neo-classicism,* strictly speaking, should be used to distinguish nineteenth-century revived classicism from the genuine classicism of antiquity. But this is a nuisance, and the differentiation is usually clear in context, so *classicism* will usually be used for both in this book.

12. DAVID: Preliminary drawing for Figure 11, 1795. Louvre, Paris.

classical reference is a double one. Like the other classicists, he used classical forms parasitically, copying them outright from fragments of painting and sculpture.* But unlike the others, David wanted through these borrowed forms to revive the supposed moral virtues of ancient Rome.

Even so, David was under one misconception as to the nature of classical art which was common to his century and to a great extent remains common to this one. A German, Johann Joachim Winckelmann (1717–1768), the first archaeologist to study the monuments of antiquity with

scientific method, had written a celebrated history of ancient art in which he defined beauty as synonymous with perfection. He codified the characteristics of classical art and insisted that all great art must be static because movement is an "accident." What Winckelmann did not understand was that classical art was warm, even sensuous. He confused its repose, its reserve, its calm, with a kind of frigidity, and his followers confused its idealization with prettification. A sculptor friend of David's in Rome, Quatremère de Quincy, introduced David to the theories of Winckelmann as a law permitting of no exception and no variation, and David retained all his life this limited and inaccurate concept of the classical spirit.

---

* In *The Oath of the Horatii* the head of the father is copied from the Roman equestrian statue of Marcus Aurelius, to name one example in a long list of specific borrowings.

David's archaeological neo-classicism reached its climax in *The Sabines* [11], which he completed in 1799 nearly five years after his trial and the brief imprisonment during which he made the first sketches for it. According to the legend, the Sabine women were abducted by the Romans, who took them to wife. Later when the fathers marched against the ravishers, the women threw themselves and their children between their Sabine fathers and their Roman husbands to stop the carnage. In David's picture the Sabine woman in the center is Hercelia; her husband Romulus is about to throw his javelin at Tatius, who bends to parry the blow. According to one story, David selected the subject because he was moved by the devotion of his wife, who returned to him when he was sent to prison. (She had left him when he voted for the death of the king.) According to another, Hercelia symbolizes France throwing herself between the warring parties in the civil conflict that tore the country after the Revolution. By the time David finished the picture, France had finally reached unity under Napoleon, and David is supposed to have agreed when the latter explanation was suggested, saying that was exactly what he had in mind. In that case, he had been extraordinarily prophetic in the first sketches five years earlier. A likely explanation is simply that the subject attracted him as a subject, all symbolism aside. It recalls his first success, *The Horatii*, in the conflicting loyalties of wives to their husbands at war with their families; also it must have given David pleasure to return to a purely classical subject after devoting himself for several years to pictures of the Revolution. Whatever his reasons for painting *The Sabines*, the uncanny dovetailing of his pictures with current political events, which had worked with *The Horatii* and *Brutus*, worked again. When Napoleon saw *The Sabines* in David's studio, he knew that he had found the man to direct French painting in his, Napoleon's, course toward empire.

In *The Sabines* David sought an extreme accuracy of archaeological truth. In addition, he modified the severity of his "Roman" classicism for a more "Greek" refine-

ment. The words have to be put in quotes because the archaeology is as faulty as the idea that Roman art was as severe as the ideals of the early Republic. Actually, all such inaccuracies or misconceptions are quite beside the point, since the neo-classical style is important only as itself, not as a re-creation of the past.

The Sabines is a fascinating picture with many faults. Even its admirers admit that it is rather chilly. For all the violence of the subject, the figures are of an extreme and even disturbing rigidity. Inspired by classical sculpture, they are not so much sculpturesque as stony. The vivacity, the sense of life, that David had once found lacking in classical art is certainly lacking here. Also, the architectural background is divorced from the friezelike grouping of women and warriors; it hangs behind them like a rented backdrop. Seen at full scale (it is a large picture, seventeen feet wide), *The Sabines* tends to break into beautifully designed studies competing with one another, although individually the passages are of great attraction. The theatrical elegance of the central standing female figure and the nude warrior to the right—Hercelia and Romulus—cannot be denied, and if a single pair of figures had to be selected to represent neo-classical types at their typically most ornamental, these might well be the ones. But the words used here are *theatrical* and *elegance*, and neither is particularly associated with the high moral disciplines that can be read into David's earlier work. He has changed. In *The Sabines* these disciplines are patently specious, although the technical disciplines of concise drawing and calculated balance are exaggerated. Classicism is again decorative style, as it was in the work of David's precursors and as it continued to be in the work of his followers, though upon its technical disciplines David insisted to the end.

Academic drawing had always been based on a study of the nude; it was standard practice to make preliminary drawings from the nude even for draped figures. In a study for the figure of Tatius in *The Sabines* David begins with the skeleton, builds the muscles on it, and finally indicates the helmet sketchily [13]. From

13. DAVID: Study for Tatius in *The Sabines*. Location unknown.

studies like this one David went ahead to refine or idealize nature to one degree or another. In *The Horatii* the anatomy is realistic, but in *The Sabines* David's stated purpose was to go beyond realism to an ideal beauty. He had wanted to leave the figures of the Horatii nude, in accordance with the forms of classical sculpture, but had dared not. Compositional studies for *The Sabines* [12] show that David still felt under this restraint when he began the picture. (They also show that the rigidity of the final scheme was imposed by degrees upon a much freer one.) But by the time he was ready to complete it, modes and manners had relaxed to such an extent that he

not only stripped the male figures but clothed the female ones in diaphanous garments that would have been altogether inappropriate to the severe conceptions of his early work.

David violated precedent by setting up *The Sabines* in his studio and charging admission to see it, a practice that had been forbidden by the Royal Academy. But there was no more Royal Academy and people flocked to see the picture as they had flocked to the Salons to see *The Horatii* and *Brutus*. As they paid their entrance fee, visitors were given a printed statement defending the admission charge. David made enough money to buy himself a comfortable country place outside Paris.

David and Napoleon

Now, under Napoleon, social Paris became a carnival. Freed from the moralistic restrictions of the Revolution and confident once more that the ground was not going to open beneath their feet or the guillotine descend on their necks, people with money indulged in pleasures as vain and often as licentious as the former excesses of the vanished world of the French court. David's influence on the mode reached a point without parallel in the history of the arts. A fashionable ball was a phantasmagoria of classical goddesses; a well-appointed room was as Greek or Roman as a working compromise with contemporary living would allow. The styles of decoration and costume called Directoire and Empire after the divisions of Napoleon's reign owe everything to David. The classical furniture he had designed and built for studio use was imitated in tens of thousands of pieces not only in Paris but everywhere in Europe and even in America. He now occupied himself with official paintings for Napoleon, plus whatever other commissions it interested him to accept. After the wild success of *The Sabines*, Madame Récamier, an ambitious charmer who put the highest premium on her position as a leader of social and intellectual Paris, was not too proud to write him, "I have arranged things so that I can sit for my portrait under the conditions you

14. DAVID: *Madame Récamier*, 1800. 68 x 85¾". Louvre, Paris.

explain. I hope that you understand the great value J attach to a work by you. I will be at your orders for the sittings; let me know when it is convenient for you to begin."

The portrait [14] is one of the most delicate of David's works, an exquisite summary of the spirit of the Directoire style at its purest. It is also one of the most painterly; because it was never finished, it never received the final polish to which David reduced the surface of his other work. Madame Récamier is not posed in costume for an archaeological costume ball but is in fashionable toilette with the exception of the bare feet, a detail David insisted on although it pushed the vogue for classical imitation beyond the point acceptable even to Madame Récamier. A more serious disagreement arose when David insisted on another point: he painted the hair light brown in harmony with the color scheme of the rest of the picture and in line with the formula for classical beauty. Madame Récamier's hair was coal black and she was

proud of it. Without telling David, she went to his most successful pupil, Gérard, who could be depended on to do the kind of portrait she wanted. Gérard reported to David, who told him to go ahead but refused to finish the first commission. Left thus, the portrait reveals the touch of David's brush as so deft, so sensitive, yet without any sacrifice of precision and assurance, that we realize how much was polished out of the rest of his work. With the exception of *Marat*, this is the only painting David regarded as a major one where his personal sensitivity as an artist is not impinged upon by the cruelly self-disciplined exaggerations of craftsmanship.

When Napoleon assumed the title of Emperor in 1804, David was given the title of First Painter. He had long since relinquished all political activity, and he painted now to commemorate the events of Napoleon's reign but not to comment on them beyond a general presentation of the Emperor in dignified and glorified terms. The spirit of the Napoleonic commissions is best

15. David: *Le Sacre*, 1805. 204 x 366″. Louvre, Paris.

summarized in *Le Sacre* [15], a vast canvas of some 500 square feet that was to have been one of a series of four (two were completed) apotheosizing the Emperor after his coronation. *Le Sacre* is the coronation scene itself, a mass portrait of superhuman dimensions. A church was commandeered to serve as a studio—similarly, in 1792, a church had been commandeered for work on *The Oath of the Tennis Court*. This was in 1805 and David was nearly sixty; he had a corps of assistants. There was a specialist in perspective, named Degotti, for the backgrounds; a pupil, Georges Rouget, was the chief of several other lieutenant painters. Even so, David did a portrait drawing for each of the heads. The assistants transferred these to the canvas and roughed them in; David finished each one himself.

Le Sacre shows Napoleon, already crowned, in turn crowning his Empress in the presence of the Pope, a host of dignitaries, and the distressingly unimpressive members of the family. Napoleon preferred to be represented at this moment rather than the one in which he knelt to be crowned by the Pope, since thus he was not put on record at any man's feet. It has been objected that the attendant figures of the court have the air of parvenus in their Sunday best. That, of course, is exactly what they were.

For this as for the other pictures David painted of him Napoleon refused to pose. "Why do you need a model?" he asked. "Do you think the great men of antiquity posed for their portraits? Who cares whether the busts of Alexander the Great look like him? It is enough that we have an image of him that conforms to his genius. That is the way great men should be painted." In *Le Sacre* the great man is painted as a handsome, almost boyish fellow, and he places the crown upon the head of an outrageously rejuvenated Josephine, for whose figure one of David's daughters posed. When an acquaintance objected to this flattering transformation of a woman who was a badly preserved forty-one, and six years older than her husband, David

16. DAVID: *Madame Sériziat*, 1795. Panel, 51½ x 37¾". Louvre, Paris.

17. DAVID: *Monsieur Sériziat*, 1795. Panel, 50¾ x 37¾". Louvre, Paris.

quashed the objection by suggesting that it be made directly to the Empress herself.

In *Le Sacre* David had a next-to-impossible assignment. It was not only that the picture had to be so large. Mythological or ancient historical references were ruled out by Napoleon's demand for a straightforward record of the event, and without them David was forced into a rather pedestrian realism, saved from dullness only by the magnificence of the staging of the actual ceremony. On the whole, *Le Sacre* is a ponderous and wearisome picture in spite of everything David could do. But it is probably the most familiar of all pictures to French school children and remains for Frenchmen the symbol of the glorious days of Napoleon's zenith.

Given the initial handicaps, David's solution was more than adequate. He solved the problem of organizing so many figures partly by grouping, but even more by a less apparent device, a consistent illumination that binds each participant into convincing relationship to the others. There is nothing subtle about this light; it unifies the picture only because it falls so logically everywhere. As a help, David studied a scaled mock-up of the scene, built for him complete with costumed miniature figures. Yet in the end *Le Sacre* is not a stirring picture except by association of ideas. In it David is the soundest of craftsmen, but he is not an artist of emotional or intellectual force.

David: The Artist

What about David as an artist of personal sensitivity, an artist who can respond to human joy and sorrow, gaiety and confusion, hope and disappointment, revery and

Amicos Antonium Mungez et Angelicam uxorem
amicus Ludovicus David. Anno MDCCCXII.

18. DAVID: *Antoine Mongez and His Wife Angelica,* 1812. Panel, 37¾ x 54″. *Musée de Lille.*

excitement, and communicate with us as other human beings?

In this respect David often denies himself, on the stoic principle that the expression of emotions of either pleasure or pain is a weakness. Even in a picture of the stature of *The Oath of the Horatii,* the observer is likely to feel that he is not so much sharing an experience or an idea as being taught a lesson—which happens to be exactly what the encyclopedist Diderot, just before the Revolution, stated as the function of painting.

But in his portraits David frequently relents, especially when the sitters are close friends and the pictures were not intended for formal public exhibition. After his release from prison he stayed for a while with his wife's sister, Émélie Sériziat, and her husband. David was a man who had been bitterly chastised, who had narrowly escaped execution, whose career seemed to be in ruins. He had always been a man with a reputation for severity, yet during his imprisonment his friends and his family had shown him loyalty and affection. During the two months he spent with the Sériziats he must have been conscious of his good

fortune, grateful for the kindness of people, perhaps even aware of and regretful for his own iciness. There was a particularly affectionate bond between David and Émélie; the portrait he now painted of her [16] is a delight and a revelation of gentle sensitivities rarely suggested in his work up until this time. The informality of the pose, the freshness of the color, the loving attention to engaging details of costume and the sweetness of the little bouquet of flowers— all these are specific attractions but they only partially account for something more elusive, a tenderness and human warmth, an intimacy of personal response between painter and subject.

The air of intimacy and informality is not accidental, for the picture is carefully composed. The placement of the child is masterly. In a more conspicuous position he would have detracted from the picture as David conceived it, since this is a portrait of Émélie Sériziat, not a picture of a mother and child. As it is, the child is very nearly crowded out of the picture, which would have been unpleasant if David had not turned the head so that we are regarded with open curiosity. The child seems almost to have slipped into the range of the picture by accident, without knowledge that he would be painted; he is held in perfect balance, neither detracting from the main subject nor altogether subjugated to it. The companion portrait of Monsieur Sériziat [17] is closer to Davidian formula, but not close enough for its precision to turn frigid.

The Sériziats were painted in 1795. Seventeen years later David painted a double portrait of his friend Antoine Mongez and his wife [18]. Like the Sériziat portraits, this one was a labor of love. It is inscribed "Amicos Antonium Mongez et Angelicam uxorem amicus Ludovicus David. Anno MDCCCXII."

The Latin is not an affectation but appropriate in a portrait of Mongez, the author of a scholarly dictionary of antiquities. His hand rests on this volume and also holds a coin, symbol of his function as an administrator in the government's department of finance. His wife Angelica had been a student of David's; she costumed the figures for his mock-up of *Le Sacre* and executed minor passages in that gigantic picture. The Mongez portrait is more formal than those of the Sériziats but no less warm, and as a presentation of two rich personalities it even surpasses them. It is as if we met the young Sériziats after a passage of years and a happy transition into middle age.

When Napoleon fell, David was exiled. He finished his life in Brussels, painting away at whatever assignments it pleased him to set himself, venerated by followers of the tradition he had established, the grand old man of French painting. In his youth, still competing for the *Prix de Rome*, he had painted a picture of *Mars Vanquished by Minerva* [19]—the forces of violence and confusion conquered by the intellect. It is a windy picture, full of the artificialities and mannerisms of eighteenth-century painting that David later annihilated with his classical style. His last work, completed in exile fifty-three years later, in 1824, the year before his death, is another version of the defeat of Mars [20]. In the early picture Venus floats near by in support of Minerva, but in the later one she replaces her. In *Mars Disarmed by Venus and the Graces* violence and confusion are conquered not by the intellect but by the heart. Cupid unbinds the sandals of the god of war, who relinquishes his sword and shield to the Graces. Venus places a wreath of blossoms on his head; a pair of doves bill and coo on his muscular thigh. The picture is a little cloying, a little overgraceful. It may be an old man's revery, but if it is, it may be also his apology for the fanatic severity of his earlier convictions.

Sculptors and Other Painters

Neo-classical sculpture has little place in a story of modern art, for sculpture found no David and followed a speciously classical formula of prettiness and high polish which, as we will see in a moment, also infected the second generation of neo-classical painters. For the record, however, the names of the Italian sculptor Antonio Canova (1757–1822), the Frenchman Antoine Denis Chaudet (1763–1810), and the pedantic

19. DAVID: *Mars Vanquished by Minerva, 1771. 45 x 55". Louvre,* Paris.

20. DAVID: *Mars Disarmed by Venus and the Graces, 1824. 118 x 103". Musée Royal des Beaux Arts,* Brussels.

21. CHINARD: *Madame Récamier*, 1802–05. Marble, life size. *Musée des Beaux Arts*, Lyon.

22. J. B. REGNAULT: *Three Graces*, Salon of 1799. 78¾ x 60¼", octagonal. Louvre, Paris.

Dane, Bertel Thorwaldsen (1770–1844), must be mentioned. Some of the most rewarding bits of neo-classical sculpture are found spotted among the works of more obscure men. An example [21] is a bust of Madame Récamier (who never tired of commissioning images of herself) by Joseph Chinard (1756–1813), where sensitive realism brings unusual life to classically derived forms of the kind that were worked to death in the majority of cases.

Among painters, David's contemporary rival was a man seldom thought of today, Jean-Baptiste Regnault (1745–1829), who won the *Prix de Rome* in 1776 two years after David. Unlike David, who was suspicious of antiquity before the "cataracts were removed from his eyes," Regnault was dedicated to classicism from the beginning, but only in its superficial aspect as a store-

house of graceful forms. He remained a painter of the eighteenth-century court with all its caprice, seductive posturings, and artifice. In his *Three Graces* [22], as a single example, he borrows an arrangement directly from a popular and often-repeated piece of classical sculpture, but the luscious girls he paints are classical in pose only; otherwise they remain the little courtesans and coquettes popularized by the eighteenth-century court painter Boucher.

As early as 1808 David was saying, "The direction I have set for the fine arts is too severe to please for very long in France." This was true, and had already become apparent before David became aware of it. We have just seen that even in his own work he did not maintain the severity of his earliest successes. The second generation of classicists paid brush-service to the

23. GÉRARD: *Psyche Receiving the First Kiss from Cupid*, 1798. 42½ x 52″. Louvre, Paris.

24. GUÉRIN: *Aurora and Cephalus*, 1810. 99¼ x 72″. Louvre, Paris.

master, imitating his technical polish without understanding the philosophical intention behind it. Their spirit is closer to Regnault's. This was true even of David's favorite pupil, François Gérard (1770–1837). At sixteen Gérard was studying in David's studio, and David remained his sponsor from then on. For a while he gave up painting when David succeeded in getting him named a member of the Revolutionary Tribunal; it is difficult to think of Gérard in this capacity after acquaintance with his sugary *Psyche Receiving the First Kiss from Cupid* [23] or for that matter any of his other pictures. It is customary to deny virtues of any kind to Gérard, as if his art were entirely detestable, and it is true that in comparison with David's strength Gérard's affectations are appalling. But if the standard of judgment is lowered to that

of the fashionable exercise, which is Gérard's proper level, he doesn't come off too badly. Some of his portraits are charming.

Gérard's reputation during his own time was so inflated that critics ever since seem to have been trying to cut him down to size. He had a series of brilliant Salon successes, of which *Psyche Receiving the First Kiss from Cupid* was the climax. He painted Napoleon's family and leading dignitaries. After Napoleon fell and David was exiled, Gérard continued his dazzling career. The statesman Talleyrand presented him to Louis XVIII, the restored Bourbon, and he became the favorite painter of the court and the world surrounding it. In 1819 he was created a baron. His father, a Frenchman, and his mother, an Italian, had been servants before the Revolution.

25. GUÉRIN: *Phaedra and Hippolytus*, 1802. 101¼ x 139¾″. Louvre, Paris.

Whatever his shortcomings as a philosophical moralist or an intellectual classicist, Gérard is a tower of strength in comparison with his immediate contemporary Pierre-Narcisse Guérin (1774–1833), a pupil not of David's but of Regnault's. Another *Prix de Rome* winner, Guérin made an exaggerated success in the Salon of 1799. The Royalist party interpreted his picture of *Marcus Sextus Returned from Exile* as a symbol of the return to France of the emigrés who had left during the Revolution, a stroke of luck. Among biographies of successful men, Guérin's is refreshing, because he was a lazy student who had not been interested in becoming a painter in the first place. Whether he ever became much of one is open to question, but everything fell into his lap, including finally the directorship of the Academy's school in Rome. Two of his paintings, *Aurora and Cephalus* [24] imitating Regnault's sensuous prettiness and *Phaedra and Hippolytus* [25] imitating David's

spareness and precision, show how well he learned to go through the classical motions and how little connection he had with the classical spirit in either direction. *Aurora and Cephalus* is incredible in its candified suggestiveness; *Phaedra and Hippolytus* is not so much a painting as it is a scene from a drama performed by some of the most incompetent actors ever to have become involved in a classical tragedy. Yet from Guérin's studio came two of the most important painters of the century, Géricault and Delacroix, with whom the next chapter of this book is concerned, as well as many competent painters of less importance who are secure enough in their small niches.

Two other students of David's must be mentioned parenthetically: Étienne-Jean Delécluze (1781–1863), because his name frequently appears as the defender of classicism when it came under attack—he stopped painting early, after a good start, to devote himself to writing—and Jean August Dominique Ingres, because he is

26. PRUD'HON: *Justice and Divine Vengeance Pursuing Crime*, 1808. 95¾ x 115″. Louvre.

one of the greatest of all French painters. Ingres quarreled with David after a close early association; he will be given a chapter in this book later on.

Finally, one man, Pierre Paul Prud'hon (1758–1823), in nineteenth-century classicism is that anomaly which turns up in every school: the painter of talent and originality who was accepted by the school yet seems to bear no relationship to it. While the other classicists were sharpening their lines to razor-edge precision and polishing their forms to tinny brilliance, Prud'hon developed a style based on soft, yielding volumes emerging from and melting into smoky shadows, a style derived from Leonardo da Vinci and, even more, from Correggio, although these late fifteenth- and early sixteenth-century Italians were not much in classical favor. Prud'hon was an enthusiastic user of the new bitumen pigments, which gave wonderful velvety depths to shadows. As it turned out, these

pigments blistered, cracked, darkened, and peeled with age, so most of Prud'hon's canvases are in ruinous condition. His best-known painting, *Justice and Divine Vengeance Pursuing Crime* [26], is a ghost of itself, but still suggests the moody poetry, a little forced sometimes, that marked Prud'hon at his best. Slightly younger than David, but within his generation, Prud'hon was befriended by David during a difficult, unsavory, and emotionally disturbed life.

Prud'hon's drawings are often more satisfying than his paintings. As an example, a nude study in black and white chalk on gray-blue paper [27] combines sound formal description with the effect of soft, spreading illumination he cultivated. Perhaps his paintings had more of this quality before they deteriorated; or perhaps the drawing is more successful than the paintings ever were simply because Prud'hon's talent was not strong enough to encompass more ambitious conceptions.

27. Prud'hon: *Nude*, date unknown. 15 x 13″. Collection Henry P. McIlhenny, Philadelphia.

The Break with Classicism

To call these men minor classicists reduces the list of major ones to a single name, David, always excepting Ingres, who was disinherited. And whatever their differences, all these men share one similarity that cuts them off from David: they all hint at connections with lyricism or personal emotionalism. This spirit was in the air. More than David's disciplined classicism, it was the spirit of the new century. It was romanticism. It was a force too strong to be held in check by the classically minded Academy, and it breaks through openly in the painting of two nominally classical artists, Girodet and Gros, whom it is now time to consider.

CHAPTER 2

Romanticism

The Romantic Spirit

David declared that "Art should have no other guide than the torch of Reason," but this dictum is opposed by a sentiment held dear by the French: "The heart has its reasons which Reason does not know." The romantic movement was a revolt of the heart against Reason, of emotion against intellect, of the mysterious against the rational, of the individual against formula—in short, of the senses and the imagination against everything else.

No art of much consequence is created without some fusion of emotional and intellectual values, and this truth the romantic artists did not deny. But they trusted their hearts before their heads, put their intellect at the service of their instincts. If a conflict between emotional and intellectual values forced them to a choice, they dropped the torch of Reason to follow their unreasonable impulse, even when they were not certain where it might lead them. They would abandon moderation for excess, when necessary, accept confusion rather than run the risk of sacrificing spontaneity to lucidity, were willing to be utterly illogical if within their hearts they felt that they might stifle emotional truth by subjecting it to analysis. The classicists had spoken rationally of "Beauty, sublime and severe, which can be defined only by theory and understood only by Reason."* But the romantics worshiped a beauty sublime and passionate, which could not be defined and could be appreciated only by the heart.

---

* Quatremère de Quincy.

For all these reasons, romanticism out of control was often turgid, bizarre, formless, hysterical—just as classicism misunderstood had grown sterile, repetitious, and frigid. Classicists and romantics accused one another of these faults in the conflict that put them at one another's throats shortly after David's death, in a struggle that took surface form as a romantic rebellion against the platitude and monotony and hampering restrictions of the classical dogma as observed by the second-rate painters in control of the Academy. But romanticism went deeper than professional antagonisms and theories of art. It was a way of life, a way of life demanding spiritual nourishment of a special kind that classicism did not offer.

Classicism assumes the existence of a perfect order, hidden but discoverable beneath the chaos of human experience. But the assumption is not often justified by the world around us, and certainly was not justified by the succession of events in France for several decades after 1789—the tumult of the Revolution, the hysteria of the Terror, the bloody grandeur of Napoleon's triumphs, the shattering disillusion after his fall, and all the subsequent corruption and dissension. Yet classical artists continued to put a premium on balance, precision, and rule in a world that was lopsided, confused, and unpredictable. The romantics would have none of their outworn formulas.

David's art had been an expression of eighteenth-century philosophy that deified Reason, but the century had also produced a philosopher who gave the romantics a different point of departure. He was Jean Jacques Rousseau (1712-1778), who preached a return to nature, the essential goodness of man, the rights of the individual. It is only a step from Rousseau's idea that man is naturally noble to the idea that his untrammeled emotions, his instincts "in the raw," are merely sterilized, not refined, by the classical process of intellectualizing. The romantics took this step. The classical artists and philosophers had stood aside from mankind's experience to see it in breadth and to create a man-made harmony from its confusions. The romantics refused to stand aside; they plunged into the midst of experience to savor its contradictions, and when the world was too much for them, when their battered souls demanded surcease, they found it not in the contemplation of synthetic order but in imagined worlds of curious and exotic invention. Like the classicists, the romantics haunted Rome, but for different reasons. To the romantic eye, the ruins of the ancient world were not reminders of Reason. They were reminders of man's mortality. Choked by vines and grasses among the crumbling stones, the broken monuments of antiquity evoked lost battles, dead loves, and mysteries. They were settings for melancholy revery, for trysts, for episodes of sweetness or of violence. For the romantic, even the classical world was fodder for emotional yearnings.

Romantic Classicism: "Atala"

In painting, the romantic spirit appeared first in classical disguise. It is hinted at in the sugar-syrup sentiment of some of David's followers, as we have already seen, and is strong in the work of Anne-Louis Girodet-Trioson (1767–1824). Girodet was a student of David's as well as a *Prix de Rome* winner (in 1789, with Gérard second). He was busy with *The Entombment of Atala* [28] while David was putting the finishing touches on *Le Sacre*. Technically *The Entombment of Atala* is a fine classical showpiece. But conceptually it belongs to the opposing camp.

This camp had hardly begun to gather its forces. The first indications of what was about to happen were literary ones, and *The Entombment of Atala* was the result of one of them. In 1801 a young aristocrat, adventurer, and romantic spirit named René de Chateaubriand published a brief novel, *Atala*, a curious compound of the fantastic, the irrational, the beautiful, and the absurd, except that in romantic conception nothing is absurd simply because it appeals to the heart at the expense of all logic. *Atala* was a great success; it was sensational on several scores. The scene was laid in the mysterious and fascinating American wilderness; the characters were

31

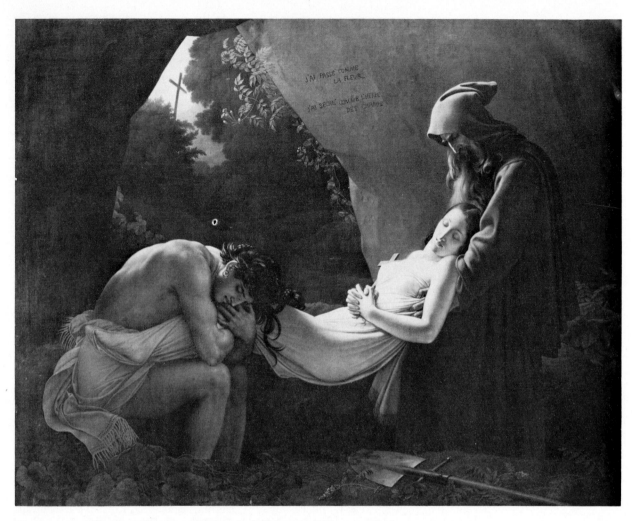

28. GIRODET: *The Entombment of Atala,* 1808. 82¾ x 105". Louvre, Paris.

American Indians (Atala, the heroine, was a half-breed girl); and the plot had a strong, if artificial, flavoring of religious sentiment. (Christianity had become fashionable with Napoleon's re-establishment of the Church after the Revolution.)

Girodet's picture was painted seven years after the appearance of the novel and illustrates its final episode. The maiden Atala has died rather than yield her virginity in marriage to her lover, in observance of a vow made not by Atala but by her mother many years before. (This is only a minor complexity in a plot that would sound ludicrous in summary.) The other characters in the picture are her lover

Choctas and a priest attached to a never-never mission in the Florida jungles. The several romantic elements here had better be examined one at a time:

First, the story of Atala is romantic because it is preoccupied with personal emotionalism. The problems faced by the Horatii, by Socrates, by Brutus, and by the Sabines may have involved personal distress, but this was incidental to the importance of a general social moral ideal. The reverse is true in Atala's case. Although she has sacrificed herself, it is not for the State or a political theory. Her difficulties were entirely personal and hence puny by Davidian standards.

29. GIRODET: *Ossian Receiving the Generals of Napoleon,* 1802. 75½ x 71½". Malmaison.

30. GIRODET: Preliminary study for Figure 29. 13 x 11¼". Louvre.

Second, the picture violates the ideal of reserve nominally demanded by classicism. Everything in it seeks to stir the observer's emotions—the exaggerated light dramatizing a moody setting, the pathetic beauty of the dead girl, the anguish of her lover.

The Christian element, being non-rational, is unclassical; and finally, the Atala story is romantic in its exoticism. A yearning for the far away and the long ago, for the high colors and fantastic peoples and curiosities of the Orient or the wilderness or of any place offering escape into the vivid and the mysterious—this yearning was a trait of the romantics in their search for release, stimulation, and fulfillment.

These romantic heresies announce themselves rather hesitantly in Girodet's picture, however, and are all but concealed beneath its classical veneer. Atala might be a beautiful Greek maiden, and her gauzy robe is inexplicable in any but classical terms. The nudity of her mourning lover is the idealized nudity of classical sculpture, not the rough nudity of a savage; Choctas might be a gladiator. And technically the painting is tight and smooth enough to satisfy any classical pedant. The dramatic light and shade is something of a departure from standard procedure, but otherwise Girodet hints at none of the technical innovations that in full-blown romantic painting were to shock the Academy more than the romantic spirit did.

The traditional recognition of *The Entombment of Atala* as a tentative romantic expression has obscured the importance of an earlier painting by Girodet, an extremely curious hybrid which, with a slightly different history, might have become the manifesto of romantic painting. *Ossian Receiving the Generals of Napoleon* [29] is a fantastic and complicated allegory celebrating the Continental Peace of 1801; it shows the ghosts of Napoleon's generals being received into a light-shot otherworld by the ghost of Ossian, a Gaelic bard of the third century. This extraordinary juxtaposition of characters is an offshoot of an audacious literary forgery. In 1760–1763 the Scotch writer James Macpherson published some grandiose and somber poems of his own invention, presenting them as translations of Ossian. The poems were received with enthusiasm, and Ossianism reached the proportions of a cult in France, an early indication that the romantic yearning for the exotic and the grandiloquent was already stirring. Girodet's Napoleonic allegory forced current events into parallel with Macpherson's forged Gaelic legends— an obvious violation of classical doctrine, which demanded parallels with ancient Rome or Greece. The picture further violates every classical regulation in its swirling, visionary composition, especially as Girodet first conceived it in a preliminary study [30]. In the final version he compromised to some extent, polishing his romantic fantasy into superficial accord with classical disciplines as far as the individual forms are concerned. Yet even this compromise is interesting as a final contradiction, between reason and fantasy, in a conception paradoxical from the beginning. Fantastical invention seems to have been natural to Girodet's talent, but *Ossian Receiving the Generals of Napoleon* was badly received at the Salon, and Girodet never attempted anything like it again. What could have been a romantic manifesto ended as the most curiously isolated and artificial concoction of the neo-classical school.

Napoleonic Romanticism: Gros

In its precision and balance, *The Entombment of Atala* implies that life is harmonious and orderly even when mildly compromised with sentiment. True romanticism could not allow such a compromise, and Napoleonic France produced a generation unwilling to accept it, a generation accustomed to violence, thirsty for strong experiences, goaded by an acute awareness of the transience of life. Anguish this generation could understand, and exaltation and despair, but not serenity nor repose. To the young officers back from the Napoleonic battlefields, the classical tragedies in the Parisian theaters and the classical paintings in the Salons seemed, somehow, not so stirring as they had remembered.

31. GROS: *Colonel Fournier-Sarlovèze*, 1812. 96¾ x 68″. Louvre.

Much more than in the tepid, graceful *Entombment of Atala*, the new ferment is at work in the painting of Antoine Jean Gros (1771–1835), a member of Napoleon's staff and a pupil of David's, by temperament a romantic of an extreme type— melancholy; brooding; impressed with the prescience of death, the suffering of man in the world, and the tragedy that not even greatness (as exemplified for Gros in Napoleon, whom he idolized) is immune to error, confusion, and malevolence. Romantic sensibility could find exaltation in suffering; melancholy was often cultivated as a pose; the voluptuousness of spiritual torment became one of the romantic pleas-

32. GROS: *Christine Boyer*, c. 1800. 84¼ x 52″. Louvre, Paris.

committed suicide in three feet of water, at the age of sixty-four. It may seem absurd to suggest that his inability to reconcile the classical ideal he yearned to believe in with the romantic one he could not help believing in was a contributing factor to his suicide. But it seems absurd only because it is difficult to imagine today the furore of the romantic–classic conflict at a time when the arts were so much a part of national life. In a France still trying to come to balance after the Revolution and the Napoleonic disaster, the exhibition of a picture or the publication of a work of fiction or the staging of a play could become a national issue.

In Italy, where his Napoleonic service took him, Gros saw works of Michelangelo, Rubens, and Van Dyck. The first two especially were the antithesis of the neo-classical ideal in their swirling movement, emotional intensity, twisting forms and, in the case of Rubens, the opulent color applied with dash and freedom. These were the men with whom the repressed romantic Gros had a natural temperamental affinity, and in spite of everything he could do to maintain his allegiance to the dogmas of classicism, their influence kept breaking through. Gros was a fine painter with a superb feeling for dramatic composition, a painterly painter with a natural painter's love for the manipulation of pigment, which he sought to repress in accord with David's dictum, "pas d'emportement du pinceau." But his brush very nearly carried him away—by Davidian standards—in some passages of his portrait of *Colonel Fournier-Sarlovèze* [31]. The romantic pose—hand on hip; head thrown back while he scans the distance; sword drawn from scabbard as he stands debonair, dashing, confident, handsome, and elegant against the dramatic background—cries aloud for equally dramatic brushwork. In the lining of the cape, the crumpled papers tossed on the ground, and especially the ornamentation of gold braid and tassels, Gros yields to temptation; the paint is thick and rich and freely applied in character with the subject's romantic flair.

The portrait of *Christine Boyer* [32] is an even greater departure from classicism, because its romantic mood is more arbi-

ures, especially when this torment could be displayed in attitudes becoming to the tormented.

But the suffering could be real, and with Gros it was. Five years after the date generally accepted as the victory year of romanticism, 1830 (when Victor Hugo's romantic drama, *Hernani*, was tempestuously presented in declared opposition to the standards of the classical theater), Gros

33. GROS: *Napoleon Visiting the Pesthouse at Jaffa,* 1804. 209 x 283″. Louvre, Paris.
Detail on opposite page.

trarily selected and the means of creating
it are more artificial. To paint a general's
portrait reflecting the color and excitement
of battle is only to capitalize upon circum-
stantial material. But the *Christine Boyer*
is deliberately romanticized. A lovely
woman in elegant indoor attire is moodily
and inexplicably posed by the side of a
stream in a shady woods. Her crimson
shawl falls on a mossy rock; a waterfall behind her tumbles into a rocky bed; the
stream flows toward us through the darkening woods from a little cave of light in
the distance. The trees are dense and dark
along the banks and behind the beautiful
quiet face. This face is turned slightly
away from us to gaze upon a single rose
floating on the current (at the extreme
lower right corner of the picture), which

in a moment will be carried beyond our
vision, and beyond hers.

The picture's exceptional quality is a
poetic mood created by romantic emphasis
on details like these to stir our sensibilities.
Romanticism is first of all a state of sensibility; the romantic temperament feels an
obligation to develop sensibilities to their
utmost rather than to discipline them. The
braggadocio and display of the *Fournier-
Sarlovèze* portrait are one manifestation of
these ideas; the feminine languor and sentimental melancholy of *Christine Boyer* are
another.

But these are portraits, where a painter
is less vulnerable to rule and regulation
than he is in official pictures. In official
subjects intended for public display the
contradiction between Gros's temperament

36 · ROMANTICISM

34. GROS: Detail from Figure 33.

35. REMBRANDT: *Christ Healing the Sick, c.* 1649. Etching, 10⅞ x 15⅜″. National Gallery, Washington, Rosenwald Collection.

and the classical style is more apparent and his struggle more painful. In 1804 he was commissioned to commemorate an incident when Napoleon, during his Near Eastern campaign of 1798–1799, visited the pesthouse in Jaffa where members of his troops were dying of the plague [33]. Actually the pesthouse was an ordinary hospital, but in the interest of dramatization Gros shifted the scene to a mosque. In doing so he reversed the approach used by David in, for instance, his *Marat:* instead of eliminating details to reduce the episode to its essentials, as David had done, and then reducing those essentials to an ultimate purity and simplicity almost abstract, Gros romantically added details and then used every possible means to increase their emotional impact. Colors are heightened, intensified, and contrasted. Whole passages are thrown into obscurity while others are pulled into strong light, reviving and going beyond David's theatrical lapse in his *Brutus* with its shadowed foreground figure. Hardly a detail has not been romanticized, but at the same time the picture clings to a token observance of the official tradition. For all their Orientalism, the arches of the mosque arranged across the background suggest the architectural flats of *The Horatii.* The nude figure lying face down in the foreground tearing at itself in agony may be romantic in its violence, but it is also a meticulous anatomical study in David's studio tradition. But the romantic focus of the picture is the nude bearded man who, dying, turns his head worshipfully toward the General [34]. The flexibility and the individualization of this figure make it the reverse of the conventionally proportioned, idealized, sculpturally modeled Davidian figure. And Gros's emotional conception of the subject, where Napoleon appears as a sort of Christ, touching the plague sores as if his bare hands would heal them miraculously, relates *Napoleon Visiting the Pesthouse at Jaffa* less closely to David than to a great romantic etching of the seventeenth century, Rembrandt's "Hundred Guilder Print," *Christ Healing the Sick* [35].

With the *Pesthouse* Gros came as close as he was ever to come to realizing his

36. GROS: *Hercules and Diomede*, Salon of 1835. 167½ x 127¼". *Musée des Beaux Arts,* Toulouse.

potential as a romantic painter on the grand scale. (His *Battle of Eylau* is a second, but not a very close second.) After the fall of Napoleon, he attempted to find in idolization of the restored Bourbons the same spiritual support he had found in idolizing Napoleon I, but if his painting from that time on is any indication of his emotional life, this life was remarkably sterile. By 1820 the romantic movement was flourishing, but Gros, still obdurate, tried to go back to the sources of the classical style in order to recultivate it in noble purity. The experiment was a debilitating one. His work became mannered instead of noble, empty instead of pure, and his last picture, *Hercules and Diomede* [36], was laughed at in the Salon of 1835, the year of his suicide.

The romantic banner Gros might have carried had been picked up in the meanwhile by the young Théodore Géricault (1791–1824), and upon Géricault's early death at thirty-three, had passed to Eugène Delacroix (1798–1863), an even younger painter whose work Gros had first admired and then, with his typical recoil from his spontaneous sympathies, disparaged.

The Romantic Declaration: Géricault and the "Raft of the Medusa"

On the 2d of July, 1816, the French frigate *Medusa* was wrecked in a storm off the west coast of Africa. When it became obvious that the vessel was lost, a raft was improvised from parts of it as it sank. Onto this makeshift were crowded 149 passengers and members of the crew. By the time they were sighted, only fifteen men had survived thirst, madness, and cannibalism. Géricault's picture of this horror [37] became for romanticism what *The Oath of the Horatii* had been for classicism a generation earlier, a public declaration of new principles and a standard around which a new school rallied in revolt.

Like David's earliest successes, the *Raft of the Medusa* attracted general attention because of its connection with exciting current events. Unlike David's, Géricault's picture actually represented the contemporary event in a contemporary way instead of allegorizing or symbolizing it in images of the past. The classicists fumed that the picture was vulgar and sensational, but this did not disturb a vulgar public interested in sensationalism. Nor was the public much impressed by the academic objection that here ordinary seamen were represented with the seriousness and on the grand scale appropriate only to the gods, heroes, and events of the ancient world. The *Medusa* had sunk in circumstances that were seized upon by the liberal party to attack the corruption of the administration (officers towing the raft from a lifeboat were accused of having cut it loose and left it adrift).

Géricault exhibited the picture in the Salon of 1819 (the official catalogue naïvely listed it only as *A Shipwreck,* to no one's confusion), and it was such an attraction that thereafter he traveled with it to England and made a considerable sum in gate receipts. The public that flocked to see the *Raft of the Medusa* came to see a sideshow novelty as much as it came to see a work of art. Certainly not one person in a hundred came to see a romantic manifesto, but this backdoor introduction of

37. Géricault: *Raft of the Medusa*, 1818. 193 x 282". Louvre, Paris.

large numbers of people to romantic paint-ing was valuable to the movement, whether or not people were conscious of the picture's revolutionary character or its merits.

These merits were considerable, but their revolutionary character was only rela-tive. To abandon David for new gods, Rubens and Michelangelo; to use color as an emotive element instead of as a decora-tive tint applied to sculpturesque forms; to subject the composition of a picture to its expressive character rather than to force expression into a standard composition—all this was counterrevolution against the Da-vidian revolution that had congealed into a formula, but none of it was innovational by historical precedent.

The composition of the *Raft of the Medusa* skips backward more than a cen-tury to recall the pictorial arrangements of seventeenth-century Italian painters, for example, Caravaggio, who made a similar revolution against the classical composi-tions of his own time. The survivors are shown in every attitude of anguish and despair. Sighting the rescue ship in the far distance, they have raised one of their number aloft on their shoulders.* He waves a shirt in a pitiable effort to attract attention. Straining, gesticulating, swoon-ing, the *Medusa's* survivors are intertwined in a turbulent mass of forms recalling the cascades of damned souls in Last Judg-ments by Michelangelo and Rubens. The

---

* This particular survivor is a Negro; his presence is justified by historical fact, but his introduction into Géricault's picture is often pointed out as evidence of the romantic interest in exotic types.

38. GÉRICAULT: Detail from *Raft of the Medusa*, Figure 37.

forms rush upward across the canvas from left to right, culminating off balance in a jagged peak like a wave about to break and topple. Such grouping is obviously more expressive of movement and excitement and confusion than David's neat seesaw in *The Sabines*, frozen forever into the classical demand for symmetrical balance—although *The Sabines* is as much a subject of movement and excitement and confusion as is the *Raft*. Géricault's departure from seesaw balance seemed outrageous to the academicians, although he quite adequately brought his composition into equilibrium, countering the strong upward left-to-right movement by reversing it in the lines of the mast and ropes, lines that are continued and echoed in various of the figures on the raft itself.

What means does Géricault use to convey emotions of pity, terror, and horror? These emotions are not merely the result of the subject. Where David would have "purified," Géricault has intensified [38]. Irregular broken forms are more suggestive of excitement than smooth, even ones. Hence Géricault exaggerates all the natural irregularities, the hollows and protrusions, of heads and bodies that David would have smoothed out in submission to a preconceived ideal. Above all, Géricault dramatizes his forms by revealing them at maximum intensity in brilliant light and dense shadow. And where David's color—rather flat, very ornamental, "tasteful"—is simply color, the turgid darks and ominous greens

39. Géricault: After Death (study), c. 1818. 17¾ x 22″. Art Institute of Chicago, Munger Collection (McKay Fund).

of the *Raft of the Medusa* are correlated to its subject. The picture is not a masterpiece of color, and it has darkened so much that we cannot be certain of its original scheme, but the conception of color as an expressive element is unquestionably present.

For his models David used the best-muscled and most perfectly proportioned human beings available to the studio, made precise imitative studies from them, and then modified his studies to bring them into correspondence with his recipe for the ideal type. Géricault abandons this idea that beauty is synonymous with perfection. A romantic, he finds beauty even in ugliness if ugliness reveals a state of soul. Instead of the athletes who posed for David, Géricault sought out the survivors of the *Medusa* and made sketches of them. One survivor was the ship's carpenter; he constructed for the artist a model of the raft.

But all this was only documentation of literal fact. Valuable as it was, it did not necessarily correspond with expressive truth. So Géricault visited hospitals and sketched men as they were dying. He sketched in morgues [39] and madhouses. According to one story, he kept corpses in his room to make studies from them—until the neighbors complained.

For all its merits the *Raft of the Medusa* has some conspicuous disharmonies. The old man with his head supported on his fist [38] near the left edge of the raft is altogether out of key; he suggests a classical philosopher strayed from David's studio into this improbable situation. The body of the nude youth he partially supports, and that of the one to the lower right, head trailing in the water, are magnificent studies in themselves and give the impression of being the parts of the picture that most interested the painter, but they are a little overconspicuous, becoming demonstration pieces. The whole picture, for that matter, may be only a first-rate studio exercise, admirable for the originality and courage of the devices it employs. But this is picking flaws in the work of a very young man whose achievement was to crystallize a new direction for painting. It is difficult to remember that Géricault was a student of Guérin, that candy-box classicist.

Géricault's reputation as a painter could rest on the *Raft of the Medusa* alone, and for that matter it very nearly does. The *Raft* was the only large or complicated composition he ever completed, although he left numerous sketches and some small versions for a similarly ambitious project, *Riderless Races at Rome* [40], races in which riderless horses were goaded into frenzies. He is an uneven painter. Sometimes his pigment has a coarse and heavy-handed quality, and his drawing may be so careless that legs and arms dangle as if shrunken or unattached within trousers or sleeves. At other times his draughtsmanship is masterful, his painting as strong and sure as it is sensitive, as in a *Portrait of a Young Man* [41] attributed to him.

Subjects of cruelty and morbidity occur so frequently in Géricault's work that his detractors hint at unhealthy preoccupations. But an interest in acute sensitivities even to the point of abnormal states of mind was inherent in romantic emotionalism. For the greatest romantics, suffering and violence may be transmuted into expressions of the human spirit struggling for release; and in exploring the dark areas of life the romantic finds beauty in unexpected places. Rembrandt was a romantic in the seventeenth century when he used derelicts and outcasts as models for tragic kings; in faces eroded by suffering he found inner beauties more expressive than the beauty of conventionally handsome sets of features or classically idealized ones. If Géricault is asked to meet such a standard, then it is true that he often seems merely a fascinated observer of madness and physical anguish for their own sakes. But his accurate studies of the insane have a special significance, because they were made

40. GÉRICAULT: *Riderless Races at Rome*, 1817. 17 x 23″. Walters Art Gallery, Baltimore.

41. GÉRICAULT (?): *Portrait of a Young Man*, after 1820. 23¼ x 18¾″. Fogg Art Museum, Cambridge, Grenville L. Winthrop Bequest.

42. DELACROIX: *Self-portrait,* 1837 or 1838. 25¼ x 20″. Louvre, Paris.

at a time when different kinds of insanity were first being recognized by a few doctors, among them Géricault's friend, Doctor Georget, for whom he did a series of paintings.

When Géricault died at thirty-three,* his friend Delacroix was twenty-five. In a lifetime of battle against pedantry, Delacroix was to bring romantic painting to fruition.

Delacroix

As a student and young painter Delacroix was closely attached to Géricault. Géricault was eight years older, wealthy, adventurous, fond of high living, and knowledgeable about the world—about several worlds, in fact. Bohemianism was a natural

---

* This was in 1824; David died the following year. Géricault, who had once had ambitions to be a jockey, died of complications following a fall from a horse.

by-product of the romantic premise that the artist's innate sensitivities are a gift so special that he is under a kind of moral obligation to develop them by indulging them to the fullest. Since these indulgences involve forays outside the bounds of the bourgeois conventions that dominated the nineteenth century, the early romantics confirmed the idea of the artist as a loose-living renegade from society—which still persists. Géricault was Delacroix's mentor as a youthful bohemian in Paris, although both men by birth were wealthy and of high social position.

But after his companion's death, Delacroix abandoned this experimental slumming for his natural habitat, the brilliant world where the upper bohemia of successful actors, writers, and painters overlapped the established order of social position and political intrigue. Here he was admired and sought after, but even while he was still a young man he began to withdraw into his work, seeing only the few people who continued to interest him as his own ideas began to crystallize. That the names of these people were great names (Chopin was his most intimate friend) was only coincidental.

Toward the end of his life Delacroix saw almost no one, remaining at work in his studio as a recluse, but still so glamorous a figure that when he did go out he was followed in the streets as a demigod by the young artists for whom he had become the symbol of revolution, independence, and integrity.

Nothing in Delacroix's life was so important to him as the theories he was developing through experiment and research. He never married, and although he had several liaisons and any number of what he described as "charming encounters," his grand passion was painting. But he was never one of those painters who could dash off a picture. He worked continually and hard; his total works are estimated at more than 12,000, although he was handicapped by various physical ailments, including a recurrent debilitating fever. The man Delacroix is well summed up in his own self-portrait [42] with its attraction, its suggestion of romantic fire, but in the end its

43. Delacroix: *The Lion Hunt,* 1861. 30 x 38⅝″. Art Institute of Chicago, Potter Palmer Collection.

hauteur. He was handsome, febrile, yet somehow unapproachable. Above all he disdained the emotional profligacy and the lack of discipline thought of as typically romantic, which was why he resented classification with such other romantic rebels as the writer Hugo, the musician Berlioz, and, above all, the painter Boulanger, who was Hugo's choice as the official leader of the romantic school. As for Aurore Dupin, the woman who called herself George Sand and led her own life with the romantic lack of discipline of the heroines of her novels, Delacroix knew her long and intimately but referred to her commiseratingly as "Poor Aurore."

Delacroix: His "Classicism"

By the standard of swooning emotionalism and self-indulgence, Delacroix was not a romantic spirit at all. By any standard he was one of the most acutely, objectively analytical men who ever painted a picture. And to understand his art in such typical pictures as *The Lion Hunt* [43] and *The Abduction of Rebecca* [44], we must recognize certain qualities that seem contradictory to romanticism. Delacroix's romanticism is theoretical rather than felt, calculated rather than inborn. He regarded himself as a true classicist, as opposed to the false classicists who merely imitated

44. DELACROIX: *The Abduction of Rebecca*, 1846. 39½ x 32¼". Metropolitan Museum of Art, New York, Wolfe Fund.

classical precedents without understanding the classical spirit. True classicism is concerned with generalizing human experience into universal symbols. Venus is not a beautiful woman, but all beauty; Minerva is not a local bluestocking, but a symbol of the majesty and power of the intellect. The kings in classical tragedy are not certain men who had certain experiences as rulers of kingdoms, but symbols of mankind in its nobility and its frailty. Romanticism, on the other hand, is concerned with the individual and his search not so much for the meaning of life as for the meaning of his own individual life. But the art of Delacroix shows us that creative genius transcends the limits of a category. Categorized as romantic, his Arabs, lions, pashas, warriors, and all the rest do not end as specific individuals represented in one dramatic moment of their lives. They are images of the total emotional life of humanity. The poet and critic Baudelaire called Delacroix's work "a kind of remembrance of the greatness and native passion of the universal man."

Delacroix's effect of romantic vehemence was achieved painstakingly; he invented ways and means to achieve it his turbulent forms in all their complexity are as carefully patterned as are David's static, stylized ones. The famous "drunken "broom" with which the classicists accused him of painting was not drunken at all. The breadth, irregularity, and apparent spontaneity of his brush stroke was produced with as much care as any classical painter took in smoothing out his surface to an impeccable polish. The colors that appear to swarm across Delacroix's canvases, as if jostling and interrupting one another, are selected and juxtaposed by no chance but in accord with theories so highly developed that alongside them the classicist's use of color as a decorative accessory is elementary. Romanticism is emotional, but Delacroix's emotionalism is achieved intellectually. This paradox must be accepted if his work is to be understood.

Delacroix: Early Works and Scandals

Delacroix's career was opened with an early success, *Dante and Vergil in Hell* [45]. This painting, showing the two poets crossing the River Styx, was exhibited in the Salon of 1822 when Delacroix was twenty-four years old. Géricault's true masters, Rubens and Michelangelo, had become Delacroix's also, and they inspired the agitated and tormented forms of the picture. The nude male in the water alongside the boat is especially Michelangelesque; he might be the Adam from the creation scene on the Sistine ceiling in a variation of pose. Delacroix's teacher Guérin was horrified by *Dante and Vergil* and advised him not to exhibit it, but Gros, who was a member of the Salon jury that year, admired it so much that he had it framed at his own expense. Delacroix could not afford a frame; he had lost the fortune he would have inherited from his parents, now dead, in a disastrous lawsuit with another family.

It was at this time that Adolphe Thiers, a shrewd statesman but a man of little taste in the arts, came to Delacroix's rescue with the "mysterious" official patronage that continued, with only occasional interruptions, throughout the artist's life. Although he was the putative son of the French minister to the Netherlands, a man well established in influential circles, Delacroix was prob-

45. DELACROIX: *Dante and Vergil in Hell*, 1821–22. 73½ x 94½". Louvre, Paris.

ably the actual son of a much more influential man, the statesman Talleyrand. Various coincidences support conclusions that could be drawn from his strong resemblance to Talleyrand, and nothing but the presence of an influential behind-the-scenes sponsor explains why Delacroix was virtually a ward of the State after his parents' deaths. His pictures were loathed and feared by Salon juries and vituperated by official critics, but again and again they appeared in the official exhibitions and were purchased by the government. Delacroix was awarded important commissions for murals in public buildings (the Palais Royal, the Palais Bourbon, the Luxembourg, and the Louvre among them) over the heads of the established hacks who would ordinarily have received these lucrative plums, as well as other semiofficial and private commissions where influence was usually more important than talent. Thus the government unwittingly acquired masterpiece after masterpiece and became, in effect, the medium for discrediting the classical hangers-on who were entrenched in its official schools. The dismay of the academicians can be imagined when Thiers manipulated the purchase of *Dante and Vergil* by the State. Delacroix was regarded as an irreverent upstart from this time forward.

46. DELACROIX: *Scenes of the Massacres of Scio,* 1824. 166 x 138½" Louvre, Paris.
47. DELACROIX: Detail from Figure 46 (extreme left of picture).

Two years later, in 1824, Delacroix came into greater prominence with his *Scenes of the Massacres of Scio* [46, 47], of which the Academy made a scandal. Even Gros, who had defended *Dante and Vergil,* reversed his opinion of Delacroix and called *Massacres of Scio* the massacre of painting.

There were routine objections to Delacroix's choice of a contemporary subject,*

---

* As an episode in the Greek-Turkish War, the population of the island of Scio, where 100,000 Greeks had lived, had just been reduced to 9,000 in one of the most terrible massacres in the history of human cruelty. *Scenes of the Massacres of Scio* was in part inspired by Delacroix's admiration of the arch-romantic spirit and romantic poet Lord Byron, whose chivalrous participation in the Greek war cost him his life at Missolonghi in the same year. Delacroix also painted a *Greece Expiring on the Ruins of Missolonghi* as a tribute to Byron and a lament for him as well as a memorial to the Greek insurrectionists.

but what really appalled Gros and the other academicians was Delacroix's use of color. *Massacres of Scio* had come to the jury as a fine example of sound, adequately conventional painting and had been accepted for exhibition. But in the interval between acceptance and the opening of the Salon, Delacroix repainted it. Painters were customarily allowed to retouch or varnish their work after acceptance, but it happened that Delacroix experienced one of the transforming revelations of his artistic life, and was impelled to transform *Massacres of Scio* as a result: he had seen a picture called *The Hay Wain* [313] sent to the Paris Salon that year by the English landscapist Constable.

Constable painted by juxtaposing spots of color rather than blending them. By French academic technique of the time, a passage changing from one tint to another would be meticulously smoothed out or "blended" (there were special brushes for this), but Constable applied his colors in strokes of graduated shades, so that the transition was made in a series of easily perceived jumps, juxtaposed rather than mushed together. The result was a greater freshness, vividness, and life to the color, as well as a sense of more immediate contact between painter and observer. The painter's presence is suggested when we can follow each stroke of his brush; whether we are aware of it or not, our participation in such a painting is greater than it is before a highly polished work where the technique is, so to speak, invisible. Delacroix once said that painting is a bridge between the thought of the painter and the thought of the observer, and Constable's bridge must have seemed to him a more direct and effective one than he had known before. In repainting *Massacres of Scio* Delacroix began the experiments with color that were to occupy him for the rest of his life and were to be enlarged upon by several generations of painters into our own century.* He freed color from the restrictions David had put on it; he revived some of its uses as he observed them in the eighteenth-century painters David had rejected, and he added new ones of his own.

By Davidian formula color is, in effect, nothing more than a decorative dye applied to carefully drawn and modeled forms, as though each object had been completely modeled without color, as though it had been carved in white stone, and the color

then washed over it as a photograph might be tinted. The color of each form—blue drapery, green leaf, gray wall—is held concisely within neat, unyielding contours. But with Delacroix the color explodes, shattering boundaries and unifying all forms with flecks and bits of pigment related to other areas. "Color is a merging of reflections," Delacroix said. An area of blue may be shot through with purples and greens and oranges; a passage of flesh (to which David would have given a smooth, uniform, pinkish tint) will be enriched with green in the shadow, blue in the highlights.

Obviously this aspect of painting is difficult to cope with in verbal description and black and white illustration. Even color illustration is not too much help with the reduction in size and loss of texture involved. But even in black and white it may be sensed that David's color exists only as an overlay. It may be bright and clear, but in Delacroix it is vivid and rich because variations are bound into variations of form; form and color enhance one another. A shift from one color to another as a form projects or recedes in painted space may either emphasize or minimize the projection or recession. Impossible as it is to demonstrate these simple points except in the presence of the paintings themselves, it is important nevertheless to remember that for Delacroix color *was* painting, it was the structure of painting as well as the basis of painting's expressive nature. All this will be more clear in retrospect as we see the painting of the century following Delacroix, because his color is the foundation of theories that build on one another in regular sequence, and are still developing.

Delacroix: His Orientalism

In 1827 Delacroix painted his largest and most ambitious demonstration picture, and the only one that was a failure with both classicists and romantics, *The Death of Sardanapalus*. The subject reflects the vogue for Orientalism that was a strong element in romantic painting and literature, offering as it did all the exotic color and savage passion denied by classical modera-

---

* *The Hay Wain* is a large picture, and loses pertinence as a technical example when reduced to the size of a page. But some of Constable's freshness and freedom as a manipulator of paint may be seen in other illustrations of his work [312, 314]. The question may be asked why Constable's picture was acceptable to the Salon jury if Delacroix's adoption of its technique was found so shocking. One answer is that *The Hay Wain* is a picturesque landscape and hence, by academic category, not a picture of first importance. A formal and pretentious subject had to observe the rules more closely. Also, *The Hay Wain* was painted by an Englishman. Frenchmen have never been able to take English painting very seriously. They find it charming but are unable to think of it as important, and in painting of little importance some eccentricity is not objectionable.

48. DELACROIX: Detail, figures about life size, from *The Death of Sardanapalus*, 1827 version. Louvre, Paris.

jects are spread around in opulent confusion. The confusion was objected to, also the "vulgarity," a favorite word with the critics, who were to continue to apply it over a period of some seventy-five years to the quality of life in any painting not classically stillborn. Oddly enough, if any shortcomings are apparent in *Sardanapalus* today, they do not lie in its confusion, which is calculated, but in the excess of this calculation, which reduces the vitality of the frenzied subject. *Sardanapalus* has passages of superb painting; the flesh of the central female figure [48], the jewels, the stuffs, are as rich as even Rubens could have made them. But the total effect, while gorgeous, is more gorgeous than passionate. Delacroix himself was dissatisfied, and seventeen years later, in 1844, he repeated the picture in much smaller dimensions [49]. In the years between the two versions he had brought his theories to maturity.

The remarkable thing about the late version is that while it was virtually seventeen years in the painting, it has all the effect of spontaneous emotional fervor. When Delacroix said, "All precautions have to be taken to make execution swift and decisive" in order not to lose "the extraordinary impression accompanying the conception" of a picture, he was denying the laborious methods of classicism. But he was denying as well, by the words *precautions* and *decisive*, the hit-or-miss improvisation by which an artist may try to capture the "extraordinary impression accompanying the conception" in the heat of the moment. Delacroix's sketches frequently have this quality of improvisation; there is a sketch in the Louvre for *Sardanapalus* that has it, but the sketch also has the formless, ambiguous passages that are inevitable at the same time. Delacroix's problem was the problem of the romantic creator in any of the arts—to give form to emotional experience without sacrificing its quality of immediacy.

In a subject of violent action the quality of immediacy cannot be retained within the seesaw balance of Davidian composition, as has already been pointed out in the *Raft of the Medusa*, where the composition was built on a strong diagonal movement. But

tion. But among the romantics only Victor Hugo liked *Sardanapalus*, which was at least consistent since, having shown little perception of Delacroix's virtues, he now found virtues in a painting where everyone else found defects.

The potentate Sardanapalus, preparing to immolate himself, is shown on his funeral pyre, which is concealed beneath cushions and a glorious rose-colored fabric, while slaves bring in his favorite wives, horses, and dogs and cut their throats in order that nothing Sardanapalus has enjoyed in life may be enjoyed by anyone else after his death. Jewels and great heaps of other ob-

49. DELACROIX: *The Death of Sardanapalus*, 1844 version. 29¾ x 37″. Collection Henry P. McIlhenny, Philadelphia.

the upward rush of Géricault's shipwrecked figures is still essentially an upward rush across the surface of the picture. In *Sardanapalus* we are led *back into* "space" created by the painter, something like the space of a large stage. The Sabines and the Horatii enact their dramas on the shallow area between footlights and curtain. In the *Raft of the Medusa* the space is hardly deeper, although theoretically the ocean background stretches to the horizon. But in *The Death of Sardanapalus* the curtain has gone up and the stage is filled with figures and trappings surging into its depths, backward and across to the climactic figure of

the dying potentate. It is fine theater, and very romantic theater. It is also composition into the picture depth on a diagonal. The advantages of this kind of composition should be apparent if the effect of turbulence in Delacroix's picture is contrasted with the rigidity of David's. Each type of composition, of course, achieves its own end. By Delacroix's aesthetic, David's composition was obvious and limited. By David's, Delacroix's would have seemed overcomplicated, overdramatic. These contrasting uses of space—shallow and defined, or deep and free—characterize, respectively, neo-classical and romantic composition.

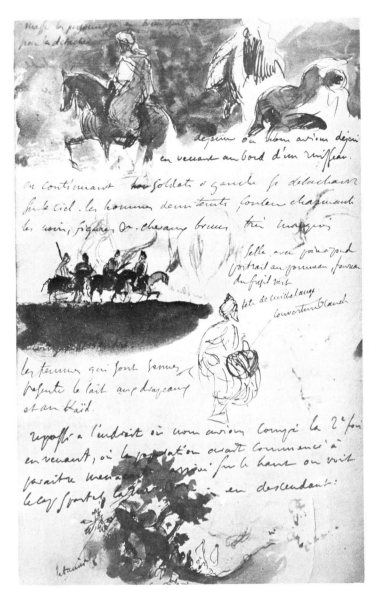

50. Delacroix: Page from his Moroccan journal, April 11, 1832. Ink and watercolor. *Bibliothèque d'Art et d'Archéologie*, Paris.

in 1832 he made a trip to Morocco.[*] From the silvery light of Paris and the civilized emotional climate of that city with its pale and cultivated inhabitants, he was plunged into a world where he was surrounded by half-barbaric figures, golden skinned or black, robed, turbaned, or naked, moving among strange vegetation and strange architecture or against the even stranger blankness of desert sand and desert sky. Everything was revealed in a blazing light where colors were vivified and contrasts were exaggerated beyond anything Delacroix had imagined at second hand.

The first entries about this trip, in the journal where for years he had kept an orderly record of his activities and theories, are the fragmentary and disconnected scribblings of a man clutching at new images so exciting that he is in terror of being unable to absorb them:

"... the sea a dark greenish blue like a fig, the hedges yellow at the top because of the bamboo, green at the base on account of the aloes ... the sons of the caid. The oldest one, his dark blue burnous; caftan of a canary yellow ... a Jewess, red skullcap, white drapery, black dress. Heads of Moors like those of Rubens, nostrils and lips rather coarse, bold eyes. Rusty cannon. Graves amid the aloes and the iris. The almond trees in flower. The Persian lilacs. The little white house in the shadow amidst the dark orange trees. The horse through the trees. The red veil. The beautiful eyes. Wax torches. Tumult."

Everywhere these notes are interspersed with sketches, quick, vivid, spotted with bright notes of watercolor [50]. Delacroix saw everything he had ever imagined, and more—fantastic banquets and entertain-

Between the two versions of *Sardanapalus* Delacroix absorbed the second determining experience of his life—second only to his discovery of color in *Massacres of Scio*. He had tried to develop his theories of color in various Oriental subjects, as offering the most appropriate raw material, but his Orientalism, as in *Sardanapalus*, was of a storybook kind, concocted from hearsay, legend, and the accumulated fantasies of other writers and painters. Then

[*] Delacroix was attached to a mission organized under a young aristocrat, the Count de Mornay. The year before, France had made its conquest of Algeria, and the sultan of Morocco was a touchy neighbor. De Mornay's mission was to conclude a treaty of good will. He had met Delacroix in the upper bohemia of the arts that they both frequented, and attached the artist to his mission at the urging of a sprightly creature named Mlle. Mars, a comédienne and an enthusiastic collector of scalps among the infatuated gallants and intellectuals of her day.

ments in the sultan's palace, local ceremonies among the people, weddings and funerals, and from a window in Tangiers the hysteria of a fanatic religious sect. Everywhere the world was strange, wild, and wonderful.

His notebooks and his recollections were his storehouse after his return. Other painters might have been content to use the exotic material for its inherent color and novelty. But Delacroix was not interested in painted travelogues. The value of the material to him was that he found through it, at last, his synthesis of human emotion and the intellectual devices for its interpretation; the picturesqueness of the material is incidental; the depth of the Moroccan experience is apparent not only in pictures directly connected with it, such as *The Lion Hunt* [43], but also in *The Abduction of Rebecca* [44], which is an incident from Scott's *Ivanhoe*, and the Biblical *Good Samaritan* [51], and in all Delacroix's other work where he realizes Baudelaire's "remembrance of the greatness and native passion of the universal man."

Delacroix: Recognition and Followers

French artists may revile the Academy and may be reviled by it, may abhor the practices of the men who control it, may oppose everything it stands for at the moment—but they continue to venerate it as an institution and as an abstract idea, a symbol of the prestige of the arts in the national life of their country. No matter what their experience of academic abuses, all Frenchmen eligible for election to the Institute of France* covet one of its chairs, and Dela-

* The Institute of France is composed of five Academies, as follows: (1) the French language, (2) literature, (3) social sciences and history, (4) mathematics and physical sciences, (5) fine arts. Each Academy is self-perpetuating; upon the death of a member a new one is elected for life from aspirants who have presented applications. Intrigue and favoritism are inevitable in the elections, and Academy membership has included some of the most trifling talents, but it has also included eventually most of the great ones who have lived long enough.

croix was no exception. He made eight applications, which were rejected, and a ninth which was accepted in 1857, six years before his death.

Even so, the official world continued to snub him on most occasions. In 1861 he completed a set of three murals in the Church of St. Sulpice, after twelve years of work filled with interruptions. The Superintendent of Fine Arts, who was the philistine Count de Nieuwerkerke, refused to look at them; the court and the world of official painting also stayed away from the opening exhibition. Such men as Théophile Gautier and Baudelaire came and admired the pictures tremendously, but whether they were admiring them as mural paintings or as a manifestation of Delacroix's perseverance and integrity in the solution of a difficult problem is a real question. Today, similarly, the St. Sulpice murals are likely to be most praised by those admirers of Delacroix who like to see, in his mural of *Jacob Wrestling with the Angel*, a symbol of the painter's struggle for the fulfillment of his admirable theories. The other subjects were *Heliodorus Driven from the Temple* and, on the ceiling vault, so small and so ill lit that it is seldom noticed, *St. Michael Killing the Dragon*. Compared with his great easel pictures, these are curiously static, dry, overstudied compositions.

Even while Delacroix was being snubbed, the romantic ideal had been vulgarized by his imitators in ways sufficiently emasculated to establish a pseudoromantic product as a standard Salon item. Thus on the coattails of second-raters he was finally accepted as the leader of a recognized school. In the important Salon of 1855, which will be described in some detail later in this book, a room was set aside for some forty of his paintings, amounting to a retrospective of his career. He was elected to the Institute two years later, and he exhibited in the Salon for the last time two years after that, in 1859, with eight pictures. The year of his death, 1863, coincides with the date of the *Salon des Refusés*, also to be treated in detail later, an event that divides the art of the nineteenth century with a boundary as sharp as the one established

51. DELACROIX: *The Good Samaritan*, 1850. 13¾ x 11″. Philadelphia Museum of Art. Anonymous loan.

52. DELAROCHE: *The Children of Edward*, 1830. 71 x 84″. Louvre, Paris.

between the eighteenth and nineteenth centuries by the Revolution and David.

Like David among classical painters, Delacroix is unapproached by any of his romantic contemporaries. This is less surprising than in the case of David, since Delacroix did not teach. But he was imitated. His most superficial imitator was a tremendous success: while Delacroix struggled to achieve his synthesis of human emotions, Paul Delaroche (1797–1856) capitalized on the romantic sentiment of the period by plagiarizing whatever elements of Delacroix's art had become generally palatable. Delaroche was not a true romantic. He was an unimaginative illustrator of historical anecdotes possessed of romantic interest. Historical novels were in great vogue, and Delaroche offered their pictorial counterparts. His pictures are quite objective reproductions of models posed in medieval and Renaissance trappings against period backgrounds. The best known are *The Children of Edward* [52], showing the two little sons of Edward IV in the Tower awaiting execution, and *The Death of Queen Elizabeth*. Both pictures are still seen now and then, and until recently they were used as illustrations in every other schoolbook on English history and literature. Delaroche, only a few months older than Delacroix, was elected to the Institute on the strength of such tepid narratives. Upon Delaroche's death Delacroix, finally elected, assumed his imitator's chair, an irony that comes to mind first when Delaroche's name is mentioned nowadays, because it is the only circumstance lending any interest to his career. He was a student of Gros.

Some other mentionable French romantic painters are listed here, in order of birth:

Alexandre Gabriel Decamps (1803–1860), a respectable painter, was trained as a classicist but revolted early against the tradition. He is discussed later in connection with the Salon of 1855, where he shared honors with Delacroix.

Eugène Devéria (1805–1865), a pupil of Girodet, for a while seemed on the point of major romantic achievement. After a great success in his Salon debut of 1827 with *The Birth of Henry IV* [53], he failed his promise and became a dry and unoriginal painter of history pictures, ending as a second-rate Delaroche. *The Birth of Henry IV* has recently been cleaned up and rehung in the Louvre. For such a huge painting, it is rather easy to pass by; perhaps the competition of *The Death of Sardanapalus* facing it on the opposite wall is too much. But upon examination it is seen to contain many passages of good solid craftsmanship. To find much more is difficult.

Prosper Georges Antoine Marilhat (1811–1847) first appeared in the Salon of 1831. Thereafter he traveled widely in Syria, Egypt, and Palestine, his special version of the Oriental vogue having to do with desert landscapes, caravans, and Oriental cities [54]. He painted with an agreeable illustrative honesty and a nice feeling for pigment.

Eugène Fromentin (1820–1876) was a painter and writer whose Orientalism was derived first from Marilhat, later from Delacroix. As a painter he had considerable facility, but as time goes on his pictures look more and more like attractive exercises in the manner of other men. His writing has retained the freshness that has begun to stale in his painting. Much of his criticism is unusually perceptive.

Alfred Dehodencq (1843–1882) had a satisfactory Salon career; his work is being revived today on a small scale.

Henri Regnault (1843–1871), as his dates show, was a long generation younger than Delacroix. In 1866, at which time Delacroix had been dead for three years, Regnault won the *Prix de Rome* with a classical subject. In Italy he painted his well-known *Automédon and the Horses of Achilles* [55], a stirring picture that might have struck Delacroix himself as promising in its romantic excitement, although it still smacks a bit of brilliant student work. With a first medal in the Salon, a brilliant colorist, intelligent and industrious, he seemed set not only to make a conventional success but, at the same time, to continue and build

53. Devéria: *The Birth of Henry IV*, 1827. 190 x 154". Louvre.

54. Marilhat: *Oriental Caravanserai*, date unknown. 10¾ x 17". Philadelphia Museum of Art, John G. Johnson Collection.

55. H. REGNAULT: *Automédon and the Horses of Achilles,* 1868. 124 x 129½". Museum of Fine Arts, Boston.

56. MICHEL: *The Old Chateau,* date unknown. 20½ x 27⅞". Philadelphia Museum of Art, John G. Johnson Collection.

upon the art of Delacroix. But Regnault was killed at the age of twenty-eight in the Franco-Prussian War.

One other name should be remembered, this time a man who was even earlier than Géricault, Georges Michel (1783–1848). He is a rather isolated painter who is frequently grouped with Géricault among the first romantics. He painted picturesque squalor, bent trees, lonely ruined towers in dramatic silhouette against golden skies [56], referring to Rembrandt for some of his strong effects of chiaroscuro. As a forerunner of romanticism, Michel is still much respected in France but is almost forgotten elsewhere.

CHAPTER 3

Ingres

The Pedant

In 1824, the year of Delacroix's romantic blast with *Massacres of Scio*, the classical school was without a leader. David was not only a very old man but in exile; Gros was floundering and compromising. Both Gérard and Guérin were alive, but neither had the qualifications for leadership. But that year a self-exiled student of David's returned from Italy. He had been working on a large religious picture, *The Vow of Louis XIII* [63], a commission for the cathedral in his provincial home city of Montauban. He brought *The Vow of Louis XIII* with him for exhibition in the Salon, much concerned as to its reception, since he had been in and out of academic favor for a long time and had no idea whether he would be attacked again or received as the prodigal son. There had been a hint that he might be in the Academy's good graces; to his surprise he had been elected its corresponding member in Florence a few months earlier.

The Vow of Louis XIII was a success. The Salon that year centered around it and the scandalous *Massacres of Scio*. Jean August Dominique Ingres (1780–1867) became the new leader of classicism, and for the rest of their lives he and Delacroix were identified as opposing generals in the classic-romantic imbroglio. At times the conflict came down to personal terms—at least on Ingres's part. Eighteen years older than Delacroix, he was an old man before he ever offered his hand to his romantic adversary. Delacroix recognized Ingres's virtues; Ingres never conceded any to Delacroix, perhaps because in his heart he felt ill equipped for the struggle he had en-

57. INGRES: *The Envoys of Agamemnon*, 1801, *Prix de Rome*. 43¼ x 61″. *École des Beaux Arts*, Paris. (Photo Giraudon.)

tered into and was jealous of the ease and flourish with which Delacroix seemed to lead his life. Ingres was a pedestrian personality, stubborn and plodding, while Delacroix was spectacular and aristocratic in contrast to Ingres's humble origin and bourgeois ambition. Delacroix painted brilliantly and theorized even more brilliantly. Ingres's pronouncements were stuffy. From all he wrote and said, it is possible to cull only here and there a phrase not embarrassing in obviousness, obtuseness, and pedantry. He was a poor talker.

But he was a great painter. His own art did not prove the validity of the dogmas he defended; it showed only that no dogma, not even one self-imposed, could stifle a creative spirit so powerful that it demanded expression on any terms. As the official leader of classical painting Ingres had to fight not only Delacroix but a second and even more formidable adversary—the romantic painter who existed within himself.

Unlike Gros, who recognized a similar conflict and subjugated his personal expression to classical doctrine, Ingres seems never to have realized where the problem lay. He was shocked and puzzled when classical painters found his work unclassical. He failed to see that romanticism goes deeper than the surface of strong light and shade, swirling action, broken color, and asymetrical composition, none of which he used. He also failed to see that classicism goes deeper than controlled outline, flat color, tight surface, and symmetrical balance, all of which he continued to use obediently. His attitude toward the Academy remained that of the brilliant student intent upon making good marks to win first prize, even when he was the Academy's leader and spokesman.

Ingres was a great painter in spite of himself. Just how this happened is best explained by examining a group of typical pictures in chronological order.

57

The Student

At seventeen Ingres came to Paris and entered David's studio. His grandfathers had been a tailor and a wig-maker; his father was a carver of sculptural ornaments. At fourteen the boy was playing the violin in an orchestra to make a little money.* Later he won prizes in drawing, and in Paris under David he continued to win them. He became David's favorite student—for a while. David painted his portrait, as affectionate, engaging, and informal a little picture as the great disciplinarian ever allowed himself to do. By 1800 Ingres was assisting David in important work. He painted, for instance, the classical standing lamp that is a conspicuous part of the portrait of *Madame Récamier* [14]. But about this time an unexplained but serious rift developed between Ingres and David. It was never mended.

Ingres had done well in preliminary competitions for the *Prix de Rome* and now, in 1801, he won it. The full subject of his competition picture was *The Envoys of Agamemnon, Sent to Achilles to Urge Him to Fight, Find Him in His Tent with Patroclus Singing of the Feats of Heroes* [57]. As an exercise in the design of male nudes, ranging from the too-muscular giant at the right to the too-lissome youths at the left,† the picture has all the artificiality, the precision, and the respect for recipe of a typical *Prix* winner. It also holds some prophecy of Ingres's future work, the germs of his originality. This originality began to appear during the next few years, to the distress of his sponsors.

The state of France's finances in 1801 was so precarious that, although Ingres had won the *Prix*, no money could be found to send him to Rome. In the five years before the money was available, the State gave him a studio and an allowance-in-disguise in the form of occasional commissions. Ingres also did a number of portraits on his own and exhibited in the Salon. But bizarre elements began to appear in his work—bizarre, that is, by the standard of conformity expected of a *Prix de Rome* man—and they culminated in his portrait of *Madame Rivière* [58], exhibited with several others in the Salon of 1806.

Madame Rivière is a masterpiece of linear design. Present everywhere, its pattern is most apparent in the folds of the gauzy scarf and the large shawl flowing through the lower half of the picture. Here sinuous, there suddenly straightening, here moving slowly, next breaking into swirls or ripples, the lines defining folds and hems have their own beauty as abstract rhythmic patterns more important than their function as description. For the first time Ingres was called "Gothic," an epithet that was to haunt him for life.

Gothic was a term of opprobrium in the classical vocabulary because it summarized the qualities antithetical to *classic*, and the classicists had never admitted the possibility of more than one standard of beauty. In late Gothic sculpture and painting, drapery was represented in exaggerated bunchings and knottings, the opposite of classical simplicity, in patterns of nervous intensity the opposite of classical repose. The intensity is not reflected in Ingres's particular and very personal use of line in the *Madame Rivière*, a graceful and seductive picture. It shares with Gothic art an interest in the edges and contours of bunched forms, but these are organized into a different, more flowing kind of pattern as a way of drawing form and composing a picture. Each line is a delight to follow individually, full of its own sensitivity, invention, and variety, yet no line exists independently. Each one mutually supports and is supported by every other one. The over-all pictorial structure is an integration of broad general movements within which the individual lines are intertwined. A major current flows in a long curve from the bottom of the picture along the hand and up the arm, then along the shoulders where it merges with a quieter, horizontal, stabilizing pattern running from one side of the frame to the other. Such "currents" may be picked up

---

* He continued to play the violin all his life, as a diversion and a solace; hence the phrase *"violon d'Ingres"* by which the French mean any cherished and sustaining hobby.

† —all identifiable according to the story in the *Iliad*, which Ingres studied carefully.

58. INGRES: *Madame Rivière*, Salon 1806. Oval 45⅝ x 35½". Louvre. (Photo Giraudon.)

anywhere in the picture; each one merges or divides along its course to flow into or serve as origin for others.

Consciously or not, Ingres violated the classical dogma of accurate or idealized proportion to create this rhythmic structure. It is true that if the lady should stand up, her arms hanging at her sides would be of grotesquely different lengths. The right one is elongated and the left one, resting on the pillow, is shortened. These distortions were dictated while the abstract pattern was being evolved from a series of natural forms. The long even curve of the right arm establishes the main direction of the linear currents eddying around it; the left one reverses these currents, checks them and brings us into quieter areas (the pillow and the bodice) that serve to relieve and accentuate the more active areas surrounding them. Except to a dogmatist the distortion would be neither noticeable nor disturbing. It is even less noticeable that the figure of Madame Rivière exists ambiguously from the waist down. The linear currents are so fascinating in themselves that it makes no difference that the disposition of the clothing describes only a token relationship between the forms of the body and the couch upon which they lie. But the academicians were outraged, especially because these heresies against academic convention were made by a young man to whom they had already awarded the *Prix de Rome*—for which funds had at last been found.

The Expatriate

With *Madame Rivière* and his other Salon pictures of 1806 labeled "Gothic," "bizarre," and "revolutionary," Ingres left for Rome hurt and confused. He was twenty-six years old; Girodet had not yet painted *The Entombment of Atala*, David was working on *Le Sacre*, Géricault was only fifteen, and Delacroix was a child of eight.

For the next fourteen years Ingres stayed in Rome, and then spent four years in Florence, with a brief excursion to Paris in between. He was thus an expatriate while romanticism announced itself tentatively in *Atala*, made its first sensation with the *Raft of the Medusa*, and found its great man with the exhibition of *Dante and Vergil* in 1822.

Ingres was more than content to stay away. He was as enchanted with Rome as he was disenchanted with Paris. Rather than return, he broke his engagement to a young woman named Anne Marie Julie Forestier, and after another abortive engagement to the daughter of a Danish archeologist he proposed by letter to Madeleine Chappell, a milliner several years older than he and a cousin of one of his

59. INGRES: *Bather of Valpinçon*, 1808. 56⅝ x 38¼". Louvre, Paris. (Photo Giraudon.)

friends in Rome. He had never seen Madeleine, who was in her thirties. She came to Rome and they met, romantically, at the tomb of Nero. The marriage was a success.

During the years in Rome between his arrival and his marriage, the "eccentricities" of Ingres's style had become more and more pronounced, which means that he had continued to develop as an original painter in spite of what he regarded as his loyal adherence to conventional classical disciplines. His *Bather of Valpinçon* [59], painted in 1808, could be Ingres's masterpiece if one picture had to be chosen from many eligible ones. It presents the typical Ingres paradox of classical derivations combined with extremely personal and, now, even sensuous responses. Nominally the *Bather of Valpinçon* has the closest classical associations, since the pose of the figure, with the cloth twisted about one arm, is borrowed from the figure of a Nereid on a Roman sarcophagus. But there all resemblance to classical sculpture ends, and although the picture is smoothly painted, with precisely defined contours, these neoclassical elements are superficial. Again, line is the picture, this time not in the complicated patterns of the *Madame Rivière* but in a reduction of the drawing of the nude body to a few subtle, almost eventless contours, suddenly contrasted with the bunched convolutions of the cloth and the turban, all played against the long straight folds of the curtain at the left, briefly echoed at the upper right. Like the contours, the modeling of the body is reduced to an ultimate simplicity and is correspondingly subtle. And a new—and thoroughly un-Davidian—element appears in the painter's sensuous response to the warmth and softness of the naked flesh.

The first series of Roman paintings reaches its climax three years later (1811) in *Jupiter and Thetis* [60, 61]. Ingres's *Prix de Rome* picture had shown Achilles and his loved friend Patroclus being called into Agamemnon's support by his ambassadors. *Jupiter and Thetis* illustrates a climactic episode later in the same story. It is certainly the most bizarre of all Ingres's paintings. The curious distortion of the woman's throat, the indescribable quality of her arms, flowering into tiny hands, the fantastic complications of the drapery falling from her body and disposed in utterly illogical folds and rills, the figure of Jupiter with its gigantic, soft torso and its diminutive face encircled by a black wreath of hair and beard—all these, with all the other curious and meticulous details, pushed just to the point of the grotesque, even to the edge of the repellent, are saved in the end by the assurance of their design and, above all,

by the sensation they convey that they are distilled from secret inner experience.

Actually, the picture follows explicitly Homer's account of how Thetis, a sea nymph, begged Jupiter to grant victory to the Trojans, to avenge an insult to her son Achilles. The request is granted in spite of the fact that in granting it, Jupiter must incur the wrath of Juno. The god had once renounced his secret love for Thetis and yielded her to Achilles' father.

In his copy of a French version of the *Iliad*, Ingres marked a passage that especially interested him; a paraphrase may give some idea of how closely he captured the essence of the episode:

"Thetis arose from the waves of the sea, and at the break of day rose through the immensity of the sky to Olympus. There she found him whose eye sees all the universe, the son of Saturn, seated far from the other gods on the highest summit of the mountain. She appeared before him and, with one hand upon his knees and lifting the other to his chin, she implored the monarch. But the god who commands the clouds answered nothing; he remained long in silence. Then this god of thunder let escape from his breast a profound sigh, and said, 'I promise you the satisfaction of your desires, and in pledge I accord you the sign of my sacred head.' Thus he spoke, and knit his black brows; the divine hair stirred upon the immortal head, and vast Olympus trembled, and Thetis, from the height of dazzling Olympus, threw herself again into the depths of the sea."

Yet, in spite of Ingres's close adherence to the text, *Jupiter and Thetis* is not a literary picture, not a mere illustration. It is complete in itself, legitimately and independently a pictorial expression. Even with no literary reference as a guide, the observer cannot but understand the drama of the moment, the nymph's hesitant temerity as she touches the face of the god, the power of the god himself, and the tension as he weighs whatever secrets must determine his response.

Jupiter and Thetis was the last of the paintings Ingres sent back to Paris under the regulation requiring an annual work

60. INGRES: Detail from Figure 61. (Photo Giraudon.)

from a *Prix de Rome* winner, and he kept a special affection for it all his life. It is the most personal of his major works, impregnated as it is with the element that most intimately characterizes Ingres's art, an element regarded dubiously by many people attempting to evaluate him: an obsessive sexuality that defies the mask of classical idealization. Basic to Ingres's conception of his subjects (in all likelihood unconsciously so on Ingres's part), sexuality is present as if by subterfuge. Where an open and virile masculine sensuousness would not be questionable, there is a suggestion of secret sensual revery. A psychiatrist might find it natural that *Jupiter and Thetis* and others of Ingres's early Roman pictures with the same quality were painted while the ar-

61. INGRES: *Jupiter and Thetis*, 1811. 130 x 101″. *Musée Granet*, Aix-en-Provence.

tist's personal life was disturbed by his two abortive engagements and the curious circumstances of his courtship of Madeleine Chappell, and equally natural that after his happy marriage in 1813 his painting took a "healthier" direction. But these same pictures can be defended as Ingres's finest work. According to one theory, all creative art is a kind of purification for the artist, and if *Jupiter and Thetis* was abstracted from Ingres's personal emotional confusions then it is a very "modern" picture of a kind frequent in the twentieth century, where the creative act becomes a kind of release and a private confessional for the artist, and the resulting work of art is only incidentally intended for the public, who is free to make of it what it will.

The Troubadour

In Rome Ingres found in Raphael a new idol among the old masters, and for him the fifteenth-century Italian replaced all other official academic deities. Ingres's nature inclined toward gentle grace, which Raphael offered; at the same time Raphael was acceptable to an avowed classicist because his derivations from classical antiquity were quite direct. But Raphael's influence on Ingres was not altogether for the best and is an element in a not very happy footnote to his total work: his troubadour pictures.

Troubadour painting was a school within a school, and although it flourished under painters who had been trained by David, classical subjects were abandoned for historical anecdotes of the middle ages and the Renaissance. Ingres, their contemporary, painted troubadour subjects when these men were having their first success, combining this kind of picture with the ones we have just seen. His troubadour subjects included a *Betrothal of Raphael*, painted in 1812, no doubt more than coincidentally the year of his own second betrothal, and *Raphael and La Fornarina*. These were the only two pictures Ingres completed in a projected series covering the life of his new idol. He repeated the second subject many times, finally with a variation as late as 1860, of which he wrote, "I hope it will cause all the others to be forgotten." He also made repeated versions of *Paolo Malatesta and Francesca da Rimini* [62]. Other subjects were *Henry IV Playing with His Children While the Spanish Ambassador Is Being Admitted, King Philip of Spain Investing the Marshal of Berwick with the Golden Fleece, The Death of Leonardo da Vinci in the Arms of Francis I,* and *Aretino in the Studio of Tintoretto.* These labored storytelling pictures seem a waste of Ingres's meticulous technique. Except for the two Raphael subjects and the *Paolo and Francesca* they hardly suggest his linear beauties.

It was specifically the vogue for troubadour painting that inspired David's complaint in 1808 that the direction he had set for the fine arts was too severe to please for very long in France. "In ten years the study

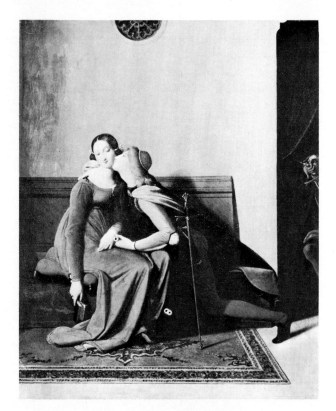

62. INGRES: *Paolo Malatesta and Francesca da Rimini, c.* 1814. Panel, 13¾ x 11". *Musée Condé,* Chantilly.

of the antique will be abandoned," he said. "I hear the antique praised on every side but when I try to find it applied, I discover that it never is. All these gods, all the heroes, will be replaced by chevaliers, by troubadours singing beneath the windows of their lady-loves, at the foot of medieval towers." The invasion of Olympus by troubadours was another of the many indications that the romantic spirit was inherent in the thought and feeling of the early nineteenth century. The troubadour subject was natural to romanticism and was much used in romantic treatments by romantic painters and dramatists, and troubadour pictures were also among the ancestors of the acres of history pictures covering Salon walls later on. As far as Ingres was concerned, the subjects offered him nothing, nor did he have anything to bring them. And there is much of their dryness in the important but essentially dull *Vow of Louis XIII.*

63. INGRES: *The Vow of Louis XIII*, 1824. (Upper portion, width 103".) Cathedral, Montauban.

64. INGRES: *Apotheosis of Homer*, 1827. 152 x 203". Louvre, Paris.

The Prodigal

But whatever its faults, *The Vow of Louis XIII* [63] was a success with everyone. After its triumphant exhibition in the Salon of 1824, the classicists, relieved to have found a new leader, welcomed the *Vow* as his inaugural address, and the romantics, including Delacroix, were glad to see the end of the Davidian formula. The classicists' approval was an about-face; they had consistently attacked Ingres's Salon pictures. Cries of "Gothic" had resounded again in 1819. By some extraordinary feats of critical gymnastics invoking as a bad example the Italian primitive master Cimabue, the academicians had managed to make the same objections to the simplicity of Ingres's Roman painting* that they had made to the complications of *Madame Rivière*.

The Vow of Louis XIII was acceptable to the academicians because it was a thoroughly derivative picture. Ingres received the commission for it in the first place on the strength of a painting of *Christ Delivering the Keys to St. Peter*, which he had completed in 1820 for the Church of San Trinità dei Monti in Rome, a lamentable picture, a pasting together, to the point of plagiarism, of elements from Raphael. *The Vow of Louis XIII*, while it remains a greatly respected work today, is really not much better on that score, although the pasted-together ensemble is more agreeable. But for the academicians this fault was a virtue. They were willing to accept the renegade who had returned to the fold with a large imitation of a certified old master. They forgave the original excesses of his youth.

Delighted to return, Ingres remained in Pairs for ten years. He received one official award after another and was named President of the *École des Beaux Arts*, the official school. He taught the academic recipes to as many as a hundred students at a time, enforcing classical dogma relentlessly (teaching beauty as one teaches arithmetic, Delacroix said), and he was even success-

* Specifically, the objections centered on a reclining nude, the *Grande Odalisque*, now in the Louvre. See [89].

ful now and then in reducing his own art to dry conformity. His major commission of the period, the *Apotheosis of Homer* [64], is an exquisitely studied demonstration of the classical rules, the picture every *Prix de Rome* contestant would have painted if he could have.

But the accord between Ingres and the world of academic success was not quite as warm as it appeared to be. He had grown increasingly irascible, and when another large religious picture, *The Martyrdom of St. Symphorien* [65], received a bad reception in the Salon of 1834, Ingres asked to be transferred back to Rome as Director of the Academy there. He was given the appointment and left again for Italy in much the same frame of mind as before. He refused all commissions, forbade henceforth the showing of any of his pictures in the Salon, and painted, among others, two pictures in which the spirit of his early Roman work is recalled with renewed and extraordinary intensity.

In both of these a languorous sexuality is expressed in forms of brilliant precision, a contrast that comes close to being jolting in one of them, the vividly tinted *Odalisque with the Slave* [66]. The other, *Stratonice* [67] repeats the subject with which David had won the *Prix de Rome* long before [5] and in spirit recalls Ingres's own *Jupiter and Thetis*. Within an elaborate Greek interior, where every mosaic, every vein of marble, every smallest detail of carved ornament, every implausible fold of drapery, is rendered with the microscopic intensity of a revelation, a dream, or a vision, the figures in the drama of repressed passion are transfixed in attitudes of extreme artificiality. Like *Jupiter and Thetis*, *Stratonice* is saved from mawkishness or absurdity by qualities that may be sensed but are not easy to explain. They have to do with the consistency of the vision, where each of a multitude of details is conceived in harmony with all the others, and conception is totally integrated with execution. It is possible to be puzzled by this conception or to be unsympathetic to it, but it is impossible not to feel that every form, every line, and every relationship of the painted images are expressions of emotional con-

65. INGRES: *The Martyrdom of St. Symphorien*, 1865. 14⅛ x 12¼". Reduced replica with minor variations from the picture for the Cathedral of Autun, 1834. Philadelphia Museum of Art, John G. Johnson Collection.

victions passionately held by the artist who created them.

Ingres completed these two pictures, after interruptions, in 1840. He was sixty years old. The following year, in bad health, he returned to Paris. The prodigal's second homecoming was triumphant with official receptions and awards. He began work on two mural commissions, *The Golden Age* and *The Age of Iron*. The first was never finished and the second was only sketched in. The fragments are not impressive. Possibly Ingres might have reached some conclusion to the struggle between sensuous forms, academic doctrine, and elaborated allegory that tears them apart, but in their present state they are like battlegrounds abandoned in fatigue.

66. INGRES: *Odalisque with the Slave*, 1842. 28 x 39⅜″. Walters Art Gallery, Baltimore.

67. INGRES: *Stratonice*, 1866. 24 x 36¼″. *Musée Fabre*, Montpellier. Variation on version of 1840. *Musée Condé*, Chantilly. (Photo Giraudon.)

In 1849 Madeleine Chappell died. The marriage that had begun with such an extraordinary courtship had been an ideal one, and Ingres was inconsolable until three years later when he yielded to the urging of friends and remarried, at seventy-one. In 1855 he was induced to relent in his determination never to exhibit again in the Salon, and like Delacroix in that year he had a gallery to himself for a retrospective collection. There were further honors at home—he was even named a senator in 1862—and his renown became international with honorary membership in the academies of other countries. When he died in 1867 he was eighty-six years old. He had outlived Delacroix, although classicism had not.

Two pictures from these last years enjoy somewhat inflated reputations. In 1820 Ingres had begun work on a standing female nude, *La Source* [68]. Now, thirty-six years later, he completed it with the help of pupils. The figure with its softened contours and cottony flesh is a superior academic studio piece, but it is a very poor second to the two great Roman nudes, the *Bather of Valpinçon* and the *Grande Odalisque*. The face, a symmetrical mask on the classical formula, has grown vapid. By most standards *La Source* is a fine picture, but not by the standard of Ingres at his greatest.

In 1862 (according to the date on the picture) or 1863 (according to a letter in which he mentions it) Ingres completed *The Turkish Bath* [69], a recombination of figures from several pictures painted in different periods. The Bather of Valpinçon, now playing a mandolin, dominates a confused arrangement of some twenty-five naked and ill-assorted harem women, ranging downward from the Bather's undiminished loveliness to the almost comical vulgarity of the squirming masses of flesh in the background. One conspicuous head, just behind the upraised arm of the reclining figure in the right foreground, with its cheek against the ear of the adjoining figure, is wedged into the composition in such a way that it would be physically impossible for a body to exist normally attached to it. *The Turkish Bath* had a difficult history, explaining some of its defects.

68. INGRES: *La Source*, 1820–56. 64½ x 32¼″. Louvre, Paris. (Photo Giraudon.)

Ingres completed it about 1852 as a rectangular composition, then reworked it several times, once after it had been returned by a purchaser, and finally changed its shape to the present circular one, with necessary additions and subtractions. He was eighty-three by the time he made this final revision.

69. INGRES: *The Turkish Bath, c. 1852–63. Diameter 42½". Louvre, Paris.

Portraits and Drawings

As a portraitist Ingres was so prolific and worked so frequently at his highest level that it is difficult to eliminate dozens of superb pictures in order to select a representative few. The early "Gothic" portrait of *Madame Rivière* has already been considered. In comparison with it, the portrait of his friend the painter *François Marius Granet* [70] is more restrained, not only because the subject is a man but because Ingres has come under new influences. He never repeated the complexity of linear flow that marked *Madame Rivière*, either because of the criticisms of it or because in

Italy he discovered the portraits of the Italian Renaissance and was attracted by their greater simplicity—or, of course, because of both. In the portrait of Granet, the head surmounts a generally pyramidal mass and is lifted above the distant horizon in order to play its lines and shapes against an eventless passage of sky. The strongest value contrasts, the white collar and the dark hair, frame the face as a further assurance that it will remain the undisputed focal point of the composition. The architectural landscape background is full of interest, but since it is reduced to small scale in the distance it emphasizes the largeness of the figure to lend it additional importance.

70. INGRES: *François Marius Granet*. Date unknown. 28¾ x 24″. Museum, Aix-en-Provence.

71. INGRES: *Comtesse d'Haussonville*, 1845. 53½ x 36¼″. Copyright The Frick Collection, N.Y.

These are all standard Renaissance devices worn threadbare in the work of any number of painters who used them in very much the way Ingres did; they are not difficult to employ skillfully. Ingres's *Granet* is a masterpiece because over this conventional framework he builds his own linear pattern, combining the sinuosities of the edges of the open cape and its thrown-back collar with the contrasting solidity of its general silhouette; contrasting equally the unqualified rectangularities of the book, the bit of wall, and the buildings in the background, with the irregular shapes of the white collar, the head, and the locks of hair patterned against the forehead. All the forms have more mass, more solidity, and are more naturalistic than those of the *Madame Rivière*, but they are still drawn in linear arabesques that have their own abstract beauty. And in both portraits the sensuousness of Ingres's response to human beauty warms and illuminates these images presented with such precision and control.

The background of the *Granet* is a specific reference to place. It shows the Villa Medici, the Renaissance palace acquired by the French Academy as its Roman base. With its gardens, its fantasy of a façade, its sculpture, its great halls, its towering position on the most beautiful of the Roman hills, looking across the most spectacular panorama of the city, the Villa Medici was a paradise for the *Prix de Rome* winners, who lived and painted there (and still do). Like Ingres, Granet was a *Prix de Rome* man. (For a while he enjoyed a success in Paris, although his work is forgotten today—which is a mercy.) Ingres's portrait of him hangs in the municipal museum in his home city of Aix-en-Provence. A few feet away *Jupiter and Thetis* covers the end

72. INGRES: *Comtesse de Tournon*, 1814. 36⅝ x 28¾". Collection Henry P. McIlhenny, Philadelphia.

wall of the gallery, a combination evoking Ingres's young manhood in Rome.

The general formula of the *Granet* served Ingres for many of his finest early portraits. In later ones, such as that of the young *Comtesse d'Haussonville* [71], done in 1845, he shows greater dependence on accessory details for their inherent interest as objects, more complication for the sake of stunning naturalistic rendering (in the stuff of the dress, for instance) at the expense of linear invention. Toward the end this tendency dominated the painter to the point where a portrait is in danger of hold-

ing more interest as a contemporary record of an interior and a lady's toilette than as a transmutation of fact into art. But Ingres never entirely succeeded in his effort to be anything but himself. Ingres the academician never quite managed to stifle Ingres the original artist.

Ingres had one great limitation as a portrait painter, if one demands that a portrait be not only a fine painting but an interpretation of character. In his average portrait whatever we learn of the sitter's character we must infer by association. Sometimes these associations are strong. The early

(1812) portrait of the *Comtesse de Tournon* [72] presents one vivid individual among Ingres's gallery of somewhat repetitious and superficially explored personalities. Yet even in this case we may feel that the old Countess was a person of such sprightly character and such characterizing features that some reflection of her individuality was inevitable in anything like an accurate reproduction of her appearance. Here the sitter seems to have imposed her personality upon the painter, where ordinarily when Ingres painted a portrait it was the other way around.

The great exception among all Ingres portraits is the one of *Monsieur Bertin* [73], the founder and director of *Le Journal des Débats*. Here it is obvious that Ingres was seeking something beyond a satisfactory "likeness" or an elegant effigy. The selection of pose, the tension in the position of the hands on the knees as the man leans forward slightly, the elimination of accessory detail, the sharp, decisive patterning of the hair—which in a preliminary drawing is shown to have been, actually, rather limp and characterless—all contribute to the impression of shrewdness and energy that would not have been present in a simple transcription of the subject's appearance as he sat patiently for the artist.

A drawing by Ingres is of such delicacy that it is brutalized in even the best reproduction. He drew constantly and made innumerable preliminary studies for his paintings. The *Musée Ingres* in his native city of Montauban is the great treasure house of these studies, but hundreds of Ingres drawings are in museums and collections elsewhere. These include especially the small portrait sketches in pencil made sometimes as preliminary studies, or often as a souvenir given in affection or in an effort at ingratiation to the aristocrats who came through Rome in steady streams. One of these is the *Comte Turpin de Crissé* [74], with the head typically modeled in more detail than the figure, which is sketched in with absolute assurance but with only an occasional light indication of shadow to enhance the form, which is otherwise revealed entirely by line. Ingres frequently catches a stronger suggestion of personality in these

73. INGRES: *Monsieur Bertin*, 1832. 45¾ x 37⅜". Louvre, Paris.

drawings than he tries for in more carefully studied paintings. Jaunty elegance, alert, sophisticated intelligence, social aplomb, and even a hint of amused cynicism are presented in the features and the pose as Ingres has transcribed them quickly here with the model before him. If Ingres seldom reflects his sitter's individuality with equal brilliance in his paintings, it is because his immediate response to a subject, which was instinctively perceptive, was not ordinarily increased and deepened by further reflection; rather it was lessened by further study of the portrait as a problem in design. If this is a limitation it must be accepted as one playing its own part, not necessarily negative, in Ingres's creation of some of the most extraordinarily effective portraits in the European tradition.

In his portraits Ingres is a great stylist; so is he, of course, in his subject pictures. But he must remain only a stylist, nothing more,

74. INGRES: *Comte Turpin de Crissé,* probably 1818. Pencil on white paper. 11⅝ x 8⅞". Collection Walter C. Baker, New York.

even in such pictures as *Jupiter and Thetis,* unless his characterizing element of hidden and even unconscious personal emotional expression is recognized. Baudelaire, who was so perceptive of the universal significance of the conceptions released through Delacroix's romantic forms, searched uneasily in the art of Ingres for meanings he seems to have suspected were concealed beneath the polished surface and fettered within the implacable contours of Ingres's style. He never convinced himself that these meanings were there. But the twentieth century, with its exploration of the hidden impulses of the creative act, has revealed Ingres as an intense, intimate, and even secret artist of the most personal kind beneath his stylizations and pedantry.

CHAPTER 4

Realism

Idealism and Disillusion

For all their differences, the classicists and the romantics held one conviction in common, and it was a basic one: they thought of life and the world as a mystery that could be explored to discover the reason for man's existence. Neither doubted the assumption that we are here for a reason and that our being is justified and meaningful. For both, nature—all the different facets of life, of the world—was what Delacroix called "a vocabulary" that could be used to study the mystery's solution. Classic or romantic, the idealist assumes that within all the conflicts and contradictions, all the ambiguities and confusions of life, somewhere there is a harmony, a discoverable truth, by which man can understand the fact that he exists. The forces around him and within him, all apparently working at odds against one another, must certainly be not accidental, as they appear to be, but animated toward meaningful order; must certainly be some part of a universal plan within which we move for some purpose toward some reward, some profound satisfaction of the human yearning to be more than an organism that is born, suffers, and dies.

The classicist sought to clarify the mystery by intellectualizing man's experience. The romantic sought its heart in the more ambiguous area of the "soul" and was willing to cultivate even life's suffering in the conviction that emotional experience holds the answer everyone seeks. But in the end —and this is the important point—both classicist and romantic were idealists, refusing to accept the world at face value, rejecting it in the end, forcing the experience of life into their respective and equally arbitrary molds in spite of repeated evidence

75. GOYA: *The Sleep of Reason Produces Monsters*, 1797–98. Etching and aquatint, 8¾ x 5⅞″. From the *Caprichos*. Philadelphia Museum of Art, gift of Smith, Kline and French Laboratories.

Goya: His World

Goya was a contemporary of David almost to the exact years, having been born two years earlier than the master of classicism and dying three years after him. Yet as a young man he discarded the classicism of his teachers, and he was never affected by the type of romanticism that developed in France. In his very old age Goya visited Paris and is said to have admired the work of the young Delacroix. But he could have told himself that the vehemence of his own work—its emotional color and its dramatic force—not only exceeded that of this Frenchman who was fifty-three years younger but that his, Goya's, art was born from a fervent experience of life that gave it a vitality alongside which Delacroix's romanticism was a theoretical demonstration.

Because of his fire and his dramatic vigor, Goya is often called a romantic painter. Because he deals so frequently with horrors and with the fantastic, he may appear to be a painter of the world of imaginative emotionalism inhabited by one type of romantic. But Goya was a realist because he saw the world without illusion. No other painter has seen it more naked of saving grace, either of reason or of sentiment, of intellect or of soul. Even when his visions are most monstrous, even when he is most outraged by what he sees and records it most violently, Goya is a realist in the basic sense: he sees the world around him for what it is and he accepts its existence as unalterable fact. The world Goya saw was not a world he could condone; but neither did he hope to change it or to discover hidden within it the classicist's order or the romantic's yearning conviction of some ultimate, if undecipherable, meaning.

The circumstances surrounding Goya in his daily life as a Spaniard offered no nourishment for idealism of any kind. While David was synthesizing an art in praise of Reason, stimulated by the French philosophers who had deified it, Goya was working at the court of Spain, surrounded by a group of human monsters who have never been surpassed for stupidity, viciousness, ignorance, greed, and corruption, in a coun-

that they could never get more than a part of it to fit.

By the middle of the nineteenth century, twenty-five years after David's death and a decade before Delacroix's and Ingres's, painters were becoming disillusioned with idealism in either form and were turning to realism, which in several forms was to dominate painting until near the end of the century. Meanwhile, the movement had been anticipated by one of the most unillusioned painters who ever lived, the Spaniard Francisco Goya (1746–1828).

75

try intellectually all but inert, with a populace brutalized by poverty, bigotry, and oppression. The national characteristics of Spain included a catalogue of all evil and misery, and Goya's observation of the world gave him no reason to believe that the eighteenth-century philosophers' dream of Reason had produced anything more than monsters. He said as much in a print showing a student asleep over his books while the air around him is filled with screech owls and bats [75]. The print has been given various interpretations, but any interpretation must accept its premise of the triumph of nightmare. Man's incapacity to think his way toward reasonable and humane existence is parabled in another print [76] in which a philosopher or teacher mouths by rote the phrases of learning to an audience deaf, dumb, and blind to thought of any kind, the whole scene taking place upon a branch so rotten that it will presently drop everyone into an abyss of which they are not even aware.

The wonder is that from such a world a man like Goya managed to emerge at all. To his common origin he owed his physical vigor and, for that matter, his intellectual vigor, which would have been stultified and corrupted if he had grown up in the world he entered later. To this world, the world of his patrons, the court and the circles surrounding it, he owed his living, the opportunity to paint, and thus eventually his fame, but he never conceded a point in his contempt for it. Goya was incapable of the kind of flattery exercised by David when he painted Napoleon's disintegrating empress as a mere slip of a girl in *Le Sacre*. Fortunately, flattery was never required of him. His portraits of the royal family are explicitly of abominable, contemptible, mediocre, or at best pathetic characters. That these portraits were accepted and that he was commissioned to repeat them is proof enough that the sitters were as stupid as he painted them to be, so satisfied with themselves that they admired their own images without seeing the ghastly revelation beneath the painted reflections.

The Family of Charles IV [77] shows a group of pompous freaks, swathed in velvets and silks and dripping with jewels. It

76. GOYA: *Ridiculous Folly*, 1813–20. Etching and aquatint. 9½ x 13¾". From the *Disparates*. Philadelphia Museum of Art, gift of Mrs. R. Sturgis Ingersoll.

has been nicknamed once and for all "the grocer and his family who have just won the Grand Lottery," a witticism hard on grocers and their families but charitable to the King of Spain and his. The monarch stands in the foreground on the right, his chest and belly ablaze with decorations. A glance is enough to substantiate the story that during the day he would ask his minister, a villain named Manuel Godoy, "how things were going" and without waiting for an answer would consider his obligations as ruler of a nation completed for another twenty-four hours. His grotesque queen stands in the center, embracing her daughter and holding the hand of her son awkwardly enough to suggest that these maternal gestures were unfamiliar ones for her. These children are presumed to have been fathered by the same Manuel Godoy, whose duties at court extended beyond the usual ministerial ones. This queen, Maria Luisa of Parma, also granted her favors to an occasional servant. There have been more vicious women in history, but they were women of greater intelligence and hence capable of greater inventiveness than this one. To the left foreground is Ferdinand, heir to the throne, who is a blank. Behind him is the face of a witch, the King's sister. Only the young couple at the

77. GOYA: *The Family of Charles IV*, 1800. 110 x 132″. Prado, Madrid. (Photo Anderson.)

extreme right seem normal. Goya has sympathetically concealed the spinal deformity with which this one of the King's children was born, translating it into a posture twisted because she carries her child in her arms. Her young husband is also a human being. But the children on each side of the Queen are devoid of innocence. The hard-faced little boy is like his father—not the King—and the girl is already an echo of her mother. Behind this collection, almost obscured in deep shadow, at the far left, Goya is at work on the picture.

In Goya's art his contempt for the men around him widens to become a horror of mankind. In his portraits of children he comes closest to relenting, yet even here, as in the *Don Manuel Osorio de Zuñiga* [78], he may see purity and innocence as nothing but fodder for corruption. From the shadows behind the utterly charming image of the little boy gleam the eyes of cats in wait to devour the fragile bird. Goya's young women are creatures of fire and beauty, but without tenderness, and he is fond of playing them in front of figures of frightful old hags. On the surface this contrast reminds us that youth and beauty are transient, but it is even more emphatically a statement that the human spirit is not only subject to

78. GOYA: *Don Manuel Osorio de Zuñiga, c.* 1787. 50 x 40″. Metropolitan Museum of Art, New York, Jules S. Bache Collection.

79. GOYA: *Que Tal?, c.* 1801. 71¼ x 48½″. *Palais des Beaux Arts,* Lille.

corruption but apparently, to Goya's way of thinking, impotent to withstand it. *Que Tal?* [79] tells us that time does not ripen humanity into wisdom, but rots and withers it into foolishness and evil.

For Goya, evil is the ultimate reality, violation and degradation are man's fate. He never condones these truths, holding them to be self-evident, but he hardly protests against them. He states vehemently that they are abominable, but he never suggests the possibility of amelioration or correction. *And Nothing Can Be Done about It* is the title of another of his prints [80], one from a series making up as horrifying a record of cruelty as has ever been set down in any medium: Goya's *Disasters of War.*

Between 1808 and 1814 Goya witnessed the Napoleonic invasions of Spain, the guerrilla warfare that followed them, the famine of 1812 that was one result of them, and the return of the Inquisition under Ferdinand VII. Even granting the different viewpoints of a Frenchman and a Spaniard on the subject of Napoleon, we must recognize that the contrast between the treatment of the Napoleonic legend in French painting and Goya's observation of terrible fact is a legitimate, if extreme, example of the difference between romantic or classical idealism and realism. There is no glory in Goya's war, no grandeur in victory or grand emotion in defeat; there are only rape, slaughter, and mutilation. His subject is human bestiality. The victims get second billing to the rapists, butchers, and mutilators; we are appalled by the perpetrators but not led to great compassion for the vic-

80. GOYA: *And Nothing Can Be Done about It* (*Y no hai remedio*), 1810–20. Etching and aquatint, 15½ x 16⅝". Philadelphia Museum of Art, gift of Smith, Kline and French Laboratories.

tims, whose agony, no matter how frightful, we must accept as a human condition beyond correction. Gros's *Pesthouse at Jaffa* [33] is by comparison an Elysium.

In such a world reality is close to nightmare, and if we have called Goya a realist we must also say that he created some of the most fantastic visions in the history of art. *The Disasters of War* are realistic in fact and in representation, lamentable as it may be that the world offers material for this realism. The set of prints called the *Caprichos* are fantasies, yet their comments on greed, superstition, stupidity, bigotry, avarice, and indifference are comments on man as a social being with responsibilities for which he is accountable, a concept that is fundamental in realistic art. The *Caprichos* are social comment made in terms of the grotesque, the monstrous, and the hallucinatory. In some of Goya's work, the hallucination passes beyond such comment and becomes a symbolical damnation of hu-

manity, as in the ghastly *Saturn Devouring His Sons* [81]. These morbidities are Goya's answer to the romantic dream of noble passions, and instead of the classicists' Olympians he shows a terrifying *Colossus* [82] dwarfing the world, a magnificent and brutish figure who dominates the universe yet looks upon it without comprehension.

Goya: His Isolation

Some of the most trenchant observations of human vanity and corruption have been made by painters or writers who have moved freely within a specific world, and have been accepted as part of it by its denizens, while within themselves they have remained separated from it by some isolating circumstance. These men remain free to observe with the objectivity of an outsider, yet with intimate access to their material. Goya was such a man. As the

81. GOYA: *Saturn Devouring His Sons*, date unknown. 57½ x 32½". Prado, Madrid. (Photo Anderson.)

82. GOYA: *Colossus*, c. 1818. Etching and aquatint, scraped, 11⅜ x 8¼". Metropolitan Museum of Art, New York.

official painter of the court he was intimately associated with the aristocratic world. His mistress was the Duchess of Alba, supposed to be the most beautiful woman in Spain and by all accounts so entrancing that she is forgiven much that would be held against a plainer woman. This was a real love affair, and in spite of the Duchess's high station, it was not so much a part of Goya's participation in the world of wealth and position as it was a continuation of his youth as a hard-working and hard-living painter in Madrid's world of brawls and the bull ring. Goya himself was an amateur bullfighter and, by legend, a good one. Later he did a series of

etchings, the *Tauromachia*, on this sport or art. Here, as in his paintings of the life of the city, its strollers, its beggars, its people of the streets, he is established historically as a realist finding material in the life around him and commenting on it in contemporary terms, without reference to ancient gods and heroes or exotic or picturesque places or customs. (If the city life he painted has an exotic flavor for us, it did not for him.)

Goya's withdrawal from this life—from life in general, for that matter—a spiritual withdrawal that left him a figure moving actively among people yet observing them from seclusion, was the result of a desperate

83. GOYA: *Portrait of His Wife, Josefa Bayeu, c.* 1798. 32 x 22″. Prado, Madrid. (Photo Anderson.)

The first years of deafness and isolation produced the *Caprichos*, a set of eighty aquatints† first announced to the public in 1797 and published two years later. *The Sleep of Reason Produces Monsters* [75] was its first plate and its theme. In the *Caprichos* unreasonable man defeats himself and tortures his fellows with every cruelty, indignity, and foolishness; the pattern of Goya's pessimism is set, and from this time on, circumstances continue to increase his paradoxical combination of vehemence and detachment. In 1802 the Duchess of Alba died. Goya was fifty-six years old. He witnessed the Napoleonic invasions and the uprisings in Madrid before the death of his wife ten years after that of his duchess. He had been married for thirty-six years to Josefa Bayeu, the sister of a painter with whom he had an early association. She was a devoted and loyal woman who bore him twenty children, some of whom lived; he painted a very sympathetic portrait of her [83].

Goya was now so cut off from human contact and so embittered that he left Madrid to go into seclusion in his country house, *La Quinta del Sordo* (Deaf Man's Villa). This was about 1814; he was sixty-eight but a man of astounding vigor. He etched the *Tauromachia*, a set of forty large plates telling the history of the bullfight and its heroes, and by 1819, at seventy-three, he had produced another set of twenty-two etchings and aquatints, the *Disparates*, and completed *The Disasters of War*, although for political reasons these latter were not published until 1863, long after his death.

The *Disparates* are the most fantastic of Goya's prints and in many ways the most

illness that left him totally deaf upon his recovery in 1793, at the age of forty-six. Whatever elements in his temperament that had predisposed him to the contemplation of human folly were now exaggerated; the isolation of deafness also coincided with his rise in official favor and his increasing contact with the world of the court.*

---

* Goya had become a court painter under Charles III in 1786 and was raised to *pintor de cámara* in 1789 by Charles IV, at about which time he seems to have studied the liberal ideas of the French encyclopedists, who were popular with Spanish intellectuals. This period of relative optimism was terminated by his illness in 1792 with convalescence and deafness in 1793. He became president of Spain's Royal Academy in 1795 and First Painter to the King in 1799.

† Aquatint is a method of acid-biting a metal plate in such a way that the effect of a graded wash is approximated, thus allowing nuances of light and shade not possible in ordinary etching. It is usually combined with etching, as in Goya's work. The process was developed as a secret one by Jean Baptiste Le Prince (1734–1781) and had become public property only shortly before Goya used it, having been revealed in a technical manual, *Encyclopédie Méthodique,* in 1791. Aquatint was particularly valuable to Goya since its wide range from deep shadow to brilliant light was so adaptable to the nightmarish illumination of the spectral regions he was creating.

84. GOYA: *El Famoso Americano, Mariano Ceballos*, 1825. Lithograph, 12¼ x 15¾".
Philadelphia Museum of Art, McIlhenny Fund.

philosophical; they are grotesque allegories whose interpretation Goya leaves up to the observer. Interpretation is not always possible in precise terms, but as the summation of all Goya's previous work the meaning of the *Disparates* is clear enough, and horrifying; Goya's deepest and bitterest experience is translated into fantasies of horror, outrage, and despair. On first publication they were given the title *Proverbios (Proverbs)* by the puzzled and no doubt frightened Academy. The title is apt, in that a proverb expresses some fundamental and enduring idea concerning man's life, disguised as humor or grotesquerie, but not apt in that proverbs grow out of the experience of a people, and the *Disparates* are Goya's own. The word means, approximately, *Fantastic Blunders.* Goya repeated the subjects in fresco on the walls of *La Quinta del Sordo;* the country villa became a compartment of hell transplanted into the Spanish countryside.

In 1824 Goya went into voluntary exile in France. Settled in Bordeaux, his eyesight failing and his vigor at last waning, he began working in the new medium of lithography* and produced four large stones continuing the *Tauromachia,* of an almost orgiastic vitality [84]. He died in Bordeaux in 1828, at eighty-two.

---

* Lithography, a process of drawing on prepared stone and then printing from it, was invented by Aloys Senefelder. It is the most direct of all the art printing processes, imposing a minimum of technical barrier between the artist's hand and the completed print. The artist draws on smooth stone just as he would do on paper; the drawing may be transferred repeatedly to paper with very little change in character. Lithographic darks are even richer than those of aquatint, and every nuance between black and white is possible. The fine-grained texture of the stone gives lithograph its particular individuality, although in modern variations of the technique other surfaces than stone are often used.

85. GOYA: *El Pelele (The Manikin)*, 1791. 105 x 63". Prado, Madrid.

86. GOYA: *Marquesa de San Andrès*, 1785–90. 33 x 22". Private collection.

Goya: His Innovations

The first influences on Goya as a painter were at odds with one another, and he was at odds with both of them. For a century Spain had been dependent on imported artists, and Goya was first subjected to the borrowed rococo forms of various Italian masters, the kind of painting that inspired David's revolt, and then to the art of Raphael Mengs, a neo-classicist of exceptional dryness, with whom he worked for a while. Goya rejected classicism on sight, but when Mengs and Francisco Bayeu used their influence to get him a place with the Royal Tapestry Works in Madrid in 1776, he produced a series of vivacious decorative paintings that easily hold their own alongside those of the eighteenth-century Italians whose tradition they follow. But even while Goya is painting within the rococo tradition of lightness and charm, sinister implications are at play beneath the artificial gaiety. The jolly girls who toss the puppet in a blanket in *El Pelele* [85] are young witches. If their victim is only a puppet, it is because they are still novices. Later they will substitute human carrion for the rag doll; this holiday in a park is only a rehearsal for a witches' sabbath.

Portrait commissions came Goya's way readily. His earliest portraits are rich technical displays with the models posed rather stiffly, a bit overweighted sometimes with incidental elaborations of costume, partly of course because the dress of the period so dictated, as in the portrait of the *Marquesa de San Andrès* [86]. The subject is not deeply explored as a personality; we make our own deductions from the lively objectivity of Goya's re-creation of the lady's features, but we are not told much about her. She regards us with an alert and vigorous glance, yet as far as Goya's characterization of her as an individual is concerned, she might be any one of hundreds like her. But a few years later Goya stands the *Marquesa de La Solana* [87] before us as a complete individual. Her homely features are presented without idealization, but never for a moment does Goya regard any detail of them, or of her costume, as incidental portions of a still-life that happens to be composed of a human being dressed in a certain way. Every element in the portrait of the *Marquesa de La Solana* contributes to the creation of a total personality, subtly projected. The earlier *Marquesa de San Andrès* is a catalogue of accessories, and the fact that styles in dress had changed between the two portraits is only a superficial explanation of their difference. In the later one the lace of the skirt and the shawl could have been played up as accessory details; instead they are all but eliminated in the reduction of the composition to large simplified areas of blacks and grays, within which the pinkish tones of the face and the bow of ribbon perched above it take on an extraordinary life. The portrait is a play between the face and the ribbon bow; the reality of the face, its rather stubborn strength, is emphasized by its existence within the disharmoniously dainty and feminine frame of the shawl and the climax of the fashionable absurdity of the bow. Larger than the face and brighter in color, elegant and dainty where the face is plain and coarse-featured, the bow is the first thing one sees in the picture. But it immediately loses its battle for attention to the face beneath it, a face that appears to tolerate the incompatible accessories surrounding it as a concession to the necessities of mode but goes on about its own more important business without giving them further thought.

This superb portrait was painted just before Goya's climactic illness. As a piece of pure painting, it reflects his discovery of Velásquez in the royal collections, now ac-

87. GOYA: *Marquesa de La Solana*, 1791–95. 71¼ x 48". Louvre, Paris.

cessible to him. It is also a prelude to his experiments in the use of color and the representation of form that were in full stride by 1800, the year of the portrait of the royal family. Historically these experiments are as important as Delacroix's later ones.

Goya was dissatisfied with the light, fresh touch of his early paintings and their clear, fresh, attractive but rather obvious decorative colors. As Delacroix was to do, he fumed against the painting methods that made a painting only a kind of tinted draw-ing. His experiments were not in the same direction as Delacroix's were to be, but he was working away from the same dissatis-factions when he complained, "Always lines, never bodies! Where does one see lines in nature? I see only forms, forms that are lighted and forms that are not, planes that are near and planes that are far, pro-jections, and hollows. I see no lines or de-tails, I don't count each hair on the head of a passerby, or the buttons on his coat. There is no reason why my brush should see more than I do."

What this means is that Goya was hunt-ing a way of painting that would present an image with the immediacy of instant vision. This, of course, is visual realism—not the search for an ideal and not the imi-tation of nature in detail, but the capturing in paint of the impact of life as we meet it head on. We see first in breadth, in masses; we receive a total impression that carries with it a certain emotional impact. Later we may examine things more closely, may relish the beauty of a line, the complexity of a part within the whole, may perceive individual hairs on a head or buttons on a coat down to the way they are sewed on. Such details may offer a great deal of inter-est or aesthetic pleasure, but to Goya's way of thinking they obscured the point, which was to capture the quality of the whole, to record it in such a way that its immediate vividness, as it impressed him, was ex-pressed with truth at maximum intensity. Since a picture cannot be painted in the space of a glance, his problem was to dis-cover a way of painting an image that would retain this immediate intensity. Of course this can always be done to some ex-tent in a quick sketch. But that, again, was beside the point, since a sketch is only sug-gestive, and dependent for its effect on its very incompleteness. Along with immediacy and intensity Goya wanted the decision and the completeness that distinguish a work of art from a fragment of nature.

To work out some of the problems in-volved in training his brush not to "see more" than he did, Goya set himself an exercise that produced two of his most celebrated paintings, the paired *Nude Maja*

[88] and *Clothed Maja** [90]. It was in-evitable that legends should accumulate around such a startling pair of pictures, which look like anything but analytical studies in technique, and inevitable too that these legends should attach themselves to the Duchess of Alba. The most popular story is that the Duchess posed for the *Nude Maja* during the Duke's absence and that the *Clothed Maja* was dashed off quickly when the lovers received word of the Duke's imminent return, an anecdote false in every factual and psychological de-tail except that the features of the girl in the *Majas* are close to those of the Duchess in Goya's several portraits of her. But since Goya used these features as a type for the spirited, vixenish young beauties who populate his work, the resemblance means nothing.

The *Majas* were painted about 1800, the year David painted *Madame Récamier* [14], a perfect contrast to the *Clothed Maja*, opposing the fashionable grace and artificiality of the neo-classical portrait with the bold vitality of Goya's realism. The *Nude Maja* and Ingres's *Grande Odalisque* [89]—the comparison is legitimate in spite of the disparity of dates—are in even more extreme and enlightening contrast. With Delacroix's *Odalisque with Parrot* [91] the classical-romantic-realistic comparison is complete. In their different ways, the Frenchmen poeticized a nude model to ac-cord with an arbitrary standard. Goya painted—magnificently—simply a naked girl, audacious, almost insolently matter-of-fact in her nakedness. If the figure is un-idealized, if the nakedness is piquant be-

---

* *Maja* and its masculine equivalent *majo* are untranslatable. Dictionaries give *fop* or *dandy* for *majo*. *Gallant* is close. *Coquette* might do for *maja* but not very well. The words carry associations of youth, good looks or prettiness, city pleasures, flirtatious display, fancy dress without high fashion, and common rather than aristocratic origin, with probabili-ties of flexible morality. As part of an inter-national movement of dandyism at the end of the eighteenth century, these Spaniards had their counterparts in England in the macaronis, and in France in the *merveilleuses,* who adopted eccentric modes of dress. The clothing worn by *majos* and *majas* eventually became the national dress of Spain.

88. GOYA: *Nude Maja, c.* 1797–98. 37⅜ x 74¾″. Prado, Madrid. (Photo Anderson.)

89. INGRES: *Odalisque en Grisaille, c.* 1813, study for *Grande Odalisque.* 32¾ x 43″.
Metropolitan Museum of Art, New York, Wolfe Fund.

cause the image seems so literal, this same literalness saves it from lasciviousness. It is too frank to be suggestive. As is always pointed out, its clothed companion piece with its gauzy, clinging, half-concealing half-revealing gown comes closer to being the suggestive one of the pair.

Technically the innovation in the *Majas* has to do with reducing the image to its essential planes, which are painted in bold, flat areas instead of being fused in subtle modulations from one to another. This does not mean a simpler, easier way of painting. Goya's boldness takes as much calculation as Ingres's subtlety; the forms and colors that seem so direct and uncomplicated are disposed in relationships as firmly integrated with one another as in any other form of picture-making. Delacroix's problem—"All precautions have to be taken to make the execution swift and decisive" in order not to lose "the extraordinary impression accompanying the conception"—is also Goya's, with the difference (in the case of the *Majas*) that where Delacroix is concerned with recording inner, emotional, impressions through exotic images, Goya pre-

sents us with what appears to be an image of brilliant external reality. The important words here are *what appears to be*, because Goya is not merely reproducing the object he sees, camera fashion. He is preserving his own vision of reality in such a way that we see it and respond to it as he did, not as

90. GOYA: *Clothed Maja, c.* 1797–98. 37⅜ x 74¾″. Prado, Madrid. (Photo Anderson.)

91. DELACROIX: *Odalisque with Parrot,* 1827. 9½ x 12½″. *Musée des Beaux Arts,* Lyon.

we might respond to the actual object if we saw it ourselves. If Goya had sought out new means of representation only in order to reproduce visual fact, the search would have been pointless. The point was to discover a new way of representation which, by preserving his own vision of the world, would be for him the best possible vehicle of expression.

The *Majas* occupy a special place in Goya's work as demonstrations, in addition to being arresting paintings in themselves. Expressively, however, they are excelled by other paintings where Goya's realism is an interpretative vehicle more than a technical process. One example is the portrait of *The Toreador José Romero* [92]. As pure painting the picture is opulent in texture and color, with the rich red lining of the cape curving up to the shoulder, the blue-green of the wide sash, the ruddy flesh tints, the blacks of the hair and the vest, and the pulsating lights everywhere on silks, velvets, and gilt embroidery. Against this brilliance Goya plays the reserved, even pensive, face of the young man. The hands, held so quietly, have an almost feminine delicacy, remindful of the precision, the refinements, the nuances, that differentiate a toreador from a butcher.

The difference between the *Majas* and a portrait like this one is the difference between an exercise in which the interest of the subject is incidental to its presentation, and an interpretation in which presentation serves expression. Goya's genius here and in other portraits lies in his revelation of the character of the sitter in what appears to be an altogether objective statement of the features. Like many other painters, Goya achieves this revelation by controlling the objective reality through selection and modification of pose and details. Where an unimaginative portraitist would have posed his bullfighter in an attitude of theatrical braggadocio suggestive of the usual connotations of the bullring, Goya cut through this overlay of convention and habit and produced, instead, a painting that not only characterizes the sitter but extends its comment into the area of philosophical speculation. Yet all this is achieved through the devices of surface realism, without symbolical clues or idealistic references. It was to this end that Goya found it necessary to discover his way of painting in which "his brush should not see more than he did." And, once discovered, this way of painting served him not only as a painter of the familiar world but also as a painter of scenes of horror, fantasy, and violence, to which the quality of "immediate vision" brings an appalling reality.

On May 2, 1808, citizens of Madrid rioted against French soldiery, and on the following day the captured rioters were taken into the countryside near the city and shot. Goya recorded both events in a pair of pictures in 1814, six years after the events. If the picture of the executions of May 3 [93] had no other virtues, it would still demonstrate that Goya's way of seeing and painting "only forms, forms that are lighted and forms that are not, planes that are near and planes that are far, projections, and hollows" gives to the subject, painted long after the event, the quality of an event that happens as we look at it. The victims, and the barren mound behind them, stand out against a dark sky in an explosion of light and blood. One man spreads his raised arms in defiance against the executioners. Another, a priest, prays; another seems only half comprehending; others clutch at themselves in terror or hide their faces in despair. Ranged in front of them, the uniformed soldiers, rifles firing, are like

92. GOYA: *The Toreador José Romero,* date unknown. 36 x 29½". Collection Mrs. Carroll S. Tyson, Chestnut Hill, Pa.

automatons. Their faces are not shown, their stances are identical, they are painted in dull grays and browns. This depersonalization accentuates the humanity of the victims, and especially it makes the central defiant figure a symbol of the individual's revolt against the forces of organized oppression, even though, in Goya's world, he is impotent before them.

Not much later, Delacroix was to commemorate a similar popular uprising in Paris, which took place in 1830, with his *Liberty Leading the People* [94]. As a romantic idealist he gives us a flurry and surge of drapery around an allegorical female figure leading other figures who thus, inevitably, lose their human identity and become allegorical symbols also. Or, if we try to regard them as human beings, they

93. GOYA: *The Executions of May 3, 1808,* 1814. 104¾ x 135⅞". Prado, Madrid. (Photo Anderson.)

94. DELACROIX: *Liberty Leading the People,* 1830. 102½ x 128". Louvre, Paris.

are at best actors in a costumed pageant. Goya's central figure of the man with arms spread wide may be, as we have just said, something like a "symbol" of the spirit of liberty unquenchable in mankind, but if Goya had such an idea in mind he delivered it in terms of the facts of this world, not in a vision of an artificial one. Both pictures can be compared with *The Oath of the Horatii* [6] as a third treatment of the same general theme: the individual's sacrifice of self to an ideal of freedom and justice. Of the three, Goya's alone meets the world on its own terms. David's by this standard (which, of course, is not the standard to which David aspires) is chilly and abstract; Delacroix's is a bit high-flown. In both of them life serves as material for art, which then becomes important for its own sake,

95. DAUMIER: *The Battle of Schools*, from *Le Charivari*, 1855. Lithograph.

Daumier: Realism and Bourgeois Culture

relegating life to second place. In Goya the raw material of life is ordered and intensified by an art that reveals, but never takes precedence over, the world in which man lives. This is why Goya is first a realist, although he is as dramatic as any romantic, as fantastic as any visionary. His art became a mine for later movements whose aims might even be at loggerheads with one another—impressionism, expressionism, even surrealism, all of which we will see. Goya demonstrates again that the arbitrary boundaries of one ism or another are never wide enough to encompass the total of a great artist's work.

This is especially true of another artist who by classification must be called a realist, a man who knew the world as well as Goya did, who painted it as literally yet more intimately, who was as aware of man's foibles and vanities as Goya was, and suffered more from them—yet who found man good where Goya found him ultimately base: the Frenchman Honoré Daumier.

Daumier (1808–1879) was born in Marseille the year of the riots in Madrid and the executions of May 3. By 1830, the year of the uprisings celebrated in Delacroix's *Liberty Leading the People*, he was working at his first job in Paris as cartoonist for a publication called *La Caricature*. During the next forty years he produced some 4,000 popular cartoons by which he made his living as well as innumerable drawings and sketches and hundreds of paintings. Daumier was the noblest realist of them all; he was one of the finest painters of any school in nineteenth-century France; and he was buried in a pauper's grave at the age of seventy-one.

Just as romanticism had been the natural expression of the turbulence of the first half of the nineteenth century in France, so realism replaced it just as naturally as an expression of the second half. Daumier

96. DAUMIER: *Boy Running*, date unknown. Crayon and Wash, 6 x 9″. National Gallery of Art, Washington, D.C., Rosenwald Collection.

lived in the era of the *Bourgeoisie Triumphant*, the practical, matter-of-fact, cautious, comfort-loving man, scornful of theory if it did not serve a tangible, profitable end (hence he was no classicist) and suspicious of passion if it threatened his security (and hence he was not a romantic). He was the realistic man, the little man of great common sense.

If his world sounds like an infertile one for the artist, that is only because we forget what an artist is: if he is truly creative, an artist absorbs the gross experience of his time and distills from it its essential meaning. In France, around the middle years of the century, creative men in all the arts ceased to yearn toward ancient Greece and Rome, returned from the long jaunt to the Orient and began to examine things as they found them at home. They discovered in the prosaic world infinite material and, above all, infinite variety. They discovered that a peasant woman was a better subject for them than Ceres, that a respectable

bourgeoise housewife offered possibilities not even hinted at by Venus, and even that a common prostitute could be painted or written about more rewardingly than a harem full of odalisques. A street in Paris was discovered to be more dramatic than an Arabian lion hunt. And if a woman choosing a hat in a millinery shop was involved in making a decision less strenuous than the ones made by the Horatii or the Sabines, nevertheless her dilemma had its own legitimacy and could be the subject of a work of art commenting on human life.

Nor need such a comment be trivial. It had, among other advantages, the great one of being a comment made at first hand, as if made on the spot instead of being trumped up in the studio. To make such comments at full force, painters invented new techniques that horrified the Academy and eventually destroyed it as a potent force in French art. Artists discovered in realism the most flexible of all approaches to expression. Freed from the restrictions and recipes of classicism, no longer goaded by the romantic obligation to theatricalize, they discovered that the world around them offered everything, that at last the individual was freed to speak as he chose about what interested him most, to interpret the world according to his own convictions instead of echoing another man's formula. Classicism had shrunk like a dried pea; romanticism had swollen until it burst; realism offered the world of everyday as the painter's lodestone.

Realism served painters of all temperaments. Within the world at hand the man of classical temperament could find images of universal truths. The romantically inclined could find the passion he yearned for. The cynic, the sentimentalist, the social theorist, the objectivist, the wit—each might create his own image from the raw material of a single subject that in itself might be the most commonplace fragment of the world, familiar to everybody. Thus in its very flexibility, realism became more demanding than either classicism or romanticism had been: without the established devices of a David or a Delacroix to follow, the realist was exposed as whatever kind of man he was, big or little of spirit, imaginative or pedestrian in his perception of the world.

Daumier is the French counterpart of Goya in his contempt for hypocrisy, falsehood, and injustice. If he is a lesser master, it is because he was never allowed to reach full stature as a painter. Goya's *Caprichos* were withdrawn a few days after they were published, and he escaped punishment by the tribunal of the Inquisition for the temerity of his subjects only because he had had the greater temerity to dedicate them to Charles IV (who could have found everything he stood for attacked in them) and to seek, successfully, the King's protection. But Daumier, on the other hand, was imprisoned for a published caricature of his king, and his serious work was curtailed in 1835 under severe restrictions of the freedom of the press. Hobbled by poverty, without a market for his kind of painting, he was unable to paint at all until he was forty, and then he painted in complete obscurity with neither the time nor the

97. DAUMIER: *Grandes Eaux à Versailles*, from *Le Charivari*, July 28, 1844. Lithograph, 9¹⁄₁₆ x 7¼". The title is a pun, *Grandes Eaux* being literally *Great Waters* but referring to Versailles's famous fountains. Collection Carl Zigrosser, Philadelphia.

money—and, for that matter, not the reason—to do the ambitious pictures that force an artist's growth and prove his mettle. But Daumier was a great painter, and certainly one of the two or three finest draughtsmen of his century. And if compassionate observation of man in his frailty and his nobility is a standard of comparison, then Daumier surpasses Goya, and only Rembrandt, in the seventeenth century, can keep him company.

Because he was a man of the nineteenth century, Daumier, unlike Rembrandt, made his most profound statements by means of the most commonplace subjects, usually the city streets and the ordinary people in them. Instead of inventing allegories, fan-

98. DAUMIER: *Saprelotte!—Full!*, from *Le Charivari*, 1848. Lithograph, 10¼ x 8⅜″. Collection Carl Zigrosser, Philadelphia.

99. DAUMIER: *Before Moreau's Picture at the Salon*, from *Le Charivari*, 1864. Lithograph, 9½ x 8¼″. Collection Carl Zigrosser, Philadelphia.

tasies, and nightmares as Goya did to reveal man's nature, Daumier observed the attitudes men assumed and the expressions on their faces and reproduced their essence, while seeming only to sketch them casually, candid-camera fashion, as they went about the routine of their daily affairs.

Daumier: Social and Political Comment

Daumier was an untrained artist. He learned to draw by observation; he never dissected a body, but he knew more about the way a body moves, the way muscles and fat are disposed upon the skeleton, than any painter who made a fetish of classical anatomy. *The Battle of Schools* [95] is a caricature comment on the revolt of the realistic painter against academic idealism. A dirty little fellow in peasant clothes, armed with a thick heavy brush, faces a skinny academician, posed in the attitude of David's Romulus from *The Sa-*

bines and armed with a palette and a mahl stick (which was an accessory to the creation of the slick finish of academic painting). The reason this burlesque of the beautiful body of David's classical athlete is so funny is that its comic exaggerations of a skinny naked man are so true, so logical. These shrunken hams and knobby joints and pipestem legs are at least as brilliant a variation on the human form as are the Davidian forms they caricature, and they are based on a more supple familiarity with anatomical fact.

Daumier learned to draw as a caricaturist, and in his transition from caricature to serious painting he held to the strict economy of statement which is caricature's essence. In a few bent lines and an area or two of wash he could capture the physical mass, the action, and the inner nature of his subject, whether a group of people waiting at a station or a frightened boy running [96]. In this way, too, he resembles Rembrandt, who was Daumier's drawing master as nearly as he ever had one.

100. DAUMIER: *Behind in the Rent*, from *Le Charivari*, 1847. Lithograph, 10⅛ x 7½″.

101. DAUMIER: *Turtledoves—Just the Way We Were*, from the series *Tout ce qu'on voudra*, 1848. Lithograph, 10½ x 9″. Both Collection Carl Zigrosser, Philadelphia.

Daumier is the only important painter of the nineteenth century in France whose development was entirely independent of the Academy and the Salon: he neither received their favors nor needed to battle their opposition. This was because he did not regard himself as a painter with a career to make and a reputation to establish. He was a professional artist with a living to earn, and he earned it by working against deadlines for periodicals.

Such work could have been a prostitution of his genius if he had curried favor by yielding to popular standards. Instead, Daumier created a new standard that lifted the cartoon of social and political comment to the level of serious art. Even when his cartoons are most humorous they are never entirely trivial. When he draws a funny face, it is also the face of a specific character, produced by a way of life acting upon a temperament. In it we recognize an individual of a social type within a complicated social system.

The favorite target of Daumier's benign exposures was the lower middle class, uncomfortable in its dutiful pretensions to gentility [97–101]. He shows its members exhausted and puzzled at Salon exhibitions, drenched in their Sunday best by sudden downpours on an excursion to Versailles, harassed by squawling brats who nullify the order and comfort of their flats, reduced to a thousand indignities by the frictions and irritations of living with their fellows who never quite recognize in them the superiorities they aspire to within themselves. Behind in their rent, they have humiliating encounters with the landlord on the stairs. The bus doesn't wait for them. Friends yawn at their funny stories; their collars are always too tight or too loose; and they realize one day that they and their mates look terrible in their bathing suits. But their lives are also full of sudden small domestic felicities. A middle-aged couple resting under a tree remember their youth as they watch birds nesting. Young parents glow

94 · REALISM

102. Guys: The King and Queen of Greece and their suite passing the base of the Acropolis, 1854. Pencil and watercolor, 10¾ x 16. Collection T. Edward Hanley, Bradford, Pa.

with pride at their little boy, although he is an absurd replica of his pompous father. Friends exchange intellectual platitudes about the Salon success of the year, impressed with one another's acumen.

The quality that raises these typical Daumier cartoons above the level of humorous journalism should be apparent when they are compared with the pictorial reporting of Daumier's contemporary, Constantin Guys (1805–1892), who is now recognized as a minor master although, like Daumier, he was seldom thought of as an artist during his lifetime. Guys seems to have been in accord with this opinion; today he would probably have been a news photographer.

Guys avoided attention and his life is not well documented, but what we know of it is fascinating enough. At eighteen he was a soldier with Byron in the Greek war, and four years later he was a dragoon in the French army. He traveled everywhere in Europe and went to the Orient. For a

while he lived in London, giving lessons in French and in drawing and selling sketches to magazines. At the middle of the century (which his life nearly spanned) he was a war correspondent for the *Illustrated London News*, one of the few journals of the time carrying pictures of current events; he covered the Revolution of 1848 and the Crimean War. Between wars he covered the ballet, opera, and the like.

His wonderful sketches, done on the spot, would be sent to the journal for wood engraving, the means of reproduction then most in use. They would lose much of their own character in this translation, but many of the originals still exist. The one illustrated here [102] shows the King in the streets of Athens, and some of the notes scribbled across the lower part of the drawing read: "For details of costumes of the parties in the Royal Cortège, the gendarmes, the people crowding the gardens, lining the street, etc. etc., see the annexed sketches. Acropolis on the right—further up in the background the new observatory—built on top of the hill. Carriages in the garden crowded with ladies with national and French fashionable costume indifferently." From notes like these the wood engravers filled in details. Sometimes a drawing would bear a note such as, "Observe all details of costume, they are entirely accurate, change background at will—make it snow if you wish."

But only a fraction of the drawings and watercolors of modes and manners for which Guys is best known [103] were done for reproduction; he seems to have drawn all the time, year after year, thousands of drawings. Pen or pencil with wash, sometimes monochrome, sometimes with a touch or two of additional color, sometimes watercolor in a few fresh clear tints, were his medium. He evokes the epoch of the Second Empire with its crinolines, its courtesans, its display, its high style flavored with a dash of vulgarity—the epoch's, not Guys's. One of his favorite subjects was the promenade in the Bois de Boulogne, with its prancing horses and its carriages filled with women in great masses of finery—hats, ruffles, ribbons, shawls, with lace-trimmed umbrellas rising above them like the smallest flowers springing out of great bouquets.

Among his contemporaries, Guys, like Daumier, had a few admirers among knowledgeable painters and critics. The great Manet (soon to be seen) was one of them, and Baudelaire published a famous article on him in the journal *Figaro* in 1863 (but written in 1859) called "A Painter of Modern Life." (Guys refused to let his name be printed, but permitted the use of his initial, which occasionally appears on a drawing.) Baudelaire recognized the elegance of Guys's style, and the deft economy with which the artist caught the visual essence of his subjects. But compared with Daumier, Guys is a reporter with exceptional vivacity and charm but not much depth. This is comparison with a giant, and does not affect the truth that Guys is an artist of stature as well as a recorder of the modes and manners of a particular society. His drawings are works of art marked by finesse and flair and infallible sensitivity to the most telling details of fashionable trap-

103. GUYS: *Une Elegante*, 1850–60. Watercolor, 15¼ x 10½". Fogg Art Museum, Cambridge, Mass., Maurice Wertheim Collection.

pings. But Daumier's cartoons are works of art rooted in the same humanitarian spirit that inspired his greatest painting.

Daumier's cartoons are based upon the assumption, never questioned, that man is good, whatever indignities, absurdities, and brutalizations life may inflict upon him. This was also Rembrandt's assumption, except that Rembrandt could not go so far as to admit the absurdities. That Daumier admits them, even cherishes them, explains the attraction held for him by a favorite subject, Don Quixote [104]. The addle-pated old man, mounted on his bony nag of a charger, his own bony silhouette topped off by the tin basin he imagines to be a knightly helmet, rides forth toward one imagined chivalric adventure after another, followed by his fat, stolid, uncomprehending and loyal lackey, Sancho Panza, who pulls his master out of one mud puddle or dung heap after another, where the old man's adventures always end. The story of Don Quixote is nominally a satire on the

104. DAUMIER: *Don Quixote and Sancho Panza,* date unknown. 22¼ x 33¼″. Collection
Mr. and Mrs. Charles S. Payson, New York.

105. DAUMIER: *The Witnesses,* 1872. Lithograph, 10 x 8¾″. Metropolitan Museum of Art.

romantic foolishness of chivalric fiction, but
it is also an undercover affirmation of the
invincibility of the spirit: after each humiliating fall the old man pulls himself together and dodders forth toward a new one,
his illusions intact. The paunchy bourgeois
who gets caught in the rain, who misses
his bus, who goes through a terrible world
sustained by a blind, unreasoning conviction of his own importance—to Daumier,
this paunchy bourgeois is noble in his absurdity if he remains an honest man.

But when Daumier is confronted with
corruption, stupidity, hypocrisy, or chican-
ery in high places, his tolerance vanishes.
The Witnesses [105] could serve as well
today as an indictment of warmongers as
it did in 1872. In fact it has done so, in
hundreds of descendants, ever since. The
politicians ranged in tiers in *Le Ventre
Législatif* (*The Legislative Belly* [106]—
usually more politely translated as *The
Legislative Body,* at the expense of Daumier's point) are individually identifiable

106. DAUMIER: *Le Ventre Législatif*, 1834. Lithograph 11 x 17″. Collection Carl Zigrosser, Philadelphia.

as Louis Philippe's henchmen, but even without this reference the caricatures stand as murderous revelations of the mentality of corrupt political opportunists anywhere, any time.

In the same year as *Le Ventre Législatif*, 1834, Daumier published the great lithograph, *Rue Transnonain* [107]. At the time of its publication the title was enough to explain the scene where a family lies murdered in the disorder of a bedroom—a father in nightshirt and nightcap, lying on the body of his child, with the body of a woman in the shadows at the left, and the head of an older man projecting into the picture at the right. The Rue Transnonain was a street in Paris inhabited by workers who were suspected of participation in the disorders of the Republican Revolt of 1834. When it was fired on from an apartment house, the civil guard broke in and shot the inhabitants, innocent or guilty.

David, as he did in *Marat* [9] would have idealized the figures in the scene as far as possible, certainly substituting a beautiful body for that of the stocky, paunchy father. The rumpled nightshirt

would have fallen into folds of classical purity. Delacroix would have chosen a different moment, perhaps the tumultuous entrance of the guard into the room, a swirl of figures, a sort of *Sardanapalus* [49] or a *Scio* [46] in a new locale. Either artist, on the evidence of similar achievements, might have produced a fine picture. But Daumier rejects these dramas to bring us into the room, in all its commonplaceness. He shows us the grossness of the father, the intimate disorder of the bed, and the woman's body sprawled and ugly, the more pathetic because it is mercilessly real.

Daumier: His Faith

Daumier turned out his lithographic cartoons for popular consumption in journals on the average of three a week, with occasional individual stones, such as *Rue Transnonain*, for general sale. In the humorous cartoons having to do with the daily scene, the faith Daumier lived by is only implied in the affectionate quality of his raillery. More searching comments would have been

107. DAUMIER: *Rue Transnonain*, 1834. Lithograph, 11¼ x 17⅜". Philadelphia Museum of Art, Bequest of Fiske Kimball.

108. DAUMIER: *After the Trial*, date unknown. Watercolor, 11 x 14¼". Philadelphia Museum of Art, Anonymous Loan.

inappropriate, wasted, and for that matter impossible, since no man can produce three major works every seven days.

But in his paintings, which were known to only a few people during his lifetime, he speaks at full strength to say that, in spite of Rue Transnonains, Legislative Bellies, and the skeletons of men killed by war and starvation, mankind is good. This is Daumier's faith. The mere fact that he held it does not make him a greater or a lesser artist than a pessimist like Goya. Optimism and pessimism are not aesthetic qualities. Nor, of course, is it "good" or virtuous to believe that mankind is "good." Pollyanna-ism is likely to be more dangerous than skepticism, sentimentalism more vicious than cynicism. But Daumier is neither a Pollyanna nor a sentimentalist, and his conviction that mankind is ultimately good must be recognized if his painting is to be understood as anything more than a representation of people going about the routine of their daily affairs.

In his paintings Daumier seldom accuses, preferring to affirm the triumph of good rather than to expose the evils standing in its way. True, there are the numerous savage representations of lawyers [108], who for Daumier, familiar with the venal courts of the period, were a compound of arrogance, pomposity, and corruption, feeding on the ills and confusions of other men. But for all their trenchancy, these pictures are exceptions. We need only compare the *Third Class Carriage* [109], with its young peasant mother and children accompanied by the old grandmother, with any young beauty and old hag of Goya's to understand that, where Goya believes that life is a process of physical and moral corruption, Daumier finds life ultimately incorruptible —by its very force of growth and continuation, if by nothing else.

Daumier states this conclusion even more universally in *Soup* [110], where the peasant mother feeds voraciously on the food she has torn from the earth while her child suckles at her breast. The two figures are bound together in a circular pattern of lines suggesting in their inevitable continuity not only the endless cycle of life but, by their fierce vitality, the triumphant force of man's constant self-regeneration.

Yet, magnificent as they are, Daumier's pictures of peasants, of people close to the soil, are not his most individual or his most subtle achievements. His peasants are still related to "nature's noblemen," not too much changed from the "noble savage" conceived in the eighteenth century. And while Daumier was working, the painter Millet (to be seen shortly) was also discovering the peasant in similar interpretations. Daumier's individual achievement rests, finally, in his discovery of human nobility in a more obscure quarter: that vast middle ground between the man of the soil at one end and the man of worldly position or intellectual achievement at the other, within the dreary reaches of undistinguished city streets where ordinary people live out their lives in rented cells. Daumier's man is the little man of good will whom he first discovered by satirizing him, the good bourgeois who for all his confusions is neither vicious nor a fool in the long run. In *The Print Collector* [111], Daumier declares his faith in this man as a rational creature.

The Print Collector is painted in a few scrubs of color dominated by grays and browns. It shows a man of no particular

109. DAUMIER: *Third Class Carriage*, c. 1862. 25¾ x 35½". Metropolitan Museum of Art, New York, H. O. Havemeyer Collection.

110. DAUMIER: *Soup*, date unknown. Wash drawing, 11 x 15¾". Louvre, Paris.

distinction or individuality, although he exists vividly, looking through a portfolio of prints in a small shop. His figure is reduced nearly to silhouette; the simplification is extreme, but an additional line of detail would be superfluous. The man is all there —the body beneath the clothes, the spirit within the body. The clothes tell us of a position in the world—not a position of any consequence; the body tells us other facts—

111. DAUMIER: *The Print Collector,* date unknown. 13⅜ x 10¼".
Philadelphia Museum of Art, Wilstach Fund.

112. DAUMIER: *First Class Carriage,* 1864. Wash drawing, 8 x
11¾". Walters Art Gallery, Baltimore.

age, and that this is a city man, for instance.
We do not need to deduce these various
facts. We are presented with them complete, in the total impression of the man's
reality, as we might understand them at a
glance, without deduction or specification,
if he passed us on the street. We can say
flatly that this is a middle-class man who
collects prints as a hobby; beyond that, we
may ponder the idea that print-collecting
is not a necessary animal function, such as
feeding and sleeping; and that, hence, it is
proof that this is a human being possessed
like other human beings of the thing that
separates him from the animals, called intellect, soul, consciousness, ego, or any of
dozens of other names. We may even point
to various means Daumier has used to say
this. We can make a symbol, for instance,
of the way the figure emerges from mysterious shadows into even more mysterious
lights. But in the end we cannot altogether
explain how Daumier says that man is part
of a miracle so good that none of his frailties
is of any importance when balanced against
the fact of his existence.

Daumier's basic premise of goodness al-
leviates the melancholy of his second one:
that within the crowds and conformity of
the city the individual is psychologically
isolated. Daumier is the first painter to express this phenomenon of modern life. He
represents his print collector alone—literally
alone in the picture, although the crowds
passing on the street, the proprietor of the
shop, and other customers are certainly
near by. And each of the people in the
First Class Carriage [112] is alone in his
own world, even while crowded side by
side with the other passengers. In some of
Daumier's pictures men establish a tenuous
bridge between themselves. An artist shows
his prints to a collector; two men ponder
a game of chess, warmed by an illusion of
intimacy through recognition of the identity of their mutual isolation; prisoners sing
together [113]; old friends share a drink at
a table in a garden [114]. These moments
of intimacy are poignant because they are
rare. In *The Drama* [115] Daumier shows
us an audience carried away by a performance on the stage, each man unconscious of
the shouldering and pressing of the other

people around him, absorbed in an illusion created by shoddy scenery and wild posturings, an illusion more real than his contact with his fellow men will be when the performance is over and he leaves the theater with the crowd.

Daumier: His Life

A few facts of Daumier's life are pertinent here. Daumier showed precocious talent as a child, but his family, which had moved from his birthplace of Marseilles to Paris, refused to let him study art. He entered painting by the back door of journalism. At twenty-two he was doing political cartoons on *La Caricature*, and it was for one of these that he was imprisoned for six months, when he was twenty-four. This was in 1832, and the cartoon was *Gargantua*, showing Louis Philippe swallowing bags of gold extracted from the people.

Daumier's drawing at this period was rather solidly modeled within closed outlines, as can still be seen in *Le Ventre Législatif* and *Rue Transnonain*. His history as a draughtsman is one of steady change toward a more broken, open, nervous, expressive line, with greater and greater economy of modeling, as evident in the other drawings just illustrated. A pen and ink drawing of a horse and rider [116] shows how far he carried this technique.

In 1835 *La Caricature* was replaced by *Le Charivari** on which Daumier worked for the rest of his professional life. The realistic novelist Balzac was also a member of its staff and commented that "this boy has some Michelangelo under his skin." Baudelaire was one of the very few others who recognized in Daumier something more than a skillful commercial cartoonist.

In 1877 Daumier's eyes failed after forty years of overwork. Corot, a saint among painters, had given him a small country cottage some years before, and Daumier retired there on a state pension awarded

_____

* A *charivari* is a mock serenade of discordant noises, made by beating on pots and pans, howling, and yelling, beneath the windows of someone who has given displeasure—a good name for a critical journal.

113. DAUMIER: *Prison Choir*, date unknown. 19¾ x 24". Walters Art Gallery, Baltimore.

114. DAUMIER: *The Good Friends*, date unknown. Wash drawing, 9¼ x 11⅞". Baltimore Museum of Art.

him by the Third Republic. The pension was more than deserved. Under the various regimes since 1830 Daumier had been unyieldingly and courageously a republican propagandist.

When Daumier died two years after his retirement the hundreds of paintings in his little house were purchased by a syndicate from his widow for almost nothing. When they were put on the market years later, plus numerous forgeries that still cause confusion, they were worth a fortune. The paintings date from 1848, when Daumier presented an allegorical figure of the Republic in a competition for mural decorations in the Hôtel de Ville—which, of course, he did not win. His first exhibition was arranged in 1878 just before his retirement, when he was seventy years old. Thus it happened that the school of realism, where in retrospect Daumier is a major figure, had been born, had fought its battles, and had given way to a new variant called impressionism before these realistic masterpieces were known.

In the meanwhile realism's battles had been fought, not expertly but with the greatest of pleasure, under the leadership of a painter who fell half by accident into that position, a man a decade younger than Daumier who died the year before Daumier's tardy exhibition, and who had left France some years before that—Gustave Courbet.

115. DAUMIER: *The Drama*, date unknown. 38 x 35″. *Neue Stadtgalerie*, Munich.

116. DAUMIER: *Rider*, date unknown. Pen drawing, 8¼ x 10½″. Private collection.

Courbet: His Theories versus His Practice

The theories of realism as advanced by Courbet (1819–1877) were not very complicated. Neither were they always very clear, since Courbet was not much of an analytical thinker. When it was necessary for him to formulate a written statement, he did so with the help of friends who were better at words than he was. Perhaps this explains why what Courbet said about painting and what he did in painting never quite agree. With the best intentions in the world his friends were likely to clarify his half-formed theories in directions expedient to purposes immediately at hand, with less regard for Courbet's painting than for their own convictions.

"Show me an angel and I will paint one" is the bluntest of Courbet's pronouncements. He held that "painting is an essentially concrete art, and can consist only of the representation of things both real and existing"—a limitation that would have ruled out all classical painting except portraits, all romantic invention, and most of the work of the old masters most admired by Courbet himself.

Nor is Courbet's own painting so objective as such pronouncements imply it should be. Although he stated that he wanted to "translate the customs, the ideas, and the look" of his own time into pictures, he added that he wanted to do so "according to his own understanding" of them. This means that while he referred directly to the world around him for his material, instead of to an imagined antiquity or a romantic Orient, he interpreted what he saw rather than merely transcribing it. And if he did not paint angels, if he painted only what he could see, what Courbet chose to see was unusually dramatic rather than prosaic. Even when a subject was nominally prosaic, he observed it more romantically than would be expected from a painter tagged "realist" and dedicated to the annihilation of the romantic ideal. His realism was conscious, but his romanticism was inborn.

It must be remembered, too, that we see Courbet's innovations in reverse perspective. We look at them from this side, across an intervening century during which realism went far beyond Courbet in the direction he set. From this distance he seems as romantic as he does realistic, but in the Salons of his own time his realism was extreme.

But all these considerations are historical. Historically it is important that Courbet was called a realist, an anti-idealist. But beyond that, beyond realism or idealism or any other ism, Courbet is a painter, in the purest sense of the word *painter*. His paint simply as paint, as a rich oily substance applied to canvas, is magnificent.

His *Young Bather* [117] is typical of many Courbets that are likely today to strike us first with the mincing artificiality of the pose. The fact that in combination with this artificiality the model is painted with a high degree of realism may even make the picture a bit ludicrous; standards in feminine beauty have changed, and we see only an overweight young woman affecting an unconvincing daintiness. The es-

117. COURBET: *Young Bather*, 1866. 51¼ x 38¼". Metropolitan Museum of Art, New York, H. O. Havemeyer Collection.

118. COURBET: *Woman with a Parrot*, 1866. 51 x 77". Metropolitan Museum of Art, New York, H. O. Havemeyer Collection.

119. COURBET: *Two Girls on the Banks of the Seine,* 1856. 66½ x 81⅛". *Petit Palais,* Paris.

sential realism of the picture is further compromised by the landscape background that has been trumped up behind the figure. The branch the model holds in her left hand is retouched with a few leaves, but it is still a studio prop not very convincingly related to the tree it is supposed to grow from. Such inconsistencies conceal the revolutionary character of the *Young Bather,* although nothing can conceal the magnificence of its painting.

In the *Woman with a Parrot* [118], painted late in Courbet's career at a time when he was having a period of fashionable success and his disciples were accusing him of compromising with conventional standards of prettiness, his innate romanticism is given full play. As an avowed realist Courbet may have painted the model very much as she looked, posed in the studio. Nevertheless, the pose is theatrical and the whole

affair several steps removed from what one would expect to encounter in the course of daily events, even if it is less so than an angel with wings. The picture is full of artificialities that contradict its realism, but all contradictions are meaningless in the face of the sumptuousness of the paint, applied with such richness and vigor as to make the flesh and the gleaming torrent of chestnut hair almost tangible.

Ultimately it is in this tangibility of the image that Courbet's realism lies. In *Two Girls on the Banks of the Seine* [119], one of the most luscious paintings of the century, the weight of languid flesh is all but palpable against the cool moisture of grass and leaves; the heavy cloth and airy lace have their own existence. In the portrait of *A Spanish Woman* [120] the hand concealed in the heavy hair exists as certainly as the visible portions of the figure, because the tangibility of the whole carries with it the feel of the palm pressed into the dark locks. This is Courbet's realism. But the mood of both pictures is romantically evocative. The dark shadows, the rich lights, the color that swells and recedes from black to brilliance, are moody and dramatic. It is a mood Courbet repeats again and again with complete independence of his subject. *Lady in a Riding Habit* (*L'Amazon*) [121] is a portrait of Louise Colet, a poetess of sorts with a spectacularly original and irritating personality. Courbet is not realist enough to present her features with objective accuracy or to explore her character; she serves him only as a figure emerging romantically from lushly romantic shadows. In his landscapes [122] Courbet goes to nature instead of fabricating a vision, but if he begins with real rocks, real streams, real trees, and real deer with their russet pelts, he ends by investing nature with an almost supernatural richness, where grottoes of foliage sink into greenish-black shadows and come forward into vitreous lights, where slabs of rock disappear from the warm sun into cool, heavy water, a nature as sensuous as flesh.

And always there is the paint, its own fat oiliness a part of the expressiveness of the painted objects. Courbet frequently applied paint with his palette knife, the thin flexible blade that is ordinarily used to mix colors on the palette. He would strike in the side of a rock with the flat of the knife, or with its tip he would flick in a sparkle of light. He painted whole pictures in this way, a technique familiar enough today, but with him an innovation.

Courbet was a natural painter. His only instruction was brief and under poor masters. He was the son of a farmer—a wealthy one—near the provincial city of Ornans, not a locality offering much opportunity for the discovery and development of a painter's talent. When he went to Paris, Courbet found his teachers on the walls of the Louvre, especially in the paintings of such seventeenth-century masters as Zurbarán, with their heavy shadows and full, rounded forms.

In effect self-trained, Courbet nevertheless had a picture accepted in the Salon of

120. COURBET: *A Spanish Woman*, 1855. 32 x 25¾". Philadelphia Museum of Art, John G. Johnson Collection.

1844, one that he had painted two years earlier when he was only twenty-three. The picture, a self-portrait with a black dog, was not much noticed. He exhibited six canvases in 1848, an exceptional year, a year of revolution, when, without a jury, the Salon was thrown open to all comers.

The following year this excessive democracy was corrected; but in one of the efforts to liberalize the Salon that occurred sporadically during the century, the new government ruled that the jury be composed of painters chosen by election rather than appointed from the academic clique. This liberal jury awarded Courbet a medal for a painting called *After Dinner at Ornans*, a picture of ordinary people sitting around a table in a simple interior. Courbet also had

121. COURBET: *Lady in a Riding Habit*, c. 1856. 45½ x 35⅛".
Metropolitan Museum of Art, New York, H. O. Havemeyer
Collection.

another self-portrait in this Salon, a romantically conceived painting in heavy chiaroscuro, called *The Man with the Leather Belt* [123]. Courbet was a handsome fellow, and until he became grossly fat he never tired of painting himself, always in the most admiring way. This self-adulation would be more bothersome if it were less naïve.

His early success did not last long in official circles. The Salon juries subsequent to the unusually liberal one of 1849 bitterly resented the fluke that had given a medal to this offensive intruder, and from that time on Courbet was mercilessly attacked by the Salon and reviled by conventional critics. One wonders what they might have said about Daumier (who was ten times the realist Courbet was), if he had offered the

irritations to the aestheticians and the competition to the established painters that Courbet did. For Courbet became a real threat. While Daumier was painting in obscurity, Courbet was seeking recognition through a declaration of war just as the romantics had done before him, choosing the usual battlefield, the Salon, for his conquest. He was a threat to the intellectual lethargy of the average critic, who had no intention of examining new ideas when the old ones were so easy to repeat year after year, and he was a potential competitor to the conventional painters who had staked out a market in the gigantic salesroom that the Salon had become.

Courbet: His "Socialism"

When Courbet won his medal he had no theories about realism. He was painting only what it appealed to him to paint. Both *After Dinner at Ornans* and *The Man with the Leather Belt* deny Courbet's later contention that the artist "does not have the right to enlarge upon" nature, that he "trifles with it at the risk of denaturing the beautiful which exists in the most diverse forms of reality." He claimed that "Beauty as given by nature is superior to all the conventions of the artist." But of course it isn't, and in these early paintings as well as in most of his later ones the conventions of the artist serve Courbet well, not so much in the direction of his "visible and tangible world" as in the expression of some poetic mystery existing beneath it. Even *Two Girls on the Banks of the Seine*, which takes art out of the studio and puts it on a familiar river bank—reflecting the kind of life enjoyed by the new middle class with its gardens, its walks in the country, and its Sunday excursions—ends not as a representation of two young bourgeois women on the banks of the Seine but as a sensuous evocation.

However, in certain pictures Courbet's departure from conventional subject matter and his relatively realistic treatment of it— relative in comparison with the derivative idealism making up the work of the rank and file of his contemporaries—offered some

122. COURBET: *The Grotto, c.* 1860. 25¼ x 31⅛″. Baltimore Museum of Art, Cone Collection.

123. COURBET: *The Man with the Leather Belt, c.* 1844. 39½ x 32½″. Louvre, Paris.

basis for the attacks that were made upon him. His trouble with the Salon began the year following his medal. Under Salon regulations any painter who had won a medal could exhibit thereafter without submitting his work to the jury. The jury of 1850, back to normal abuses, suffered from its immediate predecessor's liberality. Courbet took advantage of his position as a previous medal winner to exhibit nine pictures, including a large demonstration piece called *A Burial at Ornans* [124], showing a group of peasants and *bourgeoisie* around an open grave in the harsh countryside near his native city.

A *Burial at Ornans* is an impressive picture, huge, sober, richly and conscientiously painted, a prodigious technical demonstration without fireworks. It is irreproachable as a demonstration of the academic virtues of sound draughtsmanship, and it is more

124. COURBET: *A Burial at Ornans*, 1849. 123 x 261″. Louvre, Paris.

than adequate as a composition. But the attacks on it were virulent. Without much question the objections were quite arbitrary, being inspired more by Courbet's personal presumptuousness than by the inherent nature of the painting. Courbet had observed the simple people around the grave most sympathetically, but for the picture to have been labeled "socialistic" for this reason seems fantastic. Nevertheless this happened, and *Stonebreakers* in the same Salon, showing a laborer and a ragged boy at this work, was given the same tag. Both subjects were unusual, and in both pictures common people were represented without the sentimentality or condescension that would have made them acceptable to Salon taste. Compared with the prettified subjects alongside them on the walls of the exhibition, Courbet's peasants seemed like brutes, and the painter's normally sympathetic attitude toward them was found to be socially and politically offensive.

Courbet enjoyed the furore, especially since he soon found admirers outside the Salon. Because the aestheticians attacked his paintings as socialism, the socialists countered by defending them as art. This confusion of values was unfortunate for Courbet. Under the influence of the so-

cialist philosopher Pierre Joseph Proudhon, with whom he formed a friendship, Courbe began to take himself seriously as a political thinker. Labeled a socialist, he said that he was "not only socialist, but furthermore democratic and republican, in a word a partisan of all revolution and above all a realist, a sincere friend of the true truth." Such a statement sounds good at first, but it begins to fall apart when examined. Émile Zola, the realistic novelist and one of the great liberal spirits of the century, recognized Courbet's inadequacy as a social philosopher and said, "Oh, poor dear Master, Proudhon's book has left you with a case of democratic indigestion." Proudhon's book was the formulation of a theory of the social function of art that he set down in 1865, his *Du principe de l'art et de sa destination sociale*. Courbet boasted that *A Burial at Ornans* was the burial of romanticism, echoing Gros's remark that *Massacres of Scio* was the massacre of painting. He made an effort to bind his art to political theory, but the truth is that he was too much of a painter and not enough of a theorist to conceive a painting in anything but the shallowest of theoretical terms. In celebration of the appearance of his friend's book, Courbet painted a portrait of Proud-

125. COURBET: *Proudhon and His Daughters*, 1865. 66 x 78". *Petit Palais*, Paris.

hon with his two little daughters [125]. The socialist philosopher sits in a very pose-y pose, with books and manuscript near by, painted with acutely naturalistic precision. Courbet's "democratic indigestion" is paralleled in the images of this picture, where he forces his realistic theory into a literal application and produces the most artificial painting of his career.

Courbet enjoyed being in the public eye, where he remained dramatically as he continued to exhibit scot-free of the jury in successive Salons. At the 1853 Salon, Napoleon III did him the service of threatening to slash one of his paintings with a whip. Fortunately Courbet was wealthy enough not to have to depend upon selling his pictures to the Salon public, and when he did sell he sold for good prices to collectors with special tastes. His chief patron was Alfred Bruyas of Montpellier, but the Comte de Morny, a powerful dignitary of the Second Empire, was also his patron in secret. Courbet used to visit Bruyas in

Montpellier, and has recorded one visit in a picture of staggering arrogance, *The Encounter*, which came to be called *Bonjour Monsieur Courbet* [126], showing the painter setting out for a day's work, posed to display his handsome bearded profile at its best, while Bruyas and a manservant address him with the subservient humility appropriate to vassals before their lord. Bruyas was not the kind of man shown here —but Courbet was.

Courbet: "The Painter's Studio"

At this time the Paris cafés were becoming more and more the meeting places for discussion and exchange of ideas between artists, as the younger ones began more and more to abandon the studios of official painters to seek out the men who were in revolt against the academic system. Courbet's special cafés were the *Brasserie des Martyrs* and the *Andler Keller,* where he

126. COURBET: *The Encounter*, 1854. 50¾ x 58½". *Musée Fabre*, Montpellier.

was surrounded by admiring students. In spite of his egotism Courbet was interested in helping young painters. He visited their studios, was patient with their requests for aid, and seems generally to have given them the stimulus that they could not find in the hidebound instruction of the official schools.

Finally in 1861 there was a minor revolt within the sacred walls, and a group of students from the Academy petitioned Courbet to teach them. In a public letter, written with the help of his literary friend Castagnary, Courbet told them that he could not consent to enter into a student–teacher relationship because each man's art was necessarily his own if it was to be of any significance. But he took advantage of the opportunity to make a statement of faith, and he did consent to the setting up of a studio to give informal criticism to the students, who would be working largely on their own. The studio was not a great success, but it produced one noteworthy sketch

showing the class at work with a bull on the model stand instead of the usual nude. (The bull actually had been brought into the studio.) This was in line with the idea that realism should abandon all artificialities and deal with the coarse reality of simple things, but there is also something artificial about a bull on a model stand.

Courbet's pre-eminence as a rebel and martyr had been established a few years before this student petition. As the informally proclaimed leader of the realists, he had set about the production of a painting that would be his manifesto, standing in a corresponding position to *The Horatii* and *The Sabines* for classicism, and to *Raft of the Medusa* and *Massacres of Scio* for romanticism. The full title of the tremendous picture was *The Painter's Studio, a Real Allegory, Summarizing a Seven-year Phase of My Artistic Life* [127]. The title, and the conception of the picture, were presumptuous; Courbet never questioned for a moment that the general public would be as interested in the man Courbet as in the theory of realism, and this egocentricity is carried out literally in the composition. The artist is seated dramatically in the middle of his picture at work on a landscape. On one side of the studio are grouped the proletarian types who had served him as subjects, while on the other are various friends and well-wishers. In detail, the allegory runs something like this:

At left: a poacher and his dog (the Hunt, a frequent subject of Courbet's) seem to look with some suspicion at a sombrero, a guitar, and a dagger (Romantic Poetry—also, elements in certain very early paintings by Courbet). A death's head lies upon a copy of the periodical *Le Journal des Débats* (the Press, and perhaps a comment on censorship, or the sterility of critical journalism). A lay figure, or artist's manikin, hangs attached to a stake (either a symbol of academic art, or a reference to paintings of the Crucifixion, or both). A vine-grower (Labor) is surrounded by figures representing types who, in Courbet's half-jelled social philosophy, prey upon the people, namely, a Jewish secondhand dealer (Commerce), a buffoon (the Theater), a priest, and a prostitute.

So much for the left. At right: in the foreground, a man and woman who represent knowledgeable art lovers; a couple embracing near the window (Love? Possibly the free love of socialist liberation); the poet and friendly critic Baudelaire, reading a book and representing the Art of Poetry.* The critic Champfleury represents Prose; Proudhon himself, who probably suggested this allegorical mish-mash, represents Social Philosophy; one Promayet, Music, and one Max Buchon, Realistic Poetry. Finally, the enlightened collector and friend Bruyas symbolizes the Maecenas upon whose patronage the arts have always depended.

As for the nude model standing behind the painter, she may represent Courbet's realistic muse, but she also fulfills the unwritten law that every demonstration piece

---

* Baudelaire's friendly connection with Courbet did not last long. Later he referred to "the mob of vulgar artists and literary men whose shortsighted intelligence takes shelter behind the vague and obscure word Realism."

of this kind intended for Salon exhibition must include a nude, to show the painter's mastery, and some still life, here the magnificently painted yards of cloth she holds and the objects upon it where it tumbles onto the floor. As for the admiring small boy and the cat, their allegorical function is tenuous if it exists at all.

The absurdities of this rigmarole are so extreme that it would be unfair to enumerate them if Courbet's painting, as usual, did not make up for everything else. As a manifesto of realism the picture is as curious as it is as an allegory. Separate passages are only as realistic as Courbet usually was, which means that they are romantically presented. And when we add to this the unrealism of the arrangement, *The Painter's Studio* becomes a manifesto indeed—but not the one Courbet had in mind, proclaiming as it does the victory of his persistently romantic vision over his professed goal.

Courbet: The Pavilion of Realism

Courbet planned to exhibit *The Painter's Studio* along with a second showing of his first sensation, *A Burial at Ornans*, at the Exposition Universelle of 1855, one of the series of world's fairs staged in France at intervals during the century. For this Exposition the conditions of the Salon were modified. It was made international for the first time, with an international jury. The French entries were to summarize the preeminence of France in the arts, and in these special circumstances the *hors concours* ruling permitting medalists to exhibit without submitting to the jury was abrogated. Several of Courbet's entries were accepted, but *The Painter's Studio* and *A Burial at Ornans* were rejected by a jury that must have felt great elation in returning the *Burial* this time, in retaliation for Courbet's having inflicted it on an impotent jury in 1850.

The rejection of *The Painter's Studio* was especially disconcerting to Courbet, since Ingres, who had not entered a picture in the Salon for twenty years, had been induced to carry the banner for classicism with forty canvases, a retrospective of his career, while "modern" art was represented

127. COURBET: *The Painter's Studio*, 1855. 141 x 234″. Louvre, Paris.

by Delacroix with about the same number. Romanticism, a quarter of a century after its youthful excesses, was becoming acceptable to the general public, although again Delacroix's mysterious political affiliations may have carried some weight.

To compete with these impressive displays of idealism, Courbet decided to exhibit his rejected paintings, with others, in a special building constructed at his own expense, which he called the Pavilion of Realism. David had made a small fortune through private exhibition of *The Sabines*, and so had Géricault with the *Raft of the Medusa*, but Courbet's Pavilion of Realism was a fiasco. It attracted so few visitors that he did not even recover its costs, a hard blow in itself but not nearly so hard as the humiliating implication of public indifference. The Pavilion of Realism was deserted during most of the Exposition, but its unhappy entrepreneur might have taken some comfort if he could have read an entry in the journal of one distinguished visitor. "I

went to see Courbet's exhibition," Delacroix wrote. "There alone for nearly an hour. I discovered a masterpiece in his rejected picture. I couldn't tear myself away from it. They have refused, there, one of the most extraordinary works of our time."

And of course Delacroix was right. *The Painter's Studio* is an extraordinary picture and a fine one. Its pretentious allegorical nonsense is not important. When all is said and done, Courbet remains here, as in all his work, a pure painter in spite of his theorizing and his politicking. The art of David is richer after we know it as a demonstration of a theory of art and a statement of social dedication. The more we know about Delacroix's aesthetics and his technical processes the more we find in his pictures. But with Courbet it is the reverse. His professed realism and his professed socialism are worse than no help at all in enjoying his art; they would actually stand in the way if we had to consider them, but fortunately we do not.

128. Poussin: *The Funeral of Phocion*, 1648. 46¾ x 70½". Louvre, Paris.

Courbet was a painter-born, with neither Delacroix's intellect nor David's shrewdness. But beyond either of these men he had a capacity for responding to the everyday world, a talent of such strength that when his brush was in his hand his theories about art and society dropped away and left him purely and simply in the only capacity in which he was without question great and sure of his ground: great and sure of his ground as a man with a full-blooded love of sensuous experience and a painter who translated his world into corresponding images.

Courbet's world was a place where the literal reality of things—peasants at a funeral, deer in the green depths of a woods, a snow field, the sea, baskets of flowers, two girls lying on the grassy banks of a river—is identical with his unanalytical response to them. This response is not a complicated one but it is always present. He responds to the human warmth of simple people, to the cool secrecy of the woods and the rich waxy pelts of the deer, to the breadth of the sea or a river and the heavy sheen of its water or the tumbling foam of waves, to the opulence of healthy flesh and the heaviness of a coil of hair, to cloths and laces. In front of his paintings we need no theory, aesthetic or political, to derive the fullest satisfactions they have to offer. We are reminded of the wisest thing Courbet ever said: "There can be no schools; there are only painters."

Courbet's career, and his life, ended in a footnote beginning with the promise of glory and ending in exile. His Salon medal had coincided almost exactly with the election of Louis Napoleon as first president of the Second Republic, and the twenty years of his reign (as Napoleon III after 1852) were the great years of Courbet's life as a painter. In March, 1871, after the humiliating defeat of the Franco-Prussian War, the population of Paris rose against the government, and for a while it appeared that in the ensuing Commune Courbet was to be what David had been just after the Revolution. Suddenly his overpublicized socialism was not a liability but a recommendation, and he was elected to the body of representatives of the people, made president of an assembly of artists, and put at the head of a commission to safeguard the Louvre and other national art treasures. As David had done almost a hundred years before, Courbet now abolished the school of the Academy, as well as the Academy in Rome, and did away with Salon medals.

But these "reforms" lasted no time at all. The Commune ended in May, and reprisals began. Courbet was sentenced to prison, and after several months there he was removed to a nursing home. He was an aging man now, ill and, for the first time, defeated. During the rioting of the Commune a national monument, the Colonne Vendôme, had been wrecked. It was—and is—a giant column designed after the model of ancient Roman commemorative columns, a neo-classical tribute to Napoleon. Courbet, the anticlassicist, had once said that it should be torn down. Whether or not he had anything to do with its destruction is not certain, but he was ordered to pay the costs of its repair and re-erection. Even for Courbet, who was still a wealthy man, this was impossible. He managed to escape to Switzerland, where he died six years later.

The State of Landscape

While the partisans of Ingres, Delacroix, and Courbet were carrying on their three-cornered debate in the studios in Paris, something new was happening in the countryside near the capital. Easels were beginning to sprout among the woods, in the fields, and along the banks of rivers. For the first time, French painters were taking natural landscape seriously.

Landscape painting as the more-or-less accurate reflection of a specific scene from nature hardly existed (in France) before the second quarter of the nineteenth century. There were souvenir paintings of famous views, and occasional exceptions, such as David's view of the Luxembourg Gardens painted from the window of the room where he was imprisoned, but there was not a landscape tradition as landscape is generally thought of today, having to do with trees, streams, hills, clouds, and other components of nature in their natural combinations. A literary gentleman-collector named Deperthes, in the eighteenth century, summed up the attitude toward landscape pretty well when he defined it as "the art of composing sites after choosing the most beautiful and the most noble elements offered by nature." Deperthes warned that "If the study of nature is indispensable, it should be considered nothing more than a secondary means in a type of painting which, if it is to be properly accomplished, demands above all the inventive skill and the purity of taste which alone can give order to the inspirations of genius."

The countryside in its uncorrected state was not very highly thought of. It was accidental, unorganized, and impure. Gardens were formal; the obvious thing to do with a tree was to line it up with other trees and trim the whole row into a common shape. In his studio the painter worked in much the same way, without the uniformity but with just as much artificiality in the creation of ideal shapes from natural ones. Landscape was synthesized from harmonized trees, perfected hills, well-disciplined streams, and generic clouds. The landscape painter's job was to organize these elements into compositions of purity, nobility, serenity, and perfect proportion. This is classicism, of course. Classical landscape was idealized; it was structural; it was heroic—a fitting counterpart to the figures of gods and heroes created in much the same way.

Such landscape may fall easily into the familiar traps of the classical style: monotony, sterility, and decorative formula. But it need not do so. The finest classical landscape ever painted is probably *The Funeral of Phocion* [128] by the Academy's seventeenth-century god Nicolas Poussin (1594–1665). (If it is not the finest, then some other one of Poussin's is.) It is an extremely complicated picture, but from its complication all confusion, agitation, and uncertainty have been removed. Each of its elements—and there must be hundreds of them—is conceived less as a tree, or a branch, or a wall, or a figure, or a building or a piece of cloth or a cart, than as an abstract form that must be adjusted to take its place in balance with all the other forms in the composition.

The satisfactions to be found in *The Funeral of Phocion* have nothing to do with the pleasures to be found in nature. Neither may much interest be looked for in its nominal subject. Phocion was an Athenian general who was unjustly convicted and executed for treason, and the picture shows his sheeted body being carried beyond the city walls to unsanctified ground. But the painter is not interested in telling the story or making a parable. The subject is of incidental, less than incidental, importance. The picture's title may be *The Funeral of Phocion* but its real subject is Order. The satisfaction to be derived from it comes from the contemplation of this order in its perfection, its serenity, its abstract clarity from which all confusion, accident, and impurity has been distilled.

But we have already seen that for the romantic soul perfect order was not enough. Or, rather, it was the wrong thing. The romantic responded to nature in its untrammeled aspects, seeing trees, streams, flowers, birds, clouds, the wind, the rain, and the simple people living close to these things, as manifestations of the vague, universal mystery toward which the romantic spirit yearns for emotional fulfillment. When this yearning was most intense it demanded turbulent aspects of nature to satisfy it, even menacing ones. "Arise, ye desired storms!" was a familiar romantic cry. Nothing could be too big or too disorderly—crags in disarray, wild valleys, tempests, cataclysms—or too exotic.

This emotionalized landscape, too, was conjured up in the studio, and it too had a tradition as old as that of classical landscape. As a single example, *The Cemetery* [129] by Jacob van Ruisdael (1628–1682) is filled with storm clouds, a rainbow, shattered trees, unruly water, a ruined abbey, with mysterious dark recesses and sudden spectral lights. And it is, of course, as carefully and as artificially a concocted landscape as is *The Funeral of Phocion*.

The new landscapists who fled the studios for the countryside were thoroughly sympathetic to the classical idea that landscape painting involved problems of composition, a balanced disposition of the forms within the picture space. They were even more sympathetic to the idea that nature was full of emotional connotations which it was the painter's privilege to reveal. But they subjugated both these ideas to a third: they believed that any fragment of nature as it existed, even the most familiar and commonplace bit of field, river bank, or forest, was a legitimate subject for a work of art that could be intellectually satisfying without classical artificialities, and emotionally expressive without recourse to the usual romantic stimulants.

There was some precedent for this way of feeling also, in England. English painters were already at work from something like the same point of view, and in seventeenth-century Holland there had been similar development along with romantic examples, such as the one we have just seen.* The Frenchmen drew freely from both sources without imitating either. The important point historically is that these were Frenchmen introducing a concept of nature altogether radical to the tradition of French landscape, a concept that was to become the dominant one during the next seventy years when French painters were setting new directions for the art of all the Western world.

* The English painters receive their due later on in this book. One of them, Constable, with *The Hay Wain* [313] of the 1824 Salon, has already been mentioned in connection with Delacroix. As for the Hollanders, it is conventional to point out that the bourgeois origin of their seventeenth-century school of realistic landscape corresponds to the bourgeois origin of the French painting about to be discussed here. This is true, with the difference that the Dutch landscapes were part of a movement in painting stimulated by the Dutch love of things the good burghers proudly treasured—their houses full of possessions, their countryside, and themselves. This was less true in nineteenth-century France. As a broad statement of the difference: the Dutch landscapes are records of fact, while the French ones are records of responses to fact.

129. RUISDAEL: *The Cemetery, c.* 1660. 56 x 74¼″. Detroit Institute of Arts.

Barbizon: Rousseau, Dupré, Diaz

One of the centers for the painters who began to flee Paris to discover nature was Barbizon, a picturesque village on the edge of the Forest of Fontainebleau not far from Paris. The Forest of Fontainebleau is one of those neat, gracious woods never for a moment to be confused with a wilderness and seldom suggesting anything more savage than the upper reaches of Central Park. But it afforded vistas where the hand of rational man was as inconspicuous as it is allowed to be anywhere in France. And near the forest there were fields, peasants, and peasant cottages, which interested some of the painters, as well as chickens, ducks, and cattle, which held an unreasonable fascination for others of them. The Barbizon painters were not formally organized into a "movement," but the name of the village has attached itself to a dozen or so landscapists and painters of peasants or animals, of whom several spent a great

deal of time there. Others made occasional visits and still others worked elsewhere but in the same spirit.

The spirit is best classified as romantic-realistic. As realists the Barbizon painters made direct reference to nature and even worked directly in its presence with respectful attention to the actual disposition of its forms. It is difficult to make this sound like much of an innovation, today when everyone's idea of a landscape painter is an artist at an easel set out in the open air, but an innovation it was. Even Courbet ordinarily fabricated his landscapes indoors (as he shows himself doing in *The Painter's Studio*), although he made sketches for them out of doors (as he shows himself setting out to do in *Bonjour Monsieur Courbet*). His advice to young painters was to work from nature "even if from a dunghill." The Barbizon painters had been working from nature for years, being somewhat older than Courbet. And being much more temperate they were not interested in

130. T. Rousseau: *Under the Birches,* 1842. 16⅝ x 25⅜". Toledo Museum of Art, Gift of Arthur J. Secor.

dunghills. As romantic-realists they were interested not only in the look of nature but in discovering its "moods," the "spirit" of trees and fields and skies, "the oak wrestling with the rock," one of them said. But the mood was always discovered within the subject; the subject was never violated to serve the mood. Even when the final picture was to be painted in the studio, as it usually was, the painter subjected himself to the discipline of preliminary study out of doors, working closely within the bounds of the subject's physical identity.

These Barbizon painters were hard at work between 1830 and 1840. At first the going was difficult, upstream against the opposition of the Academy. For a while they were castigated as vulgar, but eventually most of them were accepted in the Salons and even won medals. On the whole they were quiet, unobtrusive men, and since landscape was a secondary art their deviations from the academic norm were less offensive than they would have been in the usual demonstration paintings. By the 1850's these artists were beginning to

have successes they continued to enjoy during the rest of their lifetimes while the Academy found its whipping boy in Courbet. By the end of the century, after their deaths, their vogue was tremendous, and they became stars of the international salesrooms, being collected with particular avidity in America. Their success—and while they were alive—was speeded by the aesthetic perception and the business perspicacity of a remarkable dealer named Georges Durand-Ruel (1864–1931).

In retrospect we see that it was the misfortune of the Barbizon painters to have laid so excellent a foundation for so exceptional a generation of painters—the impressionists who followed them—that their own work has suffered by comparison. By the 1920's their paintings were being pushed to less conspicuous places on museum walls, and today they have become more than anything else a storage problem. A few examples are given exhibition space as historical fillers; certain atypical paintings, on the contrary, are much sought after, for reasons that will become apparent shortly.

131. DUPRÉ: *The Hay Wagon*, date unknown. 14¼ x 18⅛″. Metropolitan Museum of Art, New York, Wolfe Bequest.

132. DIAZ: *Forest Path*, date unknown. 28 x 23¾″. Philadelphia Museum of Art, John G. Johnson Collection.

In the meanwhile, three typical Barbizon painters will do very well to represent the school: Théodore Rousseau (1812–1867), Jules Dupré (1811–1889), and Narcisse Virgile Diaz de la Peña (1807–1876). A fourth, Constant Troyon (1810–1865) made such a success in the Salon that he is taken up in the next chapter which discusses the state of that institution at mid-century.

Of the three, Rousseau is the most rewarding after continued acquaintance. He combines a sense of the monumentality of landscape with a passion for its individual forms amounting to nature worship. He is so impressed with nature as a force that every irregularity in the growth of a tree, every blade of green that springs from the earth, every cloud that scuds busily across the sky, has for him its own vigorous life as part of a purposeful scheme full of growth and activity. He sees no need to inject romantic folderol into nature because to conceal or change any part of the natural miracle would be only to weaken it. He sees no need to put it into classical order because he feels a more powerful order behind the growth of things, the turn of the seasons, the rising or setting of the sun [130]. He painted images of this cycle of omnipotent force as men have always painted images of their gods, but he did not have to fabricate an image because it was everywhere for him to see. Mystery, revery, and philosophical explanation are only incidental to his perception of the miracle around him. The miracle was tangible, self-explanatory. He accepted it at face value and gloried in it. He was a great bearded fellow—untrimmed beards were cultivated by the Barbizon painters along with other aspects of nature in its pure state—and the suave academicians enjoyed regarding him as an oaf. But during the 1850's he attained the general popularity of the school, and Salon success as well. He was not a commuting landscapist; he spent most of his life at Barbizon, and died there.

Rousseau's pantheism, for that is what it amounted to, was a kind of poetry, but it is doubtful whether the public who admired his landscapes were aware of this quality beneath the literal "picture of

133. DAUBIGNY: *River and Bridge,* date unknown. 10½ x 17⅜". Philadelphia Museum of Art, John G. Johnson Collection.

something" painted with a high degree of objective accuracy which they spontaneously respected. Poetry of a more obvious kind was cultivated by Jules Dupré [131]. He was closer to the romantic tradition than Rousseau was. (Delacroix spoke kindly of him.) He had a great enthusiasm for the English landscapists, who were also romantics who found poetry in simple aspects of the countryside. Dupré's mood, however, is more introspective than the cheerful English one. Individually his paintings are often effective in their hint of romantic pathos within the heart of nature, but he is repetitious, and after a while one suspects that his mood was continued as his trademark after it became a good thing on the market.

Narcisse Diaz is even more conventionally romantic. In fact he falls outside the realistic half of the romantic-realist classification suitable to the school as a whole. His pictures are frankly concoctions, his most typical ones being of small, secluded clearings in the forest from which the observer looks through the broken silhouettes of leaves and branches as if from a shadowed room or a grotto, at patches of light sky or open fields beyond [132]. Occasionally

these leafy cubicles are inhabited by human beings, by ideal figures such as nymphs in white robes, or even by mythological characters. It is a pleasant formula although Diaz forced it a little.

Daubigny

The truest poet of the group was neither Dupré nor Diaz, but Charles-François Daubigny (1817–1878), who discovered poetry within his subjects instead of grafting it onto them. It is a simple poetry, as direct as it is sensitive; there is never anything dramatic or high-flown about it. Daubigny's love of nature is at the opposite pole from Rousseau's fervent adoration of it. He contemplates quiet skies, gentle rivers, level, eventless fields, in calm light. Rousseau clutched with obsessed intensity upon every natural detail: the leaf was as important as the tree; he was reluctant to forego the joy of representing each blade of grass in a field. His problem was to capture the monumentality of the whole through the enumeration of an infinite number of parts.

134. MILLET: *The Sower*, 1850. 41¼ x 33″. Provident Tradesmen's Bank and Trust Company, Philadelphia.

135. MILLET: *The Gleaners*, 1857. 33 x 44″. Louvre, Paris.

Daubigny, instead, begins with the acceptance of wholeness. There is a kind of wisdom in the breadth of his vision, its calmness, its perception of the unity of natural objects which rises above their complication. His landscape is intimate and domesticated. Farm cottages rest in his countryside as naturally and as peacefully as the shrubs and trees that have grown there; so do the small stone bridges of France and the boats on the full, quiet streams [133]. Alone among the Barbizon painters Daubigny worked entirely out of doors, even adopting a little canopied rowboat as a floating studio in order to paint the banks of the river across a placid stretch of water. He loved the cool river light impregnating fresh moist air, the gentle sobriety of small farms and quiet fields in early morning or evening light. These observations, made and recorded in the open air, place Daubigny historically as the most important of the Barbizon painters; of them all, he made the most valuable contribution to the next generation, to an extent that is only beginning to be fully recognized.

As a mine for imitators, the landscape tradition of the Barbizon painters has yielded some of the most inane pictures ever turned out by commercial hacks. Their work has been deformed into countless pretty picturesque scenes of the kind used on scenic calendars, pasted on wastebaskets, and cut up for jigsaw puzzles. The resemblances of these superficial imitations are close enough to the originals to have clouded our perception of the unobtrusive virtues of the Barbizon school.

Millet

The history of art is full of drastic re-evaluations, especially in our time which is so full of shifts and upheavals and variety in points of view. Painters are especially vulnerable during the century after their death, and the reputation of Jean-François Millet (1814–1875) has tobogganed in recent years from a point high enough to make his descent very swift. A short generation ago sepia reproductions of three of his pictures, *The Sower* [134], *The Gleaners* [135], and *The Angelus* [136] hung in every classroom and Sunday school. They are typical of Millet's most ambitious work with their peasant figures generalized into large, semisculpturesque forms dominating the foreground of a deep landscape, thrown into grander-than-life eminence against the sky, meant to be symbolical of man's union with the earth. But Millet's noble poor seem a little self-conscious of their symbolical importance, a little too cleaned up to smack convincingly of the soil of which they are supposed to be an emanation. That this should be so today is striking evidence of how taste can reverse itself, since the objections to Millet during his lifetime, objections that were violent, were on the opposite score. "This is the painting of men who don't change their linen, who want to intrude themselves upon gentlemen; this art offends me and disgusts me." The speaker was a snob,* but it is still rather sad that Millet should have suffered so during his life on one score and should be discarded later on for the opposite reason.

The generations between Millet's death and his current fall from favor admired him as a painter who had achieved the ultimate statement of the nobility of the simple man, that idea begun so long ago and adapted to such a variety of expressions. The most successful example of Millet's variety was *The Sower*, which he repeated many times. The peasant is recognizable as one of Michelangelo's naked titans, descended from the Sistine ceiling, put into rough clothes, and given a bag of grain—a disconcerting blunder of miscasting. But if this initial hurdle is cleared, we see that the figure has considerable power, its gesture is a wide, generous one, harmonious with its amplitude and its symbolism.

The Sower symbolizes the turn of the seasons, the cycle of growth, fruition, and return to the soil. It may suffer in comparison with Daumier's *Soup*, but we condescend too easily to Millet. There are dozens of virtually unknown Millets, such as *The Bleaching Tub* [137], to rebuke us.

* The same Count de Nieuwerkerke, Director of Fine Arts, who refused to look at Delacroix's St. Sulpice murals.

136. MILLET: *The Angelus*, 1857–59. 21¾ x 26". Louvre, Paris.

137. MILLET: *The Bleaching Tub, c.* 1861. 17¼ x 13". Louvre, Paris.

138. MILLET: *The Quarriers,* date unknown. 29 x 23½″. Toledo Museum of Art, Gift of Arthur J. Secor.

but not, like Courbet, of a prosperous one —and was only well enough educated to envy the condition of being a gentleman without having the means to turn himself into one. Nor had he the perception to recognize that it was not important for him to be one. He became stiff and forbidding, belonging nowhere. Young painters found him difficult to approach, although certainly he must have been hungry for the appreciation they were ready to offer. Although his pictures were accepted by the Salon, after his debut in 1847 with a classical subject, his tepid successes did not counteract the sting of harsh criticisms. He avoided Paris (no doubt because he could not afford to live there in the manner he thought he should), and he and Rousseau were the only two of the Barbizon group to settle in the village permanently. Altogether he had a difficult life. He was an honest man whose art was essentially traditional, was called radical, and now seems sentimental because he is best known by his second-best pictures.

Corot: His Popular Success

The best of the Barbizon painters are excellent men who would be difficult to include in a list of the great masters of painting. Their associate Jean-Baptiste Camille Corot (1796–1875) would be difficult to omit. Since he is not a classifiable painter, Corot is always grouped with the Barbizon school because he did some work out of doors, had certain affinities with the Barbizon spirit in some of his work, and knew and was sympathetic to the Barbizon men. He belonged to an older generation, having been born in the eighteenth century, three years before Delacroix and only seven years after the Revolution. He painted just as he pleased, propounding no set of theories in opposition to others, making no belligerent pronouncements, living the eighty years of his life so quietly and painting so modestly that it is always a surprise to discover how much influence he exerted. As an isolated instance, he was on the liberal Salon jury of 1849, the one that awarded the medal to the unknown Courbet for his *After*

Here the breadth and solidity of the forms, without derivative reference, and the drama of the light are uncloyed by sentimental values. The abstract values of painting—formal relationships for their own sake —are at least as important here as are representational ones, and the representation is uncluttered by the pretentious anecdotal overlay that mars so much of Millet's work. And in an occasional atypical picture, *The Quarriers* [138] for example, Millet is suddenly released from the efforted and naïve solemnity he so often imposed upon himself and paints instead with assurance and fervor in forms of dramatic strength remindful of Daumier at his best.

Millet's failures came when he overreached himself and were inherent in his personality. He was the son of a farmer—

139. COROT: *Souvenir de Mortefontaine*, 1864. 25¼ x 34½″. Louvre, Paris.

140. DAUMIER: *Corot Sketching at Ville d'Avray, c.* 1854–56. Wash drawing, 12½ x 9½″.
Metropolitan Museum of Art, New York, H. O. Havemeyer Collection.

Dinner at Ornans to the embarrassment of subsequent juries. He was fifty years old before his own father, a prosperous merchant, realized that there was a serious painter in the family. In that year Corot was awarded the Legion of Honor, and for the first time his father stopped saying apologetically that "Camille amuses himself with painting" and said, "Well, since they have decorated Camille, he must have talent," as neat a statement as could be invented to summarize the bourgeois attitude toward aesthetic achievement.

At nineteen Corot was working in the family's business, his father having refused to give him the money to study art. Later he was given the allowance that had been allotted to a poor relation who had died, and he lived thus until his pictures began to sell, which they did when he was well along in middle age. There seems to have been no serious conflict within the family. If there were conflicts or upheavals of any kind in Corot's life, they left no mark on

141. COROT: *View at Narni*, 1826–27. 28 x 38″. National Gallery of Canada, Ottawa.

his work. He never married and seems never even to have been in love.

The pictures that began to sell so tardily were not his best ones. But they are still the ones best known and much loved by a wide public; they are also the ones connecting him most closely with the Barbizon school. Bad prints of his *Souvenir de Morte-fontaine* [139], typical of the manner that brought him into popularity and kept him there for decades, used to hang on every other living-room wall. Fluffy trees, some grasses and shrubs flecked here and there with bits of light, a sweet body of quiet water, a mild sky, and a few small, graceful figures are combined and recombined in these pictures, painted as if seen through a cool haze. They are minor lyrics of great sweetness and tenderness, overfamiliar, and weak and obvious in comparison with Corot's best work. But they are lovely pictures and need not be rejected just because they give pleasure to so many people.

Popular success came to Corot during the 1850's. The Emperor purchased one of his poetic landscapes, *Souvenir de Marcoussis*, from the banner Salon of 1855, not as official patronage but because he liked it.

Dealers were quick to add snob value to a product that had already begun to find purchasers on the strength of its popular attraction. For the rest of his life Corot could sell as many of these pictures as he was willing to paint—more, in fact, and his pictures were forged by the hundreds. There is a story that when one poverty-stricken forger was suspected and forced to go to Corot with the picture he was offering as an original, Corot signed the forgery for him. This should not be true, but it is not out of character. Corot gave money to many artists, good or bad, who needed it. It has already been mentioned that he deeded over a country cottage to the aging and destitute Daumier, who left an affectionate record of Corot sketching at Ville d'Avray [140], a locality near Paris where Corot found many of his most intimate subjects.

Corot could have made a fortune if he had wanted to. He did make a great deal of money, which he did not need. His tastes were simple and he had been perfectly happy on his allowance. In the meanwhile, along with the pictures that were clamored for, he continued to paint the kind of pictures he liked best himself.

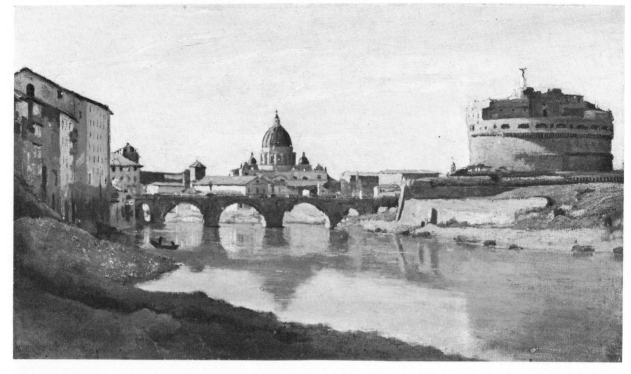

142. COROT: *Bridge and Castle of St. Angelo with Cupola of St. Peter's*, 1826–27. 10½ x 17″. California Palace of the Legion of Honor, San Francisco.

Corot and the Tradition of Landscape

Long before he hit upon his popular style, Corot was painting landscapes of an opposite solidity and definition. They are the first entirely legitimate descendants of Poussin's classical tradition after two centuries of great admiration and partial understanding. They are also among the forerunners of the modern movement, making Corot a bridge between tradition and revolution.

Corot's connection with Poussin [128] is most apparent in early pictures, such as *View at Narni* [141], where he takes an actual scene but idealizes it along Poussinesque lines. The connection is less apparent but goes deeper in pictures where he holds himself more closely to the actual appearance of the subject yet invests it with Poussin's monumental calm. As examples, his views of Rome (Rome especially, although he did similar cityscapes elsewhere)

respect objective fact with deceptive literalness. Buildings and hills are disposed approximately as they actually existed [142, 143], not juggled about at will, yet their formal relationships are as satisfying as those in a Poussin where all the forms are invented and arbitrarily combined.*

How did Corot manage to impose this perfect order on forms that in reality were combined by chance? Rome is a magnificent welter of structures and gardens, punctuated at random with some superbly organized vistas, but Corot did not choose these readymade compositions as subjects. Over-all, Rome is a hodgepodge of streets and buildings that have grown partly with-

---

* For purposes of completeness it has to be pointed out that Poussin's tradition as observed by Corot includes reference to the art of Poussin's contemporary, Claude Lorrain. But this is an unnecessary detour for getting to the main point. Lorrain's poetic devices may be echoed in *View at Narni* and are obvious in Corot's late, soft style. But Lorrain would never have painted as Corot does in the views of Rome. It is possible to imagine Poussin doing so.

143. COROT: *View of the Farnese Gardens,* 1826. 9½ x 15¾″. Phillips Collection, Washington, D.C.

out plan and partly according to a series of plans that interrupt and compete with one another. Corot takes views of this welter and brings them into classical order without appearing to depart from an approximation of photographic reality.

As an explanation of how he went about doing this, his own statement "Form and value—there are the essentials" tells everything and nothing. Form and value are part of the jargon of any tenth-rate painter. Corot's words tell us nothing we cannot see for ourselves, that like every painter working from nature he begins with the raw material presented by the forms and values as they exist, and makes his own adjustments of their relationships to achieve his own variation on the theme of the visible world. Thousands of painters do this, with varying degrees of technical skill. Some of the worst are more highly developed technicians than Corot was. But very few of them enlarge or clarify our experience. Certain of Corot's

adjustments are apparent to anyone. He avoids strong value contrasts, sticking to the middle range of half tones. He mutes color similarly. If it were possible to superimpose a photograph of the scene over one of his paintings, his variations from actual proportions and dispositions would not be extreme. But slight or great, they put the subject into order.

In this respect it may be illuminating to compare Corot's transmutation of a specific scene, a view of the Church of Santa Maria della Salute seen from across the Grand Canal in Venice [144] with the same subject as treated by one of the most commonplace spirits among nineteenth-century painters, the academician J. L. E. Meissonier [145]. One of the most successful painters of the day, Meissonier is the subject of more detailed comments later on in this book. He was a painter without technical limitations and equally without depth or sensitivity. The painting under consid-

144. COROT: *View of the Quay of the Schiavoni, Venice*, 1834. 12¼ x 11⅜". National Gallery of Victoria, Melbourne, Australia, Felton Bequest.

145. MEISSONIER: *View of Venice*, 1888. Louvre, Paris.

eration here is a muddle of gondolas, mooring masts, lanterns, water, and architecture, all painted with bright facility and a high degree of representational accuracy. From detail to detail Meissonier's collection of factual statements may be read with considerable interest by anyone with an affection for Venice, as a kind of snapshot reminder of that enchanted city, but beyond this limited function the picture does not exist. It is a parasite on its subject: it neither intensifies nor clarifies our sentiment or our understanding. At best it merely stirs up some pleasant associations and engages our attention momentarily because the representational trickery of brush and paint is so deft. It is an immediately attractive and then almost as immediately a wearisome picture. It badgers us with irrelevant details; it nags at us to admire the flashy skill with which they are represented. Oddly enough, for all its detailed accuracy it is only superficially a true picture of the scene. Looking across the Canal toward Santa Maria della Salute one is conscious of the openness of sky, the flatness of water, the isolation of beautiful monuments within these expanses. The

haphazard and accidental minutiae of the city are lost within this bigger scheme.

It is the big scheme with which Corot has concerned himself, not only by the selection of a more distant point of view but also by the arbitrary selection and placement of such elements as packing cases, barrels, and human figures, as well as moored boats, to balance and harmonize the architectural elements whose placement is predetermined. The resultant composition is more nostalgically a reminder of Venice than Meissonier's snapshot can ever be, even though it contains conspicuous elements, such as Oriental figures and sailing vessels, that none of us has ever seen there. But this evocative power is the least important aspect of Corot's achievement. Because he is an original spirit where Meissonier was a commonplace one, Corot sees Venice through a personality that invests it with the serenity and harmony of his own vision and thus enlarges our own vision of it. And quite aside from the fact that this is a picture of a certain city, it is a painting in which the disposition of forms would be deeply satisfying even if the subject were as completely an invented one as *The Funeral of Phocion*.

It is possible to discover in a general way how Corot's apparent objectivity has transcended itself, although his own comments on the quality of his objectivity are of no help at all. "I paint a woman's breast exactly as I would paint an ordinary bottle of milk," he said. No description could be more inaccurate than this one with its crassness and its implied denial of any selective response to visible reality. He could better have said, "I paint an ordinary bottle of milk as if it were a woman's breast," for every object he paints is part of a world elevated by the contemplation of this one with sentiment and dignity.

Like Poussin's, Corot's world is a quiet one where contemplation offers greater pleasures than action. Like Poussin's it is a world regarded from a distance, yet from this distance it is a world of extraordinary clarity. This clarity may be close to magical, as it is in the transformation of *The House and Factory of M. Henry* [146] and *Village Church, Rosny* [147] from commonplace-

146. COROT: *The House and Factory of M. Henry*, 1833. 33 x 41". Philadelphia Museum of Art, Wilstach Collection.

147. COROT: *Village Church, Rosny*, 1844. 21½ x 31½". Collection Mr. and Mrs. Lloyd Bruce Wescott, Clinton, N.J.

ness or pretty picturesqueness into enchantment. The eye is freed from its limitations and sees the smallest details in faraway objects. But these details are never prolix. Like everything else they are selected and adjusted into harmony and balance. Corot's world is simpler than Poussin's, more intimate because it is less complex. And where Poussin's world is created serene within a kind of crystal vacuum, Corot's has become serene surrounded by the breath of life. And in the two pictures just mentioned, the peaceful innocence so characteristic of Corot's world is emphasized by the suggestion of naïveté, almost of awkwardness, in the draughtsmanship of certain details, notably the human figures. This occurs frequently in Corot's paintings and is a larger factor in setting the character of his world than is generally recognized.

Apparently Corot never formulated a specific problem for himself, never worked toward the crystallization of any aesthetic theory. To say that he "felt his way" toward expression is misleading if it suggests fumbling. But it will do very well to describe his way of creating pictures, if by

"feeling his way" we mean the development of acute sensitivities to form and value and color relationships that must be brought into balance by a sense of their rightness without dependence on rule. When the composition of a picture is systematic (*The Oath of the Horatii*, or *Raft of the Medusa*), it is possible to define the relationship of each part to the whole without fear of misreading the painter's scheme. But when the composition is "felt," there is always the danger that an effort to analyze it by hindsight may yield conclusions that would surprise the painter who organized it in the first place.

Nevertheless, what can we find in a small Corot called *Mur, Côtes du Nord* [148], where he was free to dispose the forms compositionally in any way he chose, not being bound by the predisposition of forms existing as the buildings of a city? We might say that of the five little figures, the one to the left in the background group echoes the attitude of the corresponding one in the foreground pair, thus tying the groups together. Or reading the figures as a foreground group of two and a back-

148. Corot: *Mur, Côtes du Nord,* 1850–55. 13 x 21⅞". Philadelphia Museum of Art, John G. Johnson Collection.

ground group of three, we may enjoy the variety of this balance. On the other hand, the standing figure may be separated from the rest and we may find that the picture is composed as a kind of double seesaw with the mound of earth, center, as a pivot. One plank of the seesaw would stretch diagonally into the depth of the picture from foreground left to middleground right, balanced at either end by paired figures. The second plank on the same pivot would cross the first at right angles, balanced at either end by the standing figure and the pyramidal block centered above and behind the heads of the foreground figures.

Whether the picture is analyzed from any of these beginnings or from any one of a half a dozen other possible ones, everything in it falls reasonably into place. Yet the composition was probably not schematic in Corot's mind. *The Oath of the Horatii* and *Raft of the Medusa* are both variations on accepted schemes, the *Horatii* with icy brilliance, the *Raft* with respectable competence. But Corot could not bring himself to borrow even the elementary skeleton of an established compositional formula. "It is better to be nothing than to be the echo of other paintings," he wrote in his notebook. His quietness makes his originality inconspicuous, yet Corot was as original as any of the noisier revolutionaries who made great stirs in his lifetime.

Corot: Portraits and Figure Studies

During his lifetime Corot's portraits and figure studies were all but ignored; today they have become the most sought after of all his work. Usually these are of young women, only now and then of men or children. There are well above 300 of them, of which Corot exhibited only two, and they are the most personal work of an unusually personal artist. Like his landscapes, they are a firm bridge between tradition and contemporary painting. This is a general statement and is most important as a general one, but it may be brought down to specific terms by comparisons of Corot's *Woman with the Pearl* [150] with Leonardo da Vinci's *Mona Lisa* [149] and of

149. LEONARDO DA VINCI: *Mona Lisa, c.* 1505. 30½ x 20⅞". Louvre, Paris.

150. COROT: *Woman with the Pearl, c.* 1868–70. 27½ x 21¼". Louvre, Paris.

his *Interrupted Reading* [151] with Picasso's *Lady with a Fan* [152].

The similarity between *Woman with the Pearl* and *Mona Lisa* is too close to be accidental and, of course, Corot was familiar with the Renaissance masterpiece in the Louvre. Originally he followed it even more closely; he first painted the hair in an arrangement like Mona Lisa's and then modified it. The strands can still be seen as raised pigment in *Woman with the Pearl* although Corot has painted them out in giving his model a different coiffure. But for all its frank use of the earlier picture as a prototype, *Woman with the Pearl* is not an Italianate imitation but an original work of art. While French academic painters were

imitating the surfaces of Renaissance painting, mistaking stylistic plagiarism for philosophical union with the masters (even Ingres was guilty sometimes), Corot brushed superficialities to one side and understood the formal construction upon which the Renaissance statement was based. Like *Mona Lisa, Woman with the Pearl* is a massing of volumes building from the hands, placed parallel to the picture plane, into the masses of the torso, turned slightly away into the picture space, and returning as the head returns toward a full frontal view. These major volumes and the movement from one to another are enriched by the minor ones that compose them. Corot understands this formal structure but

151. COROT: *Interrupted Reading*, 1865–70. 36½ x 25¾″. Art Institute of Chicago, Potter Palmer Collection.

152. PICASSO: *Lady with a Fan*, 1905. 39¾ x 32″. Collection Mr. and Mrs. Averell Harriman, New York.

utilizes it for individual expression, just as an architect might understand the construction of Renaissance buildings with their arches and vaults and the nobility of their volumes but would make contemporary use of the concept without rebuilding a Renaissance palace. *Woman with the Pearl* has the tenderness and the intimacy of Corot's finest landscapes; it has also their structural subtlety of form and color which invests an apparently casual subject with a truly classical repose. Such trivial and apparently realistic details as the folds of a sleeve, a loosely fastened bodice, a fall of hair, are parts of an image so firmly integrated that trivialities are transmuted into ideal monumentality. Corot's achievement in paintings like this one was to bring into absolute harmony the apparently incompatible elements of intimacy and nobility, of sensitive vision and formal abstraction.

It is this formal abstraction that allies him to modern painting. Even more than *Woman with the Pearl, Interrupted Reading* seems casual in its pose. The pose, also, is more original and more complicated in its building up of mutually supporting and balancing volumes. The similarity to Picasso's *Lady with a Fan* is probably coincidental, but it is not very important whether the composition of the modern picture, consciously or not, stems from Corot's. What is important is that the masterful abstract construction, which in Corot is concealed beneath a deceptive appearance of inconsequential ease, is emphasized in Picasso where the pose is frankly an artificial one. In Picasso's design the abstractions of pictorial composition are exposed for their own interest, demanding at least equal attention with whatever emotional or evocative character the painting may also have. In other words, Corot's painting is traditional in that its abstractions are concealed from the lay observer even though they account for much of the painting's appeal to him; Picasso's is "modern" because these abstractions are brought to the surface and attention is called to them in order to make the most of the intellectual pleasure such abstractions afford.

This is the fundamental revolution in modern painting, and as this story goes on we will see that eventually the result is a reversal of values: in traditional painting, abstract values must be sought beneath the immediate representational and emotional or evocative ones. In modern painting, emotional and philosophical values may be deciphered within abstractions that seem at first not to offer them. But this is a parenthetical jump into the twentieth century, which the reader may feel free to forget for the moment. In the meanwhile, it is enough to remember that Corot is a formal painter as well as an artist of tender sensibility.

His *Mother and Child on Beach* [153] demonstrates both aspects with particular emphasis. The protective gesture of the young mother, which could easily have turned mawkish, is as dignified as it is gentle. The figure is designed in unusually large and simple volumes, with a broad and powerful movement initiated by the arclike fold at the bottom of the skirt, continuing in the emphatic one running along the right side up to the waist, then continuing along the back to terminate in the oval of the head. The broad sweep of this circling movement dips suddenly and flows along the long arms to terminate when it finds its goal, the figure of the child, which is painted as a solid, static pyramid, an effective brake on a movement so strong that it demands this decisive termination if it is not to carry us outside the picture. This strong static element on the left is reflected on the right by the two parallel horizontal bands of light cloth at the bottom of the picture and the triangular fold of cloth of the skirt just above them; this in turn is incorporated within the general movement of the forms first described.

It is difficult to avoid enumerating dozens of Corot's figure pictures in discussing

153. COROT: *Mother and Child on Beach*, 1868–70. 14⅞ x 18⅛". Philadelphia Museum of Art, John G. Johnson Collection.

them, since each one offers new delights and new variations on his theme. Yet this theme should seem limited, since again and again he presents us with a picture where the mood is one of gentle, inconsequential revery, touched by the faintest melancholy and a hint of languor, a mood that would pall and would certainly degenerate into trifling affectation if it were not stated in forms of such logical decision, revealed in steady, moderate light, constructed in colors dominated by the subtlest grays, grayed blues, creamy yellows, and occasional accents of rich reds. It is an art of nuances—nuances of form, of color, of mood. If the pictures have a quality of simplicity it is because these nuances are perfectly controlled to fuse form, color, and mood into a harmony so unified that it appears to have been arrived at all of a piece. One of the masterpieces is *Young Greek Girl* [155], a portrait of Emma Dobigny, a favorite model of Corot's. The Greek costume is only an accessory. Corot's "Albanian Girls," "Jewesses of Algiers," "Oriental Women," "Judiths," and "Gypsies" have nothing to do with the passionate drama of romanticism, nor do his occasional

154. Corot: *The Artist's Studio*, 1865–70. 16 x 13″. Baltimore Museum of Art, Cone Collection.

155. Corot: *Young Greek Girl*, 1868–70. 32⅝ x 21¼″. Collection Mr. and Mrs. J. Watson Webb, New York.

nude bacchantes have anything to do with revelries of the flesh.

Corot's figures are most at home costumed, and indoors. Although he frequently fabricates a landscape behind them, they remain surrounded by the quiet air, the peaceful seclusion, the intimate protection, of a simple and familiar interior. In one series of figure studies he represents models in his studio, showing a corner of the room, and his easel [154]. Corot's natural habitat is the secluded room, the quiet landscape, or the city in moments when its monuments and rivers and the spaces of its streets and squares are at rest. Yet Corot was an active man. He served on Salon juries; he traveled; he had a great success; he knew and was admired by the most conspicuous of his contemporary painters. But by the evidence of his art,

which surely may be trusted, the world of activity did not impinge upon the world of contemplation in which he lived. Corot's world is exceptional in its privacy, more exceptional in that this privacy is untouched by the morbidity or bitterness of so many worlds where people live alone.

Corot once compared Delacroix to an eagle and himself to a lark. He was satisfied, he said, with his "own little music." From anyone else the comparison would be patronizing, and even from Corot it is misleading. His art is more robust and more profound than the comparison implies. It is an art of solidity, of modesty, of dignity, of contemplation, of serenity. It is an art where reverence for simplicity is combined with mastery of civilized nuance. These are not the virtues of "little music" or of little painting.

CHAPTER 5

The Salon at Mid-century

The Academy and the Salon

By every implication in this story so far, the Academy has been cast in the role of villain. This is type-casting, and like all type-casting it is the result of one magnificent performance. In the decades just after the middle of the century, following the relatively mild persecution of Courbet, the Academy seemed determined to annihilate all French painters of genius, offering its awards, both honorary and financial, to a clique that included some of the most desperately mediocre talents ever to have made their mark in the history of art.

The Academy's motives, like the motives of other villains, seemed to itself virtuous and high-minded. Its position seemed impregnable. But its defeat, after some spectacular battles, was sufficiently ignoble to satisfy its bitterest enemies. The very word *academic* has come to mean stuffy, trite, reactionary. An introduction to this chastened institution and the painters who received its favors is in order if we are to understand why it is still so beleaguered by historians of modern art, and why it rejected and reviled the men who have become recognized as the great painters of the time.

The Academy was founded in 1648 under the patronage of Louis XIV as the Royal Academy of Painting and Sculpture. It was soon dominated by a painter named Charles Lebrun (1619–1690), whose skillful and flatulent *Louis XIV Offering Thanks* [156] is a good example of the style to which he was addicted. Lebrun was an excellent painter, in the sense that he could be depended upon to turn out a good, workmanlike job on any assignment that it can stand very well as a typical example of the kind of picture known unflatteringly as an "academic machine."

An academic machine is a technical exercise demonstrating the painter's degree of skill in manipulating the standard techniques of drawing, painting, and arranging a picture according to established formulas. And it should be said now that an academic machine is an academic machine whether the industrious hack is following Lebrun's formula or one of Picasso's. Contemporary exhibitions are full of pictures not only as meretricious as the worst of Lebrun's but fabricated on much less demanding patterns.

Because he was a pedant rather than a creative artist, Lebrun set the French Academy off in the wrong direction from the beginning. This could have doomed it to wither away into impotence, except that the Academy was maintained in a position of great power by circumstances having nothing to do with the creative genius or the creative shortcomings of the men who controlled it. The head of the Academy, in the service of the king, with fat commissions to dole out to the faithful, could dictate his own recipe as the credo of art—and those painters who were not willing to conform to his recipe could go elsewhere and do as best they could at keeping body and soul together.

The moving spirit behind the formation of the Academy was neither Louis XIV nor Lebrun, but the king's minister of finance, Colbert, who recognized Lebrun's special fitness for the job at hand and selected him for it. Colbert was one of those statesmen, appearing here and there in history, who have recognized the value of art as an instrument of national propaganda and have so employed it. Believing that a government is measured by the yardstick of the monuments created under it, Colbert conceived of the Academy as a caucus of architects, painters, and sculptors with authority to determine an appropriate national character for the arts.

The great French painter of the century was a man twenty-five years older than Lebrun, Nicolas Poussin, whose *Funeral of Phocion* [128] we have already seen.

156. Lebrun: *Louis XIV Offering Thanks,* date unknown. 190 x 104″. *Musée des Beaux Arts,* Lyon.

could be executed according to the rules. But when we have said that, we have come close to defining an industrious hack. And indeed Lebrun was frequently nothing more than that. *Louis XIV Offering Thanks* is far from his best or his worst picture, and

157. FELICIEN MYRBACH-RHEINFELD: *Candidates for Admission to the Paris Salon (Basement of Palais d'Industrie)*. Date unknown. Drawing, probably for an illustrated journal. Metropolitan Museum of Art, New York.

Poussin was fifty-four years old when the Academy was founded and had left France for the second time because he could not tolerate the intrigues of the established artists and could not prostitute himself to the grandiose projects for which Lebrun was soon to become the ideal director. Poussin spent most of his life in Italy where he was free to paint as he pleased, nourished by the monuments of classical antiquity in his creation of an art of serenity, of contemplation, of order and balance and depth.

Poussin would have been the natural leader of the Academy if its second and more admirable function had not gone begging. For in addition to regulating the character of the arts, the Academy was supposed to perpetuate all that was best in their great tradition. In truth, Colbert and Lebrun probably thought of these two functions as identical. But they could not be, because they were based on the premise that great art can be produced by formula, and it cannot. No formula can make a great artist out of a mediocre one, and any formula will restrict the expression of certain

painters, usually those with something new to say. The Academy patronized men of talent who were content to work within the formula it approved. This is all very well as far as it goes, since there was plenty of work to be done by men of conscience and discretion well-trained in their craft. This training the Academy could supply. But as a corollary, it is also true that the Academy often starved out men of genius, since by definition genius transcends formula by extraordinary powers of invention.

The artist without official standing could of course subsist on private patronage, as Poussin largely did, and during the eighteenth century the Academy's stranglehold was weakened by a class made up of individuals of wealth and cultivation in the arts, capable of recognizing original talents, who supported whatever painters pleased them, in or out of academic favor. But academic strictures remained effective in the official schools, where arbitrary standards were perpetuated and talent was disciplined into conventional channels by the prospect of material rewards for the docile student.

158. Heim: *Charles X Distributing Awards, Salon of 1824, in the Grand Salon of the Louvre.* Exhibited Salon of 1827, re-exhibited 1855. 68 x 101". Louvre, Paris.

These were the schools David cried out against, in the name of art, justice, and youth, when he annihilated the Royal Academy at the time of the Revolution.

But the new Academy under David's influence (not directly under him, for he consistently refused to accept official directorship of the school) was more vicious than it had been before. The worst aspect of the situation was that the Revolution shifted the market for paintings from a small, aristocratic, knowledgeable group of patrons to a large, common, aesthetically ignorant public. The Salon became a gigantic sales room to serve the *bourgeoisie,* who in their eagerness for the acquisition of "culture" accepted the academic stamp of approval as a guarantee of art.

The Salon was a cruel weapon. Its jury of admission held the power of professional life or death for the painter still in search of his public. The beginner who tried to bring his work to attention elsewhere was in the position of a merchant opening a store with merchandise stamped "defective" by government officials. Pictures poured in for submission to the Salon in such quantities [157] that as many as 4,000 might be rejected from a single exhibition, in spite of the fact that in the largest Salons as many as 5,000 might be hung, crowded on vast walls, frame to frame, from eye level to ceiling. The pictures in poor locations might be next to invisible but at least they had received the stamp of approval—literally the Salon stamp on the back—while rejected pictures might be returned to the artist indelibly stamped with the "R" for *refusé,* thus rendered unsaleable. A purchaser might take an option on a picture, subject to its passing the jury, or might refuse to accept one already purchased because it failed to do so. The presentation of awards at the end of the Salons were state events of solemnity and importance [158].

Although the system originated in France, it flourished vigorously, if less tempestuously, throughout Europe. England's Royal Academy was, and is, particularly respectable and its private receptions [352] were, and are, particularly fashionable. But in France the Salon became also a public battleground, with the academicians entrenched in fortified positions assaulted by rebel forces. Once they had battled their way in (as the romantic painters did) the rebels had a way of turning respectable themselves, joining ranks with the traditional painters to oppose the next wave of dissenters. During the nineteenth century, revolts followed one another so rapidly that a group of painters would hardly be established in a strategic position before it was attacked from the rear by another. The French public enjoyed the battles and took sides, mostly for the conservatives. Throngs of people crowded the exhibitions, and the Salon prize winners became the subject of vehement discussions.

Every fledgling painter hoped that from the colossal grab bag his entry would somehow emerge as the season's success, or, lacking that, even as the season's scandal—as the *Raft of the Medusa, Massacres of Scio,* and *A Burial at Ornans* had done. But these pictures were exceptions. Most of the entries fell obediently within conventional categories or failed to pass the jury. There would be the moralistic allegories; there would be the hundreds of history pictures celebrating great events in pompous terms; there would be the cute children, the sentimental anecdotes, the picturesque landscapes; and always there would be the armies of nudes—nymphs, Venuses, and bathers caught by surprise. There would be the imitations of every picture that had ever made a Salon success, warmed over and hopefully served up again. There would be the sound, craftsmanlike, first-rate work of second-rate men, and, here and there within the interminable stretches of bad, mediocre, and respectable painting would be a work of art. Almost a quarter of a million pictures were exhibited in Salons during the nineteenth century in France alone.

The painter's problem was how to compete for attention in such a field. Startling originality, by which painters may strain for attention today, was ruled out in the first place, if not by the painter's lack of imagination, then by the fact that the jury was unlikely to accept a startlingly original work. Sheer technical excellence was not much help either, since the over-all technical level of Salon pictures was very high. It is appalling to look over old Salon catalogues and see the hundreds of painters whose technical mastery seems equalled only by their aesthetic and spiritual idiocy. (Where are all these paintings now? Those in museums have sunk by degrees to the basements; the rest are in those even more mysterious limbos where unwanted paintings await an improbable resurrection.)

Subject—what the picture was "about," the story it told—took on exaggerated importance as one way of differentiating between pictures all cast in the same technical mold. Or a painter with the time, energy, and means to devote himself to the production of an unsaleable picture might stand out by means of another device: size. The Salon system produced the phenomenon of the demonstration piece painted for exhibition only, so large that it could not be lost in the crowd. But unless it was purchased by the State, a painter could do nothing with a demonstration picture after the Salon closed except roll it up and store it away in the hope that the State would eventually acquire it. This is what actually happened when the pictures were manifestos of new movements and were preserved, either by the painter or by perceptive collectors, until time had proven the importance of the movement. Courbet's mammoth *The Painter's Studio,* for instance, remained in his possession until his death, and was sold as part of the contents of his studio in 1881. After resale to another private collector, it was finally purchased for the Louvre in 1920, sixty-five years after Courbet painted it, with funds collected by public subscription.

The idea upon which the Salon system was supposed to be based was sound: the Salon was supposed to offer an annual exhibition of the best work by established painters and a proving ground for new talent. Jurors would have had to be super-human to perform their task with complete effectiveness, but they were much less than that. If a generality is ever safe, it is safe to say that for several decades beginning around 1850 the men controlling the Academy and the Salon were all but blind aes-

159. LANDSEER: *A Distinguished Member of the Humane Society,*
c. 1838. 42½ x 55". Tate Gallery, London.

thetically, and all but sadistic in their persecution of any painter who fell out of line with their goosestep. This was bad enough, but their unpardonable crime was that they debauched public taste under the pretense —or, more generously, under the illusion— that they were elevating it in their systematic program to reduce the art of painting to sterile repetitions of exhausted formulas. Yet in spite of everything, these decades were one of the most vigorous, original, and productive periods in the history of painting. This fact is a tribute to the vitality of French creative genius, which to date has always emerged victorious in its constant struggle with equally French suspicion of change.

The Salon of 1855

The Salon of 1855 was a climactic one and has already been mentioned in connection with Delacroix, who was given a large retrospective as one section of it, with Ingres, who relented after twenty years of abstention from Salon exhibition to accept a similar honor, and with Courbet, who was rejected and built his Pavilion of Realism to get a showing for *The Painter's Studio.* It

was the biggest Salon ever held and was made international as part of the great Exposition Universelle of that year. We will use it here to examine the nature of Salon art, since its awards went to painters whose work is a summary of Salon standards at the time and for the rest of the century.

Ingres was induced to exhibit by hints that the government had him in mind for special honors when the awards were announced, but these honors did not materialize. He received the Salon's highest award, a Grand Medal of Honor, but so did nine other painters, including his enemy Delacroix. The report of the jury to Emperor Napoleon III carefully listed the winners alphabetically with no comment, although in classifications other than the fine arts the various juries gave reasons for their decisions. Apparently the competition among manufacturers or engineers, who sent in tens of thousands of exhibits, was less touchy and personal than the rivalry among painters and sculptors.

Of the ten Grand Medals of Honor in painting, three went to eminent foreigners: Peter von Cornelius (Prussia), Sir Edwin Landseer (United Kingdom), and Hendrik Leys (Belgium).

Von Cornelius (1783–1867) was an inevitable choice. He was Director of the Academy of Munich, a corresponding member for his country to the Institute of France, and he was also a conventional and skilled painter of portraits and scenes from religious history. The medal was a bow to France's neighbor to the east.

Landseer (1802–1873) received a medal as a similar gesture across the English Channel. A comparative youngster of fifty-three (Cornelius was seventy-two at this time, Ingres seventy-five), he was already the dean of English painters because no other man in the history of art managed to paint animals so much as if they were human beings. With its coy title, *A Distinguished Member of the Humane Society* [159] is typical of Landseer's pictorial manipulation of the pathetic fallacy. A generation now in its fifties and sixties must still remember the picture from their primers or framed on the nursery walls, for it became universally popular. Landseer

160. LANDSEER: *Blackcock, c.* 1874. 19¾ x 26". Collection Henry P. McIlhenny, Castle Glenveagh, County Donegal, Ireland.

could paint a stag and invest it with all the dignity of an eminent conservative clubman. He also painted pictures that, like *Blackcock* [160], keep appearing as a rebuke to his wasted talent. *Blackcock* is a harmony in grays, tans, and whites, with a dash of bright blood on the snow. It is as richly painted as a Courbet, and it treats birds as birds, not as simpering human beings. Landseer was an expert draughtsman, and his drawings are beginning to interest collectors again. From the great mass of his work it would be possible to cull a small group of fine paintings.

Leys (1815–1869) was even younger but even better connected; he was a painter of history pictures, genre subjects [161], portraits, and official decorative pictures of the usual kind. There is nothing wrong with his work except that it is routine.

These three awards, however, were more concerned with international courtesy than with the art of painting. The awards made to Frenchmen give a more accurate idea of Salon taste.

Grand Medals of Honor, 1855

Although some of the award winners in 1855 now seem too bad to have been true, we can fairly use this year as an example because the awards were made with particular care to summarize France's preeminence in the arts. The sprinkling of good pictures among them shows that the jury was more perceptive than in many other years, and the inclusion of a few former heretics shows an effort toward open-mindedness. Even Courbet had some paintings accepted; it was the rejection of *The Painter's Studio* and, for exhibition a second time, *A Burial at Ornans,* that caused the excitement and in retrospect leaves the jury open to charges of bias. The 1855 jury was a good one as juries went.

Among the seven Frenchmen receiving the Grand Medal of Honor, the star was neither Ingres nor Delacroix, but a terrible little man named Jean Louis Ernest Meissonier (1815–1891), whose view of Venice [145] has already been compared with one by Corot. At twenty-five Meissonier won his first Salon medal in the lower brackets, and a year later (1841) he was awarded a higher one. After two years he went up another notch, and he repeated this success five years later. Then in the 1855 exhibition came his Grand Medal of Honor for a picture called *La Rixe* (*The Brawl*) [162], which was such a success that Napoleon III selected it from all others for purchase and presentation to Queen Victoria as a souvenir of the English sovereign's visit to the Exposition. By now Meissonier was forty years old; he lived to be seventy-six and continued to accumulate honors until new ones had to be invented for him. He was the first French painter to receive the Grand Cross of the Legion of Honor, among other things. There was no question in his mind, and there seemed to be little in the minds of many rational people, that he was

161. LEYS: *Interior of an Inn*, 1849. 28⅞ x 35¼″. Philadelphia Museum of Art, John G. Johnson Collection.

162. MEISSONIER: *La Rixe* (*The Brawl*), 1855. 17¼ x 22″. Collection H.M. Queen Elizabeth II.

163. MEISSONIER: *1814*, 1864. 19¼ x 29½". Louvre, Paris.

the Leonardo da Vinci, the Michelangelo, of modern times. In his later years he cultivated a tremendous white beard that dropped to his waist. He was fond of patterning it carefully in a series of points and posing in a black velvet robe with a jeweled belt. In this costume and with his prize beard cascading down the velvet he would assume an expression of fiercely profound and melancholy thought, as one who has transcended the intellectual limitations of mortal man, and thus he would have himself photographed or painted.

It is maddening to remember that while this mean-spirited, cantankerous, and vindictive little man was adulated, great painters were without money for paints and brushes. The typical Meissonier is a dry, pinched, painstaking illustration of some event from military history, usually Napoleonic, or a semihumorous anecdote enacted by models in costume, frequently the costume of seventeenth-century musketeers. *La Rixe* is a variation, not humorous, on this formula, and it is one of his best works, probably his best in this genre category.

Meissonier offered the new picture-buying public exactly what it wanted. In the first place, his pictures told little stories; they were easy to "understand." And the little figures enacting these stories were laboriously and accurately detailed. The public demanded that a painting be something which had quite obviously been difficult to do, like a cathedral built from toothpicks. Not only did Meissonier put every tiniest highlight on every button, but it was even possible to identify a soldier's regiment from some of these buttons. What Meissonier lacked in imagination (which is to say, everything) he would have made up in meticulous execution, if such a void could have been filled by a device so meaningless.

It was not until after 1855, about 1859, that Meissonier began his series of Napoleonic subjects. His *1814* [163], showing Napoleon in the final days of the debacle of empire, is a good example and today the best known of his many pictures of Napoleonic victories and defeats. It is an achievement of a kind to do what Meissonier did:

164. DECAMPS: *Oriental Night Scene, c.* 1840. 20¾ x 20¼". Philadelphia Museum of Art, Johnson Collection.

to take the history of military campaigns where men died in blood, or of starvation and exposure, to take events that were flung across a continent, that marked the rise and the collapse of an empire and changed the direction of history in the Western world, to take triumphs and cataclysms full of glory, terror, and anguish, to take all this and reduce it to nothing more than a well organized collection of lead soldiers accurately uniformed. Meissonier has left accounts of his efforts to create the effect of snow by spraying miniature models with borax or sugar, accounts so naïve in their enthusiasm for imitation that they would be touching if this man had not been mistaken for a great painter. Nothing he ever did suggests for a moment that he conceived of painting as anything beyond a display of manual skill, or of his subjects as anything more than pegs upon which to hang this display. In his *1814*, it might be granted that the infinite details have been neatly packed into their container, and that the picture suggests, however faintly, some

mood of sadness and regret. But these are inadequate virtues in the circumstances. The defeated Emperor's air of dejection might just as well be that of a man who has committed an embarrassing *faux pas* at an important social gathering and has been sent home in bad weather with an unusually large escort. Whatever else we can read into *1814*, whatever it says of grandeur and collapse, we must read into it for ourselves by our knowledge and associations with the pictured event. The painting is, in short, completely a parasite on what it is about. In that capacity, of course, it is perfect.

For this very reason this kind of painting pleased—and on the same terms much of it still does, for that matter. But it has nothing to do with art for all that it has to do with craftsmanship, nothing to do with expression for all its detailed illustration, nothing to do with the human spirit or with the enlargement or intensification or clarification of human experience. Even as a technical exercise it is unoriginal; its superiority to the rank and file of Salon pictures is only one of degree, not of kind. Meissonier says nothing. Behind his preoccupation with representing scenes from Napoleonic history lies the confused thinking that can attribute greatness to a painting on the strength of the greatness of the pictured event. But greatness does not rub off in this way. Meissonier manages to reduce some of the most important, dramatic, and harrowing events in history to the expressive level of a well-shined shoe. The polish is admirable, but in the long run not very important.*

After Meissonier, whose art was so spectacularly pointless, the remaining Grand Medal winners, now forgotten, are a little dull. This is too bad in the case of Alexandre Gabriel Decamps (1803–1860), a

---

* Like all painters of skill without imagination, Meissonier was at his best when he was at his least pretentious. He did some very pleasant exercises where his photographic eye and his well-trained hand combined to reproduce nicely selected bits of typical French countryside. As literal objective mementos of a scene, these can be most attractive, and if Meissonier had painted nothing else he might have been remembered as a sound landscape painter of the second rank, limited but never bothersome.

165. DECAMPS: *The Experts,* 1837. 18¼ x 25¼". Metropolitan Museum of Art, New York, H. O. Havemeyer Collection.

painter for whom one would like to find a generous word. His work retains a certain vigor and some force of color. In *Oriental Night Scene* [164], as a typical example, reds and yellows are bright and rich against a ground of browns and blacks. Although a younger man than either Ingres or Delacroix, like them Decamps was given a room to himself for the exhibition of fifty pictures, and his work was discussed by the critics as if he were of their caliber.

Decamps tried his hand at a variety of pictorial work, including some political cartoons that might look better if they did not have to stand comparison with Daumier's, which were appearing at the same time. One painting, *The Experts* [165], showing some monkeys at work judging a picture, indicates that Decamps was not entirely fooled by the Salon system. But although one would like to do so, it is difficult to find Decamps very interesting today. He is a respectable painter but not a very stimulating one. Meissonier has a morbid fascination, but Decamps is too good to be

interesting as a bad painter. As a matter of fact he was one of the earliest Orientalists. He traveled in Asia Minor before Delacroix went to Morocco. But he was content to illustrate rather than to interpret, and as an Orientalist he remains a genre painter whose subjects are taken from Turkish and Arabian locales. This is why the majority of the critics in 1855 preferred him to Delacroix. He was easier.

The other Grand Medal winners may be considered briefly:

Émile Jean Horace Vernet (1789–1863), was the son and grandson of two other Vernets, painters of some distinction. The talent was running thin by the third generation but was still adequate for the manufacture of history and military subjects by the standard recipes. Vernet was a happy, popular, successful man whose family tradition certainly helped bring him his medal.

François Joseph Heim (1787–1865), was a classical painter of the most academic kind. From his *Prix de Rome* in 1807 to his Grand Medal of Honor in 1855 his career

166. Heim: *Scene from Jewish History*, Salon of 1824, re-exhibited 1855. 154¼ x 181⅛". Louvre, Paris.

graver, Bervic, he revolted against classical technique to develop a freer, more vigorous one. Thus in his small way he is a counterpart of Delacroix, the difference being that Delacroix was a creative artist as well as a technical innovator.

If we omit Ingres and Delacroix as great painters and Meissonier as an offensive one, this is a good sound list of accomplished wielders of the brush, boring rather than vicious. Its main fault is not its inclusions but its omissions. As a list of the living Frenchmen supreme among painters in 1855 it will not do. The most conspicuous absentees are Courbet, Daumier, and Corot. No jury can be held accountable for the re-evaluations of time, and a century has elapsed since 1855. But it should not have taken a crystal ball to see that Courbet was a better painter than, say, the genial and suave Vernet. And if Daumier was painting virtually in secret, it was because the Salon standard was so inimical to his genius that he did not find a public.

Salon awards were graduated downward from the Grand Medal of Honor through Medals First, Second, and Third Class, with the usual sop of Honorable Mentions at the bottom. In the long list of winners in these lower classes more names have endured and some became even more conspicuous in the Salon than the Grand Medallists above. Yet all the winners of the Grand Medal of Honor are at least hazily familiar names to anyone who has spent much time with the history of painting, while among the other awards, even the Medals First Class, there are utter strangers even to the specialist. Occasionally some one investigates these men, hoping to discover and revive a neglected painter of merit. So far no one has struck gold.

could be used as an example to prove that slow, steady, and conventional wins the race. His *Scene from Jewish History* [166] is an exercise in Davidian style consistent enough to look for a moment like something more. Then one sees that it is nothing but an assemblage of polished but meaningless parts, an exercise indeed. It is the kind of picture that, if torn to pieces, might yield many fragments suggesting that the total might have been a neo-classical painting of the best kind, for in the fragments the Davidian disciplines are apparent, and one is free to believe that surely so much sound craftsmanship must have served some expressive purpose. Heim also painted the interior panorama of *Charles X Distributing Awards to Artists at the End of the Exhibition of 1824* illustrated in the early pages of this chapter [158]. Here he comes off better in a picture adapted to his talents, the detailed representation of an event where factual record is an end in itself.

Finally, Louis Pierre Henriquel-Dupont (1797–1892), was an engraver. He has some genuine historical importance since, after studying with Guérin as a very young man and then with an equally classical en-

Medals First Class, 1855

Corot was recognized in the second rank of awards with a Medal First Class, and one went to Théodore Rousseau (who in 1867 was even to win a Medal of Honor). The jury's report lists forty-eight Medals First Class, thirty-two of them to French painters, seven to painters of the United

167. BONHEUR: *The Horse Fair*, 1853–55. 96 x 200″. Metropolitan Museum of Art, New York, Gift of Cornelius Vanderbilt.

Kingdom, and the rest scattered around other European countries. Among the other First Medalists, several are still familiar names:

Rosa Bonheur (1822–1899), who was an unusual woman, still has a following, especially in America where her *Horse Fair* [167] is perpetually admired. She was a child prodigy and exhibited in the Salon when only nineteen years old. By 1848, when she was twenty-six, she had already won a Medal First Class. In 1853 she came conspicuously into public favor with *The Horse Fair*, which was very large to have been painted by a woman and might have attracted attention even if it had been painted by a man. There was nothing feminine about Rosa Bonheur's painting, and there were many unfeminine aspects to her deportment. Like the lady romantic writer who adopted a man's name, George Sand, Rosa Bonheur affected men's clothes upon occasion. She was an admirer of Sand, and lived her own life freely with some of the same romantic flair. She knew everyone. She painted animals with great knowledge and sympathy. In many ways her work is arresting, but in the end she is a veteri-

168. BONHEUR: *Barbaro after the Hunt*, date unknown. 38 x 51¼″. Philadelphia Museum of Art, Wilstach Collection.

narian, not an artist. She never made Landseer's mistake of trying to turn her animals into noble human beings, but now and then she showed them involved in their own emotional difficulties, as in *Barbaro after the Hunt* [168]. She painted with a heavy, rich pigment and might have found a

169. FLANDRIN: *Study of Male Nude*, exhibited 1855. 38½ x 48¾".
Louvre, Paris.

source for this in Géricault. Toward the end
of her life, which coincided with the end of
the century, she tried to bring her work into
line with that of the impressionists, who
were the modern painters of her old age.
She did not succeed, but her attempt indicates an admirable open-mindedness and
a continuation of the determinedly unfeminine vigor that was her most individual
characteristic among women painters.

Alexandre Cabanel (1823–1889), was
another *Prix de Rome* winner whose life
was a succession of triumphs. Later he
twice won the Grand Medal of Honor, in
1865 and 1867. He was an extremely fashionable painter. Since one of his paintings
[191] is considered later in some detail,
this is enough about him here.

Léon Cogniet (1794–1880), was also a
Prix de Rome man, five years older than
Delacroix and like Delacroix a student of
Guérin's. Unlike Delacroix he remained a
loyal follower in Guérin's classical manner.
Since this manner was already watered
down in Guérin's work, its further dilution
in Cogniet's leaves very little substance.
Cogniet was a weak colorist and a routine
composer. He was one of those painters

who never advance beyond the stage of
favorite pupil. Like others of this type he
spent his life as a teacher of rules just as
he had learned them. Meissonier studied
under him; so did Rosa Bonheur.

Hippolyte Jean Flandrin (1809–1864),
was a disciple of Ingres. Ingres once threatened to resign from the Academy when the
Salon jury refused one of Flandrin's paintings. Occasionally Flandrin approximated
Ingres's quality, and he left one study of a
male nude [169] of an arresting sensuousness that has made it a great favorite in the
Louvre. But in searching for a style of his
own by following a series of enthusiasms
Flandrin failed to develop very far in any
of them. And the one in which he developed farthest, a modified troubadourism,
was not the most fortunate choice he could
have made.

Federigo de Madrazo (1815–1894), a
Spaniard, dominated Spanish official art as
a history and portrait painter. He was a
brilliant success as a painter of the Spanish
aristocrats, was much honored officially in
France also, and painted in a bright, flashy
manner.

Karl Ernest Rodolphe Heinrich Salem
Lehmann (1814–1882) is less impressive
than his name. Born in Kiel, a naturalized
Frenchman, a pupil first of his father and
then of Ingres, he followed the classical
formulas with such dryness and so obses-
sively that even his contemporaries found
him limited in this way. Nevertheless he
won Medals First Class in 1840 and 1848
as well as in 1855. He founded a prize to
encourage the defense of the academic
tradition. Possibly it is still awarded.

Joseph Nicolas Robert-Fleury (1797–
1890), was a student of Girodet and Gros.
Following at a safe distance behind the romantic vanguard, he capitalized on its successes whenever they could be made palatable to bourgeois taste. His career was a
succession of official honors and sinecures
culminating in the directorship of the
Academy's School of Fine Arts and then the
directorship of the Academy in Rome.

With Constant Troyon (1810–1865) we
come to a curious phenomenon: the cow in
nineteenth-century French painting. Before
his discovery of this animal's potential as

170. TROYON: *Cows Grazing*, 1856. 24 x 32¼". Philadelphia Museum of Art, John G. Johnson Collection.

an art subject, Troyon had already put behind him a successful career as a painter of landscape in the Barbizon spirit, and as was mentioned earlier he is ordinarily grouped with that school. At twenty-three Troyon made his debut in the Salon; at twenty-nine he was awarded a Medal Third Class and at thirty a Medal Second Class. At thirty-one he had a real Salon success with a picture of Tobias and the Angel in a landscape, which was praised by the perceptive and sophisticated critic Théophile Gautier and at the same time admired by the public. In 1846 Troyon reached the award of Medal First Class. The following year he visited Belgium, where he discovered the works of two seventeenth-century painters, Albert Cuyp and Paul Potter, whose landscapes were backgrounds for various domestic animals, especially cows. From that time on, cows and, to a lesser degree, sheep preoccupied Troyon. He painted them standing in pools, grazing in meadows, entering the fold, leaving the fold, and sometimes

just doing nothing at all. He was the best—for he was an excellent painter—of a considerable group of artists dedicated to the cow. They found a ready market for their work. The cow in the living room became a familiar item. The success of these pictures may have been a result of increasing urbanization, a bourgeois nostalgia for the countryside as cities became more crowded, more complicated, more mechanized. Critics praised Troyon's mastery of the anatomy of the cow with as much seriousness as they praised other painters' mastery of the nude. Whatever the explanation for his fascination with the cow, and if we forgive him some inevitable repetitiousness, Troyon was skillful in disposing these creatures pleasantly in landscapes of grassy charm under skies of agreeable tints [170]. His Medal First Class of 1855 was his third; he won a fourth in 1859. He seems to have been a generous and agreeable man, with much of the placidity characteristic of his favorite subject.

aristocratic male elegance leading to the conclusion that European nobility of the mid-nineteenth century were a special race of unparalleled physical beauty. Winterhalter was one of those portraitists, most frequent in England, with a knack for retaining a likeness while beautifying the subject. His portraits still have great appeal in their decorative and triumphantly superficial way. Like many other painters who do not have much to say but do not pretend to be saying more than they can, Winterhalter is an enjoyable painter when accepted on his own premises.

One eminent painter, Thomas Couture (1815–1879), was awarded a Medal First Class but refused it, indignant because it was not a Grand Medal of Honor. A pupil of Gros, then of Delaroche, Couture was a *Prix de Rome* winner and made a successful Salon debut at twenty-three with a picture entitled *Young Venetian after an Orgy*. He was only thirty-two in 1847 when he won a Medal First Class with his *Romans of the Decadence* [178], another post-orgy scene that is such a perfect example of the academic concoction at its typical best that it is generally used today as an illustration when a single specimen must stand alone to typify the breed. Couture was a painter of great talent, little imagination, and a vast intolerance. We will see more of him and his *Romans of the Decadence* shortly.

Medals Second Class, 1855

In the longer list of Medals Second Class there are fewer names of importance. Two are somewhat younger men. Jean Léon Gérôme (1824–1904) lived into the twentieth century, as did Adolphe William Bouguereau (1825–1905). Just now the reputations of both these painters are at lowest ebb. With Meissonier they have become synonymous with the vicious tyranny of the academic formula in the latter half of the century, with its sterility, dogma, hypocrisy, and above all its selfishness and its blindness in the face of new developments. All this is true, so true that even the moderate virtues these men possess are usually denied them. But occasionally, and

171. WINTERHALTER: *Prince Albert of Saxe-Coburg-Gotha, c. 1846.* 94 x 61″. National Portrait Gallery, London.

Finally, among the First Medallists whose names are still familiar, there was Franz Xaver Winterhalter (1806–1873), a German by birth but a cosmopolitan by nature and experience. A portraitist, he traveled from court to court all over Europe. There was hardly a king or queen or person of great title whom he did not paint at one time or another [171]. It is easy to see why he was so sought after. His women have a melting loveliness and his men an

172. GÉRÔME: *Pygmalion and Galatea*, date unknown. 35 x 27″. Metropolitan Museum of Art, New York, Gift of Louis C. Raegner.

173. DAUMIER: *Pygmalion*, 1842. From the series *Histoire Ancienne*. Lithograph, 9 x 7½″. Collection Carl Zigrosser, Philadelphia.

most tentatively, they are given a small kind word in recent criticism. This is especially true of Gérôme.

Gérôme was a painter who pushed the slick painting surface to its limit, and he was as handy as Meissonier with highlights on buttons. According to some accounts he was also nearly as odious a personality. But he was more of an artist. He was just as fascinated with technical display in details but he was more selective in their use. He had a sense of color—for Meissonier, one color was just about as good as another—and among the multitude of his paintings (for like other successful Salon painters he was extremely productive for an insatiable market) from time to time a work of surprising attraction occurs.

The slick, tight, surface typical of so much academic painting harks back to David's, as in *The Horatii*. Gérôme, in his *Pygmalion and Galatea* [172], a wonderful

and terrible picture, is painting a classical subject with a high polish, but we are a long way from the master of the Revolution and even further from Ingres. Neither the vigorous anatomical naturalism of *The Horatii* nor the sensuous idealization of a nude by Ingres has left a mark on this descendant, although the figures have been drawn with acute naturalism and then prettified. *Pygmalion* is a consummately obvious and vulgar picture.

The story is that of the young sculptor Pygmalion. Having done a marble statue of Galatea, he falls in love with his own work, which is brought to life by Venus, who has observed the young man's plight. Gérôme's statue-woman is painted in rosy flesh pinks in the upper parts where life has suffused it, and fades out gradually to pure marble white in the feet, where the process of vivification has hardly begun. Salon audiences found this tour de force ravish-

174. Gérôme: *Prayer in the Mosque of 'Amr, Old Cairo,* perhaps 1860. 35 x 29½". Metropolitan Museum of Art, Wolfe Bequest.

jewels, and other rich stuffs and objects of the Near East. Usually he used them as knickknacks to trick out some foolish anecdote, some trivial little story for the Salon public to read, but occasionally, as in *Prayer in the Mosque* [174] he seems to become another painter and his trivia coalesce into a picture that rises above them.

Prayer in the Mosque is more than a straight reproduction of an inherently interesting subject. The colors are beautifully modulated, juxtaposed in combinations of unexpected distinction; the figures are skillfully disposed within the space, the monotony of their long stretch back into deep perspective being broken here and there most judiciously; the airy columns of the mosque have an abstract interest beyond their interest as exotic architecture. Even when we admit that these volumes are inherent in the structure and not an invention of the artist, it is still true that Gérôme has made the most of them.

Like Gérôme, Bouguereau went on from his Medal Second Class in 1855 to the Grand Medal of Honor and the whole category of official awards. The birth and death dates of these two academicians coincided within a year, and each was a resounding commercial success on both sides of the Atlantic. Even more than Gérôme's, Bouguereau's name has become synonymous with the prostitution of technical prowess to any saleable subject. Whether he was painting high-class barroom nudes or holy pictures, Bouguereau was breathtakingly adept at assuming appropriate masks to conceal the meretriciousness of his conception. Whether painting nymphs and satyrs or *Youth and Cupid* [175] to titillate bourgeois sexuality or madonnas appealing to associative religious ideas in much the same way, Bouguereau was such a skillful performer that the buying public saw no inconsistency in the work of a man who alternated between the roles of lecher and mystic. And indeed there is no inconsistency here, since in neither role was Bouguereau an expressive artist: he was a salesman with an infallible eye for the market. But he was a technician of such prowess, in a style soft and slick at the same time,

ing, but time has not been gentle with the picture. Its pretensions and affectations are mercilessly revealed and even the nude girl, once captivating, looks a little comical since fashions in feminine loveliness have changed. It is extraordinary that a public with access to Daumier's hilarious burlesque of the same subject [173] could ever take Gérôme seriously again, but they continued to do so.

Salon painters were sometimes pseudo-classical, sometimes pseudo-romantic, but always genuinely opportunistic. Orientalism had long ceased to be a scandal and was popular in all kinds of treatments. Gérôme painted Oriental subjects without any expression of their mystery, their turbulence, or even essentially of their exoticism, in paradoxical combination with his tight pseudo-neo-Davidian style. He was a master at the rendition of the silks, brasses, that anyone who is at all interested in paintings can hardly fail to respond to one by Bouguereau as a performance, no matter what he may think of it as a work of art. No matter how clearly one sees that *The Thank Offering* [176] is sentimentalized to the point of nausea, its technical aplomb remains staggering.

The wonder of a painting by Bouguereau is that it is so completely, so absolutely, all of a piece. Not a single element is out of harmony with the whole; there is not a flaw in the totality of the union between conception and execution. This, of course, is a requirement for any great work of art. The trouble with Bouguereau's perfection is that the conception and the execution are perfectly false. Yet this is perfection of a kind, even if it is a perverse kind, and Bouguereau is proof that the art of painting is so various and so complex that even "bad" pictures can be fascinating when considered as part of the whole of man's record of his own nature.

A Medal Third Class also went to Théodore Chassériau (1819–1856), who had begun as a student of Ingres and then had been attracted by the colorism and exoticism of Delacroix. He managed to fuse some of the sinuous grace of his first master with the warmth and light of romanticism; before his relatively early death he had developed a hybrid style of decorative attraction, which he displayed especially in murals.

The Salon Public

What, in summary, do all these pictures reveal as to the taste of the *bourgeoisie,* the new public of picture buyers? First of all, that a painting must in some way be ostentatious. It must pretend to a kind of profundity or sensibility, and it must do so without violating the veneer of shallow proprieties that passed for morality. If a specific moral lesson can be incorporated or implied, so much the better, but it must be a moral lesson flattering to bourgeois convenience. These components of a picture must be immediately apparent on the picture's surface; they must not be reached

175. BOUGUEREAU: *Youth and Cupid,* 1877. 75½ x 35". Louvre, Paris.

via some philosophical bridge. This ordinarily means that the picture must tell a story of some kind. It must not exist simply as a painting; it must be a picture *of* something. That is why the Salon painter was a narrator first and a painter second. The public wanted pictures they could read as they would read stories or tracts.

176. BOUGUEREAU: *The Thank Offering*, 1867. 58 x 42¼". Philadelphia Museum of Art, Wilstach Collection.

Whether or not he was conscious that he was doing so, the Salon painter sought to flatter the public. Continually, by implication, he assured them of their sensitivity, their cultivation, their intellect, their nobility of soul, their moral probity. The more this flattery was rewarded—by purchases—the more intense it became, and the more intense it became, the more it was re-warded by further purchases, in a vicious downward spiral. It must be remembered too that as the Salons became bigger and bigger the public was educated to lower and lower standards. Thousands of pictures were exhibited in each Salon, and there simply never are thousands of great painters alive at any one time, especially in any one country, even when the country is France. But all these thousands of pictures received the official stamp as great art. In these circumstances it is not surprising that by the 1860's, when the impressionists appeared, the public was offended by pictures painted in a revolutionary technique, pictures whose virtues ran counter to all the Salon vices that for so long had been mistaken for virtues of an elevated kind.

But to this summary of a depressing situation the reminder should be added that Delacroix, Ingres, and Corot were also alive and successful (Courbet, as well, was successful in his special way) and a generation of painters just then clearing their 'teens was assimilating the various contributions made by these giants of the first half of the century. Ingres's exquisite control and his respect for tradition; Delacroix's revolution of color and his insistence that the painter is independent of formula; Courbet's rejection of the ideal and the faraway in favor of the everyday world around us; and Corot's demonstration that the painter's private world could be explored to yield images of universal meaning—the young men who were to be known eventually as the impressionists were ready to build from these contributions, assimilating them without imitating the forms they had taken in the art of the great men of the first half of the century. The battle against academic dogma was a bitter one, and literally it very nearly cost some of the young impressionists their lives. But before the end of the century their victory was decisive.

CHAPTER 6

Manet

The "Salon des Refusés"

The year 1863 is the sharpest dividing line in the history of painting since the French Revolution. It is the year of the *Salon des Refusés*—the Salon of the Rejected Painters. It centered around a painter named Édouard Manet (1832–1883).

It had been almost exactly a century since David had been admitted as a student of the Royal Academy. Now, within a decade, the leaders of classicism, romanticism, and realism disappeared, as if the decks were being cleared for a new generation of painters ready to make use of everything that had been discovered during a hundred years of revolutions and counter-revolutions. Ingres and Delacroix died; so did Rousseau; Courbet was in exile. The conflicts between one ism and another no longer seemed important to a group of young men who admired Ingres for certain virtues, Delacroix for others, Courbet for yet others, without feeling that the theories these men had defended were mutually exclusive. All three were admired and followed; so was Goya; so were the eighteenth-century court painters whose artificiality Goya and David had rejected. The art of the Venetian Renaissance was studied with new excitement. The young painters were learning from everything and imitating nobody.

But the academicians had learned nothing, and were still imitating themselves. In 1863 the Salon jury finally overstepped all bounds in its spite and favoritism; the trading of votes, the reactionary prejudices, were this time too flagrant to be tolerated. More than 4,000 paintings were rejected by a jury that seems to have been dominated by a forgotten pedant named Signol, a teacher at the *École des Beaux Arts*. The rejected painters and their supporters stirred up so much agitation that the Emperor stepped into the fracas. To judge from the kind of picture he was accustomed to buying for himself and as gifts for distinguished visitors, his taste in painting was in accord with the jury's. But as a politician in a country where art was a part of national life, Napoleon III could not ignore a group of artists and intellectuals that was growing as large as the Academy and its hangers-on—and making more noise. The revolt of the students who had petitioned Courbet to open a studio had occurred only two years before, in 1861. And in 1862 a commission had been appointed to look into the organization and policies of the Academy's school in Paris, its branch in Rome, and its Salon regulations. Ignoring these straws in the wind, the jury of 1863 kept on course and now found itself in rough weather. The Count de Nieuwerkerke, who seemed triply invulnerable as Director General of Museums, Superintendent of Fine Arts, and titular president of the jury, was summoned by the Emperor and ordered to give the rejected pictures a showing.

The official announcement of this unpleasantness was mild, stated not as a rebuke to the jury but only as a decision of the Emperor's to authorize a second Salon made up of paintings rejected from the regular one, in order to give the public a chance to judge for itself the legitimacy of the complaints that had reached him. This was sensational enough. By implication it was an official admission that academic judgment was not infallible. By implication-once-removed it was even more heretical: it made way for the premise that there is no single standard of excellence, no single formula by which the excellence of a painting may be calculated.

Having thus laid themselves open to public trial, the academicians set about gathering their forces to insure the failure of the *Salon des Refusés*. Meanwhile the rejected painters were in a quandary. Under the terms of the Emperor's order, they had two weeks in which to withdraw their pic-

tures if they wanted to. At the end of that time the remaining pictures would be hung in other rooms near the Salon proper in the Palace of Industry, a vast structure built for the 1855 Exposition where the Salons were now being held. A few years before, a painter named Bonvin had arranged in his studio a small show of rejected works by various painters. This miniature preliminary *Salon des Refusés* had met with a scandalous reception, although some painters, including Courbet (whose own exhibition of rejected pictures in the Pavilion of Realism had been a failure), had spoken up for it. With this precedent the painters' dilemma was whether to risk a similar reception, whether to lay themselves open to the vindictiveness of future Salon juries, whether to exhibit in the humiliating role of a rejected painter against the odds that the exhibition would be a popular success, or whether to play safe by withdrawing. In the end most of the painters decided to risk it and only about 600 paintings were withdrawn, not a large proportion of those that had been refused.

The exhibition was both a success and a failure. Throngs crowded into it but not many people came to "judge for themselves the legitimacy of the complaints." Eager for the relaxation of a good laugh after the annual cultural exercise of the Salon proper, the public made the most of a double opportunity to demonstrate artistic perception, first by the usual appreciation of the accepted works, then by the derision—always so easy and so reassuring to the derider—of the rejected ones. The popular critics had a field day at the expense of the rejected painters, although an occasional picture was singled out for sympathetic comment even in the conventional press. The minority support was fervent; a painter and writer named Zacharie Astruc even founded a paper, issued every day during the run of the Salon, to defend the good pictures among the rejected ones, especially Manet's.

All in all, in terms of the moment, the *Salon des Refusés* was not a great success. It did not immediately impair academic prestige with the general public. But the public's easy scorn, the critical diatribes in the press, even the persecutions that the Academy continued to inflict on painters of originality, are not of importance in comparison with the fact that after 1863 the mortal illness of the academic organization was apparent to any good diagnostician. No matter that it took a long time to die, no matter that it grew increasingly vicious during its invalidism, its ultimate death as the dominant force in French painting was certain and the nature of its malady was recognized.

The *Salon des Refusés* established roots for the idea that every painter has the right to paint as he pleases and to be judged as an individual by other individuals, instead of painting according to the rules of a school whose officials have the power to grant or deny him the right to be seen. Delacroix and Courbet had fought for this idea, but they had been immune to the Salon's weapon of rejection, Delacroix by his mysterious influential connections and Courbet through the fluke of his early medal. The *Salon des Refusés* was a mass exhibition of painters who would ordinarily have been helpless against the esthetic censorship of the Salon system. Painters were achieving their own equivalent of freedom of speech.

The *Salon des Refusés* was no collection of masterpieces, and it must have included some really appalling pictures among the hundreds that legitimately had been turned down by the jury as inadequate attempts to meet academic standards. If the two exhibitions could be reassembled side by side today, they would probably look much alike, except that the technical polish of the officially accepted pictures would be higher over-all than that of the rejected ones, and the rejected ones would be studded here and there with early works of men who have become recognized as the masters of the last half of the century. The most conspicuous of these paintings would be three by Manet: *Young Man in the Costume of a Majo* and *Mlle. V. in the Costume of an Espada*, both of which would have to be borrowed from the Metropolitan Museum of Art, and *Le Déjeuner sur l'Herbe* [181], which would have to be borrowed from the Louvre.

"Le Déjeuner sur l'Herbe": Scandal

It was *Le Déjeuner sur l'Herbe* that everyone came to see and laugh at or rail against. The Emperor himself made it a four-star attraction by calling it immodest, and the critics attacked it in downright scurrilous terms. Manet suffered deeply from these attacks because the last thing he wanted was notoriety through a *succés de scandale*. Well-to-do, suave, cultivated, worldly, and socially conventional, Manet coveted a conventional success and to the end of his life he sought it in the Salon.

Two years before the *Salon des Refusés* he had seemed on the way to what he wanted. That year, at twenty-nine, he had submitted two pictures, one of them a portrait of his parents and the other a *Spanish Guitar Player* [177]. The pictures were not only accepted but attracted so much favorable attention that the *Spanish Guitar Player* was taken down and rehung in a better spot. Manet received an honorable mention (a puny award but a beginning) and by the time the Salon closed he had established himself as a young painter who would be watched.

Manet's technique in both pictures, especially the *Spanish Guitar Player*, was open to the same objections that were to be made later when his work was howled down. The public, who spontaneously enjoyed the pictures, would then no doubt have joined in the attack. The public is never very conscious of technical aberrations so long as the end result is a recognizable image of a subject it enjoys. It enjoyed Manet's portrait of his parents because portraits of an artist's parents appeal to the admirable moral sentiment of filial devotion. And the *Spanish Guitar Player* had the attraction of a picturesque subject, even though Manet had not presented it in a picturesque way. Throughout the history of Manet's lifelong struggle with the Salon, the public obviously followed the critics' cue to damn on technical grounds pictures that otherwise it would have enjoyed for their subjects, pictures that it would just as quickly have followed a cue to praise.

177. MANET: *Spanish Guitar Player*, 1860. 57 x 44⅝″. Metropolitan Museum of Art, New York, Gift of William Church Osborn.

Just two months before the 1863 Salon, which was to result in the *Salon des Refusés*, Manet made a tactical error by exhibiting fourteen pictures in the gallery of a dealer named Martinet. For some reason the critics were hostile and suspicious. They prophesied that when the Salon opened Manet would fail to repeat his first success, if he got into the Salon at all. While this should not have affected a normal jury, it is easy to believe that the reactionary jury of 1863 was already looking forward to rejecting the paintings of a young artist who had been cocky enough to exhibit so conspicuously to the public just before the Salon's pronouncements for the year. The easy thing to do was to annihilate the upstart, and the jury annihilated Manet. It is

probable that Delacroix had had something to do with Manet's good fortune in his first Salon, but in 1863 Delacroix was too ill to participate in the judging. The jury met in the spring; Delacroix died the following August.

If the jury hoped for a chance to reject him, Manet made it easy for them with *Le Déjeuner sur l'Herbe*. The other two pictures that fell under the ax with it, *Young Man in the Costume of a Majo* and *Mlle. V. in the Costume of an Espada*, were not too different from the successful *Spanish Guitar Player*, but *Le Déjeuner sur l'Herbe* is a startling picture even today. In an ordinary bit of woods, a matter-of-fact young woman has inexplicably removed her clothing while a pair of fully dressed young men lounge indifferently near by and another young woman, draped in a chemise, bathes in a pool just beyond. The picture was listed in the catalogue as *Le Bain* (*The Bath*), but immediately acquired the title by which it is still known. None of the possible translations—"Breakfast on the Grass" or "Luncheon on the Grass" which are equally used, or "Picnic" which never is —seems quite satisfactory. The subject is an adaptation in contemporary dress of the venerable tradition of demonstration pictures showing figures in a landscape, a synthesis of nudes, nature, and still life as an exhibition of skill. But Manet's painting differs from other such pictures in having not the thinnest disguise of allegory or idealization. It is extremely direct, to the point of brashness, and purely a demonstration of painting, without anecdotal or moralistic veneer of any kind. The dissociation between painter and subject is just about as complete as is possible. To the confused and offended jury, who had never seen anything like it, the directness seemed not only brash, but insolent. The total divorce from moral pretensions, being incomprehensible to people accustomed to reading moral platitudes into painting, seemed immoral in itself.

The public and critical damnation of *Le Déjeuner* is altogether indefensible in retrospect, but we might be generous and pause for a moment to try to see the picture as it looked to a startled art lover in 1863.

178. Couture: *The Romans of the Decadence*, 1847. 181 x 304″. Louvre, Paris.

In the middle of the twentieth century this demands as great an effort as would have been required in another direction in the middle of the nineteenth. As a reminder of what the public expected and had been educated to think of as the proper thing in art, an examination of Thomas Couture's *The Romans of the Decadence* [178] is chastening. The picture had been the Salon sensation of 1847 and since then had been accepted as a masterpiece that would, quite naturally in the normal course of events, take its place among the great masterpieces of the past. Manet himself had chosen Couture as his teacher and had worked with him off and on for five years. Remembering that it is always easier to scoff at pictures in their declining years than to discover in them reasons for the virtues formerly ascribed to them, let us be patient with *The Romans of the Decadence*:

It is a compendium of popular demands. For one thing, it is cultural. Something cul-tural is implied by the title, which flatter-ingly assumes that the observer is familiar with Roman history. (And what in the world could be cultural about the subject of *Le Déjeuner?*) Moralistically the subject is treated on a high plane; one is invited to disapprove of the decadence of these peo-ple, who orgiastically defile a noble hall filled with statues of their sturdier fore-fathers. (Are we asked by Manet to dis-approve of the action of his young woman who has disrobed so casually? No; he seems to accept it as the most natural thing in the world.) And *The Romans of the Decadence* is an impeccable piece of painting by a standard requiring careful drawing, com-plicated elaborations, and studio poses ac-curately rendered (whereas, once the critics had pointed it out, it was obvious that *Le Déjeuner* was painted in a way devoid of subtleties, refinements, and difficult detail; this scoundrelly artist must have turned it out in an hour or so, like a sign painter).

179. Manet: Detail from Figure 181.

180. Courbet: Detail from Figure 119.

It is easy to see now that the culture in *The Romans of the Decadence* is specious; that its moral overtones are combined with lascivious suggestion, allowing one to disapprove of the decadents while relishing vicariously their languishing indulgences; that while it obviously took hours and days and weeks to execute, it is technically static —that is, it is a repetitious exercise, copybook fashion—where *Le Déjeuner* is inventive, explorative, and far from "easy" or careless although the difficulties overcome by the painter are less apparent to the untrained eye.

They were not apparent at all to a public accustomed to taking it for granted that in a picture of *Le Déjeuner*'s dimensions the artist's job was to show how closely he could approximate the perfections of the academic formula. Not picturesque, not historical, and not anecdotal, *Le Déjeuner* seemed unexplainable except as a work of an incompetent or a madman or, worst of all, a prankster. The popular critics were no help to the public, since they made no effort to understand what Manet was doing and even went out of their way to entrench their minds against understanding.

"Le Déjeuner": Technical Innovations

And exactly what was Manet doing?

At this time he had seen very little of Goya's painting, yet he was pushing to their conclusion the same problems of representation Goya had set himself, quite as if Goya had served him as an intermediate step in the solution. Manet is more systematic and more objective than Goya, but like him Manet wants to capture the immediacy of instant vision. Like him, Manet does so by reducing the image to essential planes painted in bold, flat areas. He goes beyond Goya in the elimination of transitional areas where planes merge from light into shadow through a series of half tones, those areas that are neither light nor shadow but somewhere in between the two as the form curves away from the source of illumination. The nude in *Le Déjeuner* is all but devoid of transitional tones, and the shadows are reduced to a minimum. It is as if the lights had spread, consuming all intermediate values and compressing the shadows into areas so small and concentrated that they may even be reduced to a mere

181. MANET: *Le Déjeuner sur l'Herbe*, 1863. 84¼ x 106¼". Louvre, Paris.

182. GIORGIONE: *Concert Champêtre*, c. 1510. 43¼ x 54⅜". Louvre, Paris.

dark line along one side of the form. This is most dramatically apparent if the head of this nude [179] is compared with one of the heads from Courbet's *Two Girls on the Banks of the Seine* [180]. Courbet capitalizes on modulated half tones to give his image weight and mood; Manet eliminates them to reveal the image as the eye might receive it in one brilliant flash of light. Manet may have been influenced by effects in early photographs where the primitive emulsion, incapable of registering half tones, reduced infinite gradations to similar broad uninterrupted areas of light and sharp concentrations of dark. It would be appropriate for Manet, the most implacably objective of painters, to find a point of departure in the absolute objectivity of images

183. RAIMONDI, after RAPHAEL: *Judgment of Paris*. Engraving, 11½ x 17¼". Philadelphia Museum of Art.

produced by the operation of physical laws.

In addition to its effectiveness as formal description with a vivid immediacy, this quick, summary modeling offered advantages in the use of color. The broad light areas of Manet's forms could be painted in colors at full intensity over their whole breadth, whereas in conventional modeling the color would have had to be debased by darkening and graying where it began to turn into the intermediate tones between light and shadow. At the same time Manet frequently exaggerated the blackish and grayish tones in the shadows themselves. Reduced to such small areas, blacks and grays served to emphasize the broad expanses of color in the lights, allowing them to sing out above the darks. In comparison with the dulled tints of conventional painting or even with the bright, but broken, color of Delacroix, Manet's broad areas and large spots of color, flatly applied, seemed barbarous. Conventional painters were also deeply offended because Manet painted his forms in flat silhouettes of color and then brushed his shadows into them while they were wet. The usual way was to define the darks first and then progress into the lights, which might be painted over them. There are technical advantages to this conventional method that need not be gone into here, but it is worth mentioning that this minor deviation from standard technique

was attacked as a serious heresy, in the general condemnation of everything Manet did or did not do.

Le Déjeuner sur l'Herbe [181] is not a perfect picture. The figures are poorly integrated with their setting; they have the air of having been cut out of another picture and pasted onto this landscape where by lucky coincidence they almost fit and in a way this is what actually happened. Manet made studies from nature for the landscape but painted the models in the studio without reference to natural light. Also he has left a bothersome ambiguity in the transition between the foreground and the middleground where the second young woman bathes. The trees around her, and the rowboat just discernible at the right, where it is drawn up to the bank of the stream, are miniature ones, or else the bathing girl is a giantess. It is impossible to establish a logical relationship between the receding vista of woods in the left third of the picture, and the vista behind the bather. But if the picture does not hang together in all its parts, its major individual parts are superb. In the nude figure and the tumbled still life of fruit, bread, and discarded clothing Manet is already painting at full power in the manner that will shortly reach full integration in another painting.

"Le Déjeuner": Borrowed Elements

Le Déjeuner was not attacked for minor shortcomings like these but for its major virtues as a technical innovation, and for the "immorality" of its subject. Defending him against this latter charge, Manet's supporters pointed out that he was following the tradition of an old master, the Venetian painter Giorgione, who about 1500 had also combined nude female and clothed male figures in a landscape, and that the picture, hanging in the Louvre, shocked no one. This superficial parallel is still regarded as a defense that should have routed the opposition, but actually it is not much to the point. Giorgione's *Concert Champêtre* [182] is a harmony of sensuous textures—flesh, velvet, satin, hair, grass, crys-

184. MANET: *The Balcony*, 1869. 67¾ x 49¼″. Louvre, Paris.

185. GOYA: *Majas on a Balcony*, c. 1810–1815. 76¾ x 49½″. Metropolitan Museum of Art, New York, H. O. Havemeyer Collection.

tal, stone, and foliage. It evokes a world of idyllic dream; neither the luxuriously costumed adolescent males nor the golden-fleshed females can be compared in spirit with Manet's young boulevardiers or the well-known model who posed for the nude. This rebuttal was made at the time and is perfectly legitimate. *Le Déjeuner's* defenders further pointed out that Manet's group of three figures was taken from a trio of river gods appearing in the lower right corner of a composition by Raphael, a *Judgment of Paris* [183]. But this also is a poor defense. Raphael's figures are allegorical nudes. It is true that the Academy had honored other paintings on the basis of even more tenuous connections with its Renaissance deity, but that is still no de-

fense of *Le Déjeuner*, if it needs defense.

But of course it does not need defense of this kind. Manet was not trying to emulate either Giorgione or Raphael. He frequently borrowed compositions. This was not plagiarism any more than it was plagiarism when Ingres borrowed the pose of the *Bather of Valpinçon* from some Roman sculptor or the composition of *Stratonice* from a Greek vase painting. Manet's borrowings are closer to home—he was especially indebted to Goya—but in the end his borrowing was more superficial than, say, David's when he so meticulously incorporated classical details in his paintings. Manet neither made references to his sources nor made any attempt to conceal them. The superficial debt of *The Balcony*

[184] to Goya's *Majas on a Balcony* [185] could hardly be more apparent, but neither could the fundamental difference between the two paintings. In the Goya, two of his typical spirited young vixens are combined with sinister caped and hatted male figures in the background, ominous, half-revealed, the omnipresence of evil behind the bright façade of daily life as Goya shows it again and again. In Manet's adaptation these figures are replaced by a solid, respectable bourgeois as one of a triple portrait group. And when Manet planned a picture of the execution of Maximilian it was simpler to refer to Goya's *Executions of the 3d of May* than to do research and try to reproduce the actual scene of Maximilian's death, which was quite different from Manet's representation of it. He borrowed also from Velásquez, especially in full-length standing figures.

Must all this borrowing be apologized for? After all, most painters who borrow so directly from others are damned as eclectic or with that even more damning word *derivative*. There are all varieties of eclecticism, but at his typical worst the eclectic painter borrows from other men in the hope that something of their meaning will come along with the borrowed forms. Manet is in no way an eclectic painter, and no pardon is necessary because no offense is committed. He is no more an eclectic painter than Shakespeare was an inferior dramatist when he made use of borrowed plots.

Manet's borrowing, however, has nothing to do with new interpretation or enlargement of the subject. He is, in fact, not much interested in subject; a subject merely supplies him with forms to be painted. In *Le Déjeuner* he is not interested in the fact that some young people are having a picnic in unconventional circumstances. He is interested in a way of doing the picture, the means of representation rather than what is represented. *Le Déjeuner's* relationship to Giorgione's *Concert* or Raphael's *Judgment of Paris* need not be apologized for nor need it be used as a defense. *Le Déjeuner* need only be regarded as an effort to discover technical means to make the most direct translation of pure visual experience into the language of paint.

"Olympia"

If there is any question as to whether *Le Déjeuner sur l'Herbe* is entirely successful, or only a near-masterpiece occupying the position of a landmark, there is no question at all in the case of a picture Manet was painting the year of the *Salon des Refusés* but did not exhibit until two years later, his indisputable masterpiece, *Olympia* [186].

Le Déjeuner is startling; *Olympia* is breathtaking. *Le Déjeuner* is puzzling, here and there contradictory; *Olympia* is of the utmost clarity, brilliantly consistent in each detail, each brush stroke, each color. A young courtesan, unabashed in her nakedness, regards us with the same clinical detachment with which Manet has observed and represented her. The hard little body, the short legs, the sturdy trunk, the broad face are those of a woman of the people, but Manet makes no comment, either sentimental or sociological. He does not dramatize. The drama is in the paint—in the abrupt collision of the flat, pinkish-cream light areas of the flesh with the equally flat grayish or blackish shadows; in the expanse of white sheet where nothing seems to happen yet where the painted surface is alive; in the quick, summary notations of embroidered ornaments, of the ribbon at the neck, the bracelet; in the explosion of the bouquet of flowers.

Like *Le Déjeuner*, *Olympia* has a traditional counterpart in Venetian painting (and a closer one than Giorgione's *Concert Champêtre*), Titian's portrait of a Venetian courtesan, called *The Venus of Urbino* [187]. The parallels are direct: the general disposition of the nude figure on the white-sheeted couch, the screen or curtain in the background to the left, the two serving women in the depth to the right in the Titian and the single serving woman in the corresponding foreground position in the Manet, the little white dog in the Titian, the black cat in the Manet. But, again, the transformation is complete, from the sensuous harmonies of the Venetian painting to the flat objectivity of the Manet.

Olympia is entirely a studio product, with none of *Le Déjeuner's* disturbing am-

186. MANET: *Olympia*, 1863, Salon of 1865. 51¼ x 74¾". Louvre, Paris.

biguity in the grafting of studio figures onto a landscape, and, above all, without the inconsistent foreground–background relationships. Manet's flash-of-light vision is better adapted to the revelation of objects at close range than to the exploration of deep space. The closing up of the space occupied by the serving women in the Titian—by pulling the single serving woman of Olympia into the same plane with the rest of the subject—makes possible the unity of this vision. Manet has finally achieved the objectivity implied in Courbet's defenses of realism.

It should be obvious by now that if the term *classicism* is elastic, and *romanticism* more so, the term *realism* is most elastic of all, including the widest range of responses in the transcription of the visible world. Some critics, especially in France, differentiate objective realism like Manet's with the term *naturalism*, leaving the term *real-*

ism free to designate realistic painting which presents ideas, especially those having to do with social theories, as Courbet thought his did. Courbet's friend Castagnary, who helped him formulate some of his pronouncements, also wrote that "Courbet and Proudhon have committed an aesthetic error. Art has nothing to do with the imposition of ideas," and he was using the term *naturalism* as early as the year of the *Salon des Refusés*. Moral values are incorporated into realism; naturalism is amoral. The realist interprets what he sees; the naturalist merely paints the spectacle of life around him, its vice and ugliness, its beauty and sweetness, not preferring one to the other and commenting on neither. The realist may try to find fundamental truths in commonplace objects, but the naturalist deals with the moment only, even at its most ephemeral.

187. TITIAN: *Venus of Urbino*, 1538. 25⅝ x 46⅞". Uffizi, Florence.

The aesthetic satisfactions to be found in naturalism, then, must not be looked for in the subject. Being uninterpreted, the subject is only second best to actuality, and, furthermore, the naturalistic painter may choose to represent subjects aesthetically unpleasing in themselves. Aesthetic satisfaction must be found only in the way the picture is done, since it cannot be found elsewhere. The idea of "art for art's sake" is born, an idea leading eventually to the argument that, since subject is not important, it must be eliminated altogether and a painting must be nothing but lines, shapes, and colors. This is one of the arguments of contemporary abstract painters. Since it can be traced back directly to Manet's "art for art's sake," it makes Manet the first modern artist in a quite specific way. And it gives additional importance to the year 1863 as a dividing line.

Yet, at the risk of confusing the point and at the same time committing a heresy, we must admit that *Olympia* as a subject has an interest aside from the major one of art for art's sake. Granted that Manet does not interpret or moralize or tell a story or make a comment of any kind; granted that his own interest in the subject was incidental to his interest in painting it a certain way; granted that the fascination of this way is in itself enough to hold one in front of the picture—granted all this, it is still true that *Olympia* is not only a representation of reality but a revelation of it. Actuality is not transcribed so much as vivified, intensified, through Manet's vision of it. For close to a century now the young courtesan has regarded us with her special combination of assurance, insolence, and indifference. She still does so as if her glance and ours had just met; she holds us eternally upon the point, upon the moment, of recognition. With *Olympia* we finally reach the pole opposite classicism: the classicist sought to create images in which eternal and universal values are summarized; Manet creates images in which the moment, with whatever implications it may hold for the individual, is crystallized.

Manet before "Le Déjeuner"

How did Manet arrive at *Le Déjeuner* and *Olympia*?

He had entered Couture's studio in 1850 at the age of eighteen, after a time spent at sea and two failures to pass entrance examinations for the naval school. Before this his parents, both of them from wealthy families, had accepted the boy's choice of a naval career as an alternative to law, which was their own ambition for him.

The influence of Couture on Manet should not be discounted. Couture was a harsh and narrow man, but he was no mean painter as far as brush and color are concerned. *The Romans of the Decadence* is a tiresome exercise and its faults are easy to enumerate mercilessly, but in many small canvases—*Little Giles* [188], for instance—where he is just painting, Couture is almost as pure a painter as Manet. The color in *Little Giles* is rich, subdued, and creamy; the broad tonalities of light and darks even suggest an origin for Manet's representational processes as already described. Couture was an excellent teacher for Manet, who was able to take advantage of the good that was offered while remaining immune to the trumpery and bombast of the master's "important" work.

Manet was a realist from the start, and his student days under Couture—1850 to 1855 or 1856—coincided with the emergence of Courbet, but Manet never studied under anyone but Couture in spite of quarrels and insults in Couture's studio. Manet objected to the artificiality of the studio poses, the tight rendering that was mandatory in student work, all the academic rules and conventions. He drew and painted with such freedom that Couture told him once, "You will never be more than the Daumier of your time," which was his way of saying that Manet might pass at the level of this popular cartoonist who had a certain vulgar flair but was, of course, no artist. What Couture thought of Courbet and his followers he summed up in a painting called *The Realist*, showing a painter in rough country clothes using a monumental classical head as a stool to sit on while sketching a butchered pig.

188. COUTURE: *Little Giles*, date unknown. 25¾ x 21½". Philadelphia Museum of Art, William L. Elkins Collection.

Manet's special friend in Couture's studio was Antonin Proust, who entered it at the same time. Proust was another youth of intelligence and social position, equally eager for conventional success. Both young men admired Delacroix, who had become a legendary hero to student painters. They called on him at one time when Manet wanted to make a copy of his *Dante and Vergil in Hell*, which was then hanging in the Luxembourg Museum. Delacroix received the two young men and granted permission to copy, but his manner was so chilly and formal beneath its elegant courtesy that Manet did not follow up an association that would have been much more to his taste than the low-caste assemblies around Courbet at *Brasserie des Martyrs*.

Delacroix might have remembered the visit when he spoke up for the first picture Manet sent to the Salon jury, *The Absinthe*

189. MANET: *Lola de Valence,* 1862. 48½ x 36¼″. Louvre, Paris.

190. MANET: *Woman with a Parrot,* 1866. 72⅞ x 50⅝″. Metropolitan Museum of Art, New York, Gift of Erwin Davis.

Drinker, in 1859, of which Couture had said that the only absinthe drinker must have been the man who painted it. The jury agreed with Couture and rejected it over the head of Delacroix.

But two years later Manet made his surprising Salon success with the portrait of his parents and especially the *Spanish Guitar Player.* His interest in Spanish subjects was increased by a group of Spanish dancers who were making a great success in Paris. He painted most of them individually and also in groups on the stage. When he was not painting them he painted models and friends in Spanish costume; *Young Man in the Costume of a Majo* was posed by his brother.

The Spanish pictures were among those the critics found most offensive of the four-teen Manet exhibited with such a disastrous reception at Martinet's just before the 1863 Salon. A portrait of the leading dancer, *Lola de Valence* [189], was especially detested; it was described as a "bizarre confusion of red, blue, yellow, and black." One critic said it was as if Goya had "gone native in the middle of the Mexican pampas, smearing his canvases with crushed cochineal bugs"—these insects being the source of a brilliant magenta dye. Manet was much influenced just at this time by the colors of Spanish painting; he adopted the typical Spanish neutral gray or blackish backgrounds with spots of color played against them. The color is fairly bright when it is accented in this way, but it is hard to see a "bizarre confusion" today in *Lola de Valence,* even though Manet retouched the picture, brightening its color, after the exhibition. There are vivid passages, but only the soupy browns and obvious tints of the standard Salon product could have made them seem so outrageously raw. Many painters even imitated the darkened tones of paintings by the old masters, disfigured by coats of dirt and varnish. Today Manet's color has suffered from similar disfigurement. Recently the Metropolitan Museum of Art cleaned its group of Manets with surprising results. The *Woman with a Parrot* [190] was transformed from a pleasant, rather quiet picture into a brilliant one; the long robe, which for years had appeared to be a somewhat innocuous light tan, was revealed as a fresh luminous pink with almost white lights, combined with the woman's russet hair in which the ribbon is a bright blue accent. Such a revelation makes early criticisms of Manet more understandable, since the contrast between his color and that of the usual picture of the time was greater than it appears to have been by the evidence of Manet's uncleaned canvases today.

The Scandal of "Olympia"

With the exhibition of *Lola de Valence* and the other pictures at Martinet's and their bad critical reception, the damage was done, and when Manet submitted *Le Déjeuner* to the Salon of 1863, the events as already described occurred. After the scandal of the *Salon des Refusés* the Emperor continued his half-hearted efforts to liberalize academic practices. If he did not put his heart into it, it was because as a good bourgeois himself Napoleon III actually approved of the Academy and liked its typical product.

During the Salon's long history its juries had been elected in various ways. For a while after the Revolution of 1848, election was by the votes of all painters who had exhibited the previous year, a fairly satisfactory system although it carried with it the risk of inbreeding. But before long this system was tightened, and the jury was nominated in part by previous medal winners and in part by the Academy itself. Con-

sidering that the majority of the medal winners were academicians, it is easy to see how this system produced the situation of 1863. Jury membership had again become static and the academic caucus seemed again impregnable.

Now the Emperor made a tepid reform by which the Academy's direct nominations were reduced to one quarter of the jury members, the remaining three quarters to be elected by vote of painters—but again only painters who were also medal winners. But it was a reform of sorts, and combined with a new caution instilled by the narrow escapes of 1863, it produced a liberal jury that included Corot. In 1864 there was a petition to continue the *Salon des Refusés.* It was not granted but a room was set aside for the exhibition of some rejected pictures. They attracted little attention because more pictures had been admitted to the Salon, including Manet's. He exhibited a *Christ with Angels* and a *Bull Fight*. The criticism of the latter was so violent that he destroyed it, except for a fragment.

Then in 1865 came the exhibition of *Olympia,* with a *Christ Insulted by the Soldiers* in the same Salon. It would be repetitious to go into much detail of the vituperative attacks to which they were subjected. The critics surpassed their record of 1863 in viciousness but not often in originality. The same objections were made to Manet's "coarseness" and to the "immorality" of the *Olympia*. It was compared, among other things, to "high" game, and the crowds surrounding it to morbid sensation hunters looking at corpses in the morgue. Every indecency and corruption was read into it, nor was Manet himself spared inferences that his private character was of much the same order. Yet from the 1863 Salon the Emperor had purchased a *Birth of Venus* [191] by the academician Cabanel, as audaciously erotic a nude as has ever been put on public exhibition. The critics admitted that this studio Venus was "wanton" but were able to discover refinements in Cabanel's painting to counteract its lasciviousness. These were the same critics who called *Olympia* a dirty picture.

To escape the furore Manet went to Spain. It was his first trip to that country

191. CABANEL: *Birth of Venus*, 1863. 31½ x 53″. Pennsylvania Academy of the Fine Arts, Philadelphia, Gibson Bequest.

whose art had so influenced him. He was disappointed, not in the paintings of Velásquez and Goya, which he now saw at their best, but in the life and the aspect of the cities and people. He had expected something more picturesque, more colorful, more like the painting and the dancing that up to then had been his Spanish experience. We have the anomaly of a trip to Spain ending his Spanish period, because after that Manet turned more and more to the life around him in Paris for the subject matter of his paintings.

Manet and Zola

Upon his return from Spain, at the border, Manet received an indication of what he might continue to expect at home. The French customs inspector, seeing the name Manet on the luggage, called his family in to take a look at the eccentric artist who had painted the scandalous pictures everyone was talking about. Manet suffered intensely from this kind of notoriety, which was to continue with only temporary abatements for the rest of his life, and he never

developed a defense against it. The Spanish trip was in 1865; in 1866 the Salon refused *The Fifer*, now in the Louvre. The next year there was another of the great world fairs. Not invited to exhibit, Manet erected his own pavilion (as Courbet had done for the exposition of 1855 and as he did also this year). More scandals, more jeers. *The Execution of Maximilian*, painted for this exhibition, was withdrawn at the last minute because of the touchy political situation. The next year, 1868, Manet was finally accepted again by the Salon with two pictures, both very badly hung, *Woman with a Parrot* and a portrait of *Émile Zola* [192].

Émile Zola, of course, was to emerge as one of the dominant figures of his generation with a great block of sociological novels, a dozen crusades, and the climax of the Dreyfus case where his exposures shook the foundation of the French government. The Dreyfus case is an abomination in the history of injustice, countered only by the fact that the same nation produced a Zola to correct it. In Manet's portrait Zola is only twenty-eight years old. He was just emerging from obscurity and had not long emerged from poverty.

MANET AND ZOLA · 171

In his capacity as a critic of the arts, which is the one that concerns us here, Zola's perception did not equal his courage. He defended Manet and some of the other painters we will see, but without a clear understanding of what they were about aesthetically. Nevertheless he defended them with the conviction that they were achieving something good and were having to achieve it while suffering injustices from established hacks and pedants. The year Manet's *Fifer* was rejected, Zola wrote a series of articles on the organization of the Salon system for a paper called *L'Evénement,* including an article in defense of Manet. "A place in the Louvre is reserved for Manet," he wrote. "It is impossible, impossible I say, that he will not have his day of triumph, that he will not obliterate the timid mediocrities surrounding him." Furious objections poured into the offices of *L'Evénement* (not from everybody—some readers thought Zola was joking), and Zola, who had asked special permission to write the series of articles, lost his post as art critic of the journal. The following year he published a monograph on Manet and Manet did his portrait.

Zola is shown seated at his desk surrounded by references to the new movement in painting. A photograph of *Olympia* is on the wall. Behind it, and half covered by it, is Velásquez's *Bacchus.* The third picture in the group is a Japanese print. On the table, just behind the quill pen, the monograph on Manet does double duty as a reference to the connection between the painter and writer and as Manet's signature on the portrait.

The Japanese print is a rather special reference. These prints, today so familiar, were just becoming generally known among artists in Europe, some of the first ones having been discovered among other packing in barrels of imported porcelains. In Japan the print was a vigorous popular art form not taken very seriously by the effete aestheticians and decadent painters when prints first flourished there. After developing in a tightly closed civilization, the prints when they finally reached Europe much later bore some surprising resemblances to the painting that was beginning

192. MANET: *Émile Zola,* 1868. 57½ x 43¼". Louvre, Paris.

to develop with Manet and the impressionists. The subjects were taken from the daily world of entertainment, the theater, the transient world of actors and courtesans, teahouses, views famous with tourists, landmarks. These subjects were in opposition to the formalized art of the "fine" painters but at the same time they were not presented in an unimaginatively realistic way; they were extremely stylized and sophisticated. Manet was doing much the same thing. He painted dancers, singers, people in a public garden listening to music, the courtesan Olympia. But these subjects from the transient world were not approached emotionally, any more than were the subjects of the Japanese prints. Technically the Western painter and the Japanese printmaker were very different, the Japanese print being conceived in conventionalized

193. Torii Kiyonaga: *Shigeyuki Executing Calligraphy*, 1783. Color woodcut, 14¾ x 9⅝". Philadelphia Museum of Art, Gift of Mrs. John D. Rockefeller.

Manet and His Contemporaries

A group of painters, literary men, and dilettantes now began to gather around Manet, some of them his own age, most of them a little younger. The difference was only a few years—ten or less—but psychologically the younger painters were separated from him by a generation. *Le Déjeuner* and *Olympia* had already made Manet a name and a martyr; the younger men were just beginning their careers, and although they were meeting the same reception as Manet, his conspicuousness made him their spokesman and the symbol of their revolt. He bore the brunt of the attacks on this group of "modern" artists, who were soon to become known as the impressionists. During their formative years the *Café Guerbois* was their center, replacing Courbet's *Brasserie des Martyrs* as the winnowing place for new ideas.

Manet did not pontificate as Courbet had tended to do, nor did he ever identify himself wholeheartedly with the group around him. His cultivated manners gave an impression of greater warmth and participation than he was offering; even more than Delacroix, he barricaded himself from intimate contacts with all but a few people. The only members of the new group who knew him well were the ones whose personal backgrounds offered the same amenities as his own. The only bond that held him to the bohemian world of the struggling impressionists at the *Café Guerbois* was one of which he would gladly have rid himself: his rejection and vilification by the world he had failed to conquer. During all this time, up into the 1870's, he had sold fewer than half a dozen pictures. Sales were not vitally important to him except as a form of recognition, although even his substantial means, which he inherited, were beginning to feel some strain. He was married (after a liaison of some years, to his piano teacher) and lived quietly.

One of the more sedate members on the fringe of the impressionist group was Henri Fantin-Latour (1836–1904), a painter acceptable to the Salon and its public but sympathetic to the innovators. One of his recent successes had been a group

linear patterns having little to do with the look of actuality and *Olympia*, for example, having everything to do with one vision of it. Yet when the critic Castagnary called *Olympia* "a playing card," he referred to its composition of flat, well-defined areas of color and he could as appropriately have compared it to a Japanese print for the same reason. European artists now began to draw upon the Japanese print for compositional ideas, and in the portrait of Zola the arrangement of the background into nicely balanced rectangular areas—the pictures, the screen, the resultant rectangular areas of wall—is one reflection of Japanese print composition [193].

194. FANTIN-LATOUR: *A Studio in the Batignolles Quarter*, 1870. 68½ x 82". Louvre, Paris.

195. FANTIN-LATOUR: *Still-Life*, 1866. 23¼ x 28¾". National Gallery of Art, Washington, D. C., Chester Dale Collection.

portrait of Delacroix surrounded by friends, called *Hommage à Delacroix*. He now decided to repeat this documentary idea in a portrait of Manet in his studio, thus loyally identifying himself with the rebels in paying homage to their leader—although he left the "homage" out of the title, calling the picture *A Studio in the Batignolles Quarter* [194], where Manet then had his work place.

Manet is at his easel. Seated next to him is Astruc, the painter and writer who had been one of his most vigorous supporters during the *Salon des Refusés* and had maintained an association with the impressionists. Zola stands at Astruc's side. The young man whose head seems framed by the picture behind him on the wall is the painter Renoir; the tall one at the right is the painter

196. FANTIN-LATOUR: *Homage to Berlioz*, 1885. Pastel, 24½ x 20". Philadelphia Museum of Art, Anonymous Loan.

197. MANET: *Le Bon Bock*, 1873. 37 x 32⅝". Collection Mrs. Carroll S. Tyson, Chestnut Hill, Pa.

Bazille; behind Bazille, as if crowded in as an afterthought, appears the shadowy face of Claude Monet. These are important men and we will have a great deal to say about them. Standing behind Manet is a German painter of less consequence named Otto Scholderer who worked largely in London but made several stays in Paris and, of course, knew Fantin well. He painted still-life, some landscape, and some charming figures, bridging romanticism and impressionism, but need not be considered further. The eighth portrait is of Edmond Maître, an amateur musician and a great and loyal friend of the group*

Late Pictures and Last Days

Suddenly one of Manet's pictures made a Salon success. He had become interested in the seventeenth-century Dutch painter Franz Hals, whose free brushwork resembled Manet's own. Hals's subjects included genre ones of a convivial nature; Manet now painted a fat man enjoying a pipe and a glass of beer, *Le Bon Bock* [197], and the public loved it. No objection could be made to the violence of the color this time. It was all grays and browns and normal flesh tones, with one flash of white in the cuff of a sleeve, the most typically Manet detail in the picture. Elsewhere the painting is

* Fantin-Latour is not easy to classify as a painter. Reduced in size and printed in black and white as they are here, his portraits might be photographs. At full scale this quality is tempered by the presence of the brush, with which Fantin had a delicate touch. His still-life painting [195] is only a shade less photographic. The arrangements of the painted objects are decorative like other popular still-life, but more subtly adjusted into balances of form and color. Fantin's success in the Salon and other salesrooms was inevitable since he so completely fulfilled the first requirement: conformist subject matter represented with detailed accuracy. Occasionally he would execute a painting with the dash of Manet or the more broken technique of the impressionists, but in general he adhered to surface respect for conventional academic disciplines. However, he was without academic pretensions, even in the allegorical and literary or musical subjects that are a third group within his work [196]. In these his style can go rather soft and they are not as satisfying as the portraits and still-life.

198. MANET: *Boating*, 1874. 38¼ x 51¼″. Metropolitan Museum of Art, New York, H. O. Havemeyer Collection.

as dextrous as usual but more conventional in tonality. The face is still conceived in well-defined planes individualized by the strokes of the brush, but there are more planes, hence the forms are represented in more detail. Confronted with a subject it had always liked, painted in a more conventional technique, the Salon public was delighted.

Manet's friends were less pleased. The success of *Le Bon Bock* was based on the very values they—and Manet—regarded as false ones. *Le Bon Bock* was a success not because it was a fine painting but because it was a picture of a jolly fat man enjoying a pipe and a beer. But no one need have felt any concern. The next year two of Manet's three submissions were rejected, and the accepted one, *The Railroad Station,* received the usual scandalous press. The story continued in the same way. Manet was refused for another Exposition Universelle in 1878. Two years before his death, his old friend from Couture's studio,

Antonin Proust, was appointed Minister of Fine Arts. He forced Manet's election to the Legion of Honor with a medal in the Salon. But Manet was now suffering from locomotor ataxia and was too ill to enjoy this tardy and dubious award. He died in 1883, and when seven years later *Olympia* was purchased by subscription and offered to the Louvre,* it was accepted only reluctantly and under duress, although developments in painting had by then affirmed its indisputable pre-eminence as a landmark in the history of art.

During Manet's lifetime, impressionism was being developed by his fellow painters as an art of the out of doors, full of the shimmer of light in the open air painted in a high-keyed palette of pure tints eliminating the grays and blacks that were such an important factor in Manet's color. Manet

* Strictly speaking, to the Luxembourg Museum, the Louvre's waiting room. A painter must have been dead ten years before his work can hang in the Louvre.

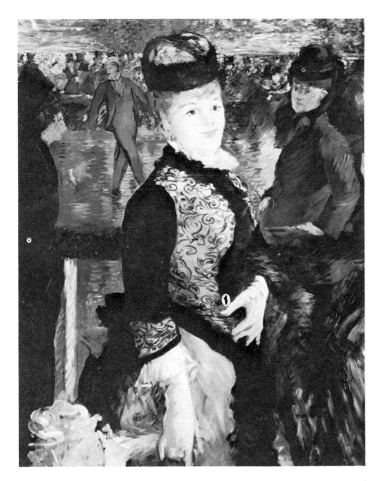

had resisted the appeal of impressionism and outdoor painting, but after 1874 he accepted it more and more. His conversion began when he watched Monet paint at Argenteuil, on the Seine, one of the impressionists' favorite spots. It was the year following the Salon success of *Le Bon Bock*, and it is typical of Manet that in order to follow a new interest he discarded the opportunity to make the kind of success he had always coveted, by repeating the successful formula. His color began to freshen, to lighten, his brush stroke increased in vivacity. But he remained Manet, the man of the boulevards and the studios. Pure landscape did not much appeal to him; when he painted the out of doors he populated it with his city folk, out of town for the day. But it was a great change. The couple enjoying themselves in *Boating* [198], the naturalness and relaxation of their attitudes, the informality of the composition suggesting that the subject has been caught snapshot fashion—all these are a long way from the couples in *Le Déjeuner*, its studied arrangement, the artificiality of its combination of figures and landscape. The couple in *Boating* exist in the full open air permeated by sunlight.

The sparkle and informality that are imposed on the outdoor painter when he

199. MANET: *Skating*, 1877. 36¼ x 28¾". Fogg Art Museum, Cambridge, Mass., Maurice Wertheim Collection.

200. MANET: Detail from Figure 199.

wants to capture effects of light and air began to show also in Manet's studio subjects. *Skating* [199], if it had been painted a few years earlier, would have been flatter, more static, its lights broader, its darks more concentrated and emphatic, its whole surface more tightly knit. Instead, it vibrates everywhere with nervous, energetic, restless, life, modeled as it is in hundreds of quick suggestive strokes which are at least as important as strokes of color as they are as definitions of form [200]. Color becomes brighter and purer, the suggestion of form even more cursory, although it remains decisive. An eye may now be nothing but an irregular star of paint; a lip or a nose or an ear may be made up of a brush of color spotted with an accent of light, another of dark. It is the kind of painting that can degenerate into the shallowest kind of tour de force. In Manet it never does. The portrait of *George Moore* [201] pushes technical showmanship just to the edge of artificiality, simultaneously transcribing the features of this talented but rather irritating young man* as a work-of-art-for-art's-sake and as a witty revelation of an exceptional character. The two aspects of the picture are inseparably present in one another.

Manet's last major work, and very nearly his last one of any kind, was *The Bar at the Folies Bergères* [202], painted in 1881 (although dated 1882) when his illness had progressed so far that it was only with the greatest physical difficulty that he could paint at all. Yet this is a large picture and it approaches *Olympia* in its certainty, in the drama of its paint, in its arresting presence. And by a perfectly logical tour de force it manages to hark back to the early style of *Olympia* in certain passages, while pushing to its limit in other passages the evanescent, shimmering, impressionist manner of Manet's last years.

The immediate foreground is the counter of a bar, with bottles, a compote of fruit,

---

* The young Irishman and professional show-off had come to Paris to study under Cabanel but soon abandoned the idea of a career as a painter. As an extremely superficial art critic and a deft novelist he drew upon French models for a career as an English man of letters.

201. MANET: *George Moore*, 1879. Pastel, 21¾ x 13⅞". Metropolitan Museum of Art, New York, H. O. Havemeyer Collection.

and a glass vase holding two roses, all painted as if Manet wanted to demonstrate finally that no one could excel him as a painter of still life. The barmaid stands behind the counter, leaning forward slightly toward an invisible customer. The silhouette is bold, of an extraordinary symmetry relieved by small interruptions and variations, climaxed in the geometrical oval of the head with its heavy cap of hair. The

202. MANET: *The Bar at the Folies Bergères*, 1881. 37¾ x 50". Collection Courtauld, London.

face, which is not Olympia's in features, re-calls Olympia's as a passage of flat tone suddenly formed and rounded by the brush-ing in of a few small, sudden concentra-tions of dark.

The rest of the picture—the entire back-ground—is a mirror. The solid, vigorously defined figure of the barmaid, as reflected from the back, is now amorphous, softened; the unseen customer is seen facing her, a few half-tone blurs; farther back the dress circle is half defined, half suggested, in merging and intermingling shapes that co-alesce here and there into a gesture, an attitude, a hat, a gloved hand holding opera glasses.

Yet, if *The Bar at the Folies Bergères* summarizes so much of Manet's accomplish-ment, it is also inventive in a new way. The complexity of its composition, the struc-tural geometry of the insistent verticals running in bands across the picture, the strong central triangle of the figure with the secondary geometrical forms included within it—all these are new in Manet. *The Bar at the Folies Bergères* is a swan song only by its coincidental date with Manet's last illness and his death. He was painting with as much inventiveness and curiosity and independence as he ever had done. And no man has ever painted with more.

Immediately after Manet's death his pic-tures began to sell at rising prices. The press discovered that he was a great painter. Before a year had gone by a memorial show was prepared. It was held in the galleries of the *École des Beaux Arts*—the fortress of the Academy.

CHAPTER 7

Impressionism

The Impressionist Group

In 1874 a group of artists with their core at the *Café Guerbois* organized a society to exhibit their work at their own expense. Such an idea had been in the air for some time, without any unanimity of opinion, but now these men saw no other way to bring their work properly before the public.

Some of the prospective exhibitors wanted to invite the friendlier older painters to show with them, for the prestige this would lend the unknowns—such men as Corot and the grand old revolutionary Courbet, who was still alive although in exile. (It was just as well that they decided against doing so, for even Corot, that man of good will, referred to them later as "that gang.") Other members wanted everyone in the group to pledge never to send to the Salon; still others, who were beginning to have an occasional picture accepted there, thought this idea bad. Manet, their great man, refused to have any part of the exhibition. So did Fantin-Latour. Even some of the painters who decided to come in did so reluctantly, still convinced that the Salon was the real field of conquest.

When the first exhibition was finally organized, it was partly a commercial venture and partly a declaration of aesthetic war. Commercially the members hoped to increase the number of private collectors who were beginning to buy their work. They were spurred on by the fact that just at this time the adventurous dealer Durand-Ruel, who had taken on some of them, was going through a financial crisis and was forced to stop all purchases until he could get his affairs in order. Aesthetically, the group was dedicated to the idea that threadbare formulas—or arbitrary formulas of any kind —could not be forced onto a painter without stifling him creatively. They demanded the right to paint as they pleased, and what they pleased, as the only means of fulfilling their creative potentials.

After considerable confusion, including quarrels and hurt feelings, an exhibition was assembled and hung in the studio of the photographer Nadar, another habitué of the *Café Guerbois*. Nadar has his own importance in the history of photography, and a cartoon by Daumier shows him in a balloon "elevating photography to the level of a fine art"; he was a pioneer in aerial views.

The thirty exhibitors were an odd combination including half a dozen names that were to be among the greatest of the century, an equal number of sound masters of the second rank, a friendly amateur or two, one popular Salon painter, and a few ghosts who would have disappeared altogether if their names had not been preserved on this historic list.* For so mixed a group no single title seemed descriptive enough, so a noncommittal name was settled on after great effort to find something more specific: *Societé anonyme des artistes peintres, sculpteurs, graveurs, etc.*

But the name did not last; an appropriate descriptive one invented itself. The exhibition of 165 pictures had hardly opened before the painters were dubbed "impressionists," a name considered as hilarious as the painting that supplied the cue for it—*Impression-Sunrise* by Claude Monet. Although the nickname was derisive, it cut through the obscuring surfaces of personal styles to the unifying element in the most original of the pictures. The impressionists accepted the new label and soon changed the name of their organization to *Peintres Impressionistes*.

Altogether the impressionists gave eight exhibitions before they disbanded, the first

in 1874 and the last in 1886, with many changes of membership during those years. By 1886 the group was full of dissensions and many of the members had grown dissatisfied with impressionism and had departed from it.

By that time, in any case, the organization had served its purpose. It had won its battle for the attention of dealers and collectors in spite of the continued insults of the Academy and its entourage of philistines and mossbacks. Resistance died hard in these circles. As late as 1893, when a great collection of impressionist painting was willed to the Louvre, it was subjected to the kind of criticism accorded *Le Déjeuner sur l'Herbe* thirty years before in the *Salon des Refusés* and was accepted only in part.* Gérôme, now seventy, described the pictures as "filth" that only "a great moral slackening" could make acceptable to the government. But this was

___

* For the record, in alphabetical order, they were: Astruc, Attendu, Béliard, Boudin, Bracquemond, Brandon, Bureau, Cals, Cézanne, Colin, Degas, Desbras, Guillaumin, Latouche, Lepic, Lépine, Levert, Meyer, de Molins, Monet, Morisot, Mulot-Durivage, de Nittis, A. Ottin, L. A. Ottin, Pissarro, Renoir, Robert, Rouart, and Sisley.

* This was the Caillebotte collection. Gustave Caillebotte was a naval architect of considerable wealth, a quiet man who discovered the impressionists before they became popular on the market and bought their pictures not as investments but because he liked them. (Many canny Americans bought impressionists early because Durand-Ruel, having been right about the Barbizon painters before their prices went up, might be right again.) Caillebotte was an amateur painter himself, made friends with the impressionists, exhibited in the second group show and four successive ones, threw his fine house on the river open to the young painters, and continued to buy their pictures during their most desperate times. He made a point of buying the kinds of pictures not saleable on the regular market—the very large ones and the ones painted to solve special problems. He did this to help the painters, but as a result he also acquired some of their most important work. The Caillebotte paintings that were finally accepted (the rejected ones included some fine Cézannes) are at the heart of the Louvre's impressionist collection.

Another friend of the impressionists was Victor Chocquet, a minor government official, the rarest and most perspicacious type of art collector. With very little money to spare, he was ready to make sacrifices elsewhere to own and enjoy the pictures he liked. As a very young man he bought watercolors by Delacroix. Like Caillebotte he discovered the impressionists for himself. Among the pictures sold by Chocquet's widow in 1899 were thirty-one Cézannes, eleven Renoirs, eleven Monets, and five Manets.

203. GOYA: *Dr. Peral, c.* 1800–10. Panel, 37⅜ x 25⅞″. National Gallery, London.

204. GOYA: Detail from Figure 203.

the last senile gasp of the old guard, and although Gérôme and Bouguereau were still coveted by one kind of collector, so were Renoir and Degas by others. Americans were buying so extensively that when *Olympia* was purchased by subscription and offered to the Louvre in 1890, one of the reasons was that the subscribers feared France would lose it as other masterpieces had already been lost to the United States.

The Nature of Impressionism

Just what is impressionism? The word *impression* had been used in art criticism off and on before Monet attached it to his picture of a sunrise. Its connotations were not flattering. The writer Théophile Gautier expressed regrets that Daubigny was satisfied to give his "impression" of a landscape and "neglect" details, although of course Daubigny was deliberately eliminating details in poeticizing his images. "Impression" suggested incompleteness, a superficial vision of the subject. When the impression-

ists made an honest word of it and sought a definition, one suggestion was "painting in terms of tone rather than in terms of the object itself." Any definition must be based on this idea, the idea that the impressionist does not analyze form but only receives the light reflected from that form onto the retina of his eye and seeks to reproduce the effect of that light, rather than the form of the object reflecting it. For instance, if a bush in the distance seen in a certain light reaches the eye only as a green blur, the impressionist paints it as a green blur, even if he happens to know the bush so well that he could reproduce its form exactly from memory. Monet, the purest of the impressionists if we accept this definition, once said that he wished he had been born blind and could have gained his sight so that he could paint without knowing what the objects before him were, since this would allow him to see them purely in terms of light. Never having seen a bush he would not know that the green blur in the distance was a bush, and would reproduce it in a matching green blur of

205. VELÁSQUEZ: *Venus and Cupid,* 1651. 48¼ x 69¾". National Gallery, London.

206. VELÁSQUEZ: Detail from Figure 205.

paint without having to forget his detailed acquaintance with it as a form.

This pushes to its ultimate Goya's idea of training his brush not to see more than his eye did. But there is the great difference that Goya wanted to train his brush to reproduce forms—"forms that are lighted and forms that are not, planes that are near and planes that are far, projections, and hollows." In his portrait of *Dr. Peral* [203] form is solidly represented, but a close detail of part of the face [204] shows how he has eliminated the "lines and details" to which he objected in classical painting. The bridge of the nose, for instance, is not defined by a line, although to the classical draughtsman lines represent the divisions between forms. The pupil of the eye is not a circular dark spot but a dark irregular area, which was all Goya allowed his brush to see since his own eye could perceive only that much from the distance at which he was painting. But Goya never goes so far as to sacrifice form to this kind of vision.

Further back, Velásquez in the seventeenth century was something of an impressionist in "painting by the tones." The reflection in the mirror in his *Venus and Cupid* [205, 206] is an extreme example. Velásquez has reproduced only the light reflected from the cloudy mirror as his eye received it from a certain distance. That light happens to carry with it the lights and darks composing the reflected face. All lines, all details, have been eliminated in this process of double reflection from the model's face to the painter's retina. Less dramatically, the other forms in the picture are painted in the same way. A host of other examples could be culled from the past to show that the impressionist idea was not altogether new, even if it had not been set up as a theory and a technique until the nineteenth century, with special departures of its own that made it revolutionary.

The quality of instant vision, the subject revealed in a momentary aspect, takes on more importance in impressionism than it ever had before. *Olympia* is seen as if in a sudden flash of light, but the the model is posed, the composition studied. The pure impressionists will paint as if they had

207. MONET: *Red Boats at Argenteuil*, 1875. 23⅜ x 31⅞". Fogg Art Museum, Cambridge, Mass., Maurice Wertheim Bequest.

caught the subject unaware, in a chance gesture. And in painting colored light— light colored because it is reflected from the varicolored objects making up the world—the impressionists will shatter the surface of their canvas into thousands of fragmented tints. Both of these innovations imply loss of form—loss of compositional form and loss of solidity in individual forms. Several members of the impressionist group will discover that this is impressionism's soft spot, and we will see them abandoning typical impressionist procedures in order to remedy it.

But whatever its definition, impressionism as a school of painting is the climactic expression of the nineteenth century. It gathers together the contributions of the conflicting schools of the first half and fuses them into a way of painting from which, in turn, the art of the twentieth century develops, partly as a continuation of impressionism, partly as a reaction against it.

The Impressionist Inheritance

From Delacroix the impressionists inherited discoveries in the theory of color upon which they enlarged. His technique of applying color in individual strokes, which he called *flochetage,* was extended to such a point that the surface of some impressionist painting became a rough texture of dots and dabs of paint. Delacroix had found greens within reds, blues and purples in the shadows of yellow. He abandoned the idea that a red object, for instance, was red all over. Any other color might exist within the red area, either because the laws of physics produced it by reflection ("Color is a merging of reflections," he said) or simply because the painter wanted it there in order to enhance or reduce the intensity of the colors stroked on near by. From this starting point, the impressionists began to use their eyes like prisms, turning white light into all its components of the spectrum, red, orange, yellow, green, blue, and violet.

From Courbet the impressionists inherited the inexhaustible mine of the everyday world. Some of them in their first days knew him in his last ones at the *Brasserie des Martyrs*. The Barbizon painters amplified Courbet's legacy, revealing landscape as a subject independent of romantic fervor or classical formality. They opened a door through which the impressionists rushed pell-mell into the open air, where they discovered their studios in fields, along river banks, and, for that matter, in the city streets.

These legacies seemed to contradict one another and all of them contradicted the art of Ingres. But the impressionists found compatibilities beneath what appeared to be antitheses. Technically the impressionists learned from all these sources and dozens of others—the English landscapists, the Japanese print, the art of Venice and of the French court, the new process of photography, perhaps too the scientific researches into the nature of light and color by such men as Chevreul, Helmholtz, Maxwell, and Rood.

Monet

Impressionism as a technique devoted to capturing effects of light out of doors is exemplified most purely in the painting of Claude Monet (1840–1926), who forced it to its limits, and then beyond.

Monet was the son of a grocer; his parents refused to support him in a career as an artist, offering to buy him out of his military service if he would abandon the idea. This he refused to do, and by the time he was sixteen he had a local reputation as a caricaturist in his home city of Le Havre. His interest in landscape was stimulated by painters who came to Le Havre to paint the port or the beaches, particularly by Eugène Boudin (who will be seen later). In Paris Monet identified himself with the impressionists although he had had an occasional Salon acceptance with a mild success in 1866. His poverty was desperate; malnutrition contributed to the death of his wife; he had to write begging letters to friends and was sometimes without money to buy paints. As late as 1888 Manet was helping him financially. (The similarity of their names sometimes caused confusion in exhibitions—to Manet's indignation.) But after 1890, when he was fifty years old, Monet was a prosperous artist.

Monet's development can be summarized in a handful of pictures that must stand for many hundreds. He was an insatiable worker. *Red Boats at Argenteuil* [207], painted in 1875, is a fully developed impressionist landscape of the period of the first group exhibition. The stretch of water is shot through with strokes of blue in many different shades. The reflections of boats and shore are struck into it freely, in bright tints of greens and pinks. On its sunny side, the largest of the boats is yellow in the highest lights, shot with lavender near the water, yet a bright rosy color overall; on its shadow side the hull is a strong violet-blue, made up of dark blues, grape colors, violet-reds, and a touch or two of vermilion. No colors are pulled together; each stroke (at close range, that is) tells individually. The boat is decorated with a stripe running around it near the gunwale. On the shadow side this stripe cuts through the purple-blue as a brilliant emerald green; on the sunny side it is bright yellow. The small clouds are flicks and dabs of pure white. On the grassy bank half a dozen greens are freely juxtaposed and intermingled, some yellowish, some bluish; the houses are pinkish with similar variations.

From a little distance these different tints and colors within single areas tend to disappear as individual strokes. The eye "mixes" them and in doing so creates colors with more vibration, more sparkle, than would have been possible if the various reds or greens or blues or pinks had been mixed on the palette and applied in large areas in the conventional way or pulled together by "blending" on the canvas. In this stage of impressionism form has not disappeared, although light, shattering against it, is already permeating and softening its surface, obscuring its details.

In black and white, the sunlit side of the red boat is all but indistinguishable from the water around it. In color, however, the

208. MONET: *Terrace at Le Havre*, 1866. 23½ x 31½". Collection the Rev. T. Pitcairn, Bryn Athyn, Pa.

contrast is quite strong. The values—that is, the lightness or darkness of the colors—are so nearly identical that in black and white the contrast disappears. This is not merely an accident of photographic translation; it is a result of the fact that Monet is painting in terms of color as light, rather than in terms of form as revealed by light and shade. As a contrast to make this point, *Red Boats at Argenteuil* can be compared with the *Terrace at Le Havre* [208] painted nine years earlier, which is still conceived in light and shadow. The forms are decisive, everywhere defined, although in color this picture is equally bright, equally sunny. The only areas where form tends to disappear are those of the clumps and sprays of flowers, painted in spots of red, green, and yellow with almost no shadow. Elsewhere the forms exist solidly in the light that strikes across their surfaces to reveal them. In *Red Boats at Argenteuil*, light is already beginning not so much to reveal the objects

as to be revealed by them. Light permeates them, they fuse with it; forms do not interrupt light, as they do in the *Terrace at Le Havre*, but are caught up in it.

Monet's preoccupation with reducing all visual experience to terms of pure light became an obsession. When his young wife died he was horrified to find himself analyzing the nacreous tints of her skin in the early morning light. As he continued to paint, wishing he could have been "born blind in order to gain his sight and be able to paint objects without knowing what they were," as he began more and more to develop the ability to see light and nothing but light, light became like a corrosive substance eating away the objects bathed in it. *Spring Trees by a Lake* [209] is all but formless. Within the twinkling strokes of blue, blue-green, pure green, yellow-green, and yellow covering most of the canvas, we barely recognize, by occasional vertical strokes of purplish and reddish tints, the

209. MONET: *Spring Trees by a Lake*, 1888. 29 x 36". Philadelphia Museum of Art, William L. Elkins Collection.

trunks of a few trees. The extreme of this progressive dematerialization of matter is reached in "effects" of certain hazy and foggy atmospheres where the canvas dissolves into mist and material forms become mists within mists.

Between the *Terrace at Le Havre* and his late pictures Monet changed from a painter responding to nature into one fascinated by an abstract problem. In the early pictures the attraction of subject is great; in the *Terrace at Le Havre*, half the observer's pleasure is his feeling of participation in a world of sun, air, flowers, and water. There is a keen and delightful sense of the fresh spanking breeze, the presence of the sparkling sea. There is also the more abstract pleasure offered by the certainty, the vigor, and the invention of the painting just as painting. In the later pictures this is the whole pleasure. It must be, for the objects from which we might have gained the sense

of participation in the scene have become devoured by a technical process.

Monet invented a name for what he was trying to achieve: *instantaneity*. In 1891 he exhibited, at Durand-Ruel's, a series of fifteen paintings of haystacks in the different lights of different times of day, analyzing the color-light relationships in various stages between half-lights of early morning and evening and the full blaze of midday. This faintly pedantic exhibition was a great success. Monet then set out on an even more elaborate analysis and painted some forty pictures of Rouen Cathedral [210] on gray days, bright days, in early light, late light, full light, light at different seasons of the year. These exercises are interesting, but they emphatically isolate the limitation of Monet's method. The monumental gray form of the cathedral is ground into a pulp of blues, oranges, pinks, and lavenders. The geometrical complications of its buttresses, windows, spires, and tracery become tottering masses of tinted fluff; they lean and waver in random placements on the canvas. A cathedral, with its mass, its organization, its logical formality, is a poor choice for dematerialization in close-range painting when it is supposed to be existing within full light. Theoretically we should be able to forget that this is a cathedral which appears to be going to pieces; practically it is difficult to do so.

But the Rouen pictures were followed by another series, this time of a perfect subject. In the garden of his house at Giverny, which Monet had bought with the proceeds from his first successful sale, there was a pool with water lilies which he had painted from time to time. Now in the 1890's he discovered in the surface of the pool, and the leaves and blossoms floating upon it, a subject with enough material to last him for the rest of his life. The shimmering, shifting translucence of the water, the delicate and even translucent petals of the blossoms, the flat shiny pads of leaves floating or half submerged in water close to the same color, with the light glancing off surfaces or striking through them onto surfaces below, repeating and reflecting on every hand, the whites and the rainbow tints—these were inexhaustible in their combinations and recombinations. Now Monet's canvases became the surfaces of pools, fragmented areas where water, light, air, and the delicate substance of blossoms all partook of one another, echoed one another, and crossed one another's boundaries until there was no differentiation between them.

The water-lily paintings supplied the motif for Monet's last work, a series of large decorative panels [211, 212]. But in these hugely expanded canvases, with large brush strokes, the forms of nature are difficult to distinguish. If the paintings are regarded as representations of lilies and water with ripples and glancing reflections of light, they never become more than great inchoate masses of opalescent color arbitrarily cut off on four sides by a frame. But if they are regarded as abstract arrangements of color applied in directed strokes, they gradually coalesce. One movement of strokes across the canvas is revealed as a

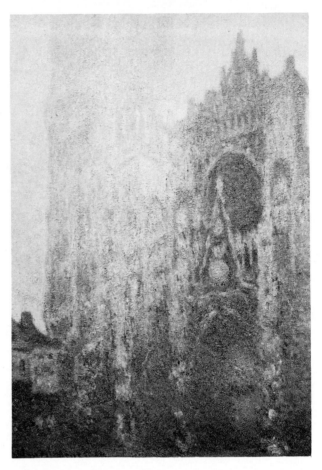

210. MONET: *Rouen Cathedral: Tour d'Albane, Early Morning*, 1894. 41¾ x 29″. Museum of Fine Arts, Boston.

check or a buttress to another; a system beginning in one section and seeming to vanish will reappear elsewhere. The colors are woven and built into a structure that is its own reason for being. The "systems" in these paintings are free inventions, felt rather than calculated, and the danger is to exaggerate their precision or to find within them a logic that does not exist. But it is safe to say that Monet, from his impressionist beginning when he painted spontaneous approximations of visual effects of light and atmosphere, gradually transformed his art into one of abstract surfaces where relationships of form and color exist for themselves in spite of the vestigial remains of a subject.

It is on this basis that Monet now seems to have anticipated a school of contemporary extremists. Jackson Pollock (1912–

211. MONET: *Water Lilies, c.* 1925. 79¾ x 221½″. Museum of Modern Art, New York, Mrs. Simon Guggenheim Fund. (Destroyed by fire, 1958.)

212. MONET: Detail from Figure 211.

1956) painted by dripping, flicking, dribbling, or pouring semiliquid colors onto a canvas (or panel) laid an the floor [213]. The pattern of different colors, densely intermingled or freely splattered, exists without even secondary reference to nature. It exists for itself as color, as line, as a complex within which movements, systems, rhythms are overlaid and intertwined. The same thing can be said about Monet's late water-lily pictures, if their starting point of light playing over the forms of nature is ignored.

213. POLLOCK: *Autumn Rhythm*, 1950. 105 x 207″. Metropolitan Museum of Art, Hearn Fund.

214. MONET: *Woman in a Garden, Springtime, c.* 1875. 19⅝ x 25¾". Walters Art Gallery, Baltimore.

Thus Monet becomes a bridge between the naturalism of early impressionist painting and a contemporary school of extreme abstraction. "Abstract impressionism" would be an appropriate term to describe Pollock's sparkling interweaving of dots, splashes, and ropelike lines of color, and the term is sometimes used as a subtle distinction within the wider "abstract expressionist" school of contemporary painting, which will be seen in a later chapter [548, 549].

Monet's landscapes and the late semiabstract paintings into which they merged are his historically important work. They obscure his portraits and figure studies, most of which were done between 1860 and the early 1870's. (He did many of his wife.) In any case, he had no great interest in human beings as personalities to be interpreted; he painted them from much the same point of view as he painted landscape —that is, as elements of nature in light. In the gentle *Woman in a Garden, Springtime* [214] the woman is more like a blossoming shrub than a person.

Sisley and Pissarro

The two other "pure" impressionists in the group were Alfred Sisley (1839–1899) and Camille Pissarro (1830–1903). Their experiments were less venturesome, within narrower boundaries, than Monet's. Hence they always fall into second place with brief consideration in books of this kind, which is too bad but inevitable.

A painter's merit cannot be gauged by the number of lines of type required to comment on it, and to comment at any length on Sisley would involve repetition of much that already has been said about Corot and Monet. His fresh and quiet art [215] has affinities with that of both these men.

Sisley resigned himself early to poverty, obscurity, and official rejections, and although he exhibited in the first impressionist show and three others, he spent very little time in Paris and finally retired to the village of Moret, where he could exist at minimum expense surrounded by subject

215. SISLEY: *Bridge at Villeneuve*, date unknown. 21½ x 29″. Philadelphia Museum of Art, John G. Johnson Collection.

matter that appealed to him—a quiet countryside and a village with old buildings, bridges, and river banks. Sisley's parents were English and he spent some time in that country. Of all French painters he comes closest to the special lyrical response to nature found in English painters and even more in English poets. Corot was his idol, and his painting has Corot's serenity beneath the more vibrant impressionist surface. Once he had discovered the impressionist palette and technique—which he never forced—his manner changed very little over the years, yet his work is not repetitious. Each picture is remarkably complete in its effect, where much impressionism seems fragmentary. Without Monet's passion for experiment, which kept the pictures pouring forth, and without a market to set a demand, which he would have worked to supply, Sisley painted with great deliberation, allowing the fullest expression of his sensibilities. He did not live to see the triumph of impressionism extend as far as his own work, but immediately

upon his death his paintings began to fetch high prices. During his lifetime he sold them for twenty-five or thirty francs.

Pissarro's impressionism has much of the sobriety of Sisley's but is less reflective. He was the oldest member of the group, being two years older even than Manet. Born in the Virgin Islands, he came to Paris the year of the great exposition of 1855. Everyone who knew Pissarro seems to have left some account of him, and by all these accounts his life and his character were a catalogue of virtues—loyalty to his friends, wisdom as the father of a large family, courage in adversity, and patience, tolerance, honesty, and industry in all circumstances.

Although Pissarro was intent upon capturing transient effects just as Monet was, he never abandoned the relative discipline of early impressionism, and for a while late in his career he joined the "neo-impressionists," who tried to solidify impressionism by systematizing its free prismatic shattering of light into a scientific application of color into minutely calculated dots [405].

Pissarro soon abandoned this extreme, but that he was attracted to it at all shows his cautiousness in the use of impressionist effects. While Monet was pushing further into exploration of effects of light in air at the expense of form, Pissarro was retreating. *The Market at Gisors* [216] is an effort to retain the atmospheric vibration of impressionism while at the same time imposing the discipline of well-defined contours on forms monumentally arranged in space.

The Market at Gisors is a late picture, but even in his early ones when he was sharing with Monet the excitement of the impressionist discoveries, Pissarro retained his respect for the material fact of the subjects he was painting. When he painted trees and fields [218], they remain trees and fields rather than becoming a multitude of small elements reflecting a characteristic spring light. In no circumstances could he have shared Monet's wish to be ignorant of the objects he saw. Of all the impressionists he is the one most closely allied to the Barbizon spirit with its love of fields, copses, and peasant huts as part of a simple life with a nobility of its own.

But his cityscapes, too, are of a great vivacity [217]. He reduces crowds, carriages, and individual figures to the merest suggestion, in scattered dots and his typical "commas" of paint, but he never allows his city buildings to decompose as Monet's cathedrals did. Pissarro is a careful painter —Monet seems careless at times. He was the only one of the impressionists to exhibit in all eight of the group shows, and during the constant squabbles he was the unofficial moderator.

More than any other member of the group, Pissarro encouraged younger men. At least three painters who were notoriously suspicious and thorny to deal with—Degas, Cézanne, and Gauguin—always retained a deep affection for him. Like Monet's and Sisley's, his financial situation was often desperate and at best difficult, but finally, at the age of sixty-two, he had the satisfaction of seeing his reputation established, not spectacularly but soundly enough, in a large retrospective exhibition organized by Durand-Ruel. It was a gratifyingly happy ending to an admirable career.

216. PISSARRO: *The Market at Gisors,* 1891. Philadelphia Museum of Art, Louis E. Stern Collection. 13½ x 10¼". Gouache.

Degas: "The Bellelli Family"

Midway during the careers of Monet, Sisley, and Pissarro, pure impressionism was abandoned by two painters who felt limited by the transient effects it imposed. One of these men, Renoir, brought impressionism directly into the tradition of the old masters by subjecting it to their disciplines. The other, Cézanne, subjected it to new disciplines, making it the point of departure for the most radical redirection of the art of painting in some six centuries.

A third, Degas, had never accepted impressionism on Monet's terms in the first place, and was its great traditionalist even while he was one of its most startling inno-

217. PISSARRO: *Avenue de l'Opéra*, 1898. 25⅜ x 31½". Collection Mr. and Mrs. Louis C. Madeira, Gladwyn, Pa.

218. PISSARRO: *Landscape with Fields*, 1885. 23⅝ x 29". Philadelphia Museum of Art, Wilstach Collection.

vators. It was never necessary for Degas to revert to traditionalism as Renoir was to do, since he had been a traditionalist from the beginning. His innovations, eccentric at first glance, are as a matter of fact brilliantly logical extensions of traditional principles.

Edgar Degas (1834–1917) was the aristocrat of the impressionists, not only by birth but in his intellectuality and reserve, his personal detachment in observing a commonplace world to record it intimately. Of all the impressionists he is the most subtle, disguised as the most direct; the most reflective, disguised as the most noncommittal; the most acute, disguised as the most casual. He is their finest draughtsman and composer; he is one of the finest draughtsmen and composers of any period. He was the only impressionist to recognize

219. DEGAS: *The Bellelli Family*, 1859. 78¾ x 99½". Louvre, Paris.

that the momentary effect—with Degas, a moment may be split to its ultimate fraction —can be used for complete revelation of individual character. He was, in fact, the only impressionist who was interested in painting individuals as psychological entities. The personalities he thus recorded exist with a completeness, a reality, that puts their portraits among the great ones of any age. Sometimes these personalities are people Degas knew; sometimes they are nobodies, a milliner's assistant at work, a clerk, a prostitute, or a vagrant. But no matter who they are, they are revealed in the most significant nuances of their inner being; and at the same time, they are

equally revealed in their relationship to the social order.

This doubly acute perception is apparent in Degas's work from the beginning. In 1856 he was only twenty-two years old. The *Salon des Refusés* was still an inconceivable event seven years in the future; Manet was just leaving Couture's studio; Pissarro was getting settled in Paris; Monet was a local boy in Le Havre doing caricatures. Degas was in Naples visiting his aunt, the Baroness Bellelli. He made sketches of her, of her husband, and of their daughters, his young cousins Giovanna and Giuliana Bellelli. During the next three or four years on subsequent visits to Florence, where his relatives were then living, he made other sketches and began to organize them into a group portrait. By 1859 or a little later he had completed the most extraordinary of all family portraits, a study of individual personalities and their interrelationships expressed through pictorial composition [219].

The family was a disturbed one, and the primary fact of the father's emotional separation from the mother and daughters is established by his unconventional placement, seated as he is with his back partly turned toward us and his face in shadow. Compositionally this isolation is defined by the strong line of the table leg that is continued by the line of the side of the fireplace—only slightly interrupted by a few papers on the corner of the table—and on up to the top of the picture by the frame of the large mirror over the mantlepiece. Thus the righthand third of the picture, containing the father's portrait, is cut off by a compositionally heretical but expressively brilliant device. In addition, this area is filled with small shapes, further differentiating it from the left two thirds where the shapes are stronger and more simple.

In contrast with the bent, indecisive attitude and silhouette of the husband, the wife stands with decision and dignity. The wide hoop skirt and the narrow shoulders form a pyramid, the stablest of all geometrical forms. Surmounting this dark silhouetted triangle and framed by her dark hair, the face of the Baroness with its calm, its sadness, and its strength, is the focal point of a composition in which we are led from one formal and psychological relationship to another, yet always back to this central focus of meaning.

The mother's arm rests on the shoulder of Giovanna, the daughter who was most like her mother and closest to her. Degas includes the smaller triangle of the figure of the little girl within the larger one of the mother's to establish this similarity and this closeness. The other daughter, Giuliana, was more volatile and more divided in her allegiance to her parents. For her Degas chooses an unconventional pose, one leg drawn up beneath her as she sits on the corner of a chair, one hand on her hip

(while Giovanna's hands are placidly folded) and her face turned from her mother and sister in the general direction of her father, although she does not quite meet his glance. Giuliana thus unites the two halves of the composition structurally, tied at once to the mother and the sister by the identity of her costume and by lines following or echoing lines in the mother-Giovanna group, and yet also tied to the father. This was Giuliana's relationship to the family: divided between its parts, although in the end (as in the picture) she was united more strongly with her mother and sister.

In its other elements the composition is unified by the repeated horizontals and verticals of the picture on the wall, the table, the door frame, the bell pull, and, for that matter, by any line or mass one wants to pick out. The rather rigid skeletal structure is relieved by the broken pattern of the rug and the sprinkling of flowers on the wallpaper.

A multiple portrait, demanding a division of attention between several individuals and yet a unity of the picture over-all, is as taxing an assignment as a painter has to cope with. *The Bellelli Family* is a masterpiece from half a dozen points of view, technically and expressively. Here in his first major picture Degas demonstrated his extraordinary combination of acute sensibility to the most personal, most private inner life of the individuals he observes, and his peculiar objectivity that allows him to stand outside these perceptions and present them in the most clinical, analytical way.

Degas: His Impressionism

Degas is one of those painters whose art is conventionally discussed chronologically.

His father,[*] a banker, had planned a career in law for his son, but this study was abandoned in 1855. This was the year of the Exposition Universelle, and Degas was much excited by Courbet's Pavilion of Realism. He was also an admirer of Dela-

---

[*] Auguste De Gas. The son changed the surname to the less aristocratic form in 1870.

220. DEGAS: Drapery study for *Sémiramis*, 1861. Black pencil and chalk on blue paper, 11⅝ x 7⅞". Louvre, Paris.

221. DEGAS: *Lady on Horseback*, 1860–65. Pencil, 12½ x 8". Louvre, Paris.

croix. But Ingres was his great man, and the Exposition gave him a chance to meet the old painter. M. Valpinçon, a friend of Degas's father, owned *The Turkish Bather*, now called the *Bather of Valpinçon* [59], but had refused to lend it to the Ingres retrospective planned for that year's vast Salon. Degas induced Valpinçon to change his mind and Valpinçon told Ingres of this. Degas and Valpinçon were invited to Ingres's studio, where Degas was given the advice to "draw lines, young man, many lines." Degas was entering the Academy's school, but as it turned out he spent most of his time studying privately under Lamothe, one of Ingres's pupils, since at that time Ingres was accepting no students.

Degas had been a precocious natural draughtsman, and his first student work makes one wonder what was left for him to learn under instruction, but he drew lines, perhaps many lines, under Lamothe. Although his allegiance to Ingres never wavered during his life, his idea was not to emulate the classical style but to capitalize on the discipline and the structural knowledge of the human body upon which it was supposed to be based. Unlike the ordinary student who imitated only the surfaces of the classical style, Degas ignored surfaces and went beneath them to the legitimate fundamentals that had been all but forgotten. He observed them from his earliest work to his last. An early drapery study

222. DEGAS: Studies of Manet, *c.* 1864–65. Pencil on pink paper, 16 x 11″. Collection Ernest Rouart, Paris.

portrait of Manet [222] is more relaxed, more inventive, yet equally disciplined. Ingres is still present, but in addition to greater warmth there is also a record and an interpretation of personality that in Ingres stopped at whatever immediately apparent suggestions were offered by the subject's face and costume. As a mature artist Degas never merely draws. He uses his crayon to probe, to explore, to discover. In a study, *Two Café Singers* [223], the transformation of classical discipline is complete; it operates now with a freedom (and in the service of a subject) that would have horrified Ingres but could never have developed in the art of Degas without the foundation of classical experience. There is not a detail, not so much as the upward bend of a singer's thumb, that is extraneous to the whole; there is not a touch of the crayon dependent on less than perfect mastery.

Degas had met Fantin-Latour and Manet, and now he began to sit in on some of the discussions that were developing at the *Café Guerbois.* By the latter 1860's he had discovered his material: the life of the city as he saw it in the drawing room, in the studio, in the shops, even in the brothel; on the boulevard, at the racetrack, in the cafés, the theater, the opera—all the places where people congregated and could be studied in a thousand expressive attitudes, attitudes spontaneously and unconsciously assumed, combined later from sketches or memory into compositions that seemed equally spontaneously and accidentally put together. In *A Carriage at the Races* [224] carriages and horses are chopped off as if by chance, and in the background a few horses and riders, trees and low buildings are scattered as if at random, while a couple of women, a sleeping boy, a man, and a dog are caught in momentary and casual attitudes as if unaware of the painter. The pose-not-posed, caught as if by good fortune at its most expressive moment, becomes Degas's major preoccupation, including the combination of these individual poses in eccentric compositions where the impression is what Degas wants it to be— that of an arbitrarily selected fragment. But if one tries to extend the fragment, one

[220] and the somewhat later, wonderfully certain, wonderfully controlled *Lady on Horseback* [221] are, respectively, an academic preliminary drawing for a large composition and a drawing in the tradition of Ingres, although neither could be confused with its prototype. *Lady on Horseback* is instinct with life as well as elegance. So, of course, is a drawing by Ingres, but there is a fullness and warmth in Degas's drawing as opposed to the cooler sparkle of his idol's. The still later drawing for a

223. DEGAS: *Two Café Singers*, 1878–80. Pastel and charcoal, 17½ x 23″. Collection
Mrs. John Wintersteen, Chestnut Hill, Pa.

224. DEGAS: *A Carriage at the Races*, 1873. 14⅜ x 22″. Museum of Fine Arts, Boston.

225. DEGAS: *Diego Martelli*, 1879. 43¼ x 39½″. National Gallery of Scotland, Edinburgh.

realizes quickly that it is not a fragment at all, but an entity complete and satisfying in itself.

Actually, as Degas himself said, no art was ever less spontaneous than his. His "snapshot" compositions are the result of reflection, study, and calculation. The portrait of Diego Martelli [225] is a direct descendant of Manet's of Zola [192]. But Zola sits formally for his portrait, while Martelli pauses long enough for the artist to sum up a composition in a quick glance— or seems to. The elements are the same—the man, the desk, the papers on it, the furniture of the room, rectangular prints or pictures patterning a wall. Like Manet, Degas draws upon the Japanese print for his composition, using in addition to the rectangular divisions of the *Zola* the bird's-eye view, the tilted perspective found in some of the prints. All this is impressionism in effect until the solidity, the balance, the contem-

plative sobriety of the picture is understood as classical.

Degas loathed the word *impressionist* with its connotation of the accidental and the incomplete, and he fought against it until he managed to get it dropped from the announcements of the fourth group exhibition in 1879, when it was replaced by the word *independent*. He was not interested in the paraphernalia of outdoor impressionism, the countryside and atmospheric effects. City streets offered him as much fresh air as he wanted; the racetrack was open country enough. Theaters and intimate interiors offered the kind of light and air he liked to paint. He needed artificial life, he said, and not for a moment would he have considered yielding to impressionist seductions to paint at Argenteuil, as Manet finally did. Degas insisted that painting was an art of convention. To imitate nature from the model was bad enough; to imitate all its accidents out of doors was unthinkable. He painted from brief notes and sketches, preferring to observe carefully and then depend upon memory. When he used a model he habitually followed a practice that had been used occasionally by some other painters: he let the model move about the studio while he observed the movement of bones and muscles, constructing his figure from this knowledge rather than by imitating the aspect of a single pose with its necessary loss of spontaneity.

Degas: His Classicism

The essentially classical nature of Degas's art and his great originality in the use of classical principles are summarized in one of his most carefully studied paintings, *Foyer de la Danse* [226] painted in 1872. By a device approaching tour de force, but familiar to the artists of classical antiquity, Degas combined a momentary scene of action with what would seem to be its impossible opposite, the imposition of classically static order. At the right of the composition are clustered the ballet master, the rehearsal violinist, and several dancers. The ballet master has just tapped on the floor

226. DEGAS: *Foyer de la Danse*, 1872. 12½ x 18". Louvre, Paris.

with his stick, and on this signal the violinist has lowered his bow. The dancer whom he has been rehearsing pauses, motionless, in the middle of a step, awaiting the master's comment or correction. Other dancers glance in her direction.

Thus, although the figures are caught in instantaneous attitudes, these attitudes are legitimately static ones between moments of action, allowing Degas to compose the various figures in classically static fashion without congealing them in Davidian posturings. The same device was used in the sculpture of antiquity. As an example, the famous *Discus Thrower* is shown just as his arm reaches the high point of the throw, at the very moment before it descends, thus allowing the sculptor to represent, legitimately motionless, a moment in a series of violent movements.

Foyer de la Danse is as nicely balanced as any classical exercise, with a variation on the seesaw principle. But the balance is not by weight, as is usual, but by a play of weight against interest. By weight the group of figures on the right, with ballet master, violinist, and dancers densely clus-

tered, is too heavy for the single figure of the dancer on the left. But by interest, isolated as she is and the object of attention from every side, she counters their weight. This kind of balance is sometimes called "occult" balance; no one has ever used it with more skill than Degas, and obviously its attraction for him is the possibility it offers of combining balance with what seems to be random placement.

In painting, classical principles dictate a "closed" composition, complete within itself, and the scene usually takes place in a boxlike space. This is true of *Foyer de la Danse*. Degas varies the restriction by turning the "box" so we see it at an angle, not only from the side but from above, but the space itself remains clearly defined. The back wall and the side wall to the left are actually seen. The wall outside the picture to the right is defined by the fact that light flows into the room from its window. In the immediate foreground a chair is set in such a way that its back parallels the side walls, and hence its side near us identifies a plane corresponding to a fourth wall between us and the dancers. The function of the chair,

227. DEGAS: *Portraits in an Office*, 1873. 29⅛ x 36⅛". *Musée Municipal*, Pau.

228. DEGAS: Detail of Michel Musson from Figure 227.

then, is to define space, yet it seems to be the most casually disposed object in the whole painting. Upon this skeleton an analysis of the picture's composition could be elaborated at length to include every object in it, since not the smallest detail is accidental. The final unifying element is light, light as it flows upon and defines the objects disposed in space. This, of course, is the opposite of the light of typically impressionist painting that consumes the objects it touches and makes of space a vibrating tinted mist.

Foyer de la Danse was completed just before Degas made a trip to New Orleans, where his mother had been born. Degas went to visit her family and his two brothers, the younger René and the elder Achille, who had entered the family's cotton brokerage firm there. Degas repeated the compositional idea of the *Foyer* picture in *Portraits in an Office* [227], where he defined space in similar ways, even including a chair in the left foreground, with his uncle Michel Musson [228] testing a sample of cotton while sitting in an adjacent chair.

229. DEGAS: *Estelle Musson (Mme. René De Gas)*, 1872–73. 29 x 36". National Gallery of Art, Washington, D.C., Chester Dale Collection.

Degas: His Humanity

Degas did several portraits of his relatives on this trip, and that of his brother René's wife [229] is one of the most exceptional among all his work. A special bond of affection had always existed between Degas and his younger brother, and now this was extended to his brother's wife, for René De Gas had married his blind cousin, Estelle Musson. The blind eyes turned to the light, the placement of the figure in the left half of the canvas with the rest of the space behind it nearly vacant, the quietness of the pose suggesting resignation, the delicacy of the colors—rose, gray, and silvery white—all have something to do with the mood of tenderness, loneliness, and affectionate sympathy pervading the picture. The composition seems to be a spontaneous one and is, of course, not a complicated one. If we cannot analyze precisely how the mood is created, we nevertheless cannot fail to be touched by it.

The portrait is an especially intimate expression of a quality for which Degas usually receives no credit. Because he defended his prejudices with a sharp tongue, anecdotes about his witticisms and his eccentricities have obscured the tenderness that was also a part of his nature. Because he never married and because he painted some unflattering pictures of women, he acquired a reputation as a woman hater, but it was not a misogynist who painted the early *Head of a Young Woman* [230]. Degas never sentimentalizes a portrait. Faced with an unpleasant subject as he frequently was—by choice as often as not—he never hesitated to record an unpleasant personality. But his model for the *Self-portrait in a Soft Hat* [231] was a young man with a face as gentle as it is skeptical. It is the face of a man who, when he painted his aged father listening to a friend's music [232], contemplated one of the most poignant aspects of human life with deep understanding and consummate tact.

230. DEGAS: *Head of a Young Woman*, 1867. 10¼ x 8¾". Louvre, Paris.

231. DEGAS: *Self-portrait in a Soft Hat*, 1857–58. Oil on paper applied to canvas, 10¼ x 7½". Sterling and Francine Clark Art Institute, Williamstown, Mass.

Degas and the Impressionists

Shortly after Degas returned from New Orleans, plans for the first group show got under way at the *Café Guerbois*. Degas was a constant irritation to the other members during its organization. He had always held himself aloof from most of them, but now he was full of ideas that met with no one else's approval. Above all he was eager to avoid any implications that this was another *Salon des Refusés*, and he confused things by insisting that as many popular painters be included as could be induced to enter. He ended by drawing in more painters than anyone else, which was helpful since it decreased each one's share of the expense (most of the group were always in financial trouble). No matter how much they admired his work, many members disliked Degas—and he seems to have given them plenty of reason. He was witty and

frequently he turned his wit against them. He could seem a snob when someone failed to interest him; unlike Manet he did not trouble to hide his feelings beneath a gloss of manners. He always showed himself at his worst in public, concealing his generosities from everyone and reserving his affection for a very few people not connected with his professional life.

Why was Degas interested in exhibiting with the impressionists? The answer redounds to his great credit. He had nothing to gain professionally from the association; he even had much to lose. He had been accepted in the Salon for six years running, 1865 to 1870 inclusive—apparently not submitting the following years—and had had compliments from influential quarters. To exhibit with so dubious a group as the unknowns of the *Café Guerbois* could only block a continuation of this mild but promising success. Degas did not need the vaguely possible financial benefits that the other members hoped against hope might develop in the form of sales. He was wealthy and he even objected to selling his pictures, although he gave away many. He might have been expected to be suspicious and disdainful of the whole thing just as Manet was, yet Degas was one of the most industrious workers in organizing the exhibition and calling it to general attention.

The fact is that Degas believed in the group and in the group show because he believed in the new painting. His relationship to impressionism was a curious one; we have already seen how many of its premises he rejected. But he did share with the other impressionists the conviction that the subject from contemporary life, presented with the quality of immediacy, was the proper field for painting in his time. It was a time so complex that man could no longer hope to achieve the expression of an ideal universal order conceivable in antiquity and reflected in the art of antiquity. Nor in such a time could such a thing as universal knowledge be imagined, as the Renaissance had imagined it and given it form, for science had begun to make a specialist of every man and no man understood more than a fraction of what surrounded him. The romantics had recognized both impossibilities in the modern world and had escaped into a never-never land of emotional stimulants. But as a man of the world fascinated by the world, Degas rejected these romantic escapes.

Denied classical serenity, Renaissance wisdom, and romantic escape, man must be content with those small and commonplace fragments of the infinitely complex world that are within the scope of his comprehension. The function of the artist, then, by Degas's idea, is to take these fragments and treat them in such a way that they afford full play to the sensibilities of anyone whose imagination can reach beyond their commonplaceness into the infinite realm of personality and association. No other painter shared the intensity of Degas's interest in the commonplace as material for painting, or his fascination with the exact description of the way people stood, sat, moved, existed in their daily round. But if

232. DEGAS: *Degas's Father Listening to Lorenzo Pagans Singing,* c. 1869–72. 31½ x 24¾″. Museum of Fine Arts, Boston.

the impressionists did not share Degas's intensity, they shared his interest in the everyday world according to their own more casual ways of seeing it. And for that reason Degas knew he was one of them.

After 1886, date of the last impressionist group show (he exhibited in all but the next to last), Degas saw few people and exhibited rarely, working in his studio as a recluse. There was a steady demand for his work. He had never liked to sell his pictures, but it now became necessary for him to do so; he had sacrificed most of his fortune in 1876 to extricate his brother from difficulties following speculations in American stocks. The exact circumstances are not known since Degas was extremely reticent about all details of his personal life.

233. DEGAS: *Ballerina and Lady with Fan*, 1885. Pastel, 26 x 30″. Philadelphia Museum of Art, John G. Johnson Collection.

234. DEGAS: *Women Ironing*, 1882. 31 x 28¾″. Durand-Ruel, Paris.

The ballet pictures that account for so much of his popularity today were produced in great numbers after the middle 1870's. His interest in the ballet was not that of a balletomane: the ballet happened to provide in one package all the elements with which he was working—indoor or artificial light, frequently unusual in source, as from footlights; eccentric angles of vision, as from a box above the stage; accessory elements of unexpected shapes, supplied by such things as bits of stage scenery, props, the rails of the orchestra pit or the curve of a box seat [233]. Above all, here were the human figures of ballet masters, wardrobe mistresses, mothers waiting for or upon their daughters, figure after figure to be caught in momentary attitudes full of variety, especially the dancers themselves with their bony, sinewy bodies and curious stances. Sometimes Degas seems to be interested in contrasting the glamor of the ballet with the unglamorous rather plain girls who learn to go through curious con-

tortions to present glamorous illusions. But ordinarily his interest in dancers is not much different from his interest in, for instance, the two laundresses [234], one ironing, one yawning, whose occupational attitudes equally fascinated him.

Degas gradually abandoned oil paints and limited himself to pastel, for which he had always had a predilection. He was essentially a draughtsman and always found the texture of oil unsympathetic. The "lines, many lines," that Ingres had advised him to draw as a student had remained the basis of his art as a painter. Line came increasingly to mean for him a boundary reduced to minimum complexity for maximum description. In *Woman Scratching* [235], the whole folded, hanging weight of breast and stomach are summed up in three rough arcs.

Pastel is ordinarily associated with filmy, airy effects because it must be applied delicately over a textured surface and not touched again if it is to retain its life. Rubbing or drawing over it deadens it. But by means of some special fixatif, the composition of which is unknown, Degas could work over his pastels without losing their grainy quality, and alone among those who have used the medium he gave it all the strength, depth, and solidity of oil. In place of its usual chalky tints he achieved a full-bodied brilliance. It was the perfect medium for him. He was drawing and, at once, painting. Toward the end of his life his sight failed, and his pastels became broader and broader in drawing. For the first time, forms tended to diffuse into something like impressionistic effects, but a lifetime of studying the construction of the human body, and its movement, had taught him where the essential hollow or bulge in a contour told most about bone, muscle, and fat. His last drawings, done when he was nearly blind, are still miracles of draughtsmanship.

In the art of Degas, tradition and innovation are so fused that they exist in identity with one another. A hundred examples could be given to continue the illustration of this point; one, *Nude Arranging Her Hair* [236], is closely allied to the *Bather of Valpinçon* [59]. Ingres's harem beauty has become a *bourgeoise*, her seraglio a boudoir in a Paris flat of which we see a corner with a somewhat blowzy chair. The beautifully patterned turban is gone; so are the svelte, lovely contours of the odalisque's body. Degas's young woman ducks her head to work vigorously at the nape of her neck with a comb. Her shoulders bunch together as she raises her arms, the lines from elbows down either side, along back and buttocks, along breast, chest, and hips, describe a series of muscular contractions and relaxations, taut here, inert there, rounded in this place, hollowed out in another, stretched across the projections of bones or resting weightily upon them. In the bourgeois century, Ingres's revery of sensuous delight has given way to Degas's factual statement of bourgeois actuality.

Technically the enameled precision of Ingres and the direct vigor of Degas may seem to contradict one another; basically they are allied. Degas's active linear contours defining forms modeled in vibrant light and Ingres's dulcet ones enclosing

235. DEGAS: *Woman Scratching*, 1881. Pastel, 15¾ x 16″. Collection T. Edward Hanley, Bradford, Pa.

236. DEGAS: *Nude Arranging Her Hair*, c. 1885. Pastel, 21¾ x 20½″. Collection Mr. and Mrs. Herbert C. Morris, Bryn Mawr, Pa.

237. Degas: *Woman Rubbing Her Back with a Sponge, c.* 1900. Bronze, height 18″. Philadelphia Museum of Art, Curt Valentine Bequest.

238. Degas: *Young Dancer,* 1880–81. Bronze with cloth accessories, height 39″. Collection Henry P. McIlhenny, Philadelphia.

forms across which light flows like a caress, are arrived at from the same tradition, which each painter reverences and observes and, each in his own way, enlarges. If Ingres depends upon the tradition of the Renaissance, so does Degas depend upon it and upon Ingres.

Degas was also a sculptor, doing occasional pieces from time to time until, in his last years, his sight failing, he did many. Theoretically there is such a thing as impressionist sculpture; actually, Degas is the only sculptor who is impressionist in anything like a pure definition. Like his paintings, his small bronzes wonderfully embody momentary aspects of unidealized figures [237], rejecting all incidentals and nonessentials to capture the essence of visible

reality. Essentially these are sketches in clay, not conceived as bronzes. Similarly, his single large piece is in effect not so much sculpture as a masterpiece of draughtsmanship in three dimensions. The bony little figure of the "ballet rat" [238], the suggested textures of hose, bodice, hair, and flesh, the vivid reality of her stance, make possible the extraordinary features of a real tarlatan skirt and a real satin hair ribbon. Astonishing at first, they take their place after a moment or two as integral harmonious parts of the reality of the figure as a whole. The only trouble is that as time has passed, the cloth has grown limp, soiled, and dusty. The reality of these real accessories is less real, in the end, than the reality of the bronze image.

239. RODIN: *The Hand of God*, 1902. Bronze, height 26¾". Rodin Museum, Philadelphia, Gift of Jules Mastbaum.

240. RODIN: *The Kiss*, 1886. Marble, height 72". Rodin Museum, Philadelphia, Gift of Jules Mastbaum.

Rodin

The impressionism of Degas's sculpture is consistent. It is impressionistic in subject, in spirit, and in the play of light over the surface of forms, forms that are realized by suggestion rather than by detailed statement. The great sculptor of the nineteenth century, Auguste Rodin (1840–1917), often uses a similar, even an exaggeratedly impressionistic technique, working in broken surfaces to reveal incompletely defined forms as if seen in flickering illumination. Purists in sculpture deny the legitimacy of this surface treatment, which confuses the visual illusionism of painting with the tactile existence of sculptural mass. Nevertheless Rodin employed it, and although his impressionism ends there, some comments on his art are best interpolated at this point.

Beneath his impressionistic surface, Rodin is sometimes a dramatic realist, sometimes a quasi symbolist, almost always a vigorously masculine romantic, but he is never an impressionist in the sense of responding to the fascination of the commonplace. A little honest commonplaceness would be refreshing in his work, as a matter of fact. The erotic mysticism of pieces like *The Hand of God* [239] is beginning to seem, nowadays, embarrassingly pretentious. And his *Gates of Hell*, which was to have been the Sistine Ceiling of sculpture but was never carried beyond the stage of preliminary studies [241] and a few completed figures, is rather a hodgepodge whether it is regarded as philosophy or as sculpture. The familiar figure of *The Thinker*, which was to have brooded over the *Gates*, can be found in the upper central portion of the preliminary study illus-

241. RODIN: *Gates of Hell*, 1880. Bronze, 18 x 12 ft. Rodin Museum, Philadelphia, Gift of Jules Mastbaum.

trated here. *The Thinker*, of course, was one of the elements completed at full scale as an independent work of sculpture, and is known everywhere. Numerous casts were made from its mold.

The bumpy, sketchy, gouged, and roughened surfaces of impressionism were so cultivated by Rodin that he seems often to have tortured his clay, punching and kneading it beyond reason. "Sculpture is quite simply the art of depression and protuberance," he once said. "There is no getting away from that." This is certainly a limited definition that would eliminate most of the world's great sculpture, but for Rodin this

violent manipulation had an expressive reason for being. A great part of the effectiveness of Rodin's sculpture comes from the plastic drama of the modeling, where the sculptor's fingers are "seen" at work. It is often objected that this is a perversion of the noble material of bronze, to ask it to be nothing more than a kind of preservative for figures conceived as clay with all clay's yielding plasticity. If this is so, it is a fundamental shortcoming in the majority of Rodin's works.

In marble, Rodin's technical impressionism takes another direction. Transitions from one portion of realistic form to others are smoothed and softened until they seem to be partially obscured by mists, as in *The Kiss* [240]. But Rodin is also acutely realistic on occasion; he spent three years in litigation to disprove the charges that an early work, *The Age of Bronze*, was not a work of sculpture at all but an actual cast from a living model. It was not, but in its reproduction of an exceptionally perfect male model it might almost as well have been.

Rodin is saved again and again by the mass and force of pieces that violate a fundamental premise of contemporary sculpture: that expressive forms must be developed from a recognition of the character of the sculptor's material, whether it is stone, bronze, wood, clay, wire, or string. Rodin's sculpture opposes this idea; his instinct is to transform his material into something else, as he tacitly stated when he said of one piece of sculpture he admired (*Venus de Medici* [243]), "You almost expect, when you touch this body, to find it warm," or when he said that "Every masterpiece of the sculptor has the radiant appearance of living flesh." This is simply not true, as a moment's reflection on Gothic sculpture, which Rodin worshiped, would have shown. But that Rodin could say this, and that so much of his sculpture is conceived from that point of view, ties him to the lesser sculptors of his century, who conceived of sculpture as the detailed imitation of nature or as three-dimensional repetitions of forms developed by painters. But it is still true that no other sculptor in the nineteenth century could have approached the massive, vital force of Rodin's study for a monument to Balzac [478], to select one example almost at random from many.

Rodin would have made an excellent painter, and his drawings are in many ways more satisfying than his sculpture. His typical manner involved a free, loose, linear description of contours, with washes of color that were allowed to run and spread beyond these contours, or might be entirely independent of them, as they are in *Imploration* [508]. Here the two bodies are drawn against a tawny color that merges with a background of russets, blues, pale greens, and grays, which have no descriptive function. Rodin drew quickly, sometimes allowing his pencil to follow the contours as he watched the model, rather than the drawing. He achieved surprising descriptions of fleshy masses with an absolute minimum of means. His subjects were erotic more often than not but are saved by his obvious conviction of the identity between physical love and spiritual fulfillment.

Degas and Renoir

Degas is not convinced of life's goodness although he never for a moment questions its fascination. Whether he is painting with as much sympathy for his subject as he does in the portrait of Estelle Musson or with the detached observation apparent in his treatment of the less attractive women in a café on the Boulevard Montmartre [247], he never stands in judgment, never makes a moral evaluation, never commits himself to a comment on the philosophical justification of man's existence in the world. If in the end the flavor of his art is pessimistic, it is not because Degas ever points out a pessimistic conclusion, but because he lets the decision go by default. The average person in "interpreting" art expects to find a positive statement of faith, an affirmation of his own hope that his existence in the world serves some ultimate good. Degas neither confirms nor refutes such an idea.

Degas's attitude toward the world—a fascination with its fragments, a refusal to comment on its wholeness—is summarized in his attitude toward women. Few painters have been more preoccupied with representing them; no painter has portrayed them more acutely as personalities. None has been more sensitive to their psychological nuances or recorded these perceptions more intimately. But Degas seems hardly conscious of women as mothers, sweethearts, or sirens. Even in *The Bellelli Family* his perception of the relationship between mother and daughters is remarkable for its analysis of human relationships rather than for sentiment. Similarly woman's body fascinates him but only as a structural entity, not as a symbol of beauty or an object of desire. His late drawings of women climbing in and out of bathtubs, drying themselves, scratching themselves, caught in every awkward and unlovely attitude that presupposes the absence of any observer—these so-called "keyhole" subjects, in which he actually was at his most objective, account for his reputation as a woman hater, along with his pictures of prostitutes and nondescript women as in, again, *Café, Boulevard Montmartre*.

In all these respects Degas's opposite is Auguste Renoir (1841–1919), the best loved of the impressionists today.

Renoir is a joyous painter, so convinced of life's goodness, which seems apparent to him on every hand, that he feels no need to philosophize or moralize about it. If he does not comment, it is only because he does not find it necessary to ponder "the meaning of life." He finds life so wonderful that simply to participate in it gives meaning to existence. He never reports on life's specific fragments, as Degas does, because life in its wholeness is present for him in every woman he paints. Where Degas individualizes women Renoir generalizes woman as a symbol. Even when he paints a portrait we are conscious of womanhood first, and only incidentally of the specific individual who is represented. And when he is not painting a portrait he repeats over and over again a facial and physical type that he adopted early and was content to vary only slightly as his art matured, not because he needed a convenient formula but because woman as a generic concept was lovelier to him than any individual set of features could be.

242. BOUCHER: *Bath of Diana*, 1742. 22½ x 28¾". Louvre, Paris.

Renoir: The Mystique of Woman

Woman is a principle so pervading Renoir's universe that everything he paints is accessory to her. Children and flowers are corollaries to his concept of woman as a kind of earth- or life-symbol who blossoms and comes to fruition. Fields, streams, trees, and skies are echoes of her fertility. When Monet painted a woman out of doors she became identified with the sward, the bushes, with nature around her, because she shared with other natural objects the faculty of reflecting light. But when Renoir paints a woman out of doors the relationship with nature is reversed. Instead of absorbing her, the impressionist shimmer and vibration is like an emanation from her, an emanation of the life she represents, animating all nature.

The mystique of woman is a constant in French art, and through Renoir impressionism makes its contribution to this tradition. The near-mystical veneration of woman in French art and life combines the simultaneous recognitions of her most direct attractions and her most profound significance. She is an object of sexual delight, a creature of unusual sensibilities in human relationships, and a reminder that no matter

how complicated man may have made himself as a civilized being, he continues to exist only through the operation of a natural force he cannot explain but which woman embodies. This concept has given woman an extraordinary position in French life and thought. Among its many different expressions one of the earliest was the medieval veneration of the Virgin coexisting with the code of chivalric love by which the knight served his lady.

Woman was never more pervasive in French life than during the eighteenth century at a court dominated by women and given over to the pursuit of lovemaking. In spite of all the dimpled affectations of eighteenth-century court art, in spite of all the furbelows and ruffles and ribbons and fantasies of dress and manners, in spite of all the viciousness and indulgence of a sociologically indefensible way of life among the aristocracy—in spite of all this, the mystique of woman was never altogether obscured by the cultivation of woman as an object of pleasure, and the art of the eighteenth-century court painters was given over to her celebration. Renoir's first contact with this art was early and quite direct.

As a boy—his father was a tailor from Limoges, poor and with a large family—Renoir was apprenticed to a decorator of fine porcelain. He copied onto cups and plates flowers and other motifs from the eighteenth-century court painter Boucher.* Their fresh pinks and blues, their vivacity, their prettiness (a word of which Renoir

---

* François Boucher (1703–1770) was also an early influence on David; some of his mannerisms are reflected in *Mars Vanquished by Minerva* [19]. But with David's shift to classicism Boucher became one of the painters he most abominated. Boucher's candified tints, his prettified girls, his great puffs and swirls of shining satins and taffetas, his hothouse flowers, his feminine elaboration, are the quintessence of the rococo style, suggesting perfumes, powders, erotic refinements. The surface of his painting is slick and shiny, his nudes sometimes seem almost rubbery. He is not much liked today but he is a delightful painter if he is regarded as a great stylist. Renoir was as much influenced by an earlier eighteenth-century painter, Antoine Watteau (1684–1721), although less obviously.

243. *Venus de Medici*, Roman copy or variation of Praxiteles' *Aphrodite of Cnidus*. Marble, life-size. Uffizi, Florence.
244. RENOIR: *Bather with Griffon*, 1870. 72½ x 45¼". *Museu de Arte*, Sao Pãolo, Brazil.

was never afraid) always remained a part of Renoir's painting. Of Boucher's *Bath of Diana* [242] he once said that he kept going back to it again and again, "as one returns to one's first love."

Boucher's painting was full of the stylish artificialities and the titillations demanded by his patrons at the court and in the demimonde. It has won for itself the unflattering designation of "boudoir painting." Renoir revivified the tradition by leaving the boudoir for the out of doors, abandoning Boucher's artificial paraphernalia for natural banks of grass and flowers. Instead of Baths of Diana he paints healthy young women bathing in country streams. Above all, he abandoned coy suggestion for a straightforward, full-blossomed sexuality that would have reduced his buxom nudes to biological specimens if he had not been

245. RENOIR: *The Swing*, 1876. 36½ x 28½". Louvre, Paris.

then as a young painter with no resources and no patrons he kept himself alive doing occasional porcelain painting and some hack commercial work, including the decoration of window blinds. Monet was having the same struggle and the two men were good friends. For a few years Renoir groped about, imitating photographs briefly and working for a while in the manner of Delacroix. He later destroyed these pseudo-romantic productions, and the earliest Renoirs we have, from around the middle 1860's, show how much he learned from Courbet. *Bather with Griffon* [244], painted in 1870 and exhibited in the Salon that year, belongs to this early group, which seem like preparatory work if they are thought of in context with Renoir's later career. But independently *Bather with Griffon* can hold its own in the company of great paintings of the nude in any time. If it lacks anything, it is the full individuality of style that marks a work of art as completely the artist's own.

Half a dozen influences are rather obviously at work here. There is the wonderful rich paint of Courbet, Courbet's feeling for the texture of young flesh expressed in pigment of an opulence that is in itself part of the expression of form. Renoir lightened this richness with the more delicate coloration, the pinks and blues of rococo painting, and lightened Courbet's spirit also by such details as the enchantingly feminine heap of discarded garments and the little dog lying on them. These are painted with a freshness and delicacy that make Courbet seem ponderous. The pose is a classical one, and significant as an indication of Renoir's early attraction to the stability of traditional forms to which he will hark back later when his art is more reflective. There are numberless Venuses of antiquity in variations of this pose, the first one probably having been Praxiteles' *Aphrodite of Cnidus* and the best known, the *Venus de Medici* [243].

But, of course, there is not the faintest suggestion of neo-classical mannerism in Renoir's use of a classical pose: *Bather with Griffon* is a realistic painting from a living model. Technically it makes superb use of the academic technical disciplines, capitalizing on their sound virtues as Renoir

so completely and naturally within a tradition wholly French—the tradition that combines the frankest delight in sexuality with the most unquestioning reverence for woman's fundamental significance as the source of all warmth and life in the world.

Renoir entered the studio of a painter named Gleyre* in 1862. As a student and

---

* Marc Gabriel Charles Gleyre (1808–1874) was a Swiss who settled in Paris as a successful painter of history and genre. He made a Salon sensation in 1840, another in 1843. When Delaroche quit teaching, Gleyre took over his studio, and altogether he trained some five or six hundred students, among them Gérôme and, as well as Renoir, the other young future impressionists, Monet, Sisley, and Bazille. Gleyre was a sound painter and had the respect of these young men although they had no ambition to follow him. He, in his turn, recognized and respected the unusual talents of Monet and Renoir. He deserves a kind word in any history of nineteenth-century painting.

246. RENOIR: *Moulin de la Galette*, 1876. 51½ x 69″. Louvre, Paris.

247. DEGAS: *Café, Boulevard Montmartre*, 1877. Pastel over monotype, 16½ x 23½″. Louvre, Paris.

248. RENOIR: *Luncheon of the Boating Party*, 1881. 51 x 68″. Phillips Collection, Washington, D.C.

learned them from Gleyre, ignoring the shallow uses to which they were ordinarily put. All these elements temper one another —classicism, realism, academicism, eighteenth-century sensibility—and all of them are bound together by Renoir's response to the idea of womanhood.

After these early paintings, Renoir's development falls into four periods, during which he discovers and practices impressionism, then rejects it, and finally returns to it with variations. These we will see in turn.

Renoir and Impressionism

By 1870 Renoir was beginning to explore, with Monet, effects of light and air, and ways of representing them with broken color. By the time of the first group exhibition his impressionist manner was fully developed, and he continued working impressionistically until 1882. *The Swing* [245] of 1876 has the dappled light, the diffused forms, the young grace, the air of courtship, typical of his work in this period. As an ambitious showpiece he painted the *Moulin de la Galette* [246] for the third impressionist exhibition of 1877. Both

these paintings have something of impressionism's momentary revelation of the subject and much of pure impressionism's haze of light fused with atmosphere. Yet Renoir is yielding only reluctantly to this cultivation of transient effects and shortly he will become thoroughly dissatisfied with them. Most of his figures are caught in repose. Like Degas in *Foyer de la Danse*, Renoir continues to feel the need for classical stability in his compositions; it finds its way into pictures of the early period almost as if without his will. His figures never quite lose their formal identity within the quivering luminosity surrounding them.*

During this first tremendously productive period, Renoir painted portraits, figures, pure landscape, landscape with figures, still-life, and street scenes. A comparison of *Moulin de la Galette* with *Café, Boulevard Montmartre* [247] demonstrates that Renoir and Degas lived in Paris as if in two different cities. For Renoir Paris was a city of light, happiness, air, movement, warmth, a city in blossom. For Degas it was a collection of human beings in haphazard juxtaposition, stratified in a system of social levels. Although the dancers in the *Moulin de la Galette* include portraits of several of Renoir's friends, they remain generic young females and their generic young male suitors, idolaters of the female principle. Only once, at the end of this delightful period, Renoir departs momentarily from the generic conceptions which are the rule in his work. In *Luncheon of the Boating Party* [248] the members are more definitely individualized by physical feature, even if not particularly so by psychological differences. Among them, at the left, holding a small dog, is the young woman who was soon to become Renoir's wife.

Renoir had by now found some patrons. An influential one was the publisher Charpentier, in whose garden *The Swing* had been painted. Renoir was beginning to find portrait commissions too, and in order to further these Madame Charpentier commis-

---

* A *galette* is a kind of cake; the *Moulin de la Galette* was a popular, inexpensive dancehall and restaurant in Montmartre, but later developed into a less savory spot than the one Renoir painted.

sioned him to do a portrait of herself and her two little girls [249]. It was submitted to the Salon of 1879 and because (in part, at least) of the social prominence of the sitter it received a good position and was a success. (Renoir never shared the attitude of aggressive hostility toward the Salon and was glad to show there when he could get accepted.) He set about deliberately in the portrait of Madame Charpentier to paint a picture that would please conventional taste without prostituting his talent. He did not regard it as a lowering of standards or a denial of principles to modify his impressionist manner to accord more closely with Salon standards. The result was a fine portrait even if it is not Renoir's most exciting work. Its limitations, however, are apparent if it is compared with Degas's portrait of the Baroness Bellelli and her two little girls [219]. It is one of the rare instances when Renoir by his own standards falls short of Degas by his.

With plenty of commissions coming his way by the end of the 1870's, when he was forty years old, Renoir had reached the point where most painters would have industriously followed up their successes. But Renoir was full of dissatisfactions with the kind of painting he was doing. The direction of these dissatisfactions is apparent in the departures made in *Luncheon of the Boating Party* from the *Moulin de la Galette*, a nearly identical subject. *Luncheon of the Boating Party* is more sharply defined in its forms, more conventional (if no more successful and not quite so interesting) in its compositional balance. Renoir was ready to abandon the light touch of impressionism just when the first collectors were beginning to be attracted to it. A trip to Italy in 1882 verified his suspicions of impressionism and put an end to his impressionist period.

Renoir: Return to Tradition

Restless, unsure of his direction, beginning to feel that in seeking effects of light he had forgotten "how either to paint or to draw," that in working directly from nature he had forgotten how to compose, that in impres-

249. RENOIR: *Madame Charpentier and Her Daughters*, 1878. 60½ x 74⅞". Metropolitan Museum of Art, New York, Wolfe Fund.

sionism a painter descended to monotony, Renoir had refused to exhibit with the group in their shows of 1879, 1880, and 1881. The Italian pilgrimage of 1882 had a definite goal: the Vatican frescoes of Raphael. They had been an academic shrine ever since Ingres had proclaimed Raphael's godhead. And they did not disappoint Renoir.

In their breadth and amplitude and definition, their "simplicity and grandeur," he said, they confirmed his dissatisfactions with impressionism. He saw too the Pompeiian paintings that had given such impetus to the classical revival a hundred years before, that had "removed the cataracts" from the eyes of David when he went to Rome as a young painter trained in the eighteenth-century tradition. And by chance Renoir also stumbled across a book now well known to painters but then obscure, a late fourteenth-century handbook on the craft of painting by Cennino Cennini, a follower of Giotto, who described in great detail the technique of egg tempera painting, a technique demanding the clearest, the most concise definition of form, allowing for no suggestion, dictating implacably closed contours. Renoir had always to draw, paint, and compose. *Dance at Bougival* [250], painted on his return from Italy, has a new solidity and definition in the two dancing figures, although the seated ones in the background are similar to those in the *Moulin de la Galette* in their softer, airier, form. Renoir was equally determined, as a matter of practical business, to make a success in the Salon instead of directing himself toward the handful of art lovers who were "capable of liking a painting without Salon approval."[*] And he would do it this time without compromising, even to the extent he had done in *Madame Charpentier and Her Daughters.*

The disciplinary problems he set himself were to be solved in a painting of bathers in a landscape [251] upon which he worked for three years, from 1884 to 1887, when it was exhibited at Petit's, a commercial gallery, with great success. Even most of the impressionists admired it, because Renoir's suspicions of impressionism as a blind alley had come to be shared by others of them—not by Monet—who were hunting their own ways out of its mists. In fact, the year before the *Bathers* was exhibited, the last group show had been held (1886), and of the major impressionists only Degas and Pissarro had participated.

The *Bathers* is a wonderful and in many ways a most inconsistent painting. It is obviously a demonstration piece, even an exercise, but the appreciation of its very sound brilliance in this capacity in no way hampers the simultaneous enjoyment of its lightness, its gaiety, and its charm. For all its Italian inspiration, Renoir's "tight" or "dry" or "harsh" period, as it is variously called, is not Italianate. The *Bathers* is closer to Boucher than it is to Raphael. These firm, pink nudes with their pouting lips, short noses, tapered hands and feet,

250. RENOIR: *Dance at Bougival*, 1883. 70¾ x 38½". Museum of Fine Arts, Boston.

admired Ingres's line, and now in the light of these Italian revelations he discovered new virtues in Ingres's meticulously controlled surfaces as well.

Renoir determined to subject himself to a period of discipline, to learn again how

[*] Renoir exhibited at the Salon for the last time in 1890 after abstaining for seven years, but his determination to make a Salon success is indicative of the whole reorientation of his way of thinking and painting. The need for Salon recognition passed when, about 1883, he reached a financial agreement with Durand-Ruel assuring him of an adequate income, and in 1892 Durand-Ruel held such a successful exhibition of his work that thereafter Renoir had no money troubles.

251. RENOIR: *Bathers,* 1884–87. 45¼ x 67″. Philadelphia Museum of Art, Mr. and Mrs. Carroll S. Tyson Collection.

252. GIRARDON: Late seventeenth-century cast of bas relief from Fountain of Diana, North Terrace, Palace of Versailles.

and swelling curves, have not changed much from the type of Diana and her attendant nymph, although the taffetas, the pearls, and the ornamental park where Diana bathed have given way to simple linen, a pin or two in the hair, and an ordinary bit of countryside. The lineage of these bathing girls goes even further back; Renoir adapted his composition from a seventeenth-century French bas-relief by the sculptor François Girardon on the Fountain of Diana in the gardens of Versailles [252].

The playful sportiveness—splashing of water and so on—of Renoir's bathing figures is belied by their static and studied design. There is a contradiction, too, between the tight modeling within unsparingly precise outlines, and the impressionistic opalescent shimmer of the background. Yet these contradictions do not matter. Renoir achieved an improbable combination of virtues: the picture is fresh, appealing, and intimate; it is also calculated and formal.

To explain the harmonious coexistence of these contradictory elements might be possible, but it is unnecessary if we accept something Renoir once said: "These days, they try to explain everything, but if a picture could be explained it wouldn't be art."* In the *Bathers* one element after another can be isolated for explanation—the echo of Ingres's line, the impressionistic vibration in the background, the eighteenth-century succulence of the nudes, the reference to Girardon who composed within a certain tradition, the vestigial realism of the figure to the lower right. Yet, in the end, there is no necessity to explain why this great picture is not a mere studio concoction, if we admit that a total painting may be more than the sum of its parts, except one part which cannot be isolated, ". . . the passion of the painter which carries everything else before it." These are Renoir's words, and in no painter's art are they more important than in his own.

---

* Renoir is not the only painter who has felt this way. Among many others, Picasso said the same thing when he was asked to analyze the symbolism of his *Guernica* and replied that if he had wanted to put it into words he would not have painted a picture, he would have written a book.

Renoir: Fulfillment

For Renoir, living and painting were indivisible. There is a steady correspondence between the changes in his way of painting and the progressive stages of his maturity and experience as a human being. His impressionist pictures with their lovely girls, their happiness, their subjects of courtship, identify his own young manhood. The shift to new disciplines in painting coincides with his acceptance of new personal responsibilities, marriage and fatherhood. But he soon relented from the severities of his reaction against the "irresponsibility" of impressionism. By the end of the 1880's he was working toward a new manner, coincident with the period in his own life when the business of settling down had been achieved, when he had established an adequate security for himself and his family, and was discovering the quiet and rewarding fulfillments of middle age.

His effort in this period is to combine formal values in painting with such virtues of impressionism as can be dissected away from its shortcomings. He frees his brush once more; his touch quickens; he allows color-as-light to flood back into his pictures, but it is an obedient light respectful of the forms it illuminates. From the Renaissance Venetians Renoir had observed that free painting, full form, and luscious color could coexist with formal order, and he went to work to establish all these elements in his personal style. At first glance the pictures of this third period look like a reversion to impressionism; at second, the color is fuller and richer; the forms, even though the edges are no longer liney, remain solid. Beneath the renewed sweetness there is a more reflective quietness, beneath the surface informality, an increased order. It is impressionism chastened by tradition, ordered by contemplation, dignified by maturity.

With the lesson of the *Bathers* behind him, Renoir returned to simple, intimate subjects, painting again his personal response to them without sacrificing what he had regained through formal discipline. Instead of the synthetic poses of the *Bathers* he paints the natural attitude of a young girl pulling on her stocking [253], but studies it as a composition of sculpturesque volumes. In the following years there are so many fine pictures that a selection at random could hardly fail to give a good example. Among them, *Two Girls at the Piano* [254] affords a double comparison with the *Bathers* and the *Moulin de la Galette*. In all three pictures Renoir employs one of his favorite motifs, consisting of a pair of figures, one seated in the foreground and the other, usually standing, behind her in an affectionate, encircling attitude.

In the *Moulin de la Galette* these two figures are conspicuous in the center foreground. A girl in a light striped dress sits on a bench with one arm over its side; behind her a girl in a darker dress stands with her hand on the first girl's shoulder, leaning forward. The grouping is extremely pleasant, the effect is there, but there are ambiguities to the forms. It is not easy to follow the volumes and they are a bit cottony. In the *Bathers* the two figures on the bank in the left half of the picture are in comparable, although far from identical, relationship. The one in back holds a cape or towel across her shoulders in such a way that it forms a kind of terminating enclosure for the interrelated masses of the two bodies. There is no ambiguity to the forms; every volume is defined in space and in its exact relationship to other volumes. In *Two Girls at the Piano* the figure relationship of the two girls in the *Moulin de la Galette* is restudied to give it the formality of the *Bathers*. The formality is disguised; it is animated by the vivacious charm of the early masterpiece, but the formality is there, and it makes of *Two Girls at the Piano* something more than a charming picture, just as it is also something more than a formal exercise.

Similarly, *Young Girls Arranging a Hat* [255] is an impressionist delight if it is savored only for its color and its subject. But if it is regarded more abstractly as a series of interrelated volumes, it builds almost sculpturally into mutually supporting masses, projecting and receding into space. The sense of weightiness, of solid form, and the reduction of the various ele-

253. RENOIR: *Nude, c.* 1888. 22 x 18¼″. Philadelphia Museum of Art, Louis E. Stern Collection.

ments in the picture to geometrical equivalents (the cylinders of the arms, the ovoids of the heads, the generally spherical derivation of all the forms) increase the generic quality of the figures. A picture of one young girl pinning flowers onto the hat of another becomes a fertility image; the swelling volumes, bursting with color, are more than ever symbols of the burgeoning generative forces of nature.

Renoir: Last Pictures

In Renoir's final period this expression surges into full undisguised statement. From the point of view of the usual painting of the female nude, the *Bather* [256] painted in 1917 or 1918, shortly before Renoir's death at the age of seventy-eight, is grotesque. The swollen belly, the massive

254. RENOIR: *Two Girls at the Piano*, 1892. 45½ x 34½". Louvre, Paris.

255. RENOIR: *Young Girls Arranging a Hat*, 1890. Pastel, 25¼ x 19½". Collection George Friedland, Philadelphia.

thighs, the great heavy feet, the billowing construction of flesh drenched in the color of strawberries and oranges against the acid greens of the tumultuous background—these are strong fare. By one standard of comparison Renoir has exaggerated his former virtues beyond the point of tolerance and to the point of absurdity; by another, he has reached the only logical conclusion to the basic conception that he stated nearly fifty years earlier in *Bather with Griffon* [244]. The heavy, rolling, glowing masses of the late paintings may be grotesque as human female figures, but they are magnificent as abstract expressions where color and form in themselves have finally become fully identified with the omnipotent and indestructible fertility of nature.

It is typical of most painters who work over a very long period of time that their late work is painted most loosely, with greatest freedom. This was true of Renoir, and the natural tendency was exaggerated by a physical malady that appeared as early as 1881 and had begun to cripple him by 1890.° In his old age rheumatism had so paralyzed him that he had to paint in a wheelchair with his brush strapped to his hand. When a foolish visitor asked him how he managed to paint such beautiful pictures under such difficulties, Renoir rebuked him with "One does not paint with one's hands." This was not altogether apt if it is taken to mean that Renoir had never considered sheer manipulation of paint of any importance, for he loved the texture of oil as much as Courbet did, and could apply it just as sensuously. But it is true that Renoir was one of those artists who

° At this time Renoir left Paris to spend the rest of his life in Cagnes, in the south of France.

paint from the heart, to such a degree that the work of the hand and the expression of the heart were identical. From time to time there is a critical flurry during which Renoir's "sentimentality" is rediscovered with disapproval. But it never takes long for such flurries to subside. In the wonderfully balanced art of Renoir, sentiment is chastened by formal order, and formal order is warmed by sentiment.

Boudin and Jongkind

There are several dozen painters whose names could be catalogued as indirect contributors to the development of impressionism, and several hundred respectable ones who discovered it at the end of the century and made it standard exhibition fare. Leaving most of them to the encyclopedia, we still must mention some fine and important painters who were second only to the men who have emerged as impressionism's giants.

Eugène Louis Boudin (1824–1898) was older than the rest of the group. His sixteen years' seniority put him in something of a fatherly position to Monet when he met that penniless and precocious youth in Le Havre, which was Boudin's native city as well as Monet's. It was Boudin who first interested Monet in landscape, to which for some reason the youngster had adopted a scornful attitude, and they worked together on landscape subjects.

The typical Boudin is a long and placid strip of beach with ladies and gentlemen ranged in front of the sea's horizon beneath a seraphic sky [257]. A figure may be indicated in three or four touches of paint in different colors—a white skirt, a red shawl, a blue umbrella—accented with bits of dark for heads and feet. But Boudin also did pure landscapes, not always involving water and beaches. He was interested in representing different weathers; these effects, and his cursory notations of form, made him a precursor of impressionism before he exhibited in the first impressionist show. He shared the impressionists' later triumphs and was also awarded a Salon medal in 1889 and the Legion of Honor in 1892. Not strictly

256. RENOIR: *Bather*, 1917–18. 20¼ x 12". Philadelphia Museum of Art, Louise and Walter Arensberg Collection.

speaking an impressionist, Boudin was acceptable on much the same terms as the Barbizon men, whose paintings by then were established commodities. He is a delightful painter, more and more sought by collectors.

Johann Barthold Jongkind (1819–1891), a Dutchman, spent his mature life in France. For a while he joined the Barbizon

257. BOUDIN: *Beach at Trouville*, 1880. Panel, 7 x 13½″. Philadelphia Museum of Art, Lisa Norris Elkins Bequest.

258. JONGKIND: *Drawbridge*, 18½ x 21¾″. Philadelphia Museum of Art, Mitcheson Collection.

painters, but for the most part he worked independently. He had a strong influence on Monet, and on Sisley and Pissarro, because he investigated transitory effects of light and painted with a quick, vibrant brush. This is his closest connection with impressionism, but since an equally important aspect of his art is not frequently enough mentioned, we may point out also that Jongkind was a romantic landscapist [258] in the spirit (if not the technical tradition) of earlier Dutchmen, especially Ruisdael.

Bazille

Frédéric Bazille (1841–1870) was a close friend of Monet's and Renoir's in Gleyre's studio and a popular member of the circle at the *Café Guerbois*. He was a tall, handsome young man with money and talent, who was still finding himself as a painter when he was killed in the battle of Beaune-la-Rolande in the Franco-Prussian War of 1870. He was born the same year as Re-

259. BAZILLE: *The Artist's Family*, 1868, retouched, 1869. 60¾ x 91″. Louvre, Paris.

260. BAZILLE: *Summer Scene, Bathers,* 1869. 63¼ x 63¼″. Fogg Art Museum, Cambridge, Mass.

noir, and in looking at the few pictures he painted before his life was cut so short, one must remember that if Renoir had been killed at this time, of the pictures illustrated in this book only *Bather with Griffon* would have been painted. Even Monet's impressionism was in its early stages, and the first group show was not held until four years later.

The characterizing feature of Bazille's work is a painstaking disposition of the elements of a nominally informal subject. A group portrait of his family on a terrace [259], a picture more than eight feet long which was exhibited in the Salon of 1868,* is filled with a curious, stiff, unnatural stillness that extends even to the leaves on the trees in the distance. It is anything but impressionistic. The yet more curious *Summer Scene, Bathers* [260], painted in 1869 and exhibited in the Salon of 1870, shows a further imposition of rigid pattern, now geometrical, on a scene filled with casual attitudes—or, at least, attitudes transfixed

* But dated, after retouching, 1869.

224 · IMPRESSIONISM

261. BAZILLE: *The Artist's Studio*, 1870. 38⅞ x 47". Louvre, Paris.

from casualness into Bazille's odd rigidity. Compositionally the picture is closer to "neo-impressionism," a movement we will discuss shortly, than to impressionism, and it is difficult to avoid pointless conjectures as to the course impressionism might have taken if Bazille had lived beyond the first period, for that is what it amounts to, of what must have been an exceptional creative life. A third painting, somewhat freer in technique, has poignant associative interest. This interior of *The Artist's Studio* [261] shows a group of young friends. Renoir is seated at the extreme left. Just above him, on the stair, is Zola. Manet stands in front of a painting on an easel. Behind him is Monet, and standing at the side of the easel is Bazille himself. Manet painted this figure, or at least Bazille's head. At the far right their musician friend Edmond Maître is at the piano.

Morisot

Berthe Morisot (1841–1895) was a granddaughter of the painter Fragonard° and the sister-in-law of Manet, but her interest in painting was not the result of this connection. Manet painted her frequently; she is the seated figure in *The Balcony* [184]. Berthe Morisot is a charming painter, and a sound one too, making her own feminine adaptation of Manet's broad style, although she first painted as a pupil of Corot's and

° Jean Honoré Fragonard (1732–1806) was the last in the three-generation trio of eighteenth-century painters — Watteau, Boucher, Fragonard—and the most facile. In line with the taste of the day, his style was feminine, coquettish, fanciful. As a successful painter he threw a commission to an unknown youngster named David. In lion-and-mouse fashion, David returned this favor by protecting Fragonard after the Revolution.

at times is a little influenced by Degas. Early in her career she appeared in the Salon, but she foreswore Salon exhibition as a declaration of faith in the impressionist cause. This faith was enduring; she continued to paint impressionistically after Renoir and others had abandoned the cause. She exhibited in all but one of the group shows and did more than her share of the hard work involved in organizing and maintaining an association of frequently difficult temperaments. Her sister Edma also painted for a while, but quit to become a wife and mother. Berthe successfully combined matrimony, motherhood, and a career.

Berthe Morisot's delightful *Girl with a Basket* [262], with its sensitivity, flourish, and style could be a particularly light and fresh late Manet. It is customary to say about any woman painter, as if it were the ultimate compliment, that she paints with almost the vigor of a man. But the beauty of Berthe Morisot's art is its femininity, which in her case is not to be confused with weakness, indecision, or an only partial achievement of a masculine standard. One would not want to "strengthen" *Woman at Her Toilet* [263] any more than one would want to endow its lovely model with the muscles of a wrestler.

Berthe Morisot was an extremely engaging correspondent. Her letters are full of illuminating comments on Manet. As a random sample, speaking of *The Balcony*, she said that Manet's paintings make "the impression of a wild or even slightly green fruit," a very neat characterization of the exotic and somewhat astringent quality of that picture in comparison with the Salon paintings of 1869 among which it appeared.

Berthe Morisot was rather jealous of another woman painter of talent who studied under Manet and followed his manner closely. This was Eva Gonzalès, the only painter Manet ever permitted to name him as teacher. She was a competent painter, although obvious in her echo of Manet. She did not exhibit in the group shows, probably because Manet did not.

The impressionist movement produced three exceptional women painters. The third was an American, Mary Cassatt.

262.   MORISOT: *Girl with a Basket*, 1892. 35¾ x 28⅛". Collection Mr. and Mrs. Louis C. Madeira, Gladwyn, Pa.

263.   MORISOT: *Woman at Her Toilet*, c. 1875. 23¾ x 31¾". Art Institute of Chicago, Stickney Collection.

264. CASSATT: *Woman Arranging Her Veil, c.* 1890. 25½ x 21½". Philadelphia Museum.

265. CASSATT: *Mother and Child,* date unknown. Pastel, 22 x 18". Philadelphia Museum of Art, Anne Hinchman Bequest.

Cassatt

Mary Cassatt (1845–1927) was an extraordinary young woman, the daughter of a wealthy Pennsylvania family, who against her parents' wishes went to Paris to continue the study of painting, which she had begun at the Pennsylvania Academy of the Fine Arts in Philadelphia. In Paris, enrolled in the studio of an established conventional painter, she found herself drawn to the art of the impressionists, particularly Degas, and in 1879 and thereafter she exhibited with them. She was a hard worker and a stern self-disciplinarian. With Degas as her early model, she had set herself, in a way, a more difficult goal than did Morisot, who modeled on Manet. The elegance of Manet, while no less masculine than the objective observation of Degas, was more susceptible to feminine modification. Although Degas's influence is frequently strong on her work

[264], Mary Cassatt was not an imitator of Degas or of anybody else. She developed a style of precision and definition that she combined with impressionist informality of subject and composition [265].

Mothers and children were a favorite subject of Mary Cassatt; she never married, and it would be easy to read into this fact something of frustration and compensation, except that the other facts of her life would not bear out such a conclusion. She was a vigorous woman, and lady, with a great many friends, and was apparently quite happy in her career as a painter without the impedimenta of a husband and children. Although she was a friend of the impressionists during their difficult days, she never for a moment participated in anything suggesting bohemianism. Her personal life, on both sides of the Atlantic, remained that of a sensible, cultivated, level-headed, and privileged gentlewoman, which makes her enthusiastic participation in the "scandalous" movement of impressionism surprising.

Mary Cassatt is an important figure in the history of the development of American taste because she introduced her wealthy American friends to the new art and urged them to collect it. The pictures bought by the Havemeyer family especially, now in the Metropolitan Museum of Art, are the American equivalent of the Caillebotte collection in the Louvre.

Mary Cassatt's most individual creative efforts were not her paintings, which were always respectable and frequently superior even by the demanding standard of the company they kept, but her prints, which were something more. For the other impressionists, prints were adjunct to painting, forms of drawing although in media somewhat more complicated than the ones ordinarily used. But for Mary Cassatt, as for all first-rate print-makers, there was an excitement in meeting the technical demands of the print and capitalizing on them to produce works of art where the medium and the expression were interdependent. Under the influence of the Japanese block prints she brought a new crispness, definition, and economy to etching and drypoint [266]. Here her achievement may stand alone, without the comparisons, inevitable in her painting, to the work of the leaders of the school.

Fin de Siècle: Toulouse-Lautrec

As impressionism began to be absorbed into the historical continuum of painting, and other isms began to develop from it, the list of painters whose art was impressionist or closely allied to impressionism a generation after the adventures of the original group could be extended indefinitely. Among this generation Henri de Toulouse-Lautrec (1864–1901) made his own special departures, but he must still be classified as an impressionist, if he must be classified at all, in bringing the story of impressionism's half-century to its end.

Lautrec's life has been used as the subject of so many biographies, some accurate,

266. CASSATT: *The Letter*, 1891. Etching and aquatint, 13½ x 9". Philadelphia Museum of Art, Louis E. Stern Collection.

some unpardonably falsified, and his art has become so familiar in debased forms through commercial adaptations of it, that it has become difficult to regard his paintings as works of art in themselves. They have become illustrative adjuncts to the story of his life and the fascination of the personalities he used as subject matter. These personalities are, in truth, fascinating enough. His greatest single source of material was the dance hall and cabaret called the *Moulin Rouge,* a phenomenon of the

267. TOULOUSE-LAUTREC: *The Salon in the Rue des Moulins,* 1894. 43⅞ x 52½". *Musée,* Albi.

end of the century in Paris without a parallel today, a place where intellectuals, performers, human curiosities, and the flotsam of bohemia intermingled. But he also painted other cabarets and the related world of the theater, cafés, restaurants, and brothels. He painted dancers, singers, prostitutes, circus performers, performing animals, actors, sportsmen, and his acquaintances and friends who ranged from noblemen to derelicts. And he was himself, of course, the most bizarre of all the creatures in the world he recorded.

Henri-Marie Raymond de Toulouse-Lautrec Monfa was descended from one of the finest houses in France. His family tree includes the names of kings and queens of both France and England. If he had not been crippled—as a child he broke both legs in two falls that left him a grotesque, dwarfish caricature of a man—he might have continued his family's tradition of hunting, riding, and provincial high living at the family seat in Albi. With these facts as a beginning, there is always a temptation to reduce any consideration of Lautrec to a series of biographies, first his own and then those of people like two of his favorite models, the dancers Louise Weber, known as *La Goulue* (the Glutton) and the nameless woman who chose for herself the name Jane Avril. Lautrec's art, as he records such people in the life of the half-world they inhabited, is partly journalism, partly an informal sociological record through the incisive presentation of specialized modes and manners, and partly, by whatever extension the observer wants to make for himself, a moral lesson. *The Salon in the Rue des Moulins* [267], which shows the reception room of a brothel frequented by Lautrec, is one of the most effective moral

268. Toulouse-Lautrec: *Oscar Wilde*, 1895. Watercolor, 23⅝ x 19¾". Collection Mr. and Mrs. Conrad H. Lester, Beverly Hills, Calif.

269. Toulouse-Lautrec: *Racing Stable Boy*, 1895. Cardboard, 26 x 20½". *Musée*, Albi.

lessons in the history of painting—if a moral lesson consists of revealing vice in its least attractive aspects. With the exception of the Madame herself, who sits almost primly erect in a high-collared morning dress, the women of the house are mere carcasses, and the wages of sin as represented here would seem to be infinite boredom.

Even more than Degas, who was his model and his god, Lautrec is first a draughtsman and second a painter. As Ingres told Degas to do, Lautrec draws "lines, many lines," but they are lines of his own kind, lines that coil and strike like serpents, jab and gash like knives, or when appropriate sag like the pouches of tired flesh they define, as in the devastating portrait of Oscar Wilde [268]. Line satisfied Lautrec; he developed very few paintings to the point where his first, direct lay-in of drawing is entirely obscured. Parts of the canvas (or the cardboard, upon which he

was fond of working) are only scrubbed over, and other parts remain bare. Sometimes his paintings are more accurately brush drawings in lines of fluid pigment, with an essential area or two covered in quick, broken strokes. He may use this technique to concentrate interest on the salient part of a picture—ordinarily the face —as Rembrandt used strong illumination to make a head emerge from surrounding obscurity [269].

Lautrec's debt to Degas is most conspicuous in his composition. One of his few highly finished paintings, *Au Moulin Rouge* [270], is an example, with its tilted perspective and the segmentation of some of the objects. It shows part of the promenade that surrounded the dance floor of the *Moulin Rouge;* at the left, the railing between promenade and dance floor cuts across the picture, separating the observer from the group of men and women at the

270. Toulouse-Lautrec: *Au Moulin Rouge*, 1892. 48⅜ x 55¼". Art Institute of Chicago, Helen Birch Bartlett Memorial.

table. Whether or not Lautrec had such an effect in mind, the effect of this separation is to put the observer at a vantage point where he watches but is not watched; it is the so-called "keyhole vision" (not altogether a savory way of putting it) of much of Degas's late work. Like Goya, Lautrec was a painter who "moved freely within a certain world and was accepted as part of it by its denizens, yet within himself remained separated from it by an isolating circumstance, remaining free to observe with the objectivity of an outsider, yet with intimate access to his material." Like Goya with his deafness, Lautrec with his deformity was thus isolated, and without pushing the analogy too far it is still safe to say that the railing between the observer and the rest of the picture helps to identify

us with Lautrec's "view," psychological and physical, of the subject.

It is redundant to insist that the composition of *Au Moulin Rouge* is not haphazard but brilliantly planned; in this case there is a special circumstance that should prove how definitely Lautrec planned it and how imperatively the haphazard, snapshot quality is calculated as the psychological basis of the picture. Originally the canvas ended without the last portion on the right side that now includes the most "haphazard" and the most telling element: the weirdly illuminated face of the woman at the extreme right edge. In order to introduce this figure Lautrec added to the canvas at the right side (and also at the bottom). If these portions are covered up we still have a fine picture, a group portrait of several of Lautrec's friends (all are identifiable) gathered around a table, but we no longer have the picture that has the strongest claims as Lautrec's masterpiece.

In color, too, the additional figure transforms the scheme from something skillful to something masterful. If the composition of *Au Moulin Rouge* owes a great deal to Degas, the color is Lautrec's own. It is dominated by the strong chemical green of the shadows on the woman's face, eerily covering the forehead, nose, and upper lip, and the violently orange hair of the woman seated at the table near by. These two colors clash and vibrate between one another within a scheme of smaller areas of sharp colors lashed by accents of black and purple. These are the colors of Lautrec's world, a world of artificial stimulations, of dreadful ennuis, a world shrill, strident, divided between avidity and indifference. Renoir's eternal values have no place in it. Instead of Renoir's young girls in meadows we have *Two Women Dancing* [271]; instead of Monet's twinkling foliage or his ponds rippled by fresh breezes, Lautrec paints the torpid atmosphere of shuttered rooms, the stale air of dance halls whipped into turbulence by the petticoats of dancers, gaslight instead of sunlight. When Lautrec paints a portrait out of doors in the small gardens of his friends in Montmartre, his sitter has the pallid air of a night creature unaccustomed to daylight. Degas, being witty at the expense of his impressionist friends who went into the country to paint streams and meadows, said that the smell of fresh air made him sick. With something closer to truth, Lautrec could have said that the air of the dance hall and the brothel was a palliative for the pains that racked his dwarfed and twisted legs. Bohemia was not his natural habitat. In the background of *Au Moulin Rouge* he shows himself moving through the world he adopted as an expedient; he is the stunted figure played against the enormous height of his companion (a cousin and his most loyal friend, Tapié de Celeyran) behind the group at the table.

In the relationship of his life to his work, the surprising thing about Lautrec is that, in spite of the alcoholism and the spectacu-

271. TOULOUSE-LAUTREC: *Two Women Dancing*, 1894. Cardboard, 23¾ x 15¾". Collection Alfred Schwabacher, New York.

lar dissipations which are too well covered by his biographers, he was tremendously productive. In spite of his personal tragedy, with whatever neuroses it might have been expected to engender, he paints with sanity, vigor, and the clearest, sharpest perception of the life around him. His detachment is never self-pitying; his comments on viciousness are never vicious, scornful, or envious; and his painting of depraved subjects is no more depraved than it is self-righteous. Conditioned by his subjects, we are more aware of the seamy world in which he moved as an artist than we are of the other

272. TOULOUSE-LAUTREC: *Seated Female Clown* (*Mlle. Cha-U-Kao*), from *Elles*, 1896. Color lithograph, 20½ x 15¾". Philadelphia Museum of Art.

rated from him by a minimum of technical barrier; we stand in front of his picture as he stood in front of it, the paint we see is the paint he applied. But in a print we must jump the gap created by the intervening process of actual printing, between the artist's work on the lithographic stone or the etching plate and the transfer of his work to paper. Lautrec closed this gap and at the same time widened the technical range of lithography by treating the stone with a new informality. He would speckle its surface with ink by flipping the ink-soaked bristles of a stiff brush above it or dab the surface in any way he chose [272]. He would combine lithographic crayon with lithographic wash in a deliberate exaggeration of textures. In short, he combined and invented variations on conventional lithographic techniques in order to give them variety; his imagination freed lithography much as the technique of impressionism released painting from academic rule. Always the closest of the print media to the intimacy of drawing, lithography in color now approached the immediacy of painting. The artist's hand became more apparent. In addition to the psychological value for the observer, this liberation widened lithography's expressive potential for the artist in ways that have been carried further ever since Lautrec pointed the way.

In the art of poster design [273] Lautrec recognized factors now accepted as so basic that it is hardly necessary to point them out. First, a poster must make its total effect immediately if it is to be effective in its primary function, since it is an announcement, not an object for contemplation. Second, since pictorial images are to be combined with type, their design must be harmonious with the flatness and boldness of type, or lettering. Both of these considerations call for simplification and virtually demand the reduction of design to two dimensions. Although tentative efforts had been made in "art" posters, Lautrec pushed these ideas to their conclusion and in applying them remained an artist as well as a designer of publicity. His posters "took possession of the street," a contemporary said, but they are also works of art.

world in which he moved with equal freedom and which was the world from which he observed the one he painted: the world of the intellectual and the aristocrat.

If Lautrec does not reach the stature of a major painter outside his century, it may be because the world he painted limited his range of comment, but within the boundaries thus set, his art is complete. In addition, he was a technical innovator in the medium of lithography and he virtually created the poster as a work of art.

Essentially, his contribution to color lithography was to close the gap between the completed print and our sense of the presence of the artist. In painting, the artist's presence is felt because we are sepa-

Lautrec's posters bear multiple relationships to the Japanese print. In the first place, these prints were ready-made ancestors as examples of patterning in areas of flat color bounded by lines ornamental in themselves. In the second, they combined, frequently, printed legends with pictorial images [193], although the ornamental character and the indecipherability of the Japanese legends obscured this fact from Western designers. Also, the Japanese prints of actors were related to the nineteenth-century theatrical poster in that they familiarized people with the physiognomy of popular performers of the day even if they were not posted as advertisements. The difference was that the Japanese prints were designed to give continued pleasure upon extended contemplation of their subtleties of line and color areas, while Lautrec's posters had to be absorbed at a glance if they were to attract the attention of busy passers-by. Lautrec met this requirement first; yet he also designed his posters to reward continued acquaintance, even if not to the extent of their Oriental prototypes.

The Post-impressionists

Lautrec died in 1901. If he can be regarded as the last of the impressionists, thus rounding out the century, it must be remembered that, in the meanwhile, impressionism had already been transformed and the direction of the art of the twentieth century had been set by the work of four men whose work was not assimilated by the nineteenth century in which they lived. These men were Georges Seurat and Vincent van Gogh who had died ten years before Lautrec, and Paul Cézanne and Paul Gauguin who were to die within the next five years.

We enter our own time with the work of these men, grouped under the accepted if not very descriptive label of "post-impressionism." They are the first "modern" artists in the sense of the word that implies a sharp departure from the natural look of the world, a distortion of visual reality

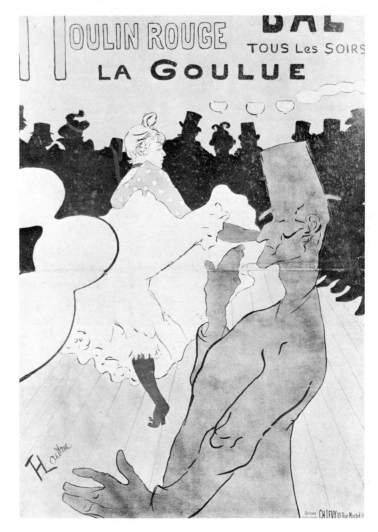

273. TOULOUSE-LAUTREC: *La Goulue at the Moulin Rouge*, 1891. Poster, color lithograph, 65 x 46". Philadelphia Museum of Art, Gift of Mr. and Mrs. R. Sturgis Ingersoll.

in whatever way the artist thinks necessary for the expression of the inner realities most important to him.

These men will be seen in their own section of this book, preliminary to the chapters on the art of the twentieth century. It is time now to recognize the fact that painters in Germany, England, and the United States were also at work while classicism, romanticism, and realism-impressionism were being formulated as theories and given pictorial expression in France.

PART II

The Nineteenth
Century Outside France

CHAPTER 8

Outside France, 1800–1850

Classicism and Benjamin West

A summary of nineteenth-century art outside France must naturally take as its point of departure the development we have just surveyed—at least it must do so in a book that intends to follow mainstreams rather than to be an encyclopedia. French artists crystallized into images the ideas that dominated the century and fought the battles for their recognition. This will not leave much point in going into detail about—for instance—a group of ten American painters* who formed an association to exhibit their work in 1898, even though three of them departed from their academic training to adopt impressionism. They were perfectly respectable impressionists, but by that date impressionism had been developed, fought for, and established by the men we have already seen. It had even been abandoned by men we have yet to see—Cézanne, van Gogh, and Gauguin—who set new directions for the twentieth century. Historically speaking, the ten Americans were in a backwater. The fact that Childe Hassam (1859–1935), to choose one of them as an example, painted American subjects instead of Parisian boulevards or meadows bordering the Seine is a small difference between him and the French impressionists whose technique he used very well. Aesthetically his pictures are no better and no worse for having been painted a generation after impressionism's victory, but historically they are footnotes. What we want to do now

---

* Frank W. Benson, Joseph R. De Camp, Thomas W. Dewing, Childe Hassam, Willard L. Metcalf, Robert Reid, Edward Simmons, Edmund C. Tarbell, John H. Twachtman, and J. Alden Weir.

is to follow classicism, romanticism, and realism-impressionism outside France with attention to painters whose personal or national character is exceptional, and to give a nod here and there to painters like Hassam who were excellent practitioners in ways with which we are already familiar. The nod is not meant to be a slight.

Outside France, then, there was no situation comparable except in the palest way to the academic stranglehold and the original painter's struggle against it, partly because the academies elsewhere were less avid for power and partly because the painters were more content to work within conventional boundaries. France was alone in regarding art as part of the fabric of national life, and her painters were very nearly alone in the kind of theorizing and technical invention that placed upon the artist a moral obligation to define and proselytize forms of painting based on aesthetic, social, and philosophical convictions.

And outside France the general public was either apathetic to the art of painting or content to follow its own taste without feeling indignant over any kind of painting it did not understand. It is impossible to imagine an *Oath of the Horatii* raising a political furore in England or Germany, even if it is possible to imagine it being produced in one of those countries in the first place, and the scandals of the *Salon des Refusés,* or the impressionist group shows, were impossible in those countries for the double reason that painters were less aggressive in their departures from tradition and that the general public regarded a picture more casually as something to be looked at with pleasure or dismissed as uninteresting, but certainly not something important enough to get very excited about one way or another. The lines between classicism, romanticism, and realism were less sharply defined; the differences between one kind of painting and another tended much more to be differences of style rather than declarations of conflicting ideas passionately held.

This was especially true of classicism, which never touched Davidian purity or intensity outside France, although its most celebrated theorist was a German and one

274. WEST: *Cleombrotus Ordered into Banishment by Leonidas II, King of Sparta, c.* 1770. 54 x 72″. Tate Gallery, London.

of the earliest painters of neo-classical historical subjects was, of all things, a provincial American youth who went to Rome and then to England where he became president of the Royal Academy. The German was Winckelmann, already mentioned with his theory that beauty is synonymous with perfection, and the American was Benjamin West (1738–1820).

Some twenty years before David completed *The Oath of the Horatii* in 1784, West was painting classical subjects of the type of *Cleombrotus Ordered into Banishment by Leonidas II, King of Sparta* [274]. While West's classical efforts do not approach the icy intensity and the disciplined simplification that are the essence of *The Oath of the Horatii,* and while they offer nothing more than obvious sentiment where *The Horatii* is charged with moral force, they do frequently anticipate David's composition on a single plane suggestive of classical bas-reliefs, the precise definition of neo-classical draughtsmanship, and the reference to classical models that were parts of David's sensational departure from French tradition.

Strictly speaking, West is not altogether an American painter. He was the son of an innkeeper near colonial Philadelphia but demonstrated such a prodigious early talent —he was painting portraits when he was thirteen—that a group of prosperous Philadelphians sent him to Rome to study. He was twenty-one years old at the time. (David was still a boy of eleven.) West was an attractive fellow with a flair for social showmanship that came to him as naturally as his talent for painting. As a handsome man and a picturesque American claiming to have had his first painting lessons from wandering Indians who had shown him how they made colors from clay to paint their faces, he became the rage in Italian society; when he went to London three years later he repeated his success. He remained an adopted Londoner for the rest of his life, was a favorite of George III, was a leader in the founding of the English Royal Academy, and its second president. But if he was a Londoner by adoption and if he became an English painter in effect, he was an important influence on American painting because two generations of American students passed through his London studio. By the time David finally won his *Prix de Rome* (in 1774) West was an established London success, and by the time *The Oath of the Horatii* set a new direction for French painting and began the story of

modern art, West was nearly fifty years old and had virtually abandoned the nascent classicism of pictures like *Cleombrotus*. West, Goya, and David died within eight years of one another, West first in 1820 at the age of eighty-two.

West as an Innovator

Except for those American writers whose judgments are affected by local pride, critics have formed the habit of condescending to West. It is true that his talents were exceeded by his success. And it is true also that he does not emerge as a great intellect or even an especially brilliant and stimulating painter. But if he had painted in hardship and obscurity, his originality might receive more sympathetic emphasis than it does.

West made his reputation in England with two paintings, *The Death of General Wolfe* [275] in 1770, and *Penn's Treaty with the Indians* [276] in 1772, both innovational. *The Death of General Wolfe* is full of trite borrowings from a variety of sources, but it was a courageous departure from convention in representing a contemporary event in minute factual detail (at exactly the time when Sir Joshua Reynolds had formulated the Academy's standards for the grand manner in painting, demanding reference to poetry or the past instead of to the present and generalization instead of particularization). West had minor precedents for his factual representation, but this was a major picture on the grand scale by a young man eager to maintain a position in academic favor. Again West anticipated David, who became the first Frenchman to approach a contemporary event in realistic detail when he relaxed the severity of his neo-classical idealizations to paint *The Oath of the Tennis Court*. David might even have known West's picture and the sensation it caused, since *The Death of General Wolfe* was such a success that it was engraved and widely distributed over France as well as England.

If there was any question now as to West's eminence, it was settled by the ap-

275. WEST: *The Death of General Wolfe*, 1770. 60 x 84″. National Gallery of Canada, Ottawa.

276. WEST: *Penn's Treaty with the Indians*, 1771. 75½ x 109″. Independence Hall, Philadelphia, on permanent loan from The Pennsylvania Academy of the Fine Arts.

277. WEST: *Arthur Middleton, His Wife and Son*, 1771. 44¾ x 66″. Philadelphia Museum of Art, lent by Henry Middleton Drinker.

pearance of *Penn's Treaty with the Indians*. *Penn's Treaty* follows the classical tenet that a painting should justify itself by propounding a moral truth or a lesson, the same idea, of course, that David would apply with such force and intensity in his stoic pictures. In *Penn's Treaty* the lesson is that conflict can be settled without bloodshed, but the lesson takes second place to the interest of the subject. The locale and the participants are sufficiently picturesque to approach genre painting, although West was only following his own precedent in presenting another recent historical event in appropriate factual terms rather than allegory. The dress of the Indians may not be entirely correct but it is as nearly so as

278. WEST: *Self-portrait, c.* 1795(?). 40 x 52½″. Royal Academy of Arts, London.

West knew how to make it from Indian souvenirs in his own collection. The picture is cluttered in spots with distracting incidentals and there is a certain—rather engaging—naïveté about it. But it is an honest picture, more original than it looks today, and its virtues plus the exotic interest of its

subject made it a tremendous success and established West in a career that never wavered for the rest of his life. Placidly enough, with no effort either to curry favor or to break new ground, West kept busy with portraits and murals, sometimes deadly dull and dry, sometimes of great charm, as in *Arthur Middleton, His Wife, and Son* [277], where the straightforward representation of the attractive young man's features, the semiclassical idealization of his wife's, and the absurd artificiality of the baby combine to produce a piquant flavor probably unplanned by a painter who was following several conventions at once without pondering any of them very deeply. On the other hand, West's *Self-portrait* [278] is perfectly consistent—a masterpiece of assurance without bravado, richly painted, and altogether an impressive demonstration by an accomplished craftsman.

Near the end of his life West's originality flared up again; he was nearly eighty when he painted the wildly romantic *Death on a Pale Horse*, exhibiting it in 1817. This was only two years before French romanticism declared itself in the Salon with the *Raft of the Medusa*, but West had caused a flurry in classical Paris seventeen years before the appearance of Géricault's roman-

279. WEST: *Death on a Pale Horse* (sketch), *c.* 1787. Oil on paper, mounted on panel, 11½ x 22½″. Philadelphia Museum of Art, McIlhenny Fund.

tic landmark by exhibiting there a study for *Death on a Pale Horse* [279]. This was in 1802, in which year Géricault was only eleven and Delacroix was a toddler of three.

With so much to his credit, and such a startling record as a forerunner of the neo-classicism and the romanticism that convulsed Paris a little later, why is West not a more important figure than he is? The answer is that his work has neither quite the technical mastery nor nearly the intellectual and emotional concentration that must combine to create paintings of the absolutely first rank. Whatever his sensitivities to nascent classicism and nascent romanticism, West never explored these sensitivities deeply enough to carry their expression beyond a hint of what was in the air. Even if he had done so, it is difficult to imagine either movement assuming in England the importance that both did in France. In England, painting had never established itself as a manifestation of national morals or policy. And if such response was unlikely in England it was impossible in America, as another American painter discovered at about the same time West was exhibiting his *Death on a Pale Horse* in London.

John Vanderlyn: The Failure of Classicism

John Vanderlyn (1775–1852) was a long generation younger than West, and where West left America as a colonial subject, Vanderlyn grew up as an American citizen. But Vanderlyn adopted a tradition even more foreign to the taste of his own country: he went to Paris for five years in 1796 (as a protégé of Aaron Burr's) and then for twelve more in 1803 and made a good Davidian classicist of himself. He returned to America with the tightest and purest example of neo-classical painting this country had seen, his *Marius amid the Ruins of Carthage* [280], which had been enthusiastically received in Paris, and the best-drawn nude, an *Ariadne* [281]. Neither painting was a success, nor was his circular panorama of Versailles. This was a tour de force of perspective painting, which placed

280. VANDERLYN: *Marius amid the Ruins of Carthage*, 1807. 87 x 68½". H. M. de Young Memorial Museum, San Francisco.

the observer directly in the center of the palace gardens, surrounding him by hedges, sculpture, palatial architecture, and strolling ladies and gentlemen. To exhibit the 3,000 square feet of canvas making up the panorama Vanderlyn had to build his own rotunda in New York, but not even the novelty of the work appealed to Americans, perhaps because they had already been left cold by the *Marius* and deeply offended by Ariadne's nakedness. Vanderlyn never recovered from this defeat and died in obscurity, an American who had made a skillful French classical painter of himself, only to fail to make the grade in his own country.

Part of the reason for the classical near-vacuum in American painting is that art

281. VANDERLYN: *Ariadne Asleep on the Island of Naxos*, 1814. 68 x 87″. Pennsylvania Academy of the Fine Arts, Philadelphia.

in America began as an offshoot of art in England, where the neo-classical disciplines as we have seen them in France never took root. This is not surprising in England, but in America circumstances arose that might have been expected to favor at least a provincial version of French classicism. At the time of the American Revolution, when the new nation's bonds with France became so close, when it was engaged in a struggle and was then creating a government drawing philosophically on some of the same ideals that inspired French thought and French political struggle—at this time one might have expected a flourishing of Franco-American classical painting. But at first the new nation was too busy pulling itself together to have much time or money or energy left over for the arts, and then whatever roots French neo-classical painting might have established in America were nipped, in the last decade of the eighteenth century, when American horror at the excesses of the Terror in France created an aversion to everything French. The didacticism of *The Oath of the Horatii* or the *Brutus*, which might have appealed to the strong moral sense of the young American republic, rang false as a background for the guillotine, and the Napoleonic career and

legend did not offer substitute attractions.

In architecture the story was different: American faith in the column and pediment as a symbol of high moral and political ideals was never shaken by disillusions with European events. When Thomas Jefferson designed the state capitol for Virginia he went directly to the architecture of ancient Rome and adapted the well-preserved temple at Nîmes into a design of great sobriety and purity. In hundreds of other examples, American architects built some of the loveliest classical structures since those of ancient Greece. But when French neo-classical painting abandoned its moral preachments and became a stylish exercise in high polish and sensuous grace, it became altogether foreign to American taste. For along with their elevated moral standard the Americans developed a provincial prudery that could not tolerate the naked gods and goddesses—or the *Ariadnes*—who replaced the stalwart warriors and the chaste matrons of David's early pictures.

These are specific reasons for the failure of neo-classicism to catch on in a country where Europe still furnished the models for most ambitious painters. But the strongest reason of all was a general one: the new country was raw. No matter what comparative felicities of good living had been developed in such centers as Boston and Philadelphia, American patrons of the arts were not ready for the aesthetic sophistications of French painting. The most cultivated Americans were earthy and practical people compared with the dilettantes and the professional intellectuals who set the pace for the intelligent layman or amateur in France.

Early German Romantics

In truth, classicism as a disciplined philosophical ideal was "too severe to please for long" even in France, as David himself had lamented. His own followers were unable to pull themselves up to it by their bootstraps even when they wanted to as much as Gros and Ingres did. If we accept the evidence of painting alone, the nineteenth century was overwhelmingly a century of romantics who were often attracted by logic and common sense and often put great faith in the literal fact of nature and the world around them, but who always ended by yielding to emotion or sentiment even when they attempted to cast themselves in the roles of classicists or realists. Outside France, those painters who followed the classical formula most closely were the ones with so little intellect or imagination that a formula was necessary to them.

Among the dozens of German classicists who are all but forgotten, Gottleib Schick (1776–1812) is better remembered than most. He produced some of the most tedious historical paintings of the century, but he also did the portrait of Frau Heinrich von Dannecker [282], the wife of the German sculptor, his teacher and friend. The picture is full of the usual artificialities and it has the rather dry and mannered drawing that might be expected, but it is also full of unclassical exceptions—the ordinary weeds that spring casually around the base of the stone, the sweetness of the little spray of flowers held in one hand, the peaceful informality of the landscape in the distance, and of course above all the direct, realistic, individualized and sympathetic representation of the face, which manages to counteract the drawing-exercise affectation of the oversmooth, excruciatingly posed arm and hand beside it. It is remindful, in its awkward way, of David's exceptional portrait of Émélie Sériziat [16].

The romantic spirit was so pervasive that it transformed the classical vision of antiquity, emotionalizing a concept which Poussin had established as a rational one. The young Germans, Englishmen, Americans, and others who converged on Rome, as the eighteenth century turned into the nineteenth, discovered the ancient world as a dream of lost beauty. Their classicism was a nostalgic revery upon a golden past. They might borrow forms from Poussin as the young American Washington Allston did in his *Italian Landscape* [283], but like him they transplanted them into a world where "perfection" was less a matter of perfection reached by distillation, less a matter of order and discipline, than a dream of a world where the hazards and deteriorations

282. SCHICK: *Frau Heinrich von Dannecker*, 1802. 46¾ x 39½".
Nationalgalerie, Berlin.

283. ALLSTON:*Italian Landscape*, 1805–08. 39 x 51". Addison Gallery of American Art, Andover, Mass.

284. SCHINKEL: *Greek City by the Sea*, 1815. 51 x 35″. *Nationalgalerie,* Berlin. Photo Stoedtner.

and the evils and misfortunes of life were unknown. When the German Karl Friedrich Schinkel (1781–1841) painted an imagined *Greek City by the Sea* [284], the world he invented was not the closed and ordered one of Poussin but a wonderful wide-flung land where pearly marble monuments rose undefiled from an undefiled landscape inhabited by men free from all vicissitude moving beneath radiant skies. All this, of course, has remained a standard dream of Hellas; it is also romantic yearning, the romantic escape into the far away, which in France took another form in Orientalism. In Germany and America, painters soon abandoned all classical reference for a vision of unspoiled nature as a mystical and often a specifically religious symbol. When the works of man appear in these landscapes they appear as monuments in ruin; to contemplate the fragments of a vanished world, the romantic finds, is more evocative of man's past than is an effort to recreate it.

Thus a ruined Gothic chapel in the snow [285] replaces the immaculate Greek temple bathed in sun; the broken trees surrounding it, gnarled, black, and frozen, rise above the crosses and headstones of abandoned graves. Or in a darkling world two friends stand beneath a half-uprooted tree [286] where the forms of nature, in disarray, are silhouetted with all their grotesque accidents and haphazard tumbling against a moon-filled sky. This romantic melancholy, this romantic contemplation of man's aloneness and his transience, this pondering of man's fate in full awareness that it is impossible for him to reach a conclusion as to its meaning or to place himself as a logical part of a universe scaled to his being, is of course pleasurable to the romantic temperament. Sometimes the romantic's world is a gentler one within which human beings may exist more placidly, sitting on rocks along the shore, for instance, while they watch a sunset or moonrise over the sea [287], aware of solemn immensities but not of threatening mysteries. There may be comfort in desolation, warmth and even a certain protection in the acceptance of frailty and mortality. The romantic is

285. FRIEDRICH: *Cloister Graveyard in the Snow*, 1810. Panel, 47⅜ x 70″. *Nationalgalerie*, Berlin, now lost.

286. FRIEDRICH: *Two Men Looking at the Moon*, 1819–20. Panel, 11¾ x 17¼″. *Staatliche Gemäldegalerie*, Dresden.

content to be received into the universal mystery, absorbed into it without examining it. He abandons himself to the idea that time and mysterious forces may shatter his works and consume his body yet at the same time must recognize his presence by the very inevitability of his inclusion within a system of laws beyond his comprehension.

French romanticism edged up to this conclusion but was never quite able to accept it. Delacroix vehemently rejected it, rightly regarding himself as a classicist in his effort to make a universal synthesis of human passions. The pictures we have just seen, by Caspar David Friedrich (1774–1840) have no parallels in French painting. Technically, they combine the sharp definition of classical draughtsmanship with the contradictory subject matter of accident

287. FRIEDRICH: *Moonrise over the Sea*, 1823. 21¾ x 28″. *Nationalgalerie*, Berlin, destroyed by fire, 1931.

288. JAMES WYATT, architect: Fonthill Abbey, 1796. Wiltshire, England, no longer standing.

and decay; they make their emotional or mystical statement in terms that are pictorially didactic, where the French romantic painter freed his brush to dash across the canvas in a way expressive of romantic excitement or agony.

Friedrich's Germanism was conscious. His twisted trees have their counterparts in German medieval painting, and his preoccupation with Gothic architecture came, in part, from his belief that it was an essentially Germanic expression. Actually, an interest in the middle ages and its arts was reviving all over Europe in reaction against the rationalism of the eighteenth century. Before that century was ended, a wild and fantastic young Englishman named William Beckford was engaged in doing the unheard of: he was building himself an abode modeled after a medieval monastery, in a country remarkable for the comfort of its domestic adaptation of classical forms. Fonthill Abbey, as Beckford called this visionary project [288], was not so much a place to live in as it was a stage set designed as a background for the romantic posturings of its owner. Impatient to see his abbey materialize, Beckford forced the builder into such an impossible schedule that he—the builder—skimped on the foundations for the central tower. On his deathbed this man is supposed to have called Beckford to his side to confess this and to warn him that the tower might collapse at any time. It did, shortly thereafter. It is symbolical of the artificiality of the nineteenth-century romantic concept of architecture that Fonthill Abbey was in ruins a few years after it was built. In this state it was, of course, more romantic than ever, but it was even less habitable.

Yet the idea of Gothic domestic architecture, as well as a rage for medieval churches, schools, postoffices, office buildings, and everything else, increased rapidly in popularity during the century. Gothic villas were built everywhere in Europe; in America they were especially popular, for they had the additional allure of creating an illusion of "Old World charm" in a country beginning to be conscious of its rawness. In France the movement was less popular. The country was so deeply ingrained with the classical tradition, and the neo-Gothic structure was so incompatible with the practicality of the French temperament, that Gothicism was largely limited to a cult of the existing monuments, which received scholarly study and restoration during the century, especially under the architect Viollet-le-Duc, who saved many structures from ruin and somewhat marred others by excessive restoration. In England, Gothicism was a passion, not only as a new reverence for the genuine monuments but in the creation of artificial ones. Builders kept on hand sets of designs for small Gothic ruins that could be built on estates not fortunate enough to have the genuine article. The built ruin is the apotheosis of the curious backing-up that characterized architecture as a romantic manifestation.

But if the idea was fundamentally absurd, it died slowly. More than a hundred years after Fonthill Abbey, in the boom days of the early 1920's, the American publisher William Randolph Hearst spent several million dollars on *La Cuesta Encantada*

289. RUNGE: *Naked Infant in a Meadow*, 1808–09. 12 x 12½". *Kunsthalle*, Hamburg.

(The Enchanted Hill), an estate on a California hilltop with a main house designed in the fashion of a Spanish cathedral including an assembly room lined with paneling from a church, a billiard room incongruously ornamented with medieval tapestries, an indoor swimming pool of vaguely Moorish design (it took three years to lay the tiles), a baronial hall, complete with banners, as a dining room and, perhaps for relief, a few Greek and Roman temples and colonnades here and there around the 120 acres. After the collapse of Fonthill Abbey, Beckford himself reverted to classical taste, perhaps oppressed by the emotional strain of living up to the atmosphere he had created. But the Enchanted Hill was quite well built, and is something of a white elephant to the State of California, which accepted it as a gift after Hearst's death and operates it, at a loss, as a park.

Of course the Enchanted Hill and smaller castles built in America at that time were

290. RUNGE: *Rest on the Flight into Egypt*, 1805–06. 38½ x 52″. *Kunsthalle*, Hamburg.

more tied up with the idea of pretentious display than with the nostalgia for the past and the taste for melancholy that inspired the early romantics like Beckford and, in painting where it more properly belonged, Friedrich. It was a cruel inconsistency that medievalism in architecture was to catch on, while Friedrich's painting was repudiated by his contemporaries, especially those who were busy following French classicism as an academic formula. Although the romantic spirit stirred earlier and more restlessly in Germany than it did in France, it somehow did not manage to come into full blossom in painting. Several factors combined to stunt it, including the early death of Friedrich's friend, Philipp Otto Runge (1777–1810), who might have joined forces with him to establish a strong romantic tradition if he had not died at thirty-three. On his sickbed Runge destroyed much of his work, and even among the few examples he left, the majority are studies for large projects he was never able to complete. But from his few remaining pictures and from his letters and notes he emerges

as a man who, as Delacroix did in France, might have imposed intellectual disciplines on German romanticism, yet who much more than Delacroix was a romantic in the most personal, emotional way.

Like Friedrich, Runge wanted to revivify German art, and he began by rejecting his own early classicism because "works of art show how mankind has changed, how a stage that has once appeared never reappears." How, then, he asked, could painters hold the "unhappy notion of wanting to revive the art of long ago? . . . of recreating a past art?" Above all, he put his faith in innocence, in nature, and in love. His startling picture of a *Naked Infant in a Meadow* [289], its eyes wide with wonder at the world around it, is his symbol of the innocence with which he would have liked to perceive the universe. It is an arresting picture, whatever its flavor of absurdity for an uninnocent eye. If not passed over as a sentimental fantasy, it may take on a magical enchantment; it is difficult to forget.

Magic is present too in Runge's *Rest on the Flight into Egypt* [290]. The tree over the holy child unexpectedly becomes an intertwining of infant angels and heavenly blossoms. At the extreme left, the ass grazes on thistly plants; the forms of his lowered head, his long neck, and the saddle chair with its drapery are silhouetted against the sky in foreshortened combinations naturalistic in detail yet fantastic in total effect. The landscape background is as meticulous as any of Friedrich's, but its mood is serenely joyful rather than sad or sinister. Runge held a theory that subject painting, history painting, was a worn-out form, and that painters who might have found themselves as landscapists had been hampered for two centuries because landscape was considered an accessory to subject rather than an independent means of expression. The revival of landscape painting in England and America, which we will see shortly, gives some support to this idea, and of course Friedrich carried it on in Germany after Runge's death. "How could a painter want for a subject," Runge asked, "when awakened to nature through what we see in ourselves, in our love, and in the heavens?"

The *Rest on the Flight into Egypt* is not first of all a religious picture in spite of its religious subject. Its air of miracle has more to do with the miracle of innocence and the miracle of landscape as a reflection of man's soul. But a group of Runge's contemporaries who flourished just after his death sought a similar return to innocence by dedicating their art to religion. They called themselves the Nazarenes and went so far as to move to Rome and set themselves up as a religious brotherhood in a former convent. The Nazarenes hoped to find spiritual grace by returning to the style of the painters of the early Renaissance. This, of course, is putting the cart before the horse.

The Nazarenes insisted on exactitude in drawing just as Friedrich and Runge had done, but unlike them they imitated old forms rather than referring to nature or inventing new ones. They ended as one of the most sterile groups in the history of painting anywhere. But their return to Christianity has some interest in early German romanticism, paralleling as it does Chateaubriand's specious Christian revival

291. BLAKE: *Zacharias and the Angel*, date unknown. Tempera, 10½ x 15". Metropolitan Museum of Art, New York, Bequest of William Church Osborn.

in France which produced, as we have seen, *Atala*. The most important of the Nazarenes was one Friedrich Overbeck (1789–1869), but the one who eventually came into honors was Peter von Cornelius, already mentioned in connection with the Salon of 1855.

Blake

Romanticism in general was a reaction against the rational thought of the eighteenth-century philosophers who made a cult of Reason. Romanticism had common bases wherever it appeared, but it also took on characterizing differences in the different countries where it put down its deepest roots. In France, the individualizing element was a yearning for personal fulfillment through sensation, through exaggerated emotionalism, through violent or swooning passions. In Germany, by the evidence of Runge's naked infant, wide-eyed in the blossoming meadow of a wondrous world, the romantics were filled with a nostalgia for innocence. By the evidence of Friedrich's Gothic ruins and moonlit forests, romanticism was a search for union with mysteries that were doors to the supernatural. The revival of Christianity (which was not much more than a fashion in France) was basic to German romanticism,

Then a Spirit passed before my face
the hair of my flesh stood up

292. BLAKE: Illustration for the Book of Job, 1825. Engraving, 7¾ x 5⅞". Philadelphia Museum of Art, Gift of Staunton B. Peck.

choly of German romanticism was never a part of Blake's art. He was fulfilled within the areas of the soul—innocence and miraculous experience—that the Germans could only look back upon as lost. Reason had corrupted them; they might cultivate innocence, but the cultivation of innocence is a contradiction on the face of it. They might theorize about the supernatural, but the supernatural, on the face of it, is self-generated and cannot be materialized by any amount of theorizing. Blake was not subject to these frustrations. His art is lyrical, joyous—a paean.

Blake is a precursor or a very early member of the romantic movement by this description, and he might be called a rebel against academic classicism because he constantly fumed and fulminated against Sir Joshua Reynolds (the head of the British Royal Academy, whom he called Sir Sloshua) and his "gang of hired knaves." But one cannot help but feel that Blake would have painted, believed, and behaved as he did no matter when he had been born, or where, and that his appearance at the beginning of the romantic movement is only an accident of chronology. And he had virtually no influence on painting until the romantic movement had matured and been replaced by other revolutions. For that matter, his influence even now, when he has become the deity of a solid, enduring cult, is vague and more closely connected with literature and bibliophilia than with painting. If he had never painted a picture, his

Tiger, tiger, burning bright
In the forests of the night

would atone for the loss. The poem is the most vivid picture he ever created.

Blake was apprenticed to an engraver at fourteen, and from that time on he painted and drew as a corollary to literature. All his work depends on its literary source; it is first poetry—including his own, Dante's, and the Bible's—and second pictorial art. He held to the idea that a dream or a vision was not a shadowy nothing but should be represented in terms more concise than those of the visual world, and he applied this idea consistently in translating words

because it supplied a God Who was beyond the formulas of Reason, Who demanded acceptance through the innocence of faith and manifested Himself through miracle.

In England there had already appeared a man who could have served Friedrich and Runge as a concrete example of their theoretical recipe for the purified human spirit. His name was William Blake (1757–1827). He was a poet and a painter, and he was an innocent. He was as innocent as a lamb, from his cradle to his grave. He lived in intimacy with the supernatural, for angels spoke to him from the branches of trees, and he accepted their shining miraculous presence as a part of his life. He was a benign eccentric to the point of madness. But the brooding, nostalgic melan-

293. BLAKE: "The Whirlwind of Lovers," illustration from Dante's *Divine Comedy*, 1827. 10⅞ x 13⅞". National Gallery of Art, Washington, D.C., Lessing J. Rosenwald Collection.

294. PALMER: *Opening the Fold*, 1880. Etching, 4⅝ x 7". Collection Carl Zigrosser, Chestnut Hill, Pa.

295. PALMER: *Coming from Evening Church*, 1830. 12 x 7¾". Tate Gallery, London.

296. FUSELI: *The Nightmare, c.* 1780–90. 40 x 50". Detroit Institute of Arts.

into his swirling, bending, twisting compositions. His forms, derived from Michelangelo and Raphael, are of the utmost clarity of definition, and his swirling, bending, and twisting arrangements are controlled in every detail of their movement. As a pictorial artist he is a draughtsman rather than a painter. The majority of his paintings are watercolors by definition, but tinted drawings in fact. His few paintings in tempera seem to refute his typical manner [291], but this is because the tempera in which they are executed has darkened, cracked, and flaked, giving a misty, conventionally "dreamy" quality to forms that must originally have been closer to his usual tight, dry contours.

Blake produced illuminated editions of his own poetry in a technique he evolved for himself, a printing method not far removed from hand coloring. He was poor all his life, but he would not accept patronage, in the custom of the day, because patronage was likely to involve compromise. He had a saint of a wife, Kate, an adoring, good, simple woman who accepted him at his own face value, and probably kept not only his body and soul but his soul and his sanity together. In the last decade of his life he attracted a small group of disciples, headed by John Linnell (1792–1882), who was thirty-five years younger than Blake, and they obtained commissions for him to illustrate, among other texts, the Book of Job [292] and Dante's *Divine Comedy* [293]. These illustrations may be the finest expressions of his eccentric genius.

The disciple Linnell was a landscape painter who did extremely pleasant, sometimes moody, pictures of the English countryside as well as some portraits and Biblical subjects. But Samuel Palmer (1805–1881), who studied with Linnell and through him was drawn into Blake's small, late circle, was a painter of great imaginative originality, unaccountably neglected today except by a few enthusiastic supporters. His tiny etchings [294] and his compact paintings [295] where a pastoral world is made half-visionary by lights sometimes spectral, sometimes golden, are the one extension of Blake's fantasy into the realm where English romanticism was find-

297. ALLSTON: *Jason Returning to Demand His Father's Kingdom*, 1807–08. 168 x 240".
University of Miami, Coral Gables, Fla., Gift of Washington Allston Trust.

ing its typical expression — landscape.
Palmer was only twenty-two years old when
Blake died at seventy, so he belongs to the
middle of the nineteenth century while
Blake belongs to its transition from the
eighteenth. In his late work Palmer lost
much of his imaginative power when he
failed to assimilate the influence of another
imaginative genius, Turner. Turner was in
mid-career at the time of Blake's death,
and we will see him shortly.

The only other artist of much importance
who is thought of in connection with Blake
was John Fuseli (1741–1825), a Swiss who
spent most of his life in London. He was an
eccentric but not, like Blake, an isolated
one. Blake was only one of many friends
who admired him, and the list included
Blake's bête noire, Reynolds. Fuseli was
a fantasist whose favorite subject, repeated
several times, was a little nightmare with
erotic overtones in which a young woman
swoons in abandon upon a couch, menaced
by a ghostly and leering horse [296], a
suggestive fantasy that has endeared Fuseli
to contemporary painters of psychopatho-
logical fantasies. Fuseli seems to have been
an honest and straightforward man, and
these qualities endeared him to Blake.

298. ALLSTON: *The Dead Man Revived by Touching the Bones
of the Prophet Elisha*, 1811–13. 156 x 132". Pennsylvania Academy
of the Fine Arts, Philadelphia.

An American Romantic: Washington Allston

While Friedrich with his broken trees and ruined cathedrals was trying to revivify a German romantic tradition, an American one was established by a man who was his contemporary almost to the years of birth and death. Washington Allston (1779–1843) was also an immediate contemporary of the unhappy John Vanderlyn who so gallicized his art that when he came home with it he found himself a foreigner. Allston was more fortunate. Although he studied in London* and in Paris in the Louvre, which had just opened, and in Rome, he never accepted any single tradition unquestioningly. He was a clear-headed fellow, well educated, an intimate of intellectuals in both England and America, not only capable of thinking for himself but determined to do so. He began with the expected dedication to classical antiquity; in Rome he painted and exhibited with Vanderlyn. We have already seen, in his *Italian Landscape* [283], that he reflected the romantic dream of the classical world, although this particular picture is somewhat more Poussinesque than other examples that might have been selected to make the point in an exaggerated way. As a matter of fact Allston had the makings of a very respectable classical painter. In Rome he began a large classical subject, *Jason Returning to Demand His Father's Kingdom* [297], where exceptional control, precision, and clarity are suggested even though the picture is unfinished. When he left Italy in 1808 the canvas was boxed for shipment but he did not recover it until eight or nine years later. By that time Allston had grown dissatisfied with classicism and had already set himself a different kind of problem, and solved it, in a contrasting picture, *The Dead Man Revived by Touching the Bones of the Prophet Elisha* [298], a subject of mystery and miracle. Instead of the classical frieze-like grouping of forms arranged across the canvas from side to side and illuminated in a clear, uniform light, *The Dead Man Revived* is constructed of forms building upward through several levels, emerging dramatically from obscuring shadows. Allston's model was no longer the art of classical antiquity but the emotionalized painting of the Italian seventeenth century.

Allston became an example of that contradiction in terms, the rational romantic. In addition to a clear intelligence he had a quick intuitive response to the world. He respected this response, but was unwilling to let it run away with him. At this time considerable theorizing went on among painters about something called "primitivism," in not quite the same sense the word has today. It had to do with the artist's abandonment to his spontaneous response to nature as opposed to the "artificialities" of civilized life. Allston rejected this idea. The world was with us, and to deny our place in it as civilized contemporary men was foolish and, for that matter, impossible. He preferred to be a part of his time and saw no reason why he should reject either it or the past. If he rejected anything, it was the skepticism of the eighteenth century, but he rejected it only as an extreme, and when he returned to religious subjects, like *The Dead Man Revived*, he was re-establishing the legitimacy of the mystical, emotional, and hence romantic Christian tradition without denying the legitimacy of an analytical one. He saw no conflict between tradition and originality. The aim of the artist, he thought, was to be true to "that within man which is ever answering to that without, as life to life—which must be life and which must be true." Allston recognized intuitive response as a basis for creation, but he was wary of a distortion away from "truth," either in the direction of blind trust in intuition or excessive suspicion denying intuition's validity.

In his theorizing, Allston was part of a new coalescence in American thought. But

---

* Allston went to England in 1801 and studied under Benjamin West; in 1803 he went to Paris with Vanderlyn. From 1804 to 1808 he was in Rome; he knew Coleridge and Washington Irving among others there, and also Vanderlyn again. In 1808 or 1809 he returned to America. Then from 1811 to 1818 he was in Europe once more, mostly in London. Thereafter he lived in Boston, where he had been educated at Harvard. He was born in South Carolina.

299. ALLSTON: *Moonlit Landscape,* 1819. 24 x 25″. Museum of Fine Arts, Boston.

300. RYDER: *Death on a Pale Horse (The Racetrack),* date unknown. 28¼ x 35¼″. Cleveland Museum of Art, J. H. Wade Fund.

all theorizing aside, his most satisfying pictures today, simply as pictures, are his moody landscapes. There is a great distance between his *Italian Landscape* and his *Moonlit Landscape* [299] painted about fourteen years later, the year after his return to America. *Moonlit Landscape* is the progenitor, or at least one of the earliest examples, of a type of moonstruck romanticism filled with an agreeable loneliness, suggestive of man's melancholy journey through the mysteries of life yet speaking comfortingly of his union with the forces behind those mysteries, that has been recurrent in American painting. This minor but persistent tradition finds variation in the art of Albert Pinkham Ryder (1847–1917), a solitary and eccentric painter who may be introduced out of chronological order here since he was one of those painters,

301. ALLSTON: *American Scenery: Time, Afternoon with a Southwest Haze*, 1835. 18½ x 24½". Museum of Fine Arts, Boston.

302. EARL: *Roger Sherman*, 1775–77. 64⅝ x 49⅝". Yale University Art Gallery, New Haven, Conn.

like Blake, whose art was essentially divorced from time and place [300].

Allston's final divorce from his European models is indicated in another revery with the elaborate title *Landscape, American Scenery: Time, Afternoon, with a Southwest Haze* [301], painted after seventeen years of repatriation. The two earlier landscapes are fantasies, but in the later one the specific references to place, time, and even the kind of day are symptoms of a revolution in landscape painting that was already flourishing in the United States.

Where Allston and other idealists fabricated their landscapes or imposed a mood arbitrarily on a free variation of an existing one, a new school of American landscapists were discovering mood and poetry as an emanation of the exact appearance of an actual scene. They were discovering American landscape as a new aspect of nature, not only scenically but psychologically differentiated from that of Europe. That they turned to American scenery for subject matter and transcribed its appearance in meticulous detail means nothing in itself except for whatever interest such representations have as factual record (which may be considerable); but that they felt and recorded new responses to landscape, and that these responses were peculiarly inspired by the American wilderness, meant that America had produced its first school independent of European inspiration.

Early "Americanism"

The typically "American" quality of painting had until then been a certain awkwardness, a dryness, a forthright honesty, in provincial approximations of more sophisticated European styles. Ralph Earl's (1751–1801) celebrated portrait of Roger Sherman [302] is a supreme example of this kind, a picture where the stiffness, the spareness, the decision, of a self-taught painter's style* accounts by coincidence for

---

* The portrait of Roger Sherman was painted before Earl went to London to study with West. Upon his return to America he was a "better" painter—that is, his naïve but forceful style was weakened by stilted elaborations.

much of the expressive power in this portrait of a man whose character was of a kind to be projected by these qualities. Even so thoroughly admirable and altogether enjoyable a painter as Charles Willson Peale (1741–1827), who can lay a strong claim to the title of "most American" of a group of painters who worked with homely sincerity as country cousins to the English tradition, is American largely on the negative score of being less European than he would have been if he could have been trained as a member of a more suave society.

This is not entirely Americanism-by-default, and it is even less so in the case of the "American primitives," whose art has been lifted in recent years from a level of interesting novelty to the respectable one of an important national art expression. The American primitives were that large body of self-trained journeyman painters who supported themselves by working for a modest market, often in the hinterlands, plus the amateur painters, equally without professional training, who painted friends and family and familiar places. Such paintings may be merely inept, or they may have a degree of awkward charm dependent on the degree of the painter's innate sensitivity to decorative color and pattern. But awkward charm may also be a genuinely expressive element, as it is in the case of Edward Hicks (1780–1849). In retrospect Hicks has become the accepted master of all the American primitives, and his *Peaceable Kingdom* [303, 304], of which he did around a hundred variations, is the summary of American primitive virtues.

In the foreground of *The Peaceable Kingdom* Hicks illustrates with faithful literalness three verses from Isaiah—

"The wolf also shall dwell with the lamb, and the leopard shall lie down with the kid; and the calf and the young lion and the fatling together; and a little child shall lead them.

And the cow and the bear shall feed; their young ones shall lie down together: and the lion shall eat straw like the ox.

And the suckling child shall play on the hole of the asp, and the weaned child shall put his hand on the cockatrice' den."

303. Hicks: *The Peaceable Kingdom, c.* 1848. 17⅛ x 23½″. Philadelphia Museum of Art, Lisa Norris Elkins Bequest.

304: Hicks: Detail from Figure 303.

—while in the background the Biblical prophecy is fulfilled as Penn concludes his treaty with the Indians. Hicks was a sign painter by trade, a Quaker by religion, and a preacher and artist by avocation. In train-

305. DURAND: *Kindred Spirits* (Thomas Cole and William Cullen Bryant), 1849. 44 x 36″. New York Public Library.

306. FRIEDRICH: *Mountain Peaks,* 1826. Panel, 51½ x 65¾″. *Nationalgalerie,* Berlin.

ing himself as an artist, he took as models the only material available to him, rather poor engravings of the old masters and, for his animals perhaps, illustrations in children's books. As far as such opportunities were concerned, he was at no greater disadvantage than the scores of other amateurs above whom he rises as an artist. His advantage was that he was gifted with a stronger feeling for design, a greater spirit of dedication, and a most conscientious industry. No apologies need be made for his naïveté or for what would be, in another kind of artist, his technical shortcomings. *The Peaceable Kingdom* is acutely limited in comparison with work in the great traditions of painting, yet Hicks's simple faith, his wonderful and innocent enthusiasm for the translation of faith into pictorial images, are not negligible virtues.

The Peaceable Kingdom is a harmonious fusion of technique and conception; as such it has an extraordinary completeness as a work of art, a character determined by circumstances that cut the painter off from the mainstreams of painting. In this limited respect it is American in an isolated way. But now, at mid-century, with the birth of a new school of landscape painting, there appeared an art where Americanism was positive, its essence flowing from native springs, even while it was allied to the great world of painting in Europe.

The Hudson River School

The paintings of the so-called "Hudson River School" are as meticulously polished, sometimes to the point of niggling detail, as Caspar David Friedrich's landscapes, but there the similarity ends. Where Friedrich's mood was nostalgic and often gloomy, even ominous, the Americans' is full of vigorous optimism. Friedrich's *Two Men Looking at the Moon* [286] are surrounded by sinister forms, even if they seem to have come to terms with a threatening world. But Asher B. Durand's *Kindred Spirits* [305] are inspired by communion with a Nature which nourishes their souls. Friedrich's *Mountain Peaks* [306] hold the observer within a menacing chasm pressing

307. Bierstadt: *Merced River, Yosemite Valley*, 1866. 36 x 50″. Metropolitan Museum of Art, New York.

upon him on either side, blocking him in the distance by harsh cliffs and cruel pinnacles, while the American peaks in Albert Bierstadt's *Merced River, Yosemite Valley* [307], equally cliffed and pinnacled, rise gloriously into an air as golden as that of any imagined Hellas. But this elysium of crags, water, trees, and rough earth is not an imagined one; the essential characteristic of these American landscapes is their reality, the fact that they are actual scenes within a country which was opening, unfolding to yield an inexhaustible sequence of new beauties for the delight, the amazement, and the enrichment of men.* The tiny figures that spot *Merced River, Yosemite Valley* here and there—standing on

a ledge of rock, moving across the shining water in a small boat—are not crushed by the immensity of the forms around them. They enter this vastness as strangers but not as intruders; their place within it may be temporary, but they are neither lost nor threatened. They are in the presence of a sublime grandeur and they breathe its air. It is a new conception of wilderness, indifferent to man's presence yet benign. It is a wilderness that never entirely yields to domestication; even at its most placid, as in Thomas Doughty's *In the Catskills* [308] it is a world infiltrated, but not transformed, by man.

The range of the Hudson River School is indicated by these three examples, from the philosophical or poetic intimacy of *Kindred Spirits* and *In the Catskills* to a passion for natural forms of supernatural grandeur, as in *Merced River, Yosemite Valley*. And it should already be apparent that "Hudson

* Even when painting imaginary landscapes, as they frequently did, the Hudson River men were more likely to concoct one from the elements of a familiar world than to try to reassemble a lost one.

308. DOUGHTY: *In the Catskills*, 1836. 31½ x 42¼". Addison Gallery of American Art, Andover, Mass.

second,* and his glorification of the West exemplifies the taste for wilder and more dramatic scenes that affected the character of the school. But there is no sharp dividing line, and both generations ranged from the intimate to the vast. It is worth mentioning that the Hudson River painters discovered American landscape at the same time that the Frenchmen were setting up their easels around Barbizon. Durand and Corot were born the same year. And as Barbizon painting became known in America, its tender, lyrical mood was fused with the more indigenous one of the Hudson River men by other landscapists, notably George Inness (1825–1894), a contemporary of the second Hudson River generation who began in their tradition, then followed more closely Corot's, and finally in his late work cultivated some of the evanescent effects of impressionism.

River" is an inaccurate blanket designation for a school spreading from one side of the continent to the other. Actually, "school" is also a loose term here. Some of the painters did know one another and did work in the Catskill Mountains near the Hudson, but they never formed an organization nor did they paint from a set of codified principles. They are unified not by place or even by time, since they covered two generations—roughly between 1820 and 1870—but rather by the optimism, the enthusiasm, the belief in some wondrously vital spirit within the American landscape, which not only remained uncontaminated by the penetration of man but endowed him with whatever portion he could absorb of its ineffable sublimity.

Durand (1796–1886) and Doughty (1793–1856) belong to the first Hudson River generation,* and the quietness of their pictures illustrated here is typical of the general temper. Bierstadt (1830–1902), who accompanied a surveying expedition into the Rocky Mountains and Yosemite Valley in 1858, belongs to the

Thomas Cole

The most individual of the Hudson River painters was a member of the earlier group, Thomas Cole (1801–1848), and he is usually thought of first whenever the school is mentioned today. The school in general is out of favor. The meticulousness of its detail, which may grow somewhat peckish and mincing; the imitativeness of its color, sometimes exaggerated into postcard gaudiness; its devotion to literal transcription rather than to pictorial theory or technical experiment make it appear humdrum alongside the brilliance and variety and complication of French painting. But because he was a fantasist as well as a landscapist, Cole has been tucked in lately with some of the strangest bedfellows in the world— the contemporary surrealist painters, who would certainly have horrified him. Two scenes [309 and 310] from the four making up his *Voyage of Life* series will give an idea of the bizarre mixture of moralizing, mysticism, melodrama, and naïve platitude that he grafted onto the Hudson River landscape with curious effect.

* Some others: Charles Codman, Samuel F. B. Morse, Alvin Fisher, Henry Inman, and Robert W. Weir.

* Some others: John W. Casilear, John F. Kensett, Worthington Whittredge, Jasper F. Cropsey, Frederick E. Church.

309. COLE: *The Voyage of Life: Youth,* 1840. 52 x 78″. Munson-Williams-Proctor Institute, Utica, N.Y.

In *Youth,* the hero of the allegory sails forth from a verdant shore where a fantastic palm tree, introduced into an otherwise fairly normal landscape, recalls certain picturizations of the Garden of Eden. Youth's guardian angel standing by the river bank and relinquishing him to the perils of life's voyage increases the resemblance of this episode to an Expulsion. In the preceding (and first) picture of the series, the Angel was at the helm of the boat as the infant hero sailed onto the River of Life where it flows from its mysterious source in a cavern. Now in charge of the tiller, Youth sails forward toward his vision of a fantastical domed and minareted concoction that rises like soap bubbles in the sky above distant mountains. The river is placid, and it flows between the banks of wooded fields where leaves, tree trunks, and ferns glitter like enamel and jewels. But in *Manhood* the river darkens and grows turbulent; it flows in rapids through canyons and gorges; the trees are blasted where they have survived at all; storms sweep through the sky and the murky gloom

is inhabited by the demons of temptation. (Barely visible in the upper center of the picture, they are demons of lust, intemperance, and suicide.) But far above, in a spot of light, the guardian Angel continues to watch, as the Man holds his hands in prayer. In the final scene the little boat has completed its hazardous passage and sails into the ocean of immortality with its now aged passenger still intact.

In the light of contemporary taste, these pictures must be accepted as the creations of an extraordinarily naïve spirit if they are not to appear pretentious. In that case, naïveté was remarkably widespread when Cole exhibited them* after their completion

---

* At the Art Union, formed to eliminate the dealer and thus increase the painter's percentage of the price of a picture. Public membership was by subscription. Members received prints and, by lottery, original paintings. Nearly 19,000 people all over the country finally joined. Oliver W. Larkin in his classic *Art and Life in America* has deftly characterized the Art Union as "joining the aesthetic with the acquisitive, and national pride with national zest for a bargain."

310. COLE: *The Voyage of Life: Manhood*, 1840. 52 x 78″. Munson-Williams-Proctor Institute, Utica, N.Y.

in 1840. Half a million people saw the pictures, and prints of them were sold by the thousands. The pictures themselves were commissioned by a wealthy banker, Sam Ward. Cole was enormously successful; *The Voyage of Life* was only one of many commissions of its kind, and his fellow artists in both painting and literature admired him (with a few exceptions) as much as did the public and his moneyed patrons. Durand's *Kindred Spirits* was painted in memory of Cole the year after his death; the kindred spirits represented in it are Cole and the American nature poet William Cullen Bryant. Bryant's poetry, like Cole's *Voyage of Life*, is at an awkward age, but it may not be long before the moral idealism in both cases becomes more conspicuous than the threadbareness and triteness that are just now so embarrassing.

But even today the two pictures we have just seen are remarkable for the consistency with which two contrasting moods are presented. Compositionally *Youth* and *Manhood* are carefully studied to make their points even if the points are obvious and labored. Cole held theories about the psychological effects of colors, believing that they corresponded to musical tones in their differences. The extremely literal detail in both pictures is more noticeable than the effort to combine these details in shapes and colors expressive in themselves. *Youth* is composed in horizontals and verticals, *Manhood* in whirls of dark around a vortex of light. Given a "modern" execution, either scheme could be abstracted into an arrangement of shape and color that might be regarded respectfully by critics who are unable to make concessions to the pictures as Cole conceived them. It is just possible that during a trip to Germany Cole became acquainted with Friedrich's pictures; there are obvious parallels between some passages in pictures like *Youth* and some in the German romantic's painting. It is certain that Cole knew and was influenced by the art of the seventeenth-century Italian romantic Salvator Rosa, in the darkly turbulent *Manhood*.

From the distance of a century that has made us suspicious of moralizing it is easy

311. COLE: *The Oxbow of the Connecticut,* 1836. 51½ x 76". Metropolitan Museum of Art, New York.

to patronize *The Voyage of Life,* but it is impertinent to extend this condescension to all of Cole's work (and indeed, as is usually done, to the whole Hudson River School). No apologies need be made for Cole where he is at his best, in his pure landscapes. The drama of his most famous one, *The Oxbow of the Connecticut* [311], is undeniable. It is broadly conceived in deep space; its minute detail is so beautifully articulated into large movements that the picture is first seen, inevitably, as a whole with its great sweeping forms, the wide swing of the river through the valley, the passage of clouds, the rise of hills across the stretch of meadows. It is only secondarily—but with further delight—that the intricate tooling of forms within forms, glittering in the sun, is discovered as one may discover through a magnifying glass unsuspected complications on the surface of a

leaf or a bit of tree bark, or with binoculars the infinite detail of meadows and hills reaching back into the distance, brought suddenly close as if they could be touched.

Cole was born in England. When his family migrated to America in 1818 he was only seventeen years old but had already worked as a textile designer and an engraver. In America he designed wallpaper and studied wood engraving; the meticulousness of this technique stayed with him as a painter and made him the most sharply detailed of the Hudson River School. When he was twenty-two Cole entered the Pennsylvania Academy of the Fine Arts in Philadelphia, the nation's first art school. He studied there for two years and then went to New York, where his landscapes were an immediate success. He made two trips back to Europe, the first in 1829–1831, the second in 1841–1842.

312.   CONSTABLE:
Stoke - by - Nayland,
1836. 49½ x 66⅜″.
Art Institute of Chi-
cago, W. W. Kimball
Collection.

English Romantic Landscape: Constable

In England Cole must surely have seen the work of a painter whose wild romantic grandeur could hardly have failed to appeal to him, Joseph Mallord William Turner (1775–1851), whose art reached its climax at just the time of Cole's second trip in such pictures as *The Slave Ship* [321] and *Steamer in a Snowstorm* [322]. He could have seen too the paintings of Turner's contemporary by birth who had died some years earlier, John Constable (1776–1837). Constable and Turner were a generation older than Cole, being contemporaries of Friedrich's and Allston's, but when Turner died at the age of seventy-six he had out-lived all these men, including Cole who had died three years before at the age of forty-seven. Chronology of this kind is not always important, but it is worth mention-ing here because Turner, dying just at mid-century, brought to its most conclusive ex-

pression the romantic spirit in landscape which we have been following in the work of these other men.

In Turner's case the nationalistic idea— Friedrich's Germanism, the Americanism of the Hudson River School, the Frenchness of the Barbizon painters—does not apply; as we will see in a moment, he abstracted from the romantic experience something like a universal expression. In the meanwhile Constable may be examined as a painter who was English through and through.

English landscape painting has charac-teristically a kind of domestic intimacy, a rich and cultivated gentleness, a warm and comfortable and not very analytical re-sponse to fields and forest and small bridges and secluded glens or open heaths where any wildness is so subdued as to resemble a garden plot in comparison with the Amer-ican wilderness, where any melancholy is so gentle as to be a happiness in comparison with the dark brooding of Friedrich's Ger-man ruins, deformed trees, and menacing

313. CONSTABLE: *The Hay Wain*, 1821. 51¼ x 73". National Gallery, London.

314. CONSTABLE: *Old Chain Pier, Brighton*, date unknown. 23½ x 38½". Philadelphia Museum of Art, Wilstach Collection.

315. CONSTABLE: Detail from Figure 314.

peaks. The people who inhabit this land-scape are thoroughly identified with its low hills, its trees, its cottages, which seem always to have been a part of it as much as its rocks and grasses. Its cathedrals, like the one on the horizon in Constable's *Stoke-by-Nayland* [312], aspire less to heaven than to peace on earth, and the clouds that move and swell through the same picture are not threatening but are a part of the fertility of drenched fields, the source of full streams and clear brooks.

This kind of Englishness, richly solid and lyrically sensitive without too heavy a metaphysical burden, received its literary expression in the English nature poets and its pictorial one in dozens of painters of picturesque landscape above whom Constable rises as a major artist surrounded by a crowd of minor attractive ones. He rises in fact as a major landscapist of any time or place, and his influence on painting beyond landscape has already been indicated in connection with the young Delacroix, who was led to new theories of color when he saw Constable's *Hay Wain* [313], which in turn were expanded by the impressionists.

Constable elaborated pictures like *The Hay Wain* and *Stoke-by-Nayland* from sketches made on the spots, usually very small and signed and dated on the back, which are not only notations of form and color but also of his immediate response to the subject. From these he elaborated the finished paintings methodically. But he was always intent, as Delacroix learned to be, upon retaining the effect of spontaneity that establishes the strongest communication between the painter and the observer. His method was brilliantly consistent. *Old Chain Pier, Brighton* [314], which was carried only into an intermediate stage of completion, reveals this consistency.

A sketch made on the spot has been enlarged and modified in whatever way seemed compositionally best, its outlines being sketched in lightly with pencil. Some of these pencil lines should be apparent in the illustrated detail [315]. The ground of the canvas itself is a warm tawny color. The major color notes have been struck in with a liberal use of paint; here and there a touch is applied with the palette knife. Constable

316. TURNER: *Falls of the Rhine at Schaffhausen, c.* 1806. 94 x 58½″. Museum of Fine Arts, Boston.

is "working the whole canvas at once"—bringing it everywhere to the same degree of completion before he goes on to the next stage in any of the parts. As a result, the picture as it is offers remarkable satisfactions, aside from its interest as a demonstration of method. It is unified by the consistency of the degree of suggestion with which its various parts are struck in, with the exception of the sail at the extreme right, which has been pushed a little further than the rest of the picture. If one part is more brilliantly struck in than another, it is the sky with its pure white clouds and its occasional spot of celestial blue. For Constable the sky with its moving clouds was the focal point of any landscape, structurally as well as expressively. In *Stoke-by-Nayland* as a typical fine example, sky, trees, and the forms of the earth are united as movements of form and light, and the sky is at once their origin and their climax.

Turner

It would be easy to go on from this point to exaggerate Constable's emphasis on such abstract elements in his art. They are present and they are important; they account for the difference between Constable and any other painter of taste, skill, discretion, and sensitive response to nature. But they do not dominate the pictures. They serve always as vehicles for the romantic interpretation of specific aspects of nature, remaining subservient to it. With Turner the case is reversed: as if to summarize the tradition of romantic landscape he reduced its elements of earth, air, water, and fire so very nearly to abstractions that the subject of a picture virtually disappears as a set of representational forms making up a scene. Nominally the subject of *Steamer in a Snowstorm* [322] is just that—a material object upon a body of water, surrounded by

317. TURNER: *Dido Building Carthage*, 1815. 60½ x 89½″. National Gallery, London.

air and revealed by light. Actually the canvas is a tempest of forms and colors that in themselves are emotionally expressive. They very nearly, if not quite, obliterate the pictorial subject to speak entirely for themselves.

Turner's progress from romantic realism toward romantic abstraction can be followed through a few pictures painted at intervals of roughly a dozen years. The early *Falls of the Rhine at Schaffhausen* [316], painted in 1806 thirty-six years before *Steamer in a Snowstorm*, is the sort of subject picturesque-romantic painters are fond of doing. It is potentially more Turneresque than some others, simply because the falls suggest the release of natural forces (an idea that preoccupies Turner later on), but on the whole this picture remains, rainbow and all, less an expressive one than a topographical souvenir with some romantic ex-

aggerations. It is one of the best pictures of its kind to be found anywhere, but it is of a fairly obvious kind. The carts, human figures, animals, barrels and bundles stretched across the lower foreground have the sort of tourist interest that is basic to the average picturesque landscape. Still, no average picture of this type would have expressed so dramatically the wild rush of water against the craggy rocks that thrust back into it.

Turner had an early success and was a prolific artist, but he found his way to completely individual expression rather slowly. *Dido Building Carthage* [317] is one of his large compositions close to the manner of Claude Lorrain, Poussin's more romantic counterpart. But Turner's semiclassical synthesis of architecture and landscape is much more than a mere skillful derivation. His first interest in the picture is in the

318. TURNER: *Ulysses Deriding Polyphemus*, 1829. 51 x 79". National Gallery, London.

319. TURNER: Detail from Figure 318.

270

320. TURNER: *Burning of the Houses of Parliament, c.* 1835. 36¼ x 48½″. Philadelphia Museum of Art, McFadden Collection.

drama of light. Turner's light is not light as the impressionists were to discover it, not a vibrant opalescent shimmer, but light as the element of fire, the fire of the sun. In *Dido Building Carthage* the sun blazes through the sky and burns a path down the center of the picture, consuming the stone bridge in the distance and impregnating the water with its brilliance.

Yet there is a contradiction here between the serenity of the picture's component forms—its temples and its trees—and the bursting energy of the sky. Turner did not hesitate long in making his choice between fire and marble. In *Ulysses Deriding Poly-*

phemus [318, 319], the sun at the horizon is an explosion of live coals spraying out across fantastic and agitated forms. Turner's romantic vision of the world as a cosmic union or struggle between the elements, dominated by fire and water, is finding its way to expression as it could not do in either *Falls of the Rhine* with its imposition of factual reference, no matter how grandiose, or in the forms of classicism, no matter how monumental or poetic.

In at least one actual event, however, Turner found a subject as good for his purpose as any invented one. He witnessed the great conflagration that destroyed the

321. TURNER: *The Slave Ship*, 1840. 35¾ x 48". Museum of Fine Arts, Boston.

Houses of Parliament in London in 1834 and recorded it in a combination of remembered fact and expressive invention [320]. The sky is a furnace; it is filled with leaping ragged areas of orange and yellow sprinkled with the vermilion flecks of floating cinders. Billows of purple smoke rise into the incandescent air; fragments of disintegrating architecture merge with it, and in the background the towers of Westminster Abbey glow as if molten. The water of the Thames is a flood of brass; boats filled with spectators lie upon it as diaphanous as shadows. The crowds on the bank are gauzy and unreal, the stone bridge melts away into the distant violence. The gas jets of the lamps surmounting its buttresses are as pale as evening lights against the sunlike intensity of the holocaust. Here Turner has reached a statement of his major theme; the dissolution of material reality into a universe where the elements are fused into one another in a way suggestive of primeval chaos. Water fuses with air, air and water fuse with fire, while earth, stone, and metal dissolve into all of them.

To express this fusion in terms of paint, Turner adopted an increasingly free technique where form was suggested by broader and broader areas of color, sometimes scrubbed in a film over the canvas, sometimes applied with heavy impasto, this latter especially in the passages where light appears most purely and most fiercely in its

322. TURNER: *Steamer in a Snowstorm*, 1842. 35½ x 47½″. National Gallery, London.

maximum concentration as fire. In a way this is impressionism, and Turner is often thought of as a proto-impressionist. He was all but unknown in France, but nearly twenty years after his death he was "discovered" by Monet and Pissarro, who were taking refuge in England during the German occupation of Paris in 1870. They seem to have been impressed, but it is difficult to say just how much direct influence Turner had on their subsequent development of impressionism as a technique for representing light; by hearsay their own statements on the question are contradictory. In the long run the question is not a very important one, since on important scores the connection is tenuous. For the impressionists, light was an optical phenomenon; for Turner, it was a cosmic force. The impressionists' light is part of a happy everyday world; Turner's is a manifestation of romantic mystery. Turner broke the surface of his painting into scrubs, films, dashes, and gobbets of color, and so did the impressionists. But for Turner color was first of all abstract and expressive; for the impressionists it was first of all descriptive of visual reality. We may make an exception of Monet's very late works, but the difference between Turner and impressionism is still the difference between *The Slave Ship* [321] and *Red Boats at Argenteuil* [207], the difference between the visionary and the commonplace, even when the commonplace is as beautiful as the impressionists discovered it could be. In other words, the impressionists were unaffected by Turner as far as any expressive factors were concerned, and as technical processes Turner's explosions of color have only incidental connections with impressionism's investigation of the spectrum on a semiscientific basis.

With *The Slave Ship* Turner's development toward a final abstract statement of romantic emotionalism was nearly complete. The title of the picture still clings to literary associations not inherent in the painting as an independent work of art, and it is with a kind of disappointment that we discover the narrative incident in the foreground right, where a shackled leg disappears into the water, surrounded by devouring fish. This bit of storytelling appears as an afterthought, a concession to popular standards in a picture that was not only complete without it but is reduced from grandeur to melodrama by its inclusion. But in *Steamer in a Snowstorm* [322] the majestic and terrible power of the elements, hinted at a third of a century before in the picturesque *Falls of the Rhine*, is at last expressed without the distractions of incidental trivia. A few blurred forms at the vortex of the composition, the ship and its mast, are a reminder that grandeur and mystery are a concept of man, that if the universe is vast and violent beyond man's comprehension, it is given meaning only because man, existing within it, has contemplated it with romantic imagination.

Popular Painting at Mid-century

Turner's grandeur is even more impressive when it is played against the limited imagination of the most popular painting of the day. Turner had established himself as a collector's painter early in his career, and he maintained that position until the end of his life. But the painting toward which the public gravitated was increasingly obvious and sentimental. This was even more true in England and Germany—and America—than it was in France; or rather, outside France the bourgeois preference for such pictures was less effectively countered by the theorizing and proselytizing of in-

323. WALDMÜLLER: *The Shattered Rose*, 1839. Panel, 25 x 19¼". *Galerie des Neunzehnten Jahrhunderts,* Vienna.

tellectuals pledged to the causes of the fine arts. In Germany especially there was an insatiable appetite for concise naturalistic statement. Already apparent in the detail of Friedrich's romantic landscapes, and insisted upon as an aesthetic principle by the Nazarenes, it persisted as an end in itself. At its lowest level it became a kind of stunt painting; at its highest it is summarized in the painting of men like Ferdinand Waldmüller (1793–1865), who may stand here as exemplifying any number of his contemporaries who painted from a similar point of view, although usually with less skill. Such painters were the darlings of popular favor during the last decades of Turner's life and on into the second half of the century after his death at its midpoint.

324. WALDMÜLLER: *The Picture Box Man*, 1847. 29½ x 36¼". *National-Museum*, Budapest.

Waldmüller was an Austrian academician who ranged over the field of portraiture, genre, and landscape. In *The Shattered Rose* [323], a better than average example of the kind of sentimental portrait with detailed accessories that was popular everywhere, the accessories are put into the service of what could be called, by stretching a point, a poetic or philosophical idea. The young girl holds in one hand a blossom that has dropped most of its petals onto the ground at her feet. For centuries the rose has been for poets the symbol of the beauty and the evanescence of youth. If Waldmüller's pretty little pictorialization of the idea is not asked to live up to its formidable literary ancestors, it may be enjoyed for its sentimental charm. The trouble is that we must suspect it of pretensions to something more than its obvious and simple-minded illustration of the familiar allegory, to which it adds nothing.

Painters like Waldmüller are at their best in the field of genre painting, where an interesting subject may most legitimately speak for itself if it is presented in recognizable detail. Within these limitations, which exclude imagination, ingenuity, or interpretive depth, Waldmüller's little account of children watching a traveling peepshow, *The Picture Box Man* [324], has everything—a lively and appealing subject, endless anecdotal proliferations, and impeccable technical finish.

In landscape also Waldmüller gave full value within the same limits. In *Morning* [325] he is so generous with detail that it seems a shame to ask that the picture be anything more than a catalogue of the facts of rustic landscape hung onto the peg of a subject of sorts, in this case the meeting of a rustic suitor and his sweetheart on a country road. And people in general, at the middle of the nineteenth century, asked nothing more. The artificiality of the scrubbed urchins in *The Picture Box Man* was preferable to Daumieresque consciousness of man as a being in the world. The pretty symbolism of the fallen petals in *The Rose* was enjoyable, while the extended implications of Goya's contrasts of pretty girls and evil old hags were disturbing. The lovers' meeting in a botanical encyclopedia, in *Morning*, involved neither the moody complications of a Friedrich nor the cosmic drama of a Turner. And in addition the Waldmüllers held for the public the appeal of stunt men; it was amazing the way they could make things look so real. A picture, then, was essentially a sleight-of-hand performance by which the painter created illusions involving jolly or sentimental anecdotes.

In England a denial of such superficial values was implicit in Turner's achievement, but he found no followers. When a group of painters organized a revolt shortly before his death, they formulated a curiously artificial aesthetic code of their own, with curious results. These were the painters of the Pre-Raphaelite Brotherhood, whose revolt we will see ushering in the second half of the century.

The American Scene: Bingham

While Turner was painting in England and the Hudson River men were revealing a new American spirit through American landscape, other painters were making explicit records of aspects of the American scene that were unique to it. Before the middle of the century John James Audubon (1785–1851) had made his magnificent collection of the *Birds of America*, where ornithological record was combined with unwavering brilliance of draughtsmanship and design. George Catlin (1796–1872) had lived with American Indian tribes in order to paint some 300 portraits of them and nearly 200 scenes from their daily life. William Sidney Mount (1807–1868) had discovered that American genre subjects could be just as picturesque, just as sentimental, and just as saleable as European ones, a discovery that was developed during the rest of the century by such painters as Eastman Johnson (1824–1906). But it remained for a man named George Caleb Bingham (1811–1879) to bring to scenes

325. WALDMÜLLER: *Morning*, 1862–63. Panel, 22½ x 27¾″. *Historisches Museum der Stadt Wien*, Vienna.

of American life the indigenous feeling that the Hudson River painters brought to its landscape.

Bingham was born in Virginia; while he was a child the family moved to Missouri. He was first a cabinetmaker's apprentice, then a student of law, then a student of theology, before he discovered that he was a painter. There is some doubt as to exactly what his earliest training was. Possibly he studied for a while with a painter named Chester Harding. But when he set himself up as a portraitist in St. Louis he was essentially self-trained. Later he studied briefly at the Pennsylvania Academy of the Fine Arts, but his style retained always a flavor of the primitivism associated with the early American tradition. He was by no means a primitive painter in the way Edward Hicks was, but the flavor is there. Much of it was lost after he studied for three years in Düsseldorf, but fortunately he did not go there until he was forty-six. In his best work he is a purely American artist of the first half of the century, although he painted for another twenty years after his return from Europe in 1859.

Bingham the painter has been compared with Mark Twain the writer. Bingham's

326. BINGHAM: *Fur Traders Descending the Missouri, c.* 1845. 29 x 36½″. Metropolitan Museum of Art, New York, Morris K. Jessup Fund.

pictures of life in the country or the towns and small cities of the Middle West draw their subject matter, and their cast of characters, from the same sources Mark Twain used in *Tom Sawyer* and *Huckleberry Finn*. A similarity, too, is the fact that both men were popular as inventors of pure narrative and humor, and came into tardy recognition for the deeper content underlying their engaging surfaces. On the face of it, *Huckleberry Finn* is an adventure story spiced with rustic humor and picturesque locale. At the same level, Bingham's *Fur Traders Descending the Missouri* [326] is a genre painting. But the story of Huck's journey down the Mississippi is also poetic and philosophical; so, too, are the evocations of Bingham's representation of a man, a boy, and a pet fox in a dugout canoe.

The quiet stretches of water and sky, the shadowy island in the distance, the spare-

ness and gentleness with which these meager elements are selected and arranged into a picture, go far beyond objective record of picturesque fact. In a special way *Fur Traders Descending the Missouri* is another statement of the relationship of man to a primal and benevolent wilderness, the theme of the Hudson River painters. But as it is treated here, the theme is at once more idyllic and more down to earth, at once more subtle and less artificial. In spite of its subject drawn from contemporary life, in spite of local picturesque details realistically shown, the picture is almost classical in its elimination of unnecessary incidentals to create a timeless image. This may be exaggerating a point, and it is improbable that Bingham thought of his picture in this way, but the point is there, and it does a great deal to account for the serenity of a picture that could be transformed into mere record or mere narrative by a few additions and complications. The figures of the youth and the rough old man, the great stretch of river and sky, are not symbolical—it would be a mistake to try to make symbols of them—but if the simplicity of *Fur Traders Descending the Missouri* is compared with the highflown trumpery of Cole's *Voyage of Life* there are certain overlappings of meaning. Cole presents his allegory in specific and didactic, and hence rigidly limited, terms. Bingham, without moralizing or allegorizing, opens up a much wider area of reflection. This does not have to mean that one picture is "better" or "worse" than another, but it does mean that where Cole was ambitious to make a grand statement, he ended with a small one, while Bingham did the reverse: in what appears to be the simple presentation of an unpretentious subject, we discover wide extensions of meaning. The two pictures, incidentally, were painted within a few years of one another, *The Voyage of Life* in 1840, *Fur Traders* about 1845.

Fur Traders Descending the Missouri is exceptional even in Bingham's work for its gentleness. But again and again he takes scenes from the life of the expanding American frontier and reveals the vitality of the epoch. His genius lay in his ability to reveal a kind of grandeur through the trivia that made it up. In *The Wood Boat* [327] he does not pretend that the boatmen who transported wood down the river were grand and noble men, although they may have been happy and roughly healthy ones. But in painting them grouped on the river bank alongside their loaded barges, he creates forms of monumental character and disposes them in logical, monumental relationships to one another in such a way that the sum of picturesque details is more than its parts. Bingham's "classicism"—it is important to keep the word in quotation marks —may be compared to that of Poussin in *Shepherds in Arcady* [415]: Poussin is a seventeenth-century intellectual synthesizing a philosophical dream of classical antiquity while Bingham is a nineteenth-century provincial recording the life around him. Yet in their integration of human and landscape forms into a monumental whole,

327. BINGHAM: *The Wood Boat, c.* 1850. 24¾ x 29⅝". City Art Museum, St. Louis.

the two painters have gone about the creation of a picture in much the same way. Bingham's relationship to three other seventeenth-century French painters, the brothers Le Nain, is even closer. Like him, they painted genre subjects and combined realism, monumentality, and a primitive flavor in pictures that rise above the temporary and specific nature of their subject matter.

Bingham's pictures were tremendously popular and were sold by the thousands in engraved reproductions. His "election series" was aimed at the popular market and these pictures [328] are full of roistering narrative incident. Here it is a bit of a strain to find the "grandeur" behind the scenes, although Bingham's most enthusiastic admirers are able to do so. Grandeur aside, the election series give vital expression to the vigor and enthusiasm of their period. Bingham shows in them that if he can compose a quiet scene of a man, a boy, and a fox in a dugout canoe, with sensitive economy, he can also manipulate dozens of figures on a crowded stage. He is so logical in his distribution of solid forms in space that a ground plan could be drawn of any one of the election pictures, with each figure and each structure occupying its own

328. BINGHAM: *The County Election*, 1851–52. 35⁷⁄₁₆ x 48¾". City Art Museum, St. Louis.

area comfortably. In other words, Bingham's control of an optical third dimension is so complete that his painted scenes could be reconstructed as physically three-dimensional ones. This is a considerable technical feat in itself, but it is given point by the fact that the arrangements are not only physically logical but characteristically expressive. Each of his characters is conceived not only as a physical mass but as a consistent personality, and the interplay of personalities is as clear as their relationship in space. The shortcoming is that the personality types are so obvious as to be trite, too true to type to be real or very interesting. In the election pictures Bingham is like a stage designer and director. He constructs a set and then fills it with expressive action. But his actors are not always talented.

Bingham was the last American painter of major stature to develop relatively free of European influence. Obviously the word "relatively" is an important one. In a civilization that began as an adjunct to Europe's it would be impossible to find a purely native tradition in colonials and their descendants. But because he was so isolated from the more sophisticated American centers, because he had to discover so many things for himself in his relative separation from European developments, and because he used what he discovered to interpret subject matter unique to his world, Bingham is emphatically an American artist. The generation of painters that followed him in the second half of the century were less so, partly because it became easier for Americans to study in Europe, as all of them wanted to do, but largely because America itself had conquered its frontiers by that time and the conditions, and the spirit, that produced Bingham, were fading,

CHAPTER 9

Outside France, 1850–1900

The Pre-Raphaelite Ideal

Romanticism as a state of mind, an emotional attitude toward life, is peculiar to no single period. Romanticism as an organized revolt to express and propagandize an attitude is peculiar to the nineteenth century. Of all the forms this revolt assumed, Pre-Raphaelitism was the most idealistic, but it was also self-defeating.

Pre-Raphaelitism was a confusion of ingredients including revolt against the times, adulation of the middle ages, noble aesthetic aspirations, religious yearning, sententious moralizing, morbid sentimentality, historical delusions, faulty archaeology, and debilitating literary preoccupations. This is a damning list, yet the Pre-Raphaelites had a unique importance in the conservative and placid world of English art. As the only group dedicated to rebellion against the *status quo*, they injected a leavening influence that has affected English painting and writing ever since, even when the Pre-Raphaelites are forgotten as its source.

Of all romantics, the Pre-Raphaelites were the ones whose obsession with the past rose most specifically from their horror of the present. England in the second half of the nineteenth century was omnipotently the center of the Industrial Revolution, swelling with wealth and wholeheartedly dedicated to materialism. The great Victorian age was under way with all its complacency and adventurousness, its practical idealism and social abuses, its elegance and vulgarity, its stolid virtue and its virtuous aberrations. The Queen had been crowned in 1837; when she would die sixty-four years later in the first year of the twentieth century, very few of her subjects would be

329. HUNT: *Dante Gabriel Rossetti*, repetition of a portrait dated 1853. 11 x 8½". Private collection, England.

able to remember clearly a time when she had not been at the head of a country devoted to materialism as a way of life. The Pre-Raphaelites questioned this way of life, and although the reform they proposed now seems misled, even pathetic, they at least exposed the problem and proposed a solution of sorts.

Fundamentally the question was whether man's spirit could flourish when his life was dominated by commerce, whether it could blossom in an air contaminated by the smoke of factories. The Pre-Raphaelites' answer was that it could not, an answer that they saw tangibly obvious in the sordidness of industrial slums, in the dreary reaches of respectable bourgeois life given over to the pursuit of money and animal comforts, in the ugliness of the objects the new machines were turning out, and in the artificiality of the fine arts, which seemed starved of nourishment. But unfortunately

they sought to answer the question by running away from it, by returning to the surface forms of past glories rather than searching out new ones. Thus they were defeated before they began, and ended by proving nothing definitely except that it is difficult to go very far forward by walking backward. In retrospect we see them floundering in a blind alley, and at the moment their art is at an excruciatingly awkward age. Their shortcomings are pathetically apparent and their virtues have become unfashionable. It is as much as a critical reputation is worth to concede them a kind word on their own terms, for their art is devoid of the kinds of abstract formal and structural values that are taken for granted today as the starting point for critical evaluations. The only element that can save them, their expressive intensity, is obscured by a factor intolerable to the contemporary aesthetic, their literary sentimentalism.

As a group, the Pre-Raphaelites were contemporaries of the older impressionists, such as Manet, Pissarro, and Degas, which means that they must stand against extraordinary competition. They were only a decade older than Cézanne, yet they might have been painting in another century. Indeed they tried to do so, and the century they had in mind was the fifteenth, in Italy, as well as the even more remote ones of Dante and the Arthurian legends. While French painters were founding a new art, the Pre-Raphaelites tried to return to the craftsmanship and (as they imagined them) the spiritual values of the late middle ages and the early Renaissance. If they were aware that the German Nazarenes had tried and failed to do the same thing, they did not profit from the warning.

The enthusiasm and the high ideals, the impracticality and the failure, of Pre-Raphaelitism were symbolized when several of the Brotherhood set out to decorate the library of the Oxford Union in 1857. Emulating, they believed, the fifteenth-century Italians who covered the walls of Florentine churches with frescoes, they set about doing so in the library, convinced that an aesthetic resurrection was at hand. The circumstances seemed ideal, since the building itself was an imitation of a medie-

How Sir Galahad, Sir Bors, & Sir Percival were fed with the Sancgreal, but Sir Percival's Sister died by the way.

330. ROSSETTI: *How Sir Galahad, Sir Bors & Sir Percival were fed, etc.,* 1864. Water-color, 11½ x 16½". Tate Gallery, London.

val one, and the Pre-Raphaelites were banded together as fellow craftsmen unified by moral principle, rather than as effete painters ambitious for conventional success in an age of industry and commerce. But their paint was hardly on the walls before it began to chip, flake, and peel. Their fresco technique was as unsound as their social theorizing. The whole thing was a disaster, from enthusiastic beginning to humiliating finish.

Rossetti

In spite of its social theorizing, Pre-Raphaelitism was a variety of escapism, having less to do with objections to the industrialized world than with a feeling of revulsion for the world on any terms, a neurotic denial of life, a yearning for a never-never land where the soul was freed from the rebuffs and responsibilities of daily living. The leader of the movement, Dante Gabriel Rossetti (1828–1882), was especially sub-

ject to the old romantic delusion that confuses emotional indulgence with spiritual nourishment. But in his poems and his swooning visionary paintings he was the most expressive member of the Brotherhood, because he was the most personal and most emotional interpreter of an ideal to which, in the end, only personal emotionalism could give a reason for being.

Rossetti was the center of the founding members—in 1848—of the secret Brotherhood, which immediately became not secret at all. The two other most important founding members were John Everett Millais (1829–1896) and William Holman Hunt (1827–1910). Hunt's portrait of Rossetti [329] with its enormously enlarged eyes seems to try to force onto a not exceptional face the exceptional quality of inward vision. This same forcing is characteristic of Rossetti's own pictures; he overplayed a minor talent. In a little picture with the enormous title *How Sir Galahad, Sir Bors, & Sir Percival were fed with the Sancgreal; but Sir Percival's Sister died by the way*

331. ROSSETTI: *Jane Burden*, 1858. Crayon, 17 x 13″. National Gallery of Ireland, Dublin.

332. ROSSETTI: *Elizabeth Siddal*, date unknown. Silverpoint, 6½ x 4½″. Collection Mr. and Mrs. Gilbert McC. Troxell, New Haven, Conn.

[330] the vision never quite coalesces although it is full of images that should be evocative. The band of haloed angels, the handsome knights, the radiant lilies, the field sprinkled with little flowers, the stuffs of the robes so conscientiously patterned, never sing together. One waits for something to happen, and nothing does. The clutter of medieval props and costumes ends as an amateur pageant. The truth is that Rossetti was technically only moderately well equipped. He was only feeble to fair as a draughtsman, and compositionally he falls into clichés. The deadly taint of amateurishness infects his art because his technical limitations are disharmonious with the sophistication of his effort.

Rossetti came closest to fulfillment when dealing with the subject that was his true obsession: the vision of a woman who was personified for him first by his wife, Elizabeth Siddal [332], then by Jane Burden [331], who became the wife of his friend William Morris. His marriage with Elizabeth Siddal was filled with quarrels and irritations, but he loved to look at her and to draw her. When he fell in love with Mrs. Morris years later, he believed that he had always been in love with her since the Pre-Raphaelites had first seen her in the audience at a theater matinee. They were working on the Oxford Union library murals at that time and asked her to pose for them; Rossetti's drawing illustrated here is probably the first he made of her. Elizabeth Siddal and Jane Burden bore some resemblance to one another, and every woman Rossetti painted, even when he used other models, resembled the two of them. He was in love with a facial type that enchanted him. Jane Burden Morris most triumphantly embodied it, with her great thick masses of undulating hair, her tremendous brooding eyes, her heavy rather swollen neck, and her small, full, exaggeratedly curling mouth. When Rossetti is fully given over to the adoration of this type he is at his best.

The fascination Jane Burden's face held for the Pre-Raphaelites must have been in part that it recalled the facial types in pictures by certain early Renaissance masters they admired, such as Fra Filippo Lippi, Verrocchio, and Botticelli. Botticelli was virtually rediscovered by the Pre-Raphaelites; the inward gaze, the long neck, the strongly defined jaw, and the sinuous convolutions of hair in Botticelli's *Venus* [1] have their counterparts in pictures like *The Bride* (sometimes called *The Beloved*) [333], although the linear rhythms so electric in Botticelli have become flaccid in Rossetti. Botticelli's vital grace is reduced to anemic languor. It would be pleasant to be able to say that as Rossetti's obsession continued his perceptions deepened and his vision took new and more profound form; instead, he followed a course of repetitious elaboration. *The Bride* even offers the type in triplicate, swathed in the complications of arts-and-crafts fabric and jewels with which Rossetti loved to bedeck his enchantresses. Even his knights are Mrs. Morris in other costumes.

William Morris and the Arts and Crafts

William Morris (1834–1896) had an importance beyond his position as the husband of Rossetti's Jane Burden. He was originally trained as an architect; as a poet he still has a respectable reputation; as a painter he worked in a manner close to Rossetti's; but as the founder of the Arts and Crafts Movement he made as enduring a contribution as any connected with Pre-Raphaelitism.

In 1851, England held the epoch-making fair called the Great Exhibition of the Works of Industry of All Nations, when

333. ROSSETTI: *The Bride*, 1865. 32½ x 30″. Tate Gallery, London.

some of the most preposterous objects ever created by man were displayed in one of the most beautiful and important structures of the century. The Crystal Palace was a sudden, brilliant, glittering, architectural sport, one of the first modern buildings, a prophecy of buildings that would not be built for another century. It was created by force of circumstance.

The problem was to erect a structure large enough to house the tens of thousands of exhibits of the fair and to construct it quickly and not too expensively. A greenhouse designer, Joseph Paxton, created an open web of cast-iron girders, wrought-iron trusses, and jointed iron pipes of standard measurements, then covered this thin, light skeleton with a skin of glass. The Crystal Palace, built in Hyde Park around great living trees [334] became, on the interior, a fantasy. Paxton's solution to the architectural problem was utterly direct

334. JOSEPH PAXTON, architect: Transept of the Crystal Palace. Color lithograph by J. Nash, 1851–54. 13½ x 19⅛″. From *Dickenson's Comprehensive Pictures of the Great Exhibition*, London, 1854.

and practical, yet the final effect was fairy-like, enchanted. The Crystal Palace was a sensation, but its architectural implications were missed. It was regarded as a wonderful and fantastic novelty rather than as the demonstration of a new aesthetic in architecture, which it was.

Among other things, the Crystal Palace was the world's first prefabricated building. The iron units were cast in foundries all over England, their lengths being determined by the largest practical size in which it was possible to manufacture the glass panes that would sheath the skeleton cage. These panes also were manufactured in many places, and the business of assembling the huge structure from the multiplication of a few unit parts was rapid and simple. After the exhibition, the building was dismantled and re-erected in Kensington, where it served as a museum and concert hall until, as late as 1936, it was destroyed

by fire (its floors and partitions having been of wood).

The Crystal Palace was potentially the source of the "functional" architecture of the twentieth century, but to English eyes in 1851 it was not, strictly speaking, architecture at all. The old Houses of Parliament that had burned (and supplied Turner with a subject for painting) were at just this time being replaced by a new structure in the Gothic style. This was *real* architecture—meaning that it drew first from the past, then forced past forms into some kind of workable arrangement with the contemporary world. In the case of the Houses of Parliament there was more justification than usual for such an idea, since the older structure had not been completely destroyed and the remaining genuinely medieval parts were to be incorporated into the new building. Also, the old structure had for a long time been synonymous with the

336. "Modernized" English Gothic project by M. P. Hapgood, Boston.

Three proposals for the completion of the Washington Monument, from *The American Art Review,* Vol. I, 1879–80. 335 *(left)*. Classical project by Paul Schulze, Washington, D.C.

337. "Modern French Renaissance with strong points of affinity with some of the better Hindu Pagodas" project by anonymous California architect.

solid tradition of English government, and the new one must be a symbolical monument as well as a usable structure. The building, as finally completed, was an impressive massing of elements—the masterpiece, certainly, of neo-Gothic architecture, and as good a defense as could be offered for the use of Gothic forms in a century to which they were foreign.

But the forms of the past were seldom so well understood. Architecture was degenerating into the ornamentation of structure, and it was even so defined in a handbook of the period. The old joke goes that the client might employ a contractor to devise a structure that would stand up and then call in a designer to "put on the architecture." This is what very nearly happened in the United States when the Washington Monument was completed after standing half finished for years because of lack of funds. (The dividing line between the early and later parts of the monument may still be seen in the slight difference of the

338. "Irish" Chair.

339. Bedstead.

Four items from *The Art Journal Illustrated Catalogue of the Great Exhibition, 1851.*

340. Baby's Bassinet.

341. Ornamental Razor.

stone.) When funds were available for its completion, ideas of architecture had "advanced" to the point where the simplicity of the original design seemed primitive. Three proposed remedies are shown here [335, 336, and 337]; respectively, they are an elaborated neo-classical design surmounted by a statue of Washington, a respectable Gothic tower surmounted by an angel, and a curious concoction of a little bit of everything surmounted by an allegorical figure. The article in *The Art Journal* accompanying the publication of these designs expressed uneasiness about the appropriateness of the Gothic design as a memorial to the father of the new country —not because it was Gothic, but because it was *English* Gothic.

But if architecture suffered through the perversion and distortion of the forms of the past, it existed in purity compared with the flood of objects now being created by machines, and even in handmade objects. Designer–craftsmen had reached the nadir of their art, and the illustrated catalogue of furniture and bric-a-brac exhibited by all nations in the Crystal Palace (with England as the chief offender) has become a standard chamber of the most hilarious horrors in the history of design. Such objects as the "Irish" chair, with its two arms in the form of Irish wolfhounds, one rising, one reclining [338]; the "rich and costly bedstead," marking the initial appearance in the English language of the adjective *costly* as one of aesthetic description [339]; the baby's bassinet made from papier-mâché, which seems to be balanced on a large brooch [340]; and such fantasies as ornamental razors [341]—these were part of the aesthetic Grand Guignol that had just inspired the formation of the Pre-Raphaelite Brotherhood.

Morris's Arts and Crafts Movement shared the general Pre-Raphaelite fault of retreat rather than advance: he tried to return to the purity of hand craftsmanship in the face of the machine. The modern style in decoration, when it finally evolved, was to be based on virtues inherent in the machine rather than on a return to virtues the machine seemed to have perverted. But the Arts and Crafts Movement at least called attention to this perversion and created objects where design and usability were more important than vulgar elaborations. Morris tried to revive the crafts of hand weaving, cabinetmaking, metal work, stained glass, even the hand printed and illuminated manuscript. But a new society demanding thousands upon thousands of repetitions of an object could not be supplied by hand craftsmanship, and Morris was able to shed only a little light in the general darkness. In the end his contribution was less in the objects he designed and made than in his stirring of an awareness that design could be a quality inherent in the material and the making of an object, as opposed to design as used in the objects we have just seen, where motifs drawn from everywhere were murderously debauched and plastered at random over any saleable object.*

Like the other Pre-Raphaelites, Morris saw the middle ages and the early Renaissance as a paradise where every object was beautiful. His vision of it in paintings, such as *La Belle Yseult* [342], filled with the kind of fabric and furniture he designed, does seem a little crowded. The same arty clutter characterizes such Morris interiors as have survived. But because the Arts and Crafts Movement respected the materials it worked with, it held the seed of a true revival. It remained for this seed to be fertilized later by designers who accepted the present instead of holding to Morris's nostalgic veneration of the past. In 1862 Morris founded his own firm, specializing in handcrafts for the decoration of churches. Here, where his medievalism was most appropriate and where handcraft could supply the market, he made his great success.

---

* The Pre-Raphaelites were not alone in their recognition of the low state of design. Even the compiler of the illustrated catalogue for the exhibition seems to have suspected that some of the objects were a little over-elaborate. And it would be chastening for anyone who enjoys laughing at the Crystal Palace exhibits to compare them with a similar quantity of furniture and bric-a-brac by modern manufacturers. These twentieth-century items would draw upon a different set of motifs—streamlined ones and so on—but many of them would be just as bad and unusable as, and much more shoddy than, their Victorian counterparts.

342. MORRIS: *La Belle Yseult*, 1858. 28⅛ x 20″. Tate Gallery, London.

343. BURNE-JONES: *The Prioress' Tale*, 1869–98, original version, 1859. Watercolor, 40½ x 25″. Wilmington Society of Fine Arts, Samuel and Mary R. Bancroft Collection.

Rossetti's Followers

Rossetti exerted enough influence to make what might be called Rossetti-ism a subdivision within the Pre-Raphaelite movement. The most immediate of his followers was Edward Burne-Jones (1833–1898), one of several painters who, like Morris, joined the founding brothers in a second wave. He was one of Morris's most enthusiastic workers in stained glass and tapestries, and the two-dimensional disciplines imposed by these techniques affected his style in painting. The ornamental flatness of *The Prioress' Tale* [343] reflects his solid professionalism as a designer. The long panel, a favorite shape with Burne-

Jones, comes of course from stained glass windows, and Burne-Jones's rich color is more like dyed wools than painted canvas. Even more than Rossetti he was unabashed in lifting elements wholesale from the painters and craftsmen who invented them so long before. But he was also a better workman than Rossetti.

Like so much Pre-Raphaelite work, *The Prioress' Tale* is a curious amalgam, combining a Chaucerian subject with Italianate forms, two vigorous if not very compatible sources of inspiration watered down with precious aestheticism. The composition was originally designed in 1859 for a cabinet belonging to William Morris, and the work was done in Morris's house at 17 Red

344. ALMA-TADEMA: *A Reading from Homer, c.* 1885. 36 x 72⅜". Philadelphia Museum of Art, George W. Elkins Collection.

345. WATTS: *Hope*, 1885. 55½ x 43¼". Tate Gallery, London.

Lion Square, a residence that served as a manifesto by demonstration of his and the Pre-Raphaelites' theories. Ten years later Burne-Jones began the watercolor replica illustrated here. Nearly thirty years after that he picked it up again and completed it, in 1898, the year of his death, and sent it to Paris, where it was exhibited in the Exposition of 1900. (The background was altered from the cabinet panel, a city scene replacing a landscape.) In her *Memorial* of her husband, Lady Burne-Jones wrote that while he was painting the poppies in the foreground of the picture someone remarked upon the importance of the first lines in a composition. "Yes," said Burne-Jones, "they come straight from the heart. You see how the flowers come at intervals like those in a tune." He sang, pointing to the poppies one after the other, "La, La, La, La." Like other romantics, the Pre-Raphaelites were fond of such analogies between the arts. Architecture was "frozen music" and so on. The American lady who later acquired *The Prioress' Tale* saw Burne-Jones at work on it in his studio shortly before his death, and reported that he had looked as if he "were seeing beyond this earth."

346. BEARDSLEY: "The Mysterious Rose Garden," from *The Yellow Book*, Vol. IV, January 1895.

clustered, there open, with its movement here quickening, there slowing, is nicely adjusted along the major curve running from top to bottom of the long panel.

Among painters not at all connected with the movement some Rossetti influence is apparent for half a century. Even so popular and conventional a man as Lawrence Alma-Tadema (1836–1912) was affected. In *A Reading from Homer* [344] the young lady in the uncomfortable position on the marble bench (Alma-Tadema was famous for his rendition of marble) is at least a cousin to Jane Burden. George Frederick Watts (1817–1904) was an acquaintance of Burne-Jones, and in his familiar *Hope* [345] he draws upon him and through him upon Rossetti. Watts shared the anti-materialist idealism professed by the Pre-Raphaelites and frequently, as in *Hope*, gave it touching expression, although he was an uneven painter who never quite found himself except for a moment in occasional pictures like this one. Toward the end of the century, Aubrey Beardsley (1872–1898) picked up Rossetti's neurotic types and the Pre-Raphaelite arts-and-crafts decor, and incorporated them into the *fin-de-siècle* preciousness [346] that was the most audacious revolt of the English intelligentsia against the now obese smugness of the Victorian age on the point of decline. And even in the twentieth century Stanley Spencer (1891–   ) echoes Rossetti and the fellow founding brothers, Hunt and Millais.

Although much of his work is nearly as dated as these mawkish aestheticisms, Burne-Jones saves himself again and again for anyone willing to look at his pictures without taking the current stand that all Pre-Raphaelite painting is ludicrous *per se*. Having been introduced to Botticelli's art by Rossetti, Burne-Jones went on to add such formidable and hard-bitten masters as Signorelli and Mantegna to those he studied. He studied them intelligently and profitably. In *The Golden Stairs* [583] he constructed a picture with more decision, variety, and subtlety than Rossetti ever commanded. The rhythmic grouping, here

Hunt, Millais, and Ruskin

William Holman Hunt demonstrated how deadly the Pre-Raphaelite formula could become in the hands of a flatly common-place intelligence; John Everett Millais showed for a while that it might have risen above itself, then he abandoned Pre-Raphaelitism to settle for a resounding academic success; the writer and critic John Ruskin (1819–1900) was the public defender of the Pre-Raphaelite cause.

Ruskin was only a little older than the Pre-Raphaelites—about ten years—but when he appeared as their champion he had already established himself as a critic. At sixteen he had discovered Turner, understanding the aspects of Turner's art that were not apparent to conventional critics or, when apparent, were puzzling or offensive to academic taste. Five years before the founding of the Pre-Raphaelite Brotherhood, Ruskin had published the first volume of his *Modern Painters*, a many-volumed series that began as an interpretation and defense of Turner. In celebration of the event (Ruskin was twenty-four years old) his father bought *The Slave Ship* for him. Turner died just as the Pre-Raphaelite movement was getting under way.

Ruskin loved medieval and early Renaissance Italy as passionately as the Pre-Raphaelites did. Unlike them, he recognized the dangers of medievalism, prophesying that if the painters' interest in the early artists led them into imitation of the past they would "come to nothing." His advice to painters to "Go to nature, rejecting nothing, selecting nothing, and scorning nothing," was misinterpreted as meaning that the painter should become as nearly as possible a sharp-focus photographer. Actually, Ruskin had offered this advice to beginners only; otherwise it is obviously altogether opposed to his understanding of Turner, and he certainly understood that the selection of detail in early Italian painting was more important than the imitation of nature. But Hunt, especially, "rejected nothing, selected nothing, and scorned nothing" in his moralistic charades.

He based his art on the idea that a *tableau-vivant* should be set up and then reproduced with excruciating complication. Added to his sentential, sentimental moralizing, this idea produced pictures like *The Awakening Conscience* [347], where a kept woman is shown rising from her paramour's lap as she experiences a sudden moral revelation. The sinful pair have been singing at the piano. Hunt even had a specific song in mind, Thomas Moore's "The Light of Other Days," and explained that "the woman is recalling the memory of her childish home, and breaking away from the gilded cage with a startled holy resolve, while her shallow companion sings on, ignorantly intensifying her repentant

347. HUNT: *The Awakening Conscience*, 1855. 29¾ x 21⅝". Collection Sir Colin Anderson, London.

purpose." As an added fillip he designed a frame to go with the picture, decorating it with marigolds, the symbol of sorrow, and ringing bells, the symbol of warning. To choose this particular picture as an example of Hunt's work, offering as it does every opportunity for a field day at his expense, would be unfair except that the picture is one of Hunt's typical productions in its meticulous muddle of pictorial detail and philosophical absurdity. By a cruel reversal, it has become an extreme example of exactly the kind of painting the Pre-Raphaelites objected to, in its artificiality and its unimaginative presentation of a narrative subject. But if it does nothing else it reveals by contrast the imaginative intensity of Rossetti and the discretion of Millais.

Millais also followed the doctrine of acutely imitative detail, but more thought-

348. MILLAIS: *Christ in the House of His Parents* (*The Carpenter's Shop*), 1850. 33½ x 54". Tate Gallery, London.

fully than Hunt. It is true that in Millais's *Christ in the House of His Parents* [348] there are too many shavings on the floor, too many sheep in the pen, too many folds in the garments, too many nicks and cracks in the table, too many microscopically executed incidentals everywhere distracting from the main point. Probably this is because the main point was foreign to the experience of the painter in the nineteenth century. The picture shows the child Christ prophetically wounded in the hands, but the nominally mystical subject becomes not much more than another piece of storytelling in a picturesque genre setting. The void left by the absence of mystical conviction must be filled with little things like shavings. But Millais has compensated as far as he can by an expert unification of the picture space into areas broad and simple enough to hold all these incidental accessories within compositional bounds, and he has tinted these areas in rich decorative colors (whereas Hunt's colors are merely bright.) The picture is admirable in every way except the way that is most important. It is too easy to see in each of the figures a model posed in the studio,

impossible to feel that any of them is a participant in a mystical event. The extreme naturalism was consciously adopted in an effort to represent the scene without the sentimental trumpery of the day, a sound idea which, if backed up by unquestioning faith rather than by the self-consciousness of an adopted theory, might have given the picture the force and conviction it lacks. But as the picture stands, it reveals Millais for what he was, a prodigious technician applying his skill to a subject foreign to his emotional experience. The literalness that is now bothersome because it serves no expressive end offended the public of the time because it seemed irreverent, and the picture's subtitle, *The Carpenter's Shop*, was given it in derision.

But technical skill at Millais's level could not fail to appeal to a public who regarded a painter first of all as a performer. And his own background of prosperous respectability and his temperamental affinity for graceful society made him an outlander in the Pre-Raphaelite camp. Millais was by nature neither a bohemian nor a dissenter; popular success was inevitable for him, and he not only achieved it but finally became

349. MILLAIS: *Mr. James Wyatt and His Granddaughter Mary*, 1849. Panel, 13⅞ x 17¾".
Private collection, England.

president of the Royal Academy. His de-
fection was a mortal blow to the Brotherhood. Popular success was badly out of key
with their dedication to revolt against the
times; it violated the fundamental concept
of the Pre-Raphaelite as a being isolated
from the vulgarities of the contemporary
world. Just as the French romantics established the bohemian concept of the artist
still current in Paris—the starveling genius
in a left-bank studio, leading a life half gay
and half tragic—so the Pre-Raphaelites initiated the tradition in Bloomsbury and
Soho, where the artist may defy convention
as a matter of principle, or of convenience,
or of habit.

As his success increased, Millais's work
became increasingly shallow, but when he
is at his best Millais is the most satisfying
of the Pre-Raphaelites because he is the
least pretentious. Occasionally he fulfills
cleanly and brilliantly his full potential as

a superb technician and an agreeable if not
profound artist. The delight of a picture
like his double portrait of *Mr. James Wyatt
and His Granddaughter Mary* [349] is its
completeness and its consistency within its
limiting boundaries. Without straining to
give more than he has to offer, Millais records sympathetically the appearance of
two people in their habitat. Since each of
the multitude of objects represented in the
picture is meaningful through its association with the sitters, the mass of detail is
pleasurable to explore, in contrast with the
cluttered paraphernalia of *Awakening Conscience* or the neatly arranged stage props
and costumes of *Christ in the House of His
Parents*. This is a comparison in one direction. In another, for instance with another
family portrait, Degas's *Bellelli Family*
[219], *James Wyatt and His Granddaughter Mary* does not come off so well. But
such a comparison might not be quite fair,

350. Frith: *Derby Day*, 1856–58. 40 x 88″. Tate Gallery, London.

351. Frith: Detail from Figure 350.

either to Millais or to ourselves. Painting offers many different kinds of pleasure, and it would be wearing if all painters were giants. In the constant shifting of critical reappraisals there is even a tendency just now to rediscover certain virtues among the popular painters against whom the Pre-Raphaelites rebelled.

The most celebrated of these men was William Powell Frith (1819–1909), whose influence on Millais was strong enough to have accounted in large part for his fall from Pre-Raphaelite grace. The nature of Frith's subject matter is revealed by a random list of a few of his picture titles: *A Village Pastor; The Railway Station; Boswell's Dinner Party; The Wedding of the Prince of Wales*, which was a command picture for the Queen; *English Merrymaking One Hundred Years Ago; Life at the Sea Side; Breakfast Time; New Ear Rings;* and above all *Derby Day* [350, 351], for which Frith received about $75,000 for the engraving rights alone. His pictures were so admired that on exhibition they had to be protected from the crowds by special railings.

Rossetti and his loyal followers admitted Frith's technical prowess, but they loathed him for his "low and common" subjects. He held the Pre-Raphaelites equally in con-

352. FRITH: *Private View at the Royal Academy, 1881.* 40½ x 77". Private collection, England.

tempt for their idealistic and hyperaesthetic ones. Frith painted the *Private View at the Royal Academy, 1881* [352] to satirize "aesthetic" fashions in dress, he said, and the "folly of listening to self-elected critics in matters of taste." On the left is "a family of pure aesthetes absorbed in affected study of the pictures." Near them "in homely contrast" stands Anthony Trollope. To the right is Oscar Wilde, "a well-known apostle of the beautiful, with a herd of eager worshippers surrounding him." Other characters appearing in the picture include Gladstone, Browning, Huxley, Du Maurier, Ellen Terry, Lily Langtry, and Frith himself.

Whatever his limitation as an aesthetician may have been, Frith did paint with zest. *Derby Day* has a natural liveliness in its exploration of a commonplace subject, a quality always admired in the art of the impressionists to which it is unfavorably compared. But of course it has no suggestion of the subtlety, the originality, and the interpretative overtones of Degas's comparable subject, *A Carriage at the Races* [224].

Frith received all academic honors as well as general acclaim. He was the English parallel (as a painter, not as a personality—for he was a genial man) of the Frenchmen Meissonier (who was five years older) and Gérôme (who was five years younger). Frith, Meissonier, and Gérôme were only three of the tremendous number of painters who, like Waldmüller, satisfied the international taste for explicitly narrated anecdote. The Frenchmen, as we have seen, were likely to bolster up their literalness with a veneer of historical reference, as in Meissonier's *1814* [163], or some other pseudo-cultural eyewash, as in Gérôme's *Pygmalion* [172]. Sir Edwin Landseer [159, 160] was also one of the gods of living English painters at this time, and if we add to the list a few of the other medal winners of the 1855 Exhibition (pp. 142–154) we have a picture of the general ambience, at its highest level, in which the Pre-Raphaelites painted.

Impressionism in England: Whistler and Others

The Pre-Raphaelite movement was well under way when the *Salon des Refusés* took place in 1863. One of the most detested pictures in that exhibition was *The White Girl* [353], by a young American, James Abbott McNeill Whistler (1834–1903), who, having been dismissed from

353. WHISTLER: *The White Girl*, 1862. 85½ x 43".
National Gallery of Art, Washington, D.C.

Without adopting Pre-Raphaelitism he became a fixture in the Pre-Raphaelite aesthetic circle and that of the younger men, like Oscar Wilde, who carried Pre-Raphaelite aestheticism on into the 1890's with even more precious and immensely more sophisticated variations. He knew the poet Swinburne and the novelist and critic George Moore. He became a great dandy and a famous wit, a bright figure among the creative talents and their admiring circle who continued the Pre-Raphaelite revolt against the materialism and stuffiness of the Victorian age.

As an impressionist, Whistler never adopted the broken strokes and the sunlit effects developed by his former French associates. He worked instead more and more in a muted palette of grays and blacks, softly blended, painting the misty tonalities of evening or gray days, sometimes flecked or splashed with red or golden lights, with strong reference to Japanese prints or Oriental ink-wash drawings with their simplification and their subtle, colorless gradations. Ruskin, who had understood Turner's art when he was a young man, was unable to accept Whistler's now that he was an aging professor. He was so infuriated by Whistler's *Falling Rocket, Nocturne in Black and Gold*, a picture which might have delighted Turner, that he wrote, "I have seen, and heard, much of cockney impudence before now; but never expected to hear a coxcomb ask two hundred guineas for flinging a pot of paint in the public's face." Whistler sued Ruskin for libel, as much for the sport of it as for any other reason, and after a well-publicized trial was awarded damages of one farthing. Poor Ruskin suffered a mental breakdown the following year (1878) and for the remaining miserable twenty-two years of his life was removed from the critical scene while Whistler continued to send up his rockets.

Because he wrote well and because he talked so wittily that his bon mots were repeated everywhere, Whistler had great influence among intellectuals and cultivated amateurs. His central idea was that of art for art's sake—the belief that abstract values in painting, such as form and color, should exist for themselves, not as accessories to

West Point (he failed chemistry), had come to Paris to study under Gleyre. In Paris he knew Courbet, Manet, Monet, Degas, and Fantin-Latour. *The White Girl*, which he preferred to call *Symphony in White No. 1*, is one of the fine pictures of nascent impressionism, and there is no good explanation as to why Whistler at this point abandoned Paris to continue his career in England. Certainly it was not because he was wounded by the reception of *The White Girl* or because he feared a good fight. For the rest of his life he was one of the liveliest scrappers in the London arena.

the imitation of nature or, especially, to storytelling. He called his pictures "symphonies," "arrangements," "harmonies," or "nocturnes" in an effort to induce the public to see a painting as a painting, not as a picture of something. The picture still popularly called *Whistler's Mother* he insisted on calling *Arrangement in Gray and Black* [354] because "that is what it is. To me it is interesting as a picture of my mother; but what can or ought the public to care about the identity of the portrait? The imitator is a poor kind of creature. If the man who paints only the tree, or flower, or other surface he sees before him were an artist, the king of artists would be the photographer." If this idea sounds elementary today, one reason is that Whistler helped to establish it as a basic tenet in modern art. His rejection of imitative effects allies him more closely with modern abstract painters than with the impressionists. In the meanwhile, the public continued to respond to nonabstract sentimental anecdotes. *The Doctor* [355] is a standard example.

Unhappily, Whistler's own painting falls a little flat in the light of his theories. It seldom goes far beyond the level of tasteful arrangements of objects that remain semiphotographically represented, even though they may be in a focus so soft that they virtually disappear. The exquisiteness and daintiness of Japanese screen painting rather than the force of the finest Japanese prints influenced him in pictures like the portrait of *Miss Cicely Alexander* [356]. To the fragile charm of the picture there can, of course, be no objection. The disappointment is only that Whistler's pictures never have the importance that a more thoroughgoing application of his theories could have given them. He paints more like a tactful follower of someone else's theories than an adventurous creative artist in his own right.

This is true also of his etchings, although he brought a new sensitivity to the medium. Beginning conventionally—which at that time meant beginning with the attitude that an etching is not much more than a drawing done on a copper plate in such a way that it can be printed many times over—Whistler eventually developed a manner dependent upon the treatment of the

354. WHISTLER: *Arrangement in Gray and Black* (*"Whistler's Mother"*), 1871. 55½ x 63⅜". Louvre, Paris. On loan to Metropolitan Museum of Art, New York.

355. SIR LUKE FILDES: *The Doctor*, 1891. 64¾ x 96". Tate Gallery, London.

plate itself. With a few lines indicating the subject, he would wipe the plate elaborately to produce infinitely subtle tonalities and gradations. Since the plate had to be inked and wiped for each impression, each impression was, in effect, an original work.

356. WHISTLER: *Miss Cicely Alexander, c.* 1873. 74¾ x 38½". National Gallery, London.

Yet this is, from one point of view, a distortion of the medium, and the etchings suffer also from the exaggerated delicacy that makes Whistler's work seem so disappointingly thin and slight. He was a great battler against philistinism, but at the same time he gave support to the philistine's conception of the artist as a rather weak and undependable fellow who may be very sensitive and all that, but is not likely to be very sound.

Whistler's personality supported the same idea. In public he cultivated affecta-

tions of dress and manner, and in private he was a difficult man, demanding a worshipfulness from his friends and students that they finally tired of giving. One of these was Walter Richard Sickert (1860–1942), who studied under Whistler until the inevitable rupture and was then self-taught. After a while virtually nothing of Whistler remained in Sickert's work. He became a solid, downright painter, as English as boiled mutton. He borrowed heavily from Degas for subject matter and composition, yet retained his earthiness in contrast to Degas's civilized mastery. It was not through Whistler, but through Sickert, a quarter of a century after it had shaken France, that impressionism was imported to England and given a national flavor.

Sickert founded an association of painters called the Camden Town Group, in 1911, to "advance" British painting, but the group was neither impressionist nor, in 1911, very advanced. A partial explanation for England's indifference to impressionism may be that so many of impressionism's most attractive elements had been anticipated, in different form, by Constable. Also, impressionist effects of light seemed pallid after Turner's blazing canvases; for that matter, English watercolor supplied the fresh tonalities offered in oil by impressionism. These factors were sufficient to take the edge off the excitement of impressionist innovations. And as for portraiture, the British tradition was not only inviolable but it, too, offered enough of the light touch of Renoir (through Gainsborough and his tradition) and even the breadth of Manet (through Reynolds and his) to make investigation of what the Frenchmen were doing seem a little pointless.

Sir William Orpen (1878–1931), who painted within the English tradition, was one of several men who modified it in the direction of French impressionism. His *Homage to Manet* [357] shows a group of English painters and literati seated beneath Manet's portrait of Eva Gonzales, which was at that time in the possession of one of them, Sir Hugh Lane, seated at the extreme right. George Moore, who keeps popping up on both sides of the channel and whose portrait by Manet has been seen [201], is seated at the table, reading. Sickert is one of the standing men, and the isolated seated figure at the table is Wilson Steer (1860–1942), who takes second place to Sickert as England's leading impressionist. All this was in 1909. Homage to Manet, by that time, was coming to be homage to an old master. Impressionism in England was a tardy and not very radical departure from traditional painting, a rather tepid compromise reached in the twentieth century long after the excitement had died down.

Germany: Feuerbach and Böcklin

In Germany after 1850, academic classicism reached the end of its road in the work of Anselm von Feuerbach, while German romanticism put forth its most flagrant bloom with Arnold Böcklin. Both men were immediate contemporaries of the founding brothers of the Pre-Raphaelites; the birth dates of Rossetti, Hunt, Millais, Feuerbach, and Böcklin are crowded into the same three years, 1827, 1828, 1829, which means that all of them were beginning their careers as the century made the turn into its second half.

Feuerbach (1829–1880) is a kind of German Ingres, struggling against the current to perpetuate the academic classical tradition. He studied at the Düsseldorf and Munich academies that paralleled the *École des Beaux Arts;* he also studied in Paris under Couture, Manet's teacher. Like Ingres and then Couture, he persisted in his allegiance to the classical subject with derivations from the Italian Renaissance. He had something of Ingres's feeling for line and much of the formal solidity and tonal harmony of Couture at his best. He was a sensitive and austere artist when he was not smothering his personal genius under excessive conformity to tired formulas. He was not altogether a success, being overshadowed by Böcklin's effulgent romanticism as well as by newer developments in vigorous realism that were fermenting at the same time in Germany, in line with Courbet's realism in France. Nor is he much remembered outside Germany today, in spite of such achievements as the portrait

357. ORPEN: *Homage to Manet,* 1909. 65 x 51″. Manchester City Art Gallery, England.

Nanna [358], with its impressive reserve and beautiful pattern, or *Orpheus and Eurydice* [359].

The latter picture especially shows why Feuerbach's reputation has grown steadily in Germany, until today he is one of the most revered of German nineteenth-century masters, while at the same time his influence on German painting has been negligible. The sensitivity and restraint of *Orpheus and Eurydice,* the elegance and clarity and control imposed upon a subject of intensely emotional nature, are foreign to the Germanic tradition of passionate or mysterious statement. Feuerbach was a truly classical artist. As such he is isolated within the Germanic tradition, which has combined such disparate ideals as passionate emotionalism and literal realism but has never absorbed much of the classical ideal that demands

358. FEUERBACH: *Nanna*, 1861. 46¾ x 38¼". *Landeskunstsammlungen*, Stuttgart.

359. FEUERBACH: *Orpheus and Eurydice*, 1869. 76¾ x 48¾". *Kunsthistorische Museum*, Vienna.

the transmutation of passion and reality into images of abstract and logical beauty. German aestheticians helped formulate that ideal but as Germany's great creative painters they have never followed it. Artistically, Feuerbach remains a foreigner, although a respected one, in his own country. Spiritually he is closest to the long classical traditions of Italy and France, but in those countries he is overshadowed because he neither initiated a school nor made a sufficiently conspicuous contribution to the one he followed. He is a painter of exceptional quality who seems destined to perpetual obscurity because his painting never followed an exceptional direction.

Feuerbach's romantic contemporary, Böcklin (1827–1901), on the other hand, was a great success. Generally regarded as a master during his own lifetime, he was virulently attacked by critics at the beginning of the twentieth century, to such an extent that his merits, which exist, were obscured by his shortcomings, which are disastrous. It takes much patience and tolerance not to pass by some of Böcklin's most serious work as gross, obvious, or even laughable. But the pendulum has swung faster for Böcklin than for most painters, and recently he has become an interesting painter historically, since critics have recognized his influence on contemporary fantastic painting, notably surrealism, which we will see in good time. Just now, Böcklin's work must be regarded with a kind of double vision. Most of it looks trite, pretentious, ludicrously ponderous in its effort to create a world of fantasy in concrete terms. But that effort is important. The only way to approach Böcklin today is to clear

360. Böcklin: *Spring, c.* 1870. 28¼ x 22¾″. *Schackgalerie*, Munich.

361. Böcklin: *Sappho*, before 1890. 37¼ x 29″. Philadelphia Museum of Art, John G. Johnson Collection.

the field by admitting first how "bad" his pictures are, in order to reach a more sympathetic understanding of how "good" they almost are.

Böcklin's work divides easily into a few categories. First, there are his sentimental classical landscapes filled with ideal allegorical figures. These are seldom worse than innocuous, and seldom better than that. One of the standard examples is *Spring* [360], a picture that suffers from having too much of a perfectly good thing, a redundance of obvious symbols—maidens, young lovers, gamboling cupids, budding trees, blossoming sward, fluffy clouds. It is typical of Böcklin to belabor his point. In *Spring* he is like a guide who takes us by the hand and insists on explaining each detail of a subject with which we are already too familiar. Except that it is obvious and insistent, *Spring* is a respectably composed picture, with passages ranging from poetic subtlety (as in the hill covered with

mingled foliage and architecture) to the most hackneyed symbolism. Böcklin wanted to capture the innocence of vision that was Runge's primary concern; this is one of several factors in his art allying him directly with the traditions of early German romanticism. Innocence of this kind escapes Böcklin (although he is naïve, which is not quite the same thing), but in the swarm of pictures he produced in this classical-sentimental-lyrical-romantic manner, an occasional one rings true enough to rebuke us. In *Sappho* [361], for instance, the lyrical mood is more effective for being simpler. *Sappho* is in an almost literal sense a less wordy picture than *Spring*. A single figure gleams magically in the dark of a forest; the expression of private revery is increased because her back is turned toward us; there is no story, no direct allegory, no symbolism already too familiar. The mood created is, in short, created pictorially. Hence *Sappho* is more satisfying

362. BÖCKLIN: *Triton and Nereid,* 1873–74. 40¼ x 75¼". *Bayerische Staatsgemäldesamm-lungen,* Munich.

than *Spring* with its conducted tour of literary clichés. Pictures in this classification make up the bulk of Böcklin's early work and they continue to appear throughout his life, with variations.

A second group of pictures shows tritons, nereids, mermaids, sirens, nature gods, evil hobgoblins, and other fantastic creatures related to Germanic legends. These appear thick and fast during the 1870's, and of course parallel Wagner's operatic use of the same material at the same time. (Wagner was fourteen years older than Böcklin.) Böcklin intersperses these Nordic creatures with Pans, centaurs, and other classical monsters, using them in the same Germanic spirit of ominous mystery and violence.

Böcklin shared coincidentally with the Pre-Raphaelites the idea that extraordinary subject matter could best be represented in realistic images. This idea is one that cropped up several times during the century. William Blake with his "spirits and visions delineated in stronger lineaments than his perishing and mortal eye could see" was one expression of it. So were Friedrich and Runge with their explicit detail in the service of nostalgic recollection. The Nazarenes and the Pre-Raphaelites "dis-

covered" that religious subject matter had been effectively presented in realistic detail by medieval artists. Böcklin differs from the painters in this list because he was not interested in sharply detailed realism so much as in full-bodied, matter-of-fact presentation of his fantasies, as if they had been set up in the studio and then painted without imaginative variation. When his "magic realism" fails to come off it is for this reason, that his most fantastic subjects seem, in the end, heavyhanded and literal. This is true, at any rate, of the pictures showing nereids, tritons, hobgoblins, and the like. One cannot help wishing sometimes that his playful water creatures would get back into their clothes and return to the beer hall where their roistering properly belongs. And it is too easy to recognize the sea serpent in *Triton and Nereid* [362] as a tube of stuffed cloth, too easy to recognize the nereid herself as a posed model on whose legs some scales have been painted. There is too much realism and too little magic; the theory is good, but the proportions are off.

Finally, there is the third group, Böcklin's dreamlike landscape inventions, like the well-known *Isle of the Dead* [363].

363. Böcklin: *The Isle of the Dead*, 1880. Panel, 29 x 48 . Metropolitan Museum of Art, New York, Reisinger Fund.

These are quite directly the continuation of Friedrich's ruined Gothic choirs, graveyards, and threatening forests and crags. At twenty, Böcklin was painting in imitation of Friedrich's subjects, if not his technique, in pictures with such titles as *Landscape with Ruined City* and *Forest in the Moonlight*. He soon abandoned such direct references to the early romantics, but fantasies of the general type of *The Isle of the Dead* crop up in his work regularly, then appear frequently in the last two decades of his life.

The three categories of Böcklin's work overlap and intermingle, but in a general way they represent chronological stages of his art—from sentimental-lyrical classicism to subjects from Germanic mythology and monstrous visions to imaginary landscapes at once serene and sinister. And in these landscapes, at last, magic and realism come close to fusion. Rocks, trees, tombs or shrines, sky, water, and lonely figures are combined in theatrical arrangements which, if they fall short of magical transformation, at least take us into a foreign land.

Later German Realism

Chronology is always confusing. (Fortunately it is not always important.) It is particularly so in the nineteenth century because of the time lag between developments in France and corresponding ones elsewhere in Europe, with further lags in America. Feuerbach was the great German academic classicist and Böcklin the culminating romantic, but it is also true that Böcklin was born the same year as Courbet. This means that Courbet's revolt against idealism, either classic or romantic, was also contemporary with the Pre-Raphaelite movement in England. And since one art revolution followed another so rapidly in France, it means further that while Böcklin was painting, the *Salon des Refusés* came and went, the impressionists held their exhibitions and disbanded, and men we have yet to see, such as Cézanne, Seurat, Gauguin and van Gogh, were at work. In fact Seurat and van Gogh died ten years before Böcklin did, Gauguin the same year as he, and Cézanne only five years after.

Realism in one form or another had always been a major element in German painting. Realism in the sense of Courbet's return to the earthiness of nature found a German protagonist in Hans Thoma (1839–1924), a man ten years younger than Courbet and for a while his student. Like Courbet's, Thoma's realism must be qualified by the term "romantic-realism." But he painted so unevenly and in such a variety of manners that a representative collection of his work would look like a group show by several painters of varying talents. He ranged from the fresh literalness of pictures like *Woodland Meadow* [364] through other landscapes concerned with the monumentality of natural forms to such romantically evocative creations as *Recollection of a Town in Umbria* [365]. The unifying factor in his work is the response to nature that took so many forms in the nineteenth century, as, indeed, it took several different ones in his own painting. He differs from earlier German landscapists in

364. THOMA: *Woodland Meadow*, 1876. Panel, 19 x 14½". *Kunsthalle*, Hamburg.

365. THOMA: *Recollection of a Town in Umbria*, date unknown. Cardboard, 20½ x 28". *Neue Staatsgalerie*, Munich.

366. LEIBL: *The Poachers*, 1882–86. 21¾ x 16½". *Nationalgalerie*, Berlin.

367. LEIBL: *The Poachers*, as it appeared before division into parts.

that his scenes, even at their most imaginative level, carry no burden of metaphysical pondering. It is this difference that finally makes of him a realist as that ambiguous term was used in the opening chapters of this book. It should be mentioned too that Thoma also turned his hand to heroic and religious themes, at which he was uniformly unsuccessful. As a portrait painter, when his sitters are close friends or members of his family he frequently delineates his subjects with a direct and straightforward clarity that can be most engaging.

Courbet's "show me an angel and I will paint one" was turned into an even flatter statement, "I paint only what I see, and only from nature," by Wilhelm Leibl (1844–1900), who observed his dictum to the letter. Like Courbet he chose peasants as subjects; unlike Courbet, he observed realistically without romantic overtones. *The Poachers* [366] shows that Leibl was a strong draughtsman and a vigorous painter. It shows little else except the con-

figuration of the faces of two Bavarian peasants. It is, however, only part of a larger picture [367] that Leibl worked on for four years and then divided into several parts because he was dissatisfied with the composition. Leibl was the true leader of the new realism in Germany; he worked in conscious opposition to Feuerbach's classicism, Böcklin's romanticism, and the art of a third and unclassifiable contemporary, Hans von Marées (1837–1887).

Although he died before 1900, Marées is more closely related to twentieth-century painting than to that of his own century. He was disturbed by the bourgeois realism of Thoma and Leibl, which seemed to him commonplace and transient. Yet he felt also that Feuerbach's traditionalism was threadbare. Without passing through the experience of impressionism, Marées felt something like the same dissatisfactions that were very soon to lead Renoir to abandon impressionism's effects for a new study of form. Marées is even more closely com-

368. DUVENECK: *Georg von Hoesslin* (sketch), 1878–79. 16 x 13¾". Detroit Institute of Arts.

parable to Cézanne. The two men, born within two years of one another and working away from the same dissatisfactions, were unknown to one another, not only as individuals but as artists. Marées appears farther on in this book [530]; he is mentioned here only to place him in chronological context.

The Americans after 1850

American painters in the second half of the century continued to look to Europe for their technical standards and, if possible, to go there to study. But now, thoroughly decolonialized, they went more often to Paris than to London; they went also to the several academies in Germany, especially the one at Munich. Some of them, like Whistler and Mary Cassatt, became expa-

triates; others came home to continue the cultivation of European academic traditions. America's art schools were modeled as closely as possible after those in Europe, with the result that the United States produced quantities of well-trained painters among its talented men, and the provincialism that characterized so much American painting of the first half of the century disappeared, except that new movements, like impressionism, were a generation late in taking root.

Some typical painters of the latter part of the century have already been mentioned in the introductory remarks to Chapter 8. It is not necessary to catalogue these excellent men here; we will see instead those American painters whose work for one reason or another has a specifically American flavor. Three of the Europeanized Americans who were most influential at home may stand for dozens of their fellows and students: Duveneck, who worked in the middle west, Chase, who worked in the east, and Sargent who worked on both sides of the Atlantic.

Frank Duveneck (1848–1919), a Kentuckian by birth, went to Munich when he was twenty-two and came under the influence of Leibl. After a dazzling student career he divided his time between Cincinnati and Munich, with schools in both places that produced a whole Duveneck group. He was a dashing brushman and could strike in a head or a figure with impressive style and assurance [368]. The general tonality of the Munich school was very dark; Duveneck's hallmark was a combination of somber color with slashing, vibrant manipulation of paint. When he is at his best the combination is extraordinarily effective. But he was so facile a painter that his brush often ran away with him in superficial display. Unfortunately, most of his students imitated his facility but missed the depth and power that still make Duveneck's best pictures stand out in the galleries of such American museums as have continued to keep them on exhibition in spite of his eclipse.

William Merritt Chase (1849–1916) was born in Indiana and studied in Munich where he knew Duveneck. His early work has the same dark Munich tonality as Duveneck's, but he was more investigative than his friend and brightened his work under the influence of Velásquez and Hals. These were painters who also influenced Manet, whose work Chase's often resembles, in a cautious way. Chase painted with less flair than either Duveneck or Manet, and, of course, when he seems to follow Manet's tradition he does so not as a revolutionary but as an intelligent and gifted painter working after the revolution was won and its innovations accepted.

John Singer Sargent (1856–1925) was the most consummate virtuoso America produced, but in the final balance he became less an American than an international portrait painter with his headquarters in London and branch offices in Boston and New York. He studied in Paris under Carolus Duran, one of the soundest of the academic professors. To the ultimate degree Sargent had the English society portrait painter's knack for catching a likeness while at the same time flattering his sitter. Anyone who posed for Sargent could be certain in advance that in the completed picture he would be perfectly recognizable yet transformed into an aristocrat no matter who he really was. It is true that Sargent painted some of the shallowest portraits of an era that was rich in them. He knew that he was often the victim of his own facility, and he often appears to fling his paint onto the canvas almost contemptuously. But his work is too easily damned. If all his commercial showpieces could be done away with, a large number of pictures would still remain where his facility is put into the service of perception [369]. And in his watercolors and drawings even those critics who habitually reject his portraits are willing to accept his technical brilliance as an end in itself. In addition, the watercolors are, of all Sargent's work, most likely to be more than technical displays. When he grew sick of portrait painting for fashionable customers he would escape for a few days into watercolor painting for himself, recording his response to informal subject matter in pictures that are as appealing in their intimacy as they are fascinating in their virtuosity [370].

369. SARGENT: *Mrs. Charles Gifford Dyer*, 1880. 24½ x 17¼". Art Institute of Chicago, Friends of American Art Collection.

370. SARGENT: *Simplon Pass: The Lesson*, 1911. Watercolor, 15 x 18¼". Museum of Fine Arts, Boston.

371. HOMER: *Gloucester Farm*, 1874. 20¾ x 30⅛". Philadelphia Museum of Art, Mc-Fadden Collection.

America: Homer and the End of an Epoch

The two painters who emerge as the ones most closely integrated with the American scene, painting it in an American spirit in the second half of the century, are Winslow Homer and Thomas Eakins. Contemporaries of the French impressionists, both men were realists of the highest order. They shared with the impressionists a preoccupation with country scenes or bourgeois life, but instead of training their own sensitivities to accord with a European vision, they remained Americans who explored their own country and, more important, the character of their fellow Americans. The fact that Homer and Eakins painted American people engaged in typically American activities is relatively unimportant. What is important is that they explored beneath American surfaces to discover and express the psychological nuances that differentiated America from Europe. Bingham had done this also, but with subject matter so picturesquely and uniquely American that

less subtle perceptions were involved. To some extent Homer capitalizes on subject matter comparable to Bingham's, but Eakins painted an American world from which the frontier had vanished. Although Homer was only eight years older than Eakins, he is something of a transition between Bingham, the painter of American frontiers, and Eakins, the painter of a matured nation.

Winslow Homer (1836–1910) made only a moderate success in the picture market; the big prices during his long life went to more conventional work than his. Yet today it takes a moment to see where his unconventionality lay. It lay in the same quarter as that of the early impressionists. Homer's first important pictures, notably *Gloucester Farm* [371], have the same interest in natural outdoor light, represented with much the same sparkle and economy, as Monet's early work (for instance, *The Terrace at Le Havre* [208]) or Boudin's. But the resemblance is coincidental; there is no real probability that Homer knew the work of either of these two men at that time.

Gloucester Farm has the formal dignity and, to a surpassing degree, the clarity of the group of pictures to which it belongs: Homer's scenes of rural life in New York and New England painted from around 1867 on into the first years of the 1880's. As genre pictures, these intimate masterpieces had sufficient attractions to make them saleable in the lower price brackets, but as "serious" paintings they were thought to lack polish, just as the impressionists were thought "crude" at the same time in France. It is, of course, precisely their lack of polish—or what was thought of as polish—that lifts pictures like *Gloucester Farm* from the rank and file of nineteenth-century genre painting, that makes them not only pictures of great pastoral charm but masterly formal compositions as well. It is apparent enough, now, that Homer has eliminated all finicky detail to create a pattern of formal masses revealed in consistent light, that he has chosen the most ordinary genre elements but has simplified them and disposed them in harmonious balance, that no touch of the brush is careless, that each stroke is as thoughtfully considered and as carefully applied as in any painting of a conventionally polished kind. But this control was not apparent to a public habituated to the enjoyment of illusionistic details in a multitude of incidental objects factually described.

While his pictures sold at low prices, Homer continued to make ends meet by commercial work, such as book and magazine illustration. His earliest work was entirely of this nature; he had covered the Civil War as a pictorial reporter for *Harper's Weekly*, and his first oil painting, *Prisoners from the Front* [372], records the experience. *Prisoners from the Front* is a surprisingly satisfactory painting in these circumstances, but in comparison with the pictures that now began to follow it, like *Gloucester Farm,* it is still pictorial journalism.

Homer went to England in 1881 and stayed there during 1882 as well, working in watercolor and developing along the tight and rather dry manner that was popular with English watercolorists just then. Upon his return he abandoned his rural

372. HOMER: *Prisoners from the Front*, 1866. 24 x 38″. Metropolitan Museum of Art, New York, Gift of Mrs. Frank B. Porter.

373. HOMER: *The Life Line*, 1884. 28¾ x 41⅝″. Philadelphia Museum of Art, George W. Elkins Collection.

pastorals, settling in Prout's Neck, Maine, and shifting his attention to the life of fishermen on the Grand Banks, which he described in a series of etchings and oils. The gentle slopes and quiet barns and peaceful country people of *Gloucester Farm* were replaced by more dramatic elements, such as raging seas, rocky shores, and the strong men and women who struggled against them. Subjects like *The Life Line* [373], one of several pictures showing wrecks or rescues at sea, had enough narrative appeal to increase Homer's popu-

374. HOMER: *The Hunter*, 1891. 28¼ x 48″. Philadelphia Museum of Art, W. L. Elkins Collection.

larity. He adapted his early, gentler style to a vigorously masculine one where the violence of nature, and man's hazardous life in contact with it, are expressed in a technique as harmonious to the subject as his earlier manner was harmonious to the

scenes of farm life. But Homer was still at his best when anecdotal elements were least conspicuous, as in *The Hunter* [374], where the relationship of man to nature is a philosophical subject rather than a narrative one. It is symbolical enough—although, of course, Homer never intended it to be— that the figure in *The Hunter* dominates the horizon, while in the wilderness of the Hudson River painters man was a tiny figure infiltrating a natural vastness. The frontiers are conquered; the giant trees of the Hudson River landscapes are felled, and *The Hunter* places his foot on this one almost as if it were a fallen enemy. He is no longer an intruder in a benign wilderness, but its benevolent conqueror.

In the Maine pictures, Homer is the last of the Americans to paint in immediate contact with the raw life of a new country.* And in his own very late work he grew further and further away from his preoccupation with the solemnities and the powerful forces of nature. He made frequent

375. HOMER: *Ship Unfurling Sails*, date unknown. Watercolor, 10¾ x 14½″. Philadelphia Museum of Art, Gift of Dr. and Mrs. George Woodward.

---

* At least, he is the last to treat this life as more than a pure genre record. Painters like Frederick Remington (1861–1909), with his cowboy pictures, continued to illustrate locally picturesque aspects of American life, often with great liveliness.

trips to the West Indies, and eventually the shining palms, the glittering clear water, the sun-drenched sails of these islands, asserted themselves over the dour coasts and the sturdy folk of the north. To paint them, Homer freed himself from the conventional niceties of his early watercolor style to work in broad, fluid areas of scintillating transparency [375], suggesting in a few essential notes the choppy surface of a bay, the degree of tension in a sail receiving the wind or hanging limp or furled, the lay of a boat in the water, the stance of a boatman, and always the pure brilliance of sun in clear air—all of these captured in a momentary aspect, as if set down in a fraction of a second. Thus, having begun, in pictures like *Gloucester Farm*, as an independent parallel to the earliest developments in French impressionism, Homer produced at the end of his career some of the purest impressionistic work of his time.

America: Thomas Eakins

Thomas Eakins (1844–1916) may well be the greatest American painter. He is certainly one of the finest painters of his century, Americanism aside.

Eakins went to Paris at twenty-two to study under, of all people, Gérôme, at the *École des Beaux Arts*. (He also studied with Bonnat there.) This was in 1866. The *Salon des Refusés* had taken place only three years before, and *Olympia* had been exhibited only the year before Eakins's arrival. Manet's art was the scandal of Paris, but nothing Eakins ever painted shows that he was affected by the twin explosions of *Le Déjeuner sur l'Herbe* and *Olympia*. It is not difficult to understand why this particular young painter was indifferent to Manet's art although he was intelligent, questioning, and thoughtful:

Eakins's passion was anatomy. For him, the human body was the most beautiful thing in the world—not the body as an object of desire, or as a set of proportions, but as a construction of bone and muscle. He had already spent two years studying anatomy by dissection at the Jefferson Medical College in Philadelphia "to in-

376. EAKINS: *Masked Seated Nude, c.* 1866. Charcoal on paper, 24 x 18". Philadelphia Museum of Art, Gift of Mrs. Thomas Eakins and Miss Marcy A. Williams.

crease his knowledge of how beautiful objects are put together" to the end that he might "be able to imitate them." Manet's experiments with the technique of capturing the quality of instant vision could be of no interest to Eakins, who found the human body beautiful because its structure and its movements were "means and end reciprocally adapted to each other." Manet's broad planes of light sacrificed the complete statement of a structure that Eakins found glorious. He was not interested in the quality of instant vision, but in a total reality where every part of the body served and depended upon every other one. This did not mean the imitation of every hair on the head, every pore in the skin, or for that matter even every small muscle, but

377. EAKINS: *Salutat*, 1898. 50 x 40". Addison Gallery of American Art, Andover, Mass.

tential. The body in *Masked Seated Nude* is alive; every bone and muscle is performing its required function in maintaining the body in the position it has assumed. Eakins never drew a living model as if it were a corpse, a statue, or a pattern of light and shade falling on an inert object. Because he studied anatomy in a medical school and analyzed the body so carefully, he is sometimes called a scientific realist, and even he called himself one. But of course he was not. His scientific knowledge of anatomy was a means to the end of expression, just as the structure of the body itself is a means to the end of movement.

But he was scientist enough to have no use for the formulas of ideal beauty, either romantic or classical. Idealization seemed to him pointless in the face of a reality so beautiful. In any case, he found that idealization—to which he held no objection when it was an "understood" idealization—was seldom based on "a thorough understanding of what is idealized." Without this understanding, idealization was merely "distortion, and distortions are ugliness." The classic and romantic idealizations current in Paris seemed to him nothing more than such distortions. He saw no point in copying casts, even those from the sculpture of the best Greek period, because nature itself was at hand for study. He worshiped the Parthenon figures, but these figures were "undoubtedly modeled from life," he thought, and he saw no reason to refer to them for models when nature was "just as varied and just as beautiful in our day as she was in the time of Phidias." "The Greeks did not study the antique." Why paint gladiators in ancient Rome when there was a boxing club around the corner? When he returned to his native Philadelphia he became the first painter to find subjects in the world of sport. The young boxer in *Salutat* [377] with his lean, hard legs, his powerfully bunched shoulders, his long arms, is built for his profession and will do better in the ring than one of David's idealized warriors could do. His body is beautiful not because its abstract proportions are harmonious—they are not, particularly—or because it can be defined by lines abstractly beautiful in themselves, like

it did mean an expression of every part of the body as a working part of a perfectly integrated structure. His academic drawing, *Masked Seated Nude* [376], introduces no muscles not actually visible beneath the model's fleshy padding, and may even omit a few that were, but its extraordinary reality comes from Eakins's knowledge of the structural function of each concealed bone, the disposition of each tensed or relaxed muscle upon the skeletal framework in any specific attitude. It is a body one can imagine shifting itself into another position. Nominally, the pose is static; actually, structure and movement were so identified in Eakins's conception of the body that movement is present even in a quiet body, if by nothing more than an immediate po-

378. EAKINS: *Musicians Rehearsing, c.* 1883. 16 x 12″. Philadelphia Museum of Art, John D. McIlhenny Bequest.

379. EAKINS: *Mrs. William D. Frishmuth*, 1900. 97 x 72½″. Philadelphia Museum of Art, Gift of Mrs. Thomas Eakins and Miss Marcy A. Williams.

those of Ingres's nudes. It is beautiful because it is a normal human body, an example of that miraculously self-contained mobile structure in good condition. In Paris, Eakins had found that he learned more by watching his fellow students when they stripped and wrestled in the studio than he did by drawing from posed models.

But of course the miracle of the human body is only a part of the miracle of a human being. Eakins's statements about his fidelity to the imitation of nature seem to deny the other part of the miracle, which is human consciousness, yet in the long run that is what Eakins is most concerned with; otherwise he might better have spent his time painting animals, whose bodies are equally miraculous as self-contained mobile structures, and even more various and dramatic than human ones. Music was a large part of Eakins's life, particularly music as

an intimate communion between friends, and the man who painted *Musicians Rehearsing* [378] was not a scientific anatomist but a man who was sensitive to the ultimate mystery in human life for which words like *soul* and *spirit* have been coined. In this picture Eakins is akin to another realist, the Daumier who painted *The Print Collector* [111]. In its subjectivity, *Musicians Rehearsing* is at one pole of Eakins's work, with the objectivity of *Salutat* at the opposite one. Most of his pictures lie in the intermediate area where imitation of visible realities and revelation of inner ones are balanced in a way uniquely his own.

In this area dozens of portraits could be cited. The one of *Mrs. William D. Frishmuth* [379], a collector of musical instruments who is shown seated among them, would be hard to surpass, either as an example of Eakins at his painterly best or as one of his typically forceful, direct, and acute revelations of personality. As a piece of objective realism the head [380] is superb beyond virtuosity. The set of the lidded eyes in their sockets, the bony projection of the irregular nose with its fleshy tip, the sag of the aging face on its strong foundation of bone, the firmness of the mouth, held decisively by an habitual contraction of the muscles, the swirl of thin soft hair away from the rather flat temples and the slightly bulging forehead—all of these features, logically integrated and existing as a magnificently solid volume in space, are presented with a tangibility approaching illusion. But the vivid emanation of character comes from something more than this masterly reproduction of a set of features extraordinary in themselves. Some of Eakins's means toward the revelation of this personality are obvious; they consist largely of the centuries-old devices of selection and accent. What Eakins has eliminated as incidental and unrevealing we cannot say, but we can see the sharp stroke that emphasizes the angle in the eyebrow at one side, the sudden emphatic shadow at the nostril, the exaggeration and breaking of the highlights in the eyes, glistening in the

380. Eakins: Detail from Figure 379.

381. Eakins: Detail from Figure 379.

382. Eakins: Detail from Figure 379.

383. EAKINS: *Miss Van Buren*, c. 1891. 45 x 32″. Phillips Collection, Washington, D.C.

384. SARGENT: *Mrs. Swinton*, 1896–97. 90 x 49″. Art Institute of Chicago, Walker Collection.

collapsing flesh around them. The delicacy of the pearls and the neckerchief accentuates the ruggedness of the head; the pose of the whole figure describes a monumental respectability, surmounted by the determined, reflective intelligence of the face.

The slight conceit of the right hand [381] resting on the piano with one finger pressing a single key, as if sounding a note, saves the pose from usualness. But counteracting any suggestion of affectation, the other hand [382] rests palm downward with massive placidity upon the strings of a viola, as if quieting them. The face and hands are the three lightest spots in the picture—not an unusual device, but exaggerated here.

They are exceptionally small and exceptionally conspicuous among the shadows, which are punctuated here and there with duller lights of polished wood and subdued metallic glints. The picture, which is very large, is dark in tonality, the dress black in the surrounding dark warm browns, with occasional russet tones in the instruments. The most conspicuous spot of color is the cool clear blue of the neckerchief; it serves as a final accent to the powerful head, making doubly sure its position as the climax of the picture.

It would be possible to go on from here and argue that in the guise of an objective image Eakins has made comments upon

385. Eakins: *Mending the Net*, 1881. 32¼ x 45¼". Philadelphia Museum of Art, Gift of Mrs. Thomas Eakins and Miss Marcy A. Williams.

386. Eakins: Detail from Figure 385.

profound and universal truths, but this would be to distort his art away from a sphere in which it is complete. His genius as a portrait painter lay in his ability to create—or, rather, to perceive and then to reveal—the psychological entity of an individual, without recourse to any but the most objective means. Any philosophical speculations stirred by the portrait of Mrs. Frishmuth must come from the observer as they might be stirred by an acquaintance with the rich personality of Mrs. Frishmuth herself, the personality Eakins has perceived, revealed, and immortalized. If a single word could describe the quality of his portraits the word would be *honesty*—honesty in the representation of externals, and honesty of characterization. It is easy to see why some of his portraits were refused after they had been commissioned, why some others were accepted only to be burned. Sitters who hoped to emerge as dukes or duchesses were mistaken when they chose Eakins to paint their portraits. Yet when Sargent, the most expert flatterer of this kind, came to Philadelphia and was being lionized, Eakins was the man he

asked to meet. His fashionable hostess had never heard of the local painter. A comparison of Eakins's *Miss Van Buren* [383] with a typical "society portrait" explains why Sargent [384] who admired the one but painted the other, made his famous remark, in self-disgust, that portraiture was "a pimp's profession." It is a remark that no portrait by Eakins could ever have inspired.

Like the French impressionists, Eakins painted the urban *bourgeoisie* on their holidays in the countryside, strolling, fishing, boating, lying in the shade. Yet it would be impossible to mistake one of his pictures in this group for a French painting, just as it would be impossible to mistake the Schuylkill River at Philadelphia for the Seine. *Mending the Net* [385, 386] is a sturdier, more masculine, more direct picture than the Frenchmen's delicious landscapes composed of color dissolved in atmosphere. Eakins's light is just as wonderfully the light of outdoors, but it is seen with a steadier eye and is painted with a firmer and more deliberate brush. Monet's boats riding at anchor at Argenteuil, Renoir's tender young

387. EAKINS: *Max Schmitt in the Single Shell*, 1871. 32¼ x 46¼". Metropolitan Museum of Art, New York, Alfred N. Punnett Fund and Gift of George D. Pratt.

people in dappled shadows, even Pissarro's sparkling fields, are feminine and evanescent (although no less delightful) by the standard of Eakins's clear skies, firm earth, heavy water, and steady light. Nor does Eakins yield to the casual, almost haphazard composition of so much impressionism; the intervals of grouping in the line of figures against the sky along the riverbank in *Mending the Net* is beautifully calculated to achieve an expression of naturalness without any loss of pictorial unity. In this particular combination of virtues—apparent spontaneity with exquisite calculation— Eakins when he is at his best is comparable to the great compositional master of impressionism, Degas, although he has no interest in Degas's brilliant innovations of the "snapshot" compositions with their eccentric angles, their objects bisected by the margins of the picture, and their figures captured in unexpected attitudes.

Eakins was interested in the relationship between photography and vision, and sometimes used photographs for reference, not as a matter of convenience but as a stimulus in solving problems of vision and representation. He was not in search of a formula; he painted sometimes in broad, simplified forms, sometimes with detailed precision, as he did in *Max Schmitt in the Single Shell* [387], an extreme example but one of his finest paintings, emulating the detailed clarity of a deep sharp focus lens capable of registering minute details with equal precision from foreground to horizon. Each twig of the trees on the river bank is shown as if at close range in miniature; this definition extends beyond the distant bridge to include a small boat and even its puff of smoke. Max Schmitt, in the scull, turning toward us as if we were holding a camera, appears to be waiting for the click of its shutter. But like Corot, who, with less complication, also represented distant details with similar telescopic clarity, Eakins has adjusted colors and values as a creative painter, not as a photographer with an exceptionally good camera. He has massed his details in acute concentrations; they seem

388. EAKINS: *The Agnew Clinic*, 1889. 74½ x 130½". University of Pennsylvania, Philadelphia.

389. EAKINS: Detail from Figure 388.

all the more wonderfully precise because they are played between the broad flat stretch of water and the even flatter expanse of sky. The effect is like that of a clear day in early spring when the world seems to emerge in magically revealing light after the obscurities of winter, when the eye is sharpened to a new sensitivity to everything it sees, as if privileged for a few hours to find new experience in familiar objects. The picture is full of the enchantment of such an experience; the oddly shaped clouds, white and scintillating in the bright sky, are a half-fantastic element further removing the scene from literalness, even though the existence of exactly such clouds at exactly such spots is conceivable as a fact of nature. No other picture of Eakins's demonstrates more absolutely his fidelity to "imitation" and, at the same time, his manipulation of imitative detail into an expressive unity that explores beneath realistic surfaces.

A limitation inherent in realism, the one that seemed its insuperable defect to the idealists, is that it is ill adapted to the synthesis of monumental compositions. The impact of a *Mrs. Frishmuth* or a *Max Schmitt* or a *Mending the Net* depends upon our feeling that the scene existed *in toto* before the eyes of the painter. If we stop to think

about it, common sense tells us that the parts were assembled on the canvas, in the studio. There is no reason to believe that Mrs. Frishmuth sat patiently while Eakins busied himself for days painting the musical instruments surrounding her, and it is obvious that in *Max Schmitt* the clouds, the light, the puff of smoke, and the man in the single shell did not remain supernaturally transfixed during the hours and days that Eakins worked on them. But this fact does not intrude itself between the image and the observer; we believe in the total simultaneous existence of all the parts. But in certain kinds of subjects, and beyond a certain point of complication, this belief becomes strained, as it does in *The Agnew Clinic* [388]. *The Agnew Clinic* represents a medical arena where the doctor lectures during the course of an operation. In addition to twenty-seven visible spectators, Eakins shows two doctors, two assistants, a nurse, and the patient under anesthesia. He makes no effort to dramatize the scene, unless the rather obtrusive variety of attitudes assumed by the spectators can be called dramatizing in a small way. The operation itself and the people performing it are described as noncommittally as a factual report, down to such details as the instrument table and even the stencilled "University Hospital" on the operation cloth beneath the patient. The report is adequately organized and is quite lucid in its separate parts, as in the head of Doctor Agnew [389], but it remains an enumeration of facts rather than a response to them.

This odd dryness, the downright stubborn objectivity, might have been the result of the unfavorable reception fourteen years earlier of a similar picture, *The Gross Clinic* [390]. Here the head of the doctor is dramatized not only by its pose and its facial expression but by its position as the climactic point of the foreground group and its isolation against the shadowed background, where the figures of the spectators are barely visible in the gloom. There is some disharmony between this dramatization and the reportorial character of the assistant figures; the artificiality of the pose of the woman at the left (the patient's mother) is also obtrusive. But on the whole it is an impressive picture whether or not it is altogether a consistent one, and a near miss, at least, in solving the problem Eakins set himself, which was the reconciliation of monumental treatment through realistic means.

The Gross Clinic had a dramatically unfavorable reception, being rejected for exhibition in Philadelphia's Centennial Exhibition of 1876, a rejection comparable to Courbet's earlier one in Paris, and for much the same reason: its realism seemed brutal. It remains a startling picture today, especially in the detail of Doctor Gross's hand holding the scalpel. The fingers glisten with blood fresh from the incision in the patient's thigh. Eakins finally arranged to have the picture hung among the medical exhibits of the Centennial. This, and subsequent discouragements, may have led him to the uncompromisingly flat statement in *The Agnew Clinic*, as opposed to the interpretative effort, in *The Gross Clinic*, to show the scientist as a towering intellectual figure beyond the limitations of ordinary men.

But it is not so much that Eakins was out of his depth in these two pictures as that he was out of his field. His field was the perception and the revelation of character, a field common to all centuries of painters, and he holds his own in that field without

390. EAKINS: *The Gross Clinic*, 1875. 96 x 78". Jefferson Medical College, Philadelphia.

apologies in any quarter. And in a field special to his own half-century, the observation of urban man in conjunction with nature, he was unique in capturing the quality of this aspect of life as it was expressed in his own country.

Postscript: The Ash Can School

At the very end of the nineteenth century in America, there appeared a group of young men who painted into and as far as the middle of the twentieth, but who are best considered as part of the century that produced realism and impressionism. These were the painters of the Ash Can School, a name given them in derision (by just whom, there is some question) because they were devoted to vigorously commonplace subjects in protest against the gentility of fashionable painting. As a group they were a short generation younger than Duveneck, Chase, Sargent, and Eakins, having been born in the 1860's and early 1870's. Coming at the end of a century studded by revolutions, the story of their own revolt is anticlimactic, especially since the essence of their heresies had been proclaimed long before by the realists and the impressionists, and had been superceded by new ones.

The most potent influences on the Ash Can School were Manet, Daumier, and other French painters related to them, men who finished their careers and died during the boyhood of the five Americans who were to form the original Ash Can group: Robert Henri (1865–1929), George Luks (1867–1933), John Sloan (1871–1951),

391. SLOAN: *Greenwich Village Backyards*, 1914. 26 x 32″. Whitney Museum of American Art, New York.

392. SLOAN: *The Wake of the Ferry*, 1907. 26 x 32″. Phillips Collection, Washington, D.C.

321

393. SLOAN: *"Professor—Please Play 'The Rosary,'"* 1913. Charcoal on paper, 18¼ x 16⅝".
Addison Gallery of American Art, Andover, Mass.

394. SLOAN: *Arachne*, 1940. 28 x 26". Philadelphia Museum of Art, Gift of Mr. and
Mrs. R. Sturgis Ingersoll.

William Glackens (1870–1938), and Everett Shinn (1876–1953). Duveneck influenced some members of the group; they
painted with a very free brush, which some
of them were likely to exaggerate into
coarse, even slipshod, technique. The
everyday subject matter of the impressionists and the social comment of one form of
realism were also somewhat coarsened in
their adaptation to the Ash Can enthusiasm
for the hurly-burly of the American city
along its main stem, in its back streets, and
in its honkytonks, bars, cheap restaurants,
and rented bedrooms.

The group was formed in Philadelphia
in the 1890's, led by Robert Henri. They
called themselves the Philadelphia Realists.
Henri's importance is hardly hinted at by
his painting, which was as facile as Sargent's but less elegant. Henri preferred
common people to aristocrats. His great
importance was as a teacher who stimulated more adventurous originality in his
students than he demonstrated in his own
work. His book *The Art Spirit* is still in-
spiring to many beginners.

John Sloan comes close to being a one-
man summary of the Ash Can School, which
changed its base to New York (and its
name to New York Realists) around 1900
and took on its typical character. *Greenwich
Village Backyards* [391] shows the kind of
subject that soon generated the nickname
Ash Can. But *The Wake of the Ferry* [392]
shows that at their best the Ash Can painters could go beyond the cheerful journal-
istic vigor of their descriptions of the city
to discover, as Daumier did, the existence
of the individual as a sentient unit isolated
within the mass of the metropolis. Sloan
was also an early practitioner of the humorous cartoon of social satire, as in *"Professor
—Please Play The Rosary"* [393], an in-
digenously American kind of humor which,
expanded and polished, was to become
"The New Yorker cartoon." In his late years,
when Ash Can realism had run its course,
Sloan abandoned it to work less successfully
in painting of a more formal nature, such as
Arachne [394].

As for the other three, William Glackens
began as an illustrator on the *Philadelphia*

395. Luks: *The Spielers*, 1905. 36 x 26″. Addison Gallery of American Art, Andover, Mass.

396. Prendergast: *Afternoon, Pincian Hill, Rome*, 1898. Watercolor, 21 x 27″. Phillips Collection, Washington, D.C.

Press and continued as a successful cartoonist in New York. After painting in the typical Ash Can manner for a while, he renounced his birthright during an extended residence in France and returned, in effect, a Franco-American impressionist. Everett Shinn followed a similar early gambit. Then, under the influence of Degas, he did theater subjects and finally turned to theatrical decoration, where his talent for rather thin and florid ornament was most at home. George Luks was by a couple of years the oldest and by all odds the gustiest member of the group. He painted with great appetite, choosing subjects from New York's east side [395], from coal mines, and also from city life in general.

Luks became a small *cause celebre* in American painting when the National Academy rejected one of his paintings, offended by his "vulgarity," that word so familiar to realists in France. Three more painters joined the Ash Can group of five to form "The Eight" around Luks as active dissenters from academic doctrine. The new trio were Maurice Prendergast (1859–1924), who eventually developed a decorative, semi-abstract, patch-work style evolved from impressionism [396]; Arthur B. Davies (1862–1928), whose wispily elongated figures in rhythmic combinations inspired by Blake were an odd combination with the low-living characters of the Ash Can family gallery; and Ernest Lawson (1873–1939), whose purely impressionist work was later affected by Cézanne. The Eight were important as protagonists in the early twentieth-century campaign to introduce radical European movements to the American public, especially in the Armory Show of 1913, which we will see later. In their own work, however, they were not strongly affected by these movements.

A younger man, George Bellows (1882–1925), became a disciple of Ash Can principles in the early 1900's (he was a student of Henri's) and produced, among other fight and sporting scenes, the painting and the lithograph [397] of *A Stag at Sharkey's*, which is as well known, probably, as any American picture within ten years either side of it. Bellows was still a very young man when it began to be evident that the Ash Can school had run its course. No other school of painting became old-fashioned more quickly;* the exhibitions of European *avant-garde* painting so enthusiastically sponsored by the Ash Can painters themselves made them out of date.

Bellows began a process of self re-education along rigidly formal lines. He studied certain elementary and arbitrary formulas for picture-making, and when he died suddenly at forty-three his painting was an odd combination of dry mechanics in conflict with his native vigor and sturdy realism. Occasionally the mechanics won out. They mar *Elinor, Jean and Anna* [398], where the intimate and affectionate nature of the subject is a little chilled by the imposition of inappropriate compositional rigidity and a touch of affectation in forms that are studied to the point of conventionalization. Here Bellows is subjecting himself to disciplines comparable to those Renoir imposed upon himself in *Bathers* [251] at very much the same stage of his career. Pointlessly but inevitably one wonders whether Bellows, if he had lived, might not have freed himself from these disciplines just as Renoir did, once they had served their purpose, to become the man who would bring American art harmoniously into the international orbit of the twentieth century without sacrifice of his indigenous character.

Bellows's Americanism was conscious and determined; he even feared European travel as a possible corruption. This kind of Chinese Wall self-consciousness has plagued some other American painters since Bellows and has been a point of departure for some critics who have failed to see that the Americanism of Allston, Bingham, Homer, Eakins, and any other painters who can be grouped with them, was an inborn Americanism, not a rejection of foreign influences.

---

* Except one, the regional school of the 1930's in America, led by Thomas Benton, Grant Wood, and John Steuart Curry, as will be seen.

397. BELLOWS: *A Stag at Sharkey's*, 1916. Lithograph, 18¾ x 24". Philadelphia Museum of Art, Gift of Mr. and Mrs. George Sharp Munson.

398. BELLOWS: *Elinor, Jean and Anna*, 1920. 59 x 66". Albright Art Gallery, Buffalo, N.Y.

PART III

Transition

CHAPTER 10

Post-impressionism: Its Classicists

The Explorers

By the end of the nineteenth century, impressionism had run its course, although Renoir, Degas, and Monet continued to work well into the twentieth. But even while impressionism was still fighting for final recognition, new directions were being followed by several men whose art was to determine the course of painting in the first generation of the new century. Fanning out from impressionism, they explored independently. More than any other painters in the history of art, they developed their theories in isolation, and in contradiction to one another. They are grouped under the catch-all designation of *post-impressionists*, a term meaning nothing except that these men departed from impressionism to find new ways of painting. The ways they found were too various to be covered by a more descriptive designation; at least so far, no better collective term has been found to describe the art of Paul Cézanne, Georges Seurat, Paul Gauguin, and Vincent van Gogh (all of whom, incidentally, died before Renoir, Degas, and Monet—even by as much as thirty-five years, to take the extreme limits between the death of Seurat, who died very young, and Monet, who died very old). The point is made at such length only to remind the reader that chapters in a book follow one another between neater boundary lines than do the birth and death dates of painters or, especially in our time, the genesis and development of new expressions in art. The trauma that led from impressionism into the plethora of isms we group under the term *modern art* was experienced by and expressed by the painters we call post-impressionists.

399. SEURAT: *A Sunday Afternoon on the Island of La Grande Jatte*, 1884–86. 81¼ x 120¼″. Art Institute of Chicago, Helen Birch Bartlett Memorial.

Neo-impressionism: Seurat

While Renoir was painting his *Bathers* in reaction against the formlessness of impressionism, a younger man named Georges Seurat (1859–1891) was attacking the same problem in a different way. With excruciating patience he was applying tiny dots of color to 67 square feet of canvas which, when the dots finally covered it, would be the painting that divides impressionism from the twentieth century, *A Sunday Afternoon on the Island of La Grande Jatte* [399, 400], which shows the strolling crowd in a public park on an island in the Seine near Paris. Both Renoir and Seurat were intent on pulling together again the disintegrating forms of impressionism, redefining their boundaries and solidifying the masses that had become ambiguous in their fusion with light and air. Renoir did so by retreating from impressionism; Seurat did so by plunging into it and putting it in order like a fanatic housewife tidying up a bachelor's apartment. By a more dignified comparison, he was like a catalyst dropped into the frothy impressionist mixture, suddenly reducing it to crystals of perfect geometrical form.

By any comparison, Seurat was the most systematic painter who ever lived, and of all painters who have tried to work on scientific principles he is the only one of major importance whose art suggests the laboratory as much as it does the studio. Since he was systematic in the extreme, his work is easy to reduce to a recipe. But like any recipe for painting, this one is deceptive since it is full of hidden variables dependent on the skill and the sensibilities of the artist.

400. SEURAT: Detail from Figure 399.

Seurat's recipe may produce a work of art as it did when Seurat used it, or a pointless exercise as it usually did in the hands of his followers. But the recipe remains:

First: Simplify all natural forms to silhouettes in accord with their basic geometrical equivalents, modifying them as necessary in accord with the taste of the artist to increase their effectiveness as pure design. Seurat's taste was for the most exquisite precision of contour; even before he added the element of geometrical reduction, this taste is evident in his academic student drawings [401], which allied him to the tradition of Ingres. He worked in the Academy's school under Lehmann, who may be remembered as a disciple of Ingres, and he studied drawings by Ingres even while he was studying Delacroix's color. But he was unaffected by Delacroix's spirit, and it should become apparent as his work is followed here that Seurat is well within the classical tradition—its purity, its balance, and even in the specifically classical-academic characteristic of insistence upon formula. Drawings in his fully developed style [402] have their own kind of formal idealization, even though Seurat insisted always upon the contemporary, everyday subjects of impressionism as opposed to the idealism of conventionally classical ones.

Second: Assemble these silhouettes into a composition (previously determined in its general expressive disposition), further modifying the individual forms and adjusting their interrelationship until they are perfectly integrated with one another and the space around them. The subject of this composition will observe the impressionists' allegiance to the world at hand, but its expressiveness will be achieved by the application of psychological values of line and color that impressionism sacrificed to "effects" of light and atmosphere and the accidental dispositions of forms in nature.

Third: Paint this composition in the technique called "divisionism" or "pointillism," in accord with theories of color held by the artist.*

It is in the second stage, the creation of the composition, that Seurat returns most obviously to French classical standards. The infinite adjustment of the parts of *La Grande Jatte* into a perfected, static interrelationship is in the tradition of Poussin. But the highly simplified forms are not Poussinesque; in their creation and their combination Seurat is equally in the tradition of the ubiquitous Japanese print, with its ornamental flatness. Of course these two traditions are contradictory, Poussin's

---

* To make a fine distinction, *divisionism* would be the breaking-up of color into its component parts, *pointillism* its application in dots of uniform size. *Chromo-luminarism* is another term sometimes met, meaning the same things.

401. SEURAT: *Male Nude*, 1877. Charcoal, 25 x 19″. Private Collection.

402. SEURAT: *Seated Woman*, 1884–86. Crayon, 12 x 7½″. Collection Louis E. Stern, New York.

being a tradition of composition of three-dimensional forms in three-dimensional space. *La Grande Jatte* can be read thus, or it can be read simply across its surface, just as its forms can be read as silhouettes, or as geometrical solids. As a composition of solid forms in classical depth the picture is more subtle, more complex, and finally more rewarding, but it is also a wonderfully effective composition if it is regarded as an enormous flat ornamental screen. This spacial ambivalence, offspring of the union between the European painters' admiration for Japanese print design and their own ingrained Western tradition, is present in

a great deal of painting during these years. And although Seurat certainly knew the prints at first hand, their influence also entered his art in a roundabout way, through the art of Puvis de Chavannes.

Pierre Cécile Puvis de Chavannes (1824–1898) occupies a curious position in French painting. A little younger than Courbet, a little older than Manet, he was unaffected by the realist-impressionist movement and is habitually thought of as one of the successful academic painters. Actually Puvis de Chavannes had a series of early rejections from the Salon and later on, when he was firmly established and served on Salon

403. PUVIS DE CHAVANNES: *The Poor Fisherman,* 1881. 59⅞ x 75".
Louvre, Paris.

404. SEURAT: *The Bridge at Courbevoie,* 1886. 18 x 21½". Home
House Society, Courtauld Institute of Art, London.

contemporary taste; his allegories are obvious and his subject pictures have a synthetic sweetness which is tiresome. But as a mural designer, as he essentially was, he simplified and flattened his forms into compositions of a decorative clarity and nicety unique in his generation.* We see more and more that he was an important influence on modern painting, not only through Seurat but, as will soon be seen, even more surprisingly through Gauguin.

Seurat so admired a painting by Puvis, *The Poor Fisherman* [403], that he made a free copy of it, shortly before he began work on *La Grande Jatte.* Whatever else *The Poor Fisherman* may be—sentimental, prettified, and ambiguous in its compromise between conventionalization and photographic realism—compositionally it is a harmonious combination of simplified forms disciplined into delicate, but decisive, balance. Upon this kind of composition Seurat imposed further disciplines, always in the direction of increased abstraction, as in the severely beautiful *Bridge at Courbevoie* [404], distilled to the geometrical essence of the subject's elements. In *La Grande Jatte,* Seurat's problem was to achieve equal clarity in the manipulation of a large number of elements in more complicated relationships.

Once the composition was established, the execution of the painting in the dot-by-dot technique of pointillism remained as a chore before which most painters would have blanched, and which demanded even of Seurat an obsessive concentration. Pointillism, as it is usually called, or divisionism as the neo-impressionists preferred to call it, is a dead end in the maze of color theories branching out from Delacroix's rediscovery of reds in greens, purples in yellows, of vibrations and countervibrations between the color elements of a painting that led, in one direction, to the even more broken color of impressionism. The work of the scientists who investigated the physi-

juries, he irritated the other members by the freedom of his judgments, and at the end of the century he was greatly respected by the generation represented by Seurat. Puvis seems both sentimental and stuffy to

* His numerous murals include *The Sacred Wood,* in the Sorbonne in Paris, the celebrated series of the life of St. Genevieve in the Pantheon near by, and some late, not entirely successful allegories for the staircase of the Public Library in Boston.

cal laws of light and color was known to the impressionists and probably influenced them to some degree in a most informal way. But there is nothing informal in the art of Seurat; he studied these theories and applied them methodically.

Where Monet would paint a large green area of foliage with many shades of green and occasional flecks of pure yellow or pure blue, allowing these tints and colors to be more or less blended by the eye, Seurat attempted to analyze the exact proportions of the components of a tint, to separate them into the colors of the spectrum, and then to apply them with scientific precision so that their optical blending would produce not only the tint but the degree of vibration he wanted. The surface of his canvas becomes a kind of "molecular dance" in contradiction to the absolute precision of the forms within which these myriads and myriads and myriads of dots spin and quiver. In his preliminary black and white studies for a picture, Seurat approximated the effect of pointillist color by drawing, in his own way, on charcoal paper with black wax crayon [402]. Charcoal paper has a fine but conspicuous grain that allows flecks of white to show through the black, to a degree dependent on the pressure of the crayon. The crayon is always pure black; grays are produced by the interspeckling of the paper's grain, just as tones and colors in the completed painting are produced by the interspeckling of calculated quantities of the component colors.

There is an essential objection to pointillist technique which was made at the time and is still legitimate in spite of the fact that Seurat's stature among recent painters makes a statement of this objection heretical. But there is no point in pretending that it is possible to look at a painting by Seurat without being first of all conscious of the novelty of its technique. One must somehow manage to cross the barrier of agonizingly meticulous and desperately sincere application of an elementary scientific principle before one is free to enjoy a work of art. Access to Seurat's studio is still through his laboratory, and one is required to watch him at work there before one is allowed to see the pictures.

405. PISSARRO: *River—Early Morning*, 1888. 18¼ x 21⅞". Philadelphia Museum of Art, John G. Johnson Collection.

But once this privilege is granted, the pictures are worth the wait. According to his own aesthetic, which he once formulated in a didactic outline, Seurat left no room for intuition in the creation of a work of art. But it is impossible to look at *La Grande Jatte* and believe that it was produced entirely by rule. If it observes rules more rigorously than painting had ever done before, these rules are still subject to the sensibilities of the artist who applied them. And for that matter, there is not very much in Seurat's rules that was new. As if it should come as a revelation, Seurat propounded a set of general principles that had been observed for centuries. Some of them were truisms that could have been picked up en route during study in any sound academic painter's studio, such as the rule that dark tones and cold colors suggest sadness, that gayety is suggested by luminous tones and warm colors. Since the Renaissance, and perhaps earlier than that, Seurat's principles had been familiar to any thoughtful painter. In reading accounts by his followers one is amazed at the long-faced reverence with which Seurat's restatement of a pedant's primer seems to have been greeted. Only the theory of optical color was new, or newish.

Seurat was also interested in discovering a scientific basis for pictorial composition, and he investigated among others a famous mathematical formula called the "golden section." Also called the "divine proportion" or "gate of harmony," it was formulated by the architect and engineer, Vitruvius, in the first century B.C. and revived in the Renaissance. In 1509 it was published in a book by a Bolognese monk, Luca Pacioli, illustrated by Leonardo da Vinci, who had made his own investigations of the mathematical bases of harmony. And we will see it picked up again in the twentieth century by certain cubists, and adopted as a name for their group. Applied as a test to many a great painting or building or art object, the "golden section" fits perfectly. Applied in the same way to some of the worst pictures or buildings or objects ever painted or built or manufactured, it works just as well. Used as a formula for creation it may yield results similar to those more effectively arrived at by a combination of general principles and intuition. Analogies may be made: in music, for instance, it is possible to create a fugue that is technically impeccable, by rule, yet an offense to the ear. In cookery it is possible to follow a recipe closely and produce a dish that is just edible where a master chef would produce a delight from what would seem to be the same preparation of the same ingredients. The point of insisting on all these objections to Seurat's fascination with formula, objections that may sound ill-tempered or uncharitable, is only to insist that *La Grande Jatte* as a work of art rises above its demonstration of codified rules. Seurat was a very young man who was investigating the whole process of creative effort, beginning with its mechanics. One can imagine him, had he lived, passing through a crisis similar to Renoir's, from the other direction. Where Renoir—rightly —mistrusted the spontaneous, unstudied effects of impressionism and recognized the need for self-discipline, so Seurat might have—rightly—relaxed his obsession with "scientific" calculation as the way to expression, putting his faith first in impulse,

and second in its discipline, as Renoir did after his period of reorientation.

As it was, Seurat produced a cycle of paintings demonstrating, systematically, the different principles of his aesthetic, before his death at the age of only thirty-two. *La Grande Jatte*, the first of the cycle, was exhibited in 1886 in the eighth, and last, impressionist group show. The group was breaking up; this was the first exhibition in four years, and neither Renoir nor Monet participated. The great problem was what to do about *La Grande Jatte* and the other neo-impressionist paintings—including those of Pissarro, who was involved just then in his brief excursion into this field [405], and those of his son Lucien, who was exhibiting for the first time, and those of Paul Signac, whose name is second only to Seurat's in neo-impressionism. Finally all these pictures were segregated in a room by themselves. The term *neo-impressionism* was coined in this year as a gesture on the part of Seurat and Signac. In spite of their departures from impressionist technique they thus acknowledged their debt to the men who had first explored the translation of light into pigment. But since the impressionist ideal was to capture the transient moment, and the neo-impressionist hope was to capture the essential quality of a scene and transfix it, the exhibition of 1886 must have been an oddly contradictory one. And it demonstrated that pure impressionism had served its purpose and reached its end, as the founding members dropped away to solve special problems, and new recruits, like Seurat, used impressionism as a foundation for new structures.

The "Salon des Indépendants"

The importance of the impressionist exhibitions had been reduced, also, because a new and more inclusive organization had been formed to allow any painter to exhibit who wanted to do so. This had occurred two years before the last impressionist show and the exhibition of *La Grande Jatte*—in 1884. Several hundred artists rejected from the Salon of that year had come together

406. Seurat: *Une Baignade*, 1883–84. 79 x 118½″. Tate Gallery, London.

to form an organization to hold no-jury exhibitions, calling themselves the *Société des Artistes Indépendants* (the same name the impressionist group had used for a while). Seurat was one of the leaders in the organization of the *Indépendants,* and in the first exhibition, 1884, he showed *Une Baignade* [406]. *Une Baignade* is obviously a forerunner of *La Grande Jatte;* it differs in that Seurat has not yet adopted the pointillist technique. It is a large, quiet picture, rather subdued in color, serenely balanced, but without the combination of formal severity and vibrant surface that would fully individualize Seurat in *La Grande Jatte*. Seurat, along with Pissarro and Signac, also exhibited in Brussels with a new group called *Les Vingt,* which was devoted to the struggle for the recognition of new art movements in that country. Similar organizations and exhibitions began to appear all over Europe and, before long, in America.

It was while Seurat was helping to arrange the *Salon des Indépendants* in 1891 that he contracted the pneumonia from which he died. It is generally accepted that he was weakened by the days and nights of laborious effort required to execute his large, carefully dotted paintings. He had not quite finished his picture for the *Salon des Indépendants* of 1891 when he died. *The Circus* [407] is an odd picture, with its thin, rather stringy forms and its immobility, which denies the theoretically lively action of its subject. In planning it, Seurat formulated a set of problems contrasting at every point with those he solved in *La Grande Jatte:* artificial light instead of daylight, an indoor setting in sharply limited space instead of an outdoor one in deeper space, a subject of action instead of one of repose. But if *La Grande Jatte* seems to demonstrate the legitimacy of Seurat's theories, *The Circus* demonstrates their limitations.

Theoretically, *The Circus* should be a successful picture. The lines swirl in a way that is theoretically correct to express action. The silhouettes, as in the rider's skirt and the hat of the clown in the foreground, are full of the theoretically expressive upward movements which should express gaiety ("Gaiety of line is given by lines above the horizontal"). The color is dominated by oranges, reds, and yellows, the "warm dominants" expressive of action and cheerfulness in Seurat's codification of rules.

But sometimes it is necessary to look at a picture not in the light of what the artist intended to do, or how successful the result should have been in view of the way he did it, but quite subjectively as to whether or not the picture speaks for itself. In *The Circus* the means are justified by theory, but there is a real question as to whether the end has been achieved, a legitimate question in spite of our knowledge that the picture is not quite complete. The truth is that as a demonstration *The Circus* is interesting, but as a work of art it remains a demonstration. Almost detail by detail it can be paired with Lautrec's picture of the *Circus Fernando* [408], even to the ringmaster's whip, the dancing clown, the scattered audience, in a comparison disastrous to Seurat's contention that picturemaking can be reduced to a science. Lautrec has observed the same general principles— active line, vivacious shapes, gay color—in

407. SEURAT: *The Circus*, 1891. 70⅝ x 58¼". Louvre, Paris.

408. TOULOUSE-LAUTREC: *In the Circus Fernando: The Ring Master*, 1888. 39½ x 63½". Art Institute of Chicago, Joseph Winterbotham Collection.

409. Seurat: *La Parade*, 1889. 39½ x 59¼". Collection Stephen C. Clark, New York.

410. Seurat: *Les Poseuses* (second version), 1888. 15½ x 19½". Collection Henry P. McIlhenny, Philadelphia.

a picture full of life not because it was painted in ignorance of method or theory, for of course it was not, but because method and theory, already mastered, were taken for granted as part of the act of creation. In Seurat's picture, method as an application of theory *is* the act of creation, or is meant to be, and this time it has not been enough.

Not only as Seurat's last work but as his least successful demonstration, *The Circus* leaves one wondering what lesson Seurat would have learned from it, and what new explorations he might have made. For with *La Grande Jatte* as a beginning and *The Circus* as a conclusion, Seurat had completed a series of five demonstrations of his systematic aesthetic. *La Parade* [409], following *La Grande Jatte* and painted in 1887–1888, attacks the problem of representing figures out of doors illuminated by

411. SEURAT: *Le Chahut* (study), 1889. 22 x 18¼″. Albright Art Gallery, Buffalo.

412. SEURAT: *La Poudreuse* (*Madeleine Knobloch*), 1889. 37½ x 31¼″. Home House Society, Courtauld Institute of Art, London.

artificial light. (The row of lotuslike shapes along the top of the composition is a line of flaring gas jets.) The depth of *La Grande Jatte's* landscape is eliminated by flat walls and screens, reduced in pattern to an abstraction of overlapping rectangles. The figures, instead of being disposed in a variety of attitudes within space, are ranged flatly and repetitiously across a plane close to the observer.

Following *La Parade*, Seurat set himself the problem of a third and last static subject, this time with the variation of his first indoor setting, and in natural light, *Les Poseuses* (*The Models*), showing three nude models posed in his studio. (Along one wall, a portion of *La Grande Jatte* was incorporated into the composition.) *Les Poseuses* is the most delicately colored, the most minutely executed, of all Seurat's pictures, exquisite to the point of thinness and dryness. His friends objected to this quality in it, attributing the picture's look of

anemia to the extreme smallness of the dots. Seurat must have agreed. In any case, he followed the disappointing large version with a small one [410] where the tiny dots of paint are harmoniously scaled to the picture area, thus transforming an arid and flavorless picture into one of gemlike precision.

Le Chahut [411] was the first of Seurat's kinetic subjects, arranged in shallow space, a preliminary to the kinetic variation of *The Circus*. Although the series of five pictures would certainly have been extended to include, for instance, a kinetic subject in natural light out of doors, they are a unit just as they stand. They are an impressive life work, yet surely they are only an introduction, a preface, to a main text that was never written.

Seurat left a single portrait, of Madeleine Knobloch, his mistress, called *La Poudreuse* [412]. Seurat's liaison, and the child of it, whom he acknowledged, were unknown

413. SIGNAC: *The Port of St. Tropez*, 1916. Watercolor, 13½ x 16¼″. Brooklyn Museum.

even to most of his closest friends until after his death. In *La Poudreuse* he originally painted his own portrait in the frame now filled by a small bouquet; it has been revealed recently by x-ray photography. Seurat's family acknowledged Madeleine Knobloch and divided the contents of his studio with her. Since Seurat had sold or given away almost nothing, this meant virtually his entire output. But no one was very interested in acquiring pictures in an eccentric technique most of which were, in any case, too large to hang except as collection pieces. They had been the subject of the usual scandals, so repetitious since the *Salon des Refusés*. Even ten years after Seurat's death his pictures were considered practically worthless, and *La Grande Jatte* was sold in 1900 for only 900 francs. A syndicate recently offered a million dollars for its purchase and return to France.

Other Neo-impressionists

Neo-impressionism attracted a large number of followers, as might be expected of a manner offering so explicit a formula. Seurat was disturbed by the size of the number, since none of them had the scientific perseverance that was prerequisite to neo-impressionism if it was to be more than formula painting. Nor did many of them have the creative sensibility that was also necessary although Seurat denied it. After Seurat's death his leadership was taken over by Paul Signac (1863–1935). Signac was four years younger but had had as much to do with the origins of neo-impressionism as had Seurat himself. Signac, in fact, had converted Seurat to the work of the impressionists, objecting to the "dull" colors of *Une Baignade* when it was exhibited in the first *Salon des Indépendants*. The two men had met at the formation of the *Société des Indépendants,* and Signac remained one of its hardest-working members and was its president for twenty-six years, beginning in 1908.

Signac was an attractive man, vigorous, enthusiastic, and as outgoing as Seurat was secretive. These qualities are reflected in his painting. He keeps bursting out of the strait jacket of neo-impressionist precision to indulge himself in the joy of painting. He executed some pen-and-ink drawings in a rather painful dot technique which was practiced by several other members of the group, including occasionally Seurat, but he was more at home with a dashing form of divisionism in which broad strokes of color are patterned freely, rather than methodically and in watercolors where vivaciously sketched lines and spots of color sparkle against white paper [413]. His book *From Eugène Delacroix to Neo-Impressionism,* published in 1889, is the classic doctrinaire reference on the school.

Among other followers, two are more distinguishable than most: Henri Edmond Cross (1856–1910), one of the founders of the *Société,* was more interested in emotional expression than in scientific theory, and sought it by using the purest, brightest colors of any of the neo-impressionists, to the point even of using them arbitrarily without regard to the actual color of the objects painted. He thus anticipated, as will become apparent later, the work of the fauvist painters, including Matisse. And Maximilien Luce (1858–1941) painted some sensitive pictures remindful of Pissarro. Like Pissarro he abandoned neo-impressionism to revert to the fresher, more intimate effects of impressionism itself.

Cézanne: His Revolution

By age and by association, Paul Cézanne (1839–1906) was one of the impressionists. He was five years younger than Degas, a year older than Monet, two years older than Renoir. He was a solitary man, but insofar as he had friends at all, he found them among his impressionist contemporaries. He exhibited in the first and third of the group shows, and when he was in Paris he frequented the *Café Guerbois* during the days when it was an impressionist center.[*] When Cézanne died at sixty-seven, Monet, Renoir, and Degas were still working. Yet by the time Renoir was setting himself to the task of painting the *Bathers,* and Seurat *La Grande Jatte,* Cézanne had already developed a way of painting as solid as Renoir's was ever to be, and more revolutionary than Seurat's. He said that he "wanted to make of impressionism something solid and durable like the art of the museums." It is a statement of intention that would have been appropriate from either Renoir or Seurat, but Cézanne's solution of the problem was so revolutionary that it takes him out of the impressionist generation except in the strictest chronological sense. Seurat was twenty years younger than Cézanne, yet without dates to guide us it would be easy to believe that the art of Seurat was a transitional step between impressionism and Cézanne. Chronology aside, Cézanne is a twentieth-century painter; that is why he is placed at this point in this book, instead of having been discussed with his impressionist friends and contemporaries, or before the younger Seurat.

Cézanne was the most revolutionary painter since the dawn of the Renaissance, which is what the critic Clive Bell meant in 1920 when he said, "If the greatest name in European painting is not Cézanne, it is Giotto." Cézanne recognized something of the same kind when he said, "I am the primitive of the way I have discovered." Together these two statements mean that European art was given a new direction in the early fourteenth century when a painter named Giotto di Bondone abandoned stylized medieval formulas of representation and turned to nature as his model; that for nearly 600 years painters followed this direction, varying and perfecting Giotto's innovation, until Cézanne appeared

---

[*] By 1877 the *Guerbois* had lost its importance as an impressionist meeting place, and the *Café de la Nouvelle Athènes* partially replaced it. The *Nouvelle Athènes,* however, became a center for literary intellectuals with only a scattering of painters.

and gave the first redirection since Giotto; and that like Giotto's achievement, Cézanne's is only a beginning, which will be varied and perfected by many generations of painters who will follow him.

No person in his right mind with more than a nodding acquaintance with the art of Cézanne approaches an explanation of it without the assumption that anything like a total and specific explanation is impossible. In the art of any great painter there is always a residue of the inexplicable after the historians and aestheticians have done their best with him. Cézanne's case is extreme. He himself complained that he had never "realized"—that is, completed, brought to concrete existence on canvas—his theories, what he had hoped to achieve. Even if we discount his statement in view of his temperament—which combined self-doubt with perseverance and allowed dissatisfaction with his own work to coexist with his conviction of its greatness—it is still true that he never managed to clarify his theories into an explainable formula. In this respect he is the opposite of Seurat. Where Seurat was certain of his formula and had only to submit himself industriously to its application, for Cézanne every brush stroke was a hazardous step and an experiment that might wreck the whole structure on the canvas. It is a mistake, often made, to analyze a painting by Cézanne as if it were a perfect and complete demonstration. And if a satisfactory analysis of one Cézanne is finally reached, it is not of much help in analyzing the next one, since Cézanne is full of variations and contradictions from picture to picture. When he said, "I am the primitive of the way I have discovered," he recognized not only the revolutionary nature of his art but also his feeling that he had gone but a short distance, and awkwardly, in the direction he set.

As a point of departure for any explanation of his art, two of Cézanne's own comments are more helpful than any others. These comments have become hackneyed for the good reason that no one has been able to invent more succinct ones to suggest the nature of the problems Cézanne set himself and the character their solution imposed on his painting. The twin statements are, "I want to do Poussin over again, after nature," and "I want to make of impressionism something solid and durable like the art of the museums."

To "do Poussin over again, after nature" sounds easier on first hearing than it does after a little thought. To do Poussin over again after nature would be to combine somehow the two opposites, Poussin's classical order and nature's immediacy. The catch is that neither must be sacrificed to the other, nor may they be mutually watered down to a compromise. How is it possible to be at once artificial and natural? To be at once orderly, like the world Poussin invented, and full of accidentals, like the world of nature? Synthetic on one hand, imitative on the other? For instance, could the problem be solved by repainting Poussin's *Funeral of Phocion* [128], charging its crystalline vacuum with effects of light and air? The suggestion is manifestly absurd since the resultant hybrid would sacrifice what Cézanne wanted from Poussin, the clarity of his order, and would not carry with it what he wanted from impressionism, its immediate contact with the reality of nature. Or, to reverse the combination, perhaps a natural landscape could be observed and modified with an eye to discovering within it the clarity and order achieved by Poussin in his invention of "unnatural" landscapes. This is an improvement. Corot, in fact, had already done this in pictures like the views of Rome [142, 143] which have been discussed.

Corot is a firm link in the tradition of Poussin, and his landscapes of the early period do combine an actual, existing scene with Poussinesque harmony of a sort. But these pictures are cityscapes; their architectural forms are half readymade for classical disposition, and when Corot painted pure landscape rather than cityscape, his sense of order was lessened, even if we forget his late, fuzzy pictures where it was even sacrificed.

Doing Poussin over again after nature did not mean, to Cézanne, adjusting the monumental forms of a great city into closer harmonies. It meant the imposition of order onto nature, without any loss of nature's vibrance, its quality of life and growth—in short, its naturalness, so dear to the impressionists that they had once been willing to sacrifice everything else to it. For this quality of life, of reality, Corot had substituted a kind of enchanted revery in pictures that were perfection in their way. But it was not the way Cézanne was seeking.

Thus to do Poussin over again after nature becomes a convenient phrase describing a problem but offering no hint of a solution. To perfect an interrelationship of forms in space, as Poussin did, yet to express the reality of their existence in nature, which is haphazard: this, Cézanne thought, must somehow be possible.

Cézanne: Color as Form

To so "make of impressionism something solid and durable like the art of the museums" is "Poussin after nature" turned around, if you wish, but an additional factor is implied—the special use of color made by the impressionists. In breaking their colors and applying the varying tints in individual strokes side by side, the impressionist conceived of color as a manifestation of light, and specific kinds of light. To begin with, Cézanne discards the idea of capturing transient effects. In the world he paints there is no time of day—no noon, no early morning or evening. There are no gray days, foggy days, no "effects" of season or weather. His forms exist in a universal light that impregnates and reveals, but it is not a light in the sense of directed rays from a single source, not even the sun. It is not light as an optical phenomenon to be investigated and experimented with. It is a uniform and enduring light, steady, strong, clear, and revealing, not a light that flows over objects and not a light that consumes them. It is a light integral to the canvas; it is "painted in" with every stroke of color. It is a static and a timeless light.

Conceiving of light in this way, Cézanne had no interest in the broken color of impressionism as a kind of optical trick to capture its shimmer in air. But the idea that impressionism's strokes of varying color could be identified with the expression of form did interest him. He began to model objects in a series of planes, each plane represented by a change of color. A round apple would be transformed into a roundish object of many facetlike planes which might change from yellow to orange, from orange to red, from red to purple, as one stroke succeeded another. In choosing these colors from facet to facet Cézanne observed—to some degree—the theory of advancing and receding color, which can be explained briefly:

A spot of yellow on a piece of blue paper appears to be in front of the blue, since yellow is optically an advancing color, blue a receding one. But a spot of blue on a sheet of yellow will look more like something seen through a hole in the paper than like something laid on top of it, for the same reason. This is because, in general, warm colors, such as yellow and orange, advance; in general cool colors, such as blue and blue-green or blue-purple, recede. But dozens of other considerations affect this generality, such as the texture of the colors, their relative intensities, their relative areas, and the effect on them of adjacent colors. And part of the problem of modeling in "plastic color" is the problem of the local color of the objects themselves, how to paint a green pear green, a red apple red, a white cloth white, yet to observe within the green, the red, and the white the color changes that will express the form. The word *express* is used instead of *describe* because the form can be "described" in black and white or with conventional use of color.

To reduce the idea of plastic color to these simple terms is immediately misleading, suggesting as it does that the objects in a picture by Cézanne are modeled on a formula that should be specifically recognizable in the painting itself. But this is almost never so. It is easy to imagine Seurat reducing the theory of plastic color to a series of equations, and then following the equations faithfully in a studio demonstration. For Cézanne this would have made the whole thing pointless. He was not a studio theorist; he insisted that the painter's first allegiance was to his subject, that he

414. Cézanne: *The Card Players*, 1890–92. 25¾ x 32″. Collection Stephen C. Clark, New York.

must work in the presence of his subject. For Cézanne, constant allegiance and reference to the subject supplied both discipline and nourishment for the process of creation. If he was painting a landscape he set up his easel out of doors, like an impressionist, not to capture the landscape's effect, as the impressionists did, but to absorb its essence. For a painter to work in his studio from sketches or from memory was to weaken his communion with the subject; to have worked entirely from theory would have been to sacrifice this communication altogether. When circumstances forced Cézanne to abandon this principle, he chafed; at work on a large composition of nude bathers he is supposed to have complained that it was impossible to find a group of models willing to pose thus out of doors, on the spot. He was exaggerating when he fretted in this way, for he did customarily synthesize figure groups from preliminary drawings and paintings made from models. But he never synthesized a pure landscape; and in all his painting the theories of form and color, which we have imagined Seurat applying within the neat boundaries of a formula, were given an additional complication by the facts of nature as Cézanne observed and respected them. There are many photographs of localities painted by Cézanne, taken from spots as close as possible to those where he must have stationed himself at work. The surprising thing about these photographs in comparison with Cézanne's paintings is always his close adherence to the subject, where one expects deviation from it.

422. CÉZANNE: *Olympia*, 1875–77. Watercolor (and crayon), 9¾ x 10½". Philadelphia Museum of Art, Louis E. Stern Collection.

During these years Cézanne met Hortense Fiquet—in 1869—and their son was born. Cézanne was in and out of Paris, where he never really felt at home. He spent the time of the Franco-Prussian War and the Commune in Aix and in the village of l'Estaque, near Marseilles, avoiding the draft, and in 1872 he worked with Pissarro at Pontoise. Under this benign influence he entered his second, or impressionist, period.

Cézanne's impressionist period runs from 1872 to 1877. By 1878 he had discovered what Renoir was to discover five years later; he was the first of the impressionists to turn away from transient effects in landscape, if indeed he can be said ever to have accepted them. His great link with impressionism was Pissarro, who himself kept a fairly tight rein on impressionism's tendency to dissolve form into tinted veils. Later, Cézanne objected even to Pissarro's impressionism, saying that if he, Pissarro, had kept on as he had started, he would have been the greatest of them all. But Cézanne felt that, instead, Pissarro had succumbed to the common failing.

The two men worked side by side at Auvers, where Cézanne painted *The House of the Hanged Man* [423], which has become the standard example of his impressionist period. It was exhibited in the first group show, to which Cézanne was admitted upon Pissarro's insistence over general objections. Manet even gave as a reason for not exhibiting that he could not afford to commit himself alongside Cézanne, who was thought of as a little freakish even by those other members who sensed his strength. And Cézanne gave them plenty of reason for feeling so. He was rough in manner, sometimes surly, always unsure of himself, and defensively contemptuous of fine manners. In a rare excursion into satire he did a take-off on Manet's *Olympia* [422], including in the background a top-hatted dandy as a jibe at Manet.

When the impressionist exhibition opened, Cézanne's pictures were the most ferociously attacked of all. (It goes without saying that all this time, and for a long time

apparent in *The Man in a Blue Cap* [419], also called *Uncle Dominic*. By hindsight or coincidence this breaking-up into planes forecasts Cézanne's later expression of planes in color sequences, but as to color itself *The Man in the Blue Cap* is not related to this idea. It is done in tans, browns, and creams and grays, punctuated by the bright blue-green of the cap, the dash of red in the scarf at the neck, and rather ruddy flesh tones. Other pictures of the period may be almost without color, in dark browns and blacks, with monochromatic lights, like the awkward but powerful portrait of *The Artist's Father* [420]. The still-lifes are also thickly painted, rather heavy in form, sometimes almost ponderous. There are many emotionalized subjects, sometimes in the form of allegories, often suggesting frustrations and confusions. There are religious subjects, including some "copies" which are very free adaptations of well-known baroque paintings. In this manner there is the odd and rather disturbing *Washing of a Corpse* [421], which at first glance seems to be a *Pietà*, or mourning of Christ.

423. CÉZANNE: *The House of the Hanged Man*, 1873–74. 22¼ x 26¾". Louvre, Paris.

after, Cézanne was regularly rejected from the Salon.) Yet, as an impressionist painting, *The House of the Hanged Man* is much more concerned with formal definition, much less with light effects, than the average. It is impressionistic in the purification and heightening of color; impressionism had released Cézanne from his heavy browns and blacks and had taught him to apply his paint more sensitively, in smaller strokes. These elements finally led to his thinking in terms of planes and volumes modeled in color.

Cézanne: Realization

The third period, in which Cézanne abandons impressionism and matures as an original artist, runs from 1878 to 1887, ending during the months of his marriage, his father's death, and the break with Zola. By now Cézanne had abandoned Paris ex-

cept for an occasional short visit. From time to time he saw Renoir, Monet, Pissarro, and Zola, but in his preoccupation with new problems he began to withdraw from his friends. After the group show of 1878 he did not exhibit again with them. If Zola had been able to understand the work of his friend at this time he might not have said, as he did about 1880, that the misfortune of the impressionists was that no artist had achieved "powerfully and definitely" the possibilities inherent in the new painting. "They are all forerunners," he said of the impressionists. "The man of genius has not arisen."

The man of genius had arisen and was at work in the steady light of the south, solidifying the shifting, quivering effects of impressionism into something solid and durable like the art of the museums, and reconciling Poussin with nature. The transformation of Cézanne's art in this "constructive" or "classical" period is revealed by

424. CÉZANNE: *View of Gardanne*, 1885–86. 31 x 25½″. Metropolitan Museum of Art, New York, and Dr. F. H. Hirschland, Harrison, N.Y.

even a superficial comparison of *The House of the Hanged Man* with a *View of Gardanne* [424]—a small town not far from Aix—where the houses rising on the steep slope are abstracted into a configuration of interlocking planes. If such a subject, like Corot's, seems half-readymade, with its

blocky houses mounting up to the climax of the steepled church, it is largely because Cézanne's statement is so clear. In the hands of most painters the picturesqueness of the jumbled houses almost on top of one another would have been exaggerated by playing up the interest and variety of the

425. CÉZANNE: *L'Estaque and the Gulf of Marseilles*, 1882–85. 25¼ x 31½". Charles R. Tyson Collection, Philadelphia, Pa.

426. CÉZANNE: *Still-life with Commode*, c. 1885. 25¾ x 31⅞". Fogg Art Museum, Cambridge, Mass., Maurice Wertheim Collection.

very confusions Cézanne eliminates when he paints planes, not walls, and volumes, not houses, and disposes them in a painting where the interest must be in created abstractions, not in imitated picturesqueness. This is what Cézanne means by "motif" instead of subject. *View of Gardanne* is a fine semiabstract pictorial structure; it would not make the best possible travel poster.

In subjects less obviously adaptable to logical disposition, the sense of organization in Cézanne's transmutation of the forms is just as great even if the means are less apparent. In landscapes like *L'Estaque and the Gulf of Marseilles* [425] all the elements dearest to the impressionists—water, sky, foliage, a scattering of small architectural forms—begin to coalesce in a new perspective, a perspective expressed by color instead of vanishing points. In talking about

427. Cézanne: *Madame Cézanne*, c. 1885. 18⅛ x 15". Collection S. S. White III and Vera White, Ardmore, Pa.

428. Cézanne: *The Man in Blue*, c. 1895. 31⅞ x 25⅝". Collection Mrs. T. G. Kenefick, Buffalo, N.Y.

his pictures to his friends, Cézanne used to point to passages where he was dissatisfied because the color remained merely color, not simultaneously color and perspective. By definition, perspective is "the science of representing on a plane surface, natural objects as they appear to the eye," with vanishing points and linear systems that create an illusion of distance. But Cézanne abandons the idea of perspective as line. "Color is perspective." He is not interested in an illusion of distance or an illusion of form. In his landscapes there is a new compactness, a deliberate limiting of space. The distance from foreground to background across trees and fields, buildings, and the gulf and on to the hills on the other side in *L'Estaque and the Gulf of Marseilles* (as in his other landscapes now) is contracted toward the observer. Instead of emphasizing the recession of plane after plane into expanding distance, Cézanne draws each plane for-

ward, compressing space and thus increasing the sense of ordered unity.

When he is not painting out of doors he is working at the same kind of problem in still-life, in front of the apples and pears that rotted during the weeks, the artificial flowers, and the ginger jar, the plate, and the few vases that appear in picture after picture. Objects assume new patterns of planes and volumes in arbitrary flattenings and tiltings, new balances and new rhythms [426]. Heads and bodies, in portraits and figure studies, are subject to similar distortions. Yet for all their revolutionary character, the paintings are first of all alive as expressions, whatever their surface of technical theory. Cézanne never loses himself in theory, a danger of which he was always conscious. Far from pure theoretical demonstrations, his landscapes are still filled with the life of growth; portraits are still personalities, even pictures of mood [427,428].

429. CÉZANNE: *Mont Sainte-Victoire*, 1885–87, 23½ x 28½". Phillips Collection, Washington, D.C.

Cézanne: Fulfillment

In the final period, the twenty years from 1886 until his death, Cézanne pushed toward a conclusion, generally in the direction of increased abstraction. To indicate the extent of this development, two views of Mont Saint-Victoire, near Aix, may be compared. The first [429] was painted just at the dividing line of the third and fourth periods; the second [430] is a work not earlier than 1904, two years before his death.

The low peak of Sainte-Victoire, rising above the countryside and familiar to Cézanne all his life, visible from his studio window, preoccupied him in painting after painting. It must have become for him something of a symbol of what he wanted to express: the grandeur, the life, the power,

yet the eternal order and stability of nature. In the earlier of the two pictures we are comparing, the peak is seen across a valley where a viaduct, roads, fields, and houses are ordered around it. We are led to its mass across a complexity of smaller volumes ordered, among other ways, by the fanning out of roads and the divisions between fields. Partly because of coincidental reasons, such as the bordering trees and the pattern of foliage against the sky, the rolling terrain mounting toward a climax and bearing many small architectural forms, this picture is especially close to Poussin, specifically to *The Funeral of Phocion* [128]. But for all its grandeur and vitality, the scene is also intimate in its sense of enclosure, of peace and order.

In contrast, the very late painting is more severe, yet it is electric in its sharp, vividly

430. CÉZANNE: *Mont Sainte-Victoire from Les Lauves, c.* 1904. 27⅞ x 36⅛″. Philadelphia Museum of Art, George W. Elkins Collection.

431. CÉZANNE: *Mont Sainte-Victoire from Bibemus Quarry, c.* 1898–1900. 25½ x 32″. Baltimore Museum of Art, Cone Collection.

colored planes. The forms now approach complete abstraction. Occasionally a house may still be distinguished as a house, or a clump of trees may tell as itself, but for the most part from plane to plane, which means from color to color, the forms exist as color-planes only. The mass of the mountain itself remains recognizable, yet it is broken into echoes and continuations of the planes that build toward it, and these planes are further continued into the sky. The compression of space is extreme. Fields, mountain, and sky are concentrated into the shallowest depth compatible with the interlocking crystallization of vivid blue, green, and orange planes.

Again and again Cézanne explored Mont Sainte-Victoire as a motif. Somewhere between these two versions, in its degree of abstraction, is a view of the mountain as

432. Cézanne: *Landscape with Mont Sainte-Victoire*, 1885–87. Watercolor, 15¼ x 19⅝".
Fogg Art Museum, Cambridge, Mass.

seen across the gash of a quarry [431]. The flat clifflike sides of orange stone impose a different order upon the composition; the peak is given a sharper elevation in harmony with the uncompromising upward rise of the quarry walls with their vertical divisions. As a final comparison, the sharp upward movement of this version contrasts with the lower forms, the gentler movement, of a watercolor painted, again, just at the turn of the third into the fourth period [432].

Cézanne's watercolors are of extraordinary delicacy. They never suggest the heaviness and the occasional fumbling that it is possible to find in some of his oils. (Other oils are painted nearly as thinly and transparently as watercolor.) The forms are indicated with a few lines lightly touched onto the paper with pencil, then these are supplemented with a minimum of plane-like washes in small areas of prismatic blue, pink, green, and violet, very pale but clear and bright.

Cézanne: "The Great Bathers"

It was after 1886 that Cézanne painted the synthesized figure studies, such as *The Card Players* which we have already seen, one of five variations on the subject, and *The Great Bathers*, the climax of a long series of compositions of bathers in landscape.

The theme of bathers in a landscape had interested Cézanne in different ways as far back as his very early "romantic" period. *The Great Bathers* [433] painted near the end of his life is a curious picture, an arresting one certainly, and for most people not a very agreeable one. Cézanne's distortion in still-life and landscape is nowadays acceptable to even casual observers; it is slight in comparison with the extreme distortion seen constantly in modern painting, familiar to everyone because it is reproduced on every hand. After the more jolting experience of Picasso's rupture and rending of natural form, the person with no formal

433. CÉZANNE: *The Great Bathers*, 1898–1905. 82 x 99″. Philadelphia Museum of Art, Wilstach Collection.

knowledge of art accepts Cézanne's trees and mountains and apples and pears without questioning their relatively mild departures from visual fact. But it is not so easy for the layman to accept the distortion of the human body with its strong associations dependent upon a standard of normal physical beauty. The female nudes in *The Great Bathers* may be no more distorted than the cloth, the bowl, and the fruit in *The White Sugar Bowl* (which belongs to the same period) but they are more disturbing because they violate a standard of beauty that is held with an emotional tenacity not at all comparable to the average person's respect for the shape of an apple or a pear.

These comments are obvious enough and would be altogether pointless except that there is a legitimate question as to whether the stock problem of nudes in a landscape is an entirely sympathetic one for Cézanne's purposes. For Renoir, yes; his *Bathers* remain delicious creatures as well as the components of a painting. They are also expressive of the theme uniting Renoir's total work: the beauty of the world as he knew and loved it and found it symbolized in women. But there is no reason why the female nude should serve Cézanne as a motif; there are even reasons why it should not, since it is known that he was embarrassed in the presence of a nude female model, suspicious and fearful of women in general. The simple, straightforward men who were his models for *The Card Players* are compatible, as motifs, with the closeness to simple values that we have called basic in Cézanne's art, with its expression of the dignity of everyday, ordinary things. From this point of view, *The Great Bathers*—Cézanne's most ambitious effort as a monumental structure—may be far down the list expressively, since its motif is so artificial, so far removed from the painter's own emotional experience. At the same time, this very removal clarifies the painting as a pure formal abstraction. Historically, *The Great Bathers* is a landmark in the development of abstract painting, the summit of Cézanne's art. Its importance in the genesis of twentieth-century painting will become apparent later in comparison with, for instance, Picasso's *Les Demoiselles d'Avignon* [560]. By itself, *The Great Bathers* may be less rewarding than most Cézannes. But in context with his total work, as a planned climax and summary, it is an important document in the history of art.

At least three of the several formal systems that are fused into the construction of the picture are apparent without much searching. First, of course, there is the powerful arched form established so emphatically by the tree trunks and echoed by at least a portion of each figure. Second, a countersystem reverses this upward thrust by a downward one climaxing where the arms of the central figures reach toward a central spot. This countersystem, also, is reflected in some portion of each figure. Finally, there is a movement into compositional depth, most apparent in the figure at the lower right lying on its stomach and facing into the picture. There are also the strong stabilizing horizontals of horizons and banks running across the center and lower portions of the composition. The picture is not finished; parts of the canvas are not covered. But the vigor and the deliberation and the consistency of the picture as it stands, the integration of every smallest part into the structural whole, are so satisfying that there is no sense of loss in our knowledge that the structural process could have continued into further complications and refinements.

In the last decade of his life, Cézanne began to be well known. By 1900, except in the usual backwater of academic intelligence, his power and the importance of his revolution were recognized beyond the specialized circle of a very few dealers, painters, and critics. In 1895 the dealer Ambroise Vollard exhibited a large number of Cézanne's paintings, reintroducing him to Paris after a lapse of close to twenty years. Vollard was only thirty years old at this time and had opened his firm only two years before. Not very certain of his own taste, he wisely accepted advice from good sources, especially from Pissarro and Degas. Pissarro, always Cézanne's good angel, brought him to Vollard's attention. It was the beginning of Vollard's career as a dealer in *avant-garde* painting, and Cézanne painted his portrait in 1899. The public was appalled by the 1895 exhibition, the conservative painters and critics were outraged, but Cézanne was immediately established as a master in the minds of the former impressionists and among the canny collectors who were beginning to gather around adventurous dealers. It did not take long for the baying of the academic hounds to recede into the distance as a meaningless racket. Within a few years, independent critics had become at least as influential as official ones, and exhibitions held by independent dealers were even more influential than the official Salon as arbiters of taste—finally to the point of abusing their prestige, in some cases, as badly as the Salon had ever done. And the Salon, considerably chastened, liberalized its standards to meet the competition of the more exciting exhibitions that had grown up all around it.

Cézanne died in 1906, at sixty-seven, after a collapse brought on by exposure when he was caught in a sudden storm while painting out of doors. In the autumn Salon of 1907 he was given a large retrospective. As a summary of a painter's development, a retrospective exhibition is associated with the idea of a winding up, a completion, a capping-off, a termination. In Cézanne's case it is impossible to make this association. His retrospective was not the terminal point of a career so much as it was a summary of a new concept of form in painting that had been brought, in the art of one man, from its genesis in impressionism to a point of departure for the generations of a new century.

434. MAILLOL: *Leda*, 1902. Bronze, height 11½". Philadelphia Museum of Art, Lisa Norris Elkins Bequest.

Sculpture in Transition: Maillol

Sculpture during the nineteenth century acted as if it were a dependent and admiring younger brother to painting, content to follow its direction rather than to set new, legitimately sculptural directions for itself. Sculpture found no Cézanne, but it found a man who re-established the validity of sculpture as an independent medium, and who did so by a renewal of classical concepts, and hence must be interpolated at this point in this narrative.

For several decades, Rodin had been the only sculptor of any declamatory force, and he dominated sculpture until well after the end of his century. But even Rodin had been exceptional more for his range as a one-man summary of principles connected with romantic and realistic-impressionist painters than as a sculptor adding legiti-

mately to the tradition of sculpture in its own right. The man who at last challenged Rodin's conception with a contrasting one was Aristide Maillol (1861–1944).

Maillol was forty before he turned seriously to sculpture. Before that, he had studied painting at the Academy under Gérôme, and under Cabanel. But he was never fascinated by painting; he had the love of handcraft that is part of every good sculptor's nature, and in 1887 he abandoned pure painting to set up a tapestry workshop. He might have spent the rest of his life happily enough at this work, carving a few wooden figures for relaxation as he did, but in the last year of the century his eyes were so weakened that he gave up tapestry design. Thus, at the age of forty, he became a sculptor and thus, also, he becomes the first artist in this story whose important work falls wholly within the twentieth century.

Maillol's beginning as a painter makes it even more surprising that as a sculptor he had no use for semipainterly modeling. He began to build the solidest, most purely sculptural forms that had appeared in a hundred years. His goddesses [434] are the stocky, full-bodied country girls who posed for him, de-individualized by formal generalizations into universal symbols. Maillol is classical (not neo-classical) because he brought back to sculpture the repose, the serenity, the balance and stability, that had been forgotten in the cultivation of accessory detail by imitative realists and the busy surfaces of Rodin and his followers.

When we say that Maillol merely rejected realism and impressionism, and returned to a kind of classicism, it may appear that his revolution was only a negative one in the first case, a reactionary one in the second. But this is not quite so. Maillol did more than clear away a great deal of debris, and his classicism had nothing to do with the imitation of classical clichés. Maillol re-established the validity of sculpture as an art of pure form, self-contained and self-sufficient; he set it on course again as an independent art. He brought back to sculpture the self-respect which, until then, no one had quite realized it had lost.

CHAPTER 11

Post-impressionism: Its Romantics

The Nature of Expressionism

Seurat and Cézanne were painters within the classical tradition by its most inclusive definition: they believed that the chaotic material of human experience could be clarified and universalized, and that the means of effecting this transmutation could be discovered through the analysis of form and structure. The fact that their forms were so innovational—especially Cézanne's—makes them no less classical. It simply demonstrates that the classical spirit need not depend for expression on images of gods and heroes foreign to the modern world, but may assume forms as original as those of gods and heroes had been when the classical Greeks invented them so long ago. The art of Seurat and Cézanne led the way for the abstract geometrical schools of the twentieth century, such as cubism, which completed the transformation of the gods and heroes into the simplest Euclidian rectangles.

But paralleling this "classical" development, the romantic spirit was forcing its own new expressions, this time with pain and violence exceptional even for romanticism. The art and the lives of Vincent van Gogh and Paul Gauguin were spectacular climaxes in the romantic tradition (which has a way of expressing itself in climaxes); their painting led in turn to the romantic art of the twentieth century, which was expressionism and its variants.

Expressionism in painting is the free distortion of form and color for the expression of inner sensations or emotions. All expressive art is a transfiguration of form to some degree, but expression*ism* is especially con-

435. DAUMIER: *Clown, c.* 1868. Composite wash drawing, 14½ x 10¼". Metropolitan Museum of Art, New York.

tional world. Less intimately, the expressionist may interpret the world for the observer by distortions revealing its essence in emotional terms peculiar to the painter. Expressionism is romanticism extended—further intensified.

Expressionism is a new term and it applies specifically to modern art, but as a general term it can apply here and there as far back as one cares to go in the history of art. In the late sixteenth century when El Greco twisted and elongated his forms and tied them together in near-hysterical patterns of swirls, angles, and lights, he anticipated the devices of expressionism, although the word was not to exist until three centuries later. And when Daumier, in one of the great drawings of the nineteenth century [435] abandoned his usual economical, realistically descriptive draughtsmanship for a tangle of agitated lines to describe a clown standing on a chair, waving his arms and shouting, he was drawing expressionistically. In the arms, recognizable form even disappears. Descriptively, the arm on the left is entirely illegible as an arm, but expressively it climaxes a pathetic and goaded figure in which Daumier makes one of his rare pessimistic statements about life, agreeing with Macbeth that it is "a tale told by an idiot, full of sound and fury, signifying nothing."

Van Gogh: "The Starry Night"

Modern expressionism stems directly from the tragic Dutchman, Vincent van Gogh (1853–1890), a man a little older than Seurat, who died a year before Seurat did. Both stemming from impressionism, these contemporaries could hardly be more unlike—Seurat with his calculation, his method, his deliberation, van Gogh with his passion, his shattering vehemence. Instead of *La Grande Jatte,* so cool, so defined, so self-contained, van Gogh gives us *The Starry Night* [436], where a whirling force catapults across the sky and writhes upward from the earth, where planets burst with their own energy and all the universe surges and pulsates in a release of intolerable vitality.

cerned with intense, personal emotions, and frequently has connotations of pathos, violence, morbidity, or tragedy. Distortion in itself is not necessarily expressionistic. Cézanne's distortions are not, because they are primarily structural, and only indirectly a vehicle for the transmission of his feelings. And these feelings in any case are not transmitted in intimate, emotionalized terms.

The expressionist opens his heart and soul and releases his deepest feelings through images intended to embrace the observer and make him a partner rather than an audience, a participant or, at least, a sympathizer within the picture's emo-

436. VAN GOGH: *The Starry Night*, 1889. 29 x 36½". Museum of Modern Art, New York, Lillie P. Bliss Bequest.

Like all the most affecting expressionist creations, *The Starry Night* seems to have welled forth onto the canvas spontaneously, as if the creative act were a compulsive physical one beyond the artist's power to restrain. "Inspiration" as a kind of frenzied enchantment visited upon a painter, a paroxysm calling forth images only half-willed, is a justifiable conception in van Gogh's case, if it is ever justifiable at all. *The Starry Night* implies that it was executed in a fever of creation, as if it had to be set down somehow on canvas in an instant, as if a pause for calculation would check the gush, the momentum, of a brush guided by a mysterious spiritual force rather than by knowledge and experience. And to a certain extent this was so. Van Gogh's letters tell of days when his painting went well, when he would work into the night without stopping to eat. In some pic-

tures the paint is squeezed onto the canvas straight from the tube, as if to reduce to a minimum the obstructions between conception and execution. Yet all this is misleading. His letters also speak of his studies for a picture that obsesses him, a picture of a starry night. There is a full preliminary drawing.

If *The Starry Night* seems to burst, to explode, to race, it does not run away. It is built on a great rushing movement from left to right; this movement courses upward through the landscape, into the hills and on into the sky, and floods into the picture like a swollen river in the galaxy beginning at the border on the upper left. But this movement curls back on itself in the center of the picture, then rushes forward again at a reduced pace, and finally curls back once more to join other rhythms instead of running out of the picture. In the rest of the sky, the moon and stars are whirlpools meshing with these major movements. The cypresses rise abruptly and lean slightly in the opposite direction as a brake; their own motion, spiraling upward, is another check to the horizontal lunge of earth and sky; a church steeple cuts less conspicuously across the sweep of a hill on the horizon, to the same effect. The moon, largest of the whirlpools of light, is itself a force that sucks the current back into the picture at a point where it would otherwise rush beyond the frame and be lost.

All of this is calculation, not in Seurat's sense certainly, but it is a scheme consciously observed. *The Starry Night* may have been painted at white heat and even with passages of improvisation. Something like "inspiration" was present and accounts for the extraordinary immediacy of the picture, but this inspiration flowed from a reservoir of study and experience even if it was released by the passionate absorption of the moment. But in the end, it is this moment that tells. Confronted by *The Starry Night* we are brought into van Gogh's presence more intimately than other painters ever quite bring us into theirs. It is a bitter kind of poetic justice that today thousands of people find van Gogh an accessible and sympathetic personality, while during his life, craving love and offering it everywhere, he was able to form only a handful of friendships, and of these half were disastrous.

Van Gogh: Early Days and Works

Indeed van Gogh must be a much easier man to read about than he was to be around. Small, ugly, and intense, without charm or wit, intelligent but narrow, socially awkward, ill dressed as a point of honor, tortured by religious confusions, yearning for affection but egotistical and stubborn, eager to please but resentful of criticism, he was one of those people who hold noble ideals too nobly, who offer their love as an embarrassing gift, whom one would like to like but whose presence is a burden. He seemed incapable of enjoying himself or of giving pleasure; in all the letters he wrote—and he wrote beautifully in them—there is no indication that he ever took anything casually for a moment.

The men of van Gogh's family were traditionally clergymen, but two uncles had a prosperous gallery in The Hague, which they sold to the international art dealer Goupil. Through this connection young Vincent, at sixteen, obtained a place with Goupil, first in The Hague, then in London, and finally in the main branch of the firm in Paris. But he failed. Never suave, always opinionated, no friend of the rich, who buy pictures, he ended by irritating so many customers that he was dismissed. Turning to religion, he failed at the theological seminary. When he sought to sacrifice himself in service as a combination evangelist and social worker among miners in a desperately depressed and gloomy area, he failed. He subjected himself to all the hardships of his poverty-stricken parishioners— their miserable quarters, their abominable diet. He slept on a hard board and a straw mattress when he could have had a comfortable bed. The miners laughed at him, their children hooted at him in the streets. Twice in love, he was twice rejected—once by his landlady's daughter in London, once by a cousin. Rejected by the women he wanted to love, rejected by the people he wanted to help, van Gogh attempted to fulfill himself on both scores by living with and caring for a prostitute he picked up on the street, ugly, stupid, and pregnant. This idyll, which could have been inspired by Dostoevski, endured for twenty months.

It was not until 1880, when he was twenty-seven years old, that van Gogh decided to be a painter. He entered this new life not as one enters a profession but as one accepts a spiritual calling, in foreknowledge of self-sacrifice.

His will, his compulsion, to paint as a direct expression of self, as a psychological need quite aside from professional ambitions or the will to fame, no matter what suffering would be involved, sets van Gogh apart from the impressionists, who had fought stubbornly in the face of every discouragement but had always been professional painters, careerists. Delacroix had established the idea of the painter's right to paint as he pleased, to enter into a pitched battle against entrenched manners of painting; Courbet had continued to fight, more as an individual than as a member of an organized school with a leader and henchmen; the impressionists had further abandoned the pre-nineteenth-century idea of the painter as a craftsman with a product to sell in satisfaction of a demand, and finally were to succeed in creating a demand by bringing public taste into line with their standards. They seemed to have culminated the idea established by Delacroix. And to all these painters, of course, art was certainly a release and an emotional satisfaction, as creation must be to any artist. But they were professionals. With van Gogh the balance swings to the other side. Although he yearned for attention, although he exhibited when he could, and finally managed to sell one painting, he was not first of all a man making his way in a profession. He was a man intent on saving his soul, in creating his very being, by painting pictures.*

Van Gogh had begun to draw at the time of his failure as an evangelist among the miners, and had attended classes for a while at the academy in Brussels. He began his serious study as an overage beginner in the academic art school at The Hague, but did not stay long. He had a cousin there, Anton Mauve, one of the most popular painters of the day. Mauve was a painter of sentimentalized humanitarian subjects in the degenerating tradition of the Barbizon school. The association did not last long,

---

* The single picture van Gogh sold, if we don't count the ones he traded for paints, was *Red Vineyards*, which was exhibited six months before his death in a group show organized by *Les Vingt*, the Brussels group with whom Seurat also exhibited. Van Gogh had exhibited in the Paris *Indépendants* shows, as anyone could do, and had organized two exhibitions in Paris restaurants, one in *Le Tambourin*, which was frequented by writers and painters, one in a huge low-priced restaurant called *La Fourche*. This was his public exhibition record during his lifetime. The year following his death he was given a retrospective at the *Indépendants*. This was in 1891. In 1935 when the Museum of Modern Art held the first big van Gogh show in New York it established the attendance record, to that date, for exhibitions of the work of a single painter.

ending as so many of van Gogh's associations did, in a quarrel. This was also the time of his association with the prostitute Sien, which had become intolerable. Van Gogh left to paint on his own in the town of Neunen, where his father was now pastor. He puzzled and frightened the townsfolk; the pastor forbade them to pose for his son.

The work from this period—from his first efforts in 1880 until the beginning of 1886 —is a continuation of the obsessive humanitarianism that had led Vincent into evangelical work, and it has the same excess of gloomy fervor that had led to his failure in it. His subjects are poor people, squalid streets or farms, miners and peasants broken by poverty and toil, the inmates of almshouses. He draws in crayon or charcoal, and in his paintings his colors are as depressing as his subjects. His first large, ambitious composition, of which there are three versions, was *The Potato Eaters* [437], painted in the dismal browns and greenish blacks of the period. "I have tried to make it clear how these people, eating their potatoes under the lamplight, have dug the earth with these very hands they put in the dish. . . . I am not at all anxious for everyone to like or admire it at once."

His taste in painting generally was also involved more with humanitarian ideas than with aesthetic values. He admired Millet, and another French painter of peasants, l'Hermitte, and the Hollander Josef Israels, although he objected when these men idealized their subjects, as they usually did. He also admired Daumier and Rembrandt, again largely for their subject matter. He read such English authors as George Eliot and Dickens, who wrote of the poor and the oppressed. The American writer Harriet Beecher Stowe was another favorite; *Uncle Tom's Cabin*, with its pathetic slaves, stirred him deeply. He read the sociological realistic novels of Zola. But he also read the aesthetic de Goncourts. He hardly knew of the impressionist painters at this time.

Early in 1886 van Gogh suddenly left Holland for Paris. It seems to have been an abrupt decision. It was certainly an important one. He had gone to Antwerp and

437. VAN GOGH: *The Potato Eaters*, 1885. 32 x 45″. Municipal Museum, Amsterdam, V. W. van Gogh Collection.

had studied for a while at the academy there, but found it dull and restricting. Academic training was intolerable to him because it seemed divorced from the earthy and simple values he was interested in. But he was a clumsy draughtsman and he knew it, and he felt the need of stimulation and excitement from other painters. If he could not tolerate the school in Antwerp, neither could he go back to working on his own in a backward rural community. His brother Theo was directing a small gallery in Paris, a branch of Goupil's. Vincent wrote him that he would be in the Louvre at a certain hour, and asked Theo to meet him there.

Later, Theo was to recognize his brother's power as an artist, but at this time Vincent was only the family problem, a maladjusted and difficult man whose drawing was nothing more than an emotional stopgap, who was reaching his middle thirties and could not hold a job, who had shown that he was impractical and unstable and would have to be either supported or abandoned to the most desperate circumstances of life, to vagabondage, starvation, the almshouse. The story of Vincent and Theo from now on is a poignant one. Their letters, up to Vincent's last unfinished one written just before his suicide, read like a fine novel and have furnished the material for several poor ones. In his letters Vincent reveals the gentleness and above all the clarity of thought that were so rare when he spoke and not at all apparent in his actions. His torment is equally revealed, and Theo's patience and love. But in their day-to-day relationships when they were together, Vincent remained a problem— stubborn, hypersensitive, and eccentric. Theo's heart must have sunk when he read Vincent's letter telling of his decision to come to Paris, but he took his brother into his flat, supported him from his own limited income, and set about helping him find his way toward a solution of his problems.

Theo's gallery handled work by all the major impressionists as well as the standard

438. VAN GOGH: *Miners, Borinage*, 1880. Pen, lightly colored. 17¼ x 21½″. Kröller-Müller State Museum, Otterlo.

Salon masters who sold much better. Theo himself, like any good dealer, was always hunting new talent and had scouted the impressionist group shows with more sympathy than most dealers risked. Vincent's arrival coincided with the final impressionist exhibition, when only a few of the original group were exhibiting and a special room had been given over to the neo-impressionists, including Seurat with *La Grande Jatte*.

The impressionists' happy, brightly tinted art did not immediately affect Vincent. He entered the studio of Cormon, a conventional painter who gave his students sound training in the imitation of the model. Here, a grown man among youngsters, Vincent labored industriously, correcting his drawings until he had erased holes in the paper, irritating everyone, the class freak. Just how he managed to get

accepted in a class limited to thirty students, with a waiting list, is a question. Theo's position as a dealer probably helped. Lautrec was among the students and Vincent came to his studio from time to time, but he was an odd ball in the effervescent company and after standing hopefully on the sidelines for a while he would disappear. Lautrec did a sketch of him at a café table; it shows a thin, bearded man leaning forward intently.

The stimulation and the new ideas Vincent had come to Paris to find, came not from the young men at Cormon's studio but from the patriarch of the impressionists, Pissarro, reappearing yet again in his constant role of saint. As he had done with Cézanne, Pissarro now induced Vincent to abandon his gloomy palette and turgid shadows for the bright, high-keyed colorism of the impressionists. But the trans-

439. VAN GOGH: *Factories at Clichy, c.* 1887. 21¼ x 28¼". City Art Museum of St. Louis.

440. VAN GOGH: *Landscape with Wall,* date unknown. Pen and ink, 8⅞ x 12½". Collection T. Edward Hanley, Bradford, Pa.

by a path along a hedge of thorns; shadows that pass, dimly visible in the twilight. In the background the large constructions of the mine, and the heaps of clinkers, stand out vaguely against the sky . . . do you think the idea good?" Good or bad, the idea was typical of his preoccupation at that time with the hard lot of common people, full of cold, gloom, and miserable hardship. But now when he paints the *Factories at Clichy* [439] he has stopped seeing and thinking in terms of oppressed workers, blackened chimneys, belching smoke, piles of cinders and slag, and sees instead a blue sky, red roofs, a foreground of slashing yellows and greens, all singing in the open air.

From the broken strokes of impressionism and the uniform dots of pointillism (Vincent had made a brief sally in this latter direction) he developed a way of painting in short, choppy strokes of bright color, like elongations of the pointillist dots, which later were to bend and writhe and to be reflected also in drawings [440] of the greatest expressive economy. Suddenly he is an artist, suddenly his own man. The contrast between *Old Shoes* [441] and the portrait of *Père Tanguy* [442] painted the same year is complete. The old shoes are vigorously painted, but the color and the implied humanitarianism are still on the dull and rather heavyhanded level that is so bothersome in *The Potato Eaters.* But *Père Tanguy* suddenly lives, as no other of Vincent's images had lived until then, and Vincent himself suddenly lives as a fulfilled painter.

Julien Tanguy, affectionately called Père Tanguy, was a color grinder who as a traveling paint salesman had met most of the impressionists during their most difficult days before 1870. When he opened his own small shop of artists' materials in Montmartre he began "buying" their paintings, which usually meant accepting them in exchange for supplies. He also kept their work on hand for chance sales, and thus grew into a collector and art dealer. He was particularly fond of Cézanne; during the years of Cézanne's obscurity as a voluntary exile in Aix, his paintings could be seen only at Père Tanguy's. There were times

formation was more than a technical one; the spirit of Vincent's art was equally changed. One of his earliest existing drawings [438], done at about the time of his decision to work seriously at art, shows, as he described it in a letter to Theo, ". . . miners, men and women, going to the shaft in the morning through the snow, when Monet and Sisley would have been without materials to paint with if it had not been for this fatherly man. Madame Tanguy did not share his confidence or his interest in those painters who, like van Gogh, used a great deal of paint but were totally unsaleable.

Psychologically, Vincent's portrait of Tanguy is a complicated picture in spite of the directness and solidity of the image. Tanguy as a personality, with his combination of naïveté and grandeur, is shown at once as a real person individualized by his bright eyes, his alert face, his simple coat and scarf and hat, and as a monumental abstraction with some of the quality of sculpture. There are few portraits where the play of personality between painter and subject is so apparent. Here, as he was to continue to do, Vincent paints his own psychological presence into the picture. The colors are vivid, with the strong dark-blue mass of the coat in the center surrounded by emerald greens and bright orange-yellows. Everywhere except in the blue coat, the painting is shot through with spots and lines of vermilion. There are lines of vermilion in the shadow on the left side of the face; a purely arbitrary line of vermilion separates the figure from the background, running from the neck on either side down along the shoulder and continuing to the bottom edge of the canvas. As Manet did in his portrait of Zola [192] van Gogh places his subject against a background of references, in this case Japanese prints. But where Manet painted a realistic image of great elegance and of great objectivity, every stroke of Vincent's brush is determined more by his reaction to the subject than by its appearance. From now on the painter who began as so dreary a colorist uses color of an intensity, both optical and expressive, beyond any use of it until this time.

Has Vincent benefited from his labors in Cormon's studio? Perhaps. In the drawing of the head and the hands of Père Tanguy there is a certainty and definition that may have been strengthened by the disciplines he inflicted on himself, but if it is examined academically the drawing fails everywhere, even where Vincent did not deliberately

441. VAN GOGH: *Old Shoes*, 1887. 19½ x 28". Fogg Art Museum, Cambridge, Mass., Maurice Wertheim Collection.

violate academic principles for expressive necessity. In the hands, the fingers of the hand on our right could not physically pass behind the others as they are supposed to do. As for Père Tanguy's right arm, from wrist to elbow, it does not exist within the sleeve, and the thigh below it is ambiguous. But these are foolish points, not to be thought of twice. Whether or not van Gogh could ever have become an academic draughtsman is beside the point, since he has now discovered where his power of expression lies, and he knows that it is not compatible with either academic regulation or impressionist vision. It is possible to think of pure impressionism as the ultimate imitative realism where the eye becomes only a lens (it was once said of Monet that he was "only an eye—but what an eye!"). And the world Vincent must transmute into images is accessible to no lens. It is an inner world of his own. While he thought of himself as the logical descendent of impressionism, actually he rejected all impressionism's values to explore this tormented inner world instead of impressionism's joyous everyday one.

In February, 1888, Vincent van Gogh left Paris for Arles, in the south of France, where this exploration was to begin in earnest.

442. VAN GOGH: *Père Tanguy*, 1887–88. 25½ x 20". Collection
Stavros Niarchos, Athens.

Van Gogh: Arles, Saint-Rémy, and Auvers

The events of van Gogh's life between his
departure from Paris in early 1888 until
his suicide in July, 1890, are well enough
known to have established him in the
popular mind as the archetype of the Mad
Genius. Not mad, he was an unstable personality who in the last two years of his life
was subject to epileptoid seizures. Not
quite a genius, he was a painter who in his
last two years produced a life work of extremest originality, combining theory with
a high degree of personal emotionalism.
Because the events of his life are dramatic
enough to be disproportionately intrusive

in a discussion of his painting, they must
be summarized first:

Vincent left Paris in a fit of despondency
to which many factors contributed. He was
irritated with the squabbling and bickering
that, he found, was the form usually taken
by the stimulating discussions he had
hoped for among painters. Not only was he
dependent on his brother Theo, but he felt
that he was in his way—as he was. And in
any case, Paris in February is not a cheerful
city in the low-income bracket. For a
painter who had suddenly discovered color
it was gray, its studios drear. By temperament Vincent was restless. He had lived
his life feeling that what he was hunting
was just around the corner. This time he
thought it lay in the brilliant sun and the
simpler life of a small Provencal city. And
this time it did.

Theo gave him an allowance and he set
himself up in Arles. For this man of thirty-
five it was like a youth's first discovery of
the world on his own. Before long he was
working so hard that he had several faint-
ing spells. Or perhaps these were the first
indication of the malady that was about to
make itself apparent. It was also just the
time of the arrival in Arles of the painter
Gauguin.

Gauguin was a fantastic and to van Gogh
a glamorous personality, with barbarous
and brutal good looks the ugly little man
must have envied, and an established reputation among avant-garde painters. The
men had met in Paris but did not know one
another very well in spite of Vincent's
strong attraction toward Gauguin. Gauguin
was somewhat older, and there is a hint of
adolescent hero worship in van Gogh's feeling for him. He urged Gauguin to visit him
in Arles; Gauguin finally consented. As far
as their painting was concerned there was
an important mutual influence. As far as
their life together was concerned there
were tensions beyond endurance, at least
beyond Vincent's, and in an incident that
apparently will never be clarified in its details there was a violent quarrel, after which
Vincent went to his room, cut off an ear,
wrapped it up, and delivered it to one of
the girls in a brothel that he had frequented
with Gauguin. This was during the last

weeks of 1888. Shortly before, he had painted a self-portrait as a present for Gauguin [443]; the words "*à mon ami Paul*" are still faintly discernable along the upper left border. The Arles experience had begun with the happiest period of van Gogh's life; but the face in the self-portrait for Gauguin is already the face of a man pushed to the limits of endurance, and the remainder of Vincent's life was torment beyond anything he had endured before.

During the first five months of 1889 he remained in Arles, with intermittent periods in the hospital as his seizures recurred. He suffered hallucinations, and his irrational behavior got him into trouble with the townspeople, as had happened elsewhere. Then for a year—May 1889 to May 1890— he was an inmate of the asylum at Saint-Rémy, near by, where he had comparative freedom and could receive immediate treatment—of a kind—during seizures. He worked passionately. *The Starry Night* was painted at Saint-Rémy.

By May the seizures seemed to have re-lented and he was thought well enough to return to the north. He went to Auvers, not far from Paris, where Pissarro lived and had worked with Cézanne. Pissarro would have taken Vincent into his own house but his wife, understandably, objected. The im-mediate reason for the choice of Auvers was the presence there of Dr. Paul Gachet* [444], a physician who had special qualifi-cations for this special case since he was a friend of Pissarro's and Cézanne's and some

443. VAN GOGH: *Self-portrait*, 1888. 24½ x 20½". Fogg Art Mu-seum, Cambridge, Mass., Maurice Wertheim Collection.

of the other impressionists—whom he had frequently treated without a fee—and was as interested in art as he was in medicine.

In Auvers Vincent experienced no fur-ther seizures. He made occasional short visits to Paris, saw Lautrec there once more, and went to the Salon and exhibitions, but he could not take much of Paris at a time. In Auvers he painted constantly. Dr. Gachet was a miracle of encouragement. But Vincent feared a recurrence of the dreadful experiences in Arles and Saint-Rémy. His consciousness of the burden his life imposed on his brother was extreme, exaggerated now because Theo had mar-ried and had just had a son.

Vincent had come to Auvers in May. Near the end of July he began a letter to Theo in which two sentences are particu-larly revealing of the nature of his art and his relationship to it:

---

* Dr. Paul Gachet (1828–1909) was himself an amateur painter of creditable skill with a special fondness for engraving and etching. Cézanne did his only plates with Gachet, and van Gogh now etched the doctor's portrait. His acquaintance with painters went back to an early one with Courbet. Like Choquet and Caillebotte he discovered the impressionists for himself and collected them along with a lot of "dark pictures" that Vincent objected to in his house. His collection is now in the Louvre. He struck Vincent as being "at least" as eccen-tric as he himself was, and there was justifica-tion for this impression. Among the free-think-ing doctor's several unusual schemes was one for a "mutual autopsy" association by which painters would leave their brains for analysis after their deaths. He had been something of a nuisance to the young impressionists but they were also genuinely fond of him.

444. VAN GOGH: *Dr. Gachet*, 1890. Etching, 7⅛ x 6".
Philadelphia Museum of Art, McIlhenny Fund.

Van Gogh: Later Work

The bulk of van Gogh's life work, the paintings that poured out during the two years and five months between his arrival in Arles and his suicide in Auvers, must be more familiar to a wider public today than the work of any other single painter. At least this is true in the United States. There are individual paintings, such as *Whistler's Mother* and the *Mona Lisa, The Blue Boy* and a Corot or two, that are better known, but in Vincent's case it is not a matter of one or two paintings. Half his work must have been reproduced in tens of thousands of color prints, offered in portfolios as inducements to subscribe to newspapers, framed up assembly-line fashion for sale in department stores and drug stores. To a vast audience on the fringe of "appreciation" he is synonymous with modern art—to which, actually, he is an excellent introduction.

This does not sound like a tragic art. Tragic art does not appeal to tens of thousands of people as a living-room decoration. The brilliance of the color, the decorative attraction of the shapes and images as they developed in Arles, are superficially cheerful. And some of the pictures are genuinely happy ones unless the pathetic associations of the painter's life are grafted onto them. But most of them take on a disquieting introspective intensity or restlessness if they are regarded as something more than spots of color on a wall.

This is true of *The Public Gardens in Arles* [445]. A twisting and writhing motion is only half repressed in the tree trunks, and it continues into the foliage and breaks through in the patch of sky, painted in a flat color yet in angular, motionful strokes. In the pictures of flowers, especially the great heavy sunflowers of Arles [446], there is the same duality. The series of sunflowers are his most popular pictures, the brightest in color, the most obviously ornamental and, being flowers, of course the most "cheerful" and nice to have around. The decorative quality was intentional. Vincent wrote from Arles in a letter to Émile Bernard that he was thinking of "decorating his studio with half a dozen paintings of

"Really, we can speak only through our paintings.

"In my own work I am risking my life, and half my reason has been lost in it."

He did not finish the letter. It was not a "suicide note," although parts of it are a summation of his relationship with Theo and have about them an air of finality. But when he stopped the letter in the middle and went out with his paintbox and his canvas he might have gone out to paint. The revolver with which he shot himself was never identified. He might have borrowed it on the way from a peasant, with the excuse that he would use it to shoot at the crows that were a nuisance in the fields. He shot himself below the heart, but managed to walk back to the inn where he was staying. Contrary to the circumstances as usually taken for granted, he did not shoot himself during an attack or in anticipation of one, and during the two days before he died he was lucid. Theo had been reached, and Vincent died in his arms.

445. VAN GOGH: *The Public Gardens in Arles,* 1888. 28½ x 35⅝". Phillips Collection, Washington, D.C.

sunflowers, a decoration in which chrome yellow, crude or broken, shall blaze forth against various backgrounds of blue, ranging from the very palest emerald up to royal blue and framed with thin strips of wood painted orange. The sort of effect of Gothic stained glass windows." The modeling of the flowers' great coarse central cushions of stamens was done in actual relief, the pigment being built up close to a quarter of an inch in some places, and textured like the rough mass of the stamens themselves. Individual petals are also defined by relief, each one existing as a mass of paint with its edge standing out prominently in front of the petals behind it. The sunflower pictures are large ones, the monstrous blossoms being painted at full size. They have a savage vehemence that is reduced to bright prettiness in the small color prints that are so popular.

An extreme flatness as far as modeling in light and shade is concerned, or even as far as the breaking of color is concerned, is characteristic of the Arles pictures in general, but their surfaces are heavily textured. The background of *L'Arlésienne* [447] is a solid yellow, the brilliant yellow that obsesses Vincent now, broken only by the texture of the broad, thick, application. Purple, its complementary, is played against it in the dress, and within the clash of the two colors the figure is transfixed. It is a composition in silhouettes, the double influence of the Japanese print and of Gauguin, who was now visiting Vincent and working with him. But even while he was painting in the dark tones of the early period, van Gogh had come upon Japanese objects and had been fascinated by their color. In Paris he knew Japanese prints well, as we see in the background in the

446. VAN GOGH: *Sunflowers*, 1888. 36¼ x 29″ Philadelphia Museum of Art, Mr. and Mrs. Carroll S. Tyson Collection.

447. VAN GOGH: *L'Arlésienne* (*Madame Ginoux*), 1887. 24 x 17″. Metropolitan Museum of Art, New York, Samuel A. Lewisohn Bequest.

portrait of Père Tanguy (where the color in the prints is exaggerated into brilliance, rather than reproduced in the softer tints of the originals), and he wrote about his trip to Arles that as he approached on the train he was so excited that he could almost believe it was Japan he was coming to. As a descendant of the Japanese print, *L'Arlésienne* has the obvious inherited characteristics of simplified silhouette and flat color, but the sinuous line of the Japanese silhouette has been replaced by a sharpened, forceful, more angular one, and the conventionalized charm has given way to a hypnotic intensity.

Madame Ginoux, a neighbor who posed in regional costume for *L'Arlésienne*, was one of several friendly people who solved for a while van Gogh's perpetual model problem. The most obliging of these were the postman Roulin and his wife. He painted five portraits of Roulin, one of them [448] showing his uniform in a strong blue

against a pale blue background, with the beard in short, straight, springing strokes of brownish and yellowish tints flecked with bits of bright blue and red. The figure is more three-dimensionally modeled than that of *L'Arlésienne,* but in the remarkable portrait of Madame Roulin called *La Berceuse* [449] the flatness is again extreme. The picture began with a sentimental idea. It was to recall lullabies to lonely men, Vincent said, and he compared its colors to common chromolithographs. He said from time to time that he wanted to make "naïve" and primitive images like those in popular almanacs or calendars that appealed to uncultivated people—another manifestation of his repeated efforts to identify himself with simple folk in whose lives he imagined that love and honesty and understanding existed in a natural state.

But it is typical of him that the intention he states in literary terms is seldom apparent in the completed picture—in most cases, fortunately not. Whether or not he began sentimentally he did not in the end paint sentimentally in *La Berceuse,* and it certainly does not suggest a chromo. Madame Roulin sits in an attitude reminiscent of Père Tanguy's, but slightly turned, and the figure is built in comparably simplified, half-primitive forms. The hands hold a rope that would be attached to a cradle, a usual means of rocking one. The lower part of the background is a solid red, against the complementary green of the skirt. The black blouse and the face are played against a background of wallpaper transformed into a dreamlike pattern of flowers, some pink ones being semirealistic alongside others that are geometrized. All are connected by odd loops and swirls, punctuated by diamond shapes, these derived from stems and leaves. The rest of the area is filled with black rings, each with a dot of vermilion in its center. The chair is defined by heavy black outlines. The resultant combination of naïveté, violence, and dream makes *La Berceuse* one of van Gogh's great canvases but it certainly does not recall a lullaby.

In van Gogh's attachment to the Roulins, psychiatrists who are interested in postmortem analyses might find a substitute parent relationship. Roulin, who was not a mail carrier but worked at loading and unloading mail from the trains, was a tremendous man, six and a half feet tall. Vincent wrote Theo that Roulin was "not quite old enough to be like a father" to him, but that he had a "silent gravity and tenderness . . . such as an old soldier might have for a young one." Thus he offered Vincent an outlet for both the dependent filial affection and the hero worship he was so eager to bestow. In another letter Vincent refers to sailors as "children and martyrs," a phrase in which there are strong elements of a psychological self-portrait, and he painted the portrait *La Berceuse* of the motherly Madame Roulin in such a way, he said, that when these sailors saw it in their cabin they would feel "the old sense of cradling come over them."

After the crisis of his first attacks, his break with Gauguin, and finally his transfer to the asylum at Saint-Rémy, Vincent's paintings take on the swirling, tempestuous

448. Van Gogh: *The Postman Roulin,* 1888. 32 x 25½". Museum of Fine Arts, Boston.

form and the more mystical expression of which *The Starry Night* is a climactic expression. But they are interspersed with milder expressions, such as *The Road Menders* [450], where the warm tones and the everyday subject modify and even for a moment conceal the compulsive writhing of the great trees whose roots must plunge into the earth with the same voracious energy that forces the trunks and branches upward. And in one exceptional moment the fields around Saint-Rémy are painted in the rain [451] and the violence fades into poetic melancholy, the twisting lines give way to a pattern of straight ones slanting across the surface of a composition recalling Japanese prints where rain over quiet landscapes was represented in the

449. Van Gogh: *La Berceuse* (*Madame Roulin*), 1889. 36¼ x 28¼". Museum of Fine Arts, Boston.

same way—an abstract linear design super-imposed over natural forms.

Then after Saint-Rémy, during the scant three months in Auvers, the twistings and knottings begin to relax. Their violence is not so much tempered as habitual, much of their true force is lost. The arabesque of lines goes limp. Movement, instead of charging through the picture, is slowed and diffused. The electric presence of *The Public Gardens in Arles* becomes a light, agreeable decorativeness in *Stairway at Auvers* [452]. There is a sense of deflation in the Auvers pictures. In color, in pattern, they share the qualities that make Vincent van Gogh one of the most popular painters in the world, but they have lost the spiritual intensity that make him a great one.

Gauguin: Early Days and Arles

As a matter of chronological tying together, it may be pointed out here that at the time of van Gogh's death Manet had been dead only seven years, and the other impressionists were at the height of their powers. Monet was fifty years old (van Gogh died at thirty-seven) and had another thirty-six years of life ahead of him. Cézanne was not to begin *The Great Bathers* until eight years later. Seurat died the year after van Gogh. Picasso was a boy of nine.

Paul Gauguin (1848–1903) was five years older than van Gogh and outlived him by thirteen years. His life was as extraordinary in its circumstances as Vincent's was, but the circumstances, which included greater poverty and privation since he had no brother Theo to support him, were more of his own making than Vincent's had been. Like Vincent's, his life has been a mine for biographers. Its central mystery is why he chose to paint.

In Vincent's case the compulsion is explicable. Anyone can accept the idea that painting is an emotional release for a man who fits in nowhere else. Since Vincent's time the idea has even been so abused that art schools are filled with students whose only qualification as potential artists consists of a demonstrated lack of qualification for being anything else. But Gauguin was a vigorous, rather brutally handsome, worldly, and self-confident man who entered a stock brokerage firm at twenty-three and did very well at his job. After a couple of years he was a successful bank agent; he married well and was soon a father. He began to draw and paint a little for relaxation, as many respectable businessmen have done without disrupting their lives. In 1876—he was twenty-eight now—he had a painting in the Salon and was buying impressionist pictures. He owned work by Manet, Renoir, Monet, Sisley and Pissarro, and even Cézanne, among others. Then the ubiquitous Pissarro appeared in person—this time not in a role Gauguin's family would have called that of a saint but rather that of a diabolic tempter, as things turned out. The two men painted together, and Gauguin exhibited in the impressionist group show of 1880 and the successive ones up through the final one in 1886. By that year he had given himself over entirely to painting as a career and was living by such hand-to-mouth jobs as pasting signs on billboards. He had expected to eke out a living as a painter, perhaps had even expected to be a successful one without too long an apprenticeship. Pissarro objected to his "commercialism" when Gauguin worried about selling, but it was not easy for a man who had been well-to-do to see his money drain away, to accept hardships that turned out to be more severe even than he had expected as part of the anticipated satisfactions of a creative life. His wife, a Danish woman, was forced at last to return to her family with Gauguin's children, a temporary measure which became permanent.

Gauguin was a sport from the romantic tradition of bohemianism, the concept of the artist as a free soul beyond the conventions of society, sacrificing such bourgeois ideals as security and respectability to the precarious but stimulating life of the studios. Gaiety and self-indulgence and moral license, which were incidental to bohemianism in its origins as a way of life dedicated to creative effort, finally became ends in themselves and created the phenomenon of the painter who does not paint, the writer who does not write, the thinker who does not think, but who make the most of the bohemian's exemption from social responsibility. Gauguin has been seen by some biographers as a man attracted by the bohemian way of life, a man who remained a Parisian bohemian even when he fled the life of the studios to paint in the South Seas. And he did have many of the qualities associated with parasitic bohemianism. He was vain, selfish, an ardent and indulgent sensualist. He loved flattery but was niggardly in recognizing the achievements of his colleagues. He was jealous of his innovations and quick to resent their adaptation by other painters. He dramatized himself, was something of an exhibitionist. The figure he cut as a personality was important to him, and he cultivated it not only by scandalizing the *bourgeoisie*, as all bohemians enjoy doing, but by creating a legend of himself among other painters. He

450. Van Gogh: *The Road Menders*, 1889. 29 x 36¼". Cleveland Museum of Art, Hanna Fund.

never hesitated to sacrifice other people to this legend or to his self-love.

But the difference between Gauguin and the armies of picayune neurotics who answer to the same description is that he made a painter of himself. If he had expected an easy success he soon discovered that he was not going to have one, and he continued to paint even when it became apparent that if he had sacrificed other people he was also going to have to sacrifice himself. He continued to paint in the face of every privation, every discouragement, in the face of humiliation, of ill health, ultimately in the face of death. If he was guilty of play-acting, these facts were very real.

From the beginning, exotic places and primitive peoples are a part of Gauguin's life, and in the end he sought a final identification with them. When he was a child his parents emigrated to Peru. Later as a recruit in the merchant marine he knew Rio de Janeiro. When he began painting seriously he hunted out spots where he could find or could imagine he found a primitive naturalness, including parts of Brittany and the island of Martinique, these before he made his visit to van Gogh in Arles. (On the way to Martinique he

451. VAN GOGH: *Rain*, 1889. 29⅞ x 36⅜". Collection Henry P. McIlhenny, Philadelphia.

452. VAN GOGH: *Stairway at Auvers*, 1890. 20 x 28". City Art Museum of St. Louis.

worked for a while as a digger on the Panama Canal.) The experience of Martinique was a determining one; after his return to France he was more than ever restless for exotic places, more than ever dependent upon them for stimulation.

After impressionist beginnings, Gauguin had theorized a great deal about what he wanted to do, and shortly before his visit to van Gogh he had summarized his ideas in a canvas called *The Vision after the Sermon—Jacob Wrestling with the Angel* [453], painted in the Breton village of Pont-Aven where he had established himself as one of the colony of artists attracted by picturesqueness and inexpensive living. It shows a group of Breton women in regional costume witnessing the struggle of

453. GAUGUIN: *The Vision after the Sermon—Jacob Wrestling with the Angel*, 1888. 28¾ x 36¼". National Gallery of Scotland, Edinburgh.

Jacob and the Angel in a field painted a solid bright red. In their simple and superstitious faith the women think of the struggle in factual terms, seeing it literally as a struggle between a man and an angel. But for the observer outside the picture—and outside the limitations of simplicity and superstition—the supernatural quality is established by the unreality of the red field. The regional bonnets are designed in almost flat silhouettes to make the most of their decorative shapes. A small cow, entirely (and deliberately) out of scale appears in the upper left quarter. The trunk of a tree cuts in a strong diagonal across the picture and separates the Biblical struggle from its peasant spectators.

The technical theories Gauguin applies here include the use of pure color, the re-

duction of all forms to their essential outlines, and the elimination of modeling within those outlines as far as possible, especially modeling by shadows. Also he insists on the painter's right to effect an entirely arbitrary arrangement of nature, although in this particular composition one does not have to look far to see that this arbitrary arrangement is closely related to the composition of Degas, which depended on arrangements the reverse of arbitrary, those discoverable in the accidental relationships of the everyday world.

Those are the technical means. The Gauguinesque spirit of the picture is in its searching out of exotic forms (the costumes of the women) in combination with what he called the "rustic and superstitious simplicity" of the subject. When he went to

454. GAUGUIN: *Women in a Garden*, 1888. 28¾ x 36″. Art Institute of Chicago, Mr. and Mrs. L. L. Coburn Memorial Collection.

455. GAUGUIN: *L'Arlésienne* (*Madame Ginoux*), 1888. Charcoal, 22 x 19″. Collection T. Edward Hanley, Bradford, Pa.

Arles, Gauguin took these ideas with him.

He arrived in Arles on the 20th of October, 1888, expecting to stay for perhaps a year. The faithful Theo had supplied money for the trip, with enough extra for first expenses, and hoped to sell enough of Gauguin's canvases to keep him in funds thereafter. Vincent was excited beyond measure. He redecorated his room in anticipation of the great visit, and after Gauguin's arrival he found their discussions "terribly electric." But Gauguin wrote to a friend that he found everything in Arles "cheap and pretty" and admitted that in these electric arguments he would say, "Corporal, you're right!" to avoid having to discuss questions with a man who seemed to like everything he detested (including the Barbizon painters) and to understand nothing that he liked (including Ingres and Degas). He found very little material that interested him, thought of leaving, changed his mind—for practical reasons, one may suspect, since Theo was virtually pensioning him as a companion for Vincent—was bored and restless. From the dark southern beauty of the Arlésiennes and their somber costumes [454], he managed to extract material for a composition suggestive of mystery and superstition, much in line with *The Vision after the Sermon* but not much in line with the life and spirit of Arles and his models. One of his fine drawings from any period is a study of the Madame Ginoux who was Vincent's model at the same time [455].

But on the whole, the visit that was such a traumatic experience for van Gogh—ending in the quarrel, the amputation of the ear, the first seizure—was only a fiasco for Gauguin. Many years later he wrote that he owed something to Vincent in the "consolidation of my previous pictorial ideas." He also congratulated himself that he had been "useful" to Vincent, and acknowledged a debt to this friend who had shown him that there were people even unhappier than himself. But he had come to Arles reluctantly and now he left it with relief. His stories about exactly what happened there are contradictory, reflecting rather more credit on himself in later versions than in his accounts immediately after the event.

456. GAUGUIN: *Self-portrait with Halo*, 1889. Panel, 31¼ x 20¼". National Gallery of Art, Washington, D.C., Chester Dale Collection.

457. GAUGUIN: *Portrait of a Woman,* 1890. 25⅝ x 21½". Art Institute of Chicago, Joseph Winterbotham Collection.

Gauguin: Pont-Aven and Le Pouldu

So Gauguin returned to Brittany, first to Pont-Aven, moving later to the similar village of Le Pouldu when Pont-Aven became tourist-ridden as such picturesque unspoiled spots always must. In 1889 and part of 1891 he was the center of a group of painters who gave the name *synthetism* to the manner of heightened color, flattened form, and heavy boundary lines he had been developing. Synthetism was a loosely formed aspect of or a secondary name for symbolism, a movement more literary than pictorial with a strong flavor of the exotic and the mysterious in reaction against realism. As far as Gauguin was concerned, though, he was following his own course and the words people attached to his art were of no concern to him except that he was flattered by the attention. He did not take synthetism very seriously, and satirized it in a self-portrait as a synthetist saint with a halo [456]. But while it is a tongue-in-cheek performance, the picture in its increased abstraction unwittingly hints at a direction another generation will follow under Gauguin's influence.

His serious work continued in the direction of *The Vision after the Sermon.* In *The Yellow Christ* he painted a medieval yellow wooden statue from the chapel of a small town near Pont-Aven, placing it out of doors and surrounding it with peasant worshipers. He was still attracted to the heavy forms of primitive and early arts, in this case those of the rough Romanesque sculpture and architecture of the region. He had even offered his *Vision after the Sermon* to the local priest, wanting to see it hung in the small church where he hoped the picture would harmonize with the ancient, rugged, and simple forms of the architecture. But the gift was refused because the priest suspected a hoax. Gauguin and the artists who gathered around him in Brittany were not remarkable for their seriousness and reverence in affairs of this kind, but this time the gift had been offered in all sincerity.

Although it seems contradictory to the flatness and unbroken color of synthetism, Gauguin was also studying Cézanne at this time, and the *Portrait of a Woman* [457] is evidence. Cézanne's faceted planes are suggested, but everywhere the forms are more neatly contained than Cézanne's, more ornamental and more graceful. Gauguin sensed Cézanne's monumentality—and he was to draw upon it—but he did not explore Cézanne's compositional premise of formal distortion in abstract spatial relationships. The woman is posed in front of a Cézanne still-life, but instead of copying it Gauguin has closed the forms in accord with his own taste.

His basic theme continued to preoccupy Gauguin: the undercurrent of superstitious fear beneath the simplicity of primitive people, the menacing whisper of the unknown permeating lives apparently simple and natural. In Le Pouldu he yearned more and more for the far away, the bizarre. Now, to find authentically exotic material *in situ*, Gauguin decided to flee civilization. An exhibition of his work was organized, and with the help of every friend with enough money to buy paintings or enough influence to attract attention to them, enough purchasers were found (including Degas) to put him in funds for a voyage to Tahiti. He left in April, 1891.

Gauguin: Tahiti and Last Years

From Gauguin's experiences in Tahiti it is possible to isolate certain facts to describe an elysium. He scorns the mean provinciality of the French colonial settlements and moves into the interior. The natives are beautiful people, the men like gods of the earth, the women like its flowers. He occupies a simple wooden hut in the midst of lovely country, surrounded by exotic birds, fruit, and foliage. He takes a young girl as his native wife; later she bears him a son. He paints all day, happily naked. He learns the native tongue, explores native myths.

The rest of the picture is less halcyon. He grows old rapidly; he spits "a litre of blood" daily for weeks at a time; he develops a persistent rash or eczema; lesions will not heal, and remain open sores; a foot broken in a brawl fails to heal properly and agonizes and immobilizes him; he runs out of funds and the money promised from France never arrives; he must beg a few francs here and there, receiving some now and then from his wife in Denmark; his daughter, at twenty, dies in Denmark, and for a man who has seen so little of her he takes it very hard and writes such a bitter letter to his wife that he never hears from her again; he humiliates himself and works for six francs a day doing hack jobs for the colonial government he detests; during periods of absolute penury he lives off boiled rice; during others, off dry bread and water; when even the Chinese storekeeper cannot give him further credit he is without bread and lives off a few mangoes; he attempts suicide with arsenic but vomits it up and has only a great agony instead; he writes abusive letters to government officials and as a result of one of them he is sentenced to a fine and three months in jail. He enters an appeal, which would have taken him to another island for a hearing, but before he leaves he suffers two slight strokes. He is helpless in his hut, abandoned except for occasional visits from natives. His sight fails. One leg is suppurating. He dies alone.

This hell was divided into two periods on either side of a return to France. Chronologically the periods are: the first Tahitian one, from his departure from Paris in the spring of 1891 to his return landing at Marseilles (with four francs in his pocket) in August, 1893; he remained in France until February, 1895; then he returned to Tahiti, stayed there until moving to the Marquesas Islands in November, 1901, where he remained until his death.

The interlude of a year and a half in France is bizarre enough in itself. The object of the trip was to collect money due him and to try for more with an exhibition of the paintings he brought back. The exhibition was a scandal and a mild success; Degas liked it. Real financial help came from an unexpected source. An uncle died and left Gauguin an inheritance. He spent it rapidly, with the assistance of a woman he attached from the studios of Montmartre, a mulatto with an Oriental cast to her features who called herself Anna the Javanese. Whatever her other attractions, Anna was a spectacular accessory to Gauguin the Exotic, who now disported himself in a long blue frock coat like a minstrel's, with large pearl buttons, a blue vest embroidered in bright colors, buff trousers, a gray hat with a blue ribbon, and a fancy walking stick he had carved for himself with barbaric figures and inlaid with a pearl. This outfit was adopted on a return trip to Pont-Aven but also made its appearance in Paris. Combined with Anna and a pet monkey, it was spectacular enough and could certainly be described as inviting attention, yet when it and Anna received more attention than Gauguin liked from a group of sailors, he got into a brawl with them and it was at this time that his foot, or ankle, was broken by a blow from a wooden shoe. These events took place in the little resort of Concarneau near Pont-Aven, and Gauguin had to be taken home on a stretcher according to some versions or trundled in a wheelbarrow according to other credible ones. As the script for a comedy these grotesque incidents would be hilarious. When one remembers that they happened in earnest, they are appalling. Anna capped the affair by abandoning Gauguin on his bed of pain and going to Paris, where she stripped the studio of all objects of value and disappeared.

The wonder is that from the misery, the confusion, the distraction, of Gauguin's life in the islands an art of any order could come. Yet it did. And in spite of his reiterations that he was a "true savage" and in spite of the fact that he was painting in a native hut instead of a mansard studio, his paintings are always sophisticated, in effect the paintings of a Parisian who has gathered material on primitive location. He

458. GAUGUIN: *Ia Orana Maria*, 1891. 44¾ x 34½". Metropolitan Museum of Art, New York, Samuel A. Lewisohn Bequest.

may have lived with the natives, may have taken a native wife, may have learned their language and their myths, but he was no primitive. He spent the end of his life in a tremendous natural reference library, acquiring a new vocabulary of motifs—dark-skinned figures, native cloths, bananas and palms and curious plants with fantastic blossoms.

Synthetism would have been an apt word if it had been coined to describe Gauguin's pictures like *Ia Orana Maria* [458], one of the earliest from the first Tahitian period. The picture is completely synthetic—divorcing the word for the moment from its associations of shoddiness. The words of the title are the equivalent of *Ave Maria* or *We Hail Thee Mary*. A native woman and

459. GAUGUIN: *Manao Tupapau—The Spirit of the Dead Watching*, 1892. 28⅝ x 36⅝". Albright-Knox Art Gallery, Buffalo, N.Y., A. Conger Goodyear Collection.

her son on her shoulder are haloed like the Virgin and Child. Two women stand in attitudes of reverence or prayer while an angel behind them points to the Tahitian Madonna. Nothing could be more artificial, much less connected with the life of the natives. It is the *Vision after the Sermon* in a new locale, except that where the Breton picture was tentative, the Tahitian one is assured in its use of rich colors and the disposition of ornamental forms into a tapestrylike unity. As a final curiosity and a final divorce from his immediate material except as studio props, Gauguin has turned to yet another source for the attitudes of the two adoring women. They are transposed directly from a bas-relief from a Javanese temple, known to Gauguin from a photograph which in all likelihood he had purchased at the Paris World's Fair two years before. A picture that refers to

a photograph of a Javanese temple, purchased in Paris and carried to the South Seas, that incorporates Javanese figures with Tahitian models into a Christian subject treated as a decorative composition to be taken back to Paris and sold in a commercial gallery for money to free the painter from the degrading commercial forces of civilization, is certainly a synthesis of some kind.

Ia Orana Maria is a richly decorative painting using an exotic vocabulary, but it would be forcing the point to pretend that it explores beneath the surface of native life. Gauguin uses Tahitian material in a way closer to its inherent character in a picture painted the following year, *Manao Tupapau* [459], usually translated as "The spirit of the dead watching," although according to Gauguin's own notes it may mean either "she thinks of the spirit of the

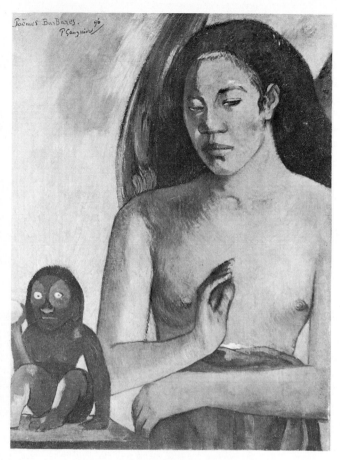

460. GAUGUIN: *Hina Te Fatou—The Moon and the Earth*, 1893. 45 x 21½″. Museum of Modern Art, New York, Lillie P. Bliss Collection.

461. GAUGUIN: *Poèmes Barbares*, 1896. 25½ x 19″. Fogg Art Museum, Cambridge, Mass., Maurice Wertheim Collection.

dead" or "the spirit of the dead remembers her." It was suggested to him when he returned late one night to discover his Tahitian wife lying on their bed waiting for him, terrified by the dark. He explained the picture in unusual detail in a letter to his wife in Denmark, telling what he wanted to express and how he went about expressing it. Instead of describing fright in a "literary way" by posing the model in the pantomimic gestures of anecdotal painting, he tried to relay the sensation by a "somber, sad, frightening" color harmony that would "sound" to the eye like a tolling death bell. Since the Polynesians believe that phosphorescence is the spirits of the dead, he painted in the background some

fantastic flowers resembling sparks. Instead of making the ghost (appearing like an idol on the left) a wild and menacing figure, he made it "like a small, harmless woman, because the girl can only see the spirit of the dead linked with the dead person, a human being like herself." At other times he made further notes on the symbolism of *Manao Tupapau*, comparing the spirit of the living soul and the spirit of the dead to day and night, and making a musical analogy to the "undulating horizontal lines" and the "harmonies of orange and blue brought together by yellows and purples."

During the first years in Tahiti Gauguin evolved a heavy-legged, narrow-hipped, square-shouldered female figure type not

462. GAUGUIN: *Whence Come We? What Are We? Whither Go We?* 1898. 67 x 177".
Museum of Fine Arts, Boston.

463. PUVIS DE CHAVANNES: *The Sacred Grove*, after 1883. 36½ x 82⅞". Art Institute of
Chicago, Potter Palmer Collection.

at all reflective of the rounded sensuous
bodies of the Tahitian women but appropriate to his idea of savage monumentality
and a fit participant in his allegories of
primitive man's union with earth, sky, and
the mystical forces behind nature. The
woman in *Hina Te Fatou—The Moon and
the Earth* [460] is a moon goddess, but a
far cry from the classical Diana and a far
cry from Ingres's *La Source* [68] (the
spring in the background suggests the com-

parison) and a far cry too from Degas's
nudes. But Degas, the worshiper of Ingres,
bought it, and it can take its place in the
long line of pictures where painters have
summarized their art in images of the female nude. With Gauguin this summary is
a compound of sophistication and primitivism, of affectation and decision, above
all a reversal of the impressionist idea that
the world must be met on its own terms
and interpreted through its own appear-

464. VUILLARD: *Le Repas, c.* 1899. 17 x 18½". Collection Henry P. McIlhenny, Philadelphia.

ance. Instead, Gauguin rejects the world; the painter's assignment becomes the exploration of universal mysteries through symbols rather than the observation of temporary fact through fragments of tangible reality. This is Gauguin's importance—no matter what affectations and insincerities and limitations may hobble him and preclude an altogether satisfactory expression of so ambitious an idea.

In the last terrible years of his life, after his return to the islands following the grotesque exhibitionism of the interlude in Paris and Pont-Aven, Gauguin's art contradicts the picture of him as a harassed and decaying man. It takes on a reserve, a

decisiveness, and a removed calm. As in *Poèmes Barbares* [461], of 1896, the gestures of his figures become hieratic and formalized. The idol and the figure are no longer part of a world of superstitious fear but exist together in a world of barbaric mysteries. In the very large and complicated picture with the cumbersome and literarily pretentious title *Whence Come We? What Are We? Whither Go We?* [462], a painted tapestry of figures, idols, and landscape neither cumbersome nor pretentious, there is an air of finality beyond that of any other of his compositions. This may be because the picture is conceived first and last as a studio summary; it is to

Gauguin what *The Painter's Studio* is to Courbet, *La Grande Jatte* to Seurat. It is also a tribute to Puvis de Chavannes, whose painting Gauguin had admired and even copied. Gauguin protested too much when he wrote of *Whence Come We?* that "By God, it is not a canvas made like Puvis de Chavannes, studies from nature, then preparatory cartoons, etc. It is all boldly done, directly with the brush, on a sack-cloth full of knots and rough spots. . . ." This may be true enough, but compositionally it is a cousin of Puvis's *The Sacred Grove* [463]. There are the same strong horizontals and verticals, the same shining water at the left, cut by a dark slanting tree in the Puvis and a slanting dark reflection in the Gauguin, the same rounding off of the corners, especially noticeable in the upper right but also noticeable in the figures at lower right and lower left. The conspicuous female figure leaning on one arm at the lower left of the Gauguin reverses a similar figure in the lower right of the Puvis. But Gauguin need not have protested. The picture is his own, and if it is directly connected with a tradition, then it places him securely within a great one, without sacrificing the originality of his contribution to it.

The Nabis

Gauguin's influence on a new generation of painters was felt at close quarters in the work of a group of youngsters twenty years younger than he, who abandoned the principles of the *Académie Julian*—virtually a preparatory class for the Academy's school —and even of the *École des Beaux Arts*, in order to follow his ideas of composing in flat, unmodeled areas as developed at Pont-Aven. By the time Gauguin left for his first stay in Tahiti his influence was apparent in the work of these young "Nabis." The word comes from a Hebrew one meaning "prophets," but it was not altogether an apt description for a group of painters who made their own adaptation of other men's innovations but were not particularly innovative themselves.

The spokesmen for the group were the painters Paul Séruzier (1863–1927), who first discovered Gauguin for the rest of them, and Maurice Denis (1870–1943), whose statement that "a picture—before being a horse, a nude, or an anecdote—is essentially a flat surface covered with colors assembled in a certain order" was the heart of the Nabi credo. He was not yet twenty years old when he wrote this, and the Nabis abandoned the principle shortly, or at least they grew less insistent about it. But it is still one of the most frequently quoted passages in art criticism and theory. There is nothing complicated about it; it is a succinct statement of the decorative principle in painting and goes no further, which is the reason the Nabis outgrew it. They outgrew it rather quickly, although Gauguin insisted on calling them, resentfully, his "followers" long after they had gone their own several ways.

The two most enduring painters of the group proved to be Pierre Bonnard (1867–1947) and Édouard Vuillard (1868–1940). Vuillard's *Le Repas* [464] of about 1899 exemplified the linearism of the first Nabi work now modified by a kind of interior impressionism suggesting the warmth and seclusion of small rooms where comfortable and affectionate lives are lived without excitement or the necessity of it, a quality that led to the coining of the term *intimism* as an offshoot of the Nabi aesthetic. A somewhat linear effect is retained here and there, as in the heads, rather surprisingly combined with a soft-focus effect in the objects in the foreground of the table. The colors are more subdued, less contrasting, than the black-and-white reproduction suggests. There are warm reddish browns, warm grays, comfortably dulled greens. In the mixture of influences, that of Degas is strong. Degas also conveyed the intimacy of small interiors, but always with a moodiness wider in its evocative reach than the gentle domesticity which pervades a typical Vuillard.

Bonnard also abandoned the restrictions of the early Nabi manner to accept a variety of stimuli. In pictures in the intimist spirit [465] he abandoned the subdued color scheme of intimism to experiment with unusual, somewhat dissonant color combinations in a way that influenced the

465. BONNARD: *After the Shower*, 1914. 37½ x 26″. Philadelphia Museum of Art, Louis E. Stern Collection.

466. BONNARD: *Bowl of Fruit*, 1933. 22½ x 21¼″. Philadelphia Museum of Art.

fauves—to be seen hereafter—and then, in turn, he was influenced by them. In his final manner, as in *Bowl of Fruit* [466], Bonnard may seem at a glance impressionist. Upon second glance the colors are seen to be forced to greater intensities, in combinations arbitrary rather than based on impressionism's optical laws. And the shapes, such as the dark shadow under the bowl, are designed more decoratively than impressionism's approximation of natural effects would have allowed.

Fantastic and Visionary Art: Redon

The post-impressionist "period," if it can be called that, was one of trauma during which impressionism, as the climax of realism, was transformed into what we call, just now, "modern art." Two other painters

are of special importance in this connection, the symbolist Odilon Redon and the primitive Henri, or "Douanier," Rousseau. Both men were contemporaries of Cézanne and the impressionists, hence a little older than van Gogh, Seurat, and Gauguin, all of whom, however, they outlived. Against the classicism of Cézanne and Seurat, the emotionalism of van Gogh, and the decorative exoticism of Gauguin, they oppose an art of fantasy.

If the reader has been a little confused about symbolism, synthetism, the Nabis, and all the other isms and painters mentioned since impressionism, it is nobody's fault. These movements were ill defined and they overlapped not only with themselves but with other movements that were developing or, like impressionism, fading. Odilon Redon (1840–1916), whose life of seventy-six years began the year before Cézanne's and ended ten years after it, is

467. REDON: *Vase of Flowers*, 1910. Pastel on cardboard, 28¼ x 18". Albright Art Gallery, Buffalo, Contemporary Art Collection.

468. REDON: *Revery*, c. 1900 (?). Pastel, 21¼ x 14¼". Museum of Modern Art, New York, Gift of Mrs. John D. Rockefeller, Jr.

usually called a symbolist. The critic Albert Aurier tried to define symbolism, in 1891, as an effort to "clothe the idea in a form perceptible to the senses," not a very helpful description since it could apply to almost any form of genuinely creative art, painting or otherwise. But all manifestations of symbolism were somewhat tied up with the idea that the painter's goal was not to investigate the world around him but to explore the world of dream and mystery. Symbolists like Gauguin, whom Aurier considered the leader of the movement, explored this mysterious world through forms connected with primitive, archaic, or exotic ones, which were presumably closer to the world of dream and mystery than the world of the Paris boulevards could ever

be. But critics today would be likely to call Redon, rather than Gauguin, the purest symbolist painter.

Redon explored a private and fantastic world, rather than Gauguin's borrowed exotic one. Redon's bias is already apparent when we read that he said that Ingres was "sterile" and "bourgeois," while Delacroix's "least scrawl" communicated life to the observer. But Redon was not interested in Delacroix's statement of the vitality of life or in Delacroix's effort to achieve a generalized statement of human emotion. He was concerned with ambiguities, and he said so, which puts a considerable disadvantage upon critics who object to his art as a rather ambiguous one. "My drawings *inspire*, and are not to be defined. They determine nothing. They place us, as does music, in the ambiguous realm of the undetermined. They are a kind of metaphor." But Redon's most famous phrase is the neat description of his intention: to "put the logic of the visible at the service of the invisible." Thus when he paints a bouquet of flowers [467] they are not flowers with scent and body, cut in the garden and put into water to be enjoyed and painted as flowers, but the blossoming of a dream, incorporeal, "a varied arabesque or maze unfolding," full of mystery and suggestion.

To the person for whom a vase of flowers is a vase of flowers, the quality of mystery in these pictures may seem to be nothing much more than a certain fuzziness combined with unusually luminous color. In that case, Redon's more completely unreal, more conventionally dreamlike compositions [468] may be more satisfying expressions of the symbolist ideal. Through such a picture, the less apparently mystical dreams of flowers and butterflies may be approached. Part of Redon's appeal, once one knows him, is that his world remains private. One may enter it, and be welcome, but one is never urged to do so. During his lifetime Redon worked quietly, not at all interested in making a great stir. But the literary symbolists, headed by the poet Mallarmé, discovered him for themselves; and such painters as Gauguin, the Nabis, and finally the young Matisse, all sought him out and were his devoted admirers.

"Douanier" Rousseau

Within the complications and intercomplications of nineteenth-century painting, the idea of giving concrete expression to supernatural mysteries or to mysterious yearnings crops up persistently. Blake, Friedrich, and Runge held it; Böcklin held it when he tried to bring the world of fantasy and dread within our grasp by representing fantasies in objectively realistic detail. The Pre-Raphaelites held it in their odd way when they tried to recapture the spiritual essence of the Biblical and medieval worlds by reproducing them—they thought—explicitly. Böcklin and other fantasists might have

said that they wanted to make "improbable beings live humanly according to the laws of the probable" or to "give the illusion of life to the most unreal creations." But these two quotations are from Redon, whose art is more conventionally visionary, in its luminous, apparitionlike quality, than the precisely defined painting of his companions in their voyages of exploration into hidden realms.

The century's most curious revelation within this shadowy territory was made half by chance, like so many discoveries, by Henri Rousseau (1840–1910), who first set about reproducing the real world as photographically as he knew how, and then discovered that he had created a world of enchantment instead. While Böcklin and Redon theorized about the interchangeability of mystery and reality, about how to make the real unreal and the unreal real, about how to dematerialize the world around us or to materialize the one we cannot see, Rousseau did not theorize at all. Yet he materialized the promised land of mystery for searchers who were more knowledgeable about it than he was.

Rousseau was a minor official in the French Customs, hence "Douanier" Rousseau, as he is most frequently called. He began as a hobby painter, the nineteenth-century phenomenon of the "Sunday painter" who might take his cheap paintbox out into the park for an afternoon's relaxation or copy a favorite postcard at home on a rainy day or try a portrait of a friend or a member of the family, preferably from a nice clear snapshot. His earliest paintings [469] have all the characteristic naïvetés of style inherent in the work of beginners feeling their way with intense interest but technical innocence. The most usual of these characteristics include extreme carefulness of outline, a smoothing out of the paint, a finicky blending of one tone into another, and a fascination with fine detail to whatever extent technical limitations may permit its execution. All of this is combined with the stiff, simple forms, the inaccurate proportions, and the skew-wise perspective of the beginner.

By most standards, these are not only shortcomings but fatal shortcomings—but

469. H. ROUSSEAU: *Village Street Scene*, 1909. 16¼ x 13".
Philadelphia Museum of Art, Arensberg Collection.

applied with rich body in spite of its smoothness. Forms which are rigid and ill drawn by conventional standards are solid and well drawn by the standard of meticulous observation and careful selection. Color that would be harsh and raw or bleached and anemic or discordant and muddy in the ordinary primitive painting, is clear and harmonious in Rousseau.

As a result of these virtues, a picture with many acute technical limitations by conventional standards may be an expressive work of art, even when the expressive quality is half accidental. Rousseau's individual deviation from the general field of primitive painting, the one that sets him apart even from such honest and expressive primitives as Hicks with his *Peaceable Kingdom* [303] is the air of enchantment that permeates his work. Every figure, every leaf, every blade of grass, seems magically transfixed within a vacuum or a crystal, magically revealed to us in its smallest element.

The unreality of Rousseau is a paradoxical combination of fantasy and factualness; the painter offers each object in his street scenes and country landscapes with unquestioning acceptance of their perfect ordinariness, yet not one of the objects is ordinary after he paints them. The human figures are so isolated and so immobile, the trees are so neatly patterned and their foliage so meticulously rigid and delicate, the streets, houses, walls are so pristine, yet so familiar as elements of daily life—everything, in short, is so commonplace and yet so uncommonly revealed, that reality and unreality reach perfect fusion and one is indistinguishable from the other. We cannot say that Rousseau shows us a new world, for we have seen all these things many times; yet we cannot say, either, that this is a world we know, for these things exist in new relationships and even in new shapes. It becomes a world of dream, whose reality the dreamer accepts without question, and whose fantasy he recognizes only upon awakening. But instead of fading, the dream is preserved like a fly in amber. And it is a curious fly, not quite like the ones we are familiar with, not quite like any other fly we have seen before.

not by quite all standards. A picture may have all these characteristics yet may combine them in a pattern of great charm or expressiveness. From the beginning, Rousseau had a sense for the agreeable or expressive placement of objects in a composition, and especially for the patterning of natural forms, such as the leaves of plants or the silhouettes of trees.

A "primitive," which in this sense means self-taught, artist may also paint with an honesty, a naïve directness, which is a transmutation of his own intensity and pleasure as he goes about the unfamiliar and exciting act of creation. This quality is inherent in Rousseau's early work to a surpassing degree. To some extent it is an intangible, yet its presence can be explained by closer examination of a painting (again [469]) which on the surface looks only "amateurish." Paint which in the run-of-the-mill picture of this kind would be thin and dry, is

To some extent all of this applies to primitive painting in general. It applies to a very large extent in exceptional primitive paintings where lucky accident is luckier than usual in transforming mere naïveté into a kind of magical vision. The difference is that in Rousseau's art it applies consistently.

Rousseau was an industrious painter and he began to show his pictures wherever he could. At the exhibitions of the *Independants* he began to attract the attention of sophisticates who recognized the decorative quality and the poetry that distinguished his work from that of the armies of other Sunday painters who resembled him superficially. He left his comfortable position with the Customs to live on a small pension and spend his time painting. This was a dangerous point for Rousseau; upon the point of becoming a professional painter rather than an enthusiastic amateur, he was ready to study under conventional teachers and to master the techniques of realistic drawing and painting, which if he had mastered them, would have cost him the original style he had developed for himself. But he was lucky enough to receive good advice. The painters and literary figures who were beginning to make something of a darling of him were not the only ones who recognized the exceptional nature of his work. According to a later statement by Rousseau, even old Gérôme, the academic tyrant who was professor at the *École des Beaux Arts*, advised him to guard his naïveté.

Rousseau did guard his naïveté. But naïveté obviously stops being naïveté once it is guarded, and false naïveté can be a most offensive affectation. Rousseau set about creating for himself a personal style based on the forms that had been spontaneous to him as a beginner. This style, as he developed it, is the paradoxical one of a highly cultivated manner based on primitive simplicities, a dangerous combination and one that has never come off very well for Rousseau's imitators. Nor have any other "modern primitives," even those who begin as genuine ones, approached Rousseau's stature. Dealers and collectors continue to scout hopefully to ferret them out, but at

470. H. Rousseau: *The Young Girl, c.* 1894. 24 x 18". Philadelphia Museum of Art, Gift of Mr. and Mrs. R. Sturgis Ingersoll.

their best they usually turn out to be charming but inconsequential, bizarre but only bizarre, or sincere yet somehow at once ponderous and shallow.* Rousseau may be charming, bizarre, and even sometimes ponderous. In *The Young Girl* [470], for instance, he is all of these. But these are secondary characteristics in a painting where the primary ones are monumentality and magic.

Rousseau was a late bloomer. His first signed pictures are from 1880, when he was already thirty-six years old, and he did not begin to exhibit with the *Indépendants*

* Some exceptions are Louis Vivin (1861–1936), Camille Bombois (1883–   ), and André Bauchant (1873–   ), all French. The Americans John Kane (1860–1934) and Horace Pippin (1888–   ), especially the latter with his intimately observed genre scenes and his engaging historical pictures, are close to the tradition of American folk art (although Kane was born in Scotland).

471. H. ROUSSEAU: *The Dream*, 1910. 80 x 118½″. Museum of Modern Art, New York, Gift of Nelson A. Rockefeller.

until he was forty-two. In the interim he possibly copied pictures in the Louvre; at any rate, there is a record of issuance of a copyist's permit to him. The jungle fantasies for which he is most widely known did not appear until 1891, when he was approaching fifty. He was a happy eccentric, part visionary and part *petit bourgeois*. He eked out his pension by giving lessons in painting, music, and harmony, and he even wrote a five-act drama, *The Revenge of a Russian Orphan*, which was produced, but demonstrated that his unusual qualities as an artist were limited to painting, even though his naïveté was not.

According to his own story, Rousseau did military service in Mexico as one of the troops in the half-hearted expedition to keep Maximilian on the throne there. If this was true—there is good reason to doubt it, since there is no proof and Rousseau was given to fabrications which he half believed himself—he would have been twenty-two at the time, and might have carried back with him the memory of exotic foliage and exotic people. But as a matter of fact he could not

have seen the wild parrots, monkeys, leopards, and other beasts, or the particular plant forms he painted, for the good reason that they did not exist in the parts of Mexico he would have seen. His experience there would have been limited to the cities and the actually not very exotic countryside in which cacti, palms, and other semitropical plants did exist, but not in the profusion of jungles and not too frequently of the types Rousseau painted. His reference sources were the zoo, the botanical gardens, and postcards and photographs of exotic creatures and places. The references are not especially important since the true source of his pictures was his own imagination, whatever actual or secondhand experience he may have had with exotic places.

In the jungle pictures [471] he is free to give full indulgence to his passion for the design of leaves, blossoms, and branches. They grow in luxuriant and unnatural profusion, ordered into clear and unnatural patterns, combining the most fantastic imagery with the most unquestioning defi-

472. H. ROUSSEAU: *The Sleeping Gypsy*, 1897. 51 x 79″. Museum of Modern Art, New York, Gift of Mrs. Simon Guggenheim.

nition. Their existence is impossible, yet undeniable. Reason tells us that these are fantasies or apparitions; our senses tell us that they are tangible fact. The conflicting halves of this paradox, formulated as a theory by Böcklin and Redon, were balanced and harmonized by Rousseau because the paradox existed in his own personality.

Rousseau was fifty-three when he created *The Sleeping Gypsy* [472], the climactic painting of his total work. In its own area, the area of fantastic and visionary art, *The Sleeping Gypsy* occupies a position comparable only to those occupied by Seurat's *La Grande Jatte*, Cézanne's *The Great Bathers*, and van Gogh's *The Starry Night*.

The Sleeping Gypsy cannot be accepted as a "primitive" painting except in the stylistic sense of the word. There is nothing unconsidered in its expressive effectiveness, no "lucky accidents," no groping, and no compromise. The pattern of the lion's mane, running in serpentine rivulets, the odd backward turning of the tuft of hair at the end of the tail, the careful sprinkling of stars in the sky, the patterned lines of hills on the horizon, the dune where the gypsy lies and the lion stands, the gypsy's robe— whatever elements, instinctive or theoretical, account for the creation of these forms, they are the creation of a born artist who has matured as a creative designer through observation and experience. Rousseau paints each of the fantastic parts of this fantastic combination with the apparently objective innocence of his streets, houses, and ordinary city trees; fantasy or nightmare are accepted as unquestioningly as the everyday world, and represented as uncompromisingly. In Böcklin, and sometimes even in Redon, the real and the unreal may still be identified as incompatible elements brought into a kind of truce with one another, but in Rousseau they cannot be separated because it was never necessary for him to combine them in the first place. In his conception of *The Sleeping Gypsy* they must have existed together, as one, from the beginning.

PART IV

The Twentieth Century

CHAPTER 12

Fauvism and Expressionism

The Position of Matisse and Picasso

Since any discussion of art since 1900 is only marking time until it reaches Matisse and Picasso, they must be introduced immediately. They are without question the two most important painters of the first half of the twentieth century. The art of these two men, sometimes overlapping and sometimes in conflict, set the pace for more painters and determined the taste of more collectors than that of any other artists during the period. The men themselves have enjoyed success during their lifetimes comparable only to that of such painters as Raphael, Titian, and Rubens, who were courted by kings and popes. Even Monet and Renoir and Degas, who lived long enough to see themselves generally successful and widely recognized, were only moderately successful and recognized in comparison with Matisse and Picasso, whose names are known everywhere, whose work is multiplied in, quite literally, millions of reproductions, and whose most casual scribbles are coveted by collectors. (Their most casual scribbles can be pretty good.) More books and articles have been published on them, already, than on any other two painters of any places or times. Even if the future should make a drastic re-evaluation of their work, it cannot alter the historical fact that Matisse and Picasso have exerted an influence as wide, apparently as deep, and certainly as revolutionary during their own lifetimes as have any painters who have ever lived.

Fifty years after the first scandals of fauvism and cubism, to which their names are respectively attached, Matisse and Picasso still shock and puzzle much of the general public, yet people come by tens of thousands to see exhibitions of their work. Matisse and Picasso are illustrated not only in every art publication, which is natural, but in every publication designed for popular consumption as well. They have found their way into elementary school-books where *The Blue Boy*, *Whistler's Mother*, and *The Sower* formerly elevated the taste of the very young. They sell in reproduction by the gross to hotels, motels, and the decorators of housing developments. Housewives who had already put *Whistler's Mother* in the attic to make room for a reproduction of a Renoir or even a van Gogh or a Gauguin, have pushed on to Matisse and Picasso, whether they understand them or not.

There are several reasons for this phenomenon of mass interest in paintings that would ordinarily appeal to only a limited audience. The educational techniques of American museums, led by the Museum of Modern Art in New York; the fact that the painters as personalities make good copy for the picture magazines, which must find new copy of some kind every week; and the new processes of color reproduction that make color so bright and attractive, even when it is inaccurate—all these factors have contributed to an impressive structure of general interest. But the foundation supporting this structure is less apparent; it is to be found in the history of the relationship of the public to the art of the impressionists and the post-impressionists. People today are aware that the painters they most enjoy—like Renoir, whom they love, and especially van Gogh and Gauguin, whom they find attractive—had to endure contumely and hardship during their lifetimes. They know the stories of the terrible lives of van Gogh and Gauguin through popular biographies and movies. On the premise that history repeats itself, they are willing to accept the chance that the painters whose art is incomprehensible to them today are the ones most likely to succeed with posterity. It is as if the public feels a sense of mass guilt for the persecutions to which late-nineteenth-century painters were subjected and is trying to atone three generations later by accepting

with humility a kind of painting it would ordinarily reject on sight.

This humility is engaging, and encouraging in its way. Less encouragingly, it is flavored by the snob value attached to the appreciation of paintings that only millionaires can afford to buy, that only intellectuals can explain, and that museums display with the same techniques used in the display of expensive merchandise. The taste for modern art, in other words, is built on false values at least as often as not. Its popularization in magazines and reproductions is usually commercial opportunism; its dissemination through museums is well intentioned, but this education concerning it is often confused with propaganda for it. It is all very curious, and the greatest tribute to the paintings of Matisse and Picasso is the fact that everyone is not sick unto death of them; the strongest proof that they are worth all the proselytization is that as works of art they have withstood the excesses of the proselytizers. And it would be ungrateful not to recognize that in spite of mistakes and abuses, the missionary work is serving its purpose: for the first time in a century, the lag between creative art and public taste, which has bedeviled original painters since the romantic revival, is beginning to shorten.

Fauvism and Expressionism

This chapter is concerned with fauvism and the related movement of expressionism, but cubism was developing at the same time. It will be necessary to refer to cubism here and there in discussing fauvism and expressionism, since all three isms impinged on one another. It would be a good idea for the reader to glance just now at some of the illustrations in the following chapter—say 560 through 569—and bear them in mind, in a general way, as examples of what cubism looks like. This will leave us free in this chapter to make occasional references to cubism in something less than a vacuum.

Fauvism, it must be said in the beginning, is a word derived from the French one meaning wild beast—*fauve*. There are other words, but not many, which could be

473. MOREAU: *The Apparition* (*Dance of Salome*) (small version), *c.* 1876. 21¾ x 17½". Fogg Art Museum, Cambridge, Mass., Grenville L. Winthrop Bequest.

the interlude during which the intimists, particularly Vuillard, had rejected bright pigmentation for a muted palette. Fauvism coalesced in 1905, two years after the death of Gauguin, and although it drew upon pointillism and from Cézanne, and from van Gogh, in the end Gauguin was the dominant influence. Fauvism and expressionism developed from the same sources on one side of their family trees; they were, so to speak, first cousins, sharing in part a common ancestry, but with differences as important as their similarities.

Matisse: Early Experiences and Discoveries

Henri Matisse (1869–1954), the central figure in fauvism, was well on his way to becoming a lawyer (as Degas and Manet, among others, had been) when he began to paint. When he was twenty-two he induced his father to let him abandon law for art, and went to Paris to study under Bouguereau, who was then an old man full of honors, an international success, and the dean of the academicians. This was in 1891 and 1892, a complicated time when Monet, Renoir, Degas, Cézanne, Lautrec, Redon, Puvis de Chavannes, Gauguin, and Douanier Rousseau were all at work. Seurat's early death had occurred the year of Matisse's arrival in Paris, and van Gogh had died only the year before. Vuillard and Bonnard, who were Matisse's age within a year or two, had begun their careers. (Most of the men who were to develop expressionism were adolescents in Germany.) The old guard of the academicians was still well entrenched; even old Meissonier had just died, at the age of seventy-five. In France the decade from 1890 to 1900 offered everything at once.

Matisse was not long in choosing his way —at least, he was not long in rejecting Bouguereau as a prelude to doing so. Although Matisse was a provincial young man he was no philistine, and he soon recognized the vulgar banality of Bouguereau's art and the sterility of his teaching. He managed to enter, instead, the studio of Gustave Moreau (1826–1898), a painter whose rather decadent exoticism [473] was

less appropriate as a descriptive name for the group of painters to whom the label was attached. The fauves included some of the most highly civilized painters ever to put color on canvas. They did use broad strong areas of pure color that seemed crude, savage, to certain shocked and puzzled critics in 1905. But not even the most offended critic could find wild-beastiness today in the later developments of the fauve painters. Objections would be safer at the opposite pole of hyperrefinement and artificiality.

Fauvism was a spontaneous development, generated in France. It slightly preceded and contributed significantly to expressionism, which had its centers in Germany. Both movements were returns to the colorism of van Gogh and Gauguin after

474. Jan Davidz de Heem (Dutch, 1606?–1684): *Still-life*, 1640. 58⅝ x 80". Louvre, Paris.

academically acceptable as a continuation of Delacroix's romanticism. Moreau had been appointed to the teaching staff of the *École des Beaux Arts*. He was an exceptional man, without much acquaintance with experimental art yet unprejudiced in any direction, alert to the special character of whatever experimental painting came to his attention, even though in his own work he stuck close to tradition. Moreau gave Matisse his first education in art, not so much as his drawing and painting instructor as his guide to the art of the past, ranging over the whole field of masters dear to the academic heart, and those who were not. Soon Matisse was copying in the Louvre, partly as a way of studying and partly because the sale of copies produced a small income. These were "free" copies rather than painstaking reproductions. Primarily, Matisse was studying pictorial structure through copying rather than meticulously imitating the surface of another man's canvas as a mechanical routine. The integration of this study into his full development as a

painter was demonstrated by his return, more than twenty years later, to a de Heem still-life [474] to restudy it in a now famous variation [475].

All this while, Matisse was hardly aware of the impressionists, much less of such painters as Cézanne, van Gogh, and Gauguin. But discovery and conversion began to come rapidly in 1896 and 1897. After a few tentative impressionist excursions he set about his first major picture, *La Desserte* [476], in pure impressionist technique, and exhibited it in the Salon of the *Société Nationale*. (This was a dissenting academic organization, created by Meissonier as the result of a quarrel within the ranks of the Salon proper in 1890, and at that time headed by Puvis de Chavannes, who had nominated Matisse for membership.) *La Desserte*, a fine impressionist painting by the most exacting standards, drew indignant criticisms from conservative painters, but Moreau defended it.

During the next few years, still regarding himself as a student and rather surprisingly

475. MATISSE: *Variation on a Still-life by de Heem,* 1915, 1916, or 1917. 71 x 87¾". Collection Mr. and Mrs. Samuel A. Marx, Chicago.

476. MATISSE: *La Desserte,* 1897. 39½ x 51½". Collection Stavros Niarchos, Athens.

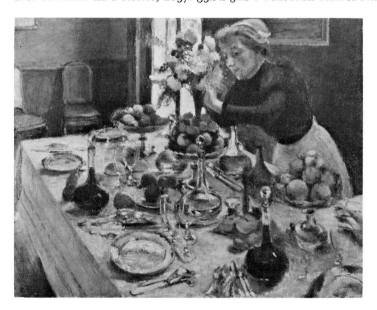

sequestered, considering the turmoil surrounding him in the Paris art world, Matisse felt his way among the crosscurrents of the end of the century. What he was learning is shown by the pictures and sculpture he acquired for himself: at considerable financial sacrifice he purchased a small Cézanne study of three bathers and a plaster bust by Rodin, and he exchanged one of his own paintings for a head of a boy by Gauguin. Rodin seems at first an odd influence on Matisse, but Matisse's *Slave* [477], a very early piece, shows how closely he followed Rodin [478], and we will see shortly that Rodin also influenced Matisse in certain drawings. Matisse had also wanted to buy a certain *Arlésienne* by van Gogh, but had given it up for the Cézanne, of which he wrote, many years later when he presented

477. MATISSE: *The Slave*, 1900–03. Bronze, height 36¼″. Baltimore Museum of Art, Cone Collection.

478. RODIN: Study for a monument to Balzac, 1895. Bronze, height 30″. Collection Mr. and Mrs. R. Sturgis Ingersoll, Penllyn, Pa.

it to the Museum of the City of Paris, "it has sustained me spiritually in the critical moments of my career as an artist." The influences of Cézanne, Gauguin, and even of Rodin are apparent in Matisse's *La Coiffure* [479] painted at this time, with its bold planes, its uncompromising force, and its emphatically defined silhouettes.

These early years of first experiment and discoveries were difficult ones for Matisse. He had abandoned a promising beginning toward conventional success, with encouraging recognition and some sales, and soon found himself in the familiar position of the experimenter—bad notices when he managed to exhibit at all, and no purchasers. He had married and had three children. But in 1905, a climactic year in his development and in the history of modern art, the situation improved dramatically, and his career as a leader among contemporary painters began in earnest.

Matisse: The Birth of Fauvism

479. MATISSE: *La Coiffure*, 1901. 37½ x 31⁹⁄₁₆″. National Gallery of Art, Washington, D.C., Chester Dale Collection.

480. MATISSE: *Olive Trees, Collioure*, 1905 (?). 18 x 21¾″. Estate of the artist.

Matisse's palette had been brightened by some essays in pointillism, and now during the summer of 1905, in the village of Collioure on the Mediterranean, he came into a sudden realization of new meanings in color. (He was nearly thirty-five years old.) *Olive Trees, Collioure* [480] at a careless glance might be dismissed as a pointillist sketch. Actually the color—pure reds, greens, oranges, violets—applied in strokes of fairly uniform size, has nothing to do with pointillist theory. The different colors do not fuse into harmonious tonalities but maintain their own intense identities, clashing against one another and setting up a "movement" of their own as color, a movement that is incorporated into the more familiar kind of movement of the rather obvious swirling linear patterns. Matisse was learning that color as pure color could have its own rhythms, its own structure, that color could be exalted for itself rather than used as a descriptive or decorative accessory to other elements of a picture.

By this idea, a tree trunk could be vermilion, a sky could be solid orange, a face could be divided down its middle by a green line with contrasting colors on either side, as part of a color structure owing no allegiance to the actual color of trees, skies, or faces but existing as an independent abstraction. Gauguin had anticipated this idea in what was now an elementary way, and therein lies his grandparentage of fauvism. But Gauguin's color, when it departed arbitrarily from the colors of nature, was arbitrary in the service of mood or of decorative effect, which is a good step removed from a full conception of abstract color structure.

What "color structure" means is well demonstrated by the famous head of Madame Matisse usually called *The Green Line* [481]. On the right the face is pink, on the left, a yellow ochre. The background is divided into three large areas of green, vermilion, and rose-violet. These areas are not screens, pictures, or any other background objects; they are purely areas of color. All three are echoed in the dress. The hair is dark blue, as are the contour lines of the dress. On the pink side of the face the contour line is red, on the left side, green. The pink and ochre have some relationship to natural color, but when we reach the light, brilliant stripe of yellow-green dividing them down the middle of the face, the purely arbitrary use of color for structure is dramatized. Without the green stripe the face would be pallid, lost in the center of the violent color surrounding it. The question may be asked: In that case, why not modify the surrounding color so that the face could compete with it, instead of introducing the arbitrary green stripe? The answer is that the painter wants to use color at maximum intensity, and since the green stripe is necessary—as color—in that particular place, he uses it instead of sacrificing color intensity elsewhere. For that matter, the shape of the stripe and its position in the composition, as well as its color, is necessary as part of the pictorial structure. If it is covered up, even in a black and white reproduction, the structure is weakened. If it is covered in the original or in a good color reproduction, the structure is destroyed. And how did Matisse arrive at this particular color for this particular stripe? Through a general knowledge of color theory in the first place, of course, but more importantly through highly developed sensibilities and instincts in its use, plus a certain amount of trial and error in preliminary studies.

The Green Line is an abstract construction of color, but it is also an arresting image. It is not to be taken as a portrait of Madame Matisse in either a realistic or an expressionistic, interpretative way, although it suggests her features. The strong masklike character of the face reflects the stylized forms of African sculpture—a new interest with Matisse, and one which was to have an even stronger impact on Picasso in the development of cubism. Matisse was twelve years older than Picasso and, for whatever interest the fact may have in the general tendency to balance one man's innovations against the other's, it is probable that Matisse introduced Picasso to African sculpture at a time when cubism was still generating as a buried seed. Picasso and Matisse had made one another's acquaint-

481. MATISSE: *Madame Matisse* (*The Green Line*), 1905. 16 x 12¾″. *Statens Museum for Kunst*, Copenhagen, Rump Collection.

ance and were being collected in the same circles; a conspicuous patron was the American, Gertrude Stein. The two men met frequently at her apartment and maintained a courteous but wary attitude toward one another, as if they already realized that they would become, during the next decades, for critics and painters and collectors, rival representatives of the two mainstreams of modern painting.

Picasso was only beginning to collect his circle, but Matisse's was already pretty well formed. Surrounding him, having varying degrees of contact with him, drawing ideas from him and contributing their own were a group of colorists who became the fauves as a result of the landmark *Salon d'Automne* of 1905. Fauvism was never systematic; it

482. Matisse: *Blue Nude*, 1907. 36¼ x 55⅛″. Baltimore Museum of Art, Cone Collection.

483. Matisse: *Reclining Nude I*, 1907. Bronze, height 13½″. Baltimore Museum of Art, Cone Collection.

had no program and no formalized theory. It was never an organized school of painting, and as a group the fauves soon lost their unity, building in their own directions from the original stimulus. And as a "school" of painting, the birth of fauvism all but took its participants by surprise.

The *Salon d'Automne* had been organized two years before the famous 1905 exhibition by a group of thoughtful painters and liberal critics, who were equally dissatisfied with the conservatism of the regular academic Salons with their ingrown juries, and the anarchy of the *Indépendants* with no juries at all. The organizers of the *Salon d'Automne* solved the jury problem by selecting its members by lot. The 1905 jury hung the work of Matisse and eleven other colorists in one room together; one critic, commenting on a small bronze in the Florentine Renaissance manner exhibited in the same room, said, "Donatello parmi les fauves!"—Donatello among the wild beasts—and fauvism as a term and the fauves as a group were born, to the usual sounds of furious hubbub familiar since the *Salon des Refusés* forty-two years before. But there was a new note in the hubbub, and a more sympathetic one. The circle of liberal critics had widened. Where one reactionary critic found that the fauve pictures had "nothing whatever to do with painting," a liberal one recognized that Matisse's art was "painting outside of every contingency, painting in itself, the act of pure painting," and while the first saw "aberrated daubs and splotches of color," the other found that "the rational mind" of the painter perfectly controlled every element introduced into the paintings. Adventurous and perspicacious collectors were also increasing in number, putting an end to stories like the youthful Monet's or van Gogh's and Gauguin's.

While the excitement of the *Salon d'Automne* was still boiling, Matisse began a large composition as a crystallization and perhaps as a manifesto of fauvist ideas. *The Joy of Life* is a faulty picture, rather flimsy and monotonous compositionally, and disturbingly mannered, although it is of historical interest in showing that Matisse was experimenting with some of the structural ideas that were to be involved in cubism, as well as elements that were to affect expressionism in its more abstract forms. The *Blue Nude* of 1907 [482] is a more successful study in the same direction, combining sinuosities of line, arbitrary color, and dislocations of form, which are of course extremely disturbing if the painting is regarded as a representation of a female nude but are extraordinarily forceful otherwise.

With pictures like the *Blue Nude* Matisse was attracting enough attention to warrant the publication of his theories the following year, 1908. Matisse was nearly forty; he is unique among painters in having reached intellectual maturity before his career as a creative artist began in earnest. In effect, he has no "youthful" period. All his pre-fauve work is essentially studious, thoughtfully preparatory.

The *Notes of a Painter* play a double theme: the importance of feeling, of pure

484. DERAIN: *Henri Matisse*, 1905. 13 x 16". Philadelphia Museum of Art, Gallatin Collection.

485. DERAIN: *The Artist's Niece*, before 1939. 37⅜ x 30⁵⁄₁₆". Private collection, France.

486. DERAIN: *Le Mas Provençal*, date unknown. 24¾ x 37¼″. Collection Robert E. McCormick, New York.

Other Fauve Painters

André Derain (1880–1954) worked with Matisse at Collioure in 1905, and painted the fauvist "portrait" of him [484] there. Derain was one of the first of the original group to depart from fauvism, and he cut off from it with exceptional completeness. When the competing cubist furore broke, Derain joined that party briefly, then for the rest of a commercially very successful career he shifted from style to style under the influence of a dozen traditional schools, as in a portrait of the artist's niece [485], where Corot, fauvism, and eighteenth-century sensibility are combined in an image of great sweetness, or *Le Mas Provençal* [486], where Corot, again, Courbet, Cézanne, and a pinch of cubism are included in the recipe.

Derain was a painter with a flair for modifying traditional styles by imposing agreeable modernisms upon them; or perhaps his flair was for modifying the radical discoveries of other painters by adapting them to acceptably traditional surfaces. He was, in either case, a painter of fashionable good taste and great discretion. His detractors think of him as a parasite on both the past and the present, but his admirers are satisfied that his middle-of-the-road art is neither a subterfuge nor an opportunistic compromise. Some critics award Derain unique stature as the only twentieth-century painter to achieve an individual compound of the great tradition of French culture as a whole with the spirit of his own time. This would place him in a position similar to the one accorded Renoir as the great traditionalist as well as one of the great innovators of the latter half of the nineteenth century. This opinion is particularly held in France—where, of course, it is most legitimate.

Maurice de Vlaminck (1876–1958) was a great friend of Derain's in their early days. They discovered van Gogh together, and it was Derain who introduced Vlaminck to Matisse. Among the cultivated and intellectual fauves, Vlaminck was an exceptional personality—more nearly *fauve* than they in his peasant vigor and his rambunctious muscularity. He was one of the

sensation, of the painter's response to the world on one hand, and, on the other, the means by which he may transmute these feelings into form and color. As a generality this is the problem of all serious painters; in the case of Matisse, the *Notes* imply everywhere a love of joyousness. He finally says, "What I dream of is an art of balance, of purity and serenity devoid of troubling or depressing subject-matter, an art which might be for every mental worker, be he business man or writer, like an appeasing influence, like a mental soother, something like a good armchair in which to rest from physical fatigue." Even granting some exaggeration and some awkwardness of expression (or of translation out of French) this is hardly the spirit of the *Blue Nude*, painted just before the notes were written, nor is it the spirit of the sculpture with which Matisse was occupying himself at the same time [483]. The *Blue Nude* and the sculpture were solutions of structural problems Matisse had set himself. Having served their purpose, their violent dislocations were soon to give way to forms no less vital but more serene or more joyous as the fauvist upheaval was assimilated.

Pure fauvism was of brief duration not only with Matisse but with the other members of the group. Before we follow Matisse's subsequent development, a few comments on the other fauves should be interpolated.

few fauves who never toyed with cubism; he rejected it on sight as overintellectualized. But he abandoned the brilliant pure colors of fauvism to develop a dramatic landscape style giving a stormy and sinister character to simple village streets or peasant cottages painted in broad spreads and slashes of Prussian blue, black, touches of acid green, and spectral lights [487]. At their most effective these landscapes have a threatening vigor. Their shortcoming is their repetitiousness; reduced to a formula, both the threat and the vigor turn back into paint.

Albert Marquet (1875–1947) was especially close to Matisse in friendship, but his connection with fauvism was not a strong one in spite of his participation in the original exhibition. He was a sober painter, and a quiet man. Rivers and bridges and harbors were his favorite subjects, and he painted them with an ordered simplicity that recalls Corot, although he simplified his compositions into the flattened color areas associated with fauvism. The color itself, however, is more likely to be subdued than vivid. Marquet is a minor painter who was content to be one. His pictures are agreeable, partly because he never tried to force himself beyond his modest potential; they are admirable because he was never content to work below it [488].

Othon Friesz (1879–1949) painted a few unusually personal and sensitive fauve works, then abandoned the movement for a reactionary and sterile style. Henri Manguin (1874–1945) and Raoul Dufy (1877–1953) capitalized in the most lighthearted way on the brightness of fauve color. Dufy, after a period of conscientious effort to build himself a solid, monumental style on the model of Cézanne, realized the true nature of his talent and accepted it. He became the most engaging painter of chic and superficial subjects since the eighteenth century. He was helped toward this decision by Paul Poiret, the influential couturier, who commissioned Dufy to design fabrics. It is usual to say that Dufy sold himself out for an easy success, but this is an injustice. To exchange his bright and sparkling pictures for the second-rate

487. Vlaminck: *Village in the Snow*, date unknown. Watercolor and gouache, 18 x 21″. Philadelphia Museum of Art, Gift of Howard A. Wolf.

488. Marquet: *Docks at Hamburg*, 1909. 27¼ x 32″. Collection Madame Albert Marquet, Bordeaux.

Cézannesque productions he might have continued to work at, would have been a very poor trade for everyone concerned. He developed a style in which swatches of decorative colors were freely applied to

489. DUFY: *Racetrack at Deauville*, 1929. 25½ x 32½". Fogg Art Museum, Cambridge, Mass., Maurice Wertheim Collection.

490. DUFY: *Threshing with a Blue Machine*, 1948. 21½ x 25¾". Toledo Museum of Art, Gift of Edward Drummond Libbey.

the canvas (or the paper—he used watercolor a great deal) and then more or less pulled together by economical calligraphic notations describing objects [489]. Racetracks, yacht basins, formal gardens, theater interiors, and other places of cheerful and expensive congregation were his favorite themes. They were most appropriate ones, too, for his manner. When he employed his fresh light colors and his bright little notations of form on less appropriate subjects—threshing machines, as one instance [490]—the style is as brilliant but the integration between means and subject is lost. This may be partly sheer association of ideas, for Dufy's manner has been plagiarized so freely by fashionable commercial artists that it has become synonymous with expensive elegance. His fecundity was extreme, and his style was one that could have become an automatically repetitive formula (as Vlaminck's did), yet Dufy retained a vivacity which suggests always that he took the greatest pleasure in what he was doing. The economy of his drawing, with its shorthand quality, conceals more variety and more observation than he is generally given credit for.

But the great names of the fauve group (unless we include Derain's) are Matisse, Braque, and Rouault. Braque turned to cubism and will be discussed with it. For Rouault, fauvism was a way station toward an intensely individual form of expression.

Rouault

Georges Rouault (1871–1958) was also a student of Moreau's, and he met Matisse in Moreau's studio. He is an anomaly in his century, a truly religious Christian painter. Perhaps it is necessary to point out that this is not the same thing as a painter of Christian subjects. There were many of these men, of course, and Rouault's earliest paintings are close to their tradition, although infused with a more visionary quality than most—thanks no doubt to the influence of Moreau.

Rouault was a devout Catholic, but his fervent Christianity is concerned less with personal redemption than with humane sociological values. He is horrified by man's inhumanity to man, appalled at poverty and misery. His Christianity is not concerned with mystical revelation but with man's spiritual union with his fellows, which is violated by every instance of cruelty or other human degradation. The expert illustration of Bible stories was not an adequate release for Rouault as a Christian painter; it was necessary for him to discover a more personal and intense expression.

By 1911 Rouault had passed through fauvism to an expressionism more remindful of the Germans than of any French tradition. He disregarded fauvism's bright colors and essentially happy mood in favor of a restricted and rather turgid palette in the service of tragic and pathetic subjects.

491. ROUAULT: *The Sirens*, 1906. Gouache, 28 x 22″. Collection Mr. and Mrs. R. Sturgis Ingersoll, Penllyn, Pa.

The Sirens [491] is painted in an oppressive tonality dominated by cold and rather sour grays, morbid gray-violets, and the blackish colors of the deliberately coarse and ugly outlines defining the swollen bodies and brutalized faces of two naked prostitutes. The women are symbols of mankind's self-corruption through the corruption of his fellows, through the cruelties, injustices, and miseries that he inflicts or whose existence he tolerates. The spirit of the picture is partly sociological, but more importantly it is religious, in the painter's identification of himself with the sufferings of humanity.

Rouault was never affected by medievalism as an imitation of the forms of medieval art (as the Pre-Raphaelites, for

492. ROUAULT: *Tragic Clowns,* 1907–10. Oil on cardboard. 29½ x 22½″. Philadelphia Museum of Art, Louis E Stern Collection.

instance, were). But in certain ways his art is a continuation of medieval forms in the idiom of the twentieth century. Rouault's heavy, simplified, powerful volumes, in pictures like *Tragic Clowns* [492], have been compared to those of Romanesque sculpture—the sculpture of the early middle ages. The reference is a little forced, however, and the resemblances may be largely coincidental. The Romanesque sculptors in their century, and Rouault in his, approached the problem of expression from opposite poles technically. The early sculptors, working at the beginning of a tradition, with virtually no reference to a body of sculpture in the past, were inventing forms whose simplicity was imposed as much by technical limitations as by any-

thing else. They were probably striving for a higher degree of imitative realism than they managed to achieve, all expressive values aside. Rouault, on the other hand, is discarding the whole tradition of imitative realism, which had become so technically expert that it was next to photographic, and is finding his means of expression through simplifications which he imposes upon himself. The common denominator between primitive medieval art and the art of Rouault is not a technical one but a spiritual one: both are concerned with the theme of mankind's frailty and his redemption. The medieval sculptors expounded the theme by illustrating the Bible story; Rouault is never so specific, but in pictures like *Tragic Clowns* the theme is implicit just as it is in *The Sirens.* The male clown with his broken face, chopped out in broad sculpturesque planes, and the young girl with her heavy, coarsening one are symbols of mankind's tragedy, which is the death of his spirit through corruption. Rouault reveals the spiritual corruption through corruption and disfigurement of the flesh. But through his identification of himself with the subjects, and by the consciousness of tragedy that he stirs in us by these images, he also makes the picture a statement of man's hope, which is redemption through compassion.

If the forms of medieval sculpture were echoed only in a roundabout way in Rouault's style, those of medieval stained glass influenced it quite directly. He had been apprenticed, at fourteen, to a maker of stained glass and had worked on the restoration of medieval windows. Even in early expressionistic pictures like *The Sirens,* the dark outlines begin to suggest the leaded joints of stained glass windows, and shortly Rouault abandoned his heavy color schemes for areas of brilliant pigments even more definitely confined and separated from one another by black outlines. In some areas the color may have the flat purity of enamel—another medieval craft; in others, heavy strokes dragged across rough surfaces may suggest the surface irregularities and the luminous variations of medieval glass. In this manner Rouault painted landscapes, Biblical sub-

ROUAULT · 411

493. ROUAULT: *Crucifixion*, 1918. 41 x 28¾″. Collection Henry P. McIlhenny, Philadelphia.

494. ROUAULT: *Pierrot with a Rose*, 1936. 36¼ x 24″. Collection S. S. White III and Vera White, Ardmore, Pa.

jects [493], and above all the clowns and other performers of circuses and pantomimes that had always interested him. He did these in great numbers, and it is a mistake to try to read emotional intensities into all of them. By implication and association these intensities may be present, if diminished, but there are also many pictures, for instance *Pierrot with a Rose* [494], where sheer decorative vigor and rich color are at least as important, and as rewarding, as whatever elements of pathos are retained by the image.

Rouault was also one of the great printmakers of the age; many people would not hesitate to give him the title of greatest. The series *Miserere* and *War* are landmarks in the development of print techniques in which expression is integrated with technical devices. They are the most

important prints from this point of view since Goya's, which they suggest in other ways also. Like Goya, Rouault reveals the whole category of man's bestiality and viciousness; unlike Goya, however, he combines recognition of these realities with the mystical convictions we have already seen in his paintings. Technically, Goya was an innovator in that he approached the print as a self-contained medium, capitalizing on its inherent character and its expressive potential rather than using it as a means of reproducing painting or as a substitute for drawing. Rouault expanded the range of the print by combining any number of techniques on a single plate, creating his printing surface not only by conventional means, such as etching and engraving with the burin, but by such roughening devices as files, sandpaper, edged rollers and

495. ROUAULT: *Dura Lex Sed Lex* (*Harsh Law, but Law*), from *Miserere*, 1926. Composite processes, 22⅝ x 17⅛". Philadelphia Museum of Art.

scrapers, and wide brush strokes of acid—upon a foundation, sometimes, of photogravure. He approached a copper plate not with the idea that he was a draftsman or a technician, but with the idea that he was an artist creating a printing surface that must yield its expressive maximum through a design created in textures. From these plates, in black and white on paper, he achieved as much depth, variety, and richness as he did in full color manipulated in relief on canvas [495].

Matisse after Fauvism

By 1907, only two years after the fauvist paroxysm of the *Salon d'Automne* of 1905, fauvism had reached its climax as a movement with some kind of unity among the men who composed the group. The more tightly organized movement of cubism was supplanting it as the most spectacular development in contemporary painting. Cubism was a more sensational departure from tradition than fauvism had been, since its distortions were more extreme, and it was more adaptable to development by a closely allied group of painters, since its theory was more objective, less dependent on personal sensitivities. The fauves began to go their own ways, as we have just seen them doing.

Of all the fauves, Matisse had always been the one most concerned with formal organization. The apparent spontaneity and the fluidity of his compositions is deceptive. Like Delacroix before him, Matisse was always intent on maintaining the impression of spontaneity in the completed canvas, even though its final organization of form and color was the result of preliminary calculation, trial, and error.

Variations on the sinuous rhythms and the fresh expression of *The Joy of Life* continued to preoccupy Matisse until they culminated in a pair of large murals, *Dance* and *Music*, commissioned by a wealthy Russian, Sergei Shchukin, to decorate the stairwell of his house in Moscow. *Dance* is a reduction, to final terms, of composition in flat color and rhythmic line. It appears to have been improvised as it was painted, but it was preceded by any number of studies [496] in which the relationships of one line and area to another were modified into final balance.

Matisse was working in other directions at the same time, attacking especially the problem of formal monumentality combined with the dynamic color of fauvism. Sometimes his experiments deviated briefly in unexpected directions. In one exceptional canvas, the portrait of *Mlle. Yvonne Landsberg* [497] of 1914, the whirling rhythms of *Dance* have been disciplined into a pattern of arcs abstracted from a powerfully static figure, which they unite with the surrounding space. The interpenetration of form and space is a characteristic of cubism, as we will see, but in rectangular planes. In the *Mlle. Landsberg* Matisse has experimented with a similar interpenetration, but in a way suggesting swelling rhythms in which space and figure echo one another in a kind of formal arabesque. *Mlle. Landsberg* is unique in its devices, although it is so effective that it might have served as the source of a whole movement in analytical painting based on curving spatial rhythms instead of cubism's rectangular structures. But Matisse did not follow up this direction; his preoccupation with vibrant areas of color would not allow the disintegration and merging of one form into another.

The diagrammatic arching lines of the *Mlle. Landsberg* are more apparent and more spectacularly innovational than the rhythms in the drawing *White Plumes* [498], but *White Plumes* is equally composed in a series of rhythmic contours which flow and build from the long sweeping arcs defining the skirt, then the arms, and then progress into the more complicated swinging, curling, and looping rhythms of the embroidery and the ribbons and plumes of the hat. The entire design is a progressively complicated variation on a flowing rhythm as the forms mount upward, climaxing in the subtly hypnotic face just as the more obvious arcs of the *Mlle. Landsberg* climax in the correspondingly harsher mask. The point made by a comparison of these two pictures is, that while Matisse was basically interested in line, form, and color as abstractions (*Mlle. Landsberg*), he is equally concerned with the creation of images (*White Plumes*). In the *Mlle. Landsberg*, abstractions come close to overpowering the image. But in *White Plumes* the image reasserts its dominance, "enriched by a wider meaning," in Matisse's words.

Five years separate the two pictures. During that time Matisse created many semi-abstract compositions, drawing upon cubism just as, indirectly, he had contributed to its origin. In 1916 he had returned to his early copy of the de Heem still-life to make his semicubist variation on it [475], and during the same period, in compositions like *The Piano Lesson* [499], his angular structures also echo cubist theories. But these angularities are a surface exaggeration of the vestigial cubism

496. MATISSE: Study for *Dance*, 1909. 108 x 144". Museum of Modern Art, New York, Gift of Nelson A. Rockefeller in honor of Alfred H. Barr, Jr.

497. MATISSE: *Mlle. Yvonne Landsberg*, 1914. 57¼ x 42". Philadelphia Museum of Art, Arensberg Collection.

498. MATISSE: *White Plumes*, 1919. Pencil, 19¼ x 14⅜″. Collection T. Edward Hanley, Bradford, Pa.

499. MATISSE: *The Piano Lesson*, 1916 or 1917. 92½ x 83¾″. Museum of Modern Art, New York, Mrs. Simon Guggenheim Fund.

in Matisse's work at this time. Basically, *The Piano Lesson* is a structure in which the linear skeleton and the pattern of geometrical areas are still dependent upon color for their life and their balance. Also, this picture, which may appear a little thin and flat at first, grows richer upon closer acquaintance. There is, for instance, the interplay between the almost jaunty little figurine of the nude in the lower left, which at first is hardly noticeable, with the elongated, angular figure at the upper right, a parent or teacher supervising the boy at the piano. There is also a kind of counterpoint between the arbitrary abstract elements and the fairly realistic representation of others—the metronome, and the music rack of the piano, where even the name, Pleyel, is shown in reverse as we see it from behind, as part of a filigree. All these balanced contradictions are in the spirit of the picture, which is an engaging, rather affectionately humorous subject contradictorily presented in a spare and carefully calculated scheme, a combination of intimacy and austerity.

Up to this point in his development, Matisse has evidently been intent upon harmonizing the joyous, intimate, and sensuous spirit that is inherent in his art with the disciplines necessary to lift it above mere charm or triviality. Around 1917, as if with a sigh of relief, he yielded himself to his "good armchair," largely abandoning the disciplines for an interim of the most relaxed, most spontaneous, and least intellectualized painting of his career. At this stage he becomes the painter of fresh, sensory delights that make him the twentieth-century inheritor of such pre-Revolutionary masters as Boucher, and of Renoir in Renoir's most intimate and informal work. His paint is applied more lusciously, and more casually, than before. His subjects have more consistently to do with pleasure, ease, and luxury. Angularities and severities of compositional structure yield to grace and, above all, to semirealism. In spite of perspective violations, *The Moorish Screen* [500] from this period could almost be a quick sketch by an impressionist or even a notation by a realist, although the emphasis on ornamental patterns would be characteristic of neither. Oriental elements, which had been a large factor in Matisse's work since a first visit to Morocco in 1911, are especially conspicuous here in the form of decorative accessories, such as carpets, screens, tiles, and the like. The whole picture is related to the glazed brilliance of Eastern patterned tiles.

Matisse was now working largely in Nice, a city dedicated to relaxation and surface attractions. His bright, comparatively naturalistic pictures pleased new collectors and even a fairly wide public, having as they did the *cachet* of approval by the most discerning critics, yet being much easier to understand than Matisse's work had been heretofore. But for all their charm, these agreeable and ornamental paintings had sacrificed much of their strength; for their grace, much of their subtlety. At this point Matisse might have followed the path of certain other fauves, notably Dufy, to settle for seduction and chic after the innovations of fauvism and the rigors of compositions like *The Piano Lesson* that had served the purpose of giving him a facile command of color and structure at less demanding levels.

Matisse was never to return to the abstractions of *The Piano Lesson* and other pictures of that period—at least, not in obvious ways. But he had never been a painter who was content to develop a formula and hold to it and he never became one. *Decorative Figure on an Ornamental Background* [501], about five years after *The Moorish Screen*, rejects the sketchy realism and rather fluid painting of the earlier picture for a return to bold definitions and more arbitrary patterning, but retains the opulence that will be characteristic of Matisse from now on. *Decorative Figure* is essentially one of Matisse's great still-life compositions rather than one

500. MATISSE: *The Moorish Screen*, 1921. 36¼ x 29″. Philadelphia Museum of Art, Lisa Norris Elkins Bequest.

of his great nudes, for the figure is like an ornamental sculpture in the ensemble of other decorative objects and patterns.

All the foregoing summaries of major stages in Matisse's development have omitted the subdivisions, the brief periods of retreat from one direction, of return to variations of earlier periods. Two years after *Decorative Figure*, for instance, paintings like *Nude by a Window* [502] may appear to differ very little from the semirealism of *The Moorish Screen*. Or the bay with its promenade, its palm tree, and quick patterns of color may go further back, as far as Collioure. In its structural skeleton of strong verticals and horizontals setting off sinuous curves, there are echoes of *The Piano Lesson*, if we want to find them. Like every painter who continues to

501. MATISSE: *Decorative Figure on an Ornamental Background*, 1927. 51½ x 38⅜".
Musée National d'Art Moderne, Paris.

502. MATISSSE: *Nude by a Window*, 1929. 25¾ x 21½". Private Collection.

grow, Matisse draws upon all that he has learned, sometimes consciously, sometimes spontaneously, but he is never content to work only in repetitions or recombinations of past successes. His first mistrust of Bouguereau, his first suspicion that that tremendous academic reputation might be an inflated one, came when he found that Bouguereau was not only making an exact copy of one of his most successful pictures but making it from another copy made some time before.

In spite of excursions in various directions, and all the divisions and subdivisions of his work into periods,* Matisse's development is, over-all, steady in the direction stated implicitly in his *Notes* when he said, "Supposing I want to paint the body of a woman: first of all I endow it with grace

* These may be followed in detail in Alfred Barr's *Matisse: His Art and His Public*.

and charm, but I know that something more than that is necessary. I try to condense the meaning of this body by drawing its essential lines. The charm will then become less apparent at first glance, but in the long run it will begin to emanate from the new image. This image at the same time will be enriched by a wider meaning . . . while the charm, being less apparent . . . will be merely one element in the general conception of the figure."

His *Lady in Blue* [503] of 1937, painted thirty years after the *Notes* were written, applies all that Matisse has learned of the artist's function as a creator who first responds to nature, then effects his own transmutation of nature in such a way that his response to it takes the form of an image revealing that response to the observer. The course of the transmutation can be followed in a series of photographs taken during the progress of the painting [504]. They show a progressive condensation and flattening of the forms, reduced to their essentials (the arms of the sofa, for instance, are finally reduced to two flat S shapes) and mutually adjusted into a balance at once decorative and expressive.

The color areas of *Lady in Blue* are quite flat, without any suggestion of modeling in light and shade. As a generality (but only as a generality) this is true of Matisse's style after about 1930. In his very late years he exaggerated this flatness in a series of brilliant conceits in cut and pasted papers of vivid color. One series of these was called *Jazz* [505]; all the more surprising, then, that their flat, bright shapes should be adapted, in Matisse's last work, to the stained glass windows of a chapel.

In the late 1940's, when he was approaching eighty, Matisse abruptly committed himself to the decoration of an entire chapel—stained glass windows, murals, ornamental tiles, altar, crucifix, confessional doors, chasubles, even the spire on the exterior—for the Dominican nuns in the little town of Vence, near Nice. Matisse underwrote some of the expense himself. Nothing in his worldly art had ever suggested that his last great work would be a religious one for which he volunteered, but everything in its ornamental character was adaptable to architectural use.

For that matter, the decoration of the chapel at Vence is not a religious work in the way it would have been if Rouault, for instance, had done it. Matisse had never been a devout man, and he experienced no conversion now, although there was a great deal of distorted publicity at the time, attributing such a reason to his decision to do the chapel. He undertook the assignment in part because of his friendship for one of the nuns but largely, it seems, in the spirit of adventurous enthusiasm that had stayed with him into his old age. "At last," he said, "we are going to have a gay chapel!" and he made no effort to synthesize any fraudulent mysticism in his preliminary designs. These were gay indeed, so gay that when a communist acquaintance of Matisse's saw them he said, "When we take over, we'll use it for a night club."

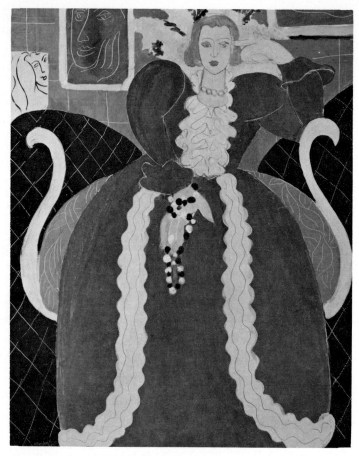

503. MATISSE: *Lady in Blue*, 1937. 36½ x 29". Collection Mrs. John Wintersteen, Chestnut Hill, Pa.

Matisse approached the decoration of the chapel as an abstract problem, a balancing of "a surface of light and color against a solid wall covered with black drawings." The scheme has little to do with the Christian mysteries except in its use of some of their familiar symbols, but it has a spareness and restraint, in spite of its bright colors, which is more appropriate to a chapel than it would be to a night club; it is pure, fresh, and joyous rather than gay and sensuous. The "murals" that balance the bright animated shapes of the windows are ceramic wall decorations in the form of thin line drawings in black on white backgrounds. They are a last statement of Matisse's development as a graphic artist, which was from elaboration (we have seen an example in the drawing *White Plumes*) to maximum simplicity.

504. MATISSE: Progressive stages of Figure 503, February 26 to April 6, 1937.

505. MATISSE: *The Knife Thrower*, from *Jazz*, 1947. Color stencil after cut paper original. 15⅞ x 25½". Philadelphia Museum of Art, McIlhenny Fund.

Girl in a Low Cut Dress [506] is a typical example of Matisse's line drawing at its most economical; it recalls Rodin, once more, in Matisse's art, especially with the bridge of *Three Friends* [507] in comparison with Rodin's *Imploration* [508], even if we grant that the resemblance between the ornamental suggestions in the background of *Three Friends* and the free washes of color in *Imploration* may be coincidental. Rodin's voluptuousness disappears in Matisse's crisper, brighter images, but the free line, capturing an immediate reaction to the model as well as describing the essence of formal contours, is common to them both. There the similarity ends. Rodin's sensuousness was always part of some mystery, some yearning, close to romantic anguish. Matisse's sensuousness is a response to the joy of the tangible world.

Expressionism: Precursors

By the definition of expressionism as "the free distortion of form and color through which a painter gives visual form to inner sensations or emotions," fauvism is a form of expressionism. But usually expressionism is concerned with "inner sensations or emotions" with connotations of pathos, violence, morbidity, or tragedy. Van Gogh is an expressionist within this definition. But by the narrowest definition of all, expressionism was a movement in twentieth-century painting that originated in Germany and continued to develop there in the work of several successive groups of painters who applied these general principles in their own intense and particular ways.

With the usual exceptions, the purest expressionist painters have been northern ones—Scandinavians, Dutchmen, Germans, and some Russians. Van Gogh was a northerner. Even though he painted in Paris and in the south of France, he was a foreigner to those places emotionally as well as nationally. He is admired and respected in France, but he has found no very close followers among French painters because he is without the qualities that temper the Frenchman's recognition of the terribleness of life—logical perception, worship of Rea-

506. MATISSE: *Girl in a Low Cut Dress,* 1939. Pen and ink, 15 x 22". Estate of the artist.

son, a sense of moderation. Nor has van Gogh the gaiety and elegance that are constants in French art and life, and so large an element in fauvism. Fauvism had secondary connections with van Gogh, but he was the natural father of German expressionism.

In addition to van Gogh, German expressionism found prophets in the Swiss Ferdinand Hodler (1853–1918), born the same year as van Gogh, the Belgian James Ensor (1860–1949), and the Norwegian Edvard Munch (1863–1944), whose birth date encloses the three men within a decade of van Gogh as to age. Ensor and Munch knew the work of van Gogh and Gauguin and were in part formed by it, but Hodler was a rather isolated painter whose connections with post-impressionism and expressionism are spotty and interrupted. They were made largely through the success of a single picture, *The Night* [509].

Hodler became a painter after making a difficult choice between art and science. The science remains apparent in his art, with its tight precise forms and what can only be called its objective quality. For in spite of the fact that *The Night* proposes a fantastic subject, the drawing of the nude

507.   MATISSE:
Three Friends, 1927.
Pen and ink, 15 x
20". *Musée National
d'Art Moderne*, Paris.

508. RODIN: *Imploration*, date unknown. Pencil with watercolor wash, 12 x 19". Collection Mr. and Mrs. Adolf Schaap, Elkins Park, Pa.

509. HODLER: *The Night*, 1890. 41¾ x 118". *Kunstmuseum*, Bern.

figures enacting it is next to scientific in the explicitness of its description. We are right back to the painting of another Swiss, then —Böcklin.* There is the same realistic-fantastic fusion, but Hodler's picture has a discipline that eliminates the beer-hall tinge so distracting in Böcklin. The discipline was a specific one invented by Hodler himself. It was compositional, and he called it *parallelism;* it dictated the arrangement of the figures in layers above one another in parallels to the picture plane. *The Night* was a great success in conventional circles in Paris when it was exhibited there in 1891, the year after it was painted. And without any question, the handsome bodies represented in it exert an eerie pull on the imagination even while one suspects that the picture is a tour de force, that it is essentially a group of *tableaux-vivants,* arrestingly combined and meticulously executed. Both its mysticism and its modernism are a little false; it is not so much mystical as it is spooky, and it is not so much an original picture as it is a streamlined version of a Salon exercise.

The Night would come off better if it were not asked to meet such strong competition from its contemporaries; as a struc-

ture the picture is an elementary exercise when we remember *La Grande Jatte* [399], painted five years before, and the tightening of contours that lifts the drawing of Hodler's figures a notch above first-rate studio exercises in the nude is only a first step in the direction Gauguin traveled. As a matter of fact, the picture hardly fits in anywhere: it is not altogether academic; its structural elements cannot quite make it post-impressionist (although Hodler belongs to a group of Germans who rejected, or never accepted, the broken forms of impressionism); and its symbolism is pedantic and seems even more so when we think of it as one of a series of pictures Hodler painted after its success, with such high-flown titles as *Disillusioned Souls* and *Glance into Infinity.* Its rather tenuous connection to expressionism has to do with its revelation of a state of mind, but it employs none of the distortions that in true expressionism give us the feeling that the revelation has been torn by the roots from the painter's consciousness and displayed, mangled and palpitating, upon the canvas.

In the cases of Ensor and Munch, the connection with expressionism is more direct. Munch summed up his art in six words so pat that they make further verbal description superfluous. "I hear the scream in nature," he said. He had firsthand experience with the brutality with which life

---

* Another Swiss forebear was Holbein the Younger (1497–1543), the Renaissance master whose polished surface and sharply defined linear contours were models for Hodler.

510. MUNCH: *Anxiety*, 1896. Color lithograph, 16¼ x 15¼". Museum of Modern Art, New York.

personal source of expressionist art, and is suggested in Hodler's *The Night;* each of the figures is spiritually isolated, even when embraced with another. And we know to what extent van Gogh's painting was a release from the aloneness he felt within himself.

It has been observed that Daumier, when he showed people in railroad carriages, or waiting in the station, or walking on the street, sometimes shows them as solitary within their own thoughts, alone in the crowd. But they share with their fellow human beings the important consolation of their common humanity. They move within the same world as their fellows and it is a world, ultimately, of warmth and meaning. But the individuals in Munch's *Anxiety* [510] are caged within their own neuroses. The forms are established as strong, thick, black and red lines or heavy, solid, black masses, except for the faces, and these are barely indicated, by the palest, most tenuous little strokes, as if obliterated by the spirit's inward turning. The pale staring eyes see nothing.°

As for Ensor, he is at least as much a fantasist as an expressionist. His typical pictures involve skeletons and masked creatures in bizarre, grotesque scenes of sinister gaiety. His color is strong and bright, so that at first glance each picture is a carnival, a group of funnyfaces or Mardi-gras revelers, for a moment. The *Skeletons Trying to Warm Themselves* [512] are puppets from a Punch and Judy show—briefly—before they become parts of a nightmare.

can treat men. His family seemed to be dogged by death and anguish; he observed, although he did not experience, the desperate poverty of the Oslo slums. He paints from a hopeless conviction of man's aloneness in the world, his vulnerability to misfortune and spiritual violation. The sense of aloneness is frequently the theme or the

° The flowing and sinuous yet oddly limp lines of *Anxiety* are a manifestation of *art nouveau,* literally the "new art," a decorative style that flourished in the decade between 1890 and 1900, not always with results that look happy today. *Art nouveau* was an effort to create new expressive patterns based on the rhythms inherent in the lines of natural forms, particularly the stems and tendrils of trailing or climbing plants. Its theory was used in the design of architectural ornament and the decorative crafts as well as in painting. The lettering in Lautrec's posters is designed in *art-nouveau* idiom. Lautrec's style as a draughtsman, strongly affected by *art nouveau,* is one of the isolated instances where it has not passed into an awkward age. The patterns of *art nouveau*

have a way of looking trite or even amateurish today, although this contemporary way of seeing them might be outgrown. Nevertheless it mars Munch's pictures for most people at the moment. In Germany, *art nouveau* was called *Jugendstil,* or the youth-style, after a magazine *Die Jugend.* In England the precious *Yellow Book* with its *art-nouveau* drawings by Aubrey Beardsley [346] was part of the movement. *Art nouveau* affected Gauguin, too, in the flowing lines of water, the patterning of plants and the like, and conspicuously in his *Self-portrait with a Halo* [456]. The background of van Gogh's *La Berceuse* [449] is related to it. And *art nouveau* infects German expressionism, as will continue to be obvious, as a congenital inheritance from Munch.

511. ENSOR: *Entry of Christ into Brussels in 1889, 1888. 101½ x 169½". Casino Communal,* Knokke-le-Zoute, Belgium. (Photo Museum of Modern Art, New York.)

Ensor's most ambitious picture was the *Entry of Christ into Brussels* [511], a canvas more than fourteen feet long, which, according to his fellow Belgian, the architect and designer, Henry van de Velde (an originator and spokesman of the theories of *art nouveau*), was an effort to create a sensation by painting a picture even larger than *La Grande Jatte.* Seurat's masterpiece had just been exhibited in Brussels and had made such a sensation that it was difficult to see for the crowds surrounding it. As a companion piece inviting comparison with *La Grande Jatte,* however, the *Entry of Christ into Brussels* is an excellent foil demonstrating Seurat's virtues. Ensor's picture is rather wearing, too loosely organized to unify so large a surface, and crowded with anecdotal detail that seems to have been piled up simply to get as much in the picture as possible. Ensor's world is more directly and disturbingly summed up in his *Self-portrait with Masks* [513]. Masks and skeletons are Ensor's symbols, respectively,

of man's falsity and his mortality. That his fantasies have this direct and conscious relationship to an interpretation of this world in personal emotionalized terms makes Ensor an expressionist as well as a painter of the other-world of dream.

Expressionism: "Die Brücke"

With these comments behind us, the flowering of expressionism in Germany can be outlined as a matter of organizations formed for its proselytization, and of personal variations on the expressionist idea. The earliest of the organizations was *Die Brücke,* meaning The Bridge, formed by a group of pupils at the Dresden Technical School and their friends. Some twenty years younger than Munch and Ensor, some thirty younger than van Gogh, they were directly influenced by these painters and also learned a great deal from the fauves, who had just declared themselves.

512. ENSOR: *Skeletons Trying to Warm Themselves*, 1889. 29½ x 23⅜″. Collection Baron Robert Gendebien, Brussels. (Photo Museum of Modern Art, New York.)

513. ENSOR: *Self-portrait with Masks*, 1889. 47½ x 31½″. Collection Cleomire Jussiant, Antwerp. (Photo Museum of Modern Art, New York.)

The Bridge was founded in 1905, began to break up with the usual internal dissensions by 1907, and was finally dissolved in 1913 while its members continued to paint along its general lines.

Emil Nolde (1867–1956) was an exception among the members of The Bridge, in being somewhat older than the others and, at the same time, something of an adopted son to them. He had passed through an early period when he did rather pretty picturesque landscapes, and had followed it with an impressionist phase, then developed an interest in stormy color. The young men who founded The Bridge recognized his color as potentially expressionist, and under their influence he developed the typical preoccupation with personal and highly emotionalized statement.

The painters of The Bridge had their individual anguishes—sociological, political, sexual, and religious—and Nolde's were religious. Like the other members of the group, he is an artist who must be accepted on his own terms, or not at all. His form of religious statement cannot be stomached if religious statement is limited to the areas of mystical reflection or miraculous revelation in which it ordinarily falls in painting, or even within the area of humanitarian compassion typical of Rouault. Nolde's *Life of Maria Aegyptiaca* [514], told in three episodes, the first showing her sinful life before conversion, the second her conversion, and the third her death, is shocking in its ugliness. But shock and ugliness, even revulsion, are Nolde's medium of religious expression. We must suppose that the painter reaches some kind of self-purification through the rejection of all grace, either spiritual or aesthetic, through embracing all baseness and grossness, reveal-

514. NOLDE: *Life of Maria Aegyptiaca*, First Episode: "Early Sinful Life," 1912. 33¾ x 39¼". Kunsthalle, Hamburg.

ing it, devouring it, and expelling it in forms of abhorrent ugliness, in forms smeared with the colors of blood and putrefaction. Here is van Gogh's personal catharsis intensified to such a pitch that it must be either embraced as profound or rejected as ludicrous.

Nolde left The Bridge as early as 1907, but his association with the group had led him to his special fulfillment in pictures of this kind. Like other expressionist painters who were still at work during the late 1930's, he was in disfavor under Hitler's regime, which sought to eliminate all "unhealthy" manifestations from German art and to create a new one out of the whole cloth. Hitlerian art was a kind of galumphing realism intended to indicate that Germany was a nation of jolly extroverts bursting with health and without a neurosis to their name, certainly an ideal opposed to the mood of The Bridge. Many of Nolde's paintings were confiscated, along with

515. SCHMIDT-ROTTLUFF: *Way to Emmaus,* 1918. Woodcut, 15½ x 19½". Philadelphia Museum of Art, Gift of Dr. George J. Roth.

those of his colleagues, and he was one of those who had the particular distinction of being forbidden to paint at all.

Karl Schmidt-Rottluff (1884–) was another of this select group. He had been a founding member of The Bridge and had even invented its name. After a beginning in which fauvist tendencies flavored his work, he shifted to a primitivism inspired by African sculpture, which was exerting influence on the expressionists, the fauves, and the cubists all at the same time for different reasons. The expressionists were attracted by its harsh primitive vigor. In France the fauves and cubists also felt the appeal of this quality, so refreshing an injection after the hyperrefinements of *fin-de-siècle* art, but they intellectualized their use of primitive forms while the Germans sought to recapture the directness of emotional statement they felt existed there. Schmidt-Rottluff's *Way to Emmaus* [515] is doubly influenced by African sculpture [1]—witness the heads—and Gothic woodcuts of a simple and crude kind. The expressionists felt that there was a minimum of technical barrier between the artist and

the observer in the earliest and most primitive woodcuts, and referred first of all to German ones, a part of their program to revitalize German art. Some of the best work of The Bridge took the form of woodcuts, but their innovation of crude cutting had been anticipated by Gauguin. He had already capitalized on crude cutting and rough printing in Tahiti, as in *Manao Tupapau* [516] (the same title as the painting already seen), although as usual with Gauguin this "primitive" directness is combined with Parisian subtleties. The woodcut *Manao Tupapau* is printed in exquisite tints of soft pinks, browns, and greens, with of course black, and in spite of the roughness of its lines it is nicely calculated, rhythmic in its organization, and as sophisticated as a Japanese print, which it suggests as much as it does primitive art. But *Way to Emmaus* is gashed out of the wood as if in fear that the slightest refinement must reduce the force of communication between artist and observer.

This force is remarkably retained, and the prints of The Bridge may end as their most distinctive achievement. The *Portrait*

516. GAUGUIN: *Manao Tupapau*, 1894. Color woodcut with touches of watercolor, 8⅞ x 18″. Philadelphia Museum of Art, Lisa Norris Elkins Fund.

517. HECKEL: *Portrait of a Man,* 1919(?). Color woodcut, 18¼ x 12¼″. National Gallery of Art, Washington D. C., Rosenwald Collection.

518. KIRCHNER: *The Street,* 1913. 47½ x 35⅞″. Museum of Modern Art, New York.

of a Man [517], possibly a self-portrait, by Erich Heckel (1883–   ) is less insistent than *Way to Emmaus,* but it wears better. With its emaciation, its introspection, its air of neurotic apprehensions, it comes as close as any single work can come to being a psychological portrait of The Bridge as a whole. In color, the print is dominated by the pale olive green of the face and hands, played against background areas of modified blue and brown, with the master block printed over them in sooty black. The woodiness of the blocks is emphasized in both cutting and printing. Woodblocks interested Heckel to such an extent that he carried their effects over into his painting, a curious reversal since color woodblocks originated as a substitute for painted pictures.

Ernst Ludwig Kirchner (1880–1938) is usually thought of as the most typical painter of The Bridge. A list of the influences at work in his art makes him sound like an eclectic: first naturalistic, then briefly pointillist, he shifted to an admiration for van Gogh and Munch, used fauvist color for a while, admired Japanese art and African sculpture like all other investigative young painters at the time, and finally adopted the angularities of cubism. Cubism was a form of spatial analysis, but it interested Kirchner only as an expression of energy. His work is the most tightly organized of any of the group, no doubt because he began as a student of architecture and even received his degree in it. With Heckel and Schmidt-Rottluff he was the third in the trio of Dresden Technical School pupils who founded The Bridge.

In early pictures, Kirchner had worked in the flat color areas of fauvism, but he is his own man in *The Street* [518], even

519. BARLACH: *Man Drawing a Sword*, 1911. Wood, height 29½″. Cranbrook Academy of Art, Bloomfield Hills, Mich.

though other influences, especially cubism, remain obvious. The rational angularities of cubism are turned into hectic, slashing patterns to express the theme that became Kirchner's major one—the tension, the neurasthenic agitation, the sinister vicious-ness, of the city. In the manner of *The Street* he painted people in gatherings where they are crowded together in an acid atmosphere, their isolation not so much a matter of melancholy aloneness as part of a cold, vicious distraction without unifying purpose. *The Street* was painted in 1913, just before World War I; Berlin at that time acted as a catalyst to fuse the various influences at work on Kirchner and make an individual painter of him.

During the war Kirchner was invalided out, not by wounds but by nervous insta-bility. He spent the rest of his life in Swit-zerland. Painting again, he lost much of his

individuality in a study of spatial cubism and rhythmic semi-fauvist landscapes. He committed suicide in 1938, partly because Hitler had condemned some 600 of his works as "degenerate." Degenerate his art may have been, but in that case Kirchner was only performing the timeless function of the painter who reveals the essence of the time and place—Germany between wars—surrounding him.*

Some members of The Bridge turned once in a while to sculpture—especially Schmidt-Rottluff and Kirchner. But the sculptor most closely allied to them in spirit was not affiliated with them or with any other expressionist group—Ernst Barlach (1870–1938). Barlach worked quite di-rectly in the tradition of German Roman-esque sculpture without being at all a para-site upon it. His bulky, vigorously chopped, often heavily textured forms have the human immediacy of some of the smaller medieval sculptures, rather than the monu-mental character of major portal figures. In medieval churches one comes on these small carvings, sometimes tucked away nearly out of sight; they are likely to be carved more freely and more personally than larger pieces in more conspicuous locations. The German examples are indi-vidualized by exceptional directness, some-times an awkwardness in their strength, an exaggerated realism that may approach caricature. Barlach draws upon this tradi-tion without reverting to it. Composition-ally his figures are most frequently marked by swinging or lunging rhythms brought into sculpturesque balance by counter-rhythms in opposing lines and masses [519].

Barlach was also one of the fine graphic artists of expressionism. His woodcuts have about them a feeling of carving; his prints retain to the highest degree the sense of the block's woodiness, the feeling of the knife or the gouge, which is typical of the prints of The Bridge.

* Otto Mueller (1874–1930) and Max Pech-stein (1881–   ) should be mentioned as the remaining important members of The Bridge. Their work is discussed by association in these remarks on other painters; it is not illustrated or further discussed here to avoid repetition, not to dismiss these two painters as negligible tal-ents.

520. KANDINSKY: *Improvisation,* 1914. 30¾ x 39⅜". Philadelphia Museum of Art, Arensberg Collection.

Expressionism: "Der Blaue Reiter"

In the expressionism of The Bridge, subject is of basic importance, no matter how violently the forms are distorted in the process of revealing inner responses to external reality. In a second German expressionist group, *Der Blaue Reiter* (The Blue Rider), subject is less important and finally disappears altogether, taking recognizable images away with it. In other words, the men of The Blue Rider are increasingly abstract and finally nonobjective painters. The term *nonobjective* (sometimes *nonfigurative* in subtle distinction) describes completely abstract art that is independent of subject even as a starting point for the derivation of forms.

The Rider group is a more cheerful one than The Bridge, more influenced by Gauguin than by van Gogh, interested in rhyth-

mical, "musical" compositions composed of sweeping curves and flowing lines rather than harsh, moody, restless, or abrupt ones. The group was not formed until the last month of 1911, some years after The Bridge, which it eventually absorbed, and it grew out of a series of exhibitions held in Munich when all the advanced art groups of the city combined to hold international exhibitions of work by men from Cézanne forward. Munich was extremely active in painting, but heretofore the sound, brownish, anecdotal academic work produced there in great quantities had not been as seriously under attack as traditional painting had been in Paris. The men of The Blue Rider broke away from the large amorphous group that was organizing exhibitions to introduce the French rebels to Germany. Their background was international rather than specifically German,

521. KANDINSKY: *Geometrical Forms*, 1928. Watercolor and ink on paper, 19 x 11". Philadelphia Museum of Art, Arensberg Collection.

had brought his work to the point of complete abstraction, as he seemed to be in the process of doing. Kandinsky is another story: the appearance of his first completely nonrepresentational work in 1910 is a historical event of great consequence, and he formulated his ideas in a treatise, *Concerning the Spiritual in Art*, which has been a handbook since its publication in 1912. He divorced painting from subject matter and tried to create mood by the psychological impact of line and color alone.

Kandinsky's various "improvisations" [520] of spontaneously applied color "mean" nothing, in the sense of direct allegory or symbol. They are based on the reasonable assumption that if a model painted in a red dress affects the observer differently from the same model painted the same way in a white dress, then the color alone accounts for the difference. In that case, simply a red shape or simply a blue shape must mean something, must strike up a "corresponding vibration in the human soul," to borrow a phrase Kandinsky used in a slightly different context. Also, if an object described in squiggly broken lines is different in psychological effect from the same object described in smooth, even, tightly defined line, then the squiggly broken lines and the smooth even ones must have their own inherent psychological quality, all subject matter aside. Thus a painting can have a mood through its lines and colors without a subject. To make the divorce from subject complete, Kandinsky ordinarily gave no titles to his paintings, identifying his improvisations by a number or by date or by some phrase to distinguish one from another but not to give a literary suggestion as to what it was "about."

In contrast to the improvisations with their expressionistically free arrangements, Kandinsky also composed in patterns of sharply defined geometrical forms [521]. These forms might be flat, regular, geometrical ones or sharp-edged ones of irregular shapes, and might be filled with color or not, and might, as in the illustration selected here, include a scattering of more accidental forms whose disposition is taken into account in the arrangement of the more calculated ones. Although he rejected

thus differentiating them from The Bridge; their influence, too, was international in contrast with the more self-contained earlier group.

The two organizing members of The Blue Rider were Franz Marc (1880–1916), a contemporary of the men we have just seen, and Wassily Kandinsky (1866–1944), somewhat older and of Russian origin, who had been a lawyer, had developed as a painter along fauvist lines, and had exhibited in Bridge shows. Marc was killed in the battle of Verdun before he

522. KANDINSKY: *Fish Form*, 1928. Watercolor and ink on paper, 12⅝ x 19⅝". Philadelphia Museum of Art, Arensberg Collection.

images, Kandinsky never thought of his nonobjective paintings as being divorced from nature, and from time to time, as in *Fish Form* [522], he allowed nature to be recognizable within extreme geometrical conventionalizations. He may or may not have been thinking of this picture when he wrote that the essential difference between a line and a fish is that "the fish can swim, eat, and be eaten. It has then, capacities of which the line is deprived. These capacities of the fish are necessary extras for the fish itself and for the kitchen, but not for painting. And so, not being necessary, they are superfluous. That is why I like the line better than the fish—at least in my painting." *Fish Form* makes a concession to image—but it remains more line than fish.

Among the painters formally and informally connected with The Blue Rider, four must be mentioned. Another Russian, Alexei von Jawlensky (1864–1941) developed a preoccupation with large, formalized, rather hieratic heads, sometimes expressionist in character and sometimes highly abstracted [523]. Heinrich Campendonck (1889–1957) painted charming peasant scenes with a fairy-tale quality re-

523. JAWLENSKY: *Looking Within—Night*, 1923. 17 x 13⅛". Philadelphia Museum of Art, Arensberg Collection.

524. FEININGER:
*The Steamer Odin,
II*, 1927. 26½ x 38½".
Museum of Modern
Art, New York, Lillie
P. Bliss Bequest.

525. DIX: *Meeting a Madman at Night,* from
Der Krieg, 1924. Etching, aquatint, and drypoint,
10¼ x 7⅝". Museum of Modern Art, New York,
Gift of Mrs. John D. Rockefeller, Jr.

flecting the naïveté of folk art. Lyonel Feininger (1871–1956), an American born of
German immigrants, returned to Europe
for study and after earlier contacts with
Kandinsky was a member of the "Four
Blues"—Kandinsky, Jawlensky, Feininger,
and Paul Klee—who constituted a secondary revival of the Rider group. Feininger's
art is a particularly distinguished one with
which cubism had a great deal to do. It is
crystal clear, precisely joined in sharp-
edged planes, sometimes defining recognizable objects, sometimes losing the object
in abstract planar extensions [524], but
always with a poetic flavor that is expressionist within the cubist variation. His construction of planes often suggests abstract
architecture, and he was an instructor in
the *Bauhaus,* the school of fine arts and
crafts centered around architecture and
established in Germany at the end of World
War I. The *Bauhaus* was probably the most
effective coordinating factor in the chaotic
picture of modern art, and it developed
teaching methods in connection with this
coordination that are now disseminated all
over the world.

Paul Klee, the fourth of the "Four Blues,"
was also a member of the *Bauhaus* staff. He

526. GROSZ: *Fit for Active Service*, 1918. Pen and ink, 14⅜ x 13⅜". Museum of Modern Art, New York, A. Conger Goodyear Fund.

527. GROSZ: *Street Scene*, date unknown. Lithograph, 10½ x 8½". Philadelphia Museum of Art, Harrison Fund.

is considered near the end of this book. And the *Bauhaus* building itself [692] was a landmark in the "International Style" of contemporary architecture, which is discussed in the Appendix.

Expressionism: "Die Neue Sachlichkeit"

During the last years of World War I and the years just following it, German painters expressed their spiritual shock in some of the most horrifying images since Goya. They rejected the intellectualism and the generally happy spirit of The Blue Rider, but they rejected also the kind of emotional intensity typical of The Bridge. Personal neurotic apprehensions like those expressed by Heckel and Kirchner now seemed puny in comparison with the horror of a world that had revealed itself as a social and

political organization given over to mass murder and moral anarchy. The new expressionism was called *Die Neue Sachlichkeit*, The New Objectivity. Objectivity is precisely the reverse of expressionist emotionalism, and the term belies the sense of outrage that animates these painters at the end of the war and immediately after it. "The New Objectivity" refers more aptly to the political and social apathy, the hopelessness, the acceptance of corruption and misery and degradation as the natural state of things which was characteristic of the later postwar years. In its turn this condition was to bring with it a nihilistic art denying the legitimacy of all logic, all order, all effort, all feeling, all plan—an art reveling in morbid nonsense in which the painters of The New Objectivity were to take a part.

Even Goya would have been appalled before the war portfolio of Otto Dix (1891–

528. Grosz: *Maid Arranging Hair of Corpulent Woman*, date unknown. Watercolor, 24⅞ x 18¾". Philadelphia Museum of Art, Gift of Bernard Davis.

529. Grosz: Detail from Figure 528.

). *The Disasters of War* as Goya reported them are a record of inhumanity and brutal folly, but Dix's *Der Krieg* shows the dissolution of matter and spirit into putrescence and senselessness. Goya is a spectator of atrocities, and we observe them with him and react as human beings capable of normal emotional and intellectual responses to them. But Dix is not an observer; he is a victim of insanity and butchery. In *Meeting a Madman at Night* [525], horror exists alone, beyond moral or social indignation, with a kind of wild idiocy. The final horror is that there is something grotesquely comical about the ghoul, like a black-face comedian gone mad.

Humor to sharpen horror was used with savage precision by George Grosz (1893–1959) in his satires of the *bourgeoisie*, the clergy, the military, and the bureaucrats who in his eyes were responsible for the war. *Fit for Active Service* [526], done in 1918 near the end of the war when German boys, old men, and broken men were being sent to the front, is funny on the surface and all the more frightful for being so. The fat, secure doctor, the trimly groomed officers with their monocles and their beast-faces raddled by vice, the kowtowing clerks and flunkies, are drawn in Grosz's typically cruel, sharp line, like a razor lancing a carbuncle, but the skeleton is contrastingly represented in macabre complications of thin, knobby bones, vestigial organs, and obscene dangling fluffs of hair and thready bits of rotten flesh. Grosz's city streets are filled with desperate, evil beings reduced to subhuman levels by vice, poverty, or corruption; the windows of his houses are vignettes of suicide, lust, and murder [527]. In his watercolors [528, 529], Grosz paints with the most delicate, the most sensitive, of techniques, in colors as sweet and fresh as the tenderest flowers, to represent obese or stunted prostitutes, shriveled harridans, starving children, pig-like profiteers, every scene of depravity, misery, and ugliness. This use of paradox—humor to enhance horror, loveliness to reveal ugliness with a new repulsiveness—is prophetic of the perversity of the irrational, nihilistic art soon to be discussed here as *dada*.

Independent Expressionists

Max Beckmann (1884–1950) was a contemporary of the three German expressionist groups just seen, falling by birth date about midway between the older and younger men. Without being strongly attached to any group he participated in their early exhibitions. He is something of a summary of the German expressionist experience and he adds to it an important element, a correlation with traditional art.

More than any of the other expressionists Beckmann studied the old masters, particularly the early Renaissance forms of Piero della Francesca, and the late medieval ones of French painting, as well as Cézanne, who was not a powerful direct influence on the other expressionists, and van Gogh, who of course was. And, most important of all, he was the direct heir of another German, Hans von Marées (1837–1887).

His dates show that as a nineteenth-century painter contemporary with the French impressionists, von Marées is introduced out of chronology here. But he painted so unobtrusively among his contemporaries that, even more than Cézanne, he is more significant as a part of twentieth-century painting than as a part of the painting of his own lifetime. He is commonly referred to nowadays as a German Cézanne, sometimes also as a parallel to Puvis de Chavannes. In either case, he rejected the imitative realism and the rather heavyhanded symbolical romanticism that surrounded him, and worked instead to translate philosophical ideas into terms of monumental form. This might mean classicism, but (again like Cézanne) von Marées believed that monumental harmonies could be fused with the direct vividness of living matter.

530. Von Marées: *Man with the Standard,* date unknown. 19⅝ x 13¾". *Kunsthalle,* Bremen.

The figure in his *Man with the Standard* [530] is typical of the solid power, the generalized statement without recourse to beautifying formula, of von Marées's art. Contemporary German painters have been happy to find in von Marées a Germanic post-impressionist, the only strong transitional figure between nineteenth-century traditions indigenous to Germanic culture and twentieth-century innovations, including expressionism, which found their major development in Germany. Beckmann is the closest of all modern Germans to von Marées, and extends to a conclusion the

531. BECKMANN: *Departure*, 1932–35. Center panel, 84¾ x 45⅜″, side panels, 84¾ x 39¼″. Museum of Modern Art, New York.

expressive Germanisms initiated or continued by the nineteenth-century painter.

Beckmann brought to expressionism von Marées's monumentality of form, and thus universalized the personalism of the other expressionists. His symbolism is social in origin rather than neurotically ingrown, and it is expressed in formally ordered compositions on the grand scale. He widened the scope of expressionism, discarded it as a vehicle for personal confession and private emotionalism or nihilistic social comment, and gave to it the strength and capacity to speak not only of one man, but of mankind.

Beckmann has never offered an explicit key to the symbolism of the three panels in *Departure* [531], but it is apparent that the two side panels are concerned with evil in their scenes of torture and foul mutilation, painted in harsh, violent, complica-

tions of form and color, while the center one is concerned with salvation, clear and serene as it is, painted in pure, brilliant, harmonious colors and broad simple forms existing in ample space. There are echoes of Christian iconography that cannot be missed. In the first place, the triptych form is that of an altarpiece. Without being at all a figure of Christ, the figure of the king in the central panel recalls Christ, partly because the net over the side of the boat recalls the miraculous draught of fishes. Beckmann said that the picture spoke to him of truths impossible for him to put into words. Whatever it meant to the painter, its theme can be sensed as a problem of good and evil common to us all.

It is in fact a rather difficult picture to absorb, but some of Beckmann's own reflections about what he wanted to achieve, to "say," in painting may be of help. Made

532. Kokoschka: *The Tempest (The Wind's Bride)*, 1914. Panel, 40¼ x 75¼". *Kunstmuseum*, Basel.

three years after the completion of *Departure* and not referring specifically to it, they are not quoted here but are paraphrased, plus parenthetical additions, in a way intended to show how fully Beckmann was an expressionist, yet how greatly he widened the expressionist boundaries:

"What I want to do in my work is to show the idea hidden behind reality, to penetrate the invisible world by means of the visible (which is the desire of most painters, and especially that of the expressionists when the "invisible world" is one of personal emotion). What helps me most in this penetration is (its technical equivalent), the penetration of space. We have to transform the three-dimensional world of objects into the two-dimensional world of the canvas (but I do not accept the idea that hence a painting must be conceived as a two-dimensional decoration. The expression of space, the organization of space on a two-dimensional canvas, need not imply decorative shallowness any more than it need imply illusions of space). The transformation is for me an experience full of magic in which I glimpse the fourth dimension, (beyond reality), which my whole being is seeking. I use color (not only to) enrich the canvas (which would be mere decoration), but to probe more deeply into the object. (But when necessary I am willing to) subordinate color to the treatment of form and space (because in the end, form and space are the abstractions in which the painter has always spoken the essential truths of human experience)."

Complicated as all this sounds—and indeed is—its general meaning is that Beckmann is an expressionist who is conscious that his personal emotional experience must be the wellspring of his art, but that it must be universalized if his paintings are to endure as something more than isolated phe-

533. KOKOSCHKA: *View of the Thames,* 1925–26. 35⅜ x 51¼″. Albright Art Gallery, Buffalo.

nomena or curiosities. He might have said: "I want to make of expressionism something solid and durable like the art of the museums."

Among other major expressionists, Oskar Kokoschka (1886–   ) was even more loosely connected than Beckmann was with expressionism as an organized movement, but like Beckmann he emerges as one of the significant painters produced by the expressionist spirit. He was an Austrian, and began his career in the last days of the old Empire, surrounded by its special atmosphere of decay, nervous sensitivity, and elegant indulgence. These elements are reflected in Kokoschka's work, but its unconventionality brought him under violent official attack. The Austrian Crown Prince said that "every bone in his body should be broken." This was in 1911; it is easy to believe, in retrospect, that Kokoschka's art gave offense because it gave expression to the spiritual morbidity of the time and its moribund culture rather than supplying cheerful assurance that all was

well, as official painting was doing. Kokoschka's *The Tempest* [532], which is also called *The Vortex* or *The Wind's Bride,* showing two lovers captured within menacing forms apparently abstracted from those of storm clouds and mountainous landscape, is a sinister and frightening picture, although at the heart of the surrounding violence the lovers have found refuge in one another. It was painted in 1914, just before the beginning of World War I.

In color *The Tempest* is expressively cold, heavy, even turgid. But by 1919, after the war, during which he was seriously wounded, Kokoschka settled in Dresden as a teacher at the Academy, and under the influence of The Bridge his color brightened, with generous use of clear vermilions, azures, and emeralds. His landscapes and particularly his cityscapes [533] combined staccato accents with flowing lines; they are ebullient, vital, and elegant. And his portraits are acute explorations of personality in which the features of the sitter seem to have been created not by the usual processes of biology but by the force of inner nature that has molded them to correspond with its own character.

The devices of expressionism were widely used by painters who, like Kokoschka, worked independently outside the centers where the expressionists developed their theories and held their exhibitions. This was natural in a form of painting placing so much emphasis on personal, intimate expression. In Paris the Lithuanian Chaim Soutine (1894–1943), working in poverty and obscurity, which he seemed actually to prefer to a conventionally prosperous career, painted in a manner recalling at once van Gogh, El Greco, and the German expressionists [546]. In Germany Käthe Kollwitz (1867–1945) was affected by expressionism in her deeply emotionalized protests against the fate of the poor, both before and after World War I. Kollwitz painted very little, but her etchings, woodcuts, and lithographs are among the most vigorous graphic productions of the early twentieth century. Unlike Grosz and other painters of The New Objectivity who observed and commented on the same desperate scene, Kollwitz was never able to protect herself within a shell of intellectualism or cynicism. Her anguish is undiminished from print to print [534].

Certain other artists even less closely connected with German expressionism, especially stylistically, are expressionist in the broad definition as using emotionally expressive distortions. One of the most conspicuous is Amedeo Modigliani (1884–1920), whose elongated forms combine a taut, wiry precision of outline with his typical neurotic languor of mood [3, 535]. Modigliani, an Italian working in Paris, has a legend exceeded in picturesqueness only by van Gogh's and Gauguin's.[*] Poverty-stricken, theatrically hand-

---

[*] Another inhabitant of Modigliani's bohemia was Maurice Utrillo (1883–1955), the son of a professional model, Suzanne Valadon, who became a respectable painter in her own right. Utrillo is unclassifiable as a painter, except as a member of the "School of Paris" of the early twentieth century. Fauvism, expressionism, cubism, may all be read into his perspectives of the streets of Montmartre or of small towns, but so may the quiet, gentle art of Corot.

534. KOLLWITZ: *Death and the Mother,* 1934. Lithograph, 20⅛ x 14⅜". Philadelphia Museum of Art.

some, tragically doomed by tuberculosis, and spectacularly dissipated, he was the culmination of the romantic tradition of the Parisian bohemian painter or poet. In spite of ill health and emotional imbroglios, Modigliani was a productive painter, working carefully in a somewhat repetitious style filled with nostalgic recalls of early Italian painting, oddly cross-bred with African sculpture. To the long list of influences that were compounded into his very personal style as a painter, Modigliani added elements from the archaic Greeks when he worked in sculpture [536], as he did particularly between 1909 and 1915. But in spite of obvious derivations, Modigliani's art is never a mere pastiche of secondhand forms. Everything serves the expression of a tender, despairing sensuality

535. MODIGLIANI: *Self-portrait*, 1919. 33½ x 23½". Collection Francisco Matarazzo Sobrinho, São Paulo, Brazil. (Photo Museum of Modern Art, New York.)

536. MODIGLIANI: *Head*, date unknown. Limestone, height 27". Philadelphia Museum of Art, Gift of Mrs. Maurice J. Speiser.

in his painting, or of a decorative hieratic reserve in his sculpture.

In Germany, living his short life during the same years as Modigliani, the sculptor Wilhelm Lehmbruck (1881–1919) began as a student at the Düsseldorf Academy, then developed a personal style under Italian and French influences. Like Modigliani's, Lehmbruck's manner is based on extreme elongations, but it is without

archaic and primitive references. Unlike the German expressionist painters with whom he is too often grouped for convenience, Lehmbruck respected the tradition of classical idealism, including its realistic elements. His *Kneeling Woman* [538] may be designed with stylistic elongations, but its modeling is not only detailed but respectful of normal anatomical structure. His surface is even an impres-

537. Lehmbruck: *Standing Woman*, 1910. Bronze, 76″ high. Museum of Modern Art, New York.

538. Lehmbruck: *Kneeling Woman*, 1911. Cast stone, 69½″ high. Museum of Modern Art, New York, Mrs. John D. Rockefeller, Jr. Fund.

sionistic one, subdued in flesh passages but marked in hair and drapery. Lehmbruck worked in Paris between 1910 and 1914, and was first influenced by Maillol. His *Standing Woman* [537], done only the year before the *Kneeling Woman*, shows how closely he followed Maillol at first. For that matter, the harmonious serenity of his fully developed style ties him at least as closely to the classical tradition as his elongations tie him to the romantic-expressionist one. His work uniquely suggests a degree of fulfillment not granted his harassed compatriots.

Expressionism in America

In America Marsden Hartley (1877–1943) was a pioneer expressionist, a bridge between the newly developing European movements and the nascent internationalization of American art. Hartley was a contemporary of the Ash Can group, but where those men were doggedly American, Hartley spent as much time as he could abroad, even exhibiting with The Blue Rider group in Munich and Berlin. Hartley was born in Maine, grew up in Cleveland, studied for

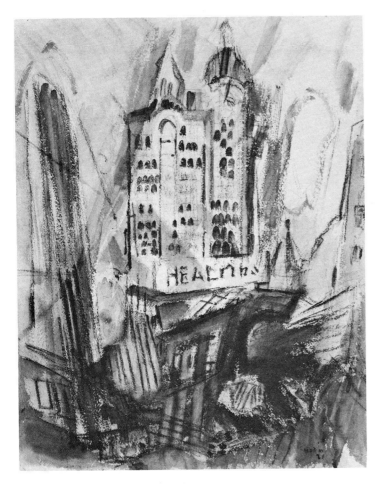

539. MARIN: *The Singer Building*, 1921. Watercolor, 26½ x 21⅝".
Philadelphia Museum of Art.

But it remained for John Marin (1870–1953) to absorb European influences and then to develop them in an art as legitimately American as it was personal.

Marin's expressionism developed through a logical sequence of creative experiences. He studied first (after a brief experience as an engineer) at the Pennsylvania Academy of the Fine Arts, where his teachers were still wholeheartedly dedicated to factual realism. This was in 1899. In Paris between 1905 and 1911 he progressed into impressionism, including etchings in Whistler's tradition. By the end of his stay in Paris he was beginning to be affected by current European developments, particularly fauvism, and shortly after that he worked in a free adaptation of cubism.

Cubism involved, as we will shortly be seeing, a disintegration of form, a shattering and reassembling of objects reduced for the most part to their rectangular equivalents. We will see too that its basis was analytical rather than emotional. But Marin fused the two apparent incompatibles—analytical cubism and emotionalized expressionism—into a vividly personal style that gave pictorial form to the clangor, the vitality, the surge, the bursting sparkling energy, of the American city.

While the Ash Can School was painting the city as a genre subject, Marin began to paint it as an idea, as a manifestation of the most exciting aspect of the American spirit, its enthusiasm, its vigor, its violent growth, an aspect that reached its climax during the years between the two world wars when Marin was working at his peak.

Marin's expressions of New York City transform the static, monolithic forms of skyscrapers, the flatness of streets and sidewalks, into abstractions of energy and excitement. In earlier pictures [539] the forms of the city tilt, break, and interrupt one another but remain at least partially recognizable. In later ones they all but disappear as recognizable objects, abstracted to the point of pure expression [540]. And in his paintings of the Maine coast the same transmutation is apparent, until finally the rocks of the earth, the water of the ocean, and the sailboats, which for Marin are an expression of the force of the

a while in New York, and then alternated between Europe and the United States. In his most typical work [542] he strives for a kind of raw power, which might be called American, through broad, deliberately crude forms, harsh color, and slashing contrapuntal arrangements. His courage and perseverance were admirable. So, frequently, is his painting, yet he seems too often to be giving an intelligent demonstration of expressionist theory, not often enough to be releasing an emotional force that demanded the use of expressionist devices. Arthur G. Dove (1880–1946), another American who studied for a while in Europe, shares Hartley's position as an eminent pioneer in his own country, and went beyond Hartley in the direction of pure abstraction and personal colorism.

movement of air, become abstractions of the vital energy of nature, just as the New York pictures are abstractions of the vital energy of the city. Homer's *Northeaster* [541], Hartley's *Hurricane Island, Vinal Haven, Maine* [542], and Marin's *Off York Island, Maine* [543] are a neat demonstration of a progression through imaginative realism, conventional expressionism, and expressionistic abstraction, each using different means toward similar ends from the same point of departure.

Marin was first of all a watercolorist. This medium is usually associated with delicate or transient effects, but Marin used it with unprecedented strength while retaining its unique sparkle, directness, and spontaneity. As all good watercolorists must do, he capitalized on the medium's transparency, fluidity, and texture. Watercolor textures

540. MARIN: *Lower Manhattan* (composition derived from top of Woolworth Building), 1922. Watercolor, 21⅜ x 26⅞″. Museum of Modern Art, New York, Lillie P. Bliss Bequest.

541. HOMER: *Northeaster*, 1895. 34⅜ x 50¼″. Metropolitan Museum of Art, New York, Gift of George A. Hearn.

444

are determined by the texture of the paper in combination with varying densities of pigments, some of which are clear and smooth in solution with water, while others are so heavy that they settle into the paper's grain. The watercolorist can control these textures by the degree of wetness and the degree of speed with which the colors are applied. Marin used a favorite heavily textured Italian paper, sometimes dragging the brush across it nearly dry, sometimes filling his brush to capacity and letting the color stream from it. He is the only major painter to have created his major work in watercolor, and in its history he brought the medium to a new stature just as Degas did with pastel.

In America, expressionism has had an influence so wide, even if it has not always

542. HARTLEY: *Hurricane Island, Vinal Haven, Maine, 1942.* 40¼ x 30″. Philadelphia Museum of Art, Gift of Mrs. Herbert C. Morris.

543. MARIN: *Off York Island, Maine, 1922.* Watercolor, 17 x 20½″. Philadelphia Museum of Art, Stieglitz Collection.

been direct, that the list of painters affected by it would extend indefinitely, ranging from the social indignation and caricature of William Gropper (1897–   ), who might be described as an expressionist Daumier [544], to the suave but introspective art of Franklin Watkins (1894–   ). Watkins won the Carnegie International Award, the most important one offered in America, in 1931 with his *Suicide in Costume* [545], a psychological allegory partly morbid and partly witty, designed with expressionistic distortions. It is in the nature of things that awards of such importance, when decided by enlightened juries, are given to paintings representing movements whose contribution to the

544. GROPPER: *For the Record*, 1940. Lithograph, 11⅝ x 16". Philadelphia Museum of Art, Harrison Fund.

545. WATKINS: *Suicide in Costume*, 1931. 33¼ x 41¼". Philadelphia Museum of Art.

mainstream of art has been tested by a certain amount of time but not ossified by too much of it. The award to *Suicide in Costume*, which was expressionistic without belonging to any expressionist school, indicated that expressionism had satisfactorily passed the initiation tests for admittance into the solid company of established ways of painting, a quarter of a century after the formation of The Bridge.

From about 1950 to the end of that decade, the most vigorous school of contemporary painting in the United States, and to a lesser degree in France, was abstract expressionism, a descendant of The Blue Rider rather than to The Bridge. Several chapters back, in the mild world of impressionism, we saw that Jackson Pollock's *Autumn Rhythm* had strong affiliations with Monet's very late work, when a passage from *Water Lilies* was extracted from context [211, 212, and 213]. A similar extraction from Soutine's *Portrait of Kisling* [546, 547] yields a fair example of abstract expressionism comparable to a paint-

546. SOUTINE: *Portrait of Kisling*, date unknown. 39 x 27¼″. Philadelphia Museum of Art, Gift of Arthur Wiesenberger.

547. SOUTINE: Detail from Figure 546.

447

ing by Willem de Kooning (1904–   ) [548], a leader among current abstract expressionist painters. This comparison is not altogether a stunt. By Kandinsky's theory that color and form can exist alone as expressive means, without reference to the imitation of visual reality, the sweeps and slashes and gobbets of color extracted from the Soutine should be expressive even though they are no longer recognizable as the description of one of the eyes in the portrait. If Soutine's colors, brush strokes, and shapes carry the expressive burden of his canvas, as they undeniably do in very large part, then they should continue to be expressive independently. De Kooning's painting is inchoate, fragmentary, and senseless unless we accept the totality of Kandinsky's premise that a painter, through talent, training, and experience (for de Kooning is talented, trained, and experienced), reaches the point where he may express himself best by attacking his canvas vigorously while improvising abstractions of form and color, painting without schematic preparations, drawing spontaneously upon all that he has learned of shape and color as expressive means. Somewhat more studiously, other abstract expressionists, for instance Philip Guston (1912–   ), may work equally without reference to visual reality, but may paint more compact, more concentrated forms [549]. (Guston's canvases may suggest enlarged fragments of Cézanne.) Each abstract expressionist who has established a reputation, as these two men have done, has also established a recognizable style. The reader could distinguish other typical de Koonings from other typical Gustons on the basis of these two examples. Other painters may work more precisely; others, even more loosely. But to multiply examples here would be pointless. The proliferations of abstract expressionism are as infinite as the difference in the personalities of the painters allows, and are at the moment familiar, even inescapable, in art magazines and exhibitions. Ultimately, however, the principle behind the variations, which may be fascinating, is the same. And for better or for worse, it all began with Kandinsky.

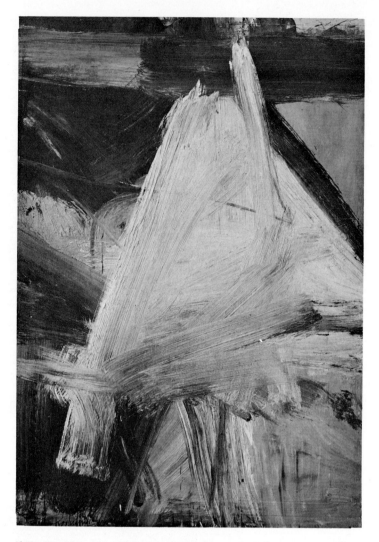

548. De Kooning: *Detour*, 1958. 59 x 42″. Sidney Janis Gallery, New York.

Or did it? It is true that Kandinsky is given credit for having produced the first entirely abstract painting in the early years of this century, but the family tree of abstract expressionism can be traced back to Delacroix, and beyond him to the traditions of which French romanticism was a continuation. When we remember Delacroix's warning that "All precautions have to be taken to make execution swift and decisive [in order not to lose] the extraordinary impression accompanying the conception," we find him stating a principle that is pushed to its limits by painters today

549. GUSTON: *The Painter's City,* 1956. 65 x 77". Sidney Janis Gallery, New York.

who appear to splash color at random, following spontaneous impulse.

Yet their "precautions" must be present behind the apparent impulsiveness, to some degree, just as in the case of Delacroix they were present to a rigidly imposed degree. And when abstract impressionism seems formless and sloppy, we may be generous and remember that Delacroix was accused of painting with "a drunken broom."

Some abstract expressionists have literally painted with brooms (while sober) on canvases laid out on the floor. By theory, when color is splashed, flipped, or shoved or swept over a surface, the artist is closest to the observer because his emotional impulse is translated into physical actions that immediately, without intermediate stages, produce shape and color. This may be going a little far, but it still goes in the direction set by early romanticism and continued through van Gogh.

But most of all, the abstract expressionists are romantic in the extreme personalism of their art. Long ago in this book we said that the romantics "would abandon moderation for excess, when necessary, would accept confusion rather than run the risk of sacrificing spontaneity to lucidity." When Guston calls his painting illustrated here "The Painter's City," he implies the most personal emotional sources for his art. Such titles attached to abstract expressionist paintings bring the school into the tradition of personal fulfillment and release, at whatever expense, which is the basis of romanticism.

CHAPTER 13

Cubism and Abstract Art

Cubism: The Early Picasso

Cubism was born unexpectedly in 1907 without benefit of theory and from curiously mixed parentage: Cézanne on one side, and the sculpture of ancient and primitive peoples on the other. It appeared first in the work of two young men named Pablo Picasso (1881–   ) and Georges Braque (1882–1963).

Picasso, a Spaniard, had come to Paris at the age of nineteen after a prodigious conquest of the academies in Barcelona and Madrid. At twelve he was a competent draughtsman [550], and thereafter as a student he ran the historical gamut of styles from academic formula straight through impressionism, mastering them all with the facility of a mimic and the understanding of an artist. Whole books have been devoted to his work during the seven years from his arrival in Paris to his first cubist painting. Here a brief summary will suffice.

During his first year or so in Paris, Picasso worked in a manner close to Toulouse-Lautrec's but bursting everywhere with restlessness, as if impatient to shift into a new direction. *Old Woman* [551] of 1901, the year of Lautrec's death, looks as if Lautrec himself might have painted it after discovering pointillism and adapting it to a violent flashing expressionism. Yet in the same year—his twenty-first —Picasso also painted the contrastingly serene *Harlequin Propped on Elbow* [552] with its controlled outlines, its decisive pattern, and broad flat areas of color, probably related to Gauguin's. This *Harlequin* is somewhat romantic in mood, decorative in arrangement, classical in its sense of control, rather affected in its selection of

550. PICASSO: Drawing from a cast, school year, 1893–94. Conté crayon, 18¼ x 25¼". Present whereabouts unknown; reproduced from *Cahiers d'Art*, courtesy of the publishers.

posture and subject, and altogether attractive in itself. Picasso is showing, as he will do again and again, that he can be everything at once.

The direction hinted at in this picture is not followed up until later. (Not only can Picasso be everything at once; he can also travel in all directions at once, seeming to abandon one direction in painting for a while and then suddenly resuming it at another level as if it had been developing of itself during the lapse of time.) During the next few years he painted in two manners called the "blue" and "rose" periods. A single example will have to suffice as typical of the blue pictures, *The Old Guitarist* [553] of 1903. Pathetic in its subject, stylized with its elongated figure posed in a cramped, angular attitude, and painted in frigid blues and blue-greens, it follows closely the basic recipe of the

551. PICASSO: *Old Woman*, 1901. 26⅜ x 20½". Philadelphia Museum of Art, Arensberg Collection.

552. PICASSO: *Harlequin Propped on Elbow*, 1901. 33 x 24¾". Collection Mr. and Mrs. Henry Clifford, Radnor, Pa.

451

553. PICASSO: *The Old Guitarist,* 1903. 37⅜ x 28″. Art Institute of Chicago, Helen Birch Bartlett Memorial Collection.

554. PICASSO: *La Toilette,* 1906. 59½ x 39″. Albright Art Gallery, Buffalo.

period. This is a style of great sophistication in which the pathos is altogether superficial, a very young man's style. Among the influences at work in it are the painting of El Greco and the early medieval French sculpture of the school of Languedoc—at least by the internal evidence of stylistic resemblance.

The blue period softens into the "circus" period and then merges in 1905 into the rose period, with the change in dominating color suggested by the tags and, above all, a change in mood. Although the figures remain delicate and elongated, they live in a happier world. Charm replaces pathos, grace takes the place of angularity; sometimes there is a strong classical flavor, as in the entrancing *La Toilette* [554] with its

references to Greek vase painting. Of all his multitudinous periods—one critic was able to subdivide them into eighty—this is the one that accounts for Picasso's widest popularity. The affectation that is an uncomfortable element in the early blue pictures, conflicting as it does with subjects of poverty and misery, is appropriate to the charming, sometimes feminine air of the later ones, as the harsh blues and greens turn into soft gray-blues and merge with rose. It is a period of brilliant technical display. Almost any picture of these years could serve as an example; a fine one is *Boy with Bouquet* [555], where we are offered a bunch of flowers by one of the adolescent harlequins, actors, acrobats, and theatrical vagabonds who replace starving

555. Picasso: *Boy with Bouquet*, 1905. Gouache, 25½ x 21⅜". Collection Mrs. John Wintersteen, Chestnut Hill, Pa.

556. Picasso: *Boy Leading a Horse*, 1905. 87 x 57¼". Collection Mr. and Mrs. William S. Paley, New York.

unfortunates as the major performers, and will continue to appear among Picasso's cast of thousands from now on.

The main areas of *Boy with Bouquet* are established in audacious scrubs and strokes of color and then, in a demonstration of infallible draughtsmanship, the features are described with a few lines struck in with almost insolent virtuosity. Had Picasso died in 1906, the charging bull of modern art would have been remembered as a delicate fellow who revived the eighteenth-century spirit at its most sensitive, a twentieth-century Watteau. During this time Picasso planned a large composition of adolescent youths and horses, *The Watering Place*. The studies [556] are consummately in this spirit.

But with the restlessness of an explorer or an inventor, Picasso changed again at the end of 1906 in a way that is important as an early step toward cubism. He began to discipline his graceful figures into new sculptural forms with an imposition of decisive geometrical regularities. Already indicated in *Lady with a Fan* [152], the new discipline is even more emphatic in *Woman with Loaves* [557], with its geometrical solids built firmly upon one another into a compact whole. The ovoid form of the torso is surmounted by the white cylinder of the cap, which is pierced to reveal the simplified sculptural forms of the head. The two loaves of bread rest on top of this structure like architectural members surmounting a column.

557. PICASSO: *Woman with Loaves*, 1906. 39 x 27½″. Philadelphia Museum of Art, Gift of Charles E. Ingersoll.

558. PICASSO: *Gertrude Stein*, 1906. 39⅜ x 32″. Metropolitan Museum of Art, New York.

Woman with Loaves was painted in the summer of 1906 (despite the date 1905, added in error beneath the signature). Earlier that year Picasso had begun a portrait of Gertrude Stein [558], the American writer who had set herself up in Paris a few years earlier and had already become a major patron, proselytizer, and practitioner in the international intellectual avant-garde. After eighty sittings Picasso had wiped out the face of her portrait. Whatever the face had been like, it is obvious that in the rest of the picture Cézanne is very much present. When Picasso returned to the picture after the summer interval during which he painted *Woman with Loaves*, the new force at work in his art produced the masklike face (painted without the model) which is so at variance with the Cézannesque forms that surround it. In his *Self-portrait* [559] painted imme-

diately afterward, the masklike quality has increased, and its severe half-primitive quality has extended to the figure also.

Cubism: Its Beginnings

By his own statement, in *Woman with Loaves*, the Stein portrait, and his own portrait, Picasso was influenced by Iberian sculpture, the archaic sculpture of pre-Roman Spain. But the two portraits look as if Picasso had already discovered African sculpture also. At any rate he discovered African sculpture at about this time, and the ingredients for cubism were assembled. These were: Cézanne, with his concept of volume and space as abstract geometry to be dealt with at whatever necessary rejection of their natural relationships; African and archaic sculpture, with their untheo-

559. PICASSO: *Self-portrait*, 1906. 36 x 28″. Philadelphia Museum of Art, Gallatin Collection.

retical but exciting reduction of natural forms to geometrical equivalents, plus an element of the bizarre and the savage that was a stimulating injection into the hyperrefinements of European painting; and, finally, the intuitive genius of Picasso and the deductive mind of Braque to merge these components with dashes of several others in their search for new expressive means.

This new expression was soon to have a name, *cubism*, and to be codified into a theory. But for the moment it manifested itself half formed in a large painting by

560. PICASSO: *Les Demoiselles d'Avignon*, 1907. 96 x 92″. Museum of Modern Art, New York, Lillie P. Bliss Bequest.

Picasso, which, although technically ambiguous, is decisively the beginning point of cubism. A composition of five nude female figures [560], the traditional bathers motif, it was later dubbed *Les Demoiselles d'Avignon* as a jape, and has continued to be called so as a convenience.

Everyone admits that these five *demoiselles* are among the unloveliest females in the history of art, and no one pretends that the picture is an unqualified success in every way, but on the other hand no student of contemporary painting denies its position as a landmark. It is a discordant picture, not only in the way it ruptures, fractures, and dislocates form with a violence that would no doubt have appalled Cézanne, but in the disharmony of its own parts. On the left the standing figure is hieratic in its formality, posed in a standard attitude of Egyptian and archaic Greek sculpture. But by the time the right side of the picture is reached, this formality has given way to a jagged, swinging, crashing line, and the African mask makes its impact with full force in the grotesque faces. For a few months during the next year, 1908, Picasso went through a "Negro" period, with close parallels to African prototypes.

456 · CUBISM AND ABSTRACT ART

The developmental period of cubism, 1907–1909, is often called its "Cézanne phase," on the basis of pictures like Braque's *Road near L'Estaque* [561], with its combination of geometrical simplification and faceted shapes. But in spirit the picture is anything but Cézannesque. The shapes themselves are bolder and more obvious than Cézanne's, and they have a nervousness, an insistence, a thrust, a harsh, angular movement that exaggerates the sense of vibrant life typical of a Cézanne landscape and sacrifices to it the classical order that also permeates Cézanne's world.

561. BRAQUE: *Road near l'Estaque,* 1908. 23¾ x 19¾". Museum of Modern Art, New York.

562. METZINGER: *Tea Time,* 1911. Panel, 29¾ x 27⅜". Philadelphia Museum of Art, Arensberg Collection.

Cubism: Analytical Phase

After 1909 and up into 1912 the introduction and development of a complication known as simultaneity brings cubism into its own as a revolutionary concept. The idea behind simultaneity is simple enough. The forms in Metzinger's° *Tea Time* [562], which suffers the unfortunate secondary title *Mona Lisa with a Teaspoon,* are broken into large facets or planes. But something else is happening too: in places these planes grow transparent in order to reveal other planes behind them; they cross and merge with these other planes. At the left a teacup and saucer are divided down their middle by a line, on one side of which they are seen head on, while on the other side they are seen from above. Theoretically we know more about the teacup because we see it from two angles at once, which is impossible when a teacup and saucer

° Jean Metzinger (1883–1956) developed certain nuances of style during this period of analytical cubism that give his work a light, gay quality quite opposed to the Spartan analytical diagrams of Braque and Picasso. Yet Metzinger was of a scientific turn of mind. Before discovering a more rewarding pseudo-science in analytical cubism, he had been attracted by the codification and systematic approach of neo-impressionism. At the end of the period of analytical cubism, he wrote its doctrinal statement, *Du Cubisme,* with his colleague Albert Gleizes (1881–1953). Both Metzinger and Gleizes were among the cubists who insisted on the use of color, while Braque and Picasso were shelving the problem in favor of pure analysis in tans, creams, and grays.

563. Picasso: *Female Nude*, 1910–11. 38¾ x 30⅞″. Philadelphia Museum of Art.

564. Picasso: *Seated Nude Woman*, 1908. 45¾ x 35″. Philadelphia Museum of Art.

are represented in conventional perspective allowing a view from only one angle at a time. Metzinger's teacup demonstrates in an elementary way the device of simultaneity—the simultaneous revelation of more than one aspect of an object in an effort to express the total image. In the case of the teacup the process is simple. Elsewhere in the picture the crossing and merging transparent planes are a more complicated application of the same idea. The left half of the head, if the right half is ignored or covered up, yields a profile. At the same time, it is included in a view of the full face. The argument that we have neither a good profile nor a good full face by usual representational standards is beside the point. The cubist is not interested in usual representational standards. It is as if he were walking around the objects he is analyzing, as one is free to walk around a piece of sculpture for successive views. But he must represent all these views at once.

This is the famous "fourth dimension" in painting. For centuries painters had been satisfied to represent an illusion of three dimensions on a two-dimensional surface by means of a systematic distortion known as perspective. The third dimension in painting is depth by perspective; the fourth dimension is movement in depth, or time, or space-time, by the simultaneous presentation of multiple aspects of an object. A new systematic distortion is necessary for this new dimension, since the old one of perspective has been outgrown.

But as the process of analytical cubism was explored, the objects subjected to its elaborations were destroyed. Picasso's *Female Nude* [563] is a fourth-dimensional complication of forms which began, no doubt, as forms similar to those in his earlier *Seated Nude Woman* [564]. But as the planes overlap, turn on edge, recede, progress, lie flat, or turn at conflicting angles, the object from which they originated is

565. LIPCHITZ: *Girl with a Braid, c.* 1914–15. Bronze, 32″ high. Philadelphia Museum of Art.

566. LIPCHITZ: *Half Standing Figure,* 1915–16. Lead, 19¼″ high. Philadelphia Museum of Art, Gallatin Collection.

lost rather than totally revealed. Cubism was also rather tentatively investigated by sculptors. What happened can be seen first in Jacques Lipchitz's (1891–   ) *Girl with a Braid* [565] and then his *Half Standing Figure* [566]. Lipchitz, like other sculptors, soon left cubism to the painters and changed to a more legitimately sculptural style—in his case—an expressionistic one.

Occasionally it is still necessary to reassure the layman as to the seriousness of cubist experiments with form, even though these experiments have long since been absorbed into the general experience of the

contemporary artist. Historically their importance is that they forced one aspect of Cézanne's revolution to a point so extreme that no painter willing to think twice about the expression of form can ever again be satisfied with its simple imitation in photographic light and shade. Theories and history aside, these analytical cubist experiments are aesthetically rewarding in themselves, even if on a somewhat rarefied level. But they soon served their purpose for the cubists, and in 1912 their severities were abandoned for a more relaxed approach, called synthetic cubism.

567. GRIS: *Dish of Fruit,* 1916. 15¾ x 9". Philadelphia Museum of Art, Gallatin Collection.

568. GRIS: *The Open Window,* 1917. Panel, 39⅝ x 29⅝". Philadelphia Museum of Art, Arensberg Collection.

Cubism: Synthetic Phase—Gris

Analytical cubism tended to lose sight of expressive values except by standards too esoteric to mean much to anyone not absorbed in the movement. Also the painters' stylistic individuality had been somewhat fettered. But synthetic cubism turned each painter loose to find his own way within the vast general field of free invention along cubist lines that was now opened up by a new way of conceiving form. Analytical cubism took its proper place as a preliminary exploratory exercise (no matter how complicated, no matter how studded with expressive exceptions). Color returned in force, sometimes related to the natural col-ors of the formal motifs, sometimes arbitrary. The shapes of objects were used as a basis for improvisations, inventions, ambitious or playful compositions in every combination and recombination of abstract shapes invented imaginatively, subject to no rule or theory. Picasso and Braque, whose analytical cubist studies had often been all but indistinguishable from one another's, diverged in opposing directions. A third young man who had shared with them in the development of analytical cubism now took his place as the poet of the movement. This was Juan Gris (1887–1927), the pseudonym of José Victoriano González, like Picasso a Spaniard who had put the academic routine behind him in his

569. GRIS: *Man at Café* (study), 1911. Pencil, 22 x 16½".
Philadelphia Museum of Art, Gallatin Collection.

own country and had come to Paris at
nineteen.

In Gris's typical *Dish of Fruit* [567] it
is easy to recognize the general shape of a
compote with its base, neck, and bowl and
to identify a couple of colored shapes as
pieces of fruit. The tabletop and even something like the bowl's shadow, to the right
of the base, are also recognizable. The
rectangular shape defined by a triple outline in the background might be a repetition of the table form or might have been
suggested by a napkin or doily. Or it could
be a picture frame on the wall. None of the
forms needs be recognizable in specific
detail, but each has been played with in-
ventively and the shapes have been colored

most ornamentally to produce a combination of forms and colors that would not
have been reached without the preliminary
puzzle-solving of analytical cubism, but
now branches away from it. In *The Open
Window* [568], it is possible to see that
the window, or what we could call a
French door, is opened onto a balcony
with a tree beyond it. We can even tell that
the long double doors are three-paned.
Along the lefthand side of the picture the
left door is represented with comparative
realism. On the right, the forms are more
broken, but a piece of cloth patterned in
large dots and gathered across the lowest
pane is immediately recognizable. The picture is filled with gentle, quiet mood, retaining as it does the connotation of a pleasant room with a window opening out to
trees, and composed as it is in simple shapes
dominated in color by soft blues, grays,
and modified whites.

In synthetic cubism, shapes and colors
may be determined by the painter's sensitivity alone; thus painting has returned to
the old basis, the painter's reaction to the
world and his interpretation of it in colored
forms. But it has returned with a new vocabulary, a vocabulary more flexible than
analytical cubism had promised. Synthetic
cubism leaves the painter unfettered by
anything except the limitations of his own
inventive ingenuity. Although to a novice
all cubist paintings may look alike, and the
idea of any one form of cubism being more
poetic than another may seem absurd,
Gris's poetic quality becomes apparent
when the surface similarities of all cubist
paintings are scratched. Even when he was
working more analytically [569], Gris always insisted that a high degree of recognizability should be retained in a painting,
in spite of the fact that the artist was involved in the cubist shattering and reassembling of forms to create new structures.
In the hands of Picasso and Braque, analytical cubism had abandoned the appeal of
subject, the response to the world, which
had been the basis of impressionism and
had been continued, with variations, in
Cézanne, Gauguin, van Gogh, and Seurat.
Subject matter was reduced to a small list
of motifs closely connected with the studio

570. GRIS: *The Violin*, 1916. Panel, 45½ x 29″. *Kunstmuseum*, Basel.

571. LÉGER: *Three Figures*, 1910–11. 76½ x 45½″. Milwaukee Art Center.

or with the café as an adjunct of the studio, such motifs as tables with bowls of fruit and glasses of wine, a few musical instruments, and posed models. But Gris frequently invested these motifs with more personal associations. *The Open Window* is one of several recollections of his quarters on the Rue Ravignan where a group of writers and painters inhabited a disreputable old building called the *Bateau-Lavoir*. Picasso lived there for a while. For the avant-garde in general, the *Bateau-Lavoir* became a kind of club, taking its place in the tradition of Courbet's *Brasserie*

des Martyrs and the impressionists' *Café Guerbois* as a center where ideas were formulated and discussed. But the associative interest of *The Open Window* is not enough to account for the poetic feeling that permeates it. This feeling is present even when the pictures are composed of the usual cubist list of motifs [570]. Typically the color is gentler, the forms are more placid, their combinations more serene than those of Gris's fellow cubists, and from these abstract elements, rather than in specific evocative elements, Gris's poetry lies. He is cubism's Corot.

572. LÉGER: *Contrast of Forms*, 1913. 51⅝ x 38⅜". Philadelphia Museum of Art, Arensberg Collection.

A Cubist Variant: Léger

Cubism's unexpected flexibility, once it was freed by the personalism of its synthetic phase, produced one of its brightest variants in the art of Fernand Léger (1881–1955). Léger, after a spell as an architect's apprentice and a brief foray into the Academy's school, discovered Cézanne and then met Braque and Picasso in 1910. Under their influence he worked for a while in facet cubism, as in *Three Figures* [571], where it is possible to discern hints of the driving, pistonlike energies that were to fascinate him later on. But Léger was always a more direct and less complicated

person than his colleagues, and he fretted under the intellectualism of formal analysis. By 1913 he had resolved the shifting, overlapping complexities of analytical cubism into a new manner, where cubes and cylinders began to appear more solidly and more boldly, painted in bright colors. *Contrast of Forms* [572], painted in 1913, is typical of a group of paintings where Léger combines strong, simple shapes in pure primary colors—red, blue, and yellow—with a great deal of white and strong defining lines in black. In spite of the crowding of the forms, which jostle and shoulder one another over the whole area of the canvas, a comparison of *Contrast of Forms* with *Three Figures* should show not only that *Contrast of Forms* is a logical continuation of the earlier picture but that it is a step in the direction of clarity and specific definition.

Even so, Léger is still feeling his way, and it was not until after World War I (during which he was mobilized and stopped painting) that he found what he wanted to do. While Gris employed cubism pensively, Léger adapted it to the clangorous mechanized life of the city. On the theory that in a mechanical age art should take on a mechanical character, he developed a style in which every form, if not actually derived from a mechanical motif, took on the character of a gear, a flywheel, a piston, or some other machine part. By his own statement, his daily contact with machines during the war might account for his new fascination with a mechanistic art, and his wartime "contact with violent and crude reality" completed his divorce from the hyperrefinements of analytical cubism.

The City [573], a large canvas, is the climax of his new style and probably the key picture in his total work. Some of the most easily identified motifs are girders, poles, puffs of smoke, and in the center a flight of steps reduced to light and dark bands behind the mechanized human figures who descend them. The colors are pure and bright, even garish and strident, dominated by several brilliant patches of lemon yellow and bright reds, cut through from top to bottom by a pole of a rosy violet color. For the most part the forms

573. Léger: *The City*, 1919. 91 x 116½". Philadelphia Museum of Art, Gallatin Collection.

are unmodeled, exceptions being the human figures, the puffs of smoke, and the pole, which are modeled into smooth geometrical ovals and cylinders.

In many ways the forms of *The City* are so obvious that they seem too easy. Subtleties must not be read into Léger; rather, a hearty vigor, a kind of primitivism. He is the most easily imitated of painters, and he has suffered from a blight of fourth-rate talents who have adopted his formula and revealed its limitations without redeeming them by his strength and enthusiasm. Léger's art is meaningless if it is distorted by a search for intellectualities that do not exist in it. His anti-intellectualism is usually refreshing; at other times it palls, and one is relieved to get away from his insistent colors, his obvious forms, and his eventually monotonous conventionalization for paintings offering less surface excitement and more contemplative depth. (Of course

574. Léger: *The Breakfast* (study), 1925. 40 x 53". Collection Mr. and Mrs. Burton Tremaine, Meriden, Conn.

575. Léger: *Divers on Yellow Background*, 1941. 75¾ x 87½". Art Institute of Chicago, Gift of Mr. and Mrs. Maurice E. Culberg.

this may be a matter of personal taste; it may be just as true that it is a relief to get away from paintings full of subtleties and enjoy Léger's single-directedness.) Sometimes, also, he forces his style onto motifs not compatible with it. In *The Breakfast* [574], unmechanistic forms are conventionalized into mechanistic molds with extraordinary results if the three women are regarded as women, although with great decorative flair if they are not. Léger once said that "One may consider the human figure not for its sentimental value but only for its plastic value. That is why in the evolution of my work since 1905 until now the human figure has remained purposely inexpressive." This is a legitimate defense and could have been stated by any of the cubists and most of the fauves, but it can still leave one wondering uncomfortably why three nudes around a breakfast table are reduced to dehumanized automatons when likelier material to serve Léger's bias was available on every hand.

There is a further possible objection to the whole mechanistic idea in painting. Léger said that "Nowadays a work of art must bear comparison with any manufac-

tured object." No statement is easier to oppose; one need only say that nowadays a work of art must give relief from the insistent mechanization of life and the monotony of manufactured objects. Furthermore, Léger's work does not bear comparison with manufactured objects if that is what he really intended to invite. Nothing he painted in pistonlike forms has the machine-perfect sleekness of a real piston; not one of his spheres has the perfection of a ball bearing. Motors and machine parts have their own abstract beauty as forms, and have it more legitimately than the less beautifully tooled conventionalizations of painters who impose these forms on nature.

In the end, Léger remains an expressive and important artist not for the theories he propounded and demonstrated, but because his own vigor and his own naïveté override theory and find their way into his work. Between 1931 and 1939 he made three visits to the United States. He was rapturous over the spectacle of energy and extroverted activity the country presented to him. He loved the skyscrapers, the Negro jazz, the noise, the lack of inhibitions (as it seemed to him), and above all the bustle and movement of New York and Chicago. The forms he had composed in *The City* had been static; now he set out to create compositions of movement with flowing lines everywhere. In a series of paintings of swimmers or divers, for which he had already found the germ in observing beach crowds in Marseilles just before sailing, he summarized his new preoccupation with contrasts of movement. Yet he reduced his compositions to rigorously controlled, ultimately balanced rhythms not at all hectic or clamorous, as is apparent in *Divers on Yellow Background* [575].

Because his work is precise and held tightly under control, Léger's "classicism" is often referred to, and in the most ambitious of his very late works, *Leisure* [576], he accepts the nomination for a post in the classical tradition of French painting. One of the figures holds a sheet of paper bearing the inscription "Hommage à Louis David." The inscription may be half mocking, but it is also at least half serious in this extraordinarily synthetic picture. To capture its

576. LÉGER: *Leisure*, 1944–49. 61⅞ x 72⅞″. *Musée National d'Art Moderne*, Paris.

flavor one must understand not only its connection with David's *The Sabines* [11] but also with modern primitive painting. In America, Léger professed the most enthusiastic admiration for the art of Edward Hicks [303], and he owed his greatest debt of all to Douanier Rousseau. The ingredients that went into the fabrication of *Leisure*, then, were of bizarre diversity: the classicism of David, the mechanistic character of the modern world, the innocence of an American Quaker minister, and the naïve-sophisticated style of an eccentric customs collector. Actually, of course, Léger is only a little classical, only speciously mechanistic, and not very innocent. He is a painter with an emphatically personal style in which native vigor and a curious affectation compete with one another —and frequently come to terms. On these

577. CASSANDRE: *L'Intran*, 1925. Lithographic poster, 43 x 59¼″. Philadelphia Museum of Art, Gallatin Collection.

578. DELAUNAY: *Eiffel Tower, c.* 1909. 38 x 27¾″. Philadelphia Museum of Art, Arensberg Collection.

579. DELAUNAY: *Eiffel Tower, c.* 1925. Lithograph, 23¾ x 17½″. Philadelphia Museum of Art, Gallatin Collection.

occasions Léger is a fine artist; on most others, he is at least a fine designer.

Directly and indirectly, Léger's style has been one of the most powerful influences on modern decorators, designers, and commercial artists. The influence has been good, although the mass of commercial work thus turned out may have drained some interest away from Léger's pictures themselves. As an example, A. M. Cassandre's effective poster for the Parisian newspaper *L'Intransigeant* [577] owes a great deal to synthetic cubism in general and to Léger in particular. A telegraph pole runs up and down through it, a coincidental resemblance, no doubt, to the one in *The City,* and is flanked with insulators simplified and modeled in Léger's manner. Wires run to an ear in a head where the eye is a series of concentric disks, and the profile, with the mouth open to shout the news, is drawn with rulers and compasses. Even the letters, interrupted before the whole word *L'Intransigeant* is spelled out, suggest the fragmentary letters in *The City* and other compositions. In the poster this is a double device, since the newspaper is ordinarily called by the nickname *L'Intran* and is shouted thus by news sellers.

Cubism: Some Subdivisions

With the liberation of cubist forms into the field of general expression, it was inevitable that the ranks of the cubists, which had grown like weeds, should break into smaller groups with their own theories. For

580. DELAUNAY: *Windows*, 1912. 13½ x 35". Philadelphia Museum of Art, Gallatin Collection.

a while one ism shouldered another in the enthusiasm for further experiment and refinements and the hope of discovery. Robert Delaunay (1885–1941), dissatisfied with cubism's static arrangements, began composing in restless planes and swinging arcs in an effort to reveal the forces inherent in static objects. He chose as his special subjects two pieces of architectural engineering where dynamic forces are brought into structural balance: the Eiffel Tower with its steel girders and the medieval church of St. Séverin with its stone vaults. His semicubist *Eiffel Tower* of about 1909 [578], compared with one of 1925 [579] demonstrates the change from static forms to ones broken up in a way suggesting movement. Delaunay similarly enlivened cubist color. In 1912, a year when cubism shot out in a dozen directions, Delaunay formulated "orphism," or color orchestration, in which he had tried to free cubism at once from the dun hues that had affected it during the analytical period and from its dependence on subject matter. As an orphist he painted a series of "window compositions" [580] in totally abstract planes something like overlapping sheets of bright colored glass. Although he did not follow up the direction these paintings set, other painters were soon to do so.

Francis Picabia (1879–1953) was also involved in orphism, but at the same time he thought that cubism could be a vehicle for the expression of ideas. He had begun as an imitator of Sisley, and he spent his life enthusiastically investigating every new

581. PICABIA: *Physical Culture,* 1913. 35¼ x 46". Philadelphia Museum of Art, Arensberg Collection.

ism that turned up, without going very deeply into any of them. The painting he called *Physical Culture* [581] is already tainted with Picabia's weakness for impertinence that later led him to use such titles as *You'll Never Sell It, I Don't Want to Paint Any More,* and *What Do You Call That?*

What might be called "dynamic cubism," apparent in Delaunay's later *Eiffel Tower* and in *Physical Culture,* is most vivaciously present in Marcel Duchamp's (1887–) celebrated *Nude Descending a Staircase* [582]. It is a painting of considerable his-

582. DUCHAMP: *Nude Descending a Staircase (No. 2)*, 1912. 58 x 35". Philadelphia Museum of Art, Arensberg Collection.

583. BURNE-JONES: *The Golden Stairs*, 1880. 109 x 46". Tate Gallery, London.

torical importance since it became the key exhibit of the Armory Show in 1913 in New York (traveling later to Chicago and Boston), which was America's first wholesale introduction to avant-garde painting. For the first time, Americans reacted with the vehemence of Frenchmen when confronted with works of art that offended them. Guards had to protect the most controver-sial paintings from attack by an enraged public. This at least was true in New York and Chicago; Bostoners retained their aplomb.

One unsympathetic critic labeled *Nude Descending a Staircase* once and for all "an explosion in a shingle factory." The jibe was perceptive, up to a point. The fig-ure is indeed shattered into shinglelike planes that merge and overlap in a pattern of great energy. But the jibe falls short in that the shattered figure is not chaotic. Contrarily, it is reassembled into a pattern of great order and vivacity, more expressive of bright descending movement than an imitative painting of a nude descending a staircase could be. But for a public that still admired Burne-Jones's *The Golden Stairs* [583], showing eighteen young women in pretty costumes descending a staircase in a series of graceful attitudes, a picture of one nude young woman descending a stair-case in many more than eighteen attitudes, overlaid, was incomprehensible and infuri-ating. The fact that after half a century *Nude Descending* has a persistent capacity to interest the sympathetic and irritate the antagonistic, while other sensational novel-ties have flared up and faded away by the dozen, is as good a proof as another that it is much more than a well-timed tour de force, as it has been suspected of being. It is an enduring landmark, and it is a work of art with extensions beyond cubism. One of these is its deliberately provocative title which, like Picabia's nonsensical ones, is allied to two other movements, dada and surrealism, where Duchamp will appear again.

Duchamp's painter brother Gaston, who adopted the pseudonym Jacques Villon (1875–1963), worked in a personal varia-tion on cubism, always rather quiet and elegant, and eventually developing into lu-cent configurations of great distinction. In the history of cubism he has a special place as the head of a group who met at his stu-dio in the early days for discussion and theorizing. In 1912 they named themselves the *Section d'Or* after the mathematical for-mula for proportional harmonies that has already been commented on in connection with neo-impressionism. The *Section d'Or* organized a huge exhibition, and all the men mentioned here—Metzinger and Gleizes, Gris and Léger, Delaunay and Picabia and Marcel Duchamp—took part in it, as well as Roger de la Fresnaye (1885–1925), Louis Marcoussis (1883–1941), André Lhote (1885–   ), and many others. As a climactic point in cubism's coming of age it summarized the forces at work before

584. BALLA: *Leash in Motion*, 1912. 35⅝ x 43¼". Collection A. Conger Goodyear, New York.

their dissemination into the general field of painting, which they have so profoundly affected. Picasso and Braque alone, the two major figures in cubism's development and the two painters who subsequently drew most significantly upon it, were not repre-sented. The immediate reason was that the exhibition was held in a commercial gallery in which they could not show, for contrac-tual reasons. But psychologically their ab-sence was appropriate, for while it is pos-sible to think of the men who did exhibit as being, first of all, cubists, it is impossible not to think of Braque and Picasso as being, first of all, painters. But before they can be further discussed here, a little attention must be given to a movement called fu-turism.

Futurism

Futurism was a parenthetical Italian move-ment that promised for a moment to be an important one but ended by draining off into cubism. The kinetic factor so apparent in *Nude Descending a Staircase*, as well as in the dynamism of Delaunay's *Eiffel*

585. Russolo: *Dynamism of an Automobile*, 1913. 41½ x 55".
Musée National d'Art Moderne, Paris.

Tower, was basic in futurism's program. *Dynamism* was their favorite word.

Futurism began as a literary movement after cubism was well under way, in 1909. An Italian litterateur named Filippo Tommaso Marinetti decided that it was the obligation of the modern creative mind to celebrate such factors in modern life as its speed and aggressiveness. He advocated tearing down all institutions dedicated to the preservation of the past, such as museums, libraries, and schools, and issued a declamatory manifesto as a call to arms. No museums, libraries, or schools were lost. (This happened in Paris, although Marinetti was Italian.) Marinetti's literary rebellion was taken up by a group of painters who were at the moment working within the general confines of neo-impressionism, and one of them, Umberto Boccioni (1882–1916), followed Marinetti's ideas in a similar manifesto exhorting the young painters of Italy to arise to the fray. The manifesto was also signed by Luigi Russolo (1885–1947), Giacomo Balla (1871–1958), Carlo Carra (1881–1966), and Gino Severini (1883–1966), and was followed by a succession of sequel manifestos. They were distributed by the thousands, sometimes by such stunts as scattering from Italian bell

towers. There was always a strong element of public theatricalism in futurist behavior, and it is difficult to read their proclamations without an uncomfortable feeling that the theories were formulated with more attention to shock value than to convictions sincerely held. Urgent and literary in tone, they are composed of such phrases as ". . . fight relentlessly against the fanatical, irresponsible, and snobbish religion of the past, which is nourished by the baneful existence of museums . . . groveling admiration for old canvases . . . criminal disdain for everything young, new, and pulsating with life . . . tyranny of the words *harmony* and *good taste*." Artists were admonished to "glorify the life of today, unceasingly and violently transformed by victorious science." Instead of the religious atmosphere that "weighed upon the souls" of their ancestors, they should draw inspiration from the liners, battleships, airplanes, submarines, and railroads that made an "iron network of speed enveloping the earth."

One way to express motion was to follow Boccioni's statement that "a galloping horse has not four legs; it has twenty." That such was also the case with dogs was demonstrated by Balla in his *Leash in Motion* [584].

The painters planned a Paris exhibition as an opening gun outside Italy after a sensational debut in Milan, but when they compared their work, full of neo-impressionist overtones, with what Braque and Picasso were doing—this was in 1910—they saw that for all their rampant modernism they were already a step behind. They performed a tactical retreat and the exhibition did not materialize until 1912, when analytical cubism had just about run its course and had been assimilated as part of futurist theory.

The simple multiple-exposure approach of *Leash in Motion* did not quite fulfill the expression of "universal dynamism," "dynamic sensation itself," "plastic dynamism," or "the translation of objects according to the *lines of force* which characterize them." The cubist idea of simultaneity was adapted to "put the spectator at the center of the picture," since the various sensations con-

586. Severini: *Dynamic Hieroglyphic of the Bal Tabarin*, 1912. Oil on canvas with sequins, 63⅜ x 61½". Museum of Modern Art, New York, Lillie P. Bliss Bequest.

verging upon him simultaneously from every side involved the same principle as analytical cubism's multiple simultaneous vision. But the futurists' adaptation of the idea also involved strong expressive color, and their shattered forms were often organized on a skeleton of strong directional lines, as in Russolo's *Dynamism of an Automobile* [585]. In Severini's *Dynamic Hieroglyphic of the Bal Tabarin* [586] the spectator is put at the center of that famous pleasure spot and is surrounded by choppy, whirling forms in extremely cheerful colors further enlivened by a scattering of real sequins.

It requires a generous effort today to see these paintings as much more than historical novelties playing second fiddle to cubism, where similar ideas were developed more exhaustively; a recent revival of interest in the futurists smacked strongly of artificial respiration. Surprisingly, futurism's contribution may end up as being made in sculpture, where it would seem least likely to succeed. Boccioni's *Unique Forms of Continuity in Space* [588] is a large, arresting bronze in which the forms seem to have been shaped by rushing air, air whose currents we can almost feel extending beyond the fluttering shapes of the

587. BERNINI: *Apollo and Daphne*, 1622–24. Marble, life size. *Galleria Borghese*, Rome. (Photo Anderson.)

588. BOCCIONI: *Unique Forms of Continuity in Space*, 1913. Bronze, 43½″ high. Museum of Modern Art, New York, Lillie P. Bliss Bequest.

metal just as they penetrate into it in other places. The dynamic "lines of force" which we have just seen as severely angular ones in Russolo's interpretation of a moving automobile now weave and twist, materializing as solids and equally extending into space suggested or defined by these solids. A striding figure is still discernible as the motif for the composition, and if *Unique Forms of Continuity in Space* is innovational, it is also linked firmly to the tradition of baroque sculpture, such as Bernini's *Apollo and Daphne* [587], where flapping draperies, wind-filled hair, and extended arms and legs fly out into surrounding space and also receive space into the hollows and voids carved into the marble. The

difference between the two pieces of sculpture is that the baroque sculptor is most apparently creating realistic forms while the futurist is most apparently creating abstract ones. But both sculptors are creating a composition where solid form and the forms of space merge and interlock. This aspect of space in connection with sculpture is considered in more detail at the end of this chapter, where another work by Boccioni, his *Development of a Bottle in Space* [632], is related to certain contemporary theories of sculpture.

World War I wrote *finis* to futurism as a potentially significant organized movement, although an army of small painters continued to go through its paces into the

589. CARRÀ: *Hermaphroditic Idol*, 1917. 25½ x 16½". Collection Carlo Frua de Angeli, Milan.

590. PICASSO: *Man with Violin*, 1911. 39½ x 28⅞". Philadelphia Museum of Art, Arensberg Collection.

1930's. To postwar Europe, futurism's theoretical advocation of destruction and violence was less attractive after four years of experience with the real thing. Die-hard futurists continued to study "dynamism" in more and more abstract form, yet futurism somehow never supplied nourishment for growth as cubism did. In retrospect its brief flourishing is revealed as a forced growth—all foliage and no roots. Of the signers of the original manifesto, Balla alone continued to develop, rather thinly, in the direction he had helped to set. Severini tried a few war motifs in 1915, including an *Armored Train*, but soon turned to doing doves, fruit, and other happy and nondynamic subjects in an adaptation of synthetic cubism that was especially popu-

lar with interior decorators. Carrà joined a dream-world school of "metaphysical" painting, which will be discussed in due time, of which his *Hermaphroditic Idol* [589] may serve here as a foretaste. We may now return to the post-analytical careers of Braque and Picasso.

Braque

The two major analytical cubists, Braque and Picasso, as has been said, worked for a while so closely that their work is distinguishable from one another's only by fine points. Picasso's *Man with Violin* [590] and Braque's *Man with Guitar* [591], both painted in 1911 at the climax of analytical

591. BRAQUE: *Man with Guitar*, 1911. 45¾ x 31⅞". Museum of Modern Art, New York, Lillie P. Bliss Bequest.

592. BRAQUE: *Musical Forms with the Words Fête and Journal*, 1913. Oil, pencil, and charcoal on canvas, 36¼ x 23½". Philadelphia Museum of Art, Arensberg Collection.

cubism, are evidence enough. Yet even here a difference appears when the two paintings are compared within the confines of analytical cubism, instead of within the context of painting in general. The Picasso shifts and vibrates within its geometrical framework, the Braque is more static, more self-contained; it is as if the multitude of planes in the Picasso have expanded to the limits of the structure they compose, while those in the Braque have contracted until the forms are compressed and ordered into stability.

The difference between the two painters indicated here will be widened as they develop in their own directions. Picasso will become the romantic of the movement—all energy, fire, restlessness, invention, emotion. Braque will develop into its classical master—controlled, reflective, harmonious, working toward an ideal of perfection within limits, as opposed to the romantic yearning for limitless expression.

With analytical cubism behind him, Braque's first departure was to restore the inherently ornamental character of the same objects that had figured in his analytical compositions—bowls of fruit, tables and goblets and compotes, and particularly musical instruments. His *Musical Forms with the Words Fête and Journal* [592]—the complication of the title is only a device to distinguish this painting from other compositions of musical forms—is a spare,

593. BRAQUE: *Musical Forms,* 1918. Collage, 30⅜ x 37⅞″. Philadelphia Museum of Art, Arensberg Collection.

open arrangement of straight lines and simple arcs or volutes derived from the shapes of a violin. A large part of the canvas is left unpainted, the design being established by crayon drawing in tones ranging from black to light gray, holding the grainy texture of the canvas. The unpainted canvas itself, in the original, serves as an ornamental surface which is lost in photography and reproduction, and it supplies an off-white that counts as a color, not as a blank area. The other colors are a grayed blue, scrubbed thinly in the rectangle in the upper left; a warm brown in the body of the violin itself; and a light tan in the rectangle of simulated wood texture above it. The area of the violin has been textured by drawing a comb or some other toothed instrument across it in a slightly wavy motion while the paint was still wet. In all, the composition achieves textural variety with economy of means, a satisfying struc-

tural balance in forms individually delicate. Its quality might be compared to that of a "dry" light wine, thinner and more subtle than a more obviously tasty sweet one.

The interest in textures and the introduction of letters in imitation of printed ones is associated with experiments Braque made in collage. The origin of collage, which is the making of pictures or compositions by pasting together bits of paper, cloth, and the like, is not certain. Like cubism it seems to have appeared spontaneously from several sources at once, but Braque certainly had a great deal to do with its origin and he used it with particular felicity. A collage of *Musical Forms* [593] extends the idea implicit in the painting we have just seen where the texture of the unpainted canvas was used as an integral part of a picture that also included simulated textures. Here all the textures are real. A banjolike instrument cut from cor-

594. BRAQUE: *The Round Table*, 1929. 58 x 45". Phillips Collection, Washington, D.C.

One value of the collage is that it opens our eyes to colors and textures we have ignored because they are commonplace. Behind the origin of collage, too, there may be ultimately the rejection of the old academic idea that painting must display technical skill of a conventional kind. By fabricating "pictures" from odds and ends of worthless material the artist makes the final denial of the validity of academic technique as an end in itself. But for Braque the value of collage was in experiments with texture, an introduction to an element that will continue to preoccupy him in other ways.

Collage soon served its purpose for Braque and its other originators, and they abandoned it. It was later taken up by experimenters and practitioners of the bizarre who used it for shock value, combining materials absurd or shocking in themselves —plumbing from toilets and the like—or cutting out portions of printed pictures and pasting them together to make irrational images. And it is a rare kindergarten nowadays that doesn't have collage in its art classes, where children have access to a heap of cloth scraps, torn paper, cellophane, wire netting, cotton, false hair, and anything else that can be pasted down. All legitimate enough in their own ways, these offshoots must not be confused with Braque's combinations of colors and textures via collage instead of via painting in the creation of synthetic cubist compositions.

Surface texture of course has always been an important part of painting, whether it is the variegated one of Rembrandt, the uniformly polished one of Ingres, the fatty, active one of Delacroix, or the congealed-confetti one of Seurat. But with Rembrandt, texture was incidental to the creation of form in light; with Ingres, part and parcel of the idea of disciplined draughtsmanship; with Delacroix, part of expression; with Seurat, the end result of a theory of the laws of light. With Braque, surface texture now becomes an integral decorative factor in painting, and from this time forward he cultivates it, sometimes mixing sand or other grainy matter with his paint to roughen it, sometimes depending only

rugated cardboard supplies the most unexpected one, but other areas are also papers of different textures. The whites are a ribbed drawing paper, the largest halftone area is a brown wrapping paper, and the black upon close examination is a paper printed with an imitation of a very fine wood grain. The upper part of the mandolin form is the kind of paper used to cover pasteboard cigar boxes, again simulating wood grain, and again a printed paper, not a simulation by the painter. The rectangles at lower right and far left center are printed with a slightly raised netlike pattern. With a few lines in crayon and a background painted blue-gray, that is the scheme. The colors of the papers have a natural ornamental harmony once their identity as cheap paper is forgotten.

on the paint's own thinness or thickness, sometimes scratching or pressing textures into it, but always incorporating texture as part of his organization of form, line, and color.

By the 1920's Braque was master of a personal cubist idiom combining spatial play with exquisitely integrated shape [594]. During the mid-1920's he began to use the human figure, usually a female nude, in addition to tables and compotes of fruit and musical instruments. *Nude* [595] of 1925, is like a decorative panel in a new substance, neither paint nor ceramic, suggesting both. It is as if the colors and textures, like those of a ceramist, were the result of the craftsman's scheme modified by the process of firing—except that here the modifications are Braque's own. His art shares the appeal of other decorative ones; *Woman with a Mandolin* [596], a synthesis of his work up until the middle 1930's, is tapestrylike in its textural richness. Braque's color here as elsewhere is indescribable, partly because no color is describable to much effect, but largely because he is the most individual decorative colorist of his generation. No color is pure; greens are olives, sages, and occasional lime greens. Modified purples are juxtaposed with citrons and blacks. When reds occur they occur suddenly and spectacularly, but also in off-shades that unify them with Braque's special family of colors. "Braque colors" have become a stock in trade for the modern interior decorator.

It is time to insert a reminder that before he was a cubist, Braque was briefly a member of the fauve group. And of all painters, he alone made a balanced fusion of fauvist principles of color with cubist ideas of form. His *Woman with a Mandolin* may eventually stand as the richest summary, within the boundaries of single pictures, of the abstract style of the first half of the twentieth century. If every painting by Picasso, every painting by Matisse, and every painting by Braque were gathered together and all but a single painting had to be destroyed, Braque's *Woman with a Mandolin* could not summarize the total, but it might come closest of them all to being the representative example.

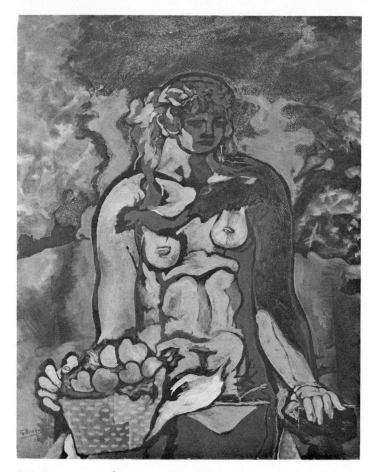

595. BRAQUE: *Nude,* 1925. 36⅛ x 28⅞". Art Institute of Chicago, Gift of Mr. and Mrs. Arnold H. Maremont.

Picasso: Cubist and Classical Variations

Picasso is certainly the most fecund painter who has ever lived. In sheer quantity his work is fantastic, which would be meaningless if he were a repetitious painter, but his invention is phenomenal, his range staggering. From his thousands of paintings, prints, and drawings it would be possible to cull several groups of work that would be creditable as the lifeworks of several painters of varying temperaments. And it would be simple to divide his total work between two classifications as the work of two tremendously productive artists, one of them a man of tender sentiments dedicated to a joyous life, the other a man appalled by

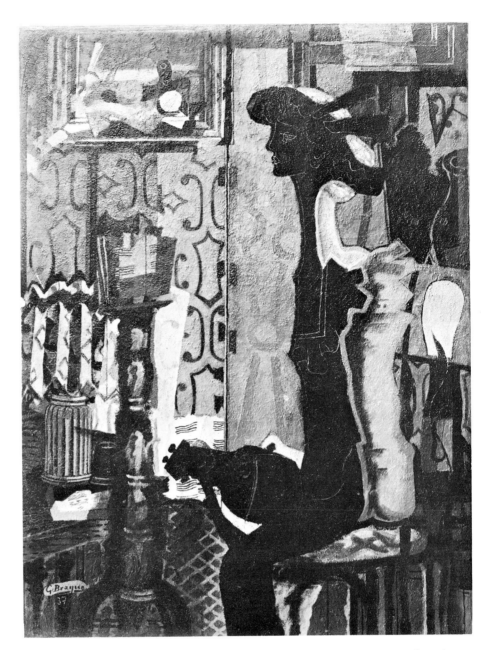

596. BRAQUE: *Woman with a Mandolin*, 1937. 51¼ x 38¼". Museum of Modern Art, New York, Mrs. Simon Guggenheim Fund.

life's terribleness and releasing his fury against it in cathartic images of horror, brutishness, and terror.

Picasso's abrupt changes of style, his sudden terminations and redirections, his harking back to principles he seemed to have exhausted years before to revive them in more vigorous forms, the sudden appear-ance from time to time of individual paint-ings that seem isolated experiments and may remain so for years, lying fallow until they are suddenly continued in a whole group of paintings—all this variation, turn-ing, and shifting would be vacillation or chaos if it were not unified by the presence of the single force which is Picasso himself.

He has a headlong vigor, an all-encompassing vitality, which refuses to accept any achievement as final or static in the expression of a world so contradictory and so rich in joy and tragedy that his experience of it must well forth in image after image patterned to record his multitudinous response to its inexhaustible excitements. No single style of image can suffice his vigor and his curiosity. It is the sense of growth and expansion, a constant pushing forward into new explorations, that gives unity to Picasso's turbulent variety when his work is surveyed as a whole.

We have already seen him as a young man influenced by Toulouse-Lautrec, then synthesizing a more individual style in his speciously pathetic images of the blue period, next relenting with the gentle harlequins, adolescents, and performers of the "circus" period, finally merging into the graceful classical echoes of the rose period —then abruptly creating *Les Demoiselles d'Avignon* and going into cubism.

Immediately after the exhaustion of analytical cubism in 1912, Picasso made some of the same adjustments we have already seen in Braque, including play with collage. For several years thereafter he explored synthetic cubism. For Picasso this was a period of fantastic eruption. The most inventive of painters exceeded himself in indicating the area over which he could range with ebullience, assurance, excitement, and often with profundity. It is necessary in understanding Picasso to remember this range. With Gris and Léger, and even with Braque, it is safe to approach each picture with some certainty that it will fall within the general boundaries of each man's characteristic expression. With Picasso, each picture must be approached individually. After one of his most profound statements he may create a piece of pure legerdemain, may indulge in a kind of pictorial horseplay. A picture like *Harlequin* [597] is as witty as it is ornamental. In his celebrated and extremely complex *Painter and Model* [598], a painter (right) works from a model (left) and both are abstracted according to free applications of cubist ideas. But the shattered and distorted head of the model appears reassembled on the painter's

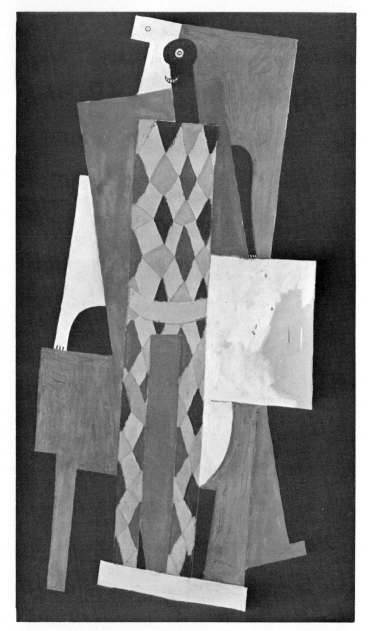

597. Picasso: *Harlequin*, 1915. 72¼ x 41⅜". Museum of Modern Art, New York, Lillie P. Bliss Bequest.

canvas in a clear profile, the only realistically identifiable element in the composition. This turnabout, a tour de force variation on the picture-within-a-picture theme, is clever enough to have been borrowed by cartoonists in popular magazines, but it is also a comment on the nature of cubist vision, and, beyond that, an informal philo-

598. PICASSO: *Painter and Model*, 1928. 51⅝ x 63⅞". Collection Mr. and Mrs. Sidney Janis, New York.

sophical reflection on the relationship of the painter's art to the visible world.

In 1921, as if to summarize the potential of synthetic cubism, Picasso painted two large compositions of *Three Musicians*, one fairly complicated [599] and one highly simplified [600]. In both of them, three masked mummers or Mardi gras celebrators are costumed as Harlequin—Picasso's ubiquitous Harlequin—Pierrot, and a monk. Each has a musical instrument. Side by side the two paintings are a lesson in synthetic cubist design. To the person who cannot see in individual pictures of this kind a harmony and integration of form, it might be enlightening to imagine transposing a single figure from one picture to the other. Not only is this impossible because of the interlockings of form, but if a figure

were torn from its compositional moorings and somehow grafted into the other painting, its forms would be disharmonious with those surrounding it—too complicated or too simple, and without adequate or harmonious interrelationship of its lines and shapes to those of its new companions.

Even while he was reaching the synthetic cubist culmination in *Three Musicians*, Picasso was working on a second group of drawings and paintings of an opposite character, a new version of the monumental classical figure type so dear to the academicians. The opposite of cubistic, Picasso's new figures are solid and unviolated as mass [601], and painted a solid dulled pink something like terra cotta, increasing their sculptural quality. The exaggerated heaviness, the overlarge hands, the extreme simplification into geometrical masses, add to their ponderous, indissoluble unity, which is a reaction against the disintegration of solids in cubism. In these pictures Picasso returns to the weighty solidity and definition of the portrait of Gertrude Stein [558], but as usual he is not so much returning, as resurrecting and transfiguring. His art is a constant series of transmigrations of the forms of one period into the forms of another. Among the sudden brilliant variations in the classical period is *Woman in White* [602], where the ponderousness is ameliorated by the delicacy of the technique. The picture is painted in thin veils of pigment with contrasting heavily loaded lights (particularly in the face) and quick, decisive lines to define the features, all capped by the most delicate calligraphic indications of the hair, suggesting Oriental painting and completing an image of great repose, alertly alive.

The next years include also a cycle of paintings stemming from cubism but involving sweeping curves and circles, often described in heavy black lines enclosing bright glassy colors. *Girl before a Mirror* [603] of 1932 has become a standard example of this "stained glass" manner. Cubist ideas of simultaneity are brought back to their earliest and simplest devices, as in the combination profile and full face of the girl, but the invention is free, subject to no restrictions cubist or otherwise, in the creation of scintillating patterns. *Girl before a Mirror,* like most of Picasso's major canvases, has been the subject of elaborate psychoanalytical interpretations. The full rounded or globular forms of the figure, their unity with the long rounded forms of the mirror, or pier glass, the simultaneous identification and transformation of figure and reflection, the suggestion of interior as well as exterior anatomical forms—all are rich material for this kind of study and could be interpreted in any one of a dozen ways by a dozen schools of psychologists. As a purely visual spectacle, *Girl before a Mirror* is one of the most vibrant and powerful of Picasso's works, with its combination, so frequent in his work from now on, of almost savage force with the extremest sophistication.

599–600. PICASSO: *Three Musicians,* 1921. *Above,* 80 x 74″. Philadelphia Museum of Art, Gallatin Collection. *Below,* 79 x 87¾″. Museum of Modern Art, New York, Mrs. Simon Guggenheim Fund.

601. Picasso: *Standing Nude*, 1922. Panel, 7½ x 5½". Wadsworth Atheneum, Hartford, Conn.

603. Picasso: *Girl before a Mirror*, 1932. 63¾ x 51¼". Museum of Modern Art, New York, Gift of Mrs. Simon Guggenheim.

602. Picasso: *Woman in White*, 1923. 39 x 31½". Metropolitan Museum of Art, New York, Rogers Fund, 1951; from The Museum of Modern Art, Lillie P. Bliss Collection.

Picasso: "Minotauromachia" and "Guernica"

Shortly after *Girl before a Mirror*, a new theme, ominous and violent, appears and soon dominates Picasso's conceptions, the double theme of the bullfight, which is a ceremony of death, and the Minotaur, that monster half bull and half man who in Greek legend devoured annually his tribute of seven youths and seven maidens delivered into his labyrinth by the Athenians. These reveries of violence correspond to a disturbed period in Picasso's own life and culminate in one of his most elaborate works, a large etching full of personal symbols, *Minotauromachia* [604]. The symbolism of the various figures may or may not have been explicit in Picasso's mind, but in a general way the symbolism is apparent without a key. The theme is, first of all, a conflict between good and evil, between innocence and corruption, between life and death. On the right the Minotaur with its

604. PICASSO: *Minotauromachia,* 1935. Etching, 19½ x 27⅜". Philadelphia Museum of Art, Gift of Henry P. McIlhenny.

powerful male human body and its grotesque beast's head advances with the sword of a bullfighter. A female figure in bullfighter's costume lies dead across the back of a terrified horse, a reference of course to the pitiful nags who are sacrificed to the horns of the bull in the early stages of the sport. But at the right a little girl holds a bunch of flowers—it might be the one offered us years ago by the *Boy with Bouquet* [555]—and holds a gleaming light, serene in her confidence of its power against the Minotaur, who shields himself from it— or is about to extinguish it. The little girl wears a tam-o'-shanter and stands as primly as a child in a storybook illustration. Behind her a male figure suggestive of Christ ascends a ladder. The conflict is witnessed by a pair of young women on a balcony where a dove perches. On one side the scene takes place against a background of

the wall of the house, on the other against a deep stretch of sea where a tiny sailboat appears like an afterthought. One may make of these symbols whatever explicit interpretation seems necessary, but beyond a certain point explicit interpretation is superfluous. The pictorial images evoke emotional associations without identifying tags.

Minotauromachia served as prototype for an explosive picture that now appears: Picasso's most deeply felt, most emotionalized, most vehement painting, probably his masterpiece if a single one must be chosen from so many candidates—*Guernica* [605, 606, 607, 608, 609, and 610].

In April, 1937, the ancient and holy city of Guernica in northern Spain was destroyed by German bombers supporting General Franco in the Spanish civil war. Guernica was not particularly a strategic

605. PICASSO: *Guernica*, 1937. 138 x 308″. Museum of Modern Art, New York, on loan from the artist.

606. PICASSO: Composition study for Figure 605, May 9, 1937. Pencil on white paper, 9½ x 17⅞″. Collection the artist.

target; its destruction was primarily a test run, the first practical application of the military theory of saturation bombing, a rehearsal for World War II. The rehearsal was successful. Most of Guernica was re-duced to rubble and its inhabitants were destroyed with it.

Picasso's outrage as a Spaniard and as a human being produced the *Guernica* in a matter of weeks. It is a large painting—

607. PICASSO: Detail from Figure 605. Approximately 66 x 63".

608. PICASSO: Detail from Figure 605. Approximately 37 x 46".

more than twenty-five feet long—painted entirely in blacks, whites, and grays. Distortions take on a new horribleness; there is a blatant and tragic ugliness to the human creatures who shriek, howl, and die. A bomb has fallen into the courtyard or barn of a farmhouse. A horse screams in the center of the composition. A bull, symbol of triumphant violence, rises immune at the left. The large space is organized on one of the oldest schemes in Western art. It is essentially a triptych on the formula of a Renaissance altarpiece with a central portion and two folding wings. Its two wing-like side elements, which would once have been occupied by flanking saints, show on one side a mother who screeches as she holds the body of her child, and on the other a woman who falls through the floor of a burning building. The triangular central motif, which in the altarpiece would

486 · CUBISM AND ABSTRACT ART

609. PICASSO: Detail from Figure 605. Approximately 34 x 43″.

610. PICASSO: Detail from Figure 605. Approximately 38 x 48″.

have built up to a madonna enthroned among adoring saints, is packed with mangled human and animal forms including a symbolical severed arm and hand still grasping a broken sword. A comparison of the completed picture with a preliminary composition study [606] shows that Picasso built the central triangular mass, and flanked it by the two "wings," by reorganizing a more chaotic scheme composed of the same elements.

Some of the impact of *Guernica* comes from the frightening combination of the ludicrous and the grotesque with the tragic. The eyes askew in heads, the hands and feet with swollen fingers and toes, like hideous mutations—all these monstrous deformities, all the ugliness, are reminders that death by the violence of war is abominable and obscene. Picasso's drawings for *Guernica* included some of the most ghastly images in the history of horror and fantasy [611].

Since *Guernica*, Picasso has varied his style with customary frequency, but elements of the grotesque and the horrible have been persistent in it. On a superficial level, *Girl with Cock* [612] of the year following *Guernica* is trivial or silly as to subject, but this silliness and even the half-comical presentation, especially of the rooster, is identified with the terrible, the irrational, violence of life. The ominous knife on the floor to the left is represented with a clarity that leaves no doubt as to the picture's implication.

Yet in the middle of nightmarish grotesqueries there will appear a drawing or a small painting recalling the tenderness of the early acrobats, harlequins, and boys leading horses, and in the last few years Picasso has been painting with revived gayety, brightness, and opulence. In December, 1954, and into February, 1955, he occupied himself with a series of studies with Delacroix's *Women of Algiers* as a basis for a set of variations [613], [614], where legerdemain, cubist derivations, stained glass color, inversions and returns, and sheer inventive play with space, pattern, and color are juggled, tossed, caught, shattered, pieced together, multiplied and divided in a prestidigious exhibition of one man's art that has dominated inventive painting for half a century. And in the same year, 1955, following Matisse's death late in 1954, there was a spurt of Matisse-like Picassos in bright flat colors with fauvist echoes that could be interpreted as a form of tribute to a worthy antagonist in an undeclared war in which, happily, both opponents were victors.

611. PICASSO: Guernica Series #37. Ink and oil on canvas, 21⅝ x 18⅛". Collection the artist.

612. PICASSO: *Girl with Cock*, 1938. 51¼ x 47½". Collection Mrs. Meric Callery, New York.

613. PICASSO: *Women of Algiers, Variation "L,"* 1955. 51⅛ x 38⅛". Private Collection.

614. PICASSO: *Women of Algiers, Variation "N,"* 1955. 44⅞ x 57½". Washington University, St. Louis, Mo.

615. MALEVICH: *White on White*, 1918. 31¼ x 31¼". Museum of Modern Art, New York.

The Nonobjective Conclusion

Picasso, Braque, and the cubists are abstract painters because, by the dictionary definition, their compositions are "creation(s) suggested by a concrete object or organic figure which is transformed by the artist into a nonrepresentational design with recognizable elements." The term *nonobjective* (or, sometimes, *nonfigurative*) has been coined to distinguish from this kind of abstraction, with its partial departure from representation, a total abstraction where representational elements are entirely eliminated.

When analytical cubism so abstracted concrete objects (such as men with violins) that only fragmentary elements were recognizable here and there, the nonobjective conclusion to the process of abstraction that had begun with Cézanne's distortion was indicated. If the object had virtually disappeared, to such an extent that the aesthetic and psychological satisfactions of painting were to be found in planes as planes, rather than as parts of objects, why bother with the objects as a point of departure? Not only why bother, but why tolerate any vestigial remains?

We have already seen how synthetic cubism responded to this question. Instead of eliminating the subject it returned to it, and Picasso even developed a symbolical and emotionalized art where the recognizability of the objects was necessary to an understanding of the picture. *Guernica* would certainly not make the sense it does if the anguished horse and the ravished and brutalized human beings were not recognizable as the victims of a frightful social crime.

But certain other painters rejected subject entirely for pure abstraction—for nonobjectivity. We have seen that Kandinsky painted his first altogether nonrepresentational composition in 1910—a record. Shortly after, a Russian cubist named Kasimir Malevich (1878–1935) made the transition from abstract to nonobjective geometrical painting in a single jump of even more spectacular decisiveness, probably after a study of Kandinsky's theories. Malevich exhibited a black square placed neatly on a white background (the black square was painstakingly filled in with pencil) as a demonstration of his theory that art must leave behind all dependence on motif. The square represented nothing at all, was an abstraction of no concrete object. It was simply a geometrical area of black against a geometrical area of white, differing from Kandinsky's painting in that it "expressed" nothing. *Suprematism* was the name Malevich gave his new theory, which limited the painter's vocabulary to the rectangle, the circle, the triangle, and the cross. The third dimension was ruled out—instead of cubes, rectangles; instead of cones, triangles; instead of spheres, circles. It was permissible to combine several of these forms in a single painting, but since the aim of suprematism was to create the ultimate work of art, the black square on a white ground was the supreme suprematist composition. At least it seemed so for five years, until in 1918 Malevich conceived a white square on a white ground [615].

616. MONDRIAN: *Landscape with Farmhouse*, 1906. 34 x 42¾". Collection Mrs. Isaac Schoenberg, Swarthmore, Pa.

Beyond that not even he could go. The trouble with an ultimate is its finality, and it was Malevich's misfortune that in two paintings he had exhausted the possibilities of suprematism as a theory, and there was not much left to do with it except to defend it in dialectics.

But during these same years, the years between the black square and the white square, another painter was involved in more subtle considerations of the same idea that had inspired suprematism. His name was Piet Mondrian (1872–1944), and his theory came to be called neo-plasticism.

Mondrian had begun as a conventional painter working in a broad form of impressionism, turning out picturesque subjects, such as boats in canals and other stock items, in his native Holland. But by 1906 he was beginning to conventionalize his landscapes into flat patterns, as in *Landscape with Farmhouse* [616], where he

hunts out the hint of natural geometry in walls and river banks and leafless branches silhouetted against the sky, and emphasizes it. But this is not Cézanne's solid geometry. It is plane geometry, as flat as a piece of painted stage scenery. From the loosely rectangular areas of the houses and, especially, their reflections in the water, it is only a few steps to the precisely geometrical lines and areas of Mondrian's typical nonobjective canvases, such as *Composition with Yellow* [617] and *Rhythm in Straight Lines* [618].

Mondrian wrote extensively and his theories include ideas like these, when they are pared down to apply to paintings like the two just mentioned:

1. All painting is composed of line and color. Line and color are the essence of painting. Hence they must be freed from their bondage to the imitation of nature and allowed to exist for themselves.

617. MONDRIAN: *Composition with Yellow*, 1936. 28¾ x 26″. Philadelphia Museum of Art, Arensberg Collection.

2. Painting occupies a plane surface. The plane surface is integral with the physical and psychological being of the painting. Hence the plane surface must be respected, must be allowed to declare itself, must not be falsified by imitations of volume, by perspective. Painting must be as flat as the surface it is painted on.

3. Painters striving for universality of expression have always simplified forms. The simpler the form, the more nearly it is universal. Hence the simplest form of all, the rectangle, must constitute the sole form if painting is to achieve universality.

4. The purer the color, the more it is appropriate to this universality. The only pure colors are the primary ones, which cannot be mixed from other colors but exist in themselves: red, yellow, and blue. Hence they alone may be used, each pure in itself.

These premises and conclusions are simple enough, but their application was not a simple process because it was subject to a universal variable:

Regarding the mechanical look of his painting, Mondrian wrote that "for the modern mentality, a work which has the appearance of a machine or a technical product" is most effective. But the artist is not a mechanic and hence his creations may not be "calculated." The artist is " a living machine capable of realizing in a pure manner the essence of art." Thus the artistic content of one of Mondrian's compositions still depends on the same qualities that have determined the artistic content of all the great works of the past—from the cave paintings on through to those of Mondrian himself—which is, simply, the artist's sensitivity to the rightness of the lines, the forms defined by those lines, and the colors of those forms, in his composition. The difference would be that until Mondrian this rightness could not exist in its purity. It was contaminated by its subservience to representation. With Mondrian this rightness can exist, at last, unsullied. Such is the theory.

Thus Mondrian is like a poet who examines *The Iliad* and *The Odyssey* and finds them powerful and wonderful but formless; who reads, let us say, a long lyric of Shelley's and finds it melodious but scattered; who discovers a sonnet by Shakespeare where the poet is forced into a rigid scheme of rhyme and meter into which he must order his expression. Here our poet-Mondrian begins to discover what he is hunting. It seems to him that within the limitations of the sonnet form Shakespeare has said as much as some writers might say in a novel, and that in the sonnet, expression benefits from compression. Our poet-Mondrian then examines the most rigid, the most arbitrary, the most demanding verse forms and, still finding them too elastic, invents a new one imposing further limitations within which he must constrict what he wants to say. Finally he goes a step further: he rejects words—just as the painter-Mondrian rejects images—and reduces his verse not only to sounds but to the half dozen sounds which he decides are the absolutely basic, the absolutely pure, the absolutely fundamental ones formed by the human voice. He then writes a poem of pure sound and pure form, freed at last from service to any other values.

If the parallel sounds too extreme, perhaps it is only because such a theory has not been applied to the art of writing. Mondrian's compositions were—and are—just as extreme in their elimination of all motif and all associative values.

Granting that Mondrian's theory is valid and that his sensitivity as an artist is adequate to apply the theory successfully, does he reach the perfection that should thus be possible? If so, then to shift a line in *Rhythm in Straight Lines* should be to throw the rhythm out of kilter, out of dynamic balance. (For Mondrian insists that the balance is dynamic; a static one would involve nothing more complicated than a generally symmetrical arrangement.) Or the yellow filling two rectangles in *Composition with Yellow* could not be changed to red or blue, and could not be shifted elsewhere in the composition, without making some other changes to bring the arrangement back into balance. And so on. While tests of this kind push the idea to the limits of absurdity, the test is implicit in the theory, and can be applied as legitimately to a Mondrian as to Seurat's *La Grande Jatte* [399], which is composed from a similar point of view except that its elements are "impure" in shape and color, subservient as they are to images of the real world no matter how conventionalized these images are. By Mondrian's standards *La Grande Jatte*, for all its impeccable order and for all its departures from visual fact, is a compromise between abstraction and photography. This compromise he refuses to make. But toward the end of his life he relented enough to introduce a few modified colors in his rectangles, and to incorporate extraneous ideas, if never images. His *Broadway Boogie Woogie* [619] accepts a subject by the title he gave it. Fascinated by the rhythms of American life when he established residence in New York, he peppered his rectangles with little cubes of dancing colors interspersed with heavier blocky forms. The parallel to the jazz music form called boogie woogie is quite direct—a lively repetitious bass pattern establishes a firm skeleton for an over-

618. MONDRIAN: *Rhythm in Straight Lines*, 1942. 28¼ x 27". Collection Mr. and Mrs. Henry Clifford, Radnor, Pa.

619. MONDRIAN: *Broadway Boogie Woogie*, 1942–43. 50 x 50". Museum of Modern Art, New York.

620. MONDRIAN: *Composition No. 10, Plus and Minus*, 1915. 33½ x 42½". Rijksmuseum Kröller-Müller, Otterlo.

621. MONDRIAN: *Horizontal Tree*, 1911. 29⅝ x 43⅞". Munson-Williams-Proctor Institute, Utica, N.Y.

lay of improvisations in sharp chords and trills. Mondrian stated the parallel by describing boogie woogie as a "destruction of melody" corresponding to his "rejection of natural aspect."

The difference between *Broadway Boogie Woogie* and other Mondrians of the same general type is apparent even to the novice on first introduction. But on closer acquaintance, even Mondrian's other apparently repetitious compositions are divisible into periods where he works at different problems. Dissatisfied because a group of compositions are "too restless" or "too static" or unsatisfactory to him in some other way, he may use more or fewer or heavier or lighter lines, more or fewer colored rectangles, sometimes no color at all. Admitting that this is variation within an extremely narrow range, the variation is still there and offers rewards of a special nature to anyone whose interest extends far enough into the problem of aesthetic disciplines. *Composition with Yellow* is a lighter, more delicate arrangement than *Rhythm in Straight Lines; Rhythm in Straight Lines* is bolder, more insistent, than *Composition with Yellow*.

In less rigidly geometrical works than rectangular patterns like these, Mondrian may be a semicubist whose connection to nature, even if several times removed, is still apparent. And if the pattern of leafless branches of the trees in *Landscape with Farmhouse* is compared with *Composition No. 10, Plus and Minus* [620] an ultimate connection with nature is apparent, especially when one of his many abstract tree studies [621] is interposed between them as an intermediate step. *Plus and Minus* is not a doodle, but the final resolution of a problem that began with a fairly realistic image.

Mondrian's goal was the classical one: perfection within imposed limitations. The danger he ran, even at best, was toward chilliness and sterility. The same goal and the same dangers have always been involved in the classical tradition; they affected David. The difference with Mondrian is that the limitations on ancient classical and nineteenth-century neo-classical artists were merely demanding, while those on Mondrian were excruciating. Whether these limitations were so extreme that they precluded the possibility of Mondrian's ever being anything more than a phenomenon fascinating to students and specialists, is a question that cannot be answered at such close range. But in the meanwhile, at mid-century, Mondrian appears to have reached the nonobjective conclusion implied by the abstract elements (but *only* the abstract elements) of a classical tradition that includes Poussin, David, Cézanne, and elements of cubism.

Mondrian was virtually a one-man school, although the painter Theo Van Doesburg (1883–1931) was associated with him for a while after 1916. Van Doesburg later made his own departure from neo-plasticism in a variation he called "elementarism." Neo-plasticism was intimately connected with the development of contemporary architectural style, and has influenced furniture design, typography, and for that matter all the decorative arts. Sporadically between 1917 and 1928 the painters, architects, designers, and theorizers connected with it published a magazine, *De Stijl*, which disseminated the ideas of the group. Their ideas were incorporated into the "international style" in architecture, which also has its affiliations with expressionism and cubism, as we will see a little further along in this book.

Other Abstract and Nonobjective Isms

In 1918, a year after the founding of *De Stijl*, and the same year as the supremacist climax in *White on White*, two architect-painter-theorist-writers named Amédée Ozenfant (1886–1966) and Charles-Édouard Jeanneret, who took the name of Le Corbusier (1887–1965), added a third variation to the investigation of geometrical abstract art, calling it *purism*. Cubism, they decided, had sold itself out to pretty invention, had degenerated into ornamental caprice, and needed purifying. They published a manifesto called *Après le Cubisme* to launch their reform, proposing an art of rigidly disciplined abstraction. Retaining the cubist idea of simultaneity but rejecting the gaiety of synthetic cubism, they returned to the hard, sharp character of analytical cubism. Above all, the forms of purism were to be of a mechanical clarity that would symbolize the twentieth century as the age of the machine. Léger, of course, held this same theory, but he applied it with a great deal of bounce in his

622. Le Corbusier: *Still-life*, 1920. 31⅞ x 39¼". Museum of Modern Art, New York.

623. Nicholson: *Relief*, 1939. Wood, painted, 32⅞ x 45". Museum of Modern Art, New York, Gift of H. S. Ede and the artist (by exchange).

brightly colored mechanistic conventionalizations. So did the futurists, but we have seen what happened to them. The forms of purism were austere, dry, and often all but devoid of color [622]. In itself purism never managed to strike very deep roots, but it

624. MORANDI: *Still-life*, 1948. 16 x 16". Collection Mr. and Mrs. Leo Lionni, Greenwich, Conn.

625. LE CORBUSIER: Savoye House, 1929–31. Poissy, France.

in the infinitely overlapping variations of contemporary painting, both Mondrian and purism may have left their mark on the reserved and pensive art of the Italian Giorgio Morandi (1890–1964), although the objects he adjusts into abstract relationships—a few ordinary bottles and bowls [624], combined and recombined in picture after picture, yet without monotony—retain their concrete reality.*

But if purism itself failed to develop significantly in painting, the cleanness of its forms and their adaptability to the design and manufacture of machine-tooled usable objects had a wide and truly "purifying" effect on industrial design. And as an architect Le Corbusier became one of the half dozen most influential men of the first part of the century, a leader in the theory and practice of design in the international style. His Savoye House [625] has become a standard example of the declaration of revolution in domestic architecture, not because it remains the most beautiful or the most livable modern residence—it is far from either—but because it was a progenitor of hundreds of designs that have adapted and developed its innovations with others in the sifting process that has created a new style. As an architectural analogy to purist theories of painting, the Savoye House is an abstract design of integrated flat and curved planes, of enclosed space and open space, defined in sharp clean lines. In a photograph, where a single static point of view is imposed, the Savoye House looks more severe than it does in three dimensions, when its elements are seen in shifting combinations from different angles. In regarding the house thus, as a composition of volumes, lines, and planes, we are regarding it less as architecture than as a piece of abstract sculpture on a large scale, and as such it is a more satisfying example of the theories of purism than were purist

contributed to the development of numerous artists, for instance the leader of abstract painting in England, Ben Nicholson (1894–   ), who has combined its principles with those of cubism and *De Stijl* in an art of great tact and distinction [623]. And

---

* Two Americans, Charles Demuth (1883–1935) and Charles Sheeler (1883–   ), worked out a compromise between cubism and straightforward representation, often called cubist-realism, in which architectural or natural forms are geometrized with a nice precision which would justify their being included within the general area of purism.

paintings. The purist theories seemed to demand a physical third dimension for completion; the yearning for pure forms that led to the formation of purist theory also led to an expression in sculpture, that of Constantin Brancusi (1876–1957).

Brancusi's *Bird in Space* [626] is known everywhere, partly because one of the sculptor's many versions of this elongated form became conspicuous as the center of a dispute between the United States Customs, who wanted to tax it as bric-a-brac, and its owner, who wanted it to enter the country duty-free as a work of art—more as a matter of principle than because of the tax involved. The contest, with its decision in favor of the owner, was an introduction to the theory of abstract art for many people who would never have picked up a book on aesthetics but who did read newspaper excerpts from the testimony of artists and aestheticians who defended Brancusi's beautifully tooled brass object.

As a work of art, *Bird in Space* is at least a highly ornamental form, but this is true, also, of fine bric-a-brac. As sculpture, it is an invented shape of great purity and a certain expressive quality depending heavily upon our knowledge of the title. Many of Brancusi's works depend, for their full effect, upon the associations of a verbal clue (*White Negress, Chimera, The Newborn, The Prodigal Son, The Fish, Bird, Penguins,* to name a few). But his *Sculpture for the Blind* [627] is an exercise in pure sculptural form. By its title, this is a piece of sculpture to be handled, to be felt for its polished surface and the infinitely subtle variations of its generally egg-shaped volume. As a piece of sculpture for the sighted, *Sculpture for the Blind*, like most of Brancusi's work, would be seen ideally as it revolved slowly, so that its contours, as defined by their edges and by the areas of shadow, light, and reflections, would reveal themselves in an uninterrupted flow. (Even more ideally, it might be seen miraculously suspended in space, turning now in one direction, now in another.)

Like his contemporaries among painters, Brancusi was also influenced by the powerful simplified forms of primitive sculpture, especially in early work. *The Kiss* [628] is

626. BRANCUSI: *Bird in Space*, 1925. Polished bronze, height 49¾". Philadelphia Museum of Art, Arensberg Collection.

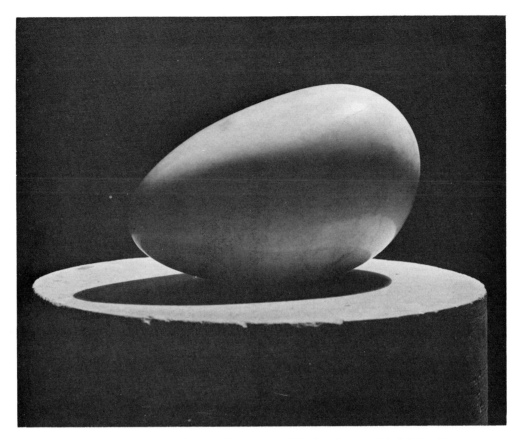

627. BRANCUSI: *Sculpture for the Blind,* 1924. Marble, height 6″. Philadelphia Museum of Art, Arensberg Collection.

628. BRANCUSI: *The Kiss,* 1908. Limestone, height 23″. Philadelphia Museum of Art, Arensberg Collection.

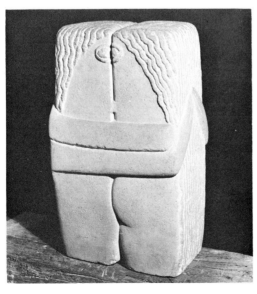

an example. Its broad heavy forms are appropriate to the grainy limestone in which it is carved, just as the polished surfaces of *Sculpture for the Blind* are appropriate to marble, and the gleaming elongations of *Bird in Space* to brass. This love of the sculptor's materials for their own sake, the adaptation of form to the expression of the materials' inherent character, is a constant in Brancusi's work—or almost a constant. A failure is a marble version of *Bird in Space,* called *Yellow Bird,* where the veined and brittle stone has been forced into a form of such character that the weight of the upper mass is too much for the narrow necklike lowest part. In marble the design has the practical failing that the neck has cracked; the psychological failing is more important, leaving us as it does with an uncomfortable feeling of violation of the material.

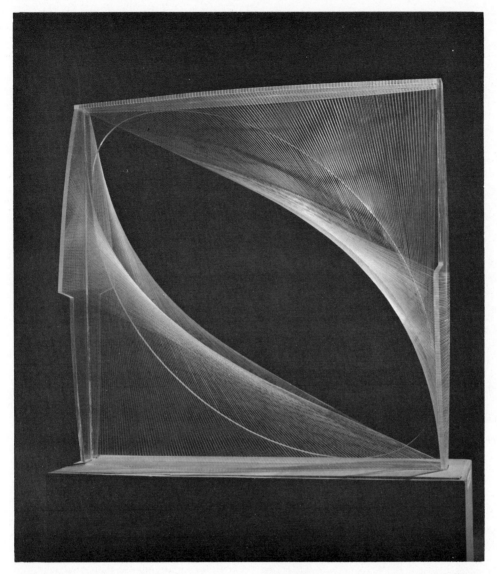

629. GABO: *Linear Construction,* 1942–43. Plastic with nylon string, height 24¼″. Phillips Collection, Washington, D.C.

Whatever else they are, Brancusi's forms are solid masses, self-contained volumes of matter. This remark may seem too obvious to be worth setting down. It would be, if it were not necessary as an introduction to the concept of form introduced in constructivism, a movement born at about the same time as neo-plasticism and purism. Constructivism was a Russian development led by Vladimir Tatlin (1885–   ), finding its major spokesmen in the brothers

Naum Gabo (1890–   ) and Antoine Pevsner (1886–1962), who brought it into the international orbit via Paris and Germany.

A first principle of constructivism was that it denied solid volumes (like Brancusi's) as an expression of space. Gabo's *Linear Construction* [629] had better be looked at for a moment before this idea is tackled by anyone not yet a little familiar with it. *Linear Construction* is built of

630. Moore: *Reclining Figure*, 1935. Elm wood, height 19″. Albright Art Gallery, Buffalo, Contemporary Art Collection.

transparent plastic. It is a piece of abstract sculpture, if you wish—more properly, however, a construction, just as it is called—which denies sculptural mass by its open design as well as by its transparent material. We have said that ideally Brancusi's *Sculpture for the Blind* would be seen in motion, so that its total mass could be examined in a flow of successive aspects. But Gabo's *Linear Construction* has no mass* and is, in effect, visible from all points of view at once. True, the object takes on variations—and fascinating ones—from different angles, but essentially it is visible as a whole, in all its complications, from any angle.

A little thought on the theories of analytical cubism will show that constructivism overlaps it. Cubist simultaneity sought to represent many aspects of the object at one time. *Linear Construction* actually does so. The "object" is not an object at all, in the

_____
* —unless one wants to be finicky about definitions. The transparent plastic has mass, strictly speaking, but psychologically it does not.

sense of being a tangible form. It is a spatial design. One enters the spatial shapes, visually; if this is sculpture, it is a molding of pure space. "Volume" and "space" now take on new meanings. Volume is no longer mass surrounded by empty space; space is no longer emptiness; space and volume are identical.

The space volumes of *Linear Construction* are arbitrary inventions by an artist, but they had a parallel in nineteenth century models rigged of string and thin metal or wood supports, which were used to demonstrate interlockings of forms in solid geometry, just as Gabo's plastic cords and plastic supports create space by defining it. The idea of space as volume instead of space as emptiness is applied in a different way by the English sculptor, Henry Moore (1898–   ), who finds his point of departure not in the man-made abstractions of geometry but in the forms of nature created by the growth of things and by the action of the elements.

Moore's hollowed-out forms [630, 631] require a new way of seeing sculpture.

To understand them, the idea of sculpture as the shaping of solid masses must be abandoned. Moore is shaping mass, but simultaneously he is shaping voids, which are equally important as design. In other words, the "hollows" and "holes" are "negative volumes" just as the masses are "positive volumes." Structurally, Moore's sculpture creates interdependencies between solids and voids. In nature, similar "negative volumes" may be of extraordinary interest. The hollow in a tree trunk or the pits and underledges and sinkholes shaped by water in river beds or even the vortex in a whirlpool of water—all these are natural voids of whose shapes we are as conscious as we are of the solids surrounding them. In Moore's sculpture there is always a strong suggestion of natural forces. Where Brancusi takes stone and carves and polishes it to emphasize its inherent characteristics as a particular kind of solid matter, Moore oftener seems to be creating the stone itself, or the wood, or the bronze, in which his sculpture exists. His figures combine a hieratic severity with a feeling of natural growth, the genesis of life within inanimate materials. Inside a house or in a museum, Moore's sculpture may be reduced to an effective demonstration of a theory or to a piece of brilliant but eccentric design. Out of doors, where it properly belongs, it shares the serene and powerful unity of trees and rocks and air, which live, and change, in nature.

Such considerations of immediately contemporary sculpture reflect new importance on the sculpture of futurism, which preceded these examples by a generation. Boccioni's *Development of a Bottle in Space* [632] might be dismissed as a tour-de-force experiment in the materialization of the painted forms of futurism and cubism, until we see its sculptured space as an ancestor of Moore's in *Internal and External Forms*. Boccioni's bottle with its hollow core is half readymade for an analysis of "negative volumes" but the idea of spatial growth, of space turned and shaped, of voids interlocking, is present even so.

It might be argued that the idea of space as volume, inherent in these several examples of sculpture, is specious because a

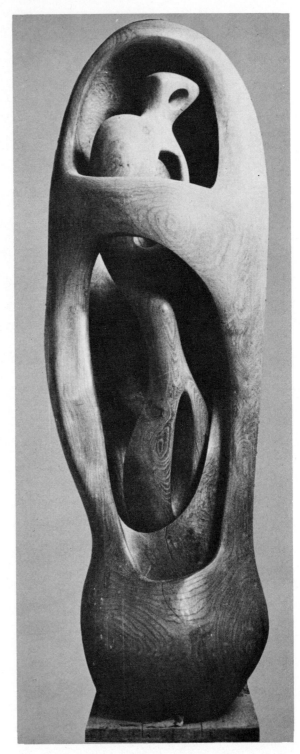

631. MOORE: *Internal and External Forms*, 1953–54. Elm wood, height 103″. Albright Art Gallery, Buffalo.

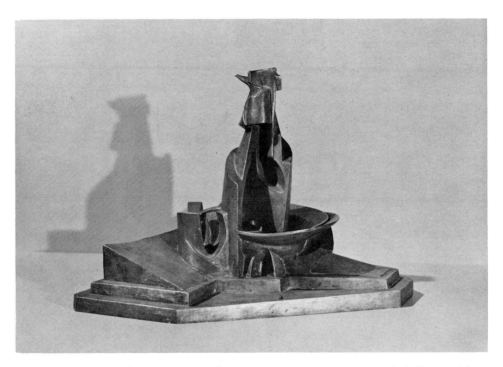

632. BOCCIONI: *Development of a Bottle in Space*, 1913. Bronze, 15 x 24″. Collection Mr. and Mrs. Harry Lewis Winston, Birmingham, Mich.

633. CALDER: *Horizontal Spines*, 1942. Steel and aluminum, height 53″. Addison Gallery of American Art, Andover, Mass.

sculptor cannot construct solid forms without constructing, by inference, corresponding voids. But the argument does not hold Brancusi's sculpture denies it. Space is only shapeless emptiness in which the solid of *Sculpture for the Blind* exists, but space lives and moves in *Internal and External Forms* just as truly as do the forms themselves. The idea of spatial movement has been given a specialized expression in the "mobile," which may be defined as a contrivance related to sculpture and composed of objects of various shapes suspended on jointed limbs in such a way that the component parts move, physically, into a variety of changing relationships when placed in a current of air. Invented by Alexander Calder (1898–), in whose hands they are never less than ingenious [633], and efficiently imitated by certain other craftsmen, mobiles are also widely prostituted as gadgets. As sculpture, the mobile is most closely related to the theories of constructivism, differing from *Linear Construction* in that it assumes a sequence of identities in space rather than revealing its total identity at one time.

CHAPTER 14

Reactions against Abstraction

The Mexican Renaissance

A rejection of abstract painting took place at about the same time in Europe and in America, but for different reasons. We are not talking here about painters who rejected abstraction on sight, but about men who examined it, even worked in it for a while, found it unsuited to what they wanted to say, and abandoned it. On both continents, anti-abstract schools flourished during the 1920's and the 1930's, while nonobjective painters were thinking their way to the logical conclusions of abstract art. In Europe the reaction took the form of extremest fantasy; on the American continent it took the opposite form of didactic social statement in the service of national or regional loyalties, first in Mexico and then in the United States.

Between 1907 and 1921, a young Mexican named Diego Rivera (1886–1957) was traveling in Europe and working in Spain and Paris. On a trip home in 1910 he held an exhibition of the painting he had done in Europe up until that time: it was a terrible group of pictures, heavy, labored, artificial, forced. But all the pictures sold because Rivera was a young man of good position, and the social patronage of the exhibition made it an event of some importance during the season.

Whatever the purchasers thought of the pictures, Rivera did not like them very much. Before going to Europe he had been trained and stimulated by three important teachers: one of them was a student of Ingres, named Reboul, who taught in the academic school in Mexico City. From him Rivera, only fourteen, had learned the exquisite draughtsmanship of the French clas-

634. RIVERA: *Head of a Woman*, 1917. Pencil, 12¼ x 9⅜". Collection Carl Zigrosser, Germantown, Pa.

635. POSADA: *Calvera Huertista*, 1913. Zinc engraving, 8½ x 8½". Collection Carl Zigrosser, Germantown, Pa.

sical tradition, which remained apparent on the surface of his early drawings [634] and, much later, continued as a basis for the control and precision of his definition of form in a more personal style. His other two masters were masters at secondhand. One of them was a popular engraver named José Guadalupe Posada (1852–1913), who was not taken too seriously as an artist at that time, when a certain stigma was attached to natively Mexican art; Posada has been recognized since as one of the powerful creative imaginations of his country. He combined macabre fantasy, passionate religious and sociological statement, and a kind of raucous wit in designs of great vitality [635]. He also kept a shop near the school Rivera attended, and the boy saw engravings of the old masters there, and Posada talked to him about them. The third teacher was the art of the ancient Mexican civilizations [636].

But Rivera's exhibition upon his return from his first trip to Europe showed none of these influences. It was sterile and derivative of poorly assimilated European models. Nevertheless he returned to Europe, where he stayed until 1921, floundering. Toward the end he discovered cubism, and he worked in it with a sharp, dry, pointless efficiency; he had some contact with Picasso, Derain, and Braque. Before he returned to Mexico again, however, he made a trip to Italy. Here he found a fourth teacher, the great frescoes of the Italian Renaissance. They acted as a catalyst, and after years of groping Rivera created, upon his return to Mexico, a nationalistic style virtually overnight. In the next ten years he covered wall after wall with frescoes that established an internationally recognized school of Mexican painting.

Nationalism of any kind in painting was unusual at that time, but Mexico was an unusual country. (The German expressionists had made an effort to revivify Germanic traditions, but these were cultural and expressive ones only.) Rivera conceived of a national art that would revive the cultural traditions native to Mexico and at the same time propagandize the new Mexican political regime. After years of inconsequential association with intellectual painters who worked on esoteric principles for the most cultivated audience, Rivera now about-faced and painted expository lessons in history and sociology for a people who, in the mass, were just emerging from illiteracy. In Mexico, the artist now became a cog in the social machine; he allied himself with his nation's welfare and made his contribution to it as a man working in the world, not as a rare and special individual in an ivory tower. With a new sense of social dedication, painters worked more in the capacity of civil servants than as individuals struggling for personal expression and recognition. Rivera and the other painters who were involved in this Mexican renaissance formed what amounted to a craftsmen's union.

Mexico was still assimilating the agrarian revolution that had dispossessed the corrupt landlords who had held the peons in feudal serfdom. The murals which now began to spread over the walls of public buildings were vividly decorative but they were also didactic, telling the story of the revolution, glorifying native traditions and festivals and legends, and excoriating the enemies of the people. The American financiers who profited from Mexico's natural resources, and the Mexican *bourgeoisie* who had tolerated their doing so were attacked in terms as obvious as comic strips, sometimes almost as exaggerated, but always with the most vehement conviction that Mexico must realize itself as a nation belonging to its people, and as a culture unique among the countries of the world. When the Mexican muralists of the 1920's descended to the most blatant propaganda and the rawest caricature, as they did again and again in intervals between lofty conceptions, it was because they were more interested in communicating with the proletariat than with aestheticians or political philosophers.

The Liberation of the Peon [637] is one of Rivera's finest compositions and his summary of the ideal of the agrarian revolution. It shows a landlord's hacienda burning in the distance while a group of revolutionary soldiers cut the peon's bonds and cover his naked body, scarred by the lash. It is a picture explicit enough for any illiterate

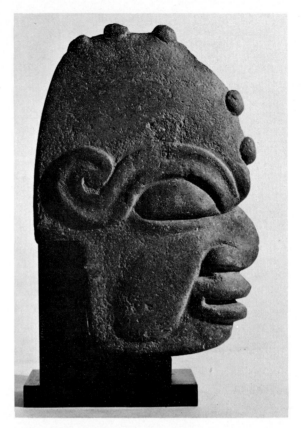

636. EAST COAST, MEXICO: *Head* (hatchet form), late Pre-Columbian. Green igneous rock, height 12″. Philadelphia Museum of Art, Arensberg Collection.

Mexican to understand as a story and as a national ideal. It is also a pictorial composition of considerable sophistication; this is the double character of Rivera's art. Technically, the painting is a pure example of *buon fresco*, or true fresco, in the great Italian tradition by which unbound pigments are painted directly onto the moist fresh plaster of a wall.* As the plaster dries,

---

* Unbound pigments are pure pigments without the "binder" of oil, glue, or other adhesive that turns them into paint. Pigments "bound" with oil become oil paint; pigments "bound" with an adhesive soluble in water become watercolor; those with any one of several albuminous substances are tempera, and so on. The fresco illustrated here was done on plaster held within a strong metal frame, rather than directly on a plastered wall as is customary, in order that this variation on one of Rivera's finest subjects could be exhibited in the United States.

637. RIVERA: *The Liberation of the Peon*, 1931. Fresco, variation of fresco in Ministry of Education, 1923–27, Mexico City. 74 x 95″. Philadelphia Museum of Art, Gift of Mr. and Mrs. Herbert C. Morris.

the pigments, incorporated into it, take on a soft grainy brilliance, combined as they are with the crystalline film that forms on the plaster's surface. True fresco is one of the oldest, the noblest, and one of the most demanding, of techniques.

Rivera's first murals under the new program were executed in encaustic, a form of painting in hot wax. In beginning his second series he experimented with the juice of the native agave plant as a binder—an idea with obvious attractions to a new nationalistic school, especially since the medium was the traditional one of pre-Columbian Mexican painting. The experiments were not successful; spots and discolorations developed, and Rivera adopted the *buon fresco* of the Italian masters he had

admired on the trip just before his return. In reviving fresco, Rivera completed the separation of painting from the studio, the dealer's gallery, and the limited audience. He re-established art as a part of the life of the people in a way that had had no parallel since the medieval cathedrals and the Renaissance churches had told the story of the Bible in sculpture, stained glass, and fresco, where everyone could read them. The buildings he decorated included the Ministry of Education, the Governor's Palace at Cuernavaca, the chapel of the Agricultural School at Chapingo [638], and, later, the Lerma Waterworks and the University and Social Security Hospital.

Rivera always tried to combine his contemporary social and political message with

638. RIVERA: *The Blood of Martyrs Enriches the Earth*, 1926–27. Fresco from Chapel of National Agricultural School, Chapingo, length approximately 160″.

639. RIVERA: *Sugar Cane*, 1931. Fresco, variation of fresco in the Palace of Cortez, Cuernavaca, 1930, 58 x 95″. Philadelphia Museum of Art, Gift of Mr. and Mrs. Herbert C. Morris.

640. South wall of court of Detroit Institute of Arts, with frescoes by Rivera, 1932–33. *Top:* two races of the continent (white and Oriental); *immediately below:* raw materials (lime and sand); *main panel:* assembly of an automobile.

another message to the Mexican people, glorifying whatever native racial and cultural roots survived the Spanish conquest, combining the story of Mexican history with illustrations of Aztec legends and of Mexican festivals and folk customs descended from the lost past. The noble figures in his murals, who may be historical or legendary characters or gods of the native earth, are likely to be painted as ethnologically pure Indian types, while his villains, if they are not North Americans, are usually Spanish ones. The Spanish-Indian hybrid we think of as the typical Mexican may serve in either capacity, but is most likely to turn up as a corrupt or stuffy little man. Rivera himself was one quarter Tarascan Indian, with a mixture of Russian, Spanish, and Portuguese Jewish ancestors making up the balance.

A first-rate mural painter is necessarily a decorator, no matter what else he may more

significantly be. In *The Liberation of the Peon* the conventionalized forms of the cartridge belts, the rope around the neck of the horse to the left, and other such decorative details are almost conspicuous enough to distract attention from subject and decrease its impact. In later work Rivera depended more and more on the decorative elements of the style he had developed, and less and less on saying very much with it as the fruits of the agrarian revolution were either harvested or irretrievably lost. Even in the early *Sugar Cane* [639] we are impressed first with the attractiveness of the picture as decoration, and have to look a second time to read its message. An anemic Nordic landowner lounges in a hammock while a sharp-featured overseer with a whip supervises some presumably oppressed but actually quite happy and healthy looking Indians who are harvesting as laborers on land, which, we presume, should belong to them. But the sociological message must be deciphered; it does not reach us at firsthand, as it does in *The Liberation of the Peon.* Eventually Rivera began repeating himself as a decorator with an effective formula.

After Rivera had established himself as an artist of major importance he was invited to the United States where he did frescoes in San Francisco, Detroit, and New York. He had never been in the United States except to pass through, and now he was impressed, as foreigners always are, with the briskness and mechanization of American life. In Detroit he adopted a mechanistic style and covered the walls of a classical court in the Detroit Institute of Arts [640] with clashing symbols of the city's industrial life. But the murals occupy the walls like a temporary exhibition which there was not quite room enough to hang, and although they are by a contemporary painter and a native of the American continent, they are less at home than are the collections of old masters and the fragments of ancient civilizations in the rooms near by. Rivera's dry and labored representation of an automobile assembly line is much less than second best to the precision and excitement and color of an assembly line itself; the mechanistic idea is not transmuted into terms that enlarge or clarify its meaning. The effort to give wide significance to the murals by such inclusions as symbols of the four races of man making up our population, and of the minerals mined and used in industry, makes an admirable outline of a project. Yet the scheme, completed, remains an outline, conscientiously worked out. The failure of the Detroit murals demonstrated, at least, the validity of the idea behind the Mexican renaissance —that art should be an integral part of the life of its country, created by artists identified with the roots of native culture.

Rivera's New York murals met with disaster of another kind. They were destroyed after he refused to make changes that would have eliminated references to communism which were unacceptable to his capitalist sponsors. (The murals were for Rockefeller Center, in New York.) The incident became a celebrated one in which the paint-

641. OROZCO: *Barricade,* 1931. 55 x 45″. Museum of Modern Art, New York.

er's right to paint what he pleased was defended as a kind of freedom of speech. However, the sponsors' legal right to destroy the works could not be questioned, whatever moral rights and wrongs were involved, and destroyed they were.

Rivera's position as the leader of the Mexican renaissance was weakened as his work grew more superficial and that of one of his fellows, José Clemente Orozco (1883–1949), matured. While Rivera was in Paris, Orozco was in Mexico doing genre scenes with a strong revolutionary flavor, involving the sordid and brutal lives imposed on common people, especially the Indians. In the first efflorescence of nationalistic murals, Orozco made a brief effort to impose Italian Renaissance forms on his style, but his native violence kept breaking through. Finally he ceased being a

642. OROZCO: *Gods of the Modern World*, 1932–34. Detail, 126 x 176″, of fresco at Dartmouth College, Hanover, N. H.

mural painter in the sense of a decorator of walls, and became a sociological expressionist who used walls to carry his message, even at the expense of violating the character of walls and the interior enclosed.

Orozco plays on the double theme of the ominousness of humanity as a dangerous mass, capable of the vilest cruelties, and the suffering of human beings as individuals. He sees humanity as at once the victim and its own victimizer, and he presents the idea in stretched, starved, and tortured forms [641]. Fantastic and grotesque figures play through his work; these are part of Orozco's native heritage from the Mexican past, from Aztec religious practices and legends that have survived in popular Mexican celebrations, as well as in some of the morbidities of Spanish customs that have fused with them. Skeletons, monsters, beasts, the whole range of the terrifying and the macabre, are inherent in Mexican folk tradition and are incorporated into its

humor and the revelry of its festivals as well as the depths of Mexican consciousness. The work of Posada [635] was a spontaneous expression of this tradition, and influenced Orozco strongly.

For Orozco, macabre fantasy was a symbol of the darkness of the human spirit, sometimes savage, sometimes blinded by prejudice or apathy, as in the scene of a skeleton giving birth [642] to another skeleton while skeleton attendants in academic robes stand by. This symbol of the sterility of academic learning cloistered from contact with life was painted for Dartmouth College as one panel in a series of overpowering murals not always flattering to the United States or to higher education, but undeniably among Orozco's finest work. Unlike Rivera, Orozco made no effort to modify his style when he was invited to the United States. Students who met him during his visit remember a man much less violent than the Dartmouth murals—a

643. Orozco: *Cortez and the Cross, and the Machine*, 1932–34. Fresco, 126 x 288″.
Dartmouth College, Hanover, N. H.

lively, genial, stocky little man wearing
glasses with enormously thick lenses, eager
to share his ideas and to understand the
people around him. Orozco's other murals
in the United States are at Pomona College,
California, and the New School, New York
City. Before these, in Mexico, he did murals
in the National Preparatory School, the
House of Tiles, and the Industrial School
at Orizaba; after his return to Mexico he
did others—and his most violent ones—in
the Palace of Fine Arts, the Governor's
Palace, and the Orphanage at Guadalajara.

In the last years of his life Orozco
adopted a machinistic and abstract style,
already prophesied in the right half of one
of the Dartmouth murals [643]. He explained that in machine forms his theme
was the same as the one that runs through
all his work—protest against oppression.
The oppression in the late works is the
oppression of the machine, sometimes the
machine as an instrument of destruction,
especially the machines of war. But these
experiments are not altogether successful;
Orozco seems to have been too intensely
human a man to have dealt successfully
with the impersonality of the machine, even
when he interpreted it as a menace to the
humanity with which he was so closely
allied.

Mexico: The Second Generation

Rivera and Orozco are one generation of
painters; they were nearing forty when the
mural program got under way. At this time
David Alfaro Siqueiros (1898–   ) and
Rufino Tamayo (1899–   ) were in their
middle twenties. Siqueiros had fought in
the revolution in his teens and he worked
with the older men in the mural program,
but in his development as a painter thereafter he was increasingly theoretical. Where
Orozco was a bridge between the old Mexico and the new, Siqueiros is part of modern Mexico as a nation with international
ties and an eye to the future, in terms of
trade unionism and industrial development
rather than the eruptive force of revolution.

Siqueiros studied in Europe for two
years, but his interest there was in discovering the means to express the potential vitality of his country in surging, heroic forms.
He returned just as the national mural program was getting under way and did his
first mural in the National Preparatory
School. He also led in the organization of
the Syndicate of Technical Workers, Painters, and Sculptors that gave definition to
the Mexican renaissance as part of the social fabric, and since then he has been
equally active as a social organizer (an ac-

644. SIQUEIROS: *War*, 1939. Duco on two panels, 48½ x 63½". Philadelphia Museum of Art, Gift of Ines Amor.

tivity that has resulted in several imprisonments) and as an artist. A man with a practical turn of mind, he has developed the use of modern materials, for instance pyroxylin and Duco for outdoor murals. *War* [644], though an easel study, is in the latter medium. It is a good example of the gigantic swelling forms, surging in and out of space, that evolved as his heroic style.

Tamayo represents the absorption of the Mexican tradition into the mainstream of contemporary painting. The cubist and fauvist principles in *Women of Tehuantepec* [645] should be obvious to the reader

by now. Coloristically, Tamayo is one of the most exciting of contemporary painters. He may paint an entire canvas in reds; his combinations of magentas, blues, oranges, lemons, pearl whites, mauves, lilacs, purples, crimsons and vermilions suggest the colors of native weaving and other crafts, colors which may be vividly ornamental or may reach a pitch of feverish intensity, especially when they are combined with subjects where the fantastic and the macabre lie threateningly beneath the surface of blazing pigments.

Yet, while Tamayo continues to use native subject matter, to incorporate echoes of pre-Columbian and popular Mexican art, he rejects the provincialism of paintings as revolutionary propaganda or history with a political or social "message." He is as closely tied to Picasso and Braque as he is to his native traditions. Thus, although he is the same age as Siqueiros, within a year, he represents the end of a tradition, the last stop on the round trip made by Mexican art in a matter of a third of a century. Before Rivera, Mexican art reflected that of Europe; Rivera rejected Europe in the 1920's and established a school of nationalistic social realism; Siqueiros accepted European isms but continued the nationalistic idea; Tamayo abandoned strong nationalism for European reference. The difference after a generation is that before 1920 the European flavor of Mexican art was European academic, while now it tastes of European modern.

645. TAMAYO: *Women of Tehuantepec,* 1939. 34 x 57". Albright Art Gallery, Buffalo, Contemporary Art Collection.

Regionalists and Social Realists

During the first years of the Mexican renaissance, the United States was engaged in the social and economic saturnalia of the 1920's, the "jazz age," which a current generation is finding rather quaint in retrospect. The country as a whole was not very art-conscious, although *Nude Descending a Staircase* was still good for a syndicated feature article from time to time, and the word *impressionistic* occurred frequently in the conversation of aspirants to culture, referring to any form of painting that was in any way puzzling. In metropolitan centers like New York, Boston, Philadelphia, and Chicago, where an artist might hope to make a living, painters fell into three general groups. There were the well-entrenched conservative men who followed such models as Chase and Sargent or branched off rashly into impressionism; there were the men who were absorbing expressionism, cubism, and fauvism—Hartley and Marin, for instance; and there was the America-first group of the Ash Can School and its descendants.

The Ash Can painters were a metropolitan group dedicated to genre subjects of city life, but by the end of the decade a post-Ash Can generation was extending its interest beyond the city limits into the American countryside, not as landscapists but as observers of people and customs. They were led there by writers like Sinclair Lewis with his *Main Street* in 1920 and Sherwood Anderson with *Winesburg, Ohio,* a year earlier, writers who had shattered the ideal concept of the United States as a country entirely dedicated to the observance of the Ten Commandments and the Boy Scout oath, and had found cruelty, injustice, stupidity, and pathological emotions existing in the hinterlands where the good, the true, and the beautiful had, by convention, been accepted as flourishing uncorrupted. There had been indications that painters were as aware as writers; as early as 1916 George Bellows produced an exceptional one, the bitter lithograph *Benediction in Georgia* [646].

In 1930 two American artists emerged who were to carry this new form of Ameri-

646. BELLOWS: *Benediction in Georgia,* 1916. Lithograph, 15 x 20". Philadelphia Museum of Art.

can consciousness into painting, first with the skeptical eye of the writers but later with a kind of defensive chauvinism for the culture of the Middle West which before long reduced their promising movement to insignificance. These painters were Thomas Hart Benton (1889–   ) and Grant Wood (1892–1942). A third was John Steuart Curry (1897–1946), who two years earlier had indicated what was about to happen with his *Baptism in Kansas* [647]. The three men and their followers came to be known as regionalists, a name in which the character and a hint of the limitations of their art is implicit.

Baptism in Kansas is a romantic genre picture, half-sociological and half-narrative; half-sympathetic to the rites pictured in it, half-uneasy about them. With a barn, a farmhouse, and a windmill in the background, a young girl with her hands clasped in ecstasy is about to be submerged in the livestock's watering trough, turned for the afternoon into a baptismal pool in the parched countryside. The neighbors who are gathered around, including other white-clad neophytes awaiting their turn, are rural types presented without idealization. Another step or two in the direction the

647. CURRY: *Baptism in Kansas*, 1928. 40 x 50″. Whitney Museum of American Art, N. Y.

picture takes to this point would have turned it into caricature. Instead, Curry painted the sky with glowing clouds and shafts of light to identify the crude ceremony with its mystical purpose. Unfortunately he also added a pair of doves circling in the radiance. These, of course, occupy the position of the dove of the Holy Spirit that hovers in radiance above the figure of Christ in pictures of the Baptism. But the introduction here of a pair of farm pigeons occupying by too-happy coincidence the space between rays of sunlight, forces the point and turns what might have been an affecting picture into a novelty, like Hamlet in modern dress, which was a popular tour de force innovated at about the same time.

Curry was born on a stock farm in Kansas and was educated at the art institutes of Kansas City and Chicago. Thereafter he made his living as an illustrator until he studied in Paris for a year. As a painter he stayed close to traditional sources; he is a descendant of Rubens and Ruisdael, appropriate ancestors for Curry's fullest expressions of the richness and sweep that he felt in the life of his native region. Of all the regionalists, Curry was the least spectacular and at first acquaintance is the least interesting. But the very eccentricities that draw first attention to Benton and Wood are also the characteristics that have come to seem so artificial that they are disharmonious to the regional idea with its rural and homely subjects. Curry may yet prove to be the tortoise who wins the race over the two local hares.

At the moment it would be difficult— probably impossible—to find a critic of established reputation who would be willing to write a really enthusiastic comment on the art of Thomas Hart Benton, although it would be easy to confront half a dozen of them with their favorable articles written some years ago. Benton became a re-

648. Benton: *Louisiana Rice Fields,* 1928. 30 x 48″. Brooklyn Museum.

gionalist by taking the long way around. He was born in Missouri, but as the son of a United States senator he spent his youth in Washington. Although he returned to the Middle West to study at the Art Institute of Chicago, he spent the five years between 1908 and 1913 in Paris, and even after his return to this country he experimented with cubism. He might have kept at it, but his painting was interrupted by a tour of duty in the Navy during World War I; thereafter he returned to the American scene, touring the country to sketch it. He came into sudden prominence in 1930 with a series of murals for the New School for Social Research in New York, followed immediately by another series for the Whitney Museum of American Art. The first murals included a few inferences that the American scene was not altogether halcyon; the second already began the jingoism that so soon infected regionalist painting. Almost any picture from that time is as good an example as the next to represent his fully developed formula, which is of an extreme repetitiousness. With Tintoretto and El Greco as his models, Benton conventionalized their mannerisms into a linear recipe for picture-making, which combined almost spastic pattern with tilted and shifting per-

spectives that remain as his only tie to cubism [648].

After skyrocketing successes in New York, Benton decided to renounce the effete East. He returned to the Middle West, but he drew no sustenance from it. Whether he was painting Kentucky hillbillies, Texas oil towns, Kansas harvesters, or genre scenes from the life of his fellow Missourians, as he did in a large set of murals for the State Capitol, he poured everything into the same mold, a mold that had the disadvantage of having no aesthetic, expressive, or traditional connection with his subjects. For a moment Benton's art seemed exciting; shortly, it became monotonous. But the flare of attention created by his first murals brought about a revival of mural painting in the United States, for Benton was the first American to take advantage of the Mexican demonstration that mural painting had not died with the Renaissance but had only been lying fallow.*

* The revival took on unexpected importance in the United States within the next few years because of an unhappy circumstance: the great economic depression of the early 1930's. The year before Benton painted his New School murals, the stock market had crashed, and within the next few years the nation suffered

649. WOOD: *American Gothic*, 1930. 29⅞ x 24⅞". Art Institute of Chicago.

650. DIX: *Dr. Mayer-Hermann*, 1926. Panel, 58¾ x 39". Museum of Modern Art, New York.

The third member in the trio of regionalist leaders was Grant Wood of Iowa, whose *American Gothic* [649] won a national award in 1930, the year of Benton's New School murals. *American Gothic* was an immediately attractive picture, and still is, to a large public that had learned to be suspicious of realistic academic painting but was fatigued by the effort to understand what the new European isms were all about. The impeccable surface was a relief to people who yearned for conventional craftsmanship in painting, and at the same time the picture was original in its piquant use of such commonplace things as gingham, rickrack braid, a pitchfork, and jigsaw carpentry as ornamental figures in a work of art. And it explored the new subject matter of rural America, not unflatteringly enough to give offense but with enough

one of the most painfully chastening experiences in its history. At the nadir of the depression, Franklin D. Roosevelt initiated the public works programs that gave employment to thousands of people in—usually—useful capacities. The inclusion of the arts program with the more practical ones of road-building and other public construction was epoch-making in a country where official art patronage on a significant scale was unheard of. The nation's schools, postoffices, and courthouses were suddenly covered with murals celebrating American history and local customs, influenced by the Mexicans on one hand and by the re- gionalists on the other. They were executed by artists ranging from students and incompetents up to artists of deserved national reputation, and they varied from excellent to daubs that have since been taken down or painted out and can be remembered only with pain. On the whole, the art program was of tremendous benefit. Aside from supplying artists with money for food—an important consideration at the time but not the most important one in the long run—it gave the painter a new professional respectability with the mass of the American public, and even gave the painter himself a new kind of self-respect as a workman.

acidity to satisfy the new self-critical consciousness stimulated by *Main Street* and its successors, since the farmer and his wife are represented as severe and narrow people. Grant Wood became a celebrity overnight (even his name was in his favor, full of sturdy connotations, exactly the name that should have been invented for the man who painted his pictures), and each new work appeared everywhere, in popular magazines as well as in the art journals. Both Wood and Benton were as widely and as favorably publicized as any American artists who have ever worked. They received a wonderful press during the 1930's.

Wood also had his European precedents, but they were more adaptable to domestication than Benton's were. Late expressionism, *Die Neue Sachlichkeit*, was among them, without the bitterness and despair of the German model, but with the smooth-surface realism of some works by Dix [650] and Grosz. So were early Flemish and German portraits, with their realistic definition and their capitalization on details of costume as ornamental design. But the virus that attacked American regionalism and drained it of significant content soon affected Wood; his style became a formula. In *The Midnight Ride of Paul Revere* [651] it is difficult to find more than an exercise in conventionalization, where a toy rider on a toy horse gallops through a toy town for no purpose.

The exploration of America proceeded in other regions than the Middle West. In New York, Reginald Marsh (1898–1954) was one of the liveliest of the painters who grew out of the Ash Can tradition. Sometimes he painted the city as objectively as the Ash Can men did, although he preferred the sordidness of the Bowery and the subway to the animation of Times Square and the intimacy of Greenwich Village, approaching such subjects in the spirit of such eighteenth-century Englishmen as Rowlandson or even Hogarth. Sometimes his satirical comment was cutting, as in *They Pay to Be Seen* [652].

Some other painters saw the American scene romantically beneath a genre surface. Charles Burchfield (1893–   ) was a Middle Westerner who anticipated the

651. Wood: *The Midnight Ride of Paul Revere*, 1931. 30 x 40″. Metropolitan Museum of Art, New York, George A. Hearn Fund.

652. Marsh: *They Pay to Be Seen*, 1934. 23¾ x 20″. Philadelphia Museum of Art, Hinchman Bequest.

653. BURCHFIELD: *Backyards in Spring*, 1946. Watercolor, 33 x 44″. Philadelphia Museum of Art, Gift of Mrs. Herbert C. Morris.

654. HOPPER: *Early Sunday Morning*, 1930. 30 x 40″. Whitney Museum of American Art, New York.

655. SHAHN: *The Passion of Sacco and Vanzetti,* 1931–32. 84½ x 48″. Whitney Museum of American Art, New York, Gift of Mr. and Mrs. Milton Lowenthal in memory of Juliana Force.

656. SHAHN: *Epoch,* 1950. 52 x 31″. Philadelphia Museum of Art, Bloomfield Moore Fund.

regionalist flurry by drawing material from his native ground, and continued quietly and sincerely after regionalism had degenerated into the exploitation of personal mannerism. Burchfield is primarily a watercolorist, although he has worked in oil, and in addition to his revelation of a romantic mood in the shabbiness of small towns [653] he has painted in semi-abstract expressionist ways. The quality of mystery and gentle resignation distinguishes his picturizations of the Middle West from the work of any other painter who can be called

regionalist. In the East, Edward Hopper (1882–   ) discovered a comparable quality in the city and in the rural refuges of New Yorkers, such as Cape Cod. He paints landscapes or cityscapes immobilized in a flat, brilliant light, whether it is the electric light of the city or the sunlight of the country. His individuals, in either setting, are lonely and isolated in a world of harsh, simplified, blocky forms represented in meticulously studied clarity [654].

Social consciousness in one form or another and to varying degrees is an element

657. SHAHN: *"Nearly Everybody Reads The Bulletin,"* 1946. Gouache and ink on masonite. 22 x 22½". Philadelphia Museum of Art, Louis E. Stern Collection.

in the conceptions of all these painters, sometimes so superficially that it becomes only a genre observation of folkways or cityways of life, sometimes so romantically that the observation of the contemporary world as a social or visual phenomenon is less important than the discovery of moods generated within it. Basically, this has been a list of conservative or even reactionary painters, implying that the artist who turns to social comment necessarily divorces himself from the various intellectualized isms of Europe. Yet the painter who has made the most searching comments among social realists is the one who has been most affected, stylistically, by abstraction.

Ben Shahn (1898–   ) was born in Lithuania, but came to this country as a child and was educated in Brooklyn schools and at New York University and City College, and in the National Academy of Design. He was thus a melting-pot American rather than a regional grass-rooter. Possibly for this reason the School of Paris made a more lasting impression on him, when he went back to Europe for a period of travel and study, than it did on Benton or, in Mexico, Rivera. He fused into his art whatever modern European influences remained valuable to him as a painter working not only in America but as an American.

There is certainly more than coincidence in the fact that while the regionalists were at the height of their popularity, the United States was dominated by the "America First" group of isolationist politicians with their stronghold in the Middle West, who believed that this country could exist free of European entanglements. The provincial chauvinism of self-consciously American painting was an expression of the same spirit. Shahn's American character is that of the contemporary international man whose examination of his own country and his own time must take into consideration the character of the world of which his country is inevitably a part, the man whose patriotism is not blind faith, but a matter of the individual's obligation to see clearly, to fight injustice and corruption and stupidity wherever they infect national life. In 1933–1934 Shahn did a series of paintings on Prohibition, beyond doubt a gross blunder in the history of American government, but not a subject that would have occurred as a possible one to any of the other painters we have been seeing. (Benton did a few picturesque moonshiners.) As a painter of protest, Shahn's position was liberal or even leftist; he worked with Rivera, for instance, on the Rockefeller Center murals that were destroyed. But he has acted on social convictions rather than arbitrary political loyalties, and the causes he has espoused, and the evils he has attacked, as in the case of Sacco and Vanzetti [655], are ones in which history and sentiment, in retrospect, have upheld liberal attitudes.

Painting as protest against specific circumstance is self-limited. The Sacco and Vanzetti series may always tell as good painting, but it must always tell first in connection with a certain event in the frame of a certain time. Probably for this reason, Shahn grew from his militant, but thoughtful protests into more generalized symbolical social observation. In *Epoch* [656] he comments on the general character of our times: a little figure who seems not too at home in his acrobatic position is balanced upside down on the shoulders of two performing cyclists, one bearing a placard "yes," the other denying him with

658. SHAHN: *Silent Music*, 1951. Silk screen stencil, 17¼ x 35″. Philadelphia Museum of Art, Harrison Fund.

a "no." The precariousness of the situation is pointed up by the bright carnivalesque shapes and colors, symbolical no doubt of the agitation and false gaiety of a world that offers a great deal of moment-to-moment distraction but very little stability. The mood is not solemn, but wry. Wry, too, and sardonic, is *"Nearly Everybody Reads the Bulletin"* [657]. The use of newspaper made into a fool's cap to cover the empty head of an inert figure who sits uncomprehending and uncaring is symbolical of the inertia with which people reject consciousness and action in a world where vigilance is the price of moral life. In other pictures the symbolism is more obscure and is probably personal. At times, too, Shahn is an artist of pure fantasy.

Shahn is one of the fine stylists of his day. The attractiveness of his economical, rather wiry draughtsmanship has led to a spate of derivations among other painters and imitations or downright plagiarisms in the field of commercial art, to such an extent that it is possible to speak of a "Ben Shahn school," although it is a false one based on the leader's technical inventiveness rather than on the significance which, in his own art, this inventiveness serves. Nor, of course, must every one of Shahn's own pictures be expected to carry a message. Among his inventions where sheer

ingenuity is sufficient in itself, there are such prints as *Silent Music* [658], where folding chairs and music stands are grouped into a rhythm of lines and spaces nearly as abstract as one of Mondrian's "plus and minus" compositions.

Surrealism

While the realist rejection of abstract intellectualisms was manifesting itself in the kind of painting we have just been seeing, fantastic and visionary painting was flourishing with equal vigor. The climax of this kind of thing came in surrealism. This does not mean that surrealism is the apogee of visionary art. It is not—not even in its own century. But it was a kind of fantasy peculiar to its century, and it will be convenient to discuss it first, and then see where it came from and what it led to.

Surrealism is based on the idea of shock through paradox, the idea of giving such a jolt to surface consciousness that it is dislocated to reveal the hidden mysteries that affect it. In surrealism these mysteries are usually morbid. Its immediate parallel outside the field of art is psychoanalysis, which probes the darkness of the pathological spirit to discover rational explanations for irrational conduct. There is a

659. DALI: *Agnostic Symbol*, 1932. 21⅜ x 25⅝″. Philadelphia Museum of Art, Arensberg Collection.

terrible rationality to surrealism, the rationality of nightmare. In the world of dream and the world of insanity, the most fantastic action is rational to the dreamer or the lunatic because it is the end result of previous experiences that dictate it. These previous experiences may be warped and out of kilter; all the same, they are present, and they demand the fantastic dream or the lunatic behavior as their logical expression.

Surrealism investigates this terrible world, this modern witches' dreambook where everything is vividly real, yet where nothing is what it seems to be. The basic paradox of surrealist painting is that every detail of every explicitly represented image is undeniably *there*. It undeniably exists—yet at the same time it cannot exist because it is outside the realm of possibility. Surrealism takes us into a world where the

impossible and the undeniable are one and the same thing—and naturally it bothers us. It is intended to do so.

As an example: everyone has seen a beach or a deep plain. Everyone has seen a spoon. Everyone has seen driftwood. Everyone has seen sky. Everyone has seen a small gold watch. But no one has seen a beach or plain upon which there rests a rectangular segment of sky, cut from its place in heaven in order to accommodate the issuance of a long-handled spoon that stretches toward us, curving around a piece of driftwood en route, and finally offers us a tiny gold watch held in its bowl and marking the hour as 6:04 o'clock. At least we have not seen it until we have seen *Agnostic Symbol* [659], in which these familiar and quite ordinary items are combined in this extraordinary way by Salvador Dali (1904–   ). The circumstance represented in this picture is preposterous, impossible, it cannot exist. But it does exist. Because there it is, explicitly, down to the last groove on the stem of the watch.

Just what the symbolism of the picture is, it is not easy to say, although one may play around in several directions with the title as a clue. Surrealism in principle denies any programmatic symbolizing, since its images are supposed to be dictated to the painter from the depths of the unconscious, the source of dreams. At least this is a tenet held to by one group of surrealists, including Dali, in a movement where personal antagonisms and contradictions have been extreme. But in Dali's most celebrated picture, *The Persistence of Memory* [660], the symbolism is clear enough. At a glance the theme is concerned with time and decay. The most obvious symbols are the watches and the dead tree, and the jellyfishlike monster melting on the beach. Scavenger ants attack one of the watches, with no success. We deduce from this that the symbolism is also concerned with immortality, the triumph of something or other over the forces of decay. The watches are a symbol not only of time, but of infinite time, eternity, impervious to the frustrated insects who would devour them. They are also limp; somebody has bent time to his will. Who? The artist, of course, since he painted them that way. Thus seen, the picture is a restatement in fantastic terms of an old idea, popular in antiquity and in the Renaissance: the idea that through creative works during his mortal life, the artist defeats time and achieves immortality.

Ordinarily, however, surrealist images take the form of free invention in whatever startling combinations the painter can work up. When he cannot invent them, he can borrow them from numerous sources, either from pictures in the past or from the textbooks of abnormal psychology. Objects selected at random and combined arbitrarily may yield the most unexpected juxtapositions, and surrealism has been the most prostituted of all twentieth-century movements in painting, the most vulnerable to charlatanism. It offers a dangerously tolerant recipe for novelty painting, by which

660. DALI: *The Persistence of Memory*, 1931. 9½ x 13". Museum of Modern Art, New York.

any painter with a skill for accurate photographic realism may do a still-life of objects rationally represented in irrational combinations, with a good chance of approximating surrealist values.

In Dali's case the qualifying factor is a special talent for diseased and disgusting imagery; the two adjectives are those of an English critic, the late George Orwell, who uses them to conclude an essay on Dali.[*] Commenting on Dali's statement, "At seven I wanted to be Napoleon. And my ambition has been growing steadily ever since," Orwell wrote, "Suppose that you have nothing in you except your egoism and a dexterity that goes no higher than the elbow; suppose that your real gift is for a detailed, academic, representational style of drawing. . . . How then do you become Napoleon? There is always one escape: *into wickedness.*" Certainly "a dexterity that goes no higher than the elbow" is the most murderous phrase in the history of criticism.

An element of charlatanism has come to be inherent in the total nature of surrealism, since its emphasis on shock values legitimizes any excess. Some of Dali's work is

[*] "Benefit of Clergy," in *Dickens, Dali, and Others*, 1946. The essay was written in 1944 as a review of Dali's book, *The Secret Life of Salvador Dali*.

661. BRUEGEL: *Allegory of Gluttony*, 1558. Engraving 8⅞ x 11½". Philadelphia Museum of Art, Phillips Collection.

saved from pornographic implication only through the exercise of great agility in aesthetic semantics. For more general consumption, his excesses run to the public buffoonery for which he has become famous, with his foot-long moustache, his recent burial and rebirth from a coffin (a stunt that received very little notice from a jaded press), his insistence that he has the fondest recollections of his life in his mother's womb, his proud claim to paranoia during his life outside it, his published "autobiography" which includes a photograph of himself nude and describes enough psycho-pathological experiences to make him the one-man madhouse of the Age of Freud. To speak this way about any man but Dali would be libelous; to speak thus about him is only to recognize his success in establishing his surrealist personality. If surrealism is built on the paradox of the rational-irrational, so is Dali's career. His irrational behavior has been directed with

acutely rational consistency—and success— toward the goal of many sane men: fame and fortune.

All other considerations aside, it is still true that up to the elbow Dali is a staggering artist. Technically *The Persistence of Memory* is a jewel, close to literally a jewel in its brilliant color, its small size, its immaculate precision. It is in the technical tradition of early Flemish and early Venetian painting; also it is parasitic on their forms. The deep distance with its sea and its rocky promontories picked out in golden light is all but a steal from the early Venetian Giovanni Bellini, whose allegories would be surrealist if their symbolism were morbid instead of poetic, and if their unrealistic combination of realistic images were disparate rather than harmonious. Surrealism has even closer affinities with the diableries and hellscapes of such Flemish painters as Hieronymus Bosch and Pieter Bruegel, who brought medieval fantasy to a climax in subjects like the latter's *Allegory of Gluttony* [661]. The concoction of monsters from vegetable, animal, and mineral fragments in these pictures served a didactic moral purpose; in hellscapes, these monsters were the torturing fiends and the persecuted damned. They have their counterparts in surrealist syntheses, such as *Geopoliticus* [662], although this hellscape has been presented opportunistically as an allegory of the geopolitical theories that were receiving enough attention in newspapers and magazines at that time to give the picture a bit of extra momentum upon its launching. But if this is a hellscape it is a twentieth-century one, the private hell of the schizoid personality.

Dada

In addition to these precursors, surrealism found models in the past wherever painters had indulged their taste for the bizarre. But the immediate origin of surrealism was in an outbreak of nihilistic art at the end of World War I, called dada, in combination with *Die Neue Sachlichkeit* and its philosophy of the objective observation of sordidness and despair. The real world surrounding the painters of *Die Neue Sachlichkeit* in Germany was nightmarish in itself. Its representation even from an objective viewpoint (which, of course, The New Objectivity painters hardly maintained) approached surrealism in giving concrete imagery to things grotesque and horrid. But even in France, a victor nation, the psychological climate after the war was sufficiently desperate to support a nihilistic art, and dada before long found its center in Paris as a cult of the absurd, the irreverent, and the meaningless.

Dada's theory was, in effect, that if the world had been unable to think its way to rational behavior in three millenniums, it was pointless for artists to pretend to find order and meaning in its chaos. Dada rejected every moral, social, and aesthetic code. (The name *dada* was supposedly found by opening a dictionary at random, but it is fortuitously apt enough to make one wonder.) The aesthetic of dada was

662. DALI: *Geopoliticus*, 1943. 17½ x 20″. Collection Louis E. Stern, New York.

that there is no aesthetic, since an aesthetic is built on reason and the world had demonstrated that it was without reason. Before the movement settled in Paris it also had centers in Berlin, Cologne, and Zurich, with a brief and artificially sustained one in New York. But everywhere the dadaists soon discovered that their movement was self-defeating by its very intention; it is simply impossible to be nothing at all. They came closest to achieving their totally negative goal in a literary way, when poems were composed by combining words at random by picking them out of a hat. The exhibitions included work by men we have already seen, such as Grosz (who formed the Berlin group), Feininger, Kandinsky, Kokoschka, Marc, Modigliani, and Picasso, who hardly fit into the dada definition, Picabia, who does, and Duchamp, who does and who doesn't, as well as others we will see shortly, such as Chirico and Klee.

The Cologne group was led by the German Max Ernst (1891–   ) and the Alsatian Jean Hans Arp (1888–1966), who had been prominent in the movement's initiation in Zurich. Their "fatagaga" pictures (the word was coined from the de-

663. DUCHAMP: *Why Not Sneeze, Rose Sélavy?* Marble blocks, thermometer, wood, and cuttlebone in small bird cage, height 4½". Philadelphia Museum of Art, Arensberg Collection.

664. DUCHAMP: *The Bride Stripped Bare by Her Bachelors, Even,* 1915–23. Oil and wire on glass, height 109¼". Philadelphia Museum of Art, Arensberg Collection.

scriptive phrase, "fabrication de tableaux garantis gazométriques") were nonsense concoctions in which cut-out pictures were combined in startling and irrational juxtapositions, enhanced by varying amounts of additional drawing or painting, and given provocative titles: *Here Everything Is Floating,* for instance. Or such things as botanical charts, anatomical engravings, or engraved illustrations for technical books would be retouched fantastically and called *The gramineous bicycle garnished with bells the pilfered greybeards and the echinoderms bending the spine to look for caresses,* or *Sitting Buddha, ask for your doctor,* or *Trophy, hypertrophied.* But even here, dada was self-defeating, since, although the images were supposedly nonsensical, psychoanalysis was demonstrating at this time that fantasy was the expression of an inner consciousness. Hence the concoction had meaning in spite of the concocter; the fact that he had chosen these particular bits and pieces to combine in this particular way, told something about his subconscious mind just as his dreams must do. This is virtually the basis of surrealism, and it is here that dada parented surrealism and merged with it.

Within the nutshell of dada the chaos became even greater than the chaos of the world. Members and groups disinherited one another so rapidly and with so many crisscrosses between cliques that no one was certain who was dada and who was not. When several dadaists proclaimed themselves communists, the communists disclaimed them in horror, while police closed dada exhibitions because the movement was antisocial as well as anti-aesthetic. Members laughed at one another and at themselves. Marcel Duchamp exhibited a urinal in New York with the title *Fountain.* The international collaboration of the American Morton Schamberg and the German Elsa von Freytag Loringhoven bore fruit in the form of a miter box combined with a plumbing trap and called *God.* Duchamp produced a quantity of "readymades," which were mass-produced objects nonsensically combined, of which the most complicated was *Why Not Sneeze, Rose Sélavy?* [663], a small birdcage filled with

665. SCHWITTERS: *Merz Konstruktion,* 1921. Painted wood, wire, and paper. 14½ x 8½".
Philadelphia Museum of Art, Gallatin Collection.

666. HARNETT: *The Old Violin,* 1886. Lithographic reproduction by Gus Ilg, 1887, with
frame continuing picture in three dimensions, 42¾ x 31¾". Philadelphia Museum of Art.

marble blocks in the shape of lump sugar, a thermomenter, and some wood and cuttlebone, with the lettering of the title underneath it. "Rose Sélavy" was a name invented as a play on the phrase "Rose c'est la vie." The list could go on for a long time.

It should also be pointed out that Duchamp's nonsense items were the logical end-result of a progression that began with the deliberately provocative title of *Nude Descending a Staircase* [582], a title with prophetic overtones of dada and surrealism. Duchamp's earlier work had been realistic, Cézannesque, and semi-expressionist in turn. The ready-mades were his last works, although he incorporated repetitions of some previous designs into a large glass

window called *The Bride Stripped Bare by Her Bachelors, Even* [644] as late as 1923. The two panes of the window were cracked during shipment, in a pattern which has added an interesting fillip not at all out of keeping with dada aesthetic.

Among other experimenters, Kurt Schwitters (1887–1948) was working with *merzbild* (trash pictures, or rubbish or litter pictures), in which he combined bits of trash such as corks, wire, odd buttons, nails, waste paper, wood fragments—anything [665]. But he was disinherited as "reactionary." After all, the cubists had done this kind of thing with collage, and Schwitters' combinations of trash elements were not random and senseless. Like collage they were designed with a nice eye to balance,

667. ARP: *Two Heads*, 1929. Painted wood relief, 47¼ x 39¼″. Museum of Modern Art, New York.

668. ARP: *Composition*, 1937. Torn paper with India ink wash, 10¾ x 8½″. Philadelphia Museum of Art, Gallatin Collection.

contrast, and textural interest.* Arp worked in bas-relief cutouts [667] or cut or torn paper [668], but his "free forms," supposedly dictated by the subconscious (or even by accident—the pieces making up his paper "designs" were often pasted down in the positions in which they fell when allowed to drop through the air) turned out to be a relaxed, curvilinear version of Mondrian's rectangular arrangements, and had

their effect on the design of useful objects, such as modernistic table tops, and even on architectural forms, where they were a harmonious contrast to the angularities of functionalism. Dada was defeated on every hand, it kept wandering off into areas that made sense. In the end, the important thing about dada was that it happened.

Dada was primarily a literary movement. So was surrealism, for that matter. Dali is

---

* The turbulence of contemporary redirections and rediscoveries brings about some surprising reappearances, as in the case of William Michael Harnett (1848–1892), a contemporary of Eakins who achieved great popularity during the latter nineteenth century with his *trompe l'oeil* paintings. Harnett received as much as $10,000 for a still-life, but his work had sunk into obscurity in this century until surrealism and *merzbild* and collage brought him back into attention. Harnett's still-lifes were admired during his lifetime for the obvious reason, considering the taste of the day— their technique of illusionism. But *merzbild*

and collage, making use of less-than-commonplace objects and materials, have revealed how skillfully Harnett contrasted the textures of commonplace ones, while surrealism has brought new attention to the supernatural life with which his microscopic detail invests a piece of polished or weathered wood, a rusted hinge, or a crumpled letter, especially when these familiar things are placed in unusual juxtaposition. One of Harnett's finest compositions, *The Old Violin*, was popular in accurate lithographic reproductions including a frame on which the picture's painted hardware was continued in three dimensions [666].

certainly the most "literary" painter since the Pre-Raphaelites, to whom he bears curious relationships. Among writers, the Rumanian poet Tristan Tzara and the Germans Hugo Ball and Richard Hülsenbeck were dada initiators, as was the French André Breton. Breton was the literary bridge between dada and surrealism, recognizing dada's ultimate dependence on the subconscious, and formulating it in the surrealist manifesto of 1924. With Louis Aragon he was the most devout theorist and practitioner of literary surrealism, of which painted surrealism is an extension. The *Cabaret Voltaire* should be mentioned here also: this combination literary club, exhibition gallery, and theater was the center of the most flagrant early shenanigans of dada. One suspects that it must have been a tiresome place. Nothing palls so quickly as excessive novelty; dada was like a costume party (come as a jackanapes), which was fun for the first half-hour while the guests were arriving but an awful bore after the first few laughs.

Mystery and Fantasy before Surrealism: Chirico

The flaw in surrealism is the self-consciousness and the trickery that are apparently implicit in the exploitation of a hidden world on an arbitrary, theoretical, didactic basis. This at any rate is its flaw in Dali as its typical practitioner, and although he was disowned by the other surrealists, his art has come to be so identified with the word *surrealism* that the word's meaning has changed to accord with Dali's use of the theory—at least, in the field of painting. But in either case, surrealism tended to become a codification of, a guide to, the laws of mystery, and even in its purest uses it was subject to the flaw that Dali exaggerated.

Fortunately, the realm of mystery was also explored (without guide books) by certain pre-surrealist and post-surrealist painters who set down their memories of their voyages in ways that enable us to share the experience, rather than the theory, of fantasy.

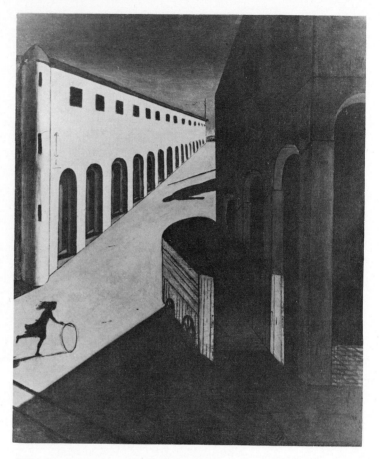

669. CHIRICO: *Melancholy and Mystery of a Street,* 1914. 34⅜ x 28¼". Collection Mr. and Mrs. Stanley Resor, New Canaan, Conn.

At the end of the nineteenth century, Douanier Rousseau was one of these men. So was Redon. Böcklin, who lived until 1901, wanted very much to be one of them, and came close to being one, in *The Isle of the Dead* [363] and pictures related to it. It will be remembered that he held to the theory of explicit representation of fantastic subjects, the basic technique of surrealism. But his pictures remained arrangements of costumed models posed in a stageset with stage props rather than figures of fantasy existing in another world.

In the early twentieth century Böcklin's hopes came to maturity in the work of an Italian born in Greece, Giorgio de Chirico (1888–   ), who reached Italy by way of Munich where, as a student, he copied some of Böcklin's pictures while he was finding his way to what he wanted to do.

670. CHIRICO: *The Soothsayer's Recompense*, 1913. 53⅜ x 71". Philadelphia Museum of Art.

After a period of Böcklinesque work, Chirico devised a dream world of his own, as tangible as Böcklin's or Dali's but free from Böcklin's fatal ponderousness on the one hand and Dali's lightweight Freudian illustrationism on the other. What Chirico wrote about the theory of his "metaphysical painting" is usually muzzy or contradictory. Why not? He was a poetic painter, not a writer or an amateur psychiatrist.

Chirico's pictures are complete without their titles, and in some cases are better off without them, but a list of some of the typical ones evokes his mood: *Melancholy and Mystery of a Street* [669]; *Enigma of the Oracle; Nostalgia of the Infinite; Lassitude of the Infinite; Melancolia; Uncertainty of the Poet; The Soothsayer's Recompense* [670]; *Joys and Enigmas of a Strange Hour; Anguish of Departure, Joy of Return.* The vocabulary of surrealism is the borrowed one of psychoanalysis, but in these pictures Chirico uses a personal vocabulary of deserted city squares, solitary figures, isolated towers, blank walls, arcaded galleries, statues, inexplicable vans, great packing cases (which, one feels, are filled with the paraphernalia of necromancy), and occasionally a rushing train or a billowing smoke stack, which in Chirico's static and enchanted world lose their association with the world of industry and engineering and become fantasms, curiosities, silent and ominous. In spite of deep clear skies and glimpses of distant landscape, we are never led into infinite space as we are in surrealism, but are held within architectural boundaries, within walled areas illuminated by flat, steady, golden light radiating across the picture from some low-lying source, casting long thin blots of shadows along pavements and against walls.

Surrealism explains everything, in perverse terms. Chirico explains nothing, yet his inexplicable cityscapes are haunted with deep memories of the grace and logic of the classical world. If we hunt an explanation of this classical echo, hanging so eerily in Chirico's sinister realm, it is easy to find it in the Renaissance-classical parentage of the simplified architecture (in its turn a reflection of Chirico's own Italian cities and towns and his memories of Greece) and in the statues, which are not invented ones but identifiable ones which have played their parts in Chirico's personal experience. These may be classical ones, but they may also be nineteenth-century ones of the most prosaic kind, transformed, like the trains and smokestacks, into images of magical suggestion. The sense of transformation is the quality that, in the end, identifies Chirico's art.

In other pictures, Chirico's classical reference is quite direct and sometimes symbolical. *The Philosopher* [671] combines a familiar classical bust which Chirico, like most academic students, probably had drawn from cast in school, with symbols of thought and learning which merge with the body of the philosopher. The head is drawn with respectful observance of conventional draughtsmanship, but there is an infiltration of cubist devices in the books. Chirico was only lightly affected by abstraction. In a series of pictures of mannequins, of which one is *The Poet and His Muse* [672] he builds geometrical forms sometimes draped, as here, in classical togas. The geometry of such pictures is less cubist than it is a genuflexion to classical mathematics, even when the togas and directly classical trappings are absent. The pictures are part Picasso and part Euclid, but entirely Chirico in their final dependence on a personal romanticism. Even the symbols of engineering and mechanical drawing that fill them are personal and romantic. Chirico's father was a construction engineer for railroads who died while his son was still a boy; Chirico's trains, smokestacks, and engineering symbols spring from emotional, not theoretical or mechanistic, sources.*

* Chirico also devised a classical subject in which mammoth sculpturesque horses with heavy luxuriant manes and tails like flowing stone rear and whinny near fragments of classical architecture. With their decorative quality,

671. CHIRICO: *The Philosopher,* date unknown. 39½ x 29½". Philadelphia Museum of Art, Bequest of Fiske and Marie Kimball.

Chirico's dream world has an air of suspension in time that makes consideration of his painting as a chronological development come as an afterthought, yet his art developed within quite concise boundaries of periods. He continued his Böcklinesque painting in Italy between 1909 and 1911; the haunted piazzas were done in Paris in 1913 and 1914 (against the current of cubism, which dominated the scene); his classical mannequins appeared in 1915, and in this same year he returned to Italy. He was in military service in Ferrara in

especially since pictures of horses are always popular, these had a great vogue and were repeated too often, not only by Chirico himself but in adaptations on fabrics and such incidentals as lamp bases, ash trays, bookends, and the like. They still have illegitimate descendants in every dime store.

672. CHIRICO: *The Poet and His Muse, c.* 1925. 35¾ x 29". Philadelphia Museum of Art, Arensberg Collection.

1917 when he and the futurist painter Carlo Carrà [589] propounded "metaphysical painting" as a school. Until that time Chirico's ideas had been stated in a general poetical way—when he set them down at all:

"Profound statements must be drawn from the most secret recesses of the artist's being, where no murmuring torrent, no bird song, no rustle of leaves, can distract him. . . . I remember one vivid winter's day at Versailles. Silence and calm reigned supreme. Everything gazed at me with mysterious, questioning eyes. And then I realized that every corner of the palace, every column, every window, possessed a spirit, an impenetrable soul. . . . I grew aware of the mystery which urges men to create strange forms, and the creation appeared more extraordinary than the creators."

Written in 1913, these words are in the unspecific and romantic mood of his dream-architectural cityscapes, and are more metaphysical than his later expositions of "metaphysical" painting. Architecture in his early work, and architecture as he saw it "gazing at him with mysterious, questioning eyes" that day at Versailles, is part of a mysterious expression of the soul. But six years later he wrote more objectively:

"Among the many senses that modern painters have lost, we must number the sense of architecture. The edifice accompanying the human figure, whether alone or in a group, whether in a scene from life or in an historical drama, was a great concern of the ancients. They applied themselves to it with loving and severe spirit, studying and perfecting the laws of perspective [—laws which, significantly, Chirico had violated in his early pictures, thus increasing the sense of other-worldliness]. . . . A landscape enclosed in the arch of a portico or in the square of a rectangle acquires a greater metaphysical value, because it is solidified and isolated from the surrounding space. Architecture completes nature."

While all this is true as far as it goes, there is nothing new here, nothing that would be foreign to any elementary academic course in picture-making, except for the metaphysical tag, which is dubiously grafted on. Chirico's painting began to lose its magic as he began to theorize so explicitly about it—perhaps because of the theorizing, more probably because some psychological change led him not only to theorizing but to a change in his way of painting. After a series of still-lifes where objects seem to enact dramas of their own, more heavily painted and with coarse outlines—pictures that are historically important as immediate precursors of surrealism but are more obvious in manufacture than his earlier work —Chirico rejected the whole modern movement and, since, has painted pictures that would have been at home in the Salon of 1855.

Chagall

The happiest fantasist of them all was another man whose visions anticipated surrealist ones in their irrational elements, and who has been claimed by surrealists as a forerunner, Marc Chagall (1887–). Chagall, a Russian, came to Paris in his early twenties and has lived in France ever since, with the exception of the years of World War I and after them until 1922. But he is a Russian painter in spite of his close association with the School of Paris. His Russia is old Russia, not the Russia of collectives but the Russia he remembers as a man who was a boy there before the revolution. Memories of Russian villages, folklore, and fairy tales impregnate his work, although such phrases as "tragic awareness" and "social consciousness" are popular with some of his admirers who feel obliged to discover in his art something more than tender and ebullient joy, as if that were not enough. One thinks first of his floating lovers, his bouquets of flowers that seem to be made of some kind of glowing powder, his sportive animals and birds —especially roosters. All these appear in his *Bouquet with Flying Lovers* [673], combined in this case with a studio window, a chair and a table, and some houses, a bridge, and a river with a boat (including two more lovers) evoking the life of bohemia at its happiest. In other pictures the couples have floated down from their Parisian flat to the south of France, which is equally Chagall's adopted habitat, with its warmth, its flowers, and its tradition of happy sensuousness and bright color. But his lovers are happy too in their snowy Russian village [674] where a small cow appears (on the left) to bless their union. This amiable creature or one of its relatives appears as an almost invisible sketch in the extreme upper left of *Bouquet with Flying Lovers*, this time as a kind of Janus with a cow's face and a human face paired, and with a body in the form of a cello, which he—it—is playing. In *I and My Village* [675] the cow dreams happily of a milkmaid, the lovers are on their way to the fields, one right side up and one upside down. These free fantasies range from the

673. CHAGALL: *Bouquet with Flying Lovers, c.* 1934–47. 51⅜ x 38⅜". Tate Gallery, London.

fairly literal fairy-tale realism of the village in the snow to the semi-abstraction of *I and My Village*, with occasional relationships to expressionism. But if there was ever a painter who should be accepted at face value rather than tied into one ism or another, it is Chagall. In *The Poet, or Half Past Three* [676], his play with cubism is particularly apparent, as well as a dash of fauvism in the patterning of flowers scattered in the upper right. But the picture's character is determined by its gay color, by the humorous symbolism of the poet's head put on upside down—poets are visionary and impractical fellows—and the happy green cat with a rosy belly who begs for attention at the poet's elbow.

674. CHAGALL: *In the Night*, 1938–43. 18½ x 20⅝". Philadelphia Museum of Art, Louis E. Stern Collection.

675. CHAGALL: *I and My Village*, 1911. 22 x 18". Philadelphia Museum of Art, Gift of Mr. and Mrs. Rudolph de Schauensee.

676. CHAGALL: *The Poet, or Half Past Three,* 1911. 77½ x 57½". Philadelphia Museum of Art.

It is still true that *The Poet*, painted in 1911, is one of the pictures which establish Chagall among those painters who, that early, were transforming cubism by rejecting the drab color of its analytical phase and, in Chagall's case especially, rejecting also its intellectualized abstraction for a return to personal, intimate, poetic or emotional statement. Chagall soon discovered that the conflict between the theoretical nature of cubism and the bubbling personalism of painters like himself—a conflict that mars *The Poet* expressively although it makes it important historically—was an unnecessary one. He solved the conflict sensibly by attempting no reconciliation but abandoning the field and going his own way in his own world.

It is true also that Chagall has done religious and literary pictures where "tragic awareness" is present at least by implication in the subject. These appeared especially in the 1940's, when racial persecutions and the death of his wife were sobering and saddening. But in the mass his art is deeply joyous, or lightly playful, above all warm and tender, in spirit. He is the only major painter of his generation who has demonstrated that the devices of expressionism are as adaptable to the translation of happy inner experience as to that of tragedy and violence, and he is the only one who has shown consistently that in the twentieth century the world of fantasy is not necessarily sinister or morbid. It is this spirit that makes his adoption as a surrealist ancestor such an artificial one.

Surrealism: Varieties and Variations

These, then, were the antecedents of surrealism—Douanier Rousseau and Redon, Chirico and Chagall, medieval hellscapes and Renaissance allegories, dada, *Die Neue Sachlichkeit,* and psychoanalysis, plus such ancestors-by-hindsight as Blake, the Pre-Raphaelites, and even Thomas Cole. With such mixed ancestry, surrealism could hardly breed true, and it did not. It produced offspring in which such unexpected recessives as social consciousness cropped up, for instance *The Eternal City* by the American Peter Blume (1906–), where each of the fantastic details, executed with the highest polish, is part of an elaborate symbolical social study of Mussolini's Italy. (The picture was painted from 1934 to 1937, when things seemed to be going well for Il Duce, but it represents him as a jack-in-the-box.)

Yves Tanguy (1900–1955) was one of the few members of the surrealist family who was unquestionably legitimate. Using the typical deep space of surrealism, he peopled it with odd forms of his own invention [677]. Although they are not the usual animal-vegetable-mineral combinations of fragments of familiar objects, they do carry hints of the musical instruments and sea forms which were combined by Bruegel and Bosch in their allegories and hellscapes. They exist in a cold blue light and as if surrounded by an invisible gas lethal to all creatures or plants but themselves. Tanguy's pictures inevitably suggest the landscape of another planet, or sometimes the floor of some strange sea from which the water has been drained.

677. TANGUY: *Shadow Country,* 1927. 39 x 31⅜". Collection **Mr.** and Mrs. Harry Lewis Winston, Birmingham, Mich.

Tanguy joined the surrealist group in 1925, the year after Breton's manifesto. But he had already discovered himself independently. He had never thought of being a painter, and had had no training as one, but when he saw a Chirico in a dealer's window, he became a painter on the instant. The suddenness and completeness of his discovery makes him, of all the surrealists, the one who most nearly qualifies as an "autonomous" creator—that is, one who paints spontaneously from internal causes or influences. Apparently these causes or influences remained static during Tanguy's career, for his paintings changed virtually not at all. The terrain of his planet did not offer much variety, but he continued to explore and record it in its pleasant monotony. Even in its repetitiousness

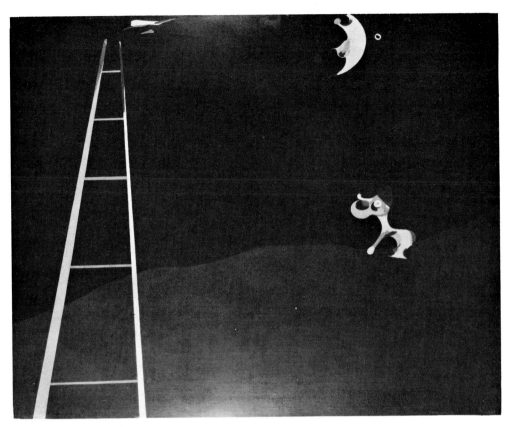

678. MIRÓ: *Dog Barking at the Moon*, 1926. 28¾ x 36¼″. Philadelphia Museum of Art, Gallatin Collection.

Tanguy's art is refreshing, as a relief from the struggle for novelty that makes Dali so wearing.

Dali and Tanguy represent the "objective" branch of surrealist painting with its tangible presentation of the impossible. In its purity the surrealist idea should dictate this tangibility, but as it happened, abstraction was too strong a force in modern painting not to affect it. Arp, with his free forms "dictated by the demands of the subconscious" has already been mentioned; another prominent name is André Masson (1896–   ), who joined the group early and drew heavily on such literary sources as Franz Kafka and the Marquis de Sade, this latter having supplied for the surrealists in general a wonderful reference index of erotic morbidities. But the most creative imagination among abstract surrealist artists belongs to Joan Miró (1893–   ). In fact, the statement may be made with-

out the limitation "abstract," for alongside Miró, Dali is a literary patchworker, and Tanguy a charming reporter in a space helmet. Miró's art is a compound of wit with nightmare, of whimsy with horror, half-delightful, half-menacing. One begins by laughing with him as he shows us a deft caprice, but if we look long enough the laughter is likely to grow thin and trail off with the uncomfortable realization that things are not as funny here as they seemed at first glance. Not always, of course: his well-known conceit, *Dog Barking at the Moon* [678] is not likely to frighten anyone, but even this bright little picture takes on an eery loneliness if it is contemplated for a few moments. And the forms in the series of pictures of which *Painting, 1933* [679] is a good example, are not bones and are not insects, not whiskered monsters or floating bladders or curious plants, although they are related to them. They are not

679. MIRÓ: *Painting, 1933.* 51 x 64″. Philadelphia Museum of Art, Gallatin Collection.

680. KLEE: *Landscape with Blue Birds,* 1919. Gouache, 8 x 10½″. Philadelphia Museum of Art, Gallatin Collection.

681. KLEE: *Jörg*, 1924. Watercolor, 9¼ x 11¼″. Philadelphia Museum of Art, Arensberg Collection.

(1879–1940). The temptation in talking about Klee is to say that he must be treated either in a sentence or two or in a long book, and settle for the sentences. No other painter of consequence seems so trivial from picture to picture; no other painter has quite Klee's characteristic of depending on his total work for his meaning. The hundredth Klee one sees enriches the first ninety-nine; the hundred and first adds to the lot. If this is also true of, for instance, Picasso, still a single picture of the blue period, or of any other period, may stand alone as an independent work of art worth while in itself. But a single picture by Klee is like a sentence from a long essay or even a phrase from it: it means something in itself but not much; it needs its place in context. If we already know the essay, a phrase from it takes on meaning from behind and before.

Klee was one of those painters who developed along the lines of historical summary. He began as a representational draughtsman, passed through the influences of Cézanne, van Gogh, and Ensor, and then met the men with whom he would be a member of The Blue Rider group of German expressionists. (Klee had a German father and a Swiss mother; his father was a musician, as were Klee and his wife.) He exhibited with The Blue Rider group in their second show, in 1911. The following year he met Picasso and Delaunay, among other

definably evil, but they are certainly not as innocent as they seem. They are hallucinations, and as such they are part of a dark and uneasy world.

Miró's background included some study of cubism, and in some of his work cubist vestiges are easy enough to find. But the painter who is most remarkable for his fusion of cubist and other abstract theories into a personal fantastic art is Paul Klee

682. KLEE: *But the Red Roof, c.* 1930. Tempera, 23⅝ x 35¾″. Philadelphia Museum of Art, Arensberg Collection.

cubists, just as analytical cubism was terminating its course. He was never a member of a surrealist group, but fantasy had always been strong in his painting; his earliest very personal works are grotesqueries with the tone of irony and the interest in abnormal states of mind which would always remain with him. But it is not the variety of these early periods that makes it necessary to know Klee through so many pictures if one is to know him at all. His early work may even be ignored; Klee is the Klee of the fantasies where cubism, free form, and inventive play are combined in what the late Francis Henry Taylor called a "fourth dimensional innocence"—an innocence, that would be, which was arrived at through sophistication. This is quite different from the yearning for innocence we saw so far back in this book when another German, Runge, painted his naked infant in a meadow [289]. Klee's "innocence" has nothing to do with inexperience and the vision of a fresh world. It is an entering into the state of mind of a child through intellectualizing experience, just as his participation in abnormal states of mind is arrived at by rational examination of these states. The philosophical amplifications of this idea, and speculations as to its worth or its viciousness as a channel for expression, have supplied material for enough books on Klee to suggest that his art is the summation of both the intellectual and the emotional redirections of painting most peculiar to the twentieth century—pure theoretical abstraction on one hand, and free invention from inner experience on the other. Many critics believe that Klee is precisely this summation. In view of all this, four pictures which seem to have been executed by a talented and careful child [680, 681, 682, and 683] may seem anticlimactic. Paul Klee is an artist's artist, a philosopher's philosopher, and, of late, most unhappily, a faddists' cult.

As surrealist concepts and surrealist mannerisms have spread beyond members of the original group, variations and recombinations have appeared everywhere. The Chilean painter Roberto Matta (1911–) derived an effective style [684] in

683. KLEE: *Diana,* 1931. Panel, 37½ x 23⅝". Collection Mr. and Mrs. William Bernoudy, St. Louis.

which Tanguy's planet is set aflame, and sinuous mutations of his chilly forms are stretched and spread into glowing gelatinous films, whirling about in luminous gases. Matta may vary this formula with more diagrammatic compositions where a kind of astral geometry organizes the holocaust. Picasso drew upon surrealism in the ghastly forms of his *Guernica* studies [606]—or perhaps this is only the overlapping of two appalling worlds, for Picasso is not investigating the surrealist world of private inner conflicts but is castigating the spiritual hideousness of which mankind in general is capable. Elsewhere in Picasso's work it

684. MATTA: *The Earth Is a Man*, 1940–42. 71⅝ x 95⅝". Collection Mr. and Mrs. William Rubin, New York.

would be difficult (and not too important) to say to what degree his grotesque fantasies are surreal in inspiration. But in one group of paintings, those of his "bone" period, he creates, essentially, a body of surrealist sculpture [685]. In his partly amusing and partly frightening and altogether powerful *Baboon and Young* [686], the surrealist double-image idea is juggled by the use of a toy automobile as the head, a large cooking vessel for the mass of the body (with its curved handle forming the tail) and the incorporation of other oddments into the clay of the model, all finally unified by casting in bronze. Picasso's sporadic forays into sculpture always carry with them a disconcerting suggestion that

he could become the great man in the field if he wanted to take the trouble.

The Englishman Graham Sutherland (1903–   ) paints hard, thorny forms of a most disquieting nature, and it is possible to find surrealist overtones in the sculpture of Henry Moore [630, 631]. The nervous, grotesquely elongated forms of the Swiss Alberto Giacometti (1901–   ) are surrealist in origin, and the American Ivan Le Lorraine Albright (1897–   ) combines the nominally objective but profoundly disturbed consciousness of social horror which was *Die Neue Sachlichkeit,* with forms of a detailed and luminous putrescence that is surrealist [687]. On the west coast of the United States, a group of painters in-

685. PICASSO: *Dinard*, 1928. 9½ x 6½". Philadelphia Museum of Art, Gallatin Collection.

686. PICASSO: *Baboon and Young*, 1951. Bronze, height 21". Museum of Modern Art, New York, Mrs. Simon Guggenheim Fund.

687 (*right*). ALBRIGHT: *Into the World There Came a Soul Called Ida,* 1927–30. 56¼ x 47". Art Institute of Chicago.

cluding Morris Graves (1910–   ) have rediscovered the romantic impulses in nature; their lyrical response to birds, small animals, and plants [688], is stated in terms of fantasy and dream that have been called surrealist. But at this point the business of dissecting out possible surrealist factors in work where their presence is incidental to more important ones, gets out of control and the boundaries of surrealism disappear.

Surrealism is a variety of romanticism, if we accept a premise on which this book is based—that classicism, romanticism, and realism are the three wide groups into which expression through painting can be divided. As a romantic subdivision, surrealism would substitute the diseased

688. GRAVES: *Guardian*, 1952. 47 x 32″. University of Illinois, Urbana.

689. BERMAN: *Bridges of Paris,* 1932. 36 x 25½″. Philadelphia Museum of Art.

psyche for the passionate mystery of the soul that stirred the romantic spirits of the early nineteenth century. Late in the 1920's, a group of painters rejected the surrealist tag and called themselves "neo-romantic." They were preoccupied with romantic revery, especially when it was concerned with poignant moods of loneliness. They echoed the deserted piazzas of Chirico and the deep space of surrealism in lonely vistas, often of city streets. Chief among the neo-romantics were Christian Bérard (1902–1949), Eugène Berman (1889–   ), and Pavel Tchelitchew (1898–1957). Berman's sleeping figures under a Paris bridge [689] are symbols of spiritual weariness rather than derelicts

finding a night's refuge. The picture would be a fairly realistic one, with its perspective of bridges and its mood established by its lonely huddled figures and the isolated silhouette of a boatman, if it were not for the unexplained ropes, running like rivulets up through the composition and dominating it. As an unaccountable and hence disturbing element, they account for the feeling of unease, the eery atmosphere, that fills the picture. They are also the picture's only specific tie to surrealism.

The division between neo-romanticism and surrealism is usually more vague than it is in this example. In the case of Tchelitchew the dividing line is hard to find in *Hide-and-Seek* [690], one of the extraor-

690. TCHELITCHEW: *Hide-and-Seek,* 1940–42. 78½ x 84¾″. Museum of Modern Art, New York, Mrs. Simon Guggenheim Fund.

dinary pictures of the first part of this century whether we are speaking of surrealism, neo-romanticism, or of no ism at all. In a wondrous tangle of membranes, blood vessels, plant forms, bodies, and suggestions of internal organs, we are led in and out of recognizability as one image merges with or is transformed into another. *Hide-and-Seek* is a section through the cancer of an anguished world where agony of spirit cannot be assuaged but must be compulsively probed—the world, in short, that produced surrealism and through it found, occasionally, its expression.

The world is not, of course, as bad as all that on every hand. Tchelitchew's special

kind of romantic agony is only part of a scene and is contemporary with Mondrian's classical meditations at the opposite pole. And in spite of the fact that "modern art" implies esoteric and inscrutable concepts, realism has held its own in this century, although with less fanfare, when it has found painters who know how to use it. One of them is Andrew Wyeth (1917–   ), whose meticulous rendering of quiet subjects is deceptive, concealing as it does—or revealing as it does, for those who know how to see a picture—the most acute perceptions of personality, of the life in inanimate objects as ordinary as a weathered door. [691].

691. Wyeth: *Christina Olsen*, 1947. Tempera on panel, 32½ x 24". Collection Mr. and Mrs. Joseph Verner Reed, Greenwich, Conn.

It would be pleasant if the last paragraph of a book as long as this one is could bring it to a neat end, against a line sharply drawn. But any line would be meaningless next year, next month, tomorrow. Nearly two hundred years ago Jacques Louis David supplied a starting point for this story, which was not altogether arbitrary (although it was arbitrary enough). But there is only one way this book can end. Having brought the reader this far, it must abandon him in midstream.

Notes on Modern Architecture

The International Style, which dominated anti-traditional architectural design during the period between World War I and World War II and has been degraded as any hack's stock in trade since then, was international indeed. It was contributed to by Austrian and German industrial architects and theorists, Russian suprematists and constructivists, the Dutchmen of the De Stijl group, the French-Swiss purists, certain Scandinavians, the American skyscraper builders at the turn of the century, and the American architect Frank Lloyd Wright who later rejected this style, to which his early work had given a point of departure.

One of the Germans, Walter Gropius (1883–   ), gave definition to the nascent style when he set up a school, the *Bauhaus,* to teach architecture, painting, and crafts. The *Bauhaus* was founded just after World War I, in 1919, at Weimar. The school moved to Dessau in 1925, and remained there as a proselytizing center for modern architecture until it closed with the advent of Hitler and his reactionary program in the arts. The building constructed at Dessau [692], familiar now in thousands of descendants, was the three-dimensional manifesto of the architectural principle of functionalism, the dominating concept of the International Style, and a principle that Gropius, as well as other architects, had already applied in earlier structures, especially factories.

By purest functionalist theory, the aesthetic content of a building will all but take care of itself if the building is designed to serve its purpose with maximum efficiency, ignoring all precedents of habitual design and construction. Nothing but the totality of the functional premise was new: the premise that the test of a good building is not only how it looks but also the degree to which it fulfills its purpose has always been basic with any good architect. Twentieth-century functionalism was a reaction against the excesses of second-rate nineteenth-century architecture in which usability was sacrificed to the romantic-pictorial "stage-set" concept of architecture designed in superficial imitation of the past. We have seen an example, as far back as the end of the eighteenth century, in the pseudo-Gothic Fonthill Abbey [288] and some ludicrous extremes of inappropriateness in projected designs for the completion of the Washington Monument and similar offenses in the field of decorative arts as exhibited in the Crystal Palace [335–341]. The functionalist idea, of course, is as applicable to pitchers, beds, and razors as it is to buildings.

In spite of eclectic excesses, the nineteenth century did not smother men's natural response to functionally determined forms. The American sculptor Horatio Greenough (1805–1852) was a classicist, but he once described a sailing ship in rapturous terms that could serve as the functionalist declaration. He wrote of "the majestic form of her hull . . . the gentle transition from round to flat . . . the symmetry and rich tracery of her spars and rigging, and those grand wind muscles, her sails." And he asked, "What Academy of Design, what research of connoisseurship, what imitation of the Greeks produced this marvel of construction?"

The answer was, no Academy and no imitation of the Greeks or of anyone else. But architects were slow to take their lead from ships and other structures (bridges among them) that were, perforce, functionally designed. Architects were finally forced into functionalism when a new age began demanding new kinds of buildings that simply could not be built in imitation of outmoded ones. The most insistent and the most dramatic of these self-dictated forms was the American skyscraper.

The skyscraper was demanded by necessity and made possible by the steel skeleton and the elevator. But its birth caught archi-tects unprepared. Buildings began to rise into the air while embarrassed designers remained earthbound. At first the best they could do was to pile one temple on top of another in an effort to coat this unprecedented stalk with a frosting of tradition. They learned better in Chicago. There, with Richardson, Jenny, Root, and Sullivan as some of the great names, contemporary architecture began, and its credo was concentrated into three words by Louis Sullivan (1856–1924) when he coined the phrase "Form follows function." The old copybooks were discarded, and each new skyscraper became a chapter in a story no one was able to put down.

Americans—and the world—have never ceased marveling at the skyscraper. During the boom days of the 1920's it was romanticized as an American symbol. Little cities where skyscrapers were not justified by practical reasons (density of population and fantastically increased real estate values) managed to erect at least one skyscraper in a fever of local pride. Even New York City fell victim to the romantic mania when the Empire State Building and the Chrysler Building, simultaneously under construction, kept adding such knickknacks as chromium spires and dirigible mooring masts (one small dirigible was finally lured into place atop the Empire State) to gain a few feet over the other in a race to become the highest building in the world. A rumor that the Chrysler spire enclosed a second and secret one, to be projected upward at the last minute, proved to be unfounded.

But the early Chicago development was a practical one, and its excitement lay in the spectacle of a tremendous architectural revolution in which science, commerce, and design made mutually interdependent demands in the creation of forms that seemed almost to be creating themselves, autonomously. After such a lesson, no architect with eyes in the front of his head and anything like an alert brain inside it could fail to understand that the problems of contemporary design could no longer be solved in terms of the buttress, the column, and the arch. They saw that a building did not have to be a skyscraper to justify a solution

692. GROPIUS: The *Bauhaus*, Dessau, Germany, 1925–26. (Photo courtesy Museum of Modern Art, New York.)

approached in terms of contemporary life, and that contemporary engineering offered solutions to every demand dictated by practical necessity.

Steel and concrete skeletons allowed buildings to leap outward or upward into space unsupported by thick foundations, did away with the idea of a building as necessarily a solid closed form, might turn a building into a mere skin of glass stretched across a light structural web. The glass cage of the *Bauhaus* workshop wing [693], dramatized a principle that began with the large windows of the Chicago skyscrapers and has been adapted to everything from week-end cottages to the vast automobile plants of Detroit. It has also been adapted to glass houses that violate privacy, to glass museums that sacrifice wall space needed for display, and to im-

693. GROPIUS: The *Bauhaus* Workshop Wing. (Photo courtesy Museum of Modern Art.)

properly designed glass office buildings that are ovens in summer and glaciers in winter. Like all other architectural styles, the functional one has been abused, and we have as much pseudo-functional nowadays as we once had pseudo-Gothic, pseudo-Renaissance, and pseudo-everything else.

Although the *Bauhaus* is a masterpiece of functional design, it makes minor concessions to the idea of architecture as arbitrary pattern. One concession is the patterned variation in the sizes of the glass panes of the workshop wing—remindful of Mondrian's painted rectangles. A major concession is the vestigial cornice, which, while it reduces the old ornamental cornice to a flat band and a small projection, is still unnecessary except as a psychological capping off. Functionally no capping off of glass and steel is necessary, as it was in stone buildings where the cornice was not only ornamental but also served to give some protection from weather to parts of the building that would have deteriorated if exposed. It would be absurd to pretend that the *Bauhaus* is not designed with an eye to harmonious combinations or that it discards all lessons learned from the past. Like a log cabin, which theoretically a functionalist may admire as much as he admires the *Bauhaus,* a modern functional building looks the way it does because it is designed to perform its function with maximum effectiveness making maximum practical use of the materials and methods available. The materials happen to be glass, steel, and concrete instead of logs and clay, and the methods happen to be contemporary engineering ones instead of hand labor. Each type of building—like Greenough's ship—takes on its special aesthetic character as the result of circumstances.

The common objection to contemporary functionalist architecture is that it is cold and graceless, no matter how practical it may be, and that its semi-automatic aesthetic is inadequate outside the workshop, the factory, or at best the low-cost public building. This idea is substantiated by many buildings designed under *Bauhaus* inspiration, and Le Corbusier's famous definition of a house as a "machine for living" is a pat, if unintentional, statement of func-

tionalist limitations. Only a fanatic would insist that man is a robot who must adopt a life harmonious to a machine in which he lives. Man is a sentient being who creates architecture in forms harmonious to his life. A problem of contemporary architects has been to reconcile the functional principle with the human desire for "unnecessary" beauty, without violating the former by continuing to borrow the latter from the past. A leader in this reconciliation has been Ludwig Miës van der Rohe (1886–   ).

Miës is at once a functionalist and a variety of classicist. He fuses the functionalist premise with a second one, that the proportions of a building may be arbitrarily controlled without conflicting with the practical necessities of its use, and a third, that the beauty of materials may opulently satisfy the need for decoration while they function simultaneously as exposed working elements.

Miës's Tugendhat House, like Le Corbusier's Savoye House [625], may no longer be the best example of its kind. But with the *Bauhaus* these two residences complete the standard historical trio of decisive landmarks in the development of the International Style. The living space of the Tugendhat House [694] is divided by polished onyx slabs, where concrete would have done the job practically but not elegantly. The chrome-plated metal supports are revealed without pretense, and are handsome. Polished woods, fine leathers and fabrics are used in the furniture, which Miës designed. The difference between the interior of the Tugendhat house and any "nonfunctional" interior where materials may be equally elegant is that in the Tugendhat house everything is ornamental yet nothing is structurally extraneous. The visual beauty of the room is not a veneer, but an integral part of the structure.

As a modern classicist determined to create harmonious proportions within the strictures of the functional ideal, Miës has returned to the classical device of the module as a basis for design. The module, in classical architecture, is a standard unit of measurement by which the proportions of the other parts of a composition are regulated. The semidiameter of the base

694. Miës van der Rohe: Tugendhat House, Brno, Czechoslovakia, 1930.

of the shaft of a column was the usual module. The height of the column would be determined by a multiple of it, as would be the size of the capital, the proportion of the entire column to the architrave above it, and so on through every element of a classical design.

If the use of a module could in itself assure a harmoniously proportioned design, any schoolboy who could multiply and divide could design a perfect building. The module serves as a regulating device, a limitation within which the designer must work, assuring a unity, a coherence, to the elements of a composition even though it is still the designer's function to combine them harmoniously. It is quite certain that in the Crystal Palace [334] the unity of an enormous building was contributed to by the "module" of the standard glass pane and the standard unit composing the iron skeleton, although these "modules" were set as a manufacturing convenience rather than as an aesthetic regulation in that wonderful and prophetic structure.

Miës van der Rohe's most recently completed building, at the time of this writing, is the Seagram Building [695], a little too effulgently dubbed the Tower of Light, in New York City. In its own way it is a skyscraper descendant of the Crystal Palace as well as the logical heir of the classical ideal of form harmonized through geometry. Selecting an arbitrary measurement as a module, the architect designed a tremendous functional commercial structure which, if the module principle is effective, should have the clarity, the purity, and the unity of a Greek temple, yet without recourse to borrowed Greek forms.

But to at least one towering architect, the architecture of the International Style remained cold, inhuman and forbidding, no matter how efficient it may be and no matter, even, how elegant. If Miës's glass skyscraper has the "clarity, purity, and unity of a Greek temple," it does not have the warmth and the recognition of humanity that are equally important in the architecture of the ancient classical world.

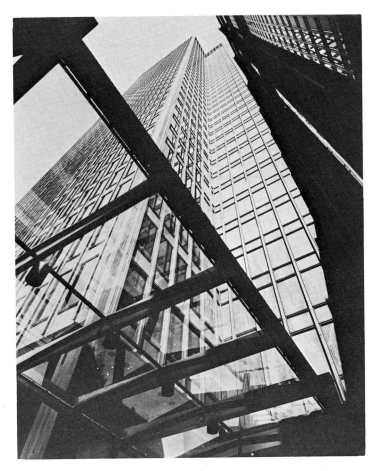

695. Miës van der Rohe: Seagram Building, New York, 1957. (Photo Ezra Stoller.)

Much of this book has been concerned with conflict between classic and romantic points of view. Frank Lloyd Wright (1869–1959), the American architect, was his country's archromantic, combining the cultivation of a rather irritatingly quarrelsome and sententious public personality with a career as the most versatile and inventive and imaginative architect of his century. He was an older man than the architects of the International Style, and as young men they found points of departure in his early work. Hence Wright was the uncle or the grandfather of the Savoye House, the Tugendhat House, the *Bauhaus*, and the spate of functional-international buildings everywhere. But he was wildly, implacably, and vehemently opposed to an architecture (he called it "flat-chested modern") that had developed only one aspect of his genius.

Wright could never have invented the phrase "a machine for living" except in derision. For him, man's house was still his cave, the place where he found shelter and seclusion, warmth, protection and intimacy. In contrast with the impersonality, the spare and chilly elegance of most modern houses, the houses Wright designed for himself were filled with objects he loved, even to the point of seeming cluttered. For Wright, a house remained man's assurance that he inhabited a benign universe. For this reason his designs are parts of the natural world in which they are built. His houses [696] lie upon the land as part of its contours, and by preference he built them of the stone on which they rest, or of warm-colored wood, or in any case of materials, in forms, that seem as native to a habitat as its plants, its rock ledges, the shape of its hills or the flatness of its planes. One of his houses, built in a gorge, incorporates a stream into its plan, while the house itself clings or rises or stretches flat in different parts, becoming an integral part of the sides of the gorge and the bed of the stream. Surrounded by trees and dappled by shadows, the house is so unified with topography that its inhabitant must surely feel not only the security and privacy of his own dwelling but, as well, the friendliness and mystery of man's union with nature.

Such romantic flights are hardly reassuring to a hardheaded businessman in need of a new, practical, economical building. Wright had a reputation, well earned, as an expensive architect whose experiments were likely to double the cost of a building. He was madly impractical from this point of view, yet his best-known work is not a residence but a group of commercial structures, the buildings he planned for the Johnson Wax Company [697]. The curious mushroom-shaped supports he designed in the administration building [698] seemed so dubious to building authorities that they demanded preliminary tests for strength—which were passed with flying colors. Typically, Wright combined this kind of engineering invention with a contradictory love of what can only be called

696. Wright: Taliesin, Spring Green, Wisconsin, 1925.

architectural fantasy. The argument that the mushroom supports are practical because they save floor space (with their tapering bases) is merely silly; more space could have been saved with any one of half a dozen familiar means of support. And any space that was saved, Wright sacrificed when he filled the interior with a forestlike repetition of the forms in areas where they spread their great supporting disks upward —and then support nothing, for only a portion of the area is covered by an upper story. It was the shape of the thing as an ornamental form, and the excitement of inventing it as an engineering one, that fascinated Wright.

The interior he thus created is next to magical in effect. The commissioning of such a building, which is at once a work of romantic art and a piece of industrial architecture, required an exceptional client who trusted an exceptional architect. The heavy additional cost has been more than made up for by the publicity Johnson's Wax has received indirectly all over the world— although this is not a consideration that can ordinarily be safely taken into account in commissioning an architect.

There has never been an architect like Wright or one of wider influence or of influence in so many directions. By forcing technological products toward the limits of new architectural forms they can assume, whether these forms are practically necessary ones or not, Wright dramatized engineering as expression and stimulated the imaginations of more hardheaded builders. His mystical veneration of such natural

697. WRIGHT: Johnson Wax Company, Racine, Wisconsin, 1949. (Photo courtesy S. C. Johnson and Son, Inc.)

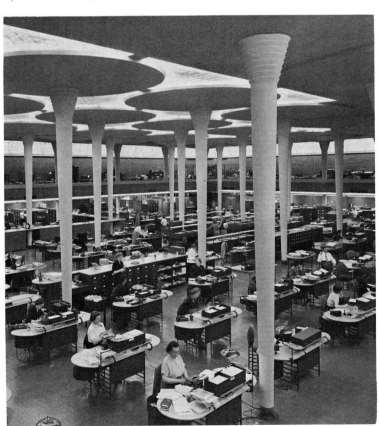

698. WRIGHT: Interior of Administration Building, Johnson Wax Company, (Photo courtesy S. C. Johnson and Son, Inc.)

551

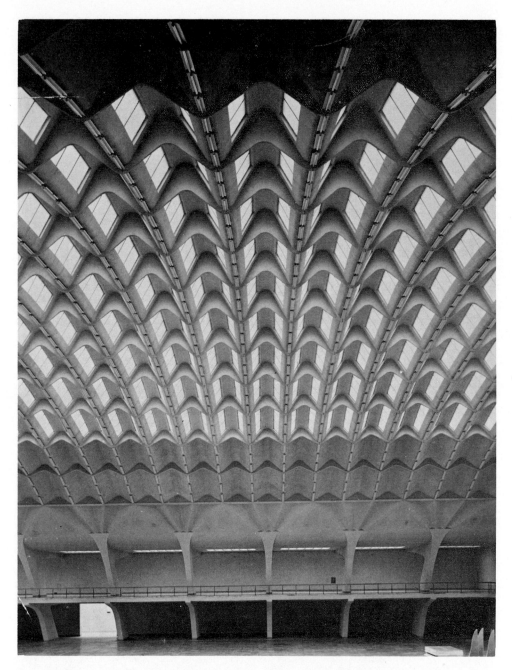

699. NERVI: Exhibition Hall, Turin, Italy, 1948–49. (From *Italy Builds* by G. E. Kidder Smith.)

materials as wood and stone, his insistence that their natural textures must not be violated, that they must be loved and respected as manifestations of the miracle of nature, has brought a new philosophical significance to domestic architecture, particuarly in America. His refusal to accept conventional plans for either domestic or public buildings, or to repeat his own, his insistence that each building must be an

700. UTZON: Opera House, Sydney, Australia, model. To be completed 1961. (Australian News and Information Bureau photograph by W. Brindle.)

individual problem in which the disposition of form and space must allow for special circumstances, was the genesis of functionalism, without its somewhat frigid objectivity. With all this to his credit, and with some of the most beautiful structures of the century bearing his name, it makes no difference in the long run that where Wright's designs have failed, they have failed disastrously. And even his unquestioning air of accepting himself as architecture's messiah in his public pronouncements, which was so irritating, must be forgiven, for after all he was far from alone in holding to that opinion.

As the second half of the century gets into its stride, it appears that Wright's rejection of "flat-chested modern" is on the verge of wholesale acceptance by generation of architects who have tired of the assembly-line character given to the International Style as it has become routine in thousands of busy contractors' offices. Especially, the use of concrete shells, molded into new and bizarre forms, is in-creasingly an exploration of engineering as the basis for structures where serviceableness fuses with fantasy. The Italian Pier Luigi Nervi (1891–) has experimented—successfully—for years with concrete as a medium adaptable to huge, incredibly light forms in which naked engineering is breathtakingly handsome [699]. His inventiveness is now being echoed by young architects everywhere in the Western world and in parts of the Eastern one as well. Wavering, flowing shapes are tending to replace functional angularities. The Danish architect Joern Utzon—as one name among many—has dramatized the concrete shell in his project for an opera house on the harbor front of Sydney, Australia [700]. It recalls "those grand wind muscles," the sails of Horatio Greenough's ship. In designs such as this, architecture is returning to the search for variety, personalism, and expressiveness after half a century of the discipline of the International Style, which begins to resemble a strait jacket.

INDEX

(The page on which an illustration appears is given in **bold-face** type.)

Daumier, Honoré (*cont.*)
    Saprelotte!—Full!, **93**, 94
    Soup, **100**, 100, 122
    Third Class Carriage, **100**, 100
    Le Ventre Législatif, **98**, 97–98, 102
    The Witnesses, **97**, 97
David, Jacques L., 3, 6–28, 31, 53, 56, 60, 75, 115, 156; art of, 31; art revolution of, 10; as artist, 22–24; balance in paintings of, 40; borrowed elements in, 164; Boucher's influence on, 211*n.*; breaks with tradition, 6; classical style of, 24; classicism of, 16–19, 20; color restrictions of, 48; and Daumier compared, 98; and Delacroix contrasted, 50; and Fragonard, 225*n.*; and French Revolution, 7–8, 14–15; and Géricault compared, 38–41; and Gros contrasted, 37; and Ingres, 27–28, 58; as landscapist, 115; last years of, 24; and Léger, 465–66; life of, 6–8; models for, 41; and Napoleon, 18, 19–22; pupils of, 25–28; quoted, 25, 30, 64; relations with Royal Academy, 6, 7, 12, 19; and troubadour painting, 64; and West, 238, 239, 240
    Antiochus and Stratonice, **9**, 8–9, 10, 11
    The Battle of the Romans and Sabines, **16**, **17**, **19**, 8, 16–19, 40, 111, 113, 466; caricatured, 93
    The Death of Socrates, **12**, 12–13, 16
    Lictors Bringing Back to Brutus the Bodies of His Sons, **13**, 13, 16, 18, 37, 243
    Marat, **14**, 14–15, 20, 37, 98
    Marie Antoinette on the Way to Execution, **7**, 7
    Mars Disarmed by Venus and the Graces, **24**, 24
    Mars Vanquished by Minerva, **24**, 24, 211*n.*
    Mongez, Antoine, and His Wife Angelica, **23**, 23–24
    The Oath of the Horatii, **11**, 9, 10–12, 13, 17*n.*, 18, 19, 23, 37, 38, 89, 111, 130, 131, 152, 238, 239
    Oath of the Tennis Court, 14, 21, 239
    Récamier, Madame, **20**, 19–20, 58, 85
    Le Sacre, **21**, 21–22, 23, 76
    Sériziat, Madame, **22**, 23, 244
    Sériziat, Monsieur, **22**, 23
Davidian formula, color in, 48; counterrevolution to, 39; end of, 65
Davies, Arthur B., 323
De Camp, Joseph R., 237*n.*
De Gas, Auguste, 195*n.*
Dead Man Revived by Touching the Bones of the Prophet Elisha, The, Allston, **254**, 255
Death of General Wolfe, The, West, **239**, 239
Death of Leonardo da Vinci, etc., The, Ingres, 64
Death and the Mother, Kollwitz, **440**, 440
Death on a Pale Horse, Ryder, **256**, 257
Death on a Pale Horse, West, **241**, 241–42
Death of Queen Elizabeth, The, Delaroche, 53
Death of Sardanapalus, The, Delacroix, **49**, **50**, 48–51, 98
Death of Socrates, The, David, **12**, 12–13, 16
Decamps, Alexandre G., 53, 145–46
    The Experts, **146**, 146
    Oriental Night Scene, **145**, 146
Decorative Figure on an Ornamental Background, Matisse, **417**, 416
Degas, Edgar, 181*n.*, 182, 192–207, 327; and classical discipline, 196–97; classicism of, 199–201; composition of, 378; and Eakins compared, 318; and Gauguin, 379, 381, 382, 385; group portraits by, 201; humanity of, 202, 210; impressionism of, 192–93, 195–99; and the impressionists, 203–07, 217; and Ingres, 196, 197; on outdoor painting, 232; pastels of, 205–06; personality of, 202, 203; pessimism of, 210; and Pissarro, 192; portraits by,

Degas, Edgar (*cont.*)
202; and Renoir contrasted, 210, 215, 216; as student, 196; subject matter of, 204; success of, 397; and Toulouse-Lautrec, 230, 231; and Vuillard contrasted, 387; women painters influenced by, 226, 227
    Ballerina and Lady with Fan, **205**, 205
    Bellelli Family, The, **194**, 194–95, 210, 216, 294–95
    Café, Boulevard Montmartre, **214**, 210, 215
    A Carriage at the Races, **198**, 197, 199, 296
    Degas's Father Listening to Lorenzo Pagans, **204**, 202
    Foyer de la Danse, **200**, 199–201, 215
    Head of a Young Woman, **203**, 202
    Lady on Horseback, **196**, 197
    Manet (studies of), **197**, 197
    Martelli, Diego, **199**, 199
    Musson, Estelle, **202**, 202
    Nude Arranging Her Hair, **206**, 206
    Portraits in an Office, **201**, 201
    Self-portrait in a Soft Hat, **203**, 202
    Sémiramis, drapery study for, **196**, 196–97
    Two Café Singers, **198**, 197
    Woman Rubbing Her Back with a Sponge, **207**, 207
    Woman Scratching, **206**, 205
    Women Ironing, **205**, 205
    Young Dancer, **207**, 207
Degas's Father Listening to Lorenzo Pagans, Degas, **204**, 202
de Heem, Jan D.
    Still-life, **400**; Matisse's variation on, **401**, 414
Dehodencq, Alfred, 54
Déjeuner sur l'Herbe, Le, Manet, **161**, **162**, 159, 160, 161–65, 170, 177, 181
de Kooning, Willem, 448
    Detour, 448
Delacroix, Eugène, 27, 38, 43–53, 60, 74, 75, 147, 155, 156, 158, 363; and abstract expressionism, 448; admitted to Institute, 52; aloofness of, 173; as a classicist, 246; color experiments and theories of, 47–48, 84, 85, 184; composition of, 50; and Constable, 47–48, 267; Corot on, 135; on Courbet, 113; and Daumier compared, 98; followers of, 52–55; and Goya compared, 75; as Guérin's pupil, 149; and Henriquel-Dupont compared, 147; and Ingres compared, 56–57; on Ingres, 65; and the impressionists, 184–85; life of, 43; and Manet, 159, 163, 168, 169; and Matisse contrasted, 413; Moroccan journal, 51–52; quoted, on immediate vision, 49, 86; and Salon of 1855, 113, 141; and Seurat, 329; State patronage for, 46; as student, 149, 347; texture of, 477
    The Abduction of Rebecca, **Pl. 2**, 52
    Dante and Vergil in Hell, **46**, 46, 47, 168
    The Death of Sardanapalus, **49**, **50**, 48–51, 98
    The Good Samaritan, **53**, 52
    Greece Expiring on the Ruins of Missolonghi, 47*n.*
    Heliodorus Driven from the Temple, 52
    Jacob Wrestling with the Angel, 52
    Liberty Leading the People, **89**, 88–89; compared with David and Goya, 89
    The Lion Hunt, **44**, 44, 52
    Odalisque with Parrot, **87**, 85
    St. Michael Killing the Dragon, 52
    Scenes of the Massacres of Scio, **47**, 47, 48, 51, 98, 109, 111, 140
    Self-portrait, **43**, 43–44
    Women of Algiers, Picasso's variations of, **488**, 487
Delaroche, Paul, 53; and Gleyre, 213*n.*; pupil of, 151
    The Children of Edward, **53**
    The Death of Queen Elizabeth, 53

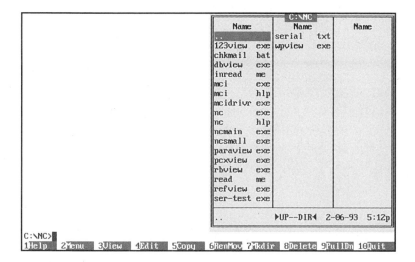

Fig. 30.1

The Norton
Commander
opening screen.

Although only the function key bar and the right panel are visible in the
initial screen, you can easily display the menu bar at the top of the
screen, and the left panel on the left half of the screen. Table 30.1 lists
the key combinations that turn the screen components on and off.

Table 30.1 Displaying the Commander Screen Components

Screen Component	Keys That Toggle the Display
Menu bar	F9
Function key bar	Ctrl+B
Left panel	Ctrl+F1
Right panel	Ctrl+F2

Using the Menus

After you press F9 (PullDn), the menu bar appears at the top of the
Commander screen (see fig. 30.2). This menu bar enables you to access
five Commander menus: Left, Files, Commands, Options, and Right.

The Left menu controls what you see in the left panel; the Right menu
controls what you see in the right panel. The Files menu enables you to
choose Commander options that deal with files. The Commands menu
contains disk-management commands that are similar to some of the

Norton Utilities commands. The Options menu contains options that enable you to control how Commander information is displayed on your computer. These menus are described in more detail in later sections of this chapter.

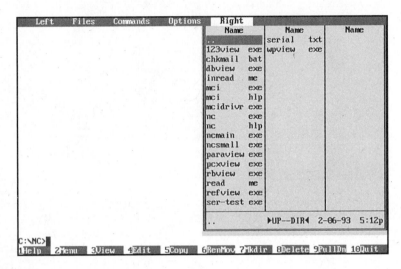

Fig. 30.2

Displaying
the Norton
Commander
menu bar.

Using the Function Key Bar

The function key bar appears at the bottom of the screen when the Norton Commander is in operation. If you are using a mouse, you can choose one of the function key options by clicking it. If you are using the keyboard, press the function key that corresponds to the menu number. To choose the Help option (1), for example, press F1. The function keys are described in the following sections.

One of the first function keys you should learn about is F10, which is the Quit key. If you want to end Norton Commander, simply press F10. A small dialog box appears in the center of the screen, asking you to verify that you want to quit. To exit Commander, choose Yes or press Enter.

Using the DOS Prompt and the History Option

The DOS prompt also appears in the Norton Commander screen, directly above the function key bar. As mentioned previously, you can use Commander menus to access commands, or you can enter DOS commands directly from the DOS prompt.

Commander offers another convenient feature for entering DOS commands. If you recently entered a DOS command and want to repeat that command, you can use the **History** option in the Commands menu to review and choose any of the last 15 commands you entered at the DOS prompt. You can access the **History** option by choosing it from the Commands menu or pressing Alt+F8. A panel then appears on-screen, listing up to 15 commands.

Using the Left and Right Panel Displays

With DOS's DIR command, you can display the contents of only one directory at a time. When you want to use one of the directory's files in a command such as COPY or RENAME, you must spell out the full file name—and you had better not make any typing mistakes.

Norton Commander's left and right panels, however, enable you to display two directories on-screen—twice as much information as you can with DOS. You can choose files or directories in these panels without worrying about typing the file or directory names. These features are among the reasons why using Commander's right and left panels is easier than using DOS commands.

The contents of the right and left panels are controlled by the options in the Right and Left pull-down menus. Depending on your preferences, these panels can contain the following information:

- A brief directory of files (names only)

- A full directory of files (including dates, times, and sizes)

- A graphic representation of the directory tree

- Information about the directory and disk

- The displayed contents of a file

When you activate the left and right panels in Commander by pressing Ctrl+F1 and Ctrl+F2, respectively, you see a display like the one shown in figure 30.3.

Usually, after you activate both panels, the left panel is set up to display the directory tree structure of the disk, and the right panel is set up to display the files in the directory that is selected in the left panel.

You can access information in only one panel at a time. When both panels are displayed, you move from one active panel to the other by pressing the Tab key (or by pointing with the mouse to a panel and clicking). When a panel is active, you can use the arrow keys or the mouse to select files or directories that you want to access or use in some way.

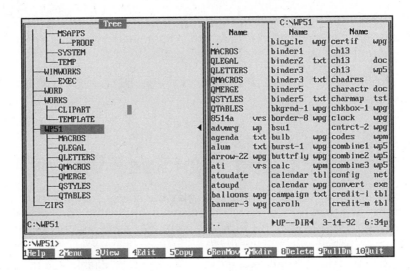

Fig. 30.3

The Norton Commander screen with both panels activated.

If you want to swap the current left and right panels on-screen, choose **S**wap Panels from the Commands menu or press Ctrl+U. The reason for swapping panels is purely aesthetic; you can perform the same operations no matter which panel holds the information. Using the **S**wap Panels option, however, is faster than swapping manually by choosing different options for each panel.

Using the Keyboard To Control the Panel Display

As mentioned previously, you press Ctrl+F1 to toggle the left panel on and off and Ctrl+F2 to toggle the right panel on and off. Commander provides several other keyboard commands for controlling the panel display and for manipulating the files and directories listed in the panels. Table 30.2 lists these keyboard commands.

Table 30.2 Keyboard Commands for Controlling the Panel Display	
Key(s)	**Description**
↑	Scrolls panel information up
↓	Scrolls panel information down
Enter	Changes to a directory if that directory name is highlighted (works like an NCD command); begins a program if a program file name (a BAT, EXE, or COM file, for example) is highlighted; has no effect if any other file name is highlighted

Key(s)	Description
Ctrl+PgUp	Changes to the parent directory
Ctrl+ \	Changes to the root directory
Gray +	Selects a group of files
Gray –	Deselects a group of files
Alt+*filename*	Speed-searches for a file
Ins	Selects or deselects file at cursor position
Ctrl+Enter	Copies file or directory name to command line
Ctrl+P	Turns inactive panel on or off
Ctrl+O	Turns both panels on or off
Ctrl+U	Swaps panels

You can change to another directory by selecting that directory with the arrow keys or the mouse, or by typing the following command at the DOS prompt:

NCD *dirname*

You press Ctrl+PgUp to change to the parent directory and Ctrl+\ to change to the root directory.

At times, you may want to select several files at the same time (for example, to copy a group of files with the F5 key). You can select a group of files with the gray + and – keys, which usually are located at the right end of the keyboard. If you press the gray + key, Commander prompts you to enter all files to be included in the selection. You can enter ***.TXT**, for example, to include all files with a TXT extension. The selected files then appear highlighted in the panel. To exclude files from the list, press the gray – key. You can press the gray – key and then enter **B.***, for example, to exclude all files that begin with the letter B. After selecting files, you can use the function key commands to copy, rename, move, or delete these files.

The Alt+*filename* command enables you to find a file in a directory quickly. Suppose that you are looking for a file named SAMPLING.TXT and you know that the directory in which this file is located contains 200 files. You can scroll through the entire directory list until you find SAMPLING.TXT, but an easier method is to press Alt+S. A small dialog box appears at the bottom-right corner of the screen. The highlight in the directory panel points to the first file in the list that begins with the letter S. After you press the second letter in the file name (A), the highlight moves to the first file name in the directory that begins with the letters SA. You soon will locate the file you want. You can then use that file in a command to copy the file, rename it, and so on.

The Ctrl+Enter command enables you to copy the name of a high-lighted file to the DOS command area quickly. Suppose that you want to enter the following command at the DOS command prompt:

WP51 FY9293RT.WP5

Instead of typing the whole command (and possibly misspelling the file name), you can highlight the file name in the directory panel, type **WP51**, and press Ctrl+Enter. The name FY9293RT.WP5 appears in the DOS command line; you have entered the command you wanted.

As mentioned previously, to control exactly what information appears in the panels (and the way that information appears), you use the options in the Left and Right pull-down menus. The following sections describe these menu options.

Displaying Files in Brief and in Full

The **Brief** and **Full** options in the Left and Right menus determine how files are displayed in a panel. The **Brief** option lists only the file names; the **Full** option (the default) also lists the file size, date, and time.

The **Brief** option enables you to display more file names at one time. Figure 30.4 shows an example of a right-panel display with the **Brief** option selected. (For an example of full mode, see the right panel shown in fig. 30.5.)

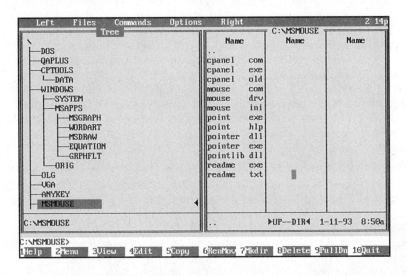

Fig. 30.4

Displaying the right panel in brief mode.

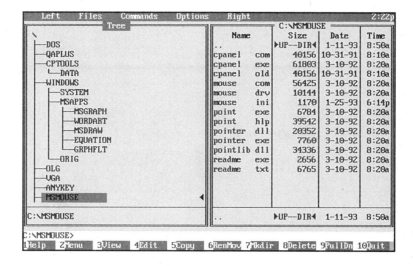

Fig. 30.5

Displaying the
full version of
the file list.

If you have many files in a directory and want to see only the file
names, use the **Brief** option so that you do not have to scroll to find
the files you want.

Displaying Summary Information

When you choose the **Info** option from the Left or Right menu, the
panel corresponding to that menu displays information about the
current drive. This information is similar to the information the
DOS CHKDSK command generates (see fig. 30.6).

The top part of the Info panel tells you the amount of memory available, the disk size and disk space available, the number of files in use,
and how much space the files occupy.

Notice that the bottom part of the Info panel shown in figure 30.6 includes the message No 'dirinfo' file in this directory. In the
DIRINFO file, you can place information about, or a brief description of,
the contents of the directory. In the WP51 directory, for example, you
can place the message This directory contains WordPerfect
Version 5.1.

If you want to create such a DIRINFO file for the current directory,
press F4 (Edit). A small edit window appears at the bottom of the Info
panel. Enter your summary information and press F10 to save the
DIRINFO file. Thereafter, whenever you display the Info panel for that
directory, your description appears at the bottom of the panel.

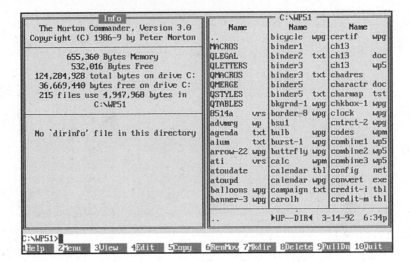

Fig. 30.6

Displaying the
Info panel.

After you examine the Info panel, you can return the panel to its previous state by pressing Ctrl+L or by choosing another panel option from the Left or Right menu.

The Info option is useful for several reasons. The Bytes Free information tells you how much RAM is available for use by programs. (Most programs have minimum memory requirements.) Commander itself uses about 13K, but Commander frees itself from memory when a program begins and then restarts itself when the program finishes. When you start a program, therefore, you have 13K more available memory than the Info panel reported.

Info also tells you how many bytes are free on a disk. This information can be important if you need to copy files to the disk. Displaying the Info panel can save you the trouble of trying to copy files that the disk cannot handle. If you don't know the amount of memory available on your floppy disks, you can get that information from the total-bytes message.

Displaying a Directory Tree

Choosing the Tree option from the Left or Right menu displays a graphic tree of the disk-directory structure, as shown in the left panel of figure 30.3. After you activate a panel that contains a directory tree, you can select a directory. If the other panel is set up to display file names, that panel displays the file names associated with the selected directory.

Sorting Files

File names displayed in the panels may be listed in various sorted orders, according to the active options in the Left and Right menus. Sort orders are helpful if you are trying to locate files by a certain criterion, such as when the files were created or what extension was used.

You can list files in order by name, extension, time of creation, or size; or you can choose to have the files listed in unsorted order, which is how they normally would appear in a DOS DIR list. After you choose the Name, Extension, Time, Size, or Unsorted option from the Left or Right menu, a check mark appears to the left of the option name.

Filtering Files

The Filter option enables you to specify which files are displayed in a panel. When you choose Filter from the Left or Right menu, the Filter dialog box appears, enabling you to choose the type of files to be displayed (see fig. 30.7).

Fig. 30.7

The Filter dialog box.

Your choices are All Files, Executable Files, and Custom. If you choose the Custom option, you then must enter a file specification; use the wild-card characters—the question mark (?) and the asterisk (*)—to describe the files to be included. If you want to list only files with the PIX extension, for example, choose the Custom option and then enter the file specification *.PIX.

Changing Drives

The **Drive** option in the Left and Right menus enables you to specify which drive should be used for the panel. When you choose this option, a dialog box displays a list of drive names. Choose a drive and press Enter. The panel then reflects the change.

Rereading and Updating File Information

The **Re**-read option in the Left and Right menus makes Commander reread file information from the disk and then update this information in a panel. The program often performs this operation automatically when you make a change. If you change a disk in a drive or modify a file with a memory-resident program, however, you should choose the **Re**-read option to make sure that Commander has up-to-date knowledge about the files on disk.

Choosing **Re**-read when the directory tree is activated ensures that Commander has current information about all directories on disk.

Displaying a Quick View of Files

The Left and Right menus' Quick View option displays the contents of a file that is highlighted in the other panel. You can view the contents of files from programs such as Lotus 1-2-3, WordStar, WordPerfect, and dBASE III, even if you don't have those programs. In addition, you can view graphic files that match the ZSoft PCX standard.

The Quick View option is similar to the F3 (View) key (see the section "Viewing Files with F3" later in this chapter). This option, however, initially displays only half a screen rather than the full-screen F3 view.

Figure 30.8 shows a Quick View panel of a Lotus 1-2-3 spreadsheet file. Notice in the function key bar that the F3 key, which previously was called View, now is called Zoom. When a Quick View panel is displayed, you can press F3 (Zoom) to expand the view from half a screen to a full screen.

Use the arrow keys to move the cursor on-screen and to scroll the spreadsheet in any direction. If you use a mouse, move the pointer to any edge of the spreadsheet until you see the pointer change to an arrow. Then click to scroll the screen in the direction of the arrow.

Managing Directories with Norton Commander

Norton Commander enables you to access and manage your directories on disk. Using Commander, you can make new directories by pressing a function key, access a command similar to the Norton Change Directory (NCD) command, and compare directories.

```
┌─────── 1-2-3 View ───────┐┌──────C:\NC───────────────────┐
│A1: 'IANLP Membership Analysis - Janu││ Name   │ Size │ Date │ Time │
│     A        B        C     ││chkmail bat│   342│10-23-89│ 3:00p│
│1 IANLP Membership Analysis - Janua  ││dbview  exe│ 61026│10-23-89│ 3:00p│
│2                            ││inread  me │  1312│10-23-89│ 3:00p│
│3                            ││mci     exe│103396│10-23-89│ 3:00p│
│4                            ││mci     hlp│ 27050│10-23-89│ 3:00p│
│5        A        M          ││mcidrivr exe│ 71272│10-23-89│ 3:00p│
│6 Region                     ││nc      exe│  3100│10-23-89│ 3:00p│
│7    1       59       85     ││nc      hlp│ 45727│10-23-89│ 3:00p│
│8    2       57       56     ││nc      ini│   476│ 2-23-93│12:42p│
│9    3      127       87     ││ncmain  exe│139274│10-23-89│ 3:00p│
│10   4       36       27     ││ncsmall exe│  2804│ 9-16-88│ 2:01p│
│11   5       38       44     ││nlpjan93 wk1│ 13796│ 2-12-93│ 7:44p│
│12   6       78       55     ││paraview exe│ 62596│10-23-89│ 3:00p│
│13   7       67       31     ││pcxview exe│ 46094│10-23-89│ 3:00p│
│14   8        6        5     ││rbview  exe│ 67966│10-23-89│ 3:00p│
│15   9       10       40     ││read    me │   974│10-23-89│ 3:00p│
│16        ──────── ──────── ││refview exe│ 63492│10-23-89│ 3:00p│
│17          478      430     ││ser-test exe│  4480│10-23-89│ 3:00p│
│                             ││                              │
│nlpjan93.wk1      13,796     ││nlpjan93.wk1  13796  2-12-93  7:44p│
└─────────────────────────────┘└──────────────────────────────┘
C:\NC>
1Help 2Menu 3Zoom 4Edit 5Copy 6RenMov 7Mkdir 8Delete 9PullDn 10Quit
```

Fig. 30.8

Using the Quick
View option.

Table 30.3 summarizes the commands you use to perform these tasks.

Table 30.3 Commands for Managing Directories

Task	Key(s)	Menu Command
Make directory	F7	**M**ake Directory option (Files menu)
Access NCD program	Alt+F10	NCD Tree option (Commands menu)
Compare directories		**C**ompare Directories option (Commands menu)

Creating Directories

The F7 (Mkdir) key enables you to make a new directory on disk. After you press F7, you are prompted to enter the name of the new directory. Enter the full path name. To make a directory named KWIKSTAT as a subdirectory of the root directory, type the path name **\KWIKSTAT** and press Enter. To make a directory named LETTERS as a subdirectory of the WP51 directory, type **\WP51\LETTERS** and press Enter.

When you press F7 (Mkdir), the Norton Commander and Norton Utilities information file TREEINFO.NCD is updated so that the NCD command works properly without having to rescan the disk to update the directory tree.

You also can make a directory by using Norton Commander's NCD command and pressing F7. See the following section for details.

Navigating Directories with NCD Tree

The NCD Tree option in the Commands menu is similar to the Norton Utilities Norton Change Directory (NCD) command. (Chapter 23 contains a detailed description of that command.) The NCD Tree option enables you to navigate among the directories on disk. This capability becomes more useful as your directory structure grows more complex.

Choose the NCD Tree option from the Commands menu or press Alt+F10. You see a display similar to the one shown in figure 30.9.

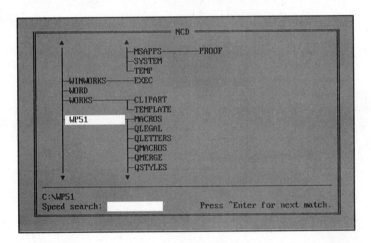

Fig. 30.9

Displaying a directory tree.

After the directory tree is displayed, you can change directories simply by selecting a new directory.

Table 30.4 lists the specific direction keys available when working with the NCD Tree display.

Table 30.4 NCD Tree Keys

Key	Description
↑, ↓, ←, →	Moves in direction of arrow
PgUp	Moves up the tree one page (19 directories at a time on a standard 25-line screen)

Key	Description
PgDn	Moves down the tree one page (19 directories at a time on a standard 25-line screen)
Home	Moves to beginning of tree
End	Moves to end of tree
Gray +	Moves forward (down) one directory entry
Gray –	Moves backward (up) one directory entry

Other keyboard shortcuts are available when you are working with the NCD Tree display. To select a directory, for example, you can type its name. You may not have to type the entire directory name for it to be highlighted. When you begin typing, NCD begins a speed search, matching the letters you type to the directory names. You need to type only enough letters to make the name unique.

To choose the \WP51\QLETTERS directory from the tree displayed in figure 30.9, for example, you can press W at the Speed search prompt. After you press W, the directory name WINWORKS is highlighted on-screen. If more than one directory name begins with the letter you press, as in this example, the first matching directory in the directory list is highlighted. To search for the next match, press Ctrl+Enter or the next letter of the directory name. For this example, press P.

Table 30.5 summarizes the NCD Tree shortcut commands.

Table 30.5 NCD Tree Keyboard Shortcuts

Key(s)	Description
Any letter	Begins speed search to select a directory
Ctrl+Enter	Searches for next match
Enter	Changes directory
F2	Rescans and rebuilds TREEINFO.NCD file
F6	Renames a directory
F7	Makes a directory
F8	Deletes a directory
Esc or F10	Quits NCD

Notice that table 30.5 lists several function keys. These keys are located at the bottom of the NCD Tree display and are described in more detail in the following list:

- *Rescanning a disk with F2.* Pressing F2 (Rescan) causes NCD to rescan a disk in order to update the directory structure and the TREEINFO.NCD file, which contains the tree-structure information. If you make or remove a directory with the DOS MD or RD command rather than the NCD command, the TREEINFO.NCD file becomes out-of-date. When you rescan to make sure that this file contains current information, the NCD Tree command works faster. The Rescan option (F2) has the same function as the Re-read option in the Left and Right menus.

- *Renaming a directory with F6.* The F6 (Rename) key enables you to rename a directory. DOS has no equivalent feature. To rename a directory, highlight the directory in the NCD Tree, press F6 (Rename), type a new name, and then press Enter.

- *Making a directory with F7.* The F7 (Mkdir) key enables you to make a new directory. First point to the directory that will be the parent directory of the new directory; then press F7, type the new directory name, and press Enter. For example, to create a subdirectory of MISC named TMP, point to MISC in the tree, press F7, type **TMP**, and press Enter. The result is a directory named \MISC\TMP. To create a subdirectory of the root directory, highlight that directory before pressing F7. When you use F7 to create a directory, the TREEINFO.NCD file is updated automatically.

  F7 creates a new directory only in the NCD Tree screen. If you press F7 in other screens, a dialog box appears, prompting you for the name of the new directory.

- *Removing a directory with F8.* The F8 (Delete) key enables you to remove a directory that contains no files or subdirectories. To delete a directory, simply highlight the directory name and press F8. When you use this method to delete a directory, the TREEINFO.NCD file is updated automatically.

Using the Compare Directories Option

The Compare Directories option in the Commands menu enables you to compare the contents of two directories. Before you use this command, you must display one directory in the right panel and the other directory in the left panel.

Any file in one directory that has the same name as, but a more recent date than, a file in the other directory is highlighted. This feature can be helpful if you want to compare similar files. Suppose that you want to make sure that a directory on a floppy disk contains all the latest files from the hard disk directory. You can use the Compare Directories option. You then can make both directories identical by copying unmatching files to the other directory with the COPY command (see the section "Copying Files" later in this chapter).

Figure 30.10 shows a comparison of two directories (NU and NU7) on drive C. Any files that do not appear in both directories appear in a different color or highlight.

```
┌─ C:\NU ──────────────────────┐  ┌─ C:\NU7 ──────────────────────┐
│  Name     │ Size   │ Date   │ Time │  │  Name     │ Size   │ Date   │ Time │
│ ..        │▶UP──DIR◀│2-15-93│ 9:19p│  │ ..        │▶UP──DIR◀│1-28-93│ 8:25p│
│20fig11a pcx│  27367 │2-17-93│ 7:21p│  │FIGS       │▶SUB-DIR◀│1-29-93│10:19p│
│advise   hlp│  69081 │1-19-93│ 1:00a│  │TEMP       │▶SUB-DIR◀│2-12-93│11:41a│
│be       exe│  19033 │1-19-93│ 1:00a│  │10fig01 pcx│  17784 │1-29-93│10:54p│
│calibrat exe│  52900 │1-19-93│ 1:00a│  │advise   hlp│  78156 │2-02-93│ 1:00a│
│calibrat hlp│  15108 │1-19-93│ 1:00a│  │askit      │    240 │2-21-93│ 9:53p│
│config   sav│     17 │2-18-93│10:21p│  │be       exe│  19049 │2-02-93│ 1:00a│
│config   sec│   2048 │2-18-93│10:26p│  │calibrat exe│  51192 │2-02-93│ 1:00a│
│config   sys│     41 │1-19-93│ 1:00a│  │calibrat hlp│  15108 │2-02-93│ 1:00a│
│config1  npc│    143 │1-19-93│ 1:00a│  │color      │    119 │2-21-93│ 9:44p│
│config2  npc│    143 │1-19-93│ 1:00a│  │config   sys│     41 │2-02-93│ 1:00a│
│config3  npc│    143 │1-19-93│ 1:00a│  │config1  npc│    143 │2-02-93│ 1:00a│
│diskedit exe│ 128439 │1-19-93│ 1:00a│  │config2  npc│    143 │2-02-93│ 1:00a│
│diskedit hlp│  78352 │1-19-93│ 1:00a│  │config3  npc│    143 │2-02-93│ 1:00a│
│diskmon  exe│  16811 │1-19-93│ 1:00a│  │daily      │    454 │2-21-93│10:08p│
│diskmon  hlp│   8514 │1-19-93│ 1:00a│  │diskedit exe│ 129867 │2-02-93│ 1:00a│
│diskreet exe│  50132 │1-19-93│ 1:00a│  │diskedit hlp│  78352 │2-02-93│ 1:00a│
│diskreet hlp│  21469 │1-19-93│ 1:00a│  │diskmon  exe│  16767 │2-02-93│ 1:00a│
├──────────────────────────────┤  ├──────────────────────────────┤
│ 32,166 bytes in 6 selected files │  │3,658,487 bytes in 98 selected files│
└──────────────────────────────┘  └──────────────────────────────┘
C:\NU7>
1Help  2Menu  3View  4Edit  5Copy  6RenMov  7Mkdir  8Delete  9PullDn  10Quit
```

Fig. 30.10

Comparing directories.

Managing Files with Norton Commander

Along with facilitating management of your directories, Norton Commander enables you to manage your files on disk with options that exceed DOS's capabilities. You can use Commander to copy, rename, move, and delete files. You can also set file attributes and find files on disk.

Table 30.6 summarizes the options you use to perform these tasks.

Table 30.6 Commands for Managing Files

Task	Function Key(s)	Menu Command
Copying files	F5	Copy (Files menu)
Renaming files	F6	Rename or Move (Files menu)

continues

Table 30.6 Continued

Task	Function Key(s)	Menu Command
Moving files	F6	**R**ename or Move (Files menu)
Deleting files	F8	**D**elete (Files menu)
Setting attributes		File **A**ttributes (Files menu)
Finding files	Alt+F7	**F**ind File (Commands menu)

These options are described in the following sections.

Copying Files

You can access the **C**opy option by pressing F5 (Copy) or by choosing **C**opy from the Files menu. This option, which is similar to the DOS COPY command, enables you to copy one or more files to another disk or location. When you use the Commander Copy option, however, you are prompted for the information on which files to copy and where to copy them. You therefore do not have to remember the correct DOS COPY command syntax.

When you are working with a disk that contains many files, you may want to limit the files that appear in a panel. You can do so by setting the filter to display files that match a certain file specification. If you are working only with *.EXE files, for example, set the filter to display only those files (refer to the earlier section "Filtering Files").

To copy a file, follow these steps:

1. Display in a panel the files that you want to copy.

2. Select the file in the Commander panel. To select multiple files, use the gray + and – keys or the mouse.

3. Choose **C**opy from the Files menu or press F5. Commander prompts you for a destination (see fig. 30.11).

4. Enter the name of a disk drive (such as **A:**), a path name (such as **\WP51**), or a combination (such as **C:\WP51**). When you are specifying the destination, you can press F10 to display a tree of the available directories. From this tree, you can highlight the directory to which you want to copy the files.

5. After you type or select the destination, press Enter. The copy operation begins.

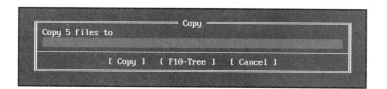

Fig. 30.11

A prompt for a
copy destination.

Another way to copy a file (regardless of the panels displayed) is to
press Shift+F5 at the DOS prompt. Commander asks you for the file
specification and the destination (see fig. 30.12).

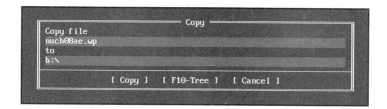

Fig. 30.12

Using the manual
copy process to
specify the
destination file.

You also can press F10 to display a directory tree. Highlight a directory
name in the tree and then press Enter to select that directory as the
destination. (You also can use the mouse to select a directory.)

Renaming and Moving Files

The **R**ename or Move option, which you access from the Files menu or
with F6 (Rename), enables you to rename one or more files in the same
directory or to move files from one location on a disk to another location on the same disk or a different one. The rename process works
much like the copy process but changes the name of a file in a directory instead of copying the file. You use the move process to specify a
destination other than the current directory. A move operation copies
the file to the new destination and erases the original file. DOS offers no
equivalent MOVE command.

To rename or move a file, follow these steps:

1. Select the file.

2. Choose **R**ename or Move from the Files menu or press F6.
   A prompt appears for you to enter the destination (or new
   name) for the file.

3. To rename the selected file, specify the destination as a file name or a file specification containing the wild-card characters * or ?. If you want to select all files with the WP extension (*.WP), type ***.BAK** as the destination. This operation renames all files with the WP extension to files with a BAK extension.

   To move the selected file, enter the name of a different destination disk or directory, or press F10 to display the directory tree and then select the destination. If you specify a different directory or drive, the selected files are moved to the new location under their original names. If you choose a destination and also include a file specification, the files are moved and renamed. If, for example, you select all files with the WP extension in the WP51 directory in drive C, and you specify the destination A:\WP51*.BAK, the files move from the original C:\WP51 directory to the A:\WP51 directory and are renamed from WP files to BAK files.

4. If the file that you want to copy or move already exists in the target directory, Commander displays the following message:

   ```
   Do you wish to write over the old file?
   ```

   Choose **Overwrite**, **All**, or **Skip**. **Overwrite** enables you to copy or move the current file. With **All**, you can use the copy and move operations for all other files to be copied or moved (no more prompts will appear). **Skip** means that you want to skip this particular copy or move operation.

To perform a rename or move operation manually, press Shift+F6. Commander prompts you to enter the name of the file to be renamed or moved and to enter the destination. You can press F10 to select a destination directory in the directory tree.

Deleting Files

The **Delete** option, which you access from the Files menu or with F8, enables you to delete one or more files.

To delete a file, follow these steps:

1. Select the file.

2. Choose **Delete** from the Files menu or press F8 (Delete). The Delete dialog box appears (see fig. 30.13).

3. Choose the **Delete** option to delete the files or choose **Cancel** to cancel the procedure.

To delete a file manually, press Shift+F8. Commander prompts you to enter the file specification of the file to be deleted. To delete all files with the BAK extension, type ***.BAK** and press Enter.

Fig. 30.13

The Delete
dialog box.

Setting File Attributes

File attributes enable you to set the read-only, archive, hidden, and system attributes for files. These attributes are the same as those described for the Norton Utilities File Find and File Attributes programs (see Chapter 9). You can set file attributes in Norton Commander by choosing the File **A**ttributes option from the Files menu.

To set file attributes, follow these steps:

1. Select the file or files for which you want to set attributes.

2. Choose File **A**ttributes from the Files menu. The Attributes dialog box appears (see fig. 30.14).

 If you selected only one file, the Clear column does not appear in the Attributes dialog box; only the Set column appears.

Fig. 30.14

The Attributes
dialog box.

3. Choose the attributes you want by highlighting a check box and pressing the space bar or clicking the appropriate check boxes.

4. Highlight the Set option at the bottom of the dialog box and press Enter to activate the settings, or choose Cancel or press Esc to cancel the procedure.

Finding Files

The Find File option in the Commands menu is similar to the File Find command in Norton Utilities. Find File enables you to locate files on disk by searching for matching file specifications.

To find a file, follow these steps:

1. Choose Find File from the Commands menu or press Alt+F7. The following prompt appears:

   File(s) to find:

2. To search for one file (such as REPORT.93), type the full file name at the prompt. To search for a group of files, type a file specification that includes wild-card characters (for example, type ***.PCX**).

3. Press Enter to initiate the search. If Commander finds a file that matches the file specification, Commander displays the directory, the file name, the size, and the date and time when the file was created. If Commander finds many files that match the specification, it lists them on-screen, grouped in their respective directories.

Figure 30.15 shows the results of a Find File search for all files matching the specification *.PCX.

Fig. 30.15

Results of a Find File search.

To move to the directory containing the file in which you are interested, use the up- and down-arrow keys to highlight the file and then press Enter. If you want to change to the directory for a particular file, highlight that file name and then choose the Chdir option at the bottom of the dialog box. If you want to begin a new search, choose the New Search option. Choose Quit FF to end the Find File procedure.

Viewing Files with F3

The F3 (View) key is one of the handiest features of Norton Commander. This function key enables you to examine the contents of a file without using the program in which that file was created. To look at a dBASE IV database, for example, you normally have to start the dBASE IV program, enter a command to get the file you want, and then enter another command to display the contents of the file. With Commander, however, you simply highlight the file name on-screen and press F3. If you want to enter the name of a file manually, press Shift+F3. Commander then prompts you for the name of the file you want to view.

You can use the View option to display files created in several major software programs. (See table 30.7 for a list of compatible programs.) Keep in mind that this information is not exhaustive, however, because several other programs create files that use the file formats of the popular programs listed in table 30.7. The programs PC-FILE:db (Buttonware) and Kwikstat (TexaSoft), for example, create and use dBASE III-type files. Thus, you can view PC-FILE:db and Kwikstat files with Norton Commander's View option.

Table 30.7 Programs Compatible with Commander's View Option	
Program Type	**Programs**
Database programs	dBASE II, III, III PLUS, and IV
	dbXL
	FoxBASE
	FoxPro
	TexaSoft Kwikstat
	Microsoft Works
	Nantucket Clipper
	Paradox
	R:BASE
	Reflex
Graphics programs	All programs that create ZSoft standard PCX-type (Paintbrush) files

continues

Table 30.7 Continued	
Program Type	**Programs**
Spreadsheet programs	1-2-3 (Releases 1.x, 2.x, and 3.x) Quattro, Quattro Pro Excel Microsoft Works Mosaic Twin Multiplan 4.0 Symphony VP-Planner Plus Words & Figures
Word processing programs	Microsoft Word 4.0, 5.0, and 5.5 Microsoft Windows Write Microsoft Works MultiMate WordPerfect 4.2, 5.0, and 5.1 WordStar Pro, WordStar 2000 XyWrite All word processing and editing programs that create ASCII text files

 NOTE Your use of the View option in some graphics programs may be restricted by your monitor's capability to display colors and by your computer's memory.

The following sections describe how to use the View option to view databases, spreadsheets, and word processing files.

Viewing Database Files

Norton Commander recognizes common database files for the programs listed in the preceding section. To view the contents of a database file—a dBASE IV file, for example—highlight the file name in a panel and press F3 (View). Figure 30.16 shows the screen that appears when you select a database file named MAGAZINE.DBF. The information displayed is the first record of the database.

By using the arrow keys, you can page through the database records and examine them one at a time, or you can use the mouse to scroll the records. You cannot change any of the information in the database, however, when you use the Commander View option.

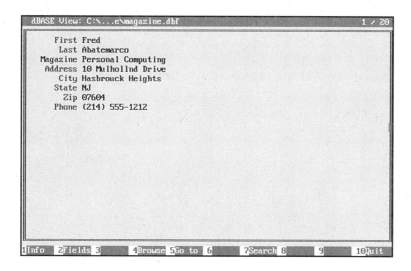

```
dBASE View: C:\...e\magazine.dbf                         1 / 20

    First Fred
     Last Abatemarco
 Magazine Personal Computing
  Address 10 Mulhollnd Drive
     City Hasbrouck Heights
    State NJ
      Zip 07604
    Phone (214) 555-1212




 1Info   2Fields 3        4Browse 5Go to  6       7Search 8        9        10Quit
```

Fig. 30.16

Using the View option to view a dBASE IV database file.

At the top of the view screen, you see information about which view method is being used to display the contents of a file. Figure 30.16 indicates dBASE View.

The number of the record being viewed and the total number of records in the database appear in the top-right corner of the screen. In figure 30.16, the message 1 / 20 means that the database contains 20 records and that you are viewing record 1.

Notice also the function key options at the bottom of the dBASE View screen. Table 30.8 lists these function keys and other command and direction keys that you can use when you view database files.

Table 30.8 Keyboard Commands in Database View

Key(s)	Description
↑ or Ctrl+E	Goes back one field
↓ or Ctrl+X	Goes forward one field
PgUp or Ctrl+R	Moves up one page or to preceding record
PgDn or Ctrl+C	Moves down one page or to following record

continues

Table 30.8 Continued

Key(s)	Description
Gray –	Goes to preceding record
Gray +	Goes to following record
Ctrl+Home or Ctrl+PgUp	Goes to first record
Ctrl+End or Ctrl+PgDn	Goes to last record
F1	Displays file information
F2	Displays field information
F4	Browses
F5	Goes to specified record
F7	Searches
Shift+F7	Continues a search
Ctrl+Pause	Stops a search
Esc or F10	Exits view and returns to Commander menus

When you first view a database, a single record is displayed on-screen. If you press F4 (Browse), the display changes to look much like a browse in dBASE, with one record displayed per line. Figure 30.17 shows this display for a magazine database.

By using this method, you can see multiple records at one time. Notice, however, that only the first three fields of the record are displayed. To view the information off the screen to the right, press the right-arrow key until the information in the other fields appears. To return to viewing a single record at a time, press F4 again.

Suppose that you want to find information—the phone number of Sam Jones, for example—in a particular record. If you press F7 (Search), the Search dialog box appears. In this dialog box, you can enter a *search key* (the text you want to search for). Figure 30.18 shows how you enter the information necessary to search for the name *Jones*.

After you enter the search key and press Enter, the first record containing that key in any field appears on-screen. If the record shown is not the one for which you are looking, you can press Shift+F7 to continue the search.

```
 dBASE View: C:\...e\magazine.dbf                         1 / 20
 First          Last            Magazine
 Fred           Abatemarco      Personal Computing
 Negash         Abdurhman       Administrative Management
 Eric           Adams           Business Software
 Russ           Adams           ID Systems]
 Dennis         Allen
 Anita          Amirrezvani     PC World
 Alvin          Anderson        Physicians and Computing
 Darcy          Anderson        PC Times
 John           Anderson        Computer Shopper
 Michael        Antonoff        Personal Computing
 Christine      Aumack          Micro Market World
 Michael        Azzara          Computer Systems News
 Ted            Bahr            AI Expert
 Richard A.     Baker           Online Today
 Robert         Baker           Baker Enterprises
 Eric           Baldwin         Macworld
 Deke           Barker          PC Times
 Chris          Barr            PC Magazine
 Theresa        Barry           Datamation
 Mike           Bayajian        Computer Graphics Today
1Info  2Fields 3       4Record 5Go to 6      7Search 8      9      10Quit
```

Fig. 30.17

Viewing a record from a magazine database.

```
                 ┌───── Search ─────┐
                 │ Enter data to search for: │
                 │ Jones              │      │
                 └────────────────────────────┘
```

Fig. 30.18

Searching records for the name *Jones*.

If you know the number of the record you want to view, you can press F5 (Go to). Commander prompts you to enter the record number, and then the program displays that record.

At times, you may need to know the structure of a database. You may be working on a program to merge information from the database, for example, and you need to know field names and widths. When you are viewing a database, you can press F2 (Fields) to display the structure of the database in the Field Information dialog box, as shown in figure 30.19.

The dialog box lists the field names, types, lengths, and decimals used (if any) in the database. When you press the F1 (Info) key, information about the database size, number of fields, and records appears.

To exit the view screen and return to Commander, press Esc or F10.

Fig. 30.19

The Field
Information
dialog box,
displaying a
database
structure.

```
================ Field Information ================

   Name          Type            Length Decimals

   First         Character         15
   Last          Character         15
   Magazine      Character         30
   Address       Character         20
   City          Character         30
   State         Character          2
   Zip           Character          5
   Phone         Character         14
```

Viewing Spreadsheet Files

Norton Commander recognizes common spreadsheet files for the programs listed earlier in table 30.7. To view the contents of a spreadsheet
file—a Lotus 1-2-3 file, for example—highlight that file name in a panel
and press F3 (View). Figure 30.20 shows the screen that appears after
you select a spreadsheet file named NLPJAN93.WK1.

```
1-2-3 View: C:\123rZZ\nlpjan93.wk1
A5:
        A       B       C       D       E       F       G       H
        A       M       F       MC      P       Total
5
6    Region
7       1      59      85      35      20      55     254
8       2      57      56      19      12      58     202
9       3     127      87      18      24      59     315
10      4      36      27       9       2      20      94
11      5      38      44      26       5      35     148
12      6      78      55       9       3      39     184
13      7      67      31      25      11      42     176
14      8       6       5       4       0       7      22
15      9      10      40      40       2      17     109
16  --------------------------------------------------------
17             478     430     185      79     332    1504
18
19
20           BOA      CA      MP      EA      MA    T_NLP     RA
21   Region
22      1      28      38      13      26      13      45       8
23      2      29      27      16      17       9      27       6
24      3      42      36      12      18       8      25       3
1Help  2    3    4    5Goto  6    7Search 8    9    10Quit
```

Fig. 30.20

Using the View
option to view a
spreadsheet file.

At the top of the screen, you see information about which view method
is being used to display the contents of a file. In figure 30.20, the first
line indicates 1-2-3 View. The second line of the screen shows the
name and contents of the highlighted cell being viewed (in this example, cell A5 is empty).

In this screen, the F1 (Help) key displays information about cursor movements and the function key commands. The F5 (Goto) key enables you to choose the area of the spreadsheet to be displayed. With the F7 (Search) key, you can search for text in the spreadsheet. F10 (Quit) exits the view and returns you to Commander.

Table 30.9 lists the function keys and other command and direction keys you can use when you view spreadsheet files.

Table 30.9 Spreadsheet View Keyboard Commands

Key(s)	Description
Home	Goes to top-left cell
End	Goes to last active cell
← or Ctrl+S	Moves one cell to the left
→ or Ctrl+D	Moves one cell to the right
↑ or Ctrl+E	Moves one cell up
↓ or Ctrl+X	Moves one cell down
PgUp or Ctrl+R	Moves one page up
PgDn or Ctrl+D	Moves one page down
Tab or Ctrl+ →	Scrolls one page to the right
Shift+Tab or Ctrl+ ←	Scrolls one page to the left
F5	Goes to specified record
F7	Searches
Shift+F7	Continues a search
Esc or F10	Exits view and returns to Commander menus

If you want to search the spreadsheet for specific information, you can use the F7 (Search) key. If, for example, you want to find a label containing the word *Taxes*, you can press F7 and then enter the search word in the View dialog box, as shown in figure 30.21.

After you press Enter, the first cell containing a match is highlighted in the spreadsheet. If the highlighted cell is not the one for which you are looking, press Shift+F7 to continue the search. If you already know the name of the cell you want to view, press F5 (Goto) and then enter a cell address (for example, enter **A5** or **N50**). Press Esc or F10 to exit the view and return to Commander.

Fig. 30.21

The View
dialog box.

Viewing Word Processing Files

Norton Commander recognizes common word processing files created
in the programs listed earlier in table 30.7. To view the contents of a
word processing file—a WordPerfect file, for example—highlight that
file name in a panel and press F3 (View). Figure 30.22 shows a view of a
WordPerfect file.

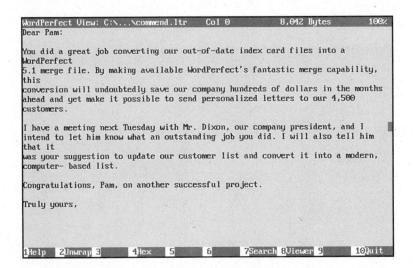

Fig. 30.22

Using the View
option to view a
WordPerfect file.

At the top of the screen, you can see information about which view
method is being used to display the contents of a file. The top line in
figure 30.22 indicates WordPerfect View. The top line of the word processing view screen also displays the file name, the current column
location of the cursor, the size of the file in bytes, and a percentage that
represents the amount of the file that has been paged off the top of the
screen.

Table 30.10 lists the function keys and other command and direction
keys you can use when you view word processing files.

Table 30.10 Word Processing View Keyboard Commands

Key(s)	Description
↑ or Ctrl+E	Scrolls up
↓ or Ctrl+X	Scrolls down
← or Ctrl+S	Scrolls left
→ or Ctrl+D	Scrolls right
Ctrl+ ← or Ctrl+A	Scrolls left 40 columns (a half screen)
Ctrl+ → or Ctrl+F	Scrolls right 40 columns
PgUp or Ctrl+R	Moves one page up
PgDn or Ctrl+C	Moves one page down
Home, Ctrl+Home, or Ctrl+PgUp	Goes to beginning of file
End, Ctrl+End, or Ctrl+PgDn	Goes to end of file
F2	Toggles word wrap on/off
F3	Returns to Quick View panel (available only if the view screen originally was a Quick View panel)
F4	Enables you to view a file in hexadecimal code
F7	Searches for text
Shift+F7	Continues search
Ctrl+Break or Esc	Stops a search
F8	Selects view type
Esc or F10	Quits

In the WordPerfect View screen, the F2 (Unwrap) key enables you to toggle the word-wrap feature on and off. When word wrap is on, text that would exceed the right margin is wrapped around to the next line. When word wrap is off, text is permitted to exceed the right margin. You can use the direction keys to display information past the right margin.

The F4 (Hex) key enables you to examine a file in hexadecimal code. This feature may be useful if you are looking for special character codes that normally are not displayed on-screen. These *ghost characters* can cause problems when you try to edit or print the file. If you display the file in hexadecimal format, you can locate these unusual characters and edit them out of your file.

When you select a database or spreadsheet file to view, the extension tells Commander what kind of file you selected. DBF files are dBASE databases, for example, and WK? files are Lotus 1-2-3 spreadsheets. Word processing programs, however, usually enable you to use any extension when you name files. Commander often can figure out what kind of file you are attempting to display, and thus uses whatever view type the program thinks is most appropriate. If Commander is wrong, however, you have to press F8 (View) and then select the correct view type.

Figure 30.23 shows the Select Viewer dialog box that appears when you press F8.

Fig. 30.23

The Select Viewer dialog box.

Because many word processing documents are long, scrolling through a document to look for a specific piece of information may take time. If you know that some key word is located in or near the paragraph for which you are looking, you can use F7 (Search) to help locate the information. Suppose that you are looking for a paragraph about a virus. To find this paragraph, press F7 (Search). A dialog box appears (similar to the ones previously discussed for database and spreadsheet views). Type the key word **virus** and press Enter. The text that includes the first occurrence of *virus* appears on-screen. If this paragraph is not the one for which you are looking, press Shift+F7 to continue the search until you find the right information. To end a search, press Ctrl+Break or Esc.

Press Esc or F10 to exit the view and return to Commander.

Editing ASCII Text Files

In addition to giving you another way to view files, the Edit command in the Files menu enables you to edit ASCII text files. You can use this command to edit files that contain up to 25K (about 25,000 characters). The command is ideal if you need to create or modify batch files (such as AUTOEXEC.BAT) or other ASCII text files.

Using the Commander Editor

The Commander editor is a full-screen editor similar to a word processing program's editor. To use the Commander editor to edit an existing
file, highlight the file name in a Commander panel and then choose **E**dit
from the Files menu or press F4. If you want to enter the name of the
file you want to edit, press Shift+F4. Commander then prompts you to
enter the file name.

Figure 30.24 shows the editor being used to edit CONFIG.SYS.

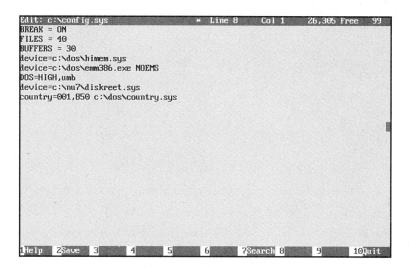

Fig. 30.24

Editing the
CONFIG.SYS
file.

Most of the commands in the editor, particularly the cursor-movement
commands, are the same as in any full-screen editor. Several editor
commands, however, deserve some added explanation.

You use Ctrl+Q to enter special characters into a file. Suppose that you
want to enter the ASCII Esc character in a file as part of a printer code.
Normally, if you press Esc, you quit the editor and return to Commander. If you press Ctrl+Q and then press Esc, however, the Esc
character is placed in the file as though you had typed it.

If you want to search for a particular word or phrase in a long file, you
can press F7 (Search). Commander then prompts you to enter the
search word. If the first word that Commander finds is not the one for
which you are looking, press Shift+F7 to repeat the search.

To end the editor, press Esc or F10. Remember to save the file before
quitting if you want your changes to be saved to disk. Press F2 to
save the edited file under the original file name you chose from the
Commander panel. If you want to use a new name, press Shift+F2.
Commander then prompts you to enter a new name.

Table 30.11 lists the direction keys and editing keys you can use in the Commander editor.

Table 30.11 Direction and Editing Keys

Key(s)	Description
↑ or Ctrl+E	Scrolls up
↓ or Ctrl+X	Scrolls down
← or Ctrl+S	Scrolls left
→ or Ctrl+D	Scrolls right
Ctrl+ ← or Ctrl+A	Moves one word to the left
Ctrl+ → or Ctrl+F	Moves one word to the right
Home	Goes to beginning of line
End	Goes to end of line
PgUp or Ctrl+R	Moves one page up
PgDn or Ctrl+C	Moves one page down
Ctrl+Home or Ctrl+PgUp	Goes to beginning of file
Ctrl+End or Ctrl+PgDn	Goes to end of file
Backspace	Deletes character to left
Del or Ctrl+G	Deletes character at cursor location
Ctrl+Backspace or Ctrl+W	Deletes one word to the left
Ctrl+T	Deletes one word to the right
Ctrl+Y	Deletes line
Ctrl+K	Deletes to end of line
Ctrl+Q	Causes the next character(s) you press to appear on-screen
	For example, if you press Ctrl+Q and then press Ctrl+F, that command is not activated; instead, the ASCII character associated with Ctrl+F appears on-screen. (Because F is the sixth letter in the alphabet, ASCII character 6 —a spade—would appear.)
F1	Accesses help
F2	Saves file
Shift+F2	Asks for file name
F7	Searches for text

Key(s)	Description
Shift+F7	Continues a search
Esc or F10	Quits the editor and returns to Commander
Shift+F10	Saves file and quits the editor

Using a Substitute Editor

Normally, when you choose an editing option, Commander uses a built-in editor. You may, however, prefer to use your own editor if you are more comfortable with it.

You can specify that Commander use a substitute editor of your choice. Choose Editor from the Options menu. You then are prompted to choose Built-in (the built-in editor) or External (an external editor).

If you choose the External option, Commander prompts you to enter the command used to begin the editor. Enter this command, followed by an exclamation mark (!) if you want to use only a file name when editing, or type !.! after the command if you want to use a file name plus an extension. If you are using the WP (WordPerfect) editor in the WPROC directory, for example, you should enter the following command to indicate that you want the full file name used during editing:

    \WPROC\WP !.!

The path name (\WPROC) is necessary if you must use the path name to start the editor from the DOS prompt. If you do not specify ! or !.!, Commander uses !.! as the default.

Other editors that you may use include DOS 5.0 Editor, WordStar, Boxer, and PC-Write.

Customizing the Norton Commander Screen Display

Norton Commander has several options that you can use to customize how the program looks on your screen. You can, for example, change the number of lines displayed (if you have an EGA or VGA monitor), enabling Commander to display more information per screen. The following sections describe these options in detail.

Controlling the Number of Lines Displayed

The EGA Lines command enables you to set your EGA or VGA monitor to display more than the normal 25 lines per screen. You can access this command by choosing EGA Lines from the Commands menu or pressing Alt+F9. The command is a toggle. If you have an EGA monitor, choosing the command toggles between normal 25-line mode and 43-line mode. If you are using a VGA monitor, you toggle between 25- and 50-line mode.

Displaying more information on-screen may simplify your access to files and directories. The only problem with the 43- and 50-line modes is that the characters are smaller than normal and may be more difficult to read.

NOTE If your CONFIG.SYS file in the root directory contains the command line DEVICE=ANSI.SYS, you can display only 25 lines on-screen. (See Appendix A for more information.) Thus, even if you enter 43-line EGA mode or 50-line VGA mode, your monitor still displays only 25 lines. You can remove the DEVICE=ANSI.SYS command from the CONFIG.SYS file to enable your monitor to display more lines per screen. If you are using DOS 4 or a later version, you can include the /L switch in the command instead. Before you decide to remove the ANSI.SYS command, be aware that some programs need it to work properly. You need to check your programs to determine whether they require ANSI.SYS.

Choosing Other Screen Options

The Options menu provides several other screen options. Like the EGA Lines option, these options operate as toggles, turning the features off and on. When an option is on, a check mark appears beside the option name in the menu.

The following additional options are available in the Options menu:

■ **Auto Menus** is an advanced feature that enables you to create custom menus, which are covered in the section "Automating Menus" later in this chapter.

- **P**ath Prompt controls whether the DOS prompt includes a path name. If you are in the WP51 directory with the **P**ath Prompt option turned off, for example, the DOS prompt (on drive C) is C>. When **P**ath Prompt is turned on, the prompt is C:\WP51>. Most users prefer the second version of the prompt (which includes the path) because it displays the current directory.

- **K**ey Bar determines whether the function key bar appears at the bottom of the screen.

- **F**ull Screen determines whether the right and left panels extend from the top to the bottom of the screen or are only half that size.

- **M**ini Status controls the status line at the bottom of each panel. When the **M**ini Status option is turned on, the status line shows the name, size, date, and time of the highlighted file or directory. If you have selected files in the panel, the status line displays the number of files selected. If the **M**ini Status option is off, the status line does not appear.

- **C**lock determines whether a clock appears in the upper-right corner of the Commander screen.

- Another option in the Options menu is **C**onfiguration. When you exit Norton Commander, the screen display reverts to the display that was in effect when you started Commander. The **C**onfiguration option enables you to save any changes so that they are in effect the next time you use Commander. To save your changes, choose **C**onfiguration from the Options menu and then choose Auto Save Setup in the Configuration dialog box (by default, this option already is on).

See the following sections for more information on the **C**onfiguration option.

Setting Commander's Configuration

After you choose the Configuration option from the Options menu, the Configuration dialog box appears (see fig. 30.25).

This dialog box contains five sections: Screen Colors, Screen Blank Delay, File Panel Options, Tree Panel Options, and Other Options. The following sections describe these areas in detail.

Fig. 30.25

The Configuration dialog box.

Setting Screen Colors

In the Screen Colors section of the Configuration dialog box, you can tell Commander whether you are using a color monitor, a black-and-white monitor, or a laptop monitor. Use the arrow keys or the mouse to select the monitor type.

Setting Screen Blank Delay Options

The Screen Blank Delay options enable you to choose how long Commander waits until automatically blanking out your screen. Blanking out the screen saves your monitor from possible burn-in of an image. (On some screens, if you leave an image on-screen for a long time, a trace of the image remains on-screen, like a ghost.) The default delay is five minutes.

When Commander blanks out the screen, you see a random pattern of white dots on a black background, resembling stars in the sky. The dots come and go, so that you can tell whether the computer is working. When the screen is blanked out, you can press any key or move the mouse to bring back the working screen. Commander blanks out the screen only when you are at the DOS prompt, not when you are working in a program.

You can choose to turn off the blanking feature or to specify a delay of 1 to 40 minutes by using the arrow keys to highlight the appropriate option in the Screen Blank Delay section and then pressing the space bar to lock the option into place. If you are using a mouse, just point to the option and click.

Setting File Panel Options

In the File Panel Options section of the Configuration dialog box, you indicate whether you want hidden files to appear in directories. You can also choose the meaning of the Ins key when selecting files.

If you choose the Ins Moves Down option, you can select files in a panel by repeatedly pressing the Ins key. Each time you press Ins, the cursor moves down to the next file. If you do not choose Ins Moves Down, you have to select options with the arrow keys and the space bar or with the mouse.

Controlling Automatic Display of Directory Files

The Tree Panel Options section contains one option: Auto Change Directory. If you turn on this option, you tell Commander that when you highlight a directory in a tree, you want the other panel to display the files contained in the highlighted directory. This option does not affect the NCD command (Alt+F10).

Setting Other Configuration Options

The following options are also available in the Configuration dialog box:

- Menu Bar Always Visible enables you to specify whether the menu bar always appears at the top of the screen. By default, this option is off.

- With Auto Save Setup, you can save any changes you make in the screen configuration during a Commander session. By default, this option is on.

- Left-Handed Mouse enables you to specify whether you are using a left-handed mouse and to reverse the functions of the left and right mouse buttons. By default, this option is off.

- Fast Mouse Reset, when on, enables Commander to return from a command faster if you are using a COMPAQ or PS/2 computer with a mouse port.

Choose OK to return to the Commander screen and save these settings, or choose Cancel to exit this dialog box without saving any changes.

Defining File Extensions in Commander

Another element of Norton Commander that takes some of the work out of accessing programs is the file extension feature, which you can use to define meanings for file extensions. After Commander knows the definition of a file extension, you can choose any file with that extension from a panel, and Commander begins the appropriate program.

Recall that a file specification has the format *filename.ext*. If you defined WP as an extension for WordPerfect, for example, and later choose the file REPORT.WP from a panel, Commander begins WordPerfect with the file REPORT.WP on-screen and ready to edit.

To tell Commander the meanings of various extensions, you must enter information into the file NC.EXT in the NC directory. To create or edit this file, follow these steps:

1. Choose Extension File Edit from the Commands menu. You see a screen similar to the one shown in figure 30.26. The Help box at the bottom of this screen summarizes the format of an extension command. You are now in the Commander editor.

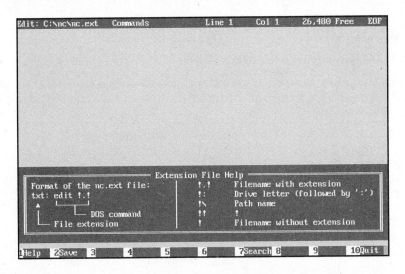

Fig. 30.26

Editing the extension file in the Commander editor.

2. For each extension that you want to define, type a line of information, using the following format:

    ext: *command* !.!

The *ext*: is the extension that you are defining. This parameter could be DOC: for Microsoft Word files using the DOC extension, FOR: for FORTRAN programs using the FOR extension, and so on. The *command* is the command required to begin the program associated with the defined file extension. You can include a path to the command, if necessary. The !.! parameter means that the command is to be followed by a file name with an extension, causing WordPerfect to load the selected file into the program for editing.

To tell Commander to use the command WP from the WP51 directory to edit a file with a WP extension, for example, use one of the following specifications:

WP: C:\WP51\WP !.!

WP: C:\WP51\WP !.WP

The !.! specification is part of Norton Commander's extension definition, similar to DOS's *.* wild-card specification. In the preceding example, you can use !.WP or !.! because both keep the extension WP in the file specification.

Table 30.12 describes !.! and related specifications.

Table 30.12 Specifications Used in the Extension Definition

Specification	Meaning
!.!	File name with extension
!	File name without extension
!:	Drive letter, followed by a colon
!\	Path name

You must choose the specification in the command line according to what the program expects in order for the selected file to be accessed. Thus, the specification ! indicates that the file name is to be placed in the command line without an extension, and the specification !:!.! means that the drive name and a colon appear before the file name and extension. If you do not place a !.! or ! specification in the extension-definition line, Commander begins the program but does not access the selected file automatically.

Suppose that you define the following specification:

CAI: \CAI\CAI !:!\!

If you later choose the file DEMO.CAI, the command generated contains the current drive (!:), the current path name (!\), and the file name without the extension (!). Therefore, if you are in the C:\TMP directory when you choose this file, the DOS command used to start the program is \CAI\CAI C:\TMP\DEMO.

Figure 30.27 shows an extension file containing a variety of definitions. The first definition is for WordPerfect. The second definition specifies that an editor named Edit be used to edit files with FOR (FORTRAN) extensions. The third definition begins the CAI program (PC-CAI, a computer-aided instructional program).

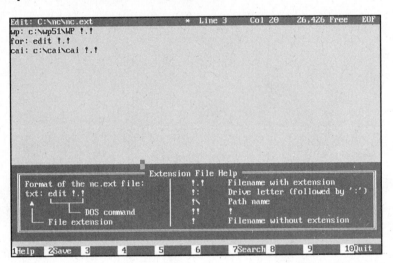

Fig. 30.27

Extension
specifications.

After you enter your extension definitions, save them by pressing F2 (Save). End the editor by pressing F10 (Quit). To abandon the edit without saving, press Esc or F10 without first pressing F2.

You can then choose a file from a Commander panel and begin using that file in the proper program. To return to the extension file (\NC\NC.EXT) to change, add, or remove any of your definitions, choose Extension File Edit from the Commands menu again.

Performing Advanced Norton Commander Operations

The Norton Commander commands covered in the preceding sections are straightforward commands you can use without any advanced computer knowledge. Although the topics in the following sections require more knowledge about how a computer works, they also introduce you to some of the more exciting features of Norton Commander. You learn how to use menus to customize your computer so that it works the way you think it should work. You also discover how to use Commander Mail to send messages by electronic mail (e-mail) and how to use Commander Link to transfer information quickly from one computer to another.

Creating and Using Menus in Commander

Not all computer users have the same programs. You may use WordPerfect, Microsoft Excel, and dBASE IV, for example; another person may use PC-FILE, PROCOMM, Kwikstat, and 10 other programs. To begin any of these programs on your computer, you may need to enter several commands. For example, you may have to change to a different directory and run a preliminary setup program before you run the actual program.

If you use your computer infrequently or have many different directories and programs, you may forget the command sequences for all your programs. You may wish that you had a menu of programs so that you could choose a program and automatically issue all necessary commands to begin the program. Norton Commander's user menus make this procedure possible.

Like a dialog box, a user menu displays options on-screen. A series of commands (usually DOS commands) is associated with each option in a user menu. After you choose a user-menu option, Commander acts like a DOS batch file, issuing these commands in sequence as though you had entered them from the DOS prompt.

Two kinds of user menus are available: *main* and *local*. You use the same commands to create both menus. The primary physical differences between main and local menus are the directories in which the menus are stored. The main menu is stored in the NC directory; local menus are stored in other directories. The primary functional difference between main and local menus is that local menus usually contain options that deal with programs in one directory, whereas main menus usually contain selections that pertain to programs in several different directories.

You activate a user menu by pressing F2 while the Commander program is running and the DOS prompt is on-screen. If a local menu is located in the current directory, that menu appears. If no local menu exists, Commander accesses the main menu from the NC directory. If no menu is available in either place, you get an error message after you press F2.

Thus, the first (and perhaps the only) menu you usually need to create is the one in the NC directory: the main menu. If the main menu is the only user menu, you can access it whenever you press F2. If you want different menus in other subdirectories, however, you need to create local menus. (You can have local menus without having a main menu.)

You may want to have a local menu in a subdirectory that contains several programs you want to access. In your accounting directory, for example, you may want a menu of options for running programs that do posting, end-of-month runs, trial balances, and so on, but you do not want all these options cluttering up the main menu. You can create user menus in such a way that when you choose the broad topic Accounting from the main menu, a local menu containing the detailed accounting choices appears.

Alternatively, because many people may use one computer, you may want to create different menus that start programs. You can create one batch file that causes WordPerfect to load with a particular data-file directory, for example, and another batch file that causes 1-2-3 to open a particular spreadsheet.

Creating User Menus

You create a user menu in Norton Commander by choosing **M**enu File Edit from the Commands menu. You then enter lines of information in a file to tell Commander which selections you want to display in the menu and what should happen when a user chooses any of those menu items.

You can place four basic kinds of lines in the menu file:

■ *Comment lines* begin with an apostrophe ('). These lines do not influence how the menu looks or functions. Comment lines are optional and are provided only so that you can document a menu file's function. Comments are helpful to other users who may have to change the file in the future, (and may be helpful to you if you have to return to the file a year later).

■ *Menu items* begin with a hot key, followed by a colon (:). To create a menu item called Begin WordPerfect that a user can choose by pressing W, enter this command in the menu file:

W: Begin WordPerfect

The W (the hot key) must be in the far-left column of the file (flush left). If you enter a line flush left (any line without a letter and a colon or without an apostrophe that is flush left), that line becomes a menu item without a hot key.

■ *DOS commands* or other commands are listed in the lines following a menu item. These commands must not be flush left. To in-
dent these commands, place a tab or one or more blank spaces in
front of the text.

■ *Blank line separators* should be inserted after each menu item.
To create a blank line, press Enter.

To create a typical user menu, follow these steps:

1. Choose **M**enu File Edit from the Commands menu. The User Menu
dialog box appears (see fig. 30.28).

Fig. 30.28

The User Menu
dialog box.

2. The options in this dialog box enable you to create a main menu,
create a local menu, or cancel the command. For this example,
choose **M**ain. The User Menu edit screen appears (see fig. 30.29).

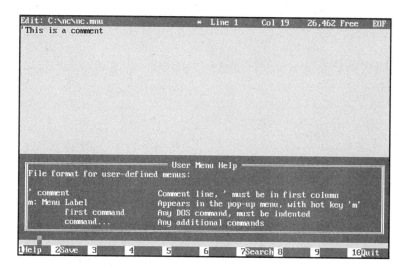

Fig. 30.29

The User Menu
edit screen.

This screen is a version of the Commander editor (discussed earlier in this chapter). The file named NC.MNU in the NC directory is
displayed and ready for you to edit. (If you choose to edit a local
menu in another directory, the edit screen displays the NC.MNU
file for you to edit in the specified directory.)

Notice the help box at the bottom of the edit screen in figure 30.29. This screen summarizes the file format for creating a user menu.

3. In the menu file, enter lines that define your user menu. For example, the lines associated with beginning the WordPerfect program are these:

```
W: Begin WordPerfect
       NCD \WP51
       WP
```

Notice in this example (and in fig. 30.30) that the menu-item line— W: Begin WordPerfect—is flush left in the file and that the other lines are indented.

Figure 30.30 shows an example of information entered in the editor to create a menu with three options. Each option consists of a letter and a colon, a brief description, and some DOS commands that invoke the appropriate program. The PROCOMM program, for example, begins with two commands. First, the NCD \PROCOMM command changes to the \PROCOMM directory, and then the PROCOMM command begins the PROCOMM program.

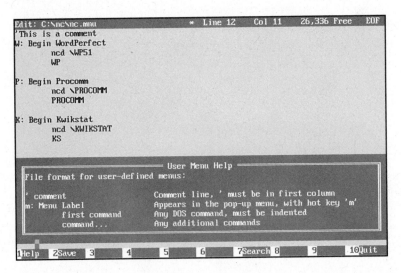

Fig. 30.30

Menu entries in the User Menu edit screen.

4. Save the menu file by pressing F2 (Save).

5. Quit the menu editor by pressing F10 (Quit).

Invoking User Menus

After you create a menu, you can open it by pressing F2 (Menu) in the Norton Commander screen. Remember that if a local menu exists in the current directory, Commander opens that menu. If no local menu exists, Commander opens the main menu located in the NC directory.

Figure 30.31 shows how the menu created in figure 30.30 looks on-screen.

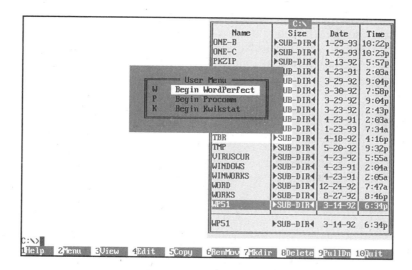

Fig. 30.31

The menu in use.

To exit the user menu without choosing an option, press Esc.

Automating Menus

If you are taking advantage of Commander's menu capabilities, you may want to set up the program to display your user menu whenever you start Commander. You could create a series of menus, for example, to help a novice use a variety of programs without issuing a DOS command.

You can automate the user menu system by choosing Auto Menus from the Options menu. When Auto Menus is turned on, the local or main menu (whichever is appropriate to the current directory) opens whenever you begin Commander. Keep in mind, however, that after you end the menu by pressing Esc or choosing some other menu option, the user menu disappears. You must press F2 to redisplay the menu.

You can design local menus so that they always come back to the main menu, however. You could use the following commands, for example, in the main menu to begin WordPerfect:

```
W: Begin WordPerfect
      NCD \WP51
      WP
      NCD \NC
```

The first line tells the program that the W hot key is associated with the menu item Begin WordPerfect. The second line begins the commands that execute if a user chooses this option from the menu. In the preceding example, the second line changes to the \WP51 directory, which contains the WordPerfect program. The third line begins the WordPerfect program, and the fourth line changes back to the \NC directory so that the main menu again appears. Thus, after you exit WordPerfect, the command NCD \NC is issued automatically, bringing you back to the \NC directory and the main menu.

Using Commander Mail

The Commander menu and extension features enable you to access information in your computer. Commander Mail enables you to send and receive information through the MCI electronic network, MCI Mail.

You can perform the following tasks with MCI Mail:

- *Send and receive electronic mail (e-mail).* Electronic mail is a message that is sent electronically from one user's computer to one or more other computers. You write a message on your computer and send the message to someone who has an MCI account. You can also send ASCII text files as e-mail. The message is routed electronically to the specified address (the recipient's computer).

- *Send a letter through Commander Mail to MCI Mail and have that letter printed and mailed to a designated address.* You write the letter on your computer and then send the letter and the recipient's address to the MCI network. MCI prints and mails the letter.

- *Send information to a fax machine through MCI Mail.* You create a letter on your computer and then send the letter and the recipient's fax number to the MCI network. MCI sends the letter to the appropriate fax machine.

- *Send messages through other services.* This feature is useful if you want to send electronic mail to someone who is not an MCI subscriber but does subscribe to a service such as CompuServe or Telemail X.400.

MCI Mail is a convenient way to communicate quickly and is particularly well suited for members of an organization or for colleagues who live in diverse places. Messages can be sent at the sender's convenience and read at the recipient's convenience. Electronic mail messages also arrive much faster than express mail and have the clarity of a letter as opposed to the possible misinterpretations that characterize voice messages. Using MCI Mail, salespeople can send orders to the home office at the end of each day, and journalists can send messages and stories to their offices quickly. The possibilities for improved communication are endless.

Using Commander's MCI interface rather than MCI's interface (which you can use if you dial MCI) means that you do not have to use a communications program (such as PROCOMM or Crosstalk). You can do all the work of preparing and reading communications off-line (which reduces actual connection time). You also have the benefit of Commander's simple pull-down user interface.

Reviewing the Requirements for Using MCI Mail

To use MCI Mail, you need an MCI account and some computer hardware. To get an MCI account, call (800) 444-6245. MCI assigns you a user name and a password, which you will receive by mail within several days.

You also need to have a modem hooked up to your computer. Generally, personal computers use either internal or external modems. An *internal modem* fits inside your computer in one of the expansion slots. An *external modem* is connected to a communication port on your computer by a serial cable.

If your computer has an internal modem, all you see from the outside are phone jacks on the back of the computer. One of these jacks is labeled To Line. To hook your modem into the phone system, you must run a phone line from the To Line jack in the back of the computer to the phone wall jack. Usually, another jack in the back of the computer is called To Phone. You can use this jack to hook up a normal telephone. Figure 30.32 illustrates the proper hookup.

An external modem is hooked into your computer through a serial port—normally, the COM1 or COM2 port. Your COM port usually is a 25-pin (RS-232) connector. IBM AT-type machines use a 9-pin connector. Figure 30.33 shows both kinds of connectors.

A cable connects the modem to the COM port on the back of the computer. A phone line is then hooked into the modem (in the To Line jack) from the phone wall plug. Optionally, you can have a regular phone hooked into the modem's To Phone jack. Figure 30.34 shows this hookup.

Wall jack

Fig. 30.32

Hooking up an
internal modem.

Serial Connectors

9-pin
connector
(used on ATs)

25-pin
RS-232 connector

Fig. 30.33

25-pin and 9-pin
serial connectors.

Back of computer

External modem

Modem is connected to computer with serial cable

To jack To phone

To computer

Serial connector

Wall jack

Fig. 30.34

Hooking up an external modem.

MCI supports modems that operate at speeds of 300, 1200, and 2400 baud. The *baud rate* is the speed at which your computer modem transmits and receives information. Although a baud rate of 300 is very slow, 1200 and 2400 baud are acceptable. Speeds of up to 9600 baud are quite common.

The advantage of using an internal modem is that it does not need a communication port, which you may want to use for something else. Using an internal modem makes changing from computer to computer difficult, however, because you have to take your computer apart to remove the modem. An external modem has an important advantage: you can use it with more than one computer simply by unplugging the modem from one computer and plugging it into another. The disadvantage of using an external modem is that it takes up room on your desk. Other than these convenience considerations, the internal and external modems operate the same way.

As soon as your computer is set up with a modem and you have an MCI account, you can start sending and receiving messages.

> **T I P**
>
> If you do not have a modem, look for one with a fast baud rate. The faster the modem, the faster you can send and receive messages over phone lines; and the quicker the communication, the shorter the phone call. Because services like MCI charge you by actual connection time, shorter connection time usually saves you money. Probably the most commonly used modems today are 2400 baud. If you are on a tight budget, however, you can buy a 1200-baud modem for less than $100. Using a slow 300-baud modem is not a good idea.
>
> You also need a *Hayes-compatible* modem. Modems operate through a command language in much the same way that a PC DOS computer operates through DOS commands. Hayes-compatible modems operate on the AT command set, which Norton Commander is set up to use.

Setting Up Commander Mail To Communicate with MCI Mail

To set up Commander Mail, choose Commander Mail from the Commands menu. The first time you choose this command, you see a screen like the one shown in figure 30.35.

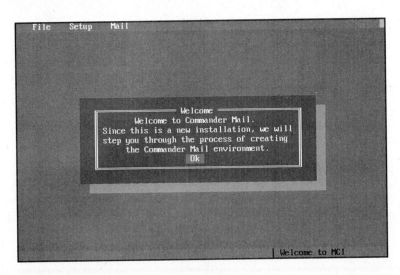

Fig. 30.35

The Commander Mail setup message.

This screen tells you that you must go through a setup procedure before you can use Commander Mail. You need to have your MCI account information handy. If you do not want to set up Commander Mail (for example, if you do not have your account number yet), press Esc. Otherwise, press Enter to proceed with the setup.

Adding, Deleting, and Modifying Accounts

If you proceed with the Commander Mail setup, the Account 1 dialog box appears when you press Enter (see fig. 30.36).

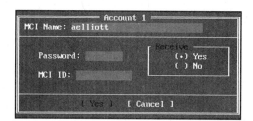

Fig. 30.36

The Account 1 dialog box.

In this box, you enter information about your MCI account. First enter your MCI account name (often, the first letter of your first name, followed by your full last name). No spaces are included in the MCI account name. Then enter your password and MCI ID number, both of which you will find in the Welcome to MCI Mail kit that you receive in the mail after you subscribe.

After you enter your account information, indicate whether you want to receive mail. In the Receive area of the dialog box, choose Yes if you want to be able to send *and* receive MCI electronic mail; choose No if you do not want to receive mail and you plan to use MCI Mail only to send information. Then choose Yes at the bottom of the dialog box to confirm the information for this account. The MCI Account List dialog box appears.

If more than one person with an MCI account will be using Commander Mail on this machine, you can add additional accounts by choosing the Add option. (If you choose Add, an Account 2 dialog box appears, showing basically the same dialog box as for Account 1.) If you need to change or remove one of the accounts after you enter it, highlight the account and choose Modify (to make changes) or Delete (to remove the account). When you finish making additions, modifications, or deletions, choose Ok to save the list.

After you choose Ok, the MCI Account List dialog box appears again (see fig. 30.37), this time displaying information about your account.

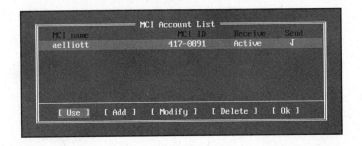

Fig. 30.37

The completed
MCI Account List
dialog box.

Highlight your MCI name and choose Use to tell Commander Mail
to charge your account for the messages you send. Commander will
charge this account every time you use MCI Mail unless you add
another account to the account list.

Specifying Directories for Message Storage

After you choose OK from the MCI Account List dialog box, a Directories dialog box appears, indicating the directories where MCI messages
will be stored (see fig. 30.38).

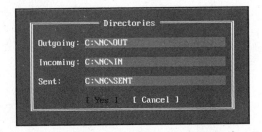

Fig. 30.38

The Directories
dialog box.

The default directories are \NC\OUT, \NC\IN, and \NC\SENT. The OUT
directory stores outgoing mail, the IN directory stores incoming mail,
and the SENT directory stores copies of messages you have sent. You
can type new names for these directories or accept the defaults. To
enter new names, highlight the directory you want to change, type a
new directory name, and press Enter. When the directory names are
the way you want them, choose Yes.

Specifying Your Modem Setup

Next, you must tell Commander Mail about your modem setup.
Figure 30.39 shows the Modem dialog box, which appears when
you choose Yes in the Directories dialog box.

Fig. 30.39

The Modem
dialog box.

The Port setting indicates the serial port to which your modem is connected. If you have only one serial port on your machine, you probably are using COM1. If you have two serial ports, you need to check your system's documentation to determine which port you are using. Usually, the COM1 port is any built-in port on your computer, and the COM2 port is a port added with an expansion card.

The Dialing setting indicates whether your telephone exchange uses tone or pulse dialing. Some older exchanges use only pulse dialing. If you must use a rotary-dial telephone, your exchange supports only pulse dialing. If you can use a touch-tone phone, your exchange supports tone dialing. (To find out whether your exchange supports tone dialing, call your telephone company.)

The Modem Sound setting determines whether you hear the dialing process when your modem tries to make a connection. (If your modem does not have a speaker, you will not hear the dialing even if you choose this option.) The advantage of hearing the dialing process is that you can tell whether the call is going through properly—for example, you can hear busy signals. If you have a speaker modem but do not hear the dialing taking place, you may have selected the wrong COM port. Wait for a message from the computer. Usually, this message appears within 30 seconds.

The Baud Rate setting indicates the speed at which you want your modem to operate. For the fastest communication, choose the highest baud rate your modem can support. (Check your modem documentation for the highest baud rate.)

The Modem Initialization String field appears at the bottom of the Modem dialog box. The *modem initialization string* is a code that Commander Mail uses for a modem. The code shown in figure 30.39 is for a Hayes-compatible modem, which is the most common type of modem. If you are using a Hayes-compatible modem, you do not have to know which initialization string to use; Commander Mail automatically supplies the necessary code. If you are using a non-Hayes-compatible modem, you need to check your documentation for the proper initialization string.

After you choose the appropriate options in the Modem dialog box, choose Yes to save the settings.

Specifying the Phone Number

The next setup dialog box asks for the phone number you will be using to communicate with MCI Mail (see fig. 30.40).

Fig. 30.40

The Phone Number dialog box.

Your Welcome to MCI Mail kit contains the phone numbers you can use:

■ (800) 234-6245 for 300- and 1200-baud modems

■ (800) 456-6245 for modems up to 2400 baud

■ (800) 967-9600 for 9600-baud modems

Type the appropriate number in the Phone Number dialog box.

The Prefix entry is any number or series of numbers that you must type to get an outside line. In many businesses, this prefix is 9. After you enter the phone number and any necessary prefix, choose Yes to save this information.

At this point, the Commander Mail setup program begins creating the directories you specified in the Directories dialog box. A New Directory dialog box appears in sequence for each of the three new directories: IN, OUT, and SENT (or for another three directories, if you changed the default names).

Figure 30.41 shows the New Directory dialog box that asks whether you want Commander to create the \NC\IN directory.

Fig. 30.41

Creating
the \NC\IN
directory
during setup.

Choose Mkdir to create these directories on your hard disk or Cancel
to cancel the operation. If you cancel the creation of a directory, you
return to the DOS prompt. Later, if you try to run MCI Mail, you will be
prompted again to make the necessary directories. You cannot run MCI
Mail until these directories exist.

After you create the directories, you have reached the end of the setup
procedure. A dialog box appears, displaying the following message:

```
Commander Mail has now created the parameter file,
MCI.INI, required to run the communications driver,
MCIDRIVR.EXE.
```

This message tells you that the settings you chose during the setup
procedure are stored in the file MCI.INI and that you can begin using
MCI Mail.

After you set up your system to support MCI Mail, a screen like the one
shown in figure 30.42 appears when you choose Commander Mail from
the Commands menu.

Fig. 30.42

The In
Box screen.

The In Box screen displays any messages that you have received. The first time you use Commander Mail, no messages appear in this screen.

Customizing Commander Mail

The menu bar at the top of the In Box screen lists three pull-down menus: File, Setup, and Mail. The File menu contains three options: Help, About MCI, and Quit. The Help option (which you can activate by pressing F1) provides information about how to use Commander Mail. The About MCI option lists the phone numbers for MCI phone support and the MCI support mailbox. The Quit option ends your Commander Mail session.

The Setup menu contains six options—Address Book, MCI Accounts, Schedule, Phone, Modem, and Directories—that enable you to customize Commander Mail. The following sections discuss these options in detail. The Mail menu is described in the section "Managing Messages" later in this chapter.

Entering and Editing Addresses

The Address Book option enables you to create a list of addresses of people to whom you plan to send messages. After you choose this option, the MCI Address Book dialog box appears.

Figure 30.43 shows an Address Book dialog box that contains only one address.

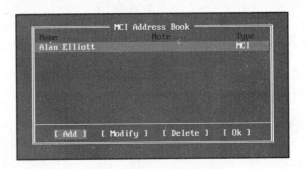

Fig. 30.43

The MCI Address Book dialog box.

At the bottom of the box are command buttons for the following four options:

Option	Description
Add	Adds a name to the address book
Modify	Changes the highlighted address
Delete	Deletes the highlighted address
OK	Exits the Address Book dialog box and returns to the Setup menu

When you choose Add, the Address Type dialog box appears (see fig. 30.44).

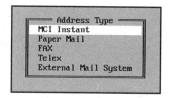

Fig. 30.44

The Address Type dialog box.

In this dialog box, you specify how you want to send messages to the address that you are adding. You have five options:

> MCI Instant
> Paper Mail
> FAX
> Telex
> External Mail System

If you will be sending messages to the same person but using different methods each time (MCI or a fax, for example), you must enter a separate address for each way that you want to send messages.

To choose an option in the Address Type dialog box, highlight the option and press Enter or click the option. If you choose MCI Instant, the MCI Subscriber Address dialog box appears (see fig. 30.45).

In this box, you enter the information about the MCI account to which the message will be sent. You must know the MCI user name or the MCI account number for this address. (If you know one but are unsure about the other, enter the one you know.) The information that you enter in the Name, Note, Location, and Organization fields appears in the electronic messages you send. As you move the cursor in this dialog box, a highlighted area next to each part of the address indicates how many characters you can enter.

Fig. 30.45

The MCI Subscriber Address dialog box.

After you enter information in the Name field, press Enter to move to the next field. (You also can use the arrow keys to move from field to field.)

If your message recipient does not have an MCI account, you can choose Paper Mail in the Address Type dialog box. You may want to use MCI Paper Mail rather than send the letter yourself for several reasons. You may like the important-looking, telegramlike style of MCI letters. You may find this method easier than writing and printing a letter. And if you are away from your office, you may want to write and send letters directly from your computer—from a hotel room, a conference room, or wherever you can plug your computer into a phone jack.

When you choose the Paper Mail option, you see a dialog box similar to that shown in figure 30.45, but with a different list of fields:

> Name
> Note
> Country
> Title/Company
> Addr.Line1
> Addr.Line2
> City
> State
> ZipCode

Type the necessary information in each field. The information that you enter is used to address the letter that MCI sends by regular mail. You must make entries in the Name and Addr.Line1 fields; entries in the Note, Addr.Line2, and Title/Company fields are optional. You can place any identifying information that you want in the Note Field, or leave it blank. When you finish entering the information, choose Ok.

If you want to send your messages to a fax machine, you can choose the FAX option in the Address Type dialog box. When you choose this option, you see a dialog box similar to the one in figure 30.45, but with a different list of fields:

Name
Note
Phone #
Retry

You must make entries in the Name and Phone # fields; entries in the Note and Retry fields are optional. In the Retry field, you can enter the number of hours that MCI should keep trying to send the message if it cannot get through. The default setting is 4 hours; you can enter a number between 0.5 and 12. If you cannot reach the fax number (the line may be busy, for example), MCI continues to try to send the fax for the length of time specified in the Retry field.

After MCI has sent the fax or has exhausted all attempts (for example, if the specified retry time has expired), you receive an e-mail message from MCI, telling you whether the message was sent.

If you want to send a message to a telex address, choose Telex in the Address Type dialog box. You see a dialog box similar to the one in figure 30.45, but with a different list of fields:

Name
Note
Country
Telex Number
Answerback

You must make entries in the Name and Telex Number fields; entries in the Note, Country, and Answerback fields are optional. If you leave the Country field blank, Commander Mail uses USA as the default. Do not use the Answerback field unless you know your recipient's answerback code. (*Answerback* is a verification code that some telex subscribers use as a safety feature.)

 You also can receive telex messages through MCI Mail. Your telex number is 650 plus your MCI ID number. If your MCI ID is 123-4567, for example, your telex number is 6501234567. Messages sent by telex appear in your MCI Commander Mail In Box as electronic messages.

To send a message to a person who uses an e-mail service other than MCI, you must choose External Mail System in the Address Type dialog box. You see a dialog box similar to the one in figure 30.45, but with a different list of fields:

Name
Note
Mailsystem
MBX Info 1
MBX Info 2
MBX Info 3

You must make entries in the Name, Mailsystem, and MBX Info 1 fields; entries in the Note, MBX Info 2, and MBX Info 3 fields are optional. The Mailsystem field contains the name of the e-mail service, such as CompuServe. (Norton Commander currently does not support e-mail services other than MCI Mail and CompuServe.) The MBX Info 1 field contains the ID number for that service (for example, CompuServe ID number 12345,789). The MBX Info 2 and 3 fields are reserved for future use, because MCI periodically adds new services. Your correspondence from MCI will explain any future uses for these fields.

After you add addresses, they appear in the MCI Address Book dialog box whenever you create a message. You then can highlight the address to which you want to send the message.

Eventually, you will probably need to modify or delete some addresses. To modify an address, choose Address Book from the Setup menu. When the MCI Address Book dialog box appears (refer to fig. 30.43), highlight the address that you want to change, and then choose the Modify option. The address appears. Make the necessary corrections in the address and then choose Ok to save the changes.

To delete an address, choose the Address Book option from the Setup menu. When the MCI Address Book dialog box appears, highlight the address that you want to delete, and then choose the Delete option. Choose Ok to save the change.

Specifying MCI Accounts

The MCI Accounts option in the Setup menu enables you to choose which account should be charged when you send messages. You can add new accounts, modify current accounts, or delete accounts by following the procedure you used to add your first account. See the section "Adding, Deleting, and Modifying Accounts" earlier in the chapter.

To modify an account after you complete the initial setup, choose MCI Accounts from the Setup menu. The MCI Account List dialog box appears (refer to fig. 30.37). You can highlight the account that you want to change, and then choose Modify. Commander Mail displays the information on-screen so that you can edit it. Choose Ok to save the modified account list. Choose Cancel to exit the list without saving your changes.

Deleting an existing account is similar to modifying one. To delete an account, choose the MCI Accounts option from the Setup menu. When the MCI Account List dialog box appears, highlight the account that you want to delete, and then choose Delete. Choose Ok.

Setting Up Commander Mail To Run Automatically

The Schedule option in the Setup menu enables you to specify when (and whether) Commander Mail automatically calls MCI. You can set up Commander Mail to send and receive messages unattended during the night, for example, when rates are lower. Any messages that you receive overnight appear on your computer the next day.

Suppose that you have salespeople who send in orders daily. You can set up Commander Mail to call MCI several times during the day to collect messages and to send your salespeople confirmation that their orders were received.

After you choose the Schedule option, the Schedule dialog box appears (see fig. 30.46).

Fig. 30.46

The Schedule
dialog box.

In this dialog box, you have two choices: On Demand and Use Schedule Below. The On Demand option means that you choose when to contact MCI Mail. If you choose the Use Schedule Below option, MCI Mail initiates calls at specified times. You can type up to eight times in the dialog box. When you finish, choose Yes to close the Schedule box and return to the Setup menu.

For Commander Mail to operate in automatic mode, you must begin the MCIDRIVR program from the DOS prompt. After you set up the times in the Schedule dialog box for Commander to call MCI Mail, load the MCIDRIVR program by entering the following command at the DOS prompt:

MCIDRIVR

After you enter this command, the Commander Mail program becomes a background program, and you return to the DOS prompt, from which you can run other programs. Even if you are using another program at the time, Commander Mail initiates a call at the scheduled times, sends all messages that are in your Out Box, and receives any messages that are waiting for you.

When you enter the MCIDRIVR command at the DOS prompt, you can include several switches that control various features of this program. Table 30.13 lists the switches available for the MCIDRIVR command.

Table 30.13 Switches for the MCIDRIVR Command	
Switch	**Description**
/A	Aborts the current communications session.
/D	Leaves MCIDRIVR in memory but temporarily disables it.
/E	Activates the driver. (You use this switch if the MCIDRIVR program is in memory but disabled.)
/N	Initiates a session. The program immediately dials the MCI phone number and then sends and receives messages. The command MCIDRIVR/N, for example, begins an MCI session immediately, even at a time not specified in the Schedule dialog box.
/S	Sets DOS errorlevel to 0 if the driver is waiting for a scheduled event, or sets errorlevel to 1 if the driver is participating in a communications session. (You also can use this switch in a batch program. For more information, see Chapter 24.)
/X	Exits the current session and removes the driver from memory.

Changing the MCI Phone Number

The Phone option in the Setup menu enables you to change the phone number and prefix that you use to call MCI Mail. (MCI will contact you if the number you use to access MCI services changes.)

The Phone Number dialog box appears when you choose the Phone option. This dialog box is the same one you used during the setup procedure to specify the MCI phone number (refer to fig. 30.40).

Changing Modem Settings

The Modem option in the Setup menu enables you to change the settings for your modem, which you may need to do if you install a different modem. (Your new modem may run at a different speed from that of your original modem, for example.) The modem settings include communications port, tone or pulse dialing, modem sound, baud rate, and initialization string.

The Modem dialog box appears when you choose the Modem option. This dialog box is the same one you used during the setup procedure to specify modem settings (refer to fig. 30.39).

Changing Message Directories

The Directories option in the Setup menu enables you to change the names of the directories that you use to store outgoing messages, incoming messages, and delivered messages. Remember that these directories usually are listed as \NC\OUT, \NC\IN, and \NC\SENT during the setup procedure. You may want to change directories, for example, from drive C to another disk if drive C is getting full and cannot store all the messages you are receiving.

The Directories dialog box appears when you choose the Directories option. This dialog box is the same one you used during the setup procedure to specify directories (refer to fig. 30.38).

Managing Messages

You use the Mail menu in the Commander Mail menu bar to manage your incoming and outgoing messages (see fig. 30.47).

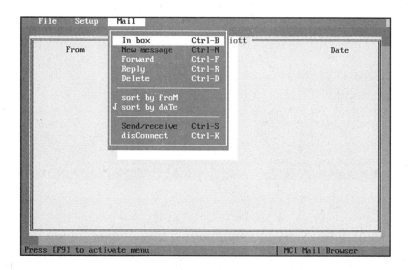

Fig. 30.47

Commander Mail's Mail menu.

The four basic tasks that you perform from this menu are creating, sending, receiving, and reading messages.

To mail an electronic message, you use these steps:

1. Choose New Message from the Mail menu.

2. Select the destination of your message in the MCI Address Book dialog box.

3. Write the message, using the Commander editor, and save it to disk.

4. Send the message by choosing Send/Receive from the Mail menu.

This general procedure is the one you probably will use most of the time. The following sections discuss how to use the options in the Mail menu to manage your incoming and outgoing messages.

Creating Messages

After you choose New Message from the Mail menu, you see a screen similar to the one shown in figure 30.48.

Fig. 30.48

The New
Message screen.

In the fields at the top of the New Message screen, you enter information that tells MCI where to send the message. These fields are To, CC (carbon copy), Subject, Attach, and Handling.

The To field is the only field in which you must make an entry. To enter information, highlight the field and then press Enter. The Edit Send List dialog box appears (see fig. 30.49).

Fig. 30.49

The Edit Send List
dialog box.

You use this dialog box to specify the recipient of your message.
Choose the List option to display the MCI Address Book dialog box
(see fig. 30.50).

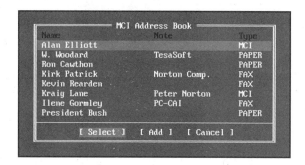

Fig. 30.50

The MCI Address
Book dialog box.

Select an address in the MCI Address Book dialog box and then choose
Select. You return to the Edit Send List dialog box, which now displays
the selected address. Choose List again and repeat this process for as
many addresses as you want to select.

If you choose the New option in the Edit Send List dialog box, you are
prompted to enter all the information needed to send a message. First,
you are prompted to select the address type from the Address Type
dialog box (refer to fig. 30.44). After you select an address type, you are
asked whether you want to add this name to your address book. Then
you see a dialog box similar to the one in figure 30.45, with a list of
fields appropriate to the address type you have chosen. After you enter
the information, the new address is added to the Edit Send List dialog
box.

The Remove option enables you to delete a name from the list. The
Handling option enables you to choose several ways of handling your
message. After you choose the Handling option, a dialog box appears,
displaying the following four options:

Option	Description
Receipt	Indicates that you want a receipt verifying that the recipient has received the message.
4hour	Specifies priority delivery of the message.
Charge	Specifies a charging code. This code, which is for your own use, can be anything you want but cannot contain spaces.
Alert	Notifies the recipient by telephone that an MCI message has been sent. You must supply the recipient's phone number.

You can select names for the CC field in the New Message screen in the same way that you select names for the To field. You can type any information in the Subject field.

The Attach field specifies the name of a file to be included with the message. This file must be an ASCII text file. If you want to include the SALES.TXT file from the C:\REPORT directory, for example, type the following line in the Attach field:

C:\REPORT\SALES.TXT

You use the Handling option to specify the same handling for all recipients in the send list. When you choose a Handling option for this message, the option is in effect for all addresses in the list. You cannot specify the Alert option for one address, for example, and not for another.

After you enter all the necessary information at the top of the New Message screen, type the actual message in the bottom half of the screen. (In this screen, you are using the Commander editor.) After you type the message, press F10. You are given the option of saving the message. If you choose to save the message, the message goes to your \NC\OUT directory, from which you can send it later.

Sending and Receiving Messages

After you create a message, you need to connect to the MCI network to send and receive messages. Choosing the Send/Receive option from the Mail menu instructs Commander Mail to begin a communications session. A communications session performs the following tasks:

■ Calls the MCI Mail service

■ Sends any messages you have in the Out Box

■ Receives messages from MCI and displays them in your In Box

If you use the Schedule feature to have Commander Mail automatically send and receive mail, your system performs this entire Send/Receive procedure without any human intervention. When you manually choose the Send/Receive option, you see the Send/Receive MCI Mail screen, from which you can monitor the progress of the communication to MCI Mail and the sending and receiving of messages.

The box in the upper-left corner lists the six activities that will be taking place:

> Initializing
> Dial Service
> Get into MCI
> Send Mail
> Receive Mail
> Terminate Session

While an activity is taking place, a dot blinks to the left of the activity name. When Commander Mail completes an activity, a check mark appears next to the activity name.

During the *initializing* process, your computer establishes contact with your modem. During the *dial-service* activity, your modem calls the MCI phone number. If your modem has a speaker and you chose the Modem Sound option in the Modem dialog box, you should hear the dialing process.

The bottom-left box in the Send/Receive MCI Mail screen also displays information about what is happening, including messages about your modem setup—the baud rate or the MCI name of the phone number being dialed, for example. While you are connected to MCI, the message `Connected to MCI` appears. When the session is over, the message `Hanging Up` appears, and then a message stating the length of the session appears.

Boxes on the right side of the screen provide information about the progress of the session. The Total Session box is a bar graph that shows the elapsed time of the session. The Current Activity graph shows the progress of an activity, such as sending or receiving messages. The MCI and Commander Activity area displays modem-activity messages such as `Wait`, `Receive`, and `Send`.

After connecting to MCI, Commander Mail sends your account name and password to MCI. If this information is correct, you are logged on to MCI. After you log on, any messages in your Out Box (the \NC\OUT directory) are sent, and any messages from MCI are placed in your In Box (the \NC\IN directory). Then the session ends automatically.

The Sent and Received messages in the bottom-left corner of the screen tell you how many messages were sent and how many were received. The time you spent logged on to MCI appears in the Current Timer area of the screen. When the session is over, you can go to your In Box to read any messages.

Reading Messages

You use the In Box option in the Mail menu to examine incoming messages. The In Box dialog box appears, containing messages to be read. To read a message in the list, highlight it and press Enter, or double-click the message name. The message then appears on-screen. If the text is too long to fit in one screen, you can use the PgUp and PgDn keys to scroll the message. Press Esc to exit the message and return to the In Box dialog box.

Using Other MCI Mail Options

In addition to creating, sending, receiving, and reading messages, you can forward, reply to, delete, sort by sender (from), sort by date, print messages, and disconnect.

Forwarding Messages

If you choose the Forward option from the Mail menu, you can select a message in your In Box and forward it to a person in your address list. This option enables you to send to a third party a message that you received from someone else.

Replying to Messages

The Reply option in the Mail menu enables you to choose a message from your In Box and reply to that message. When you choose to reply, the To field in the message editor contains the name of the person who sent you the message.

After you type the message, Commander Mail stores it in the Out Box to be sent the next time you choose Send/Receive from the Mail menu.

Deleting Messages

The Delete option in the Mail menu enables you to delete a message that is in your In Box. You should delete messages periodically to make more space available on your hard disk.

Another way to delete messages from the In box is to move those files to another directory. You can use the Commander Move command (F6), for example, to move all files in the directory \NC\IN (your In Box) to another directory.

Sorting Messages

Commander Mail sorts the messages in your In Box by the name of the sender or by the date. To designate a sort option, choose Sort by From or Sort by Date from the Mail menu. A check mark appears next to the option for the chosen sort in effect. If you typically have only a handful of messages in your In Box, either sort option is acceptable because you can easily see all the message names in one screen.

Printing Mail Messages

Commander Mail does not contain an option that enables you to print a message directly from Commander Mail. Because the messages are ASCII text files, however, you can use the DOS PRINT command to print messages from your IN, OUT, or SENT directory. To print an In Box message called ELLIOTT.U00, for example, you would type the following command at the DOS prompt:

    PRINT \NC\IN\ELLIOTT.U00

Disconnecting Communications

You may begin a communications session and realize that you specified the wrong messages to be sent. You can cancel an MCI Send/Receive session at any time by choosing Disconnect from the Mail menu or by pressing Esc or Ctrl+K.

Using Commander Link

Commander Link enables you to link two local computers and then copy or move files between them. This feature also enables you to rename or delete files on either computer. Link may come in handy if you are upgrading from one computer to another and want to copy your old files to the new computer.

The feature also can be helpful if you use both a desktop computer and a laptop. In many cases, laptops use 3 1/2-inch floppy disks, and desktop computers use 5 1/4-inch floppy disks. Commander Link enables you to access files from the laptop without the interim step of copying the file to a computer that has both 3 1/2-inch and 5 1/4-inch drives.

Commander Link has two requirements:

- The two computers must be attached by a serial null modem cable connected to the COM1 or COM2 port of each computer.

- Norton Commander must be running on both computers.

A *null modem cable*, which basically is a serial cable with some of the wires crossed, feeds a signal from one computer to another. You can buy a null modem cable at a computer supply store for about the same price as that of a normal serial cable.

After you attach a null modem cable to the serial ports of both computers and start Norton Commander on both computers, you are ready to use Commander Link. Figure 30.51 shows how a null modem cable is connected to two computers.

Fig. 30.51

The null modem cable connected to two computers.

Serial port

Serial port

Null modem cable

To begin Commander Link, choose the Lin**k** option from the Left or Right pull-down menu. A dialog box like the one shown in figure 30.52 appears.

Fig. 30.52

The Commander Link dialog box.

The Mode options in this dialog box are Master and Slave. You must designate one computer the master machine, from which all commands will be given; the other computer is the slave. Using the arrow keys, highlight the Master or Slave option for each computer and then press the space bar.

The Port options are COM1 and COM2. For each computer, choose the Port option that corresponds to the serial port where you attached the cable.

The Turbo Mode option maximizes the speed of communication between the master and slave computers. If you have trouble with the communication, turn off this option on both computers and then try again.

To begin the link procedure, choose the Link option at the bottom of the Commander Link dialog box. You can then access files in the slave machine or the master machine by choosing the **C**opy, **R**ename or Move, and **D**elete options from the Files menu of the master machine. You cannot use DOS commands to access files across the link.

After you set up the link on the master and slave machines, you see panels showing the master and slave directories. You can use the menu bar in the panel containing the slave machine's directory listing to display a full or brief listing. Because of the way the Link program operates, none of the other settings work for the slave machine. The slave machine's keyboard does not respond when the machine is set to slave mode.

You can also change directories on either machine. If the slave machine is set to a subdirectory, you can choose the parent directory (. .) at the top of the directory list to switch to the root directory. Choosing . . moves you up one directory in the tree. You follow the same procedure to choose a directory on the master machine.

You can copy, delete, and rename files between machines. Where the files are copied, moved, deleted, or renamed is determined by the panel in which you are operating. If you are operating from the link panel, which represents the linked (slave) machine, deleting a file in that panel deletes a file on the slave machine. If you delete a file in the nonlink panel, you are deleting a file on the master machine. Because Commander makes deleting files so easy, you need to be careful when you delete. Think of the link panel as being a directory, even though that directory happens to be on another machine.

In Commander Link, you use the Norton Commander **C**opy, **R**ename or Move, and **D**elete commands in essentially the same way you always do, as though you were using two directories on the same hard disk.

To copy files from the slave machine to the master machine, follow these steps:

1. Select the file or files to be copied.

   If you want to copy one file, highlight that file in the Commander panel. You may have to change directories in the link (slave) panel to locate the file.

   If you want to copy multiple files, move your cursor to the link panel and press the gray + key. You are then prompted to specify files. Enter a file name or a file specification, which can include the asterisk (*) or question mark (?) wild-card characters, and then press Enter. The specified files are highlighted. (You also can press the gray + key to specify files to be excluded from the selection.)

   You can add files to the selection list by highlighting the file name and pressing Ins.

2. Press F5 (Copy). Commander prompts you to specify where to copy the files in the master machine.

3. Select the destination.

    A default destination often appears on-screen. To accept that destination, press Enter. Otherwise, enter the name of a disk drive (such as **A:**), a path name (such as **\WP51**), or a drive/path combination (such as **C:\WP51**).

    When you specify the destination, you can press F10 to display a tree of the available directories on the master machine. From this tree, you can highlight the directory to which you want to copy the files.

4. Press Enter to start the copy operation.

5. End the link by choosing Lin**k** from the master machine's Right or Left menu. This step disables the link and returns the master and slave machines to normal operation.

To give you an idea of how quickly operations can occur in linked machines, a test copy of a 90,794-byte file took 18.27 seconds. In other words, the file was copied at about 5,000 bytes per second.

Summary

This chapter covered basic and advanced features of Norton Commander. You learned how to use Commander as a substitute for DOS commands. Norton Commander's NCD command enables you to choose directories from a graphic tree, create new directories, change directories, remove directories, and rename directories. You can use the View file options to view the contents of word processing, spreadsheet, and database files. You can use Commander also to set screen colors and blank your screen.

Commander's advanced options generally take a little more time to learn and use, but they represent some of the most exciting aspects of the program. The menu options enable you to customize Commander menus to fit your particular needs. The communications features—Mail and Link—enable you to communicate around the world or with the computer on the next desktop. In all, Norton Commander provides several powerful features that enable you to make better use of your computer's resources.

Norton Utilities 7 Command Reference

This Command Reference lists the commands in Norton Utilities 7 in alphabetical order and provides essential information about their use. If you already know what a command does but you need a reminder of how to use it, this Command Reference is an easy-to-use resource. Commands from earlier versions of Norton Utilities (4.5, 5.0, and 6.0) are listed also, with references to the new Version 7 commands that replace old commands. In addition, this Command Reference provides references to the chapters of this book that contain complete descriptions of commands.

Many Norton Utilities 7 commands include switches and other options. In this book, the following conventions apply to the way those options are presented in the command syntax examples:

- Items enclosed in brackets ([]) are optional.

- For words printed in *italic*, substitute the appropriate parameter. To use the DISKREET [*switches*] syntax, for example, you could type the following command:

        DISKREET /ON

■ The [*d:*] option represents the disk drive name (for example, A:, B:, C:, or D:).

■ The [*filespec*] option represents a file specification. Unless noted, this specification can include a path name. The file specification for the MYFILE.TXT file in the \WP51 directory is \WP51\MYFILE.TXT. You usually can use the DOS wild-card characters—the asterisk (*) and question mark (?)—in file specifications. For example, *.TXT specifies all files with the TXT extension.

■ The [*color*] option refers to a selection of colors. A color designation in a command line, for example, could be WHITE ON BLUE. (For more information, see Chapter 24 on using batch files.)

■ A vertical bar (I) between two options (such as ON I OFF) means that you can choose one option or the other, but not both at the same time.

■ When specified, the /DEBUG option causes the command to display the DOS errorlevel value returned. Some Norton Batch Enhancer commands use this errorlevel for branching control.

When you use a Norton command from the DOS prompt, several global switches are available. You should place the following switches in the command line after the command:

Switch	Description
/BW	Specifies a monochrome display so that the command displays black-and-white screens rather than color screens.
/G0	Controls EGA and VGA monitor settings. Disables use of a graphic mouse pointer and graphics symbols.
	To use the /G0 switch with the Disk Tools utility, for example, enter **DISKTOOL /G0**.
/G1	Controls EGA and VGA monitor settings. Disables use of the graphic mouse pointer and enables dialog boxes to use graphics symbols instead of character-based symbols (for example, buttons rather than check boxes).

Switch	Description
/LCD	Specifies an LCD (laptop computer display) so that the command uses colors that Norton specifically chose for this kind of display.
/NOZOOM	Disables zoom-style dialog boxes. This switch cuts screen-redrawing time and is particularly useful for slower computers.

Batch Enhancer (BE)

The Batch Enhancer (BE) command consists of a series of sub-commands intended to supplement the DOS batch commands. With Batch Enhancer, you can create batch files and menus. The following sections describe the Batch Enhancer subcommands.

Syntax

BE *subcommand*

BE *filespec*

If a list of subcommands is stored in a file, use the second version of the BE command (BE *filespec*) to cause the subcommands in that file to execute (as in a DOS batch file). You also can enter a BE command from the DOS prompt, as in the first version of the command (BE *subcommand*).

Note

■ You must include either a subcommand or a file specification in the BE command line.

For more information, see Chapter 24.

ASK

The BE subcommand ASK waits for a response from the user and then stores the response in the DOS errorlevel variable. You usually need to use the DOS IF ERRORLEVEL GOTO LABEL command after ASK.

Syntax

BE ASK *prompt* [*keys*] [DEFAULT=*key*] [TIMEOUT=*n*]
[ADJUST=*n*] [*color*] [/DEBUG]

Example

The following command displays the prompt Enter Menu
Choice: and waits for your input:

BE ASK "Enter Menu Choice:" ABCD DEFAULT=D
TIMEOUT=60

When the user presses a key that represents a menu choice (for
example, A, B, C, or D), the BE ASK command sets the errorlevel
code; the first key becomes ERRORLEVEL 1, the second key is
ERRORLEVEL 2, and so on. If you do not provide a menu-choice
key list (such as ABCD), ASK accepts any key the user presses.
If the user does not press a key during the TIMEOUT period
(60 seconds), the command uses the DEFAULT option (D).

Note

■ As the ASK subcommand runs, it displays the prompt on-
screen and waits for the user to enter an answer. Design the
prompt to display a list of correct responses or to refer to a
list of responses in a displayed menu.

Tip

■ The DOS IF command can use the ERRORLEVEL values
returned by ASK, enabling you to create menus. (See the
section "Using the ASK Command" in Chapter 24.)

BEEP

The BE subcommand BEEP causes a beep or musical tone to
sound from the PC's speaker.

Syntax

BE BEEP [*switches*]

BE BEEP [*filespec*] [/E]

Switches

Switch	Description
/D*n*	Specifies the duration of a tone, where *n* is in measurements of 1/18 of a second. For example, /D3 specifies that the tone sounds for 3/18 of a second.
/E	Echoes the text in the file to the screen (when used with a file specification).
/F*n*	Specifies the frequency of a tone, where *n* is cycles per second (Hz). The switch /F440, for example, plays a tone at 440 cycles per second.
/R*n*	Specifies that the tone repeat *n* times.
/W*n*	Specifies a wait (pause) in durations of 1/18 of a second. The switch /W3, for example, causes a wait of 3/18 of a second.

Example

The following command creates a sound at a frequency of 440 Hz, pauses for 10/18 of a second, and sounds the tone again:

BE BEEP /F440 /R2 /W10

BOX

The BE subcommand BOX draws a box on-screen. You can use this box to display a message or create a menu.

Syntax

BE BOX *top,left,bottom,right* [SINGLE|DOUBLE] [*color*]

Parameters in uppercase are key words in the command; these words appear in the command as written here. The parameters in lowercase italic represent a number or option to be placed into the command—for example, *top* = 3 and *left* = 2.

Here are descriptions of the BOX parameters:

Parameter	Description
top	Specifies the row number of the upper-left corner of the box.
left	Specifies the column number of the upper-left corner of the box.
bottom	Specifies the row number of the lower-right corner of the box.
right	Specifies the column number of the lower-right corner of the box.
SINGLE	Produces a box with single lines (the default).
DOUBLE	Produces a box with double lines.
color	Specifies the color of the text. For more information about this option, see the section on the Screen Attributes (SA) command.

Example

The following command draws a box on-screen with the upper-left corner positioned 2 lines from the top of the screen and 10 columns from the left:

   BE BOX 2,10,20,70 DOUBLE

The lower-right corner of the box is 20 lines from the top of the screen and 70 columns from the left. The box has double lines.

CLS

The BE subcommand CLS clears the screen and (optionally) sets the screen color.

Syntax

   BE CLS [*color*]

Following is a list of the color choices:

Setting	Command
Intensity	BRIGHT or BOLD (these commands are identical) BLINKING
Main Setting	NORMAL REVERSE UNDERLINE
Colors (either foreground or background)	WHITE BLACK RED MAGENTA BLUE GREEN CYAN YELLOW

Example

The following command clears the screen and causes on-screen characters to appear in bold white on a blue background:

    BE CLS BOLD WHITE ON BLUE

Note

■ The color selections you can use are the same as those used in the BE SA subcommand.

Tips

■ Often color choices are an option in a Norton BE subcommand. Whenever the *color* option is available, you can use the color choices described for the CLS subcommand.

■ The BE SA subcommand has a /CLS option, so you can also use that command to set colors and clear the screen.

DELAY

The BE subcommand DELAY causes the batch file to delay for a specified time, measured in 1/18 of a second.

Syntax

BE DELAY [*time*]

Example

The following command delays the execution of the batch file for one second:

BE DELAY 18

The execution of the batch file continues after the delay time has elapsed.

Note

■ The *time* option is measured in 1/18 of a second, so a *time* entry of 9 causes a delay of half a second, 18 causes a delay of a second, and 36 causes a delay of 2 seconds.

EXIT

The BE subcommand EXIT terminates a Norton script file (not a DOS batch file). Use this subcommand to stop a script at any point. The subcommand has no options.

Syntax

BE EXIT

GOTO

The BE subcommand GOTO enables you to branch the flow of the script to another part of the file.

Syntax

BE *filespec* [[GOTO] *label*]

The *filespec* parameter is a script file, and *label* is a label on its own line, starting in column 1 of the script file. A label is a statement that begins with a colon (:).

Example

Note the following label:

:THISISALABEL

To send the flow of the script to this label, use this command:

BE *filespec* GOTO THISISALABEL

JUMP

The BE subcommand JUMP enables you to incorporate conditional branching into a script file (not for use in a DOS batch file). Unlike GOTO, which always branches to a specified label, JUMP can branch to any of several labels, based on the current value of the exit code.

Syntax

BE JUMP *label1*, [*label2*[,...*labeln*]] [/DEFAULT:*label*]

The *label1* parameter is the name of the label to which the flow of the script should be sent if the exit code is 1, *label2* is the name of the label to which the flow should be sent if the exit code is 2, and so on. If no label matches the exit code, the flow is sent to the label specified by the /DEFAULT switch. If no label matches the exit code and no default label exists, execution continues with the command following the JUMP command.

Tip

■ See the next subcommand, MONTHDAY, for an example of how to use JUMP.

MONTHDAY

The BE subcommand MONTHDAY returns the day of the month as an exit code, which you then can use in a BE JUMP subcommand or in a DOS IF ERRORLEVEL command.

Syntax

BE MONTHDAY [/DEBUG]

The /DEBUG option displays the exit code on-screen.

Example

To perform a backup on the first day of the month, you can use the following commands:

BE MONTHDAY
BE JUMP BACKUP /DEFAULT:NOBACKUP

Because the BACKUP label is the first label in the BE JUMP command, it corresponds to the first day of the month. On the first day of the month, the batch file goes to the label :BACKUP (which contains instructions for performing a backup). On other days, the flow of the script is to the :NOBACKUP label.

Tip

■ You can use the related command WEEKDAY in the same way to design batch files that are sensitive to specific days of the week.

PRINTCHAR

The BE subcommand PRINTCHAR prints a character a specified number of times. You can use this subcommand to create interesting menus or diagrams on-screen.

Syntax

BE PRINTCHAR *character,repeats* [*color*]

The *character* parameter can be any ASCII character (including extended ASCII), and you can specify any number of *repeats* up to

80. The *color* parameter specifies the color of the text on-screen. For more information about color, see the section on the BE Screen Attributes (SA) command.

Example

The following command prints the asterisk (*) character 20 times in a single line on-screen:

BE PRINTCHAR *,20

REBOOT

The BE subcommand REBOOT enables you to warm-boot the computer—that is, to cause a reboot as though you had pressed Ctrl+Alt+Del.

Syntax

BE REBOOT [/VERIFY]

When the /VERIFY switch is included in the command, you (or another user) are prompted to confirm whether the reboot should take place.

Note

■ If your batch file alters an entry in your AUTOEXEC.BAT or CONFIG.SYS file, or in any other file that may be accessed when you boot your computer, you may want to include the REBOOT command at the end of your batch file to cause the changes to take effect.

ROWCOL

The BE subcommand ROWCOL places the cursor at a designated location on-screen and (optionally) displays text at that location.

Syntax

BE ROWCOL *row,col*[*,text*] [*color*]

The *row* parameter represents the number of the row (usually, 1 to 25) in which you want the cursor and any specified text to appear; *col* is the number of the column (usually 1 to 80). If you include a *text* parameter in the command, that text is written to the screen at the designated location. The *color* parameter specifies the color of the text. For more information about the color option, see the next section on the BE Screen Attributes (SA) command.

Example

The following command places the cursor 10 lines from the top and 5 columns from the left of the screen. At that location, the command prints the text specified in quotation marks:

BE ROWCOL 10,5, "Make a selection using the cursor keys."

The cursor ends up *after* the printed text, not at *row,col*.

Screen Attributes (SA)

The BE subcommand SA sets color attributes for the screen—that is, specifies which colors are used for the background and the text that appears on-screen.

Syntax

BE SA *main-setting* [*switches*]

BE SA [*intensity*] [*foreground*] [ON *background*] [*switches*]

The options for *main-setting* are NORMAL, REVERSE, and UNDER-LINE.

Example

The following command is simple and easy to remember:

BE SA NORMAL

This command changes the text to whatever the current monitor's default colors are.

The second version of BE SA is more complicated but more powerful. Choices for *intensity* are BRIGHT, BOLD, and BLINKING. (BRIGHT and BOLD are identical.) Choices for *foreground* and *background* colors are WHITE, BLACK, RED, MAGENTA, BLUE, GREEN, CYAN, and YELLOW. For example, the following command changes colors to high-intensity white on a blue background:

BE SA BRIGHT WHITE ON BLUE

Switches

Switch	Description
/N	Instructs the SA subcommand not to set border color
/CLS	Clears the screen after setting the screen attributes

Following is a list of the color choices for SA:

Setting	Command
Intensity	BRIGHT or BOLD (these commands are identical) BLINKING
Main Setting	NORMAL REVERSE UNDERLINE
Colors (either foreground or background)	WHITE BLACK RED MAGENTA BLUE GREEN CYAN YELLOW

Example

The following command causes characters to appear in bold white on a blue background:

BE SA BOLD WHITE ON BLUE /CLS

This command also clears the screen. For more information, see the earlier section on the CLS command.

SHIFTSTATE

The BE subcommand SHIFTSTATE examines the status of the left and right Shift keys, the Alt key, and the Ctrl key (the command determines whether the key is *shifted*, or pressed), and returns an exit code that indicates where those keys are in the shift state. Then you can use the exit code to cause the script to branch with the JUMP subcommand or the DOS ERRORLEVEL command. See Chapter 24 for information on creating script files.

Syntax

BE SHIFTSTATE [/DEBUG]

The /DEBUG option displays the exit code.

This command returns the following exit codes:

Key in Shift State	Returned Code
Right Shift	1
Left Shift	2
Ctrl (left or right)	4
Alt (left or right)	8

Tip

■ You can use the shift state to create several versions of the same command. You can write a script file in which BE MYCMD performs one set of commands, but performs another set of commands if Shift, Alt, or Ctrl is pressed.

TRIGGER

The BE subcommand TRIGGER halts the execution of a script file until a specified time. This command enables you to set up your script so that it stops and then waits until the specified time to continue execution. For information about creating script files, see Chapter 24 on using batch files.

Syntax

BE TRIGGER *hh:mm* [AM] [PM]

The *hh:mm* parameter is the hours and minutes in 24-hour clock time. (In 24-hour clock time, 14:00 is 2:00 p.m.) Use the AM or PM designation in the command line to specify 12-hour clock time, as in 2:00 PM. In this designation, 12:00 AM is 0:00 (midnight), and 12:00 PM is noon.

Example

You can use the TRIGGER subcommand to begin executing a communications program early in the morning, when telephone rates are lowest. The following command causes the script to pause until two o'clock in the morning before it continues:

BE TRIGGER 2:00 AM

WEEKDAY

Like the MONTHDAY subcommand, the BE subcommand WEEKDAY returns the day of the week as an exit code. You can use the WEEKDAY subcommand in a JUMP subcommand or in an IF ERRORLEVEL command.

Syntax

BE WEEKDAY [/DEBUG]

The /DEBUG option displays the exit code.

Example

To execute a backup on the second day of the week (Monday), use the following commands:

BE WEEKDAY
BE JUMP NOBACKUP, BACKUP /DEFAULT:NOBACKUP

Because the BACKUP label is the second label in the BE JUMP command, it corresponds to the second day of the week. On the first day of the week, the command branches to NOBACKUP. On the second day of the week, the batch file goes to the label :BACKUP (which contains instructions for performing a backup). On other days, the flow of the script is to the :NOBACKUP label.

Tip

■ You can use the related command MONTHDAY in the same way to design batch files that are sensitive to specific days of the month.

WINDOW

The BE subcommand WINDOW draws a window on-screen, with optional shadow and zoom features.

Syntax

BE WINDOW *top,left,bottom,right* [*color*] [SHADOW] [ZOOM]

Following are descriptions of the WINDOW parameters:

Parameter	Description
top	Specifies the row number of the upper-left corner of the window.
left	Specifies the column number of the upper-left corner of the window.
bottom	Specifies the row number of the lower-right corner of the window.
right	Specifies the column number of the lower-right corner of the window.
SHADOW	Adds a shadow to the right and bottom edges of the window.
ZOOM	Zooms the window onto the screen; the window starts as a small rectangle and grows to full size. (You can use EXPLODE instead of ZOOM; these parameters are identical.)

Example

The following command draws a window on-screen with the upper-left corner positioned 2 lines from the top and 10 columns from the left of the screen:

BE WINDOW 2,10,20,70 SHADOW ZOOM

The lower-right corner of the window is 20 lines from the top and 70 columns from the left of the screen. The window zooms onto the screen, with a shadow.

Note

■ The main difference between the BOX and WINDOW command is that the BOX command does not overwrite any text on-screen. The WINDOW command blanks out the window, erasing any text on-screen.

Calibrate (CALIBRAT)

To optimize the speed and reliability of reading and writing information to your hard disk, use the Calibrate command. Calibrate performs a nondestructive low-level format, enabling you to check your disk for reliability without destroying the information on it.

Syntax

CALIBRAT [*d:*] [*switches*]

Switches

Switch	Description
/BATCH	Does not prompt for input from the user. Returns to DOS when finished.
/BLANK	Blanks the screen during the test.
/NOCOPY	Does not make a duplicate copy of the track being tested.
/NOFORMAT	Performs pattern testing only and skips the low-level format.
/NOSEEK	Skips the seek tests. Use this switch when you do not want CALIBRAT to test the disk's head-positioning mechanism. Usually, you should use CALIBRAT once without /NOSEEK to test the mechanism. Then you can include /NOSEEK in subsequent tests.
/ISMFM	Specifies that the interleave test be performed on an MFM-type hard drive. You can determine whether you have an MFM drive by using the SYSINFO command.
/PATTERN:*n*	Specifies which testing level (*n*) to use. The parameter *n* can be 0, 5, 40, or 80. The higher the number, the more thorough the test; the higher the number, however, the longer CALIBRAT takes to test the disk.
/R:*file*	Generates a report and writes it to the file name specified in the switch. You must use the /BATCH switch when you use /R:*file*.

continues

Switch	Description
/RA:*file*	Performs the same function as the /R:*file* switch but adds the information to the file instead of creating a new file.
/X:[*d*][*d*]	Excludes named drives from the test. The switch /X:DE, for example, excludes disks D and E from testing. If your computer has allocated nonexistent drives, you must use this switch to exclude those drives from the tests.

Note

■ When you use this command, make sure that no memory-resident programs (TSRs) are loaded and that only essential device drivers (in your CONFIG.SYS file) are in use.

For more information, see Chapter 20.

Directory Sort (DS)

You use the Directory Sort (DS) command to sort the names of files in a directory by name, extension, time, date, or size.

Syntax

DS [*sortkeys*] [*pathname*] /S

The *pathname* parameter is the directory to be sorted. If you do not include sort keys, the program runs in interactive mode. Here are the sort keys that are available:

Key	Sorts By
N	Name
E	Extension
D	Date
T	Time
S	Size

Adding a minus sign (–) to any sort key reverses the sort order. The –N switch, then, tells the command to sort by name in reverse alphabetical order. The /S switch tells the command to include subdirectories in the sorting.

Example

To sort by name and extension order, use the following command:

DS NE

For more information, see Chapter 26.

Disk Editor (DISKEDIT)

Norton Disk Editor enables you to view and edit information on the entire floppy disk or hard disk, including system areas, boot records, file allocation tables, and data areas. Disk Editor is useful when you cannot recover information with Norton Disk Doctor or UnErase. To use this program effectively, however, you must understand how disks work.

Syntax

DISKEDIT [*d:*][*path*][*filename*] [*switches*]

Switches

Switch	Description
/M	Operates in maintenance mode, enabling Disk Editor to bypass DOS and directly view the contents of a disk.
/SKIPHIGH	Does not load into high memory. Use this switch if you are using a memory manager that already occupies high DOS memory.
/W	Uses write-access mode. Otherwise, the command is in read-only mode, in which you cannot write information to disk.
/X:[*d*][*d*]	Excludes certain drives from processing. The switch /X:DE, for example, excludes disks D and E from testing. If your computer has allocated nonexistent drives, you must use this switch to exclude those drives.

Note

■ Disk Editor is an interactive program that you operate from the Norton main screen.

For more information, see Chapter 17.

Disk Information (DI)

The Disk Information command in Norton Utilities 4.5 has been integrated into the System Info command in Versions 5, 6, and 7. For more information, see the section on the System Info (SYSINFO) utility later in this Command Reference.

Disk Monitor (DISKMON)

Disk Monitor contains three main features:

■ Disk Protect prevents unauthorized use of your files on disk.

■ Disk Light places a disk-access light on your monitor so that you can see when your disk is being used.

■ Disk Park moves the read/write head on your hard disk to a safe location so that you can move your computer.

Syntax

DISKMON [*switches*]

Switches

Switch	Description
/LIGHT+|−	Turns on (+) or off (−) the Disk Light feature.
/PARK	Parks all drives.
/PROTECT+|−	Turns on (+) or off (−) the Disk Protect feature. When this feature is on, protection is set to the selections that were stored in DM.INI when you ran the command interactively.

Switch	Description
/SKIPHIGH	Does not load into high memory. Use this switch if you are using a memory manager that already occupies high DOS memory.
/STATUS	Displays a summary of Disk Monitor status.
/UNINSTALL	Uninstalls the Disk Monitor program from memory if that program was the last TSR (terminate-and-stay-resident) program loaded into memory.

Note

■ Run Disk Monitor interactively (enter **DISKMON** at the DOS prompt) the first time you use this command to choose the type of protection you want (files, system areas, entire disk, and floppy format). Disk Monitor stores your selections in a file named DM.INI. After you set up the command the way you want it, you can use Disk Monitor and its switches from the DOS prompt.

For more information, see Chapter 6.

Disk Test (DT)

The Disk Test (DT) command for Norton Utilities 4.5 has been incorporated into the Norton Disk Doctor command for Versions 5, 6, and 7. For more information, see the section on Norton Disk Doctor (NDD) later in this Command Reference.

Disk Tools (DISKTOOL)

Disk Tools is a set of four utilities containing data protection and recovery features. These tools enable you to perform the following tasks:

■ Make a disk bootable

■ Recover from DOS's RECOVER command

- Revive a defective floppy disk
- Mark a cluster

Syntax

DISKTOOL [/MAKEBOOT] [/SKIPHIGH]

DISKTOOL [/DOSRECOVER] [/SKIPHIGH]

DISKTOOL [/REVIVE] [/DEVICEDRIVEN] [/SKIPHIGH]

DISKTOOL [/MARKCLUSTER] [/SKIPHIGH]

Switches

Switch	Description
/DOSRECOVER	Skips the Disk Tools menu and proceeds to the Recover from DOS's RECOVER option.
/MAKEBOOT	Skips the Disk Tools menu and proceeds to the Make a Disk Bootable option.
/REVIVE	Skips the Disk Tools menu and proceeds to the Revive a Defective Diskette option.
/DEVICEDRIVEN	Tells the command that the drive being used is device-driven.
/MARKCLUSTER	Skips the Disk Tools menu and proceeds to the Mark a Cluster option.
/SKIPHIGH	Does not load into high memory. Use this option if you are using a memory manager that already occupies high DOS memory.

Notes

- The Disk Tools program is designed primarily for interactive use. By including switches in the command line, however, you can choose which tool to use and tell the program not to use high DOS memory.

- Previous versions of the Disk Tools command included Rescue Disk options. To create or use a rescue disk in Version 7, use the RESCUE command (see Chapter 14).

For more information on Disk Tools, see Chapter 13.

Diskreet (DISKREET)

Diskreet is a program that enables you to protect files or disks by using a password. Files stored by Diskreet are encrypted so that they are unreadable, even by Disk Editor. An *NDisk* is an area of your hard disk that operates like a separate disk; this area contains encrypted information that is password-protected.

Syntax

DISKREET [*switches*]

Switches

Switch	Description
/CLOSE	Closes all disks
/D:*filespec*	Decrypts the specified files
/E:*filespec*	Encrypts the specified files
/HIDE[:*d*]	Hides the specified drive (NDisk)
/OFF	Disables use of the Diskreet driver
/ON	Enables the Diskreet driver
/P:*password*	Specifies *password* to use for encryption or decryption
/T:*filename*	Specifies a target name for the encrypted file
/SHOW[:*d*]	Shows the hidden drives (disks) being used to store files

Note

- For the Diskreet program to work, the following line must be in your CONFIG.SYS file:

  DEVICE=*path*\DISKREET.SYS

  The *path* is the name of the directory in which your Norton files are stored. When you boot your computer, this line tells DOS to make the Diskreet driver available for use.

For more information, see Chapter 7.

Duplicate Disk (DUPDISK)

The Duplicate Disk (DUPDISK) program is similar to the DOS DISKCOPY command but has more features. Like DISKCOPY, DUPDISK copies the contents of a disk to a disk of similar size (that is, 360K, 720K, and so on).

Syntax

DUPDISK d: [*d:*]

If a second disk drive is not specified, DUPDISK assumes that the disk duplication occurs on the same disk.

Example

To duplicate a disk from drive A to drive B, use this command:

DUPDISK A: B:

For more information, see Chapter 26.

Notes

■ Unlike DISKCOPY, DUPDISK enables you to make multiple copies of the same disk quickly, without having to reread the master (source) disk. If you use a single floppy drive, DUPDISK often enables you to swap disks only once during a copy instead of several times, as usually required by DISKCOPY.

■ When DOS formats a disk (beginning with Version 4), it assigns the disk a unique volume serial number. (This number appears when you perform a directory listing of the disk.) So when DOS performs a DISKCOPY and formats the target disk, it also gives the target disk a unique serial number. DUPDISK, however, places an exact copy of the source disk on the target disk, including the serial number.

■ Because DUPDISK is designed to copy only disks of similar size, you cannot use this command to copy a 360K source disk to a 720K target disk. To copy to a disk of another size, use the DOS COPY command.

File Attributes (FA)

The File Attributes (FA) command enables you to display, set, or reset the archive, hidden, read-only, and system file attributes.

Syntax

FA [*filespec*] [*switches*]

Switches

Switch	Description
/A+ | −	Sets archive attribute on (+) or off (−)
/CLEAR	Removes (clears) all the attributes
/DIR+ | −	Sets hidden directory on (+) or off (−)
/HID+ | −	Sets hidden attribute on (+) or off (−)
/P	Pauses after each displayed screen
/R+ | −	Sets read-only attribute on (+) or off (−)
/SYS+ | −	Sets system attribute on (+) or off (−)
/S	Includes subdirectories
/T	Displays only file and directory totals
/U	Lists all "unusual" files (those for which some attribute has been set)

Example

The following command sets the read-only attribute on for all BAT files in the current directory:

FA *.BAT /R+

Note

■ You also can use the Find File command to set file attributes.

For more information, see Chapter 9.

File Date (FD)

The File Date (FD) command enables you to change a file's date and time stamp.

Syntax

FD [*filespec*] [*switches*]

Switches

Switch	Description
/D[*date*]	Sets the date (in the format *mm-dd-yy*)
/P	Pauses after each screen is displayed
/S	Sets the date in files in subdirectories
/T[*time*]	Sets the time (in the format *hh:mm:ss*)

Example

To set all files on the disk to the date of 1-1-93 and the time of 12:00, use this command:

FD *.* /D:1-1-93 /T:12:00

Note

■ You also can use the File Find command to set the date and time stamp for files.

For more information, see Chapter 26.

File Find (FILEFIND)

The File Find command helps you find files by name in any directory on disk, search for text in files, set file attributes, and set dates and times for files. This command also tells you whether enough room exists on a disk to copy a group of files from another disk. See also the Text Search (TS), File Size (FS), and File Locate (FL) commands.

Syntax

FILEFIND [*d*:][*filespec*] [*search-text*] [*switches*]

The *filespec* option can include wild-card characters—the question mark (?) and asterisk (*).

Switches

Switch	Description
/A+ | −	Sets (+) or unsets (−) the archive attribute. If neither + nor − is included, the command lists files that have the archive attribute set.
/BATCH	Exits the program automatically and returns to the DOS prompt.
/C	Includes the current directory in the search.
/CLEAR	Clears all file attributes.
/CS	Makes the search case-sensitive.
/D[:][*date*]	Specifies the date to be placed on the files that match the file specification. The date should be in the format *mm-dd-yy*. (The date format may differ if your computer uses a non-United States country code.)
/HID+ | −	Sets (+) or unsets (−) the hidden attribute. If neither + nor − is included, the command lists files with the hidden attribute set.
/NOW	Sets the time and date to the current system time and date.
/O:*file*	Saves output lists from the command to the specified file.
/R+ | −	Sets (+) or unsets (−) the read-only attribute. If neither + nor − is included, the command lists files that have the read-only attribute set.
/S	Includes all subdirectories in the search.
/SYS+ | −	Sets (+) or unsets (−) the system attribute. If neither + nor − is included, the command lists files that have the system attribute set.
/T[:][*time*]	Specifies the time to be placed on the files that match the file specification. The time should be in the format *hh:mm:ss*. (The time format may be different if your computer uses a non-United States country code.)
/TARGET:*d*	Determines whether the files specified will fit on the target drive *d*.

Example

The following command sets the date and time to 1-1-93 and noon for all files on the floppy disk in drive A:

FILEFIND A:*.* /D01-01-93 /T12:00:00

The following command produces a list of the files stored on drive C that match the *.DRV file specification:

FILEFIND C:*.DRV

This list reports the file name, size, date, time, and file attributes.

Notes

- For more information on setting the time and date, refer to the section on the File Date (FD) command earlier in this Command Reference.

- For more information on setting file attributes, refer to the earlier section on the File Attributes (FA) command.

For more information, see Chapters 9 and 25.

File Fix (FILEFIX)

To diagnose and repair damaged dBASE, Clipper, Quattro Pro, WordPerfect, Lotus 1-2-3, Symphony, or compatible files, you use the File Fix utility. File Fix examines the contents of damaged files and attempts to reconstruct those files. Many files can be repaired automatically, but some require the user to intervene and make decisions about how to fix the file.

File Fix runs in interactive mode.

Syntax

FILEFIX [*filename*]

The *filename* option is the name of the file you want to fix.

Example

FILEFIX MYFILE.DBF

File Fix determines from the DBF extension that this file is a dBASE-compatible file and begins the File Fix procedure for that file type.

Note

■ File Fix determines the file type by the file extension.

For more information, see Chapter 15.

File Info (FI)

The File Info (FI) command for Norton Utilities 4.5 is not included in Version 5, 6, or 7.

File Locate (FL)

The File Locate (FL) command is similar to the File Find utility, but FL operates only from the DOS prompt and does not include the date-, time-, and attribute-setting functions of File Find.

Syntax

FL [*filespec*] [*switches*]

Switches

Switch	Description
/A	Searches for files on all drives
/F[*n*]	Finds the specified number (*n*) of files that match the file specification (the default for *n* is 1)
/P	Pauses after each screen
/T	Searches the directories in the PATH statement only
/W	Lists files in wide format on-screen
/E:*name*	Search for files in a path specified by an environment variable

Example

To locate all files on all drives that match the file specification *.XYX, use the following command:

FL *.XYX /A

Note

■ If you omit the *filespec* parameter, File Locate finds all files on the drive, which is equivalent to displaying a directory (DIR) for each directory on the drive and is a way to display a list of all file names on a disk.

For more information, see Chapter 25.

File Save

The File Save command in Norton Utilities 5 was renamed SmartCan in Versions 6 and 7. For information on this command, see the section on SmartCan later in this Command Reference.

File Size (FS)

The File Size (FS) command enables you to list the size of a file or the total size of a group of files. File Size lists also the slack space. Use File Size to determine whether a target disk has enough space to receive copies of files.

Syntax

FS [*filespec*] [*target drive*:] [*switches*]

Switches

Switch	Description
/P	Pauses after each screen
/S	Includes subdirectories in the file list
/T	Displays only the total size of a specified group of files, not the sizes of individual files

Examples

To find out the sizes of all files in the current directory, use one of the following commands:

FS *.*

FS

To display the sizes of all files in the current directory and all subdirectories, use this command:

FS /S

To find out whether you have enough room to copy all files with a WP extension to disk A, use the following command:

FS *.WP A:

For more information, see Chapter 26.

Format Recover (FR)

The Format Recover (FR) command in Norton Utilities 4.5 has been integrated into the UnFormat command in Versions 5, 6, and 7. For more information, see the section on the UnFormat command later in this Command Reference.

Image (IMAGE)

The Image program captures important information about the files on your hard disk and saves that information to a file named IMAGE.DAT. If you accidentally format your disk, the information in the IMAGE.DAT file can help the UnFormat program restore your files.

Syntax

IMAGE [*switch*]

Switches

Switch	Description
/NOBACK	Instructs the command not to create the backup file IMAGE.BAK
/OUT	Instructs the command not to display a message that the IMAGE file has been updated

Note

■ To keep the IMAGE.DAT file current, place the IMAGE command in your AUTOEXEC.BAT file so that IMAGE.DAT is updated each time you boot your computer.

For more information, see Chapter 4.

Line Print (LP)

The Line Print (LP) command enables you to print a text file to the printer and to choose print options.

Syntax

LP [*filespec*] [*output*] [*switches*]

The *output* option tells LP where to print the file. The default is PRN:. Some common output designations are LPT1:, LPT2:, COM1:, and COM2:.

Switches

Switch	Description
/80	Sets page width to 80 columns.
/132	Sets page width to 132 columns.
/A	Adds the file to the specified output file. If an output file exists, the new information is added to the end of that file; otherwise, LP creates a new file. (This switch works only if you specified an output file.)
/B*n*	Sets bottom margin to *n* lines (the default is 3).

Switch	Description
/CONFIG:*file*	Prints a file according to the information in the specified file. Use the NUCONFIG command to create this configuration file.
/EBCDICT	Tells Line Print that the original file is in EBCDIC format.
/HEADER*n*	Sets the type of header (*n* is a number): 0 = no header 1 = header that consists of current date and time on line 1 (the default) 2 = current date and time, plus file date and time on two lines
/HI*n*	Sets page height to *n* lines (the default is 66).
/L*n*	Sets left margin to *n* spaces (the default is 5).
/N	Turns on page numbering.
/PA*n*	Sets starting page number at *n* (the default is 1).
/PR:*xx*	Tells LP what kind of printer you are using. Here are the available options for *xx*: TT = Teletype (TTY) GE = Generic (the default) EP = Epson dot matrix PR = ProPrinter QU = Quietwriter TO = Toshiba LA = LaserJet PO = PostScript
/R*n*	Sets right margin to *n* spaces (the default is 5).
/SET:*filespec*	Tells Line Print that a printer setup string is in the file specified by *filespec*.
/SP*n*	Sets line spacing to *n* lines (the default is 1).
/TAB*n*	Sets tab spacing to *n* spaces (the default is 8).
/T*n*	Sets top margin to *n* lines (the default is 3).
/W*n*	Sets page width to *n* spaces (the default is 85).
/WS	Tells Line Print that the original file is in WordStar format.

Example

To print the file REPORT.TXT (which was created in WordStar) to the printer, use this command:

LP REPORT.TXT /WS

For more information, see Chapter 26.

List Directories (LD)

The List Directories (LD) command in Norton Utilities 4.5 has been integrated into the Norton Change Directory command in Versions 5, 6, and 7. For more information, see the section on Norton Change Directory later in this Command Reference.

Norton Cache (NCACHE2)

The Norton Cache program enables you to specify how much random-access memory (RAM) in your computer should be used as a buffer when the computer reads information from disk. The larger the cache, the faster disk access tends to be.

Syntax

To place the Norton Cache program in your AUTOEXEC.BAT file, you can use the following syntax:

path\NCACHE2 [*parameters*]

The *path* refers to the directory name in which the NCACHE2 file is stored. To place the program in your CONFIG.SYS file, you can use the following syntax:

DEVICE=*path*\NCACHE2 [*switches*]

Switches

Drive Switch	Description
/+	-A	Activates or deactivates caching. Use this switch if you need to deactivate caching to run a program in which you do not want to use caching.

Drive Switch	Description
/+I–C	Enables or disables caching of additional information. When this switch is disabled, no new information is cached.
/+I–I	Enables or disables IntelliWrites. When on, this switch accelerates disk writes and returns control to the program before the write operation ends.
/+I–P	Enables or disables write protection for drives.
/+I–S	Enables or disables SmartReads.
/+I–W	Enables or disables write-through caching. When write-through caching is disabled, writes are written directly to the disk, bypassing the cache.

Additional Switch	Description
/BLOCK=n	Sets the size of the cache blocks; n is a number (in K). Use large blocks if you are accessing large files and your disk is unfragmented. Use smaller blocks if you are accessing small files or your disk is fragmented.
/DELAY=$ss.hh$	Delay writes to the disk in seconds or hundredths of a second (for example, 00.10 is one-hundredth of a second). The default is 00.00. Slight writing delays can improve the speed of write-intensive programs.
/DISKRESET=ON I OFF	Specifies that all data be written to disk when a program makes a disk reset request.
/DOS=n or /DOS=$-n$	Specifies how much DOS (conventional) memory the cache uses. Use this switch only when you do not have any expanded or extended memory. A negative value tells the command to leave that much memory free for other programs to use.
/DUMP	Writes to disk all information that currently is in the cache.

continues

Additional Switch	Description
/EXP=*n* or /EXP=–*n*	Specifies how much expanded memory (in K) the cache uses. A negative value tells the command to leave that much memory free for other programs to use. (/EXP=750, for example, tells the command to use 750K of expanded memory for the disk cache.) Any expanded memory used must be compatible with LIM 4.
/EXT=*n* or /EXT=–*n*	Specifies how much extended memory (in K) the cache uses. A negative value tells the command to leave that much memory free for other programs to use. (/EXT=256, for example, tells the command to use 256K of extended memory for the cache.)
/G=*n*	Limits the caching of group sector reads for specified drive(s).
/INI=*filespec*	Indicates where to look for the file that contains installation options. If your installation options are in your NORTON directory in a file named NCACHE.INI, for example, use the parameter INI=\NORTON\NCACHE.INI.
/INSTALL	Installs Norton Cache with all default values, including the use of all available expanded and extended memory for the cache. This switch often is the easiest and quickest way to execute the command.
/MULTI ON|OFF	Specifies whether the multitasking feature of IntelliWrites is on or off.
/OPTIMIZE=[S|E|M]	Optimizes for speed, efficiency, or memory.
	The S (Speed) option sets the following parameters:
	/BLOCK=8K
	/DELAY=1.0
	/READ=8K
	/WRITE=*x*, where *x* is the largest track (in K) of all tracks being cached

Additional Switch	Description
	The E (Efficiency) option sets the following parameters:
	/BLOCK=s, where s is the smallest block size for the current cache (usually 512K to 1M)
	/DELAY=1.0
	/READ=8K
	/WRITE=8K
	The M (Memory) option sets the following parameters:
	/BLOCK=8K
	/DELAY=0.0
	/READ=0 (disables the read-ahead feature)
	/WRITE=0 (disables IntelliWrites)
/QUICK=ON|OFF	ON displays the DOS prompt even when information is being written to disk. OFF displays the DOS prompt after all writes to the disk are finished.
/QUIET	Specifies quiet mode; only errors are reported.
/R=Dn	Specifies how many sectors ahead should be read. A specification of /R=0 or /R=D0 disables read-aheads. /R=n specifies read-aheads always; /R=Dn causes read-aheads only when the file being read is not a random file. n is the number of sectors ranging from 0 to 15.
/READ=n	Sets the maximum size (in K) for read-aheads. For n, use a whole number from 8 to 64.
/REPORT=ON|OFF	Displays status information (ON) or does not display status information (OFF).
/RESET	Resets the cache by writing all pending disk writes, flushing all the data from all drives.
/SAVE	Saves current cache settings in the file specified by the /INI switch (or NCACHE.INI).

continues

Additional Switch	Description
/STATUS=ON|OFF	Displays a condensed version of the cache report. If the OFF switch is used, the report is not displayed at install time.
/UNINSTALL	Removes the NCACHE2 (TSR) program from memory and discontinues caching. You can uninstall only if the program was loaded from your AUTOEXEC.BAT file, not from your CONFIG.SYS file.
/USEHMA=ON|OFF	Uses the XMS high memory area to reduce the use of DOS RAM (if set to ON). This option is available only if you have an extended memory manager.
/USEHIGH=ON|OFF	Minimizes the use of conventional (low) DOS memory if high memory is available (if set to ON). The default setting is OFF.
/WRITE=n	Sets maximum size (in K) of the IntelliWrites buffer. For n, use a whole number from 8 to 64.

Example

To install the cache by using default conditions, enter the following command:

    NCACHE2 /INSTALL

To install the cache by using all but 64K of extended memory and using read-aheads of 32K only for drive C, enter this command:

    NCACHE2 /EXT=–64 /READ=32K /–A C:/+A

The /–A switch deactivates caching for all drives, and then C:/+A activates caching for drive C. Thus, only drive C is cached.

Notes

- If your computer currently uses the Microsoft Smart-Drive cache, you must remove that cache from your AUTOEXEC.BAT or CONFIG.SYS file before you use the NCACHE2 program.

- When you install NCACHE2 without specifying a cache size, the default setting is /EXT=4096, 2048K.

For more information, see Chapter 21.

Norton Change Directory (NCD)

The Norton Change Directory (NCD) command enables you to manage your directories on disk, change quickly from directory to directory, and print a directory tree. NCD gives you more control of directory names than the normal DOS commands do. The NCD command is particularly suited for use interactively, but you can also use it from the DOS prompt.

Syntax

When you enter the NCD command from the DOS prompt, the syntax can be any of the following:

NCD [*dirname*] [*switches*]

NCD [*d*:] /V:*label*

NCD [*d*:] /L[:*output*] [/G|/NG|/T] [/P] [/A]

NCD MD [*dirname*]

NCD RD [*dirname*]

NCD SIZE [*dirname*]

NCD COPY *source destination* [/DELETE]

NCD GRAFT *source destination*

NCD RMTREE *dirname* [/BATCH]

The *dirname* parameter is the name of the directory to be changed, created, removed, or displayed. The *source* and *destination* parameters tell the command the original location of the directory to be copied or grafted (*source*) and the target location (*destination*) for the directory.

COPY copies a directory to a new location. The following command copies all files from the directory named MYDIR to the directory named YOURDIR:

NCD COPY \MYDIR \YOURDIR

Including /DELETE (described in the "Switches" section) deletes copied files from their original locations.

GRAFT automatically deletes files from the old location. RMTREE removes a directory and all associated files.

The MD and RD versions of the NCD command are similar to the DOS MD and RD commands. You use these commands to make a new directory or remove an empty directory. The SIZE command displays the amount of space taken up by the files in the directory.

To use the COPY, GRAFT, and RMTREE options, you first must enable them in the NCD configuration dialog box, which you access with the Directory Configure option.

Switches

Switch	Description
/A	Displays the directory tree for all drives except floppy drives.
/BATCH	Skips all prompts and exits to DOS when finished.
/DELETE	Deletes copied files from their original directory.
/G	Displays the directory tree graphically.
/L:*output*	Prints the directory tree to the specified output file.
/N	Does not write to the file TREEINFO.NCD. If you are using NCD on a write-protected disk, you need to use this switch.
/NG	Displays the tree using nongraphic characters. Use this switch when you are using a printer that does not support graphic characters.
/P	Pauses after each screenful of information is displayed.
/R	Updates the file TREEINFO.NCD, which contains information about your directory tree structure.
/T	Totals the number and size of all files.
/V:*label*	Places a volume label on the disk.

Examples

To create a directory named \WP51\REPORTS, use this command:

NCD MD \WP51\REPORTS

To use the NCD command to change directories, enter **NCD** plus the name of the directory to which you want to change. To change to the directory \ONE-A\TWO-A\THREE-A\FOUR-A, use the following command:

NCD FOUR-A

For more information, see Chapter 23.

Norton Control Center (NCC)

Norton Control Center (NCC) enables you to control hardware settings, including display colors, keyboard rates, and clock settings. You can use Norton Control Center in command-line or interactive mode.

Syntax

NCC [*filespec*] [*switches*]

The *filespec* variable refers to a file that contains system information specifications. Before you use this version of the command, you must create this file by using NCC in interactive mode to choose the settings you want and then saving the information to a file.

Switches

Switch	Description
/CURSOR	Reads the information in the file named by *filespec* but sets only the cursor size
/DOSCOLOR	Reads the information in the file named by *filespec* but sets only the previously chosen DOS colors for foreground, background, and border
/PALETTE	Reads the information in the file named by *filespec* but sets only the palette colors
/SET	Reads the information in the file named by *filespec* and sets all the parameters

If you have not created a settings file with the NCC command in interactive mode, you can set a few options with certain quick switches:

Switch	Description
/25	Places the monitor in 25-line mode (same as /CO80)
/35	Places the monitor in 35-line mode (supported only by EGA monitors)
/43	Places the monitor in 43-line mode (supported only by EGA and VGA monitors)
/50	Places the monitor in 50-line mode (supported only by VGA monitors)
/BW80	Places the monitor in black-and-white mode with 25 lines and 80 columns
/CO80	Places the monitor in color mode with 25 lines and 80 columns
/FAST	Sets the keyboard rate to its fastest possible value

You can use Norton Control Center also to set system stop-watches. The following switches are available:

Switch	Description
/C:*comment*	Displays the text string *comment* after you execute the command. This switch is useful for documenting which timer is being reported. If the comment contains blanks, you must enclose the entire comment in quotation marks.
/L	Displays the time and date on left side of monitor.
/N	Suppresses display of the current time and date.
/START:*n*	Begins stopwatch number *n*, which is a number ranging from 1 to 4.
/STOP:*n*	Stops stopwatch number *n*, which is a number ranging from 1 to 4.

Example

To set your VGA computer so that 50 lines are displayed on-screen and the keyboard rate is the fastest value, use this command:

NCC /50/FAST

Note

■ To access Norton Control Center interactively, enter **NCC** at the DOS prompt without using any file specification. The Norton Control Center menu appears, enabling you to choose interactively the same options you can set with switches from the prompt.

For more information, see Chapter 22.

NDOS

NDOS is an alternative command processor that replaces COMMAND.COM, providing several new and enhanced DOS commands.

Syntax

NDOS [*switches*]

You can begin the NDOS processor at any time by entering the NDOS command at the DOS prompt, but the program usually is installed in the CONFIG.SYS file with the NUCONFIG command (see Chapter 2).

Here is the normal command for installing the program in CONFIG.SYS:

SHELL=C:\NU7\NDOS.COM /P

The /P switch specifies that NDOS is loaded as the primary command processor. This version of the command assumes that you have the Norton Utilities 7 program stored in the directory called \NU7 on drive C. Include also the following command in CONFIG.SYS:

DEVICE=C:\NU7\KEYSTACK.SYS

You need this command if you want to use the NDOS KEYSTACK command.

Switches

Switch	Description
@d:*filespec*	Uses commands in the designated file as options for loading NDOS.
/A:*n*	Sets the alias list size to *n*, which is a number ranging from 256 to 32000.
/C *command*	Loads a transient copy of NDOS. This switch usually is used by programs to start the command processor, execute a command, and then return to the program.
/E:*n* or /E+*n*	Sets the environment size. If :*n* is used, the size is set to *n* for the primary shell; *n* is a number ranging from 256 to 512 (the default is 256). If the +*n* option is used, the environment is set to its current value plus *n*.
/H:*n*	Sets the history size. *n* is a number ranging from 512 to 8192 bytes.
/L:*d*:*path*	Used with secondary shells, /L specifies where to find the NDOS.OVL file. You must use this switch if the NDOS.OVL file is not in the default directory.
/P	Loads NDOS as the primary command processor.
/S:B[*d*:*path*]	Sets NDOS swapping mode to the default. NDOS first tries XMS memory, then EMS, and then disk swapping (to the specified directory).
/S:E	Sets NDOS swapping mode to EMS memory.
/S:N	Turns off NDOS swapping mode.
/S:X	Sets NDOS swapping mode to XMS memory.
/U	Moves the resident portion of NDOS to XMS UMB (upper memory block) to reduce the size of the resident portion in low memory. You can use this switch only with 286 and later computers.

Note

■ Many NDOS commands have the same names and syntax as DOS commands but usually include additional features. NDOS also includes Batch Enhancer commands.

For more information, see Chapter 28.

Norton Disk Doctor (NDD)

Norton Disk Doctor (NDD) finds and corrects, if possible, physical or logical problems on a disk.

Syntax

NDD [*d*:][*d*:] [*switches*]

The *d*: options are disk drive names.

Switches

Switch	Description
/COMPLETE or /C	Tests for bad cylinders on the disk; also tests the partition table, boot record, root directory, and lost clusters.
/DT	Tells the program to perform only the surface test.
/FIXSPACES	Tells the program to fix file names that contain spaces.
/NOCOMP	Omits tests on compression structures (common when you are running file compression programs such as Stacker).
/NOHOST	Omits tests for the host drives of compressed volumes. Drive D, for example, often is the host drive when the disk contains a compression program such as Stacker.
/QUICK or /Q	Omits the test for bad cylinders, but tests the partition table, boot record, root directory, and lost clusters.
/R:*file*	Outputs to the named file a report on the result of the test. Use with /Q or /C.
/RA:*file*	Adds the report to the named file instead of creating a new file (otherwise, this switch is the same as /R). Use with /Q or /C.
/SKIPHIGH	Does not load into high memory. Include this command if you are using a memory manager that already occupies DOS high memory.

continues

Switch	Description
/REBUILD	Rebuilds the entire disk.
/UNDELETE	Undeletes a DOS partition that was skipped when a user chose not to undelete the partition during a previous run of NDD.
/UNDO	Causes the program to undo repairs made in earlier runs of the program.
/X:d	Excludes drive d from the test.

Example

To run a quick check of a disk, use NDD with the /QUICK switch:

    NDD /QUICK

You can place this command in your AUTOEXEC.BAT file to specify that a quick check of your disk be performed each time you boot your computer.

Notes

■ Use Norton Disk Doctor whenever you experience problems accessing a file or when you get a DOS error message concerning the operation of a disk. NDD is your first line of defense against these problems, enabling you to keep the problems from getting worse and to solve the problems before any data is lost.

■ If you enter the NDD command with no switches, you operate in interactive mode. The Disk Doctor menu appears. From this menu, you can choose options that diagnose the disk or attempt common solutions (making a disk bootable, reviving a defective disk, or recovering from DOS's RECOVER command).

For more information, see Chapter 12.

Norton Integrator (NI)

The Norton Integrator (NI) command in Norton Utilities 4.5 has been integrated into the NORTON (Norton Utilities main screen) command in Versions 5, 6, and 7. For more information, see the section on the Norton Utilities main screen (NORTON).

Norton Utilities Configuration (NUCONFIG)

The Norton Utilities Configuration (NUCONFIG) command enables you to change the way the Norton Utilities program works. You can set passwords, edit menus, change video and mouse settings, set up Norton Cache, include commands in AUTOEXEC.BAT and CONFIG.SYS, assign alternative utility names, and uncompress the program's EXE files. From the Norton main screen, you can access these items from the **C**onfiguration menu. From the DOS prompt, you can display the **C**onfiguration menu by entering **NUCONFIG**.

For more information, see Chapter 2.

Norton Utilities Main Screen (NORTON)

The NORTON command opens the Norton Utilities main screen, which contains a list of all the utilities. From this screen, you can run any of the Norton Utilities programs. From the menu bar, you can access brief help files that describe the purpose and syntax of each utility.

To open the Norton Utilities main screen from the DOS prompt, enter **NORTON**.

Norton Utilities Main Program (NU)

The Norton Utilities main program (the NU command) in Norton Advanced Utilities Version 4.5 has been integrated into the DISKEDIT command in Versions 5, 6, and 7. For information on DISKEDIT, refer to the section on Disk Editor (DISKEDIT) earlier in this Command Reference.

Quick UnErase (QU)

The Quick UnErase (QU) command in Norton Utilities 4.5 has been integrated into the UnErase command in Versions 5, 6, and 7. For more information, see the section on UnErase (UNERASE) later in this Command Reference.

Safe Format (SFORMAT, SF, or FORMAT)

The Safe Format command prevents you from accidentally formatting a disk that contains important information, and writes UnFormat to disk as a safety check for those times when you do format a disk.

Syntax

SFORMAT [*d*:] [*switches*]

You may have renamed the SFORMAT command as FORMAT to replace the DOS command of the same name. If so, you use the following syntax for the SFORMAT (FORMAT) command:

FORMAT [*d*:] [*switches*]

(SFORMAT.EXE is renamed FORMAT.EXE.)

To shorten the name, you can rename Safe Format as SF and then use this syntax:

SF [*d*:] [*switches*]

Use the NUCONFIG program (see Chapter 2) to rename the Safe Format program as FORMAT or SF.

Switches

Switch	Description
/1	Formats the disk as single-sided.
/4	Formats the disk as 360K (in a 1.2M drive).
/8	Formats the disk with eight tracks per sector.

Switch	Description
/B	Leaves space on the disk for system files.
/F:*size*	Specifies the size of the disk in K (360 or 720) or M (1.2, 1.44, or 2.88). *size* can be 360, 720, 1.2, 1.44, or 2.88.
/N:*n*	Specifies the number of sectors per track. *n* can be 8, 9, 15, or 18.
/S	Places system files on the disk.
/T:*n*	Specifies the number of tracks. *n* can be 40 or 80.
/V:*label*	Places a volume label on the disk.

Following are the switches that are unique to Norton's Safe Format command:

Switch	Description
/A	Uses automatic mode (in batch files)
/D	Uses DOS format mode
/Q	Uses quick-format mode
/U	Unconditional format; no warnings

Example

To format a disk with system files and place the volume label MYDISK on the disk, use this command:

SFORMAT B: /S /V:MYDISK

Note

■ You can use the Safe Format command in interactive mode by entering **SFORMAT** (or **FORMAT**) with no switches. From the Safe Format dialog box that appears, you can choose the drive to format, the size of the disk to format, whether to copy system files to the disk, which (if any) volume label to put on the disk, and which format mode to use (safe, quick, or DOS).

For more information, see Chapter 4.

SmartCan (SMARTCAN)

The SmartCan command moves deleted files to a less-used part of the hard disk so that those files remain recoverable for a longer period. After you use the part of the disk that contains a deleted file, any deleted files that occupy that space become unrecoverable.

Syntax

SMARTCAN [*switches*]

Switches

Switch	Description
/OFF	Disables the SmartCan command so that deleted files are not affected. The SmartCan command remains in memory but does not function until you use the /ON switch.
/ON	Enables the SmartCan command to move deleted files to a safe area.
/CONVERT	Causes the program to search for and convert old Erase Protect trash cans. Erase Protect is the name of SmartCan for earlier versions of Norton Utilities.
/SKIPHIGH	Does not load into high memory.
/STATUS	Displays the status of the SmartCan command.
/UNINSTALL	Removes the SmartCan command from memory if the command was the last memory-resident (TSR) command loaded.

Notes

- Usually, you should include the Smartcan command in your AUTOEXEC.BAT file so that the command is in effect whenever you delete files.

- The SmartCan command is a memory-resident (TSR) program.

- For information about unerasing deleted files, see the section on the UnErase command later in this Command Reference.

For more information, see Chapter 5.

Speed Disk (SPEEDISK)

The Speed Disk command reorganizes your disk so that fragmented files can be unfragmented. You can use this command to pack and rearrange files to help your disk run at top speed.

Syntax

SPEEDISK [*d*:] [*switches*]

Switches

Switch	Description
/B	Reboots after the command finishes.
/F	Performs a full optimization of the disk.
/FD	Performs a full optimization with directories first.
/FF	Performs a full optimization with a file reorder.
/Q	Unfragments free space and fills unused gaps (quick compression).
/SD[–]	Sorts file by date. If you include the minus (–) parameter, the sort is from most recent date to oldest date.
/SE[–]	Sorts files by extension. If you include the minus (–) parameter, the sort is in descending alphabetical order.
/SN[–]	Sorts by file name. If you include the minus (–) parameter, the sort is in descending alphabetical order.
/SS[–]	Sorts by file size. If you include the minus (–) parameter, the sort is from largest to smallest.
/U	Unfragments as many files as possible without moving parts of the directory structure. Some damaged files may not be capable of unfragmenting.
/V	Uses verify-after-write data verification. That is, each time information is written to the disk, the information is then read from the disk to verify that it was correctly written.

Example

To optimize drive C with a full optimization and then reboot the computer after the optimization, use this command:

SPEEDISK C: /F/B

Note

■ You can run Speed Disk in interactive mode by entering **SPEEDISK** with switches. In interactive mode, you can choose options from the Speed Disk menus. You can also choose which files not to move and which files to place on the disk first (closest to track 0).

For more information, see Chapter 19.

System Info (SYSINFO)

The System Info (SYSINFO) command provides information about your computer (computer type, peripherals in use, ROM-BIOS information, and so on) and performs tests that enable you to compare your computer's performance with the performance of other computers.

Syntax

SYSINFO [*d:*] [*switches*]

Switches

Switch	Description
/AUTO:*n*	Operates in automatic mode. The *n* parameter specifies a delay of a certain number of seconds between screens.
/DEMO	Operates in demo mode.
/DI	Produces the Drive Information Summary dialog box only.
/NOHDM	Tells the program not to attempt to detect the hard drive model.

Switch	Description
/N	Skips the live memory probe. On some computers, this probe forces you to reboot after the SYSINFO test. Use the /N switch to get around this problem.
/REP:*filespec*	Causes the program to print a report to the specified file.
/SPEC:*filespec*	Causes the program to use settings saved in the specified file.
/SOUND	Produces a beep between CPU tests.
/SUMMARY	Produces the System Summary dialog box only.
/TSR	Shows all TSR (terminate-and-stay-resident) programs in memory.

For more information, see Chapter 18.

Text Search (TS)

The Text Search (TS) command enables you to search for text in files anywhere on disk, including erased space.

Syntax

TS [*filespec*] [*string*] [*switches*]

The *filespec* option names the files to be searched, such as *.BAT. If this parameter is missing, all files are searched. The *string* option is the text to be located in those files (for example, TEXAS).

Switches

Switch	Description
/A	Automates the search and ignores prompts.
/C*n*	Begins the search at the cluster specified by *n*.
/CS	Performs a case-sensitive search. Thus, if you specify the search string as *Alan*, the command does not find *ALAN*.
/D	Searches the entire disk.

continues

Switch	Description
/E	Searches only the erased portions of the disk.
/EBCDIC	Specifies that the files being searched are in EBCDIC format.
/LOG	Creates output suitable for a log file or printer.
/S	Includes subdirectories in the search.
/T	Sets the noninteractive summary total.
/WS	Specifies that the files being searched are in WordStar format.
/F:*filename*	Specifies the output file to hold the disk clusters.

Example

To find occurrences of TEXAS in files with a TXT extension, use the following command:

    TS *.TXT TEXAS

For more information, see Chapter 25.

Time Mark (TM)

The Time Mark (TM) command in Norton Utilities 4.5 has been integrated into Norton Command Center (NCC) in Versions 5, 6, and 7. For more information, refer to the section on Norton Command Center (NCC) earlier in this Command Reference.

UnErase (UNERASE)

The UnErase command enables you to recover erased (deleted) files. You can unerase only files that have not been overwritten by other files.

Syntax

    UNERASE [*filespec*] [*switches*]

Switches

Switch	Description
/IMAGE	Uses the information in the IMAGE file to aid in recovery.
/MIRROR	Uses the information in the MIRROR file to aid in recovery. (The MIRROR file is created by the MIRROR command in DOS 5.0.)
/NOINFO	Causes the program not to use the IMAGE and MIRROR information.
/NOTRACK	Does not use DOS delete-tracking information to aid in file recovery.
/PROTECTED	Causes the program to recover only files protected by SmartCan or DOS's Delete Sentry.
/NOPROTECTED	Causes the program to exclude from recovery those files protected by SmartCan or DOS's Delete Sentry.
/SKIPHIGH	Does not load into high memory. Include this command if you are using a memory manager that already occupies DOS high memory.

Example

The following command looks for all erased files with the BAK extension:

        UNERASE *.BAK

The UnErase command may prompt you to provide the first character of the name of the file to be unerased. Follow the prompts on-screen after entering the command.

Notes

- ■ For information on how to protect erased files, refer to the section on the SmartCan command earlier in this Command Reference.

- ■ By default, the command uses the most current of the IMAGE or MIRROR files and also uses DOS delete-tracking information, if that information is available.

■ You can use the wild-card characters ? and * to specify which files you want to unerase.

For more information, see Chapters 10 and 16.

UnFormat (UNFORMAT)

You use the UnFormat command to bring back information on a formatted disk that has been reformatted accidentally.

Syntax

UNFORMAT [*d*:]

The *d*: option is the name of the disk to be unformatted.

Switches

Switch	Description
/IMAGE	Tells the command to use the IMAGE recovery-information file
/MIRROR	Tells the command to use the MIRROR recovery-information file

If you do not specify the IMAGE or MIRROR file, UnFormat uses the most recent of the files, if they exist.

Notes

■ This command works best if you used the Image (or DOS MIRROR) command to store a copy of the system areas of your disk or if you formatted the disk with Safe Format. (For more information, refer to the sections on the Image and Safe Format commands earlier in this Command Reference.)

■ If your hard disk has been formatted, do not copy anything to the hard disk before you attempt to use UnFormat. In this case, you should run the UnFormat program from a floppy disk. (For more information, see Chapter 14 on using a rescue disk.)

For more information, see Chapter 11.

Unremove Directory (UD)

The Unremove Directory (UD) command in Norton Utilities 4.5 has been integrated into the UnErase command in Versions 5, 6, and 7. For more information, refer to the section on the UnErase (UNERASE) command earlier in this Command Reference.

Volume Label (VL)

The Volume Label (VL) command in Norton Utilities 4.5 has been incorporated into the NCD command in Versions 5, 6, and 7. For more information, refer to the section on the Norton Change Directory (NCD) command earlier in this Command Reference.

Wipe Disk

The Wipe Disk command in Norton Utilities 4.5 has been integrated into the WipeInfo command in Versions 5, 6, and 7. For more information, see the section on the WipeInfo (WIPEINFO) command.

Wipe File

The Wipe File command in Norton Utilities 4.5 has been integrated into the WipeInfo command in Versions 5, 6, and 7. For more information, see the section covering the WipeInfo (WIPEINFO) command.

WipeInfo (WIPEINFO)

The WipeInfo command overwrites information on disk in such a way that the information cannot be recovered. You can use this command to wipe certain files or the entire disk.

Syntax

WIPEINFO *d*:[*disk switch*] [*common switches*]

WIPEINFO *d*:[*filespec*] [*file switches*] [*common switches*]

Switches

Disk Switch	Description
/E	Overwrites only information that is unused or that is in erased files (files marked for erasure by the DOS ERASE command but otherwise recoverable).

File Switch	Description
/K	Also wipes any slack space allocated to a file.
/N	Uses no-wipe mode, which causes the WipeInfo command to behave like the DOS ERASE command. The file is marked as erased but is not overwritten.
/S	Wipes out files that match *filespec* in subdirectories also.

Common Switch	Description
/GOV*n*	Uses a government-standard overwriting procedure. The default for *n* (number of overwrites) is 3. Although the default normally is 0, the /GOV switch overrides this default. When you include the /GOV switch, the value written to disk is ASCII value 246.
/R*n*	Overwrites the disk *n* times (the default is 1).
/V*n*	Selects the value that is to be used to overwrite information on the disk. The *n* value is a number ranging from 0 to 255.
/BATCH	Executes the command without prompts (for batch files).

Example

To wipe disk D (adhering to the government standard), enter the following command:

WIPEINFO D:/GOV

For more information, see Chapter 8.

A DOS Review

D OS, which stands for *d*isk *o*perating *s*ystem, is a software program that manages the resources of your computer. On the IBM PC, this operating system is called PC DOS. IBM-compatible computers use a nearly equivalent DOS called MS-DOS, which stands for Microsoft DOS. Microsoft is the company that designed DOS for the IBM family of personal computers.

Items are stored and retrieved in many everyday activities, such as banking, filing, or checking a coat. Information is just one more thing that needs to be stored somewhere so that it can be retrieved later. Because the computer handles information, having a "manager" place information somewhere and later retrieve it makes sense. On the computer, DOS is the manager. You tell DOS what to do with the information, and DOS stores it and retrieves it as directed.

For DOS to understand what you want it to do, you must speak its language. This appendix covers the basic concepts and commands—the *language*—of DOS. If you are a new computer user, read this entire appendix before you use the book, because the book frequently references DOS concepts and commands. If you are familiar with some parts of DOS, you may not need to read the entire appendix. Instead, you can study only the topics that you want to learn more about and those that will be helpful to you as you use this book (and your computer). The topics covered in this appendix include the following:

- Learning how DOS works
- Reviewing commonly used DOS commands
- Managing a hard disk with DOS commands

■ Using batch files and system files

■ Using DOS to back up information on your hard disk

■ Using DOS 5 and DOS 6

Understanding How DOS Works

Before you learn what specific tasks DOS can do, you must first understand how DOS works. To understand that, you must understand the
concept of computer files. You can relate computer files to paper files
used in the workplace. You are undoubtedly familiar with folders in a
file cabinet. Each folder contains information about some person, item,
contract, and so on. Computer files operate similarly. Like a physical
file, a computer file contains information. This information may be your
resume, your monthly budget, an economics report, or a software
program. Instead of having physical pieces of paper, you have electronically stored information on the disk.

The computer needs to keep track of all the files on disk somehow, and
you need to be able to make copies of files, erase files, and perform
other managerial functions concerning the resources of the computer.
DOS manages these resources under the direction of you—the
computer operator.

This appendix begins with a summary of the changes DOS has
undergone since its inception. You then learn how DOS gets your
computer going, how to name and use DOS files, and how to issue
DOS commands.

Reviewing the Evolution of DOS

When the IBM PC was first introduced in October, 1981, it operated
under the PC DOS operating system, Version 1.0. Since that time, PC
DOS has undergone several changes, and newer versions have been
released. In any business or university, you are likely to find several
versions in use, so knowing some of the differences among the various
versions is helpful. Some earlier versions of PC DOS are not fully
compatible with the newer versions.

DOS has been continually changed so that it can support new storage
devices introduced on new versions of the PC. Usually, these changes
involve advancements in disk storage. When first introduced, the PC

supported only single-sided floppy disks—disks that stored information on one side only. When double-sided disks were introduced, a new version of DOS was required, and DOS 1.1 was released. Besides supporting new disk devices, later versions of DOS contain new and improved features, such as support for new kinds of monitors and other peripherals.

Various changes in PC DOS are outlined in table A.1. Changes in DOS are typically considered upwardly compatible. That is, new versions of DOS can usually read information from disks created with old versions of DOS—but not always. For example, a major change in the way information is stored on disk was made in DOS 2.0. The result is that a computer that uses DOS 1.1 or DOS 1.0 cannot read a floppy disk formatted with DOS 2.0. Hard disks were first supported with DOS 2.0. The Norton programs covered in this book are based on the assumption that you operate with DOS 2.0 or a later version. The currently popular 1.44M disks were first supported with DOS 3.3. Norton Utilities requires DOS 3.3 or later to run.

Table A.1 Versions of PC DOS

Version	Primary Feature(s)
1.0	Supports single-sided floppy disks (160K)
1.1	Supports double-sided floppy disks (320K)
2.0	Supports hard disks and a subdirectory file structure (double-sided disks, now 360K)
2.1	Supports the half-height floppy disks on the IBM PCjr
3.0	Supports the 1.2M disk and other new functions of the IBM PC AT
3.1	Supports networking
3.2	Supports 720K 3 1/2-inch floppy disks, laptop computers, and networking
3.3	Supports 1.44M 3 1/2-inch floppy disks and the PS/2 series of computers
4.0	Features pull-down menus and supports drive use past the previous 32M limit
5.0	Supports 2.88M 3 1/2-inch floppy disks, provides better memory management, and adds some data recovery features
6.0	Adds disk compression, virus checking, and more utility programs

Booting Your Computer

By itself, the computer hardware does not "know" how to do many tasks. It can match patterns of 0s and 1s and use those patterns to follow commands that programmers stored in the computer's memory. Because the computer knows so little, you need a quick way to "teach" it what to do. That teaching process occurs when the computer is booted.

Within the PC, a small amount of information is always present in ROM (read-only memory). This memory contains the BIOS (basic input-output system) and some other diagnostic and language programs. This memory does not contain DOS.

How, then, can the computer operate? When you turn on your computer, it has only the most primitive instructions. The computer knows enough, however, to look for DOS on a disk in the disk drive. The computer "pulls itself" to life by reading its instructions from the DOS program on disk. In computer jargon, loading DOS into memory is called *booting* the machine. This booting process occurs whenever you turn on the computer.

After you load DOS into memory from your floppy disk or hard disk, the computer can perform many management functions. Most of these functions are ways to access and manipulate information on disk.

At times, you may need to reboot the computer. A program bug, for example, may cause the computer to freeze so that it no longer responds to program commands. Your only chance for recovery may be to reboot. One obvious way to reboot is to turn off the computer and then turn it back on. This process is called a *cold boot*. Electronic equipment is particularly sensitive, however, to being turned on and off. The computer's electronics stabilize when the power is turned on. Many times, if an electronic component fails, it does so after you first turn it on—when it gets the initial burst of power.

Because of this danger of failure, the system gives you a built-in way to restart the computer without turning off the power. This method of rebooting is called a *warm boot*. To perform a warm boot, hold down the Ctrl and Alt keys and press Del. Hold down all three keys for a second, release all keys, and the computer reboots. Some computers have restart buttons that perform warm boots. With Norton Utilities, you can enter **BE REBOOT** to cause the computer to perform a warm boot.

Naming and Using DOS Files

As mentioned previously, files stored on a computer are like folders stored in a file cabinet. Some identifying name is usually written on each folder's tab. If the folder contains the budget for May, 1993, for example, the tab may say *BUDGET MAY 1993*. If the folder contains a copy of the annual report, the tab may say *ANNUAL REPORT*. The name on the tab gives a short description of the contents of the file.

Usually, you do not place folders in file drawers at random. All the budget files may be in one drawer, and all the report files may be in another drawer. In fact, you may reserve an entire file cabinet for reports, and another cabinet may contain only financial information. You should name and organize files on the computer in the same way.

Specifying File Names

Like the name tab on a paper folder, each computer file has a name, called a *file name*. A file name should briefly describe the contents of the file. Your resume may be named RESUME, for example, and the May, 1993, budget may be named BUDMAY93. When you create related files, select names that are similar. If you are writing a three-part paper, you may want to create three separate files named PART1, PART2, and PART3. If you are collecting monthly data, you may want to name the files containing the information MAY93, JUN93, and JUL93.

Although you usually create files from applications rather than from DOS, the file names you use must obey DOS guidelines. A DOS file name can contain up to eight characters, including all letters (upper- and lowercase) and numbers, but it cannot contain spaces or any of the following characters:

> . ' \ / [ ] : | < > + = ; * ? ,

Some programs enable you to use a space in a file name, but not on the DOS level, so avoid using spaces.

Using File Extensions

In the case of computer files, the file name includes a second part, called the *extension*, which you can use to specify the type of file— whether it is a word processing file, database file, letter, or budget.

You can include up to three characters in the extension, which you separate from the file name with a period. You can use the name RESUME.WP for a resume file you create with the WordPerfect word processing program, and you can use the name PROJECT.LET for a letter you write about a certain project. This extended form of the name is called the *file specification*, or *filespec* for short. You also may include a drive name, such as drive C or A, in your file specification. Examples are C:MYFILE.DOC and C:\MYFILE.DOC.

DOS and other software programs commonly follow certain conventions for file extensions because extensions often tell the computer what kind of information is in the computer file. Files on disk that contain DOS commands usually end with the extension COM.

BASIC language programs end with the extension BAS. Application programs also use certain extensions. Lotus 1-2-3 worksheets, for example, may end in WKS, WK1, or WK3. Table A.2 lists some common file extensions. You need to be aware of the extensions that DOS uses so that you can choose your own without conflicting with these predefined extensions.

Table A.2 Common Extensions

Extension	Description
BAS	BASIC language program
BAT	Batch command file (a type of DOS file)
BMT	Norton batch-to-memory file
COM	Command program (DOS command)
DBF	dBASE database file
EXE	Executable program (software)
PRN	Lotus print-to-disk file
SYS	File containing system information
TXT	Text file (standard ASCII)
WKS, WK1, or WK3	Lotus 1-2-3 worksheet file

Using Wild-Card Characters

If you select similar names for related files, you then have the ability to manipulate those files simultaneously as a group. If the files are named similarly, DOS (and Norton) commands enable you to refer to more than one file with wild cards or global file characters. These wild-card characters are the asterisk (*) and the question mark (?). Like a wild card in a poker game, * and ? may be substituted for any characters—the asterisk for any number of characters, and the question mark for any one character.

To copy all your data files from one disk to another, you must tell DOS which files to copy. Suppose that your files are named JAN, FEB, MAR, and so on, through DEC. To copy all 12 of these files requires 12 commands, each specifying one file to copy. However, if you name the files JAN.DAT, FEB.DAT, MAR.DAT, and so on, through DEC.DAT, you can copy all the files with the single file specification *.DAT. This specifies files with the extension DAT, regardless of the file name. In this case, you use the DAT extension to remind the user that these files contain data.

Because the ? wild card replaces only one character, the specification ???.DAT substitutes for up to three characters in a file name. This file specification selects J.DAT, JA.DAT, and JAN.DAT, but not JANU.DAT or JANUARY.DAT. The wild-card specification *.* matches all files—all file names and all extensions. As this appendix introduces DOS commands, it gives you specific examples of wild cards. Norton commands also use wild cards extensively. Norton's NDOS provides more flexible use of wild cards. See Chapter 28 for more information about NDOS.

Issuing DOS Commands

DOS—whether PC DOS or MS-DOS—is similar to a language. DOS performs management functions on the IBM PC (and compatibles), but not until you instruct it to do so. You, the user, typically give those instructions in the form of a DOS command. A DOS command is usually a word (often a verb) that tells DOS what you want it to do. Sometimes the command is followed by one or more words, or *parameters*, that clarify which task the command performs. These parameters are called *options* or *switches*.

The command CLS (Clear Screen), for example, tells DOS to blank the screen. CLS requires no other parameters. However, the command COPY requires that you also specify what file(s) to copy and where to copy them. Therefore, you must include additional information in the command.

When the DOS prompt is on the computer screen, the operating system is waiting for you to enter a DOS command or the name of an executable program. The DOS prompt usually is a letter (A, B, C, and so on) followed by the > symbol. The following prompt, for example, means that DOS is waiting for instructions and that drive A is the currently active drive or the default drive:

```
A>
```

If DOS needs to look on disk for some information, it automatically looks on the default drive unless you direct the system to look elsewhere. If you use a hard disk system, the default drive is usually C, with the following prompt:

```
C>
```

This prompt indicates that you are logged on to drive C. To change drives, type the drive letter followed by a colon and press Enter. (You may have variations of these two prompts, such as A:\> and C\:>.)

DOS consists of a number of commands, which are categorized as two types: *internal* and *external*. Internal DOS commands are copied into the computer's memory when DOS is loaded as you boot the computer. These commands stay in memory until you turn off the computer; you can use these commands whenever the DOS prompt appears on-screen. Internal commands covered in this appendix include ATTRIB, CD, CLS, COPY, DEL, DIR, ERASE, FIND, MD, PATH, PROMPT, RD, RENAME, and TYPE.

If you stored every DOS command in memory, however, not enough memory would be left for application programs. Some DOS commands, therefore, are not copied onto the computer's memory at boot time but are stored on disk in a file until they are needed. These external DOS commands on disk are usually identified by the COM extension. The FORMAT command, for example, is stored on the DOS disk as the file FORMAT.COM. If you use an external command, it must be available on disk. After you enter the FORMAT command, for example, DOS looks on the default (currently active) disk to find the file FORMAT.COM. If the file is not found, the following message appears on-screen:

```
Bad command or file name
```

This error message indicates that the command you requested was not found on disk. External commands covered in this appendix include BACKUP, CHKDSK, DISKCOPY, FORMAT, PRINT, RECOVER, RESTORE, and TREE. To learn how to access external DOS commands, see the section "Working with Directory Path Names," later in this appendix.

Norton commands are much like DOS external commands. Each command constitutes a program that resides on disk until you enter the command name at the DOS prompt. Then the program is entered into memory and run.

To issue a DOS command, type it at the DOS prompt and press Enter. For example, to use the DIR command to display a list of the files located in the default directory, type the following command and press Enter:

> DIR

To have DOS display a directory of a disk other than the default disk, you must add more information to the DIR command. To display a directory of the files on the floppy disk in drive A, use this command:

> DIR A:

Reviewing Commonly Used DOS Commands

Although dozens of DOS commands are available, this review of DOS is limited to the commands you commonly refer to or may need to know so that you can understand the information in this book. This appendix covers selected options and switches for each command. For a more complete list of command parameters, consult your DOS manual or Que's *Using MS-DOS 6,* Special Edition.

 NOTE In the syntax descriptions of DOS commands, items enclosed in brackets ([ ]) are optional. Items that appear in italics are command variables. You should replace the *filespec* variable, for example, with a real file specification when you enter the command at the DOS prompt.

ATTRIB

The ATTRIB command lists or sets the read-only and archive attributes of files. You cannot write to, change, or erase a read-only file. The *read-only* attribute protects the file from accidental or unauthorized change. The *archive* attribute indicates whether the file has been backed up and is used for some backup procedures. ATTRIB is available in DOS 3.0 and later versions. Here is the syntax of this command:

> ATTRIB [+|–R] [+|–A] *filespec* [/S]

The +R option sets the file or files indicated in the *filespec* to read-only, and –R turns off the read-only attribute. The +A option sets files to archive (archive is set on), and –A turns off the archive attribute. When you back up a file, the archive attribute setting is switched off, indicating to the system that the file has been backed up.

If you use the /S switch, the files in all subdirectories that match the *filespec* are also affected. If you do not use the + I –R or + I –A option, ATTRIB lists file names that match the *filespec*, and reports the current archive and read-only settings for those files. Norton's NDOS provides an ATTRIB command with additional features beyond the DOS ATTRIB command (see Chapter 28 for more information on NDOS commands).

CHKDSK

With the CHKDSK command, you can examine a floppy or hard disk to determine how much space is being used and whether the disk has any problems. CHKDSK, for example, may detect lost clusters in files on disk. CHKDSK summarizes the amount of available memory on disk and also reports the amount of RAM available to the computer. CHKDSK is an external DOS command and has this syntax:

CHKDSK [*d*:] [/F]

The *d*: designation specifies the floppy disk or hard disk to check. To check the disk in drive B, use this command:

CHKDSK B:

The /F switch tells CHKDSK to fix any problems found with the file allocation table. If you do not use the /F switch, CHKDSK still tells you how much space would be fixed if the /F switch were used, but it does not fix the problems. Instead of using CHKDSK, use Norton Disk Doctor (NDD) to find and solve these kinds of disk problems. For more information on NDD, see Chapter 12.

CLS

The CLS command clears the screen. No options or switches are available. CLS has the following syntax:

CLS

Norton's NDOS provides a CLS command with additional features beyond the DOS CLS command (see Chapter 28 for more information).

COPY

The COPY command is a powerful, frequently used DOS command. COPY copies one or more files to another disk or to the same disk under a new name. You use this syntax:

COPY [*d:*]*filespec* [*d:*][*filespec*]

Here is a more easily remembered syntax:

COPY *source destination*

To copy the file named REPORT.TXT from the current default disk (A) to disk C, use the following command:

COPY REPORT.TXT C:REPORT.TXT

In this command, the source is the file REPORT.TXT, and the destination is C:REPORT.TXT. Note that you do not have to specify a drive letter if the file is on the default drive. Furthermore, you can omit the name of the destination file if it is the same as the source file. The following command, used from the A> prompt, performs the same copy as the preceding command:

COPY REPORT.TXT C:

The source file does not have to be on the default drive. To copy files from a drive other than the default to another drive, include the drive specification in both the source and destination file names. You can also change the name of a file during a copy.

Suppose that the default drive is C and you want to copy a file from drive A to drive B and rename the file at the same time. Use the following command:

COPY A:REPORT.TXT B:RPT.TXT

Another way to use the COPY command is to copy a file on the same disk to a different file name. To make a duplicate copy of the file REPORT.TXT and call the duplicate copy REPORT.DUP, you can use this command:

COPY REPORT.TXT REPORT.DUP

If you attempt to copy a file to itself, an error results. The following command produces an error message:

COPY REPORT.TXT REPORT.TXT

You can copy multiple files simultaneously with the wild-card characters (* and ?). To copy all DAT files from the default drive C to drive A, use this command:

COPY *.DAT A:

To copy a file from a directory to another directory, you must include the directory name in the command (unless the file is in the current default directory). The following command copies the file named MYFILE.TXT in the C:\MYDIR directory to the \YOURDIR directory:

COPY C:\MYDIR\MYFILE.TXT \YOURDIR

Norton's NDOS provides a COPY command with additional features beyond the DOS COPY command (see Chapter 28 for information on NDOS).

> **CAUTION:** The COPY command allows you to overwrite an existing file with a new file—without giving you a warning that the old file is about to be overwritten. Norton Disk Monitor (see Chapter 6) can prevent accidental overwrites of files.

DIR

The DIR command displays names of files on disk, file sizes, and dates and times the files were created. You use the following syntax:

DIR [*d:*][*filespec*] [/P][/W]

Here is the simplest version of this command:

DIR

The DIR command gives you a list of all files on the default drive.

To list files located on another drive, specify the drive letter. To obtain a listing of files on drive B, use this command:

DIR B:

If you include a file specification in the command, DIR lists only those files that match the specification. To view a directory of just the files with DAT extensions, use the following command:

DIR *.DAT

To list all files that begin with the letter R, use this command:

DIR R*.*

The switches in the DIR command are /P and /W. The /P switch instructs DOS to pause after a screen of file names is displayed. If more than 22 file names are in a directory, the names usually scroll off-screen during a directory listing. With the /P switch, the first 22 files are listed, and the following message appears at the bottom of the screen:

```
Press a key to continue. . .
```

After you press a key, the next 22 files are displayed. This process continues until all files are listed.

The /W switch stands for *wide listing*. In this version of the list, only the file names appear, with several file names listed on each line. This format enables you to display more file names on one screen.

You can combine the DIR command's options and switches. The following command lists all the files on drive B with a DAT extension, in wide format:

```
DIR B:*.DAT /W
```

To display a list of files from a directory that is not the current default directory, place the directory name in the command. The following command displays a list of files in the \MYDIR directory:

```
DIR \MYDIR
```

Norton's NDOS provides a DIR command with features beyond the DOS DIR command (see Chapter 28 for information on NDOS).

DISKCOPY

Many times, you may want to make an exact copy of a floppy disk. In fact, when you get new software, always copy all the original disks and use copies instead of originals in your work. Use the DISKCOPY command to copy the contents of an entire floppy disk from one disk to another of equal size. Note the syntax of this command:

```
DISKCOPY d1: d2:
```

The *d1*: designation is the source disk, and *d2*: is the destination disk. To copy the disk in drive A to the disk in drive B, use the following command:

```
DISKCOPY A: B:
```

If the destination disk is not formatted, the DISKCOPY procedure formats the disk. DISKCOPY makes an exact copy of a disk. If the source or destination disk contains any bad sectors, the DISKCOPY procedure may not work. Furthermore, both source and destination disks must be the same size. You cannot use the DISKCOPY command to copy from the hard disk to a floppy, for example, because the hard disk is a different size from the floppy disk.

If you use a system with only one floppy disk drive, you still can perform a DISKCOPY procedure. From the A> prompt, use this command:

DISKCOPY A: A:

DOS prompts you to insert the source disk in the drive; then the system prompts you to place the target disk in the drive. You may have to swap disks several times during each DISKCOPY procedure.

Norton Utilities 7 provides a replacement to the DOS DISKCOPY command. See Chapter 26 for information on the Duplicate Disk (DUPDISK) command.

CAUTION: The DISKCOPY command erases everything on the target floppy disk. Be sure that the target disk does not contain anything important, because it cannot be recovered once new information has been copied to it with DISKCOPY.

ERASE and DEL

The ERASE and DEL commands remove files from the disk. These commands are identical and use the same syntax:

ERASE [*d:*][*filespec*]

DEL [*d:*][*filespec*]

Pay attention to what is on your disk and how much space you have used. Running out of space on disk is a common problem. The ERASE and DEL commands can remove unneeded files from disk and free up that space for other files to use. Like most DOS commands, these commands may be used on a single file or multiple files and with wild-card characters in *filespec*. To erase the single file named REQUEST.LET, enter one of the following:

ERASE REQUEST.LET

DEL REQUEST.LET

To erase all files with the extension DAT, use this command:

ERASE *.DAT

To erase all files, use the following:

ERASE *.*

After you enter the ERASE (or DEL) command followed by *.*, DOS prompts you with this question:

Are you sure (Y/N)?

DOS is offering you a chance to change your mind before it erases everything on your disk. Press Y and Enter to continue with the erase, or press N and Enter to cancel the procedure.

> **CAUTION:** Be very sure that you know what you are doing when you enter the ERASE or DEL command. Check to make sure that you are logged on to the correct disk drive and directory. (If you accidentally erase a file, however, you may be able to recover it with the Norton UnErase command. See Chapter 10 for more information.)

Norton's NDOS provides ERASE and DEL commands with features beyond the DOS ERASE and DEL commands. See Chapter 28 for more information on NDOS. In addition, Norton Utilities 7 provides a more thorough way to erase a file (so that it can't be unerased). See Chapter 8 for information about the WipeInfo command.

FDISK

The FDISK command prepares your hard disk (fixed disk) for formatting. Usually, you need to execute this command only once—when you first get a new computer. Occasionally, you may need to start over with the FDISK command again. FDISK begins a program that prompts you with questions about how you want to set up your hard disk.

> **WARNING:** If you use FDISK on a hard disk, all information on that disk may be lost. Use FDISK only when you are sure that you want to start from scratch on the disk. Refer to your DOS manual for details. If you are not an experienced user, do not use FDISK until you verify with an experienced user that it is the correct command to use.

FIND

The FIND command, also called a *filter*, searches for a string of characters in a file (or files) and lists each line in the file containing text that matches the string. The FIND command can help you look for a file that contains particular information. You use the following syntax:

FIND *string* [*filespec*] [*filespec*] [*filespec*]...

To determine whether the string *1993 REPORT* is in the files REPORT.1, REPORT.2, and REPORT.3, use this command:

FIND "1993 REPORT" REPORT.1 REPORT.2 REPORT.3

The results of the find may look like this:

```
---------REPORT.1
---------REPORT.2
THE 1993 REPORT ON SILVER PRICES
---------REPORT.3
```

In this example, the phrase *1993 REPORT* was found only in the file named REPORT.2. The line that contains the phrase is listed below the name of the file being searched. The other files had no finds associated with them.

The Norton's Text Search (TS), File Locate (FL), and File Find commands are powerful alternatives to the DOS FIND command. See Chapter 25 for more information on these commands.

FORMAT

The FORMAT command prepares floppy disks and hard disks for use. After you purchase floppy disks, you cannot just put them into the disk drive and use them. You must first format them. Formatting specifies how information is stored on disk. The FORMAT procedure also analyzes the entire disk for defective tracks and prepares the disk to accept DOS files. Here is the syntax of the FORMAT command:

FORMAT [*d:*] [*switches*]

Suppose that you use a computer with a hard disk drive and you are logged on to drive C. To format a new floppy disk in drive A, the simplest command is the following:

FORMAT A:

After you enter the FORMAT command, DOS responds with this message:

```
Insert new diskette for drive A:
and press ENTER when ready. . .
```

This prompt gives you a chance to back out of the command if you discover that you do not want to format that floppy disk. If you want to cancel the command at this point, press Ctrl+Break.

WARNING: You can destroy all information on a floppy disk or hard disk drive by using the FORMAT command incorrectly. If you do not enter the name of the drive to format, the FORMAT command uses the default drive. Thus, if you enter the following command from the C> prompt, DOS assumes that you want to format the hard disk drive C:

FORMAT

Be careful not to do this (unless you want to erase everything on your hard disk)!

The FORMAT command has a number of switches. Only the most common one, /S, is described here.

The /S switch causes the FORMAT procedure to create a system disk— one that contains the files necessary to boot the computer. To format the disk in drive A with a label and the system files, use the following:

FORMAT A: /S

The Norton Safe Format (SFORMAT) command is a safer, faster alternative to DOS FORMAT. In addition, the Norton UnFormat (UNFORMAT) command enables you to unformat a formatted hard disk, but with some restrictions. (For more information on Safe Format, see Chapter 4.) DOS 5 (and later) contains an UNFORMAT command also. And beginning with DOS 5, formatting a floppy disk with the FORMAT command in DOS 5 (or later) is similar to using the Norton Safe Format— it is possible to unformat the disk by using the DOS or Norton UNFORMAT command. If you format a disk with DOS FORMAT in a version earlier than DOS 5, however, it is impossible to recover information from that floppy disk by using the DOS or Norton UNFORMAT command.

PRINT

The PRINT command enables you to print the contents of a text file to the printer. The PRINT command has this syntax:

PRINT [*d:*]*filespec* [/T]

To print a file in drive B called EXAMPLE.TXT to the line printer, enter the following command:

PRINT B:EXAMPLE.TXT

The computer responds with this prompt:

```
Name of list device (PRN):
```

Press Enter to print the file to the standard print device (PRN=Printer), or enter another device name, such as LPT1 or LPT2 (parallel ports), or COM1 or COM2 (serial ports).

You can queue several files to print at once by entering several PRINT commands; DOS remembers each of the files and prints them in the order of the PRINT commands. If you decide to stop the print job, reenter the command with the /T switch. To terminate the current print job, enter the following command:

PRINT /T

This command terminates all print jobs in the print queue. A cancel message is displayed, the page in the printer is advanced to the top of the form, and the printer's buzzer sounds. See Chapter 26 for a description of the Norton Line Print (LP) command.

RECOVER

The RECOVER command recovers files that have been damaged somehow. You can misuse this command easily, so consider using the Disk Tools (DISKTOOL) command instead. For more information on Disk Tools, see Chapter 13.

RENAME or REN

The RENAME or REN command changes the name of a file on disk. Suppose that you save a file named REPORT with your word processor, but you misspell the file name by typing **REPOTR**. When you are back in

DOS, you can correct the problem with the RENAME command. Use the following syntax:

RENAME [*d:*]*filespec1 filespec2*

Notice that the command REN is an acceptable abbreviation of the RENAME command. Basically, the RENAME command has the following form:

RENAME *oldname newname*

The *oldname* variable is the current name of a file, and *newname* is the name you want the file to have. Include a space between the *oldname* and *newname* specifications. To rename the file REQUEST.LET as REQUEST.TXT, use this command:

RENAME REQUEST.LET REQUEST.TXT

You can use wild-card characters to rename a group of related files. To rename the files JAN.DAT through DEC.DAT on drive A to the new names JAN.OLD through DEC.OLD, use the following command from the A> prompt:

RENAME *.DAT *.OLD

You cannot rename a file to a file name that currently exists on that disk. If you try this, you see the following error message:

```
Duplicate file name or file not found
```

Note that RENAME is not a COPY command, which means that you cannot rename a file from one disk drive to another. The following command, for example, does not work:

RENAME A:REQUEST.LET B:REQUEST.LET

If you attempt to use this command, this error message appears:

```
Invalid parameter
```

Norton's NDOS provides RENAME and REN commands with features beyond the DOS RENAME and REN commands. See Chapter 28 for more information on NDOS.

SYS

The SYS command transfers system files from a bootable disk to another disk. Use the following syntax:

SYS *d:*

The *d*: designation is the drive name of the disk in which you want to place the system files. The SYS command does not transfer the file COMMAND.COM to the destination disk. You can use the regular COPY command to copy the COMMAND.COM file to the disk. For more information, see the FORMAT /S command in the FORMAT section earlier in this chapter.

The system files are hidden files. You cannot access them by using the normal COPY command, nor do they appear when you issue a DIR command. You must place the system files at a certain spot on disk, so unless you formatted a disk by using the /B switch, SYS cannot transfer a copy of the system files to the disk. The Make a Disk Bootable option in Norton Disk Tools (discussed in Chapter 13) enables you to transfer system files to a disk that has not been prepared to accept them.

TYPE

The TYPE command prints the contents of a file to the screen. TYPE has the following syntax:

TYPE [*d*:]*filespec*

To display the contents of the EXAMPLE.TXT file located on drive B, use this command:

TYPE B:EXAMPLE.TXT

The file to be printed should be a text file. If you attempt to use TYPE to print the contents of a non-ASCII file, the result probably will be a series of meaningless characters on-screen.

Norton's NDOS provides a TYPE command with features beyond the DOS TYPE command (see Chapter 28 for more information on NDOS).

Managing Your Hard Disk

Most microcomputers sold today include a hard disk storage device. A *hard disk* (also called a *fixed disk*) is a permanent disk usually housed in the computer; the hard disk is capable of storing many times the amount of information that a single floppy disk can hold. The size of most hard disks is measured in megabytes (M), or millions of bytes. A 100M hard disk can store 100 million characters of information.

Using a computer with a hard disk creates several challenges. The fact that a hard disk can store more information can be an advantage as well as a disadvantage. With a hard disk, you don't need to keep up with a mile-high stack of floppy disks, but you need to plan more. Managing more than 1,000 files stored on a hard disk can be a huge task. When you run the DIR command, the information could take several minutes to scroll by.

Understanding Directories

You can solve this problem by dividing the hard disk into several directories, each of which contains related information. One directory may contain all DOS files. Another directory may contain word processing files. Yet another directory may contain database files. Each directory functions almost like a separate disk.

DOS sets up directories in a particular way. When you format a disk (including a floppy disk), the format procedure automatically creates one directory, called the *root directory*. You can create other directories to branch off the root, thereby building a directory tree. You must choose which directories to create, and you must develop the philosophy behind the structure. Figure A.1 shows one possible directory tree. This tree is organized by task. The top directory is the original or root directory. Branching off are directories (or subdirectories) that contain the task-oriented partitions of DOS, Word Processing, Database, and Spreadsheet.

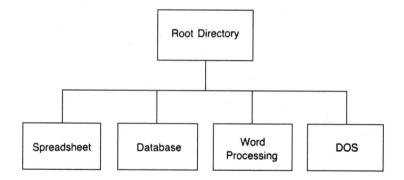

Fig. A.1

A directory structure.

Creating directories according to a planned directory tree can help make your work more efficient. You can move from branch to branch, depending on the tasks you want to complete. If you are doing word processing, for example, you can move to the word processing directory, which gives you access to all your word processing files. Working from this directory also separates you from the unrelated files in other directories. If you are in the word processing directory and enter **DIR**, you get a list of files in that directory only.

How do you create a directory? How do you move from one directory to another? How do you get rid of a directory? These questions are answered by a series of DOS commands, which enable you to create, use, and remove directories as necessary:

Command Name	Abbreviation	Description
MKDIR	MD	Makes a directory
CHDIR	CD	Changes directories
RMDIR	RD	Removes a directory

Before learning how to use the DOS commands to manage your hard disk, you should understand how the names of the directories relate to file specifications. Use the NCD (Norton Change Directory) command instead of the DOS commands (see Chapter 23 for information on NCD). This command provides a graphic interface that makes creating, changing, and removing directories more intuitive. NCD also has additional capabilities, such as renaming directories.

Working with Directory Path Names

Each directory has a name. The root directory always is designated as the \ directory, but you assign your own names to the directories you create that branch off the root directory. A directory name can include up to eight characters (see "Specifying File Names" earlier in this appendix).

When referring to a directory name, most people use the entire path name. A directory's path name describes the path that DOS can take through the directory tree structure to find the directory. The WP directory that branches off the root directory is usually referred to as \WP. The directory named LETTERS that branches off the WP directory is specified by the path name \WP\LETTERS. So a backslash (\) is used for two purposes:

- The first backslash (\) specifies the root directory.

- The second backslash (\) separates the names of subdirectories.

A directory path becomes a part of the file specification of any file in that directory. The path appears between the drive specification and the file name and always contains a beginning and an ending backslash. Generally, a complete file specification consists of the following:

d:\path\filename.ext

This specification represents a drive name, a path, a file name, a period, and an extension. Here is the complete file specification for a file named MYFILE.TXT on drive C in the \WP directory:

C:\WP\MYFILE.TXT

Norton's NCD command provides features beyond the DOS MD, CD, and RD commands. See Chapter 23 for more information on NCD.

Creating New Directories

You use the DOS MKDIR command, often abbreviated as MD, to make a new directory. Either of these versions will work:

MD *path*

MKDIR *path*

The following command creates a directory named \WP on the current drive:

MD \WP

The new \WP directory branches directly off the root directory. To make a directory named LETTERS that branches off \WP, use this command:

MD \WP\LETTERS

Changing Directories

Every hard disk has one or more directories, beginning with the root directory. The CHDIR command (or CD for short) changes from the current directory to another directory on the same disk drive. While in a particular directory, you can enter such commands as DIR or RENAME that apply only to the files in the current directory. You can use either of the following versions of this command:

CD *path*

CHDIR *path*

To change to the directory named \WP, enter this command:

CD \WP

To go back to the root directory, enter this command:

CD \

With CD, you can move from any directory to any other directory by entering the command and the complete path of the directory to which you want to change.

Here is another version of the CD command:

CD..

This command takes you to the next higher directory in the tree structure. Suppose that you are in the directory \WP\LETTERS. Typing **CD..** changes you to the \WP directory.

Removing Empty Directories

Sometimes you need to remove a directory from the hard disk to make room for other, more important files. Use the RMDIR or RD command for that purpose. You cannot remove a directory that contains any user files, though, so you must first erase or move all files in the directory first. You can use either of the following versions:

RD *path*

RMDIR *path*

To remove the directory named \MYDIR, use this command:

RD \MYDIR

Listing Directories

When your hard disk contains a number of directories, you may want to view a list of which directories are available. The DOS command to perform that task is TREE. The TREE command displays a listing of all the directories on the specified drive. TREE has the following syntax:

TREE [*d*:]

To see which directories are on your entire disk, enter this command:

TREE \

The Norton Utilities NCD command enables you to look at the directory tree and interactively change, rename, make, and remove directories. For more information on NCD, see Chapter 23.

Giving Paths to Programs

At this point, you are undoubtedly familiar with the concept of the path as part of a file specification. PATH also is a DOS command. The PATH command tells DOS where to look for programs not in the current directory. Many applications require you to know how to create or modify a PATH command. Use the following syntax for this command:

PATH [*path*];[*path*];[*path*]...

The TREE command, for example, requires that the file TREE.COM be on disk. Under normal circumstances, if you enter TREE in the \WP directory, you get this message:

```
Bad command or file name
```

The reason is that the TREE.COM command file is not in the \WP directory and DOS cannot find and execute the command. To avoid the need to keep copies of all programs in all directories or to type a full path name each time, you can tell the computer where to find a program when you request it from a directory in which the program does not reside. This function is the responsibility of the PATH command.

The PATH command gives the computer a priority list of directories to search for executable program files. The PATH command causes DOS to search for only three kinds of executable files: COM (command), EXE (program), and BAT (batch) files.

A common directory setup includes a directory named \DOS. This directory generally contains all the DOS files as well as external DOS commands. In addition, you may have a \NORTON directory that contains all the Norton commands. Note the following example:

PATH C:\;C:\DOS;C:\NORTON

This command indicates that if the NORTON command is given in any directory and the command is not found in that directory, DOS looks first in the root directory (specified in the PATH command as C:\). If the command is not there, DOS looks in the next directory listed in the PATH command—in this case, the C:\DOS directory. Finally, if the command still has not been found, DOS looks in the C:\NORTON directory. When the command TREE is entered in the \WP directory, then, the command file TREE.COM is found in the \DOS directory, and the command is successful. Notice that each directory name in the PATH command is separated from the preceding directory name by a semicolon (;).

When a PATH command is given, it remains in effect until you reboot the computer or turn it off. Therefore, you usually enter the command only once each time you boot the computer. As you learn in the discussion of the AUTOEXEC.BAT file later in this appendix, you can automate the entry of the PATH command.

Controlling the DOS Prompt

When you switch from directory to directory, you may have difficulty keeping track of which directory you are in. To solve this problem, you can use the PROMPT command to customize the DOS prompt, which is normally C> on a hard disk. PROMPT has the following syntax:

PROMPT [*prompt commands*]

The various prompt commands are listed in table A.3. Each command must be preceded by a dollar sign ($). Any text following the PROMPT command that is not preceded by a $ is displayed literally.

Table A.3 PROMPT $ Commands

Command	Displays
_ (underscore)	Carriage return, line feed
B	|
D	The system date
E	The Esc character
G	>
H	The Backspace character
L	<
N	The default drive letter
P	The current path/directory
Q	=
T	The system time
V	The version of DOS

The following DOS command causes the DOS prompt to include the path as part of the prompt:

PROMPT PG

The $P is the prompt command for the path, and the $G is the prompt command for the greater-than sign. While you are in the root directory, the prompt is therefore C:\>. The \ between the C: and the > tells you that you are in the root directory. If you enter the command **CD \DOS**, the prompt becomes C:\DOS>, indicating that you are in the DOS directory.

The PROMPT command offers a variety of ways to customize the DOS prompt. To display any text, include it in the PROMPT command without a preceding $. To display a unique prompt, you can use a command like the following:

   PROMPT This computer belongs to Bill!$_$P$G

The text This computer belongs to Bill! is output literally. The $_ command (a dollar sign and an underscore) tells PROMPT to perform a carriage return and a line feed, which means that the cursor moves to the next line. On that line, the prompt appears, specified by the PG prompt commands. When you are logged on to the root directory, this prompt appears as the following:

   This computer belongs to Bill!
   C:\>

Norton's NDOS provides a PROMPT command with features beyond those of DOS PROMPT. See Chapter 28 for more information on NDOS.

Using Batch and System Files

A BAT file extension indicates that a file is a batch file—one that contains several DOS commands you want executed in a particular order. A system file often is designated by the SYS extension. A common system file that you need to know about is CONFIG.SYS, which tells the computer certain information about how to operate.

Creating Batch Files

If you have a series of DOS commands that you perform repetitively, you can create a file that contains these commands and have DOS execute all of them in sequence. Suppose that you often use these two commands:

   CLS

   DIR /W

These commands clear the screen and perform a directory command in wide mode. You can place these two commands in a file, such as WIDE.BAT. Then, instead of remembering exactly how to type these commands each time you need them, you can run that batch file by just entering **WIDE**. With this command, you tell DOS to execute the two commands contained in the batch file WIDE.BAT.

You have several ways to create this kind of file. The most common method is to use a file editor. A simple file editor named EDLIN is included as a part of DOS. Most word processing programs can create batch files also. In later versions of DOS (beginning with DOS 5), a full-screen editor named EDIT is available.

Here is one way to create a batch file without using a text editor:

1. Enter the following command:

   COPY CON WIDE.BAT

   This command tells DOS that you will enter (copy) information from the console; the command indicates also that the information is to be placed in the file named WIDE.BAT.

2. Enter the commands you want to include in the batch file. You may want to enter these commands:

   CLS
   DIR /W

   You do not see the DOS prompt.

3. To end this procedure, press the F6 key or Ctrl+Z. The lines you typed are now stored in the file called WIDE.BAT.

Creating an AUTOEXEC.BAT File in DOS

Each time you boot the computer, DOS looks for a special batch file called AUTOEXEC.BAT. If you want a series of commands to execute each time you boot the computer, place them in the AUTOEXEC.BAT file. If, for example, you always want the PATH and PROMPT commands to be activated when the computer is booted, you can create an AUTOEXEC.BAT file that contains these commands, as for the WIDE.BAT file you created earlier. Then whenever you boot your computer, your path is set up, and your prompt is customized automatically. The PATH and PROMPT commands are frequently included in the AUTOEXEC.BAT file.

Creating a CONFIG.SYS File

Another file that DOS looks for each time you boot the computer is CONFIG.SYS. Like AUTOEXEC.BAT, CONFIG.SYS is not a required file. If you do have a CONFIG.SYS file in your root directory, however, DOS looks in the file to see how you want the computer configured. You rarely need to decide for yourself what goes into the CONFIG.SYS file, because the software you install usually has instructions about its requirements for the file. DOS, for example, usually enables software to communicate with eight files at once on disk. This sounds like a great many files, but some complicated programs like dBASE IV need more access to the disk than DOS usually provides. Therefore, the dBASE IV installation manual tells you to place the following lines in your CONFIG.SYS file:

    FILES=20
    BUFFERS=15

These commands allow more files and more *disk buffers* (reserved portions of RAM that temporarily hold data to be written to disk) than are usually available. These lines are the two most common settings in the CONFIG.SYS file. Other items that you can set in this file include the following:

Item	Description
COUNTRY	Specifies which country you are in. This item pertains to how dates are displayed.
DEVICE	Specifies certain kinds of input and output devices, such as monitors, plotters, and memory disks.
LASTDRIVE	Specifies the maximum number of disk drives on your computer (the normal setting is E).

CAUTION: Unless your program documentation directs you to set or change the information in CONFIG.SYS, you should change or add to this file only under the guidance of someone familiar with its use. For more information, see Que's *Using MS-DOS 6, Special Edition.*

You can create the CONFIG.SYS file with a word processor (using text file mode), the Edlin editor, or the DOS Edit program. The Norton NUCONFIG command also enables you to add or remove drivers and program commands to the CONFIG.SYS and AUTOEXEC.BAT files.

Remember that DOS executes the AUTOEXEC.BAT and CONFIG.SYS files at boot time. If you change one of these files, you must reboot the computer to have DOS act on the information in the files.

Using DOS To Back Up Your Hard Disk

Another important feature of DOS is its capability to back up the information on your hard disk. You can easily destroy data on disks. In fact, sometime during your use of the computer, you are likely to lose some data. With caution, you will experience such a loss only rarely—and if you have a backup procedure, you should be able to recover from the loss with little grief. Although Norton Utilities can help you recover information in a number of ways, keeping backup copies of your work is still a good idea.

One of the simplest ways to back up your information is to make multiple copies of everything you do. If you are writing a paper, for example, you should keep at least two copies, each on a separate disk. If your original copy is on a hard disk, copy the file to a floppy disk each time you finish working on the file.

Save your work often. Never work on a document for hours without making copies. If the electricity goes off or the computer has problems, you can easily lose an entire day's work. How often you should save your work is determined by how much time you are willing to lose. If you do not mind possibly losing a few hours' worth of work, save and back up your work (just the files you are working on—not the entire disk) every few hours, or at least once a day.

In addition to backing up a single file (which you can do easily with the COPY command), you can take advantage of a DOS procedure for backing up an entire hard disk: the BACKUP command.

Using BACKUP

The most common way to back up a hard disk is to copy it to floppy disks. The DOS BACKUP command (for DOS before Version 6) enables you to copy files from the hard disk to any number of floppy disks. You can copy the entire disk or just portions of it to floppy disks. You may need 30 or more floppy disks to back up an entire hard disk. BACKUP has the following syntax:

BACKUP *source destination* [*switches*]

Here is the simplest form of the BACKUP command:

        BACKUP C: A:

This command tells DOS to back up all files on drive C to floppy disks in drive A. After you issue the command, the computer prompts you to insert disk #1 in drive A. Information is copied to the floppy disk until it is full. Then you are prompted to insert disk #2 into the drive. This procedure repeats until all the files are backed up onto the floppy disks. Note, however, that this form of the command backs up only the files from the currently active directory.

If you are using DOS 3.2 or earlier, all backup disks must first be formatted. Unfortunately, this requirement means that you must have some idea of how many floppy disks you need for the backup. To back up a 10M hard disk to 360K floppy disks, you need 28 floppy disks (10,000,000/360,000=27.7). If you are using a version later than DOS 3.3, you do not need to format floppy disks to use for backup. The procedure formats the disks during the backup (if you used the /F switch).

Usually, you have no reason to back up copies of executable programs from the hard disk, because you have those programs on the original floppy disks (which you could reload in a crisis). You do want to back up the files that contain your work. To back up specific files, you can enter the names of those files by using wild-card characters. Suppose that you name all your data files with a DAT extension and you want to back up all those files. Use the following command:

        BACKUP C:*.DAT A:

This command backs up DAT files only in the active subdirectory. To back up all directories, make sure that your file specification begins with the root directory (\) and add the /S switch to the command:

        BACKUP C:*.DAT A: /S

To back up all files in all directories and all subdirectories, use this command:

        BACKUP C:\ A: /S

The following switches may be used with DOS BACKUP:

Switch	Description
/A	Adds more files to a set of already backed-up files
/D:mm-dd-yy	Backs up all files modified on or after a specified date
/F	Tells BACKUP to format disks used in the backup if those disks were not formatted

continues

Switch	Description
/M	Backs up files that have been modified since the last backup
/S	Backs up all subdirectories, starting with the specified or current directory
/T:*time*	Backs up all files modified at or after the specified time (*hh:mm:ss*)

DOS 6 contains a backup program that is essentially the same as the Norton Backup utility, described in Chapter 29.

Using RESTORE

To use one or more of the files that you have backed up with the DOS BACKUP command, you must use the RESTORE command to copy these files from the backup floppy disks back to the hard disk. RESTORE has this syntax:

RESTORE *source destination* [*switches*]

Note the following example:

RESTORE A: C: /S

This command restores all files from floppy disks in disk A (source) to the fixed disk C (destination), including all subdirectories (/S). Other options for the RESTORE command are listed in your DOS manual. A particularly helpful one is the /P or PROMPT switch. When you use this switch, the computer prompts you before restoring a file and enables you to choose the files to restore.

Creating a Disaster Recovery Plan

Set up a procedure to back up your hard disk—or portions of it—regularly. Here is an example of a good procedure:

1. After you initially load your hard disk, back up the entire hard disk twice. Place backup set #1 off-site. Keep backup set #2 on site for quick restores. Set #1 is for recovery from a major disaster, such as the entire room burning down—including your computer and set #2.

2. Back up the entire disk daily, using the /M and /A switches. This is an incremental backup, which uses additional disks. This backup, along with set #2, provides you with a current backup of the computer.

3. Back up the entire disk once a week. Place this new weekly backup off-site and bring back the old off-site backup so that you can reuse its disks for the incremental backups (step 2) and the next weekly backup.

This procedure results in two backups: one weekly backup stored away from the office in case of an emergency (such as a fire or flood), and one "working" backup at the office that you can use daily.

Keep a copy of this book and Norton Utilities handy in case a disk accidentally is formatted. See Chapters 3 and 4 on how to prepare for and recover from a potential disk-related disaster.

Because backups take up so much disk space, you should keep your hard disk clear of unneeded files. Unneeded files on a disk can clutter the directories, limit the amount of disk space for other uses, and prolong the backup procedure. In addition to the backup procedure, another good idea is to set aside time once a week to erase any unneeded files from the hard disk, or to copy them to floppy disks on a semipermanent basis.

Alternatives to the DOS BACKUP command (particularly for DOS 5 or earlier) are available. Commercially available programs such as Norton Backup (see Chapter 29) and FastBack provide a quicker way to back up your hard disk. Backup devices such as tape drives and optical disk drives enable you to back up an entire hard disk to a single tape or disk in a few minutes.

Using DOS 5

DOS 5 is a recent version of DOS. Although the commands described in the preceding review of DOS are still in DOS 5, the new version contains additional features that relate to data protection and recovery.

DOS 5 contains the commands UNDELETE and UNFORMAT, which are similar to Norton's UnErase and UnFormat commands. These Norton and DOS commands are compared in Appendix B.

In addition, DOS 5 contains the MIRROR program, which is similar to Norton's Image program. MIRROR saves information about your FAT, directory, and system information to help in format and file recovery. In fact, to help with the recovery of files or in unformatting a disk,

Norton programs use information in the DOS MIRROR file, if it is available. If you use the Norton Image program, you do not need to use the DOS MIRROR program.

The DOS 5 FORMAT command now formats floppy disks in a way similar to Norton's Safe Format command. Instead of wiping out all information on a disk (which is what the DOS FORMAT command in DOS 4.0 and earlier versions does), DOS 5 FORMAT, in its default mode, clears only the directory and FAT, enabling you to use the UNFORMAT command to recover the floppy disk if needed.

Another important feature of DOS 5 is its use of RAM (random-access memory). In many cases, using DOS 5 can free up a significant amount of conventional memory, which gives programs more space to operate.

DOS 5 also provides a replacement for the outdated EDLIN line editor. The new Edit program is a full-screen editor, which behaves much like a word processor.

Using DOS 6

Version 6 of DOS was released in 1993. It contains a number of new features and improvements over earlier versions of DOS. One major new feature is data compression. This feature (called DoubleSpace) enables you to store more information on your disk. DOS automatically compresses the information written to disk and uncompresses it when it is read back. After you install the compression, it is transparent to the user, although it may cause some degradation in the speed of disk access.

DOS 6 also contains a small version of the Norton Speed Disk program. The DOS version is called Defrag. If you have both versions, use the Norton version. Another improved feature is MEMMAKER. This DOS 6 program enables you to manage your computer's memory and fine-tune your system to work best with the types of programs you are using.

As mentioned previously, the DOS 6 BACKUP command is essentially a version of Norton's Backup program. This gives you added flexibility in backing up your program in an interactive environment instead of using a command line. The Anti-Virus program in DOS 6 is a version of the Central Point Anti-Virus program. This program checks your system for viruses and cleans infected files. The DOS UNDELETE command can be used from Windows in DOS 6. Previously, this command could be used only from the DOS prompt. DOS 6 also has an enhanced Help system, more support for Windows and networking, and support for workgroup computing.

Comparing DOS and Norton Utilities Commands

This appendix contains an alphabetical list of frequently used DOS commands and their descriptions. Each DOS command is compared to a similar Norton Utilities command. (The DOS commands are listed first in the headings for each section and are also discussed first in each section.) In most cases, the Norton commands have advantages over the DOS commands. These advantages are described briefly, and examples of DOS commands and corresponding Norton commands are given. For more information on the available options and switches for each Norton command, consult the alphabetical list of Norton Utilities commands in the Command Reference in this book. NDOS commands that are similar to DOS commands, however, are not listed in this chapter. You can find a list of NDOS commands in Chapter 28.

ATTRIB versus File Find and File Attributes

The DOS command ATTRIB displays or sets read-only and archive attributes for a file. DOS Versions 5 and 6 also enable you to set the system and hidden attributes.

To set all *.TXT files to read-only, enter the following command:

    ATTRIB +R *.TXT

To display the current attributes for all files with the TXT extension, use this command:

    ATTRIB *.TXT

The Norton commands File Find and File Attributes (FA) enable you to set all four attributes, including read-only, archive, hidden, and system. The FA command also can display a directory of files and attributes. It can clear all attributes at once with the /CLEAR switch.

To set all files with the TXT extension to read-only (including files in subdirectories), enter the following command:

    FA *.TXT /R+

With the File Find command, you can set attributes interactively from menu options.

The FA and File Find commands are described in Chapters 9 and 25.

CHDIR or CD versus Norton Change Directory

CHDIR or CD enables you to change to another directory. To change to the \WP\LETTERS directory, enter this command:

    CD \WP\LETTERS

With Norton Change Directory (NCD), you can use a partial name (when it is unique) to change directories. You can use the NCD command in command-line mode or interactive mode. In interactive mode, you can switch to a directory by moving the cursor to the directory name displayed in a tree diagram.

To change to the directory named \WP\LETTERS, enter the following command:

 NCD LET

The NCD command is discussed in Chapter 23.

CHKDSK versus Norton Disk Doctor

CHKDSK enables you to check your disk for errors within the file allocation table (for file fragmentation or lost clusters, for example) and the DOS directory, and report the status.

To test a disk and attempt to fix any logical problems in the directory or file allocation table, enter the following command:

 CHKDSK A:/F

Norton Disk Doctor (NDD) performs a more thorough check of the disk than CHKDSK. NDD searches the disk for bad sectors and attempts to correct both physical and logical problems. You also can use NDD in interactive mode.

To test the partition table, boot record, root directory, and lost clusters, enter this command:

 NDD /QUICK

The NDD command is discussed in Chapter 12.

DATE versus Norton Control Center

The DOS DATE command enables you to set the system date for your computer. This command often does not change the *internal clock* (which keeps track of date and time even when the computer is turned off) in the computer. Thus, when you reboot, you may have to reset the date. To set the date permanently, you must use the SETUP command on some computers.

To reset the date to October 24, 1993, for example, enter the following command:

>   DATE 10-24-93

The Norton Control Center (NCC) Time and Date option enables you to set the system date. For many computers, this command also sets the internal clock.

The NCC command is discussed in Chapter 22.

DEL or ERASE versus WipeInfo

DEL or ERASE deletes one or more files. To delete files with the BAK extension in the default directory, enter the following command:

>   DEL *.BAK

 NOTE   You can unerase these files with the Norton UnErase command. Or, if you are using DOS 5.0 or a later version, you can use the DOS UNDELETE command.

WipeInfo erases files so that you cannot recover them—not even by using Norton UnErase operations. Optionally, WipeInfo can mimic the DOS ERASE command and erase files so that you can unerase them. WipeInfo has the advantage of being able to erase files across subdirectories.

To wipe out all files with the BAT extension in the current directory and all subdirectories, enter the following command:

>   WIPEINFO *.BAK /S

The WipeInfo command is discussed in Chapter 8.

DISKCOPY versus Duplicate Disk

DISKCOPY copies an entire disk to another disk of the same size. For example, to copy a disk in drive A to a disk of the same size in drive B, use the following command:

>   DISKCOPY A: B:

Norton Duplicate Disk (DUPDISK or DD) performs the same task but allows you to choose interactively (from drop-down list boxes) the source and destination disks if you do not specify them in the command line. To copy a disk in drive A to a disk of the same size in drive B, use this command:

DUPDISK A: B:

Note that drives A and B could physically be the same disk drive because you are prompted to swap disks during the copy procedure. Unlike DISKCOPY, DUPDISK uses extended or expanded memory to store the disk image during copy; thus, less disk swapping occurs than when you use DISKCOPY.

If the destination disk is not formatted, DISKCOPY formats the disk, giving it a unique volume serial number (for DOS 4 and later versions). DUPDISK, however, gives the new disk the identical serial number. When you are using DUPDISK and the destination disk is not formatted, you are asked whether you want the destination disk formatted.

When you make multiple copies of a disk, DUPDISK does not reread the contents of the source disk, although DISKCOPY does. Faster duplicating is the result.

The DUPDISK command is discussed in Chapter 26.

DIR versus File Find and File Attributes

DIR lists selected file names on-screen. For example, to display all files with the BAT extension, enter the following command:

DIR *.BAT

File Find enables you to display selected file names from a list box, a directory, or an entire hard disk. File Attributes (FA) can list a directory of files along with their file attributes, which are not listed with the DIR command.

To list all files on the disk that match the specification, including those files in subdirectories, enter the following command:

FA *.BAT

FIND versus File Find and Text Search

FIND enables you to find and report the existence of specified text in selected files. You must explicitly list all the files that you want to be searched; you cannot use wild-card characters in the search for file names.

To list on-screen any lines in REPORT.DOC that contain the string *text*, enter the following command:

    FIND "text" REPORT.DOC

File Find enables you to search files in subdirectories and to search erased spaces on the disk for the specified search string. You can also make the search case-sensitive.

When searching *erased space*, you are actually searching information on disk that was once the information in a file. When a file is erased, only the reference to the file is really deleted. The actual contents of the file remain on disk in erased space until that space is overwritten by another file.

To search all files having the DOC extension in the current directory and subdirectories or to search for the character string specified by *text*, enter the following command:

    FILEFIND

The File Find interactive search screen appears. You then enter the criteria for your search. Specify to search *.DOC in the search entry area and choose to search the entire disk, the current directory, or the current directory and its subdirectories. Then choose the Find option on the menu, and the search begins. After File Find locates files that contain the desired text, you can select a file from the list and choose to view its contents.

The Text Search (TS) command enables you to perform a text search from the DOS prompt. To search for the word DEFICIT in all files on disk that match *.RPT, enter the following command:

    TS *.RPT "DEFICIT" /S

The searching capabilities of File Find and Text Search are described in Chapter 25.

FORMAT versus Safe Format

DOS FORMAT prepares a disk to store files. To format and place a volume label on a disk in drive A, enter the following command:

    FORMAT A:/V

Beginning with DOS 5, the default method of formatting a disk with the DOS FORMAT command is similar to the Norton Safe Format option.

Safe Format (SFORMAT) formats disks. The Safe Format command has several safety features not available with the DOS FORMAT command. Safe Format saves format information in case the format is an accident, for example. This feature enables you to unformat the disk with the Norton Utilities UnFormat command. Safe Format provides several format modes, including Safe Format, the normal DOS FORMAT, and a quick format. Quick format mode places a new system area on an already formatted disk—effectively erasing all records pertaining to directory and file locations on disk. You also can run Safe Format in interactive mode and choose options from menus rather than remember command-line switches.

To format and place the label MYDISK on a disk in drive A, enter this command:

    SFORMAT A: /V:MYDISK

Safe Format is described in Chapter 4.

MIRROR versus IMAGE

The DOS MIRROR command saves information about files on disk to support the use of the DOS UNDELETE and UNFORMAT programs. Usually, you place the MIRROR command in your AUTOEXEC.BAT file so that a copy of the file information is saved each time you boot your computer. MIRROR is available in DOS beginning with Version 5.

The Norton Image (IMAGE) command is similar to the MIRROR command. For use in DOS recovery commands, the IMAGE command is preferable to the MIRROR command. IMAGE saves information about the files on your disk and is used to support the Norton UnErase and UnFormat commands. The Norton UnErase and UnFormat commands will use MIRROR information if IMAGE information is missing and MIRROR information is available. Usually, you place the IMAGE command in your AUTOEXEC.BAT file so that a copy of the file information is saved each time you boot your computer.

The Image command is discussed in Chapter 4.

MKDIR or MD versus Norton Change Directory

MKDIR or MD makes a directory. To make a subdirectory named LETTERS in the WP directory, enter the following command:

MD \WP\LETTERS

Norton Change Directory (NCD), when used with the MD option, also makes a directory. In addition, this command updates the NCD directory file, which gives you quicker access to directories when you later use the NCD command in interactive mode. In interactive mode, you can add a directory by highlighting the directory name on-screen and pressing F7. The NCD command also has a **R**ename option (F6), which enables you to rename a directory. DOS has no equivalent command.

To make a subdirectory named LETTERS in the WP directory and update the NCD directory file, enter this command:

NCD MD \WP\LETTERS

The NCD command is discussed in Chapter 23.

MODE versus Norton Control Center

MODE specifies communications port settings (among other features). To set up the communication port 1 as 1200 baud, for example, enter one of the following commands:

MODE COM1 BAUD=1200

MODE COM1:1200

Norton Control Center (NCC), when used with the **S**erial Ports option, enables you to set up the parameters of a serial port interactively by choosing options from a menu.

The NCC command is discussed in Chapter 22.

PRINT versus Line Print

The DOS PRINT command prints the contents of an ASCII file to a printer or other output device. To print the file MYSTUFF.TXT, you use this command:

> PRINT MYSTUFF.TXT

The Norton Line Print (LP) command includes options not available in PRINT. You can choose to include line numbers or a header in the printout, to print WordStar files, and so on. To print the file MYSTUFF.TXT and include line numbers, use the following command:

> LP MYSTUFF.TXT /N

The Line Print command is discussed in Chapter 26.

RECOVER versus Disk Tools

RECOVER tries to reclaim disks or files with defective sectors.

WARNING: The RECOVER command is dangerous because the slightest misuse can be devastating. Files often are renamed machine-generated names, and you can easily lose perfectly good files. Do not use this command unless you know exactly what you are doing.

Norton's Disk Tools command (DISKTOOL), when used with RECOVER, attempts to reclaim files and directories that have been renamed and removed by the DOS RECOVER command. Instead of using RECOVER to reclaim files, use the NDD command in interactive mode and choose the **D**iagnose Disk option or Disk Tools' Revive a Defective Diskette option.

Chapter 13 discusses Disk Tools.

RMDIR or RD versus Norton Change Directory

RMDIR or RD removes a directory. To remove the WP directory, enter the following command:

    RD \WP

Norton Change Directory (NCD), when used with the RD option, removes a directory. This command also updates the NCD directory file. You can run NCD in interactive mode, enabling you to remove a directory by pointing to the directory name on a graphic tree and pressing F8 (**D**elete).

To remove the WP directory, enter this command:

    NCD RD \WP

The NCD command is discussed in Chapter 23.

SYS versus Disk Tools

SYS places system files (but not the COMMAND.COM file) on disk if the disk was prepared to receive system files when it was originally formatted.

To place the system files on drive C, enter the following command:

    SYS C:

Disk Tools, when used with the Make a Disk Bootable option, places the system files on a disk even if the disk was not prepared for these files when it was formatted. This option also copies the COMMAND.COM file to the disk to make it bootable.

Chapter 13 discusses Disk Tools.

TIME versus Norton Control Center

DOS TIME enables you to set the system time on your computer. For many versions of the PC, however, the DOS time setting does not reset the internal clock. Thus, when you reboot, your time setting may have disappeared. To set the internal clock, you may have to use the SETUP command.

To set the system time to 10:40 a.m., enter the following command:

TIME 10:40

The Time and Date option in Norton Control Center (NCC) enables you to set the system time. For many computers, this option also sets the internal clock.

The NCC command is discussed in Chapter 22.

TREE versus Norton Change Directory

TREE displays information about directories on the disk. Beginning with DOS 4, this command displays directories in a graphic tree structure.

To display directory names for the entire disk, enter this command:

TREE \

 NOTE Be sure to include the space between TREE and the backslash (\).

In interactive mode, Norton Change Directory (NCD) displays directories in a tree structure, and NCD enables you to point to directory names on-screen and choose to add, rename, delete, or change the directories.

The NCD command is discussed in Chapter 23.

UNDELETE versus UnErase

The DOS UNDELETE command restores a previously deleted file. If you used ERASE or DEL to delete the file named MYFILE.WK1, you can use the command

UNDELETE *.WK1

to search for all erased files with a WK1 extension. You then are prompted to enter the first letter of the name of each deleted file found. The UNDELETE command is available beginning with DOS 5.

The Norton UnErase command is similar to UNDELETE. UnErase presents a list of possible files to undelete. This list also predicts the success (poor, fair, good, or excellent) that UnErase will have with undeleting the files. You may view the contents of a file before undeleting it. Norton also contains a manual unerase feature that enables you to piece together an erased file that you cannot unerase automatically. The Norton UnErase command uses information in the MIRROR or IMAGE file to assist in recovering files.

The UnErase command is discussed in Chapter 10.

UNFORMAT versus UnFormat and Disk Tools

DOS UNFORMAT enables you to restore a formatted disk or a disk that has been restructured with the DOS RECOVER command. UNFORMAT uses information from the MIRROR file created when the DOS MIRROR command was last run. To unformat the disk in drive C, enter the following command:

UNFORMAT C:

The DOS UNFORMAT command is available beginning with DOS 5.

The Norton UnFormat command also enables you to restore a formatted disk. This command can use information in the DOS MIRROR file or the Norton IMAGE file to restore a hard disk. Norton UnFormat can unformat a disk even when this information is not present; however, files in the root directory will be lost and directories under the root will be named DIR0, DIR1, and so on. You can use the Norton Disk Tools command to recover from the DOS RECOVER command.

The UnFormat command is discussed in Chapter 11, and the Disk Tools command is discussed in Chapter 13.

VOL versus Norton Change Directory

VOL displays the volume label for a disk. To display the name given to a disk in drive B when the disk was formatted, enter this command:

VOL B:

The Norton Change Directory (NCD) command enables you to change a volume label. In interactive mode, this option is on the NCD **D**isk pulldown menu.

The NCD command is discussed in Chapter 23.

Installing Norton Programs

This appendix covers installation procedures for Norton Utilities 7, Norton Commander 3, and Norton Backup 2. You learn how to install these programs on a hard disk system. Installation of Norton Utilities 7 also includes creation of an emergency floppy disk (a rescue disk).

NOTE In this appendix, it is assumed that you are installing each program on a hard disk (drive C) from a floppy disk (drive A). If your configuration is different, specify a different drive designation when you enter commands—for example, substitute D if your hard disk is drive D, B if your floppy disk is drive B, and so on.

Installing Norton Utilities 7

Norton Utilities 7 includes three 3 1/2-inch high-density disks (which you can exchange for 5 1/4-inch disks if necessary). Disk #1 is labeled *Install*, Disk #2 is labeled *Emergency/Data Recovery*, and Disk #3 is labeled *Utilities*.

The full Norton Utilities 7 program takes about 4M of actual disk space, although the user's manual accompanying the software recommends a minimum of 5M. Because one of Norton Utilities' primary functions is to enable you to manage your hard disk better, you probably will not install the full system on a floppy disk computer. For these installation instructions, therefore, it is assumed that you will be installing the full program on a hard disk.

> **WARNING:** Before beginning the installation, be certain that you have backed up all crucial files located on your hard disk. If your disk contains deleted or erased files that you might want to recover, you must recover them before installing Norton Utilities. During the installation, this advice appears in an information screen; you have the option to return to DOS and perform any necessary backup or recovery procedures.

Viewing the READ.ME and WHATS.NEW Files

On the Install disk for Norton Utilities 7, you may find the file READ.ME, which contains last-minute notes about the program. Assuming that the Install disk is in drive A of your computer, you can print the READ.ME file with the following command:

COPY A:READ.ME LPT1:

If you inserted the Install disk in a different drive, substitute that drive letter for A in the command. To use this command, you need to have a printer installed on printer port 1. If you do not have a printer, use the following command to display the READ.ME file on-screen:

TYPE A:READ.ME | MORE

If the file is several screens long, the message -- MORE -- appears at the bottom of the first screen; press any key to move from one screen to the next. When you finish reading the file, press Ctrl+C or Ctrl+Break to return to the DOS prompt.

You can also examine this file by using Norton Commander (the Edit or View option) or your word processing program. Or you can use the Norton Utilities LP command to print the file after you install the program. To learn more about the LP command, see Chapter 26, which covers the Norton command-line utilities.

You may find another file, called WHATS.NEW, on the Install disk. WHATS.NEW enables you to view information about the new features of this release of the program. Follow the procedures described in the preceding paragraphs to view the contents of this file.

To send the file to the printer, use the following command:

    COPY A:WHATS.NEW LPT1:

To view the file on-screen, enter this command:

    TYPE A:WHATS.NEW | MORE

Installing the Program

To install Norton Utilities 7 on your hard disk, follow these steps:

1. Turn on your computer and boot it in the usual way. End any programs that started automatically (such as a menu) so that you are at the DOS prompt (usually C:\> on a hard disk).

2. Insert the Norton Utilities Install disk in drive A.

3. Switch to drive A by typing **A:** and pressing Enter. Your prompt now should be A>, A:\>, or an equivalent.

4. To begin the installation procedure for Norton Utilities, type **INSTALL** and press Enter.

5. The first dialog box that appears prompts you to choose the display colors. The options are **C**olor, **B**lack & White, **L**aptop, and **R**eturn to DOS (see fig. C.1).

    Use the up- and down-arrow keys to choose the option that matches your monitor; then press Enter. Alternatively, press the highlighted letter associated with your choice, or point to the option with the mouse and click once.

Fig. C.1

The Choose
Display Color
dialog box.

6. After you make your color choice, the Install program scans for a previous version of the software on your hard disk. If an old copy exists on your disk, Install defaults to that directory to install the new version. Otherwise, the installation directory is NU. (You can choose a different directory later.)

NOTE If a previous version of Norton Utilities exists on your computer and you choose to install the new version in the same directory, all old files will automatically be removed before installation.

After the scan for an old version, a warning box appears, telling you not to install Norton Utilities if you accidentally formatted your hard disk or if you want to recover some files from that disk (see fig. C.2). To unformat the disk or to recover files, use the emergency floppy disk included in the software package.

Fig. C.2

Norton Utilities'
preinstallation
warning.

7. To cancel the installation procedure, choose **Return** to DOS. To continue the installation, press Enter or choose **Continue**.

The next dialog box that appears summarizes the installation process (see fig. C.3). The installation program does the following tasks:

■ Copies Norton Utilities files to your hard disk

■ Enables you to place certain Norton Utilities commands in your AUTOEXEC.BAT and CONFIG.SYS files

■ Enables you to set the configuration of your computer (screen colors, mouse, and graphics)

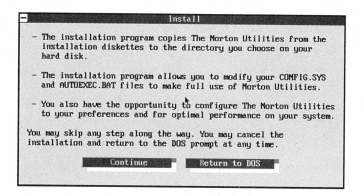

```
┌─────────────────────────────────────────────────┐
│ ─                    Install                     │
├─────────────────────────────────────────────────┤
│                                                  │
│   - The installation program copies The Norton Utilities from the │
│     installation diskettes to the directory you choose on your    │
│     hard disk.                                   │
│                                                  │
│   - The installation program allows you to modify your CONFIG.SYS │
│     and AUTOEXEC.BAT files to make full use of Norton Utilities.  │
│                                                  │
│   - You also have the opportunity to configure The Norton Utilities │
│     to your preferences and for optimal performance on your system. │
│                                                  │
│   You may skip any step along the way. You may cancel the         │
│   installation and return to the DOS prompt at any time.          │
│                                                  │
│        ▃▃▃▃ Continue ▃▃▃▃      ▃▃▃▃ Return to DOS ▃▃▃▃            │
└─────────────────────────────────────────────────┘
```

Fig. C.3

A summary of the installation process.

8. Choose Continue or press Enter. You then see the dialog box shown in figure C.4.

```
┌──────────────────────────────────────┐
│                                      │
│        Personalize your copy of      │
│            Norton Utilities          │
│                                      │
│  Enter Your Name:                    │
│  [.................................] │
│                                      │
│  Enter Your Company:                 │
│  [.................................] │
│                                      │
│             ▃▃▃ OK ▃▃▃               │
│                                      │
└──────────────────────────────────────┘
```

Fig. C.4

Personalizing your copy of Norton Utilities.

9. You must enter your name in this dialog box; the company information is optional. After you enter the necessary information, choose OK or press Enter.

10. Install asks you to specify the type of installation you want (see fig. C.5). Choose the appropriate type of installation by pressing the first letter of the option, using the up- and down-arrow keys to select the option, or clicking the option. Notice that the full installation requires 4M of disk space. If you choose Full Install, the installation procedure will copy all Norton Utilities to your hard drive. Choosing Custom Install gives you the opportunity to pick and choose which utilities will be installed, and offers you information on the amount of disk space required by each utility.

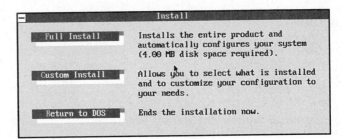

Fig. C.5

Specifying the type of installation.

11. After you select an installation type, a new Install dialog box appears, requesting information about where you want to install Norton Utilities (see fig. C.6). Choose the directory in which the program will be installed.

    If you want to accept the default directory, press Enter to continue the installation. To change the directory, press Backspace to delete the C:\NU entry and then enter a new directory.

Fig. C.6

Specifying the directory for Norton Utilities.

12. After you specify the directory name, press Enter or choose Continue. (As noted previously, if an old version of Norton Utilities exists in this directory, that version will be deleted before the new

version is installed.) If you chose **C**ustom Install in step 10, the Install Program Files dialog box appears. This dialog box enables you to specify what portions of the program to install. A check mark appears to the left of every option that is to be installed (see fig. C.7).

Fig. C.7

Selecting files for a custom installation.

13. Use the up- and down-arrow keys or your mouse to move from option to option, and press the space bar to select or deselect options (or use your mouse). Whenever you select or deselect an option, an odometer (located directly below the Install **G**roups list box) keeps a running tally of the space available on the destination drive, the combined size of all files selected, and the disk space that will remain after you install your selected options. Unless you do not have space to install the entire program, you probably will want to accept the full installation.

14. After you make your selections, press Enter or choose **I**nstall. A dialog box similar to that in figure C.8 appears, enabling you to select what programs are to be added to your AUTOEXEC.BAT. You make these selections by using the up- and down-arrow keys to highlight the programs you want added and then pressing the space bar, or you can double-click each program name. A check mark appears next to each item you select. After you have made your selections, choose **C**ontinue or **R**eturn to DOS. The install program begins copying files from the Install disk. You are prompted to change disks during the installation process.

When the installation process is complete, the program displays the Save System Files dialog box, where you specify the changes you want to make in your system files to accommodate Norton Utilities. The following section describes the options in this dialog box.

Fig. C.8

The Select
Configuration
Options dialog
box.

Modifying AUTOEXEC.BAT and CONFIG.SYS

After you install Norton Utilities, you have the option of modifying your
AUTOEXEC.BAT and CONFIG.SYS files. Although the default option is
Make Changes to Startup Files, you may want to save the changes in an
alternative file, or you may elect not to save the changes at all. If you
choose **R**eview in the Save System Files dialog box, you can preview the
changes before the program actually writes them to disk (see fig. C.9).
If you accept the changes, backup copies of your original files are saved
as AUTOEXEC.NU7 and CONFIG.NU7.

Fig. C.9

The Save System
Files dialog box.

Some of the changes that will occur, if you elect to make them during
the installation process, include adding the newly installed software
to the PATH statement in your AUTOEXEC.BAT file and setting the

environment variable NU to the subdirectory where Norton Utilities is installed. Automatic changes might include changes to your CONFIG.SYS file. If your FILES and BUFFERS statements are not adequate to allow Norton Utilities to run efficiently, it will offer to make the necessary changes for you.

Other options available are **S**ave Changes in Alternate Files and **D**o Not Save Changes. Electing to save changes to an alternative file will create the files AUTOEXEC.TMP and CONFIG.TMP and place them in the directory where Norton Utilities is installed. Should you decide later that you want to implement the changes recorded in these alternative files, you may simply copy them to the root directory and reboot your computer; the changes take effect immediately. Should you elect not to save the changes, the screen for the next installation step, creating a rescue disk, is displayed.

Creating a Rescue Disk

Regardless of whether you chose to modify your AUTOEXEC.BAT and CONFIG.SYS files, Install prompts you to create a rescue disk (see fig. C.10). The floppy disk that you create during this process contains the files you may need if your hard disk is formatted accidentally or develops problems that make it unusable.

Fig. C.10

The Create Rescue Disk dialog box.

 NOTE Have a floppy disk ready for this process (formatted or unformatted). A new disk or one that contains no useful information is recommended. This process automatically formats the disk, thus deleting any information stored on it.

To create the rescue disk, follow these steps:

1. Activate the **S**ave Rescue Information To list box by pressing Tab until the list box is active, pressing S, or clicking the triangle.

2. Press PgDn or click the triangle to open the drop-down list box, from which you can choose options. For the **S**ave Rescue Information To option, you must specify the disk drive to which you want to save the rescue files (such as A, B, or C).

3. Repeat steps 1 and 2 for the Rescue **D**iskette Type list box. For the Rescue **D**iskette Type option, you must indicate the type of disk you are using.

4. Choose the **F**ormat Rescue Diskette option if you didn't format the rescue disk before starting this process. If you want to add files to the rescue disk, other than those displayed in the **R**escue Disk Contents list box, you can choose **B**rowse. This option enables you to select files that you think are important to the reconstruction of your hard drive should some catastrophic act occur. In the lower-left corner of the screen, you will see a message indicating the amount of disk space required to store the selected files. If the space required exceeds the amount of space available on your destination drive, you need to determine which files you can do without, and remove them from the list.

5. After you are satisfied with your selections in this dialog box, choose **C**reate or press Enter.

6. If you elected to format the rescue disk, you receive one last warning (see fig. C.11). If you are sure that the right disk is in the drive, choose **O**K or press Enter. If you have any doubt, choose **C**ancel or press Esc.

Fig. C.11

The last warning before Install reformats the rescue disk.

7. When the process of creating the rescue disk is complete, a dialog box appears, providing three options (see fig. C.12).

   If, during the installation process, you elected to modify your AUTOEXEC.BAT and CONFIG.SYS files, choose the **R**eboot option

so that the changes recorded in those files will take effect. Otherwise, choose **G**o to Program to use Norton Utilities 7, or choose
Return to **D**OS.

Fig. C.12

Ready to start
Norton Utilities.

8. If you elected to return to DOS in step 7 and you want to begin
   Norton Utilities, enter **NORTON** at the DOS prompt. If you get an
   error message, check that you are in the proper directory—NU7.
   If you are not, change to that directory by entering **CD \NU7** and
   then reissuing the NORTON command. (If you installed Norton
   Utilities in a different directory, replace NU7 with the appropriate
   directory name.)

 Be sure to keep your rescue disk and your installation disks
in a safe place in case you need to use them later.

Installing Norton Commander 3

The Norton Commander 3 package consists of two 360K 5 1/4-inch
disks and one 720K 3 1/2-inch disk. If drive A is a 720K or 1.44M drive,
use the 3 1/2-inch disk. If drive A is a 360K or 1.2M disk drive, use the 5
1/4-inch disks.

Norton Commander takes about 850K of disk space. Because one of the
Commander's primary functions is to enable you to manage your hard
disk better, you probably will not install the program on a floppy disk
system. For these installation instructions, therefore, it is assumed that
you are installing Norton Commander on a hard disk system.

Viewing the READ.ME and INREAD.ME Files

Before beginning the installation process, you may want to read or print the READ.ME and INREAD.ME files that come with Norton Commander. The INREAD.ME file contains helpful information about what to do if the installation process does not work. The READ.ME file contains last-minute notes about the program.

Assuming that the installation disk is in drive A of your computer, you can print the READ.ME and INREAD.ME files with the following command:

COPY A:*.ME LPT1:

To use this command, you need to have a printer installed on printer port 1. If you do not have a printer, use the TYPE command to examine these files on-screen. To examine the contents of the INREAD.ME file, enter the following command:

TYPE A:INREAD.ME

To examine the contents of the READ.ME file, enter this command:

TYPE A:READ.ME

Neither command requires the | MORE switch (described earlier in this appendix) because both files display a single screen of information.

Installing the Program

To install Norton Commander 3, follow these steps:

1. Turn on your computer and boot it in the usual way. Exit any programs that started automatically (such as a menu) so that you are at the DOS prompt (usually C:\> on a hard disk).

2. Switch to drive A by entering **A:** at the DOS prompt. Your prompt now should be A>, A:\>, or an equivalent.

3. Insert the Norton Commander Program Disk in drive A.

   If you are using a 5 1/4-inch drive, insert the first 5 1/4-inch Commander disk (Disk #1) in drive A.

   If you are using a 3 1/2-inch drive, insert the 3 1/2-inch Commander disk in drive A.

4. To begin the installation process, type **INSTALL** and press Enter.

5. You are prompted to select the drive from which you want to install Norton Commander (A or B). Type the letter, click the drive letter, or use the arrow keys to highlight the appropriate drive letter of the drive that contains the Installation disk. Then press Enter.

6. You see a screen similar to the one shown in figure C.13, summarizing the installation process.

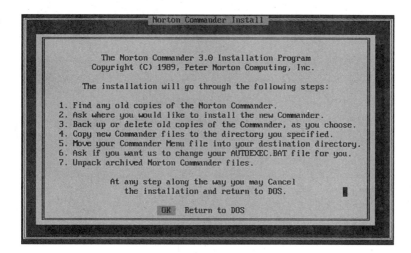

```
┌────────────────── Norton Commander Install ──────────────────┐
│                                                              │
│  ┌────────────────────────────────────────────────────────┐ │
│  │                                                        │ │
│  │      The Norton Commander 3.0 Installation Program     │ │
│  │      Copyright (C) 1989, Peter Norton Computing, Inc.   │ │
│  │                                                        │ │
│  │      The installation will go through the following steps: │
│  │                                                        │ │
│  │  1. Find any old copies of the Norton Commander.       │ │
│  │  2. Ask where you would like to install the new Commander. │
│  │  3. Back up or delete old copies of the Commander, as you choose. │
│  │  4. Copy new Commander files to the directory you specified. │
│  │  5. Move your Commander Menu file into your destination directory. │
│  │  6. Ask if you want us to change your AUTOEXEC.BAT file for you. │
│  │  7. Unpack archived Norton Commander files.            │ │
│  │                                                        │ │
│  │      At any step along the way you may Cancel          │ │
│  │          the installation and return to DOS.       ▌   │ │
│  │                                                        │ │
│  │             OK    Return to DOS                        │ │
│  └────────────────────────────────────────────────────────┘ │
└──────────────────────────────────────────────────────────────┘
```

Fig. C.13

The initial installation screen for Norton Commander.

At the bottom of the screen are two options: OK and Return to DOS. OK is highlighted. To continue with the installation, press Enter. To return to DOS, press R.

7. The Install program next looks at your disk to see whether a current copy of Norton Commander is installed in a directory named NC. If you have an old copy, you are given a chance to delete the old copy or back it up to some other location on disk.

    You can choose one of three options:

    ■ The Overwrite option writes the new version to the old directory, overwriting the old version.

    ■ The Back Up option causes the installation program to write the old files to a backup directory named NC.BAK.

    ■ The Return to DOS option cancels installation.

    Use the arrow keys to point to the option you prefer, and then press the space bar to lock in your choice; or just click the option.

After you choose an option, press Enter or click OK to continue with the installation.

8. Install next asks you to enter the name of the disk and directory to which Commander should be copied (see fig. C.14).

The default directory for Commander is C:\NC, which appears in the text box. If you accept this directory, press Enter to continue the installation. To change the directory, press Backspace to delete the C:\NC entry and then type a new directory. If this is the first time you are installing Norton Commander, a message appears directly above the default directory, indicating that Norton Commander was not contained within your PATH statement.

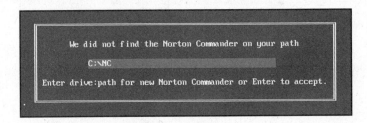

Fig. C.14

Specifying the directory for Commander.

9. The installation program prompts you once more before the copy operation begins, giving you a chance to return to DOS and cancel the installation (see fig. C.15).

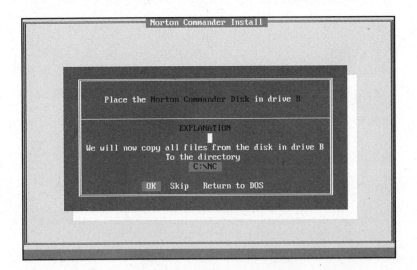

Fig. C.15

Preparing to copy Norton Commander files.

To continue the installation, press Enter to accept the highlighted OK option. To cancel the operation and return to DOS, press R.

10. The Install program asks whether you want the path to the Commander directory to be placed in the PATH statement of your AUTOEXEC.BAT file (see fig. C.16).

    Again, if you are installing Commander for the first time, choose OK. The path to the directory where Norton Commander resides will be added to your AUTOEXEC.BAT file, and a backup of the original file will be created (named AUTOEXEC.BAK). If you already have a path to the Commander's directory, you can press S to skip this part of the installation.

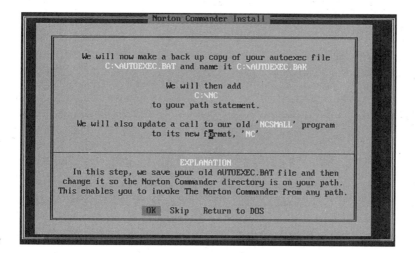

Fig. C.16

Indicating whether you want Install to change your AUTOEXEC.BAT file.

After all the files are copied to disk and modifications are made to AUTOEXEC.BAT, the installation is complete. To begin Norton Commander, enter **NC** at the DOS prompt.

If you want Commander to run each time you boot your computer and you elected to skip the automatic update performed during the installation, you can place the NC command as the last line in your AUTOEXEC.BAT file. (See Appendix A for an explanation of the AUTOEXEC.BAT file and how to edit it.)

Installing Norton Backup 2

Two versions of Norton Backup for DOS have been released (Versions 1.1 and 2.0). The versions function in essentially the same way. If the instructions provided in this section differ from what appears on your screen during the installation process, you should consult the instructions accompanying the version of Norton Backup that you are attempting to install.

Depending on your version, the number of disks associated with your software may vary. For this procedure, it is assumed that you are installing Norton Backup 2.

Installing the Program

The Norton Backup 2 program comes with three 3 1/2-inch disks and two 5 1/4-inch disks. If you are using a computer with a 3 1/2-inch disk (720K or 1.44M) drive, use the 3 1/2-inch disks to install the program. If you are using a computer with a 5 1/4-inch disk (360K or 1.2M) drive, use the 5 1/4-inch disks.

The Backup program requires that you have two blank floppy disks to test the program. Be sure that you have these disks handy when you begin the installation. If you have 3 1/2-inch and 5 1/4-inch disk drives, you can use either size for the test. You do not need to format the disks before the test; the disks are automatically formatted during the procedure, if necessary.

The Norton Backup installation program performs several tasks:

- ◼ Copies necessary files to your hard disk.

- ◼ Modifies your AUTOEXEC.BAT file to place the Norton Backup directory in your PATH command.

- ◼ Examines your computer system to determine which disk drives your computer contains and which disks can be used as backups.

- ◼ Runs several tests on your computer to determine the most efficient way to perform the backup. These tests deal with the speed of your computer and your disks.

To install Norton Backup, follow these steps:

1. Insert Disk #1 in drive A.

2. Switch to drive A by typing **A:** at the DOS prompt and pressing Enter. Your prompt now should be A>, A:\>, or the equivalent.

3. At the DOS prompt, type **INSTALL** and press Enter.

4. The Install program asks you a series of questions about your computer. Choose the default settings or make changes as necessary. (Usually, you should choose the default settings for installation; you can change these settings later.)

   The first decision you must make pertains to the display type. As illustrated in figure C.17, you must select the type of display connected to your computer.

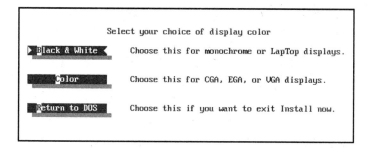

Fig. C.17

Norton Backup
display options.

Immediately following your selection of a display type, the installation routine scans the disk for previous versions of Norton Backup and then presents a brief description of what is about to occur (see fig. C.18). If, for any reason, you want to discontinue the installation, choose **R**eturn to DOS. Otherwise, choose **C**ontinue.

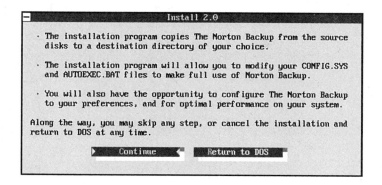

Fig. C.18

A description of the installation procedures.

5. You are prompted to tell the installation program where you want to install Norton Backup. The default is C:\NBACKUP (see fig. C.19). If another version of Norton Backup is found, you will see a message indicating that a copy of the program has been found in C:\NBACKUP. If Norton Backup exists and you want to overwrite the existing version, or if this is a first-time installation and you want the files copied to the default directory (C:\NBACKUP), choose **C**ontinue.

If you want to change the location where the files will be installed, simply type the new location, specifying the drive and path, and then choose **C**ontinue.

If old files exist, you will see a message momentarily appear on the screen to indicate that existing files are being deleted. Otherwise, the install routine begins copying the necessary files from the disks.

Fig. C.19

Choosing where
to install Norton
Backup.

6. After the files are copied, you are asked whether you want to add
   the Norton Backup to your DOS help file. DOS 5.0 and later versions have a Help facility, enabling you to access help on the commands incorporated into Norton Backup. You can choose **A**dd
   Help or **D**on't Add Help (see fig. C.20).

Fig. C.20

The dialog box
for adding
Norton Backup
to your DOS
help file.

7. You are prompted to personalize your copy of Norton Backup
   (see fig. C.21). You must enter your name. The company name is
   optional.

Fig. C.21

The dialog box
for personalizing
your copy of
Norton Backup.

8. After you choose your basic options and the files are copied, the installation procedure runs a series of tests, using two floppy disks that you supply. Follow the instructions on-screen, which prompt you to place the disks in the disk drive at certain times during the tests.

   If your computer fails any of these tests, Norton Backup attempts to reset its options to compensate for the problem. If your computer fails certain tests, the backup program will still work, but it will not be able to back up at its highest speed.

Configuring the Backup Program

You must configure Norton Backup before you start using it. Configuration, performed during installation, involves telling Norton Backup the program level and the type of backup device you use. Then Norton Backup performs tests to determine how the device is used.

When you install Norton Backup, the program automatically performs the configuration, with some input from you. You can reconfigure when you add a new backup device or change devices. If, for example, you have been using disks for backup and then buy a tape backup system, you must reconfigure Norton Backup to use the tape backup system. Reconfiguring Norton Backup is discussed in Chapter 29.

The configuration portion of the installation program first configures itself to your system by running several tests. These tests determine the default setup and tell Norton Backup how fast it can perform the exchange of information. The tests consist of the following steps:

- Selecting the program complexity level
- Configuring the screen and mouse
- Selecting backup devices
- Configuring and testing backup devices
- Making changes to CONFIG.SYS and AUTOEXEC.BAT

This section explains the three levels of operation within Norton Backup, the screen and mouse configuration, and the two tests that help determine how Norton Backup will work with your computer. This section also discusses the proposed changes to your computer's AUTOEXEC.BAT and CONFIG.SYS files.

The first item you can choose is how complex you want Norton Backup to be. Choose one of three levels:

■ The **B**asic level is a versatile selection. You can create and change setup files, create and change catalog files, change some options, select specific files, and use Backup Scheduler.

■ The **A**dvanced level is for advanced users. This level includes all the Basic level features plus additional option settings, the creation of include and exclude scripts, and the use of special exclusions. Figure C.22 shows the Program Level dialog box.

 NOTE Include and exclude scripts are lists that you can build to include or exclude files in a backup automatically. Special exclusions are files that you exclude when selecting backup files. You can, for example, exclude files outside a date range, exclude hidden files, and exclude system files.

Fig. C.22

The Program
Level dialog box.

■ The **P**reset level is the easiest and best suited for beginners. You can select preset backups, choose backup catalogs, select files for restoration or comparison, and use macros.

After you select the level of complexity, you can configure the screen with the following options:

■ The **S**creen Colors option enables you to choose one of the predefined screen palettes or customize the screen colors yourself.

■ With the **D**isplay Lines option, you can change the number of lines displayed.

■ With the **G**raphical Display option, you can display graphic elements that emulate Microsoft Windows, or you can display simple text elements.

■ The **R**educe Display Speed option eliminates snow that appears on some video monitors.

■ The **E**xpanding Dialogs option changes the size of dialog boxes.

To select or deselect a check box option, highlight the option and press the space bar, or just click the option. A check mark or x in the box indicates that the option is selected.

You can change the following mouse options:

- The Double-Click option changes the speed at which you must click the mouse button twice in succession to choose an item.

- The Sensitivity option changes the speed that the mouse pointer moves on-screen when you move the mouse.

- The Acceleration option changes how quickly the mouse pointer moves on-screen in relation to the speed changes of the mouse.

- The Left-Handed Mouse option switches the actions of the mouse buttons.

- Choose the Hard Mouse Reset option only if you are experiencing erratic problems with your mouse. Such problems may include a lack of mouse pointer response to mouse movement, or mouse clicks with no results.

Figure C.23 shows the Video and Mouse Configuration dialog box, where you can make all of these selections. After you make all your changes for the screen and mouse, choose OK.

Fig. C.23

The Video and Mouse Configuration dialog box.

The most important step in configuration is selecting the backup devices. The automatic configuration searches for all possible devices— that is, Norton Backup detects disk drives and tape drives. While detecting devices, Norton Backup even determines the maximum capacity of the device; for example, the program determines whether drive A is a 3 1/2-inch high-density drive. After Norton Backup determines the types of drives available for backup purposes, it will perform a Floppy Drive Change Line test to see whether your system is capable of using the fastest and most reliable method to determine when a disk has been removed and replaced in your floppy drive. To begin this test, choose **S**tart Test (see fig. C.24).

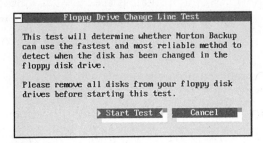

Fig. C.24

The Floppy Drive Change Line Test dialog box.

After you are sure that Norton Backup has made the correct choices, continue by choosing OK in the Backup Devices dialog box that appears. Figure C.25 illustrates the results of its search of all drives.

```
                    Backup Devices
  Floppy Drive  :
  3½" 1.44Mb High Density            ▶    OK
  Floppy Drive  :
  Not Installed                          Cancel
  tape drive:
  Not Installed                         Auto Config
```

Fig. C.25

A list of backup devices detected.

Norton Backup must know how to access your hard disk and floppy disk or tape drive. The Backup program makes this determination by a direct memory access (DMA) test. Most computers enable Norton Backup to access the hard disk and the floppy disk or tape drive at the same time, which greatly increases backup speed. In the DMA Test dialog box (which appears after you specify the backup devices), choose **S**tart DMA Test or press Enter to start the DMA test, which takes just a moment (see fig. C.26). After the test is finished, the results are displayed (see fig. C.27). Press Enter or choose **O**K to continue the testing process.

Fig. C.26

The DMA Test dialog box.

Fig. C.27

The results of a successful DMA test.

> **CAUTION:** During the DMA test, your computer may *hang*, or stop working. If the message `Testing DMA` appears for more than 30 seconds, your computer has hung. If this problem occurs, restart your computer and Norton Backup. This time, the DMA is set to Low Speed. Don't try to set it to High Speed. (Low Speed and High Speed determine the rate at which data can be transferred.)

Norton Backup next runs a compatibility test to verify the configuration (see fig. C.28). This test does an actual backup and comparison. Be prepared to insert two disks sequentially during the test. Press Enter to start the test. Watch the screen as Norton Backup makes backup choices. Insert the disks and press Enter as the program prompts you during the test.

> You can skip the compatibility test, but the test is beneficial because it confirms the setup configuration (see fig. C.29).

T I P

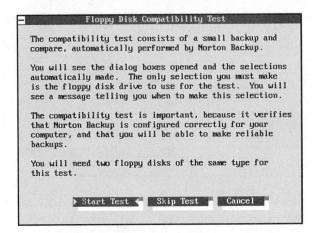

Fig. C.28

The Floppy Disk
Compatibility
Test dialog box.

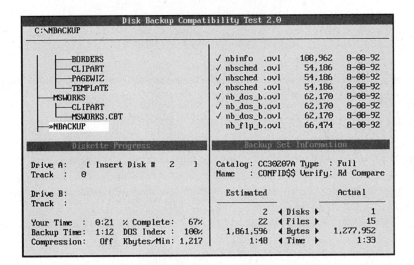

Fig. C.29

The compatibility
test in progress.

After the compatibility test is finished, Norton Backup prompts you to
change your CONFIG.SYS and AUTOEXEC.BAT files. The changes in
CONFIG.SYS pertain to the FILES and BUFFERS statements. For optimum performance, you should have FILES and BUFFERS set to at least
30. If your current CONFIG.SYS statement is less than 30, the program
prompts you to make the change.

Norton Backup then displays your computer's CONFIG.SYS file with the
changes you selected. You can choose **M**ove Line (to change the order
of commands in the CONFIG.SYS file), **S**ave Changes, or **C**ancel (to cancel the changes). If you want to move a line, select the line to move
with the arrow keys or mouse. Then press Enter or choose **M**ove Line

and use the arrow keys to move the line to the correct location. After you select a line and choose **M**ove Line, the **M**ove Line command button changes to **D**rop Line. When the line is in the correct position, choose **D**rop Line or press Enter. Choose **S**ave Changes to save the changes made to the CONFIG.SYS file.

Norton Backup enables you to change the AUTOEXEC.BAT file by adding the Norton Backup directory to your PATH statement, setting up a DOS environment variable called NBACKUP, and loading the Backup Scheduler TSR. You are asked whether you want to schedule backups at this time. Your options include the following:

- Perform a complete backup the next time you turn on your computer

- Perform a complete backup every Friday at 4:00PM

- Perform incremental backups Monday through Thursday at 4:00PM

If you want these events to occur automatically, choose **Y**es. Otherwise, choose **N**o.

As with the changes you made to CONFIG.SYS, mark the check boxes for the changes you want to make, and then press Enter. You next see your computer's AUTOEXEC.BAT file. You can move the lines in AUTOEXEC.BAT or save the changes.

Now automatic installation is almost complete. You can save your choices by choosing **S**ave, or you can return to any part of the configuration to make additional changes.

The Norton Backup opening screen is again displayed. Norton Backup is now ready to back up your data.

Verifying the Backup Configuration

After you install Norton Backup, you should back up all or a portion of your hard disk and then restore your backed-up files to verify that the program is installed and working correctly.

After saving your changes, Norton Backup automatically begins a backup session, prompting you to insert Disk #1. If you are prepared to perform a backup, insert your first backup disk in the appropriate drive. The drive light will be active, indicating the drive where the program expects you to insert a disk. If you want to wait and perform a backup at a later time, press Esc, and you are presented with a screen that offers the options **R**eboot, **G**o to Program, and Return to **D**OS.

Reboot reboots your computer, invoking changes made to your AUTOEXEC.BAT and CONFIG.SYS files. **G**o to Program goes to the Norton Backup 2.0 main menu. Return to **D**OS takes you back to the DOS prompt without invoking the changes to your AUTOEXEC.BAT and CONFIG.SYS files.

If you elected to reboot your computer or you returned to the DOS prompt, you can begin the program by entering **NBACKUP** at the DOS prompt. If Norton Backup fails to start, be certain that you are in the directory in which Norton Backup was installed (for example, C:\NBACKUP). If you chose to have the installation program modify your AUTOEXEC.BAT and CONFIG.SYS files, simply reboot your computer and enter **NBACKUP** at the DOS prompt.

Dealing with Disk-Related Problems

Norton Utilities 7 provides a number of commands for fixing disk problems that you cannot fix by using DOS commands alone. Many disk problems occur when bad spots develop on the magnetic surface of a disk. The magnetic signal on the disk gradually weakens until DOS cannot read the information. Other problems occur when a disk gets nearly full of files and they become so fragmented that DOS loses track of critical information. If these problems begin to appear, you may experience computer difficulties ranging from the inability to read one file to the inability to access your entire hard disk.

The first part of this appendix describes some common problems and suggests how you can use Norton Utilities commands to diagnose and solve these problems. Sometimes, however, a disk may be irreparable with these methods. You may have to perform a low-level format on the hard disk, which is explained in the section "The Hard Disk Needs a Low-Level Format" in this appendix.

Another problem is computer sabotage. The data on your computer may be damaged by a computer virus or the deliberate act of an individual. For information on handling these types of problems, see the section "The Threat of Viruses and Sabotage" in this appendix.

For suggestions on how to respond to common DOS error messages, see the final section, "Responding to DOS Error Messages." A DOS error message is usually the result of a problem related to a DOS command. For example, if you enter a command that DOS does not recognize (perhaps you incorrectly spell it), DOS responds with the message Bad command or file name. Knowing the meaning of a DOS message can be valuable in figuring out how to deal with the problem.

Diagnosing and Fixing Disk Problems

This section presents several common disk problems and gives suggestions for solving them by using Norton Utilities and DOS commands.

The Computer No Longer Boots from the Hard Disk

If your computer has booted from the hard disk in the past but now it does not, you must boot from a floppy disk in drive A. Make sure that the disk contains the same version of DOS that is on the hard disk.

One condition that can cause a hard disk to fail to boot is that the correct COMMAND.COM file is no longer in the hard disk root directory. After you boot your computer, examine the hard disk's root directory to determine whether it contains the correct COMMAND.COM—you should be able to tell by looking at its date and size. If they do not match the date and size on the original DOS disk, copy the correct COMMAND.COM to the hard disk and try booting again.

If the COMMAND.COM file is OK, your system files may have become corrupted. You can use the DOS SYS command to transfer a fresh copy of the system files to the hard disk or, better yet, you can use the Make a Disk Bootable option in Disk Tools. This option places COMMAND.COM and the system files on your disk. If one of these approaches does not work, your hard disk may be damaged physically, and you probably need to have it repaired.

You should keep a floppy disk handy that contains the files necessary to boot your computer in case it becomes unbootable from the hard disk. This floppy disk should be formatted with the System (/S) FORMAT option. It should contain the DOS programs FDISK and DEBUG, the Norton programs Disk Tools and Disk Doctor, and the files AUTOEXEC.BAT and CONFIG.SYS. The floppy disk should also include any device drivers (for the mouse or plotter, for example).

The Rescue Disk program provided with Norton Utilities 7 creates such a disk; you can specify which files you want to store on the rescue disk for use in an emergency. See Chapter 14 for details on this program.

The Hard Disk Cannot Be Formatted as a System Disk

The hard disk, like a floppy disk, uses track 0 to store system information. If that track is bad on a hard disk, the DOS FORMAT command will not create a bootable hard disk. You have several alternatives for circumventing this problem, however. After you boot the computer from a floppy disk in drive A, use Norton Disk Doctor to diagnose the hard disk and then attempt to fix the problem (see Chapter 12). If that approach does not work, you may need to perform a low-level format of the disk. If the disk contains valuable information, you need to use a nondestructive program such as SpinRite from Gibson Research or Norton's Calibrate utility. See the section "The Hard Disk Needs a Low-Level Format" later in this appendix for more information.

The DISKCOPY Command Results in Errors

If you use the DOS DISKCOPY command to copy a disk, you may get write errors, read errors, or both. Write errors are associated with writing data to the destination disk. If the destination disk has a bad or unreadable spot, a write error occurs. If you get a write error, change to another destination disk. Read errors are associated with reading data from the source disk. If the source disk has a bad or unreadable spot, a read error occurs.

Of the two types of errors, the read error is of more concern because it occurs on the disk that contains the original data. If you get a read error, use Norton Disk Doctor to examine the source disk. Disk Doctor determines whether the read error is in an area that contains a file and then attempts to correct the problem by moving the file to a safer part of the disk.

The Hard Disk Needs a Low-Level Format

When a hard disk is manufactured, it contains random magnetic signals. To make the disk usable, the manufacturer of the hard disk drive or disk controller performs a low-level format on the hard disk. This format is much more thorough than the procedure performed by DOS FORMAT. A low-level format prepares the surface of the hard disk to receive a DOS format and detects bad spots on the surface.

Occasionally, a working hard disk develops problems that cannot be corrected except by a low-level disk format. Some machines have low-level formatting programs built into their ROM software. You can use the DOS DEBUG program to tell the formatting program to begin operating. This low-level format usually is a completely destructive format, however, and nondestructive low-level formatting programs are available. Examples are SpinRite from Gibson Research and the Calibrate program in Norton Utilities 7. By using one of these low-level formatting procedures, you may be able to recover some information from the disk.

> **WARNING:** Do not perform a low-level format of your disk unless you are an experienced computer user. Before performing the low-level format described here, try the low-level (nondestructive) format described in Chapter 20.

To use the computer's built-in program to perform a low-level format (which is destructive to data on the disk), follow these instructions:

1. Boot the computer, using the original DOS disk in drive A.

2. Begin the DEBUG program, which is located on the DOS disk, by entering **DEBUG** at the DOS prompt.

3. A – prompt should appear on-screen. At this prompt, type **G=C800:5** and press Enter. If nothing happens within a minute or two, your computer probably does not have a built-in low-level formatting program. You must reboot the computer and use a nondestructive low-level formatting program.

4. If a low-level formatting program does exist in ROM, another prompt appears. At this prompt, enter an interleave number, which controls your hard disk access time.

The *interleave* determines how much information is read from the disk on each pass. Use an interleave number from 3 to 6. On most AT-type computers, enter an interleave of **3**. On most PC- or XT-type computers, enter an interleave of **6.** If your PC-type computer is a turbo, you may be able to choose a lower interleave than 6 and therefore make your disk access faster. If you choose an interleave that is not optimum, however, your disk access will be too slow. If, after performing the low-level format and some tests (such as running SYSINFO), you feel that your disk access is too slow, try a higher interleave number.

> Running the Norton Calibrate program gives you the best interleave ratio for your disk. Using Calibrate, you can change the interleave without having to redo a destructive low-level format such as the one originally performed on the disk by the manufacturer.

T I P

The low-level format may take several hours to perform. After it is finished, you need to run the DOS FDISK command before formatting the disk.

The Threat of Viruses and Sabotage

At some time, you may become the unfortunate victim of deliberate destruction of computer data. Someone may sabotage your data by destroying, changing, or erasing data on your computer disk. Or your computer may become infected by some type of computer virus program. Virus programs have been known to come from pirated software and from demos that appear in the mail, but rarely from commercial software. Some virus programs are nondestructive and simply give you a message (and a scare). Other virus programs may attempt to destroy all the data on your disk.

You can take a few precautions to lower your chances of having your computer sabotaged. First, load software only from reputable sources and limit other users' access to your computer. You can also set the attributes of important files to read-only. These files should include at least the COMMAND.COM, AUTOEXEC.BAT, and CONFIG.SYS files in your root directory. Be sure to compare the size of your copy of COMMAND.COM on your hard disk with the size of the copy on your original DOS disk. If the sizes differ, your COMMAND.COM may be infected.

You can also purchase and load a virus protection package such as Norton AntiVirus (NAV). Using this program, you can scan your disk for viruses and correct some kinds of virus destruction. You can place the NAV command in your AUTOEXEC.BAT file to verify each time you boot that your disk is free of viruses.

Another important step in being prepared for data destruction is to have current backups of your system, program, and data files. You particularly may want to keep a backup disk of the files in your root directory. Keep also a current copy of your original DOS disk and a copy of your Norton Utilities rescue disk (see Chapter 14).

Virus programs continue to get more complicated and destructive. Depending on the nature of the attack, you may not be able to recover any of your data. If your computer's disk has been compromised by a virus or sabotage, however, Norton Utilities offers some hope of recovery. The following sections provide possible solutions to various problems arising from virus programs or sabotage.

Files or Directories Have Been Erased

Use the Norton UnErase command to recover erased files before you write new information to your disk. You can also use the UnErase command to recover each directory and any associated files that have been erased.

System Files Have Been Altered

Virus programs often attempt to change the COMMAND.COM file or other system files. If you suspect a virus, compare the date and time of the COMMAND.COM file in your hard disk's root directory with the original (or backup) copy of COMMAND.COM. If you notice any difference, replace the infected file on the hard disk.

To replace not only COMMAND.COM but also the other system files, boot your computer from a copy of your original DOS disk in drive A. Use the Make a Disk Bootable option in Disk Tools to copy a fresh version of the system to the hard disk. If a virus program caused the problem, examine your hard disk to find and remove that program. Until you are sure that you have corrected the problem, quarantine all files from the computer and the floppy disk you used to reboot the computer; do *not* distribute any files (particularly program files) from the computer or floppy disk to any other computer.

The AUTOEXEC.BAT File Has Been Altered

If you discover that your AUTOEXEC.BAT file has been changed, try to determine when and why the change was made. Some software installation programs change this file and the CONFIG.SYS file as part of the installation process. Some virus programs, however, may change the AUTOEXEC.BAT file in order to run a destructive program or a counter program that will eventually release a destructive virus. A *counter program* counts the number of times your computer is booted or a program is run, and then activates on a preset count. You should examine your AUTOEXEC.BAT and CONFIG.SYS files and understand the reason for each command. If you notice a suspicious command, replace the old AUTOEXEC.BAT with your backup copy or delete the unknown command. If AUTOEXEC.BAT calls an unknown program, determine where the program is and what it does. Remove the program from your computer if you do not know its purpose. One well-publicized virus that was sent to hundreds of persons in the guise of a demo program used a command in the AUTOEXEC.BAT file to trigger its main counting mechanism.

The Hard Disk Has a Hidden File or Directory

Some legitimate programs create hidden files or directories on disk as part of a file-protection scheme. Some virus programs also create hidden files and directories in which destructive programs may reside. Using Norton Control Center (the NCC command), you can see any hidden directories that reside on your disk. If you notice one directory that looks suspicious, investigate it (for example, examine the file by using Disk Editor). You can also discover any hidden files on disk by using the Norton File Find utility. Again, if you do not know why the files are on your disk, investigate to find out whether a legitimate program placed them there or whether they were created from an unknown source. If you suspect sabotage, be sure to keep copies of all important files on backup disks until you are sure that the danger is past.

The Hard Disk Has Been Erased

If your hard disk looks as if it has been erased completely or reformatted, you have several options:

- Boot your computer from the original DOS disk (or your Norton rescue disk) and then use the Norton UnErase command to see whether any directories and files can be saved. Some attacks have been known to rename files and directories. You may have to examine recovered files individually to determine their contents.

- If the disk was formatted, you can try to unformat it with the Norton UnFormat command. If you recently ran the Image command, recovery will be easier.

- Virus attacks are becoming smarter and more destructive. Having backups of your files is important because some attacks completely destroy data. For these problems, recovering your files from backup disks is the only solution.

Responding to DOS Error Messages

This section contains information about what to do if you encounter DOS error messages. Not all DOS error messages are covered, only the most common disk-oriented messages.

Abort, Retry, Ignore, Fail?

This message may appear if you attempt to read or write something to a disk, a printer, or another device. If a disk is bad or not positioned properly in the disk drive, DOS displays this error message. You have four choices for responding to the prompt: press A to abort, R to retry, I to ignore, or F to fail. The following list gives the meanings of these options:

Option	Description
Abort	Cancels the procedure.
Retry	Tries the procedure again.
Ignore	Ignores the error and proceeds. During a copy, for example, the Ignore option continues the copying operation, but the resulting file may have missing information that could not be copied correctly.
Fail	Skips the problem, and DOS tries to continue with the procedure. If the problem is that the computer cannot access a disk drive, you may be prompted to enter a new current disk drive name. (Fail is similar to Ignore.)

The message `Abort, Retry, Ignore, Fail?` may appear for disk- or device-related problems.

Disk-Related Problems and Solutions

Sometimes if you choose Retry, DOS can read or write to the disk on the second or third try. Even if this approach works, though, you may need to correct the problem by running Norton Disk Doctor to fix files or running Norton Speed Disk to unfragment files.

If the problem is with a floppy disk, verify that you have the disk positioned properly in the disk drive. Make sure that the disk is not upside down, for example, and that the disk drive door is shut.

Sometimes the magnetic media in the disk jacket gets stuck because of a jacket flaw or because the media is out of alignment. Remove the floppy disk from the drive and tap the disk on its side to attempt to loosen it; do not touch the magnetic media. Place the disk back in the drive and try the read or write operation again.

You should make sure that the disk is formatted and that it is formatted so that it can be read on the disk drive you are using. If, for example, you are using a 360K drive and have inserted a disk originally formatted as a 1.2M disk, the drive cannot read the disk.

If you cannot readily solve the problem, choose the Abort option and examine the disk by using Norton System Info (the SYSINFO command) or Norton Disk Doctor (the NDD command).

If you are convinced that the disk is formatted properly for this drive but DOS is still having trouble reading a file, try to correct the problem with Norton Disk Doctor.

Problems Caused by Other Devices

Make sure that your printer is turned on and that it is on-line. Check that a cable is attached properly to the device. Correct any problems and choose Retry.

DOS may be trying to communicate with some other device that is not turned on or attached properly. If so, choose Abort by pressing A and correct the problem.

If DOS is attempting to communicate through a COM port, make sure that it is set up correctly. You can use the DOS MODE command or Norton Control Center (NCC) to set up a communications (serial) port. Abort the current procedure and fix the problem.

Access Denied

This message appears if you attempt to change (or write to) a file that has its attribute set as read-only. You can change this setting by using the DOS ATTRIB command or the Norton File Find utility. Make sure that you want to change this file before you remove the read-only status.

`Access denied` may appear if you attempt to use a subdirectory as a file, such as trying to edit the subdirectory.

Bad Command or File Name

This message appears if you enter at the DOS prompt a command that DOS does not recognize—for example, if you misspell the command. If you see this message, first check your spelling.

Another possibility is that you entered a correct command but you were not in the proper directory or did not have your PATH command set up to find the command in its directory. Correct your PATH command (usually in your AUTOEXEC.BAT file) or change directories by using the DOS CD command or Norton Change Directory (the NCD command).

Bad or Missing Command Interpreter

If the file COMMAND.COM is not on the boot disk or if DOS has a problem reading this file, you get this message. If you attempted to boot from a floppy disk, perhaps it was not a boot disk. If you were booting from a hard disk, you need to correct the problem by rebooting from drive A with a correct version of DOS and then fixing the problem on your hard disk. You may have to copy COMMAND.COM back to the hard disk's root directory. If your hard disk still has problems, you may need to use Norton Disk Doctor (NDD).

Cannot Find System Files

This message appears if DOS cannot find the hidden system files required to boot the computer. You cannot make a disk bootable simply by placing the COMMAND.COM file on it. You must use the DOS SYS command or the Make a Disk Bootable option in Disk Tools to place these hidden files on a disk.

Cannot Read File Allocation Table

This message may appear if you use the DOS RECOVER command. Instead of using this DOS command, use Norton Disk Doctor (NDD) to attempt to recover damaged files. If you already have used RECOVER, use Norton Disk Tools to recover from the RECOVER command.

Data Error

This message usually means that a disk has a bad spot and that DOS is trying to read or write to that spot. You can attempt to locate and correct this problem by using Norton Disk Doctor (NDD).

Drive Not Ready Reading/Writing Device

If the drive door is not fully closed, you get this message. Verify that you have inserted your floppy disk properly in the drive and that the drive door is fully closed. The problem also may be caused by a defective drive. If so, you need to have a qualified technician correct the problem.

Error in Loading Operating System

This message may appear if DOS is unable to find the proper system information while attempting to boot the system. Turn off your computer and try again. You may need to boot the computer from a DOS disk in drive A and then correct the problem by using DOS SYS to write a fresh copy of the system files to your boot disk (usually disk C: for a hard disk). Alternatively, you can use the Make a Disk Bootable option in Disk Tools to correct the problem.

Error Writing Fixed Disk

This message may appear if DOS cannot write system startup information to a disk. Use Norton Disk Doctor (NDD) to analyze and correct the problem. If the problem persists, attempt to copy as much information from this disk as possible. You may need to boot from a floppy disk in drive A, and you may need to perform a low-level format of the disk. See the section "The Hard Disk Needs a Low-Level Format" earlier in this appendix.

Error Writing Partition Table

This message may appear during the FORMAT procedure and may be caused by a hardware problem or a physically damaged disk. The boot record at the beginning of the disk probably cannot be read from or written to. A possible solution is to reformat the boot record. You can use Norton Disk Doctor (NDD) to attempt to fix your disk and recover information. You may need, however, to replace your disk, get a technician to correct the hardware problem, or perform a low-level format on your disk. For more information, see the section "The Hard Disk Needs a Low-Level Format" earlier in this appendix.

File Allocation Table Bad

If this message appears, DOS has lost information about where files are stored. This information is usually kept in the file allocation table (FAT). Two copies (normally identical) of the FAT usually reside on a disk. By using the Norton Disk Doctor's **D**iagnose Disk option, you may be able to recover information from the duplicate FAT.

File Cannot Be Copied to Itself

If you omit a required destination in the COPY command, you get this message. For example, the following command produces this error message because DOS does not allow the file to be written to itself:

    COPY MYFILE.TXT

File Creation Error

This message appears if DOS is unable to write a file to a directory. The directory or disk may be full. Use the DIR command to list files to see how much space is available on disk. If the directory or disk is full, you can delete unnecessary files to make room for the file. This error message can also appear if you attempt to write to a read-only file. If you want to write to a file that has the read-only attribute set, you need to change the file's attribute (use the DOS ATTRIB command or Norton File Find) or save the file under another name.

Furthermore, the disk may be physically damaged, and DOS may have tried to write the file to a bad spot on the disk. You can verify whether the disk has bad spots by running Norton Disk Doctor. NDD marks bad spots so that they cannot be used to store files.

File Not Found

You get this message if you attempt to access a file that is not in the current directory or is not in the directory of the specified path. You may have misspelled the file name or included an incorrect path. You can use Norton File Find to see whether the file is located in another directory.

If you still get this message, the file space on the disk may be damaged. You then should try to reclaim the file by using Norton Disk Doctor's **D**iagnose Disk option.

General Failure

This message appears if DOS cannot figure out why a problem has occurred. In this case, you may have to do your own fishing for the culprit. If you are attempting to access a disk in a drive, you may want to make sure that the disk is readable. Are you, for example, attempting to access a 1.2M 5 1/4-inch disk in a 360K drive, or a 1.44M 3 1/2-inch disk in a 720K drive? You can also check to see that you have inserted your floppy disk correctly in the disk drive and that the disk drive door is closed all the way.

A damaged disk or disk drive can cause the problem. Try moving the disk to another disk drive or use Norton Disk Doctor to attempt to read the disk.

Incorrect DOS Version

You get this message if you attempt to use a DOS external command from a version of DOS other than the one under which the computer was booted—for example, you attempt to use the PRINT command (PRINT.COM) for DOS 3.3 when the machine was booted with DOS 4.0. You should make sure that all your DOS commands on disk are from the same version of DOS. To find out which version of DOS you are using, enter the VER command at the DOS prompt.

Incorrect (or Invalid) Number of Parameters

This message appears when you enter a DOS command that has an incorrect number of parameters or invalid parameters. Check your DOS command syntax and reenter the command.

Insufficient Disk Space

If you attempt to write a file to a disk that is full or does not have enough free space to hold the file, you get this message. To correct the problem, erase unneeded files and retry writing to the disk. You can use the File Size utility to see whether the destination disk has enough space to receive one or more files.

Invalid Drive Specification (or Invalid Drive or File Name)

This message appears when you use a drive specification that does not exist. If you use drive D in a DOS command when you have no drive D, for example, DOS gives you this error message.

Invalid Partition Table

If DOS attempts to boot the computer from your hard disk and finds something wrong with the computer's partition information, this message appears. This information should be on your disk at track 0. If this area is bad, you can use Norton Disk Doctor to attempt to diagnose and recover the partition information for you, or you can use the Make a Disk Bootable option in Disk Tools to refresh the boot information on the disk.

Invalid Path, Not Directory, or Directory Not Empty

This message appears if you attempt to remove a directory that contains files or that does not exist. If you want to remove an existing directory, you first must erase all files and subdirectories contained in that directory.

Memory Allocation Error

You get this message if a program that you are running overwrites the area in the computer's memory that stores important DOS information, or if the disk does not have enough available memory to load portions of DOS. This command may freeze your computer and cause you to have to reboot. A possible solution to this problem is to lower the number of buffers and/or device drivers specified in your CONFIG.SYS file or to remove some memory-resident programs (also called TSR, terminate-and-stay-resident, or pop-up programs).

Missing Operating System

You get this message if DOS attempts to boot the computer from a disk the system perceives to be bootable, but some or all of the system information is missing. To correct the problem, you can copy all files to floppy disks and then reformat the disk with DOS FORMAT or use the Make a Disk Bootable option in Disk Tools. With Norton, none of the files on disk are removed, so you do not have to back up the disk first.

No Room for System on Destination Disk

This message appears if you attempt to use DOS SYS to place a copy of the system files on a disk that has not been prepared during the format procedure to receive those files. To make the disk bootable with DOS, copy all files from the disk and then reformat the disk with the /S switch. Alternatively, use the Make a Disk Bootable option in Disk Tools to create a bootable disk without destroying files, even on a disk that was not formatted to be a system disk.

Non-System Disk

If you attempt to boot from a disk that does not contain the full DOS system or that has damaged system files, you get this message. If you are using a hard disk system, make sure that you do not have a disk in drive A when you boot the computer because the computer then attempts to boot from that disk. If your disk should be bootable but is not, you can attempt to fix the disk by using the Make a Disk Bootable option in Disk Tools.

Not Ready

When DOS attempts to read or write information to a device and cannot do so, this message appears. The problem may be that the disk drive door or knob is not closed completely, the disk is not formatted, the printer is not turned on or is not on-line, or another device is not ready to receive information. Determine the problem, correct it, and try again.

If a drive becomes overheated, it may produce the Not ready message. Check to see whether the computer is getting proper ventilation. (You may need to vacuum the vents around the edges of the computer.) If your computer has an exhaust fan, make sure that it is working properly. Turn off the computer and let the disk cool down. If the problem continues, consult a technician for further assistance.

Probable Non-DOS Disk

This message appears when DOS has problems reading the FAT or the disk media descriptor during a CHKDSK command. This problem may occur particularly on a hard disk larger than 32M that is partitioned into several drives. You can usually fix the problem by running Norton Disk Doctor's Diagnose Disk procedure.

Read Fault Error

If DOS is unable to read information from a disk, you get this message. You may have improperly seated the disk in the drive, or the drive door may not be closed properly. You also will probably get the message Abort, Retry, Ignore, Fail?

Abort the procedure and reseat the disk. To reseat the disk, take the disk out of the drive and tap the disk on its side to loosen it up. On a 5 1/4-inch disk, you can carefully place two fingers in the center hole and move the disk in the cover to loosen the disk. Place the disk back in the drive and close the drive door. If other disks work in the drive but this one cannot be read, try the Revive a Defective Diskette option in Disk Tools.

Required Parameter Missing

This message appears if you enter a DOS command that has too few parameters entered on the command line. Check your DOS command syntax and reenter the command.

Sector Not Found

If DOS attempts to read from or write something to a disk when the sector on the disk cannot be accessed, this message appears. You also will probably see the message Abort, Retry, Ignore, Fail? Abort the current command by pressing A.

If the problem occurs with a floppy disk, try to read the floppy disk in a different drive. Copy all the files you can from the disk. Use Disk Doctor to find and mark bad spots on the disk. Also try the Revive a Defective Diskette option in Disk Tools. Reformat the floppy disk or discard it.

If the problem occurs with a hard disk, use Disk Doctor to find and mark the bad sectors. If the problem persists on the hard disk, you need to back up all the files you possibly can and then perform a low-level format on the disk. For more information, see the section "The Hard Disk Needs a Low-Level Format" earlier in this appendix.

Seek Error

If DOS is unable to find the track on disk that is needed to read from or write data to the disk, you receive this message. You also get the message Abort, Retry, Ignore, Fail? Choose to abort the process by pressing A.

If this message appears while you are trying to access a floppy disk, take the disk out, tap it on its side, and reinsert it correctly into the drive. If the problem continues, use the Revive a Defective Diskette option in Disk Tools. Copy all possible information from the disk and then discard the disk or reformat it.

If the problem occurs when you are trying to access a hard disk, attempt to copy as many files off the disk as possible. You may try to use Disk Editor to restore the usefulness of the bad sectors. After you have recovered as many files as possible, perform a low-level format on the hard disk. For more information, see the section "The Hard Disk Needs a Low-Level Format" earlier in this appendix.

Too Many Parameters

This message appears if you enter a DOS command that has an invalid number of parameters. Check your DOS command syntax and reenter the command.

Top Level Process Aborted, Cannot Continue

If a DOS command failed when you were trying to access the disk, this message appears. Reboot and run Disk Doctor to locate and attempt to fix any bad sectors.

Write Protect Error

You get this message if you attempt to write data to a disk that is write-protected. On a 5 1/4-inch floppy disk, you set write protection by placing a piece of tape over the notch on the side of the disk. A 3 1/2-inch disk is write-protected when you move the write-protect tab so that an open hole appears in the corner of the disk. Before removing write protection, make sure that you want to change information on the disk.

Symbols

A

H

handles, 306
hard disks, 65-68, 432
    accessing, 116
    backing up, with BACKUP
        command, 714-716
    calibrating, 343-349
    computers, booting, 760-761
    directories, 705-706
        changing, 707-708
        hidden, 765
        path names, 706-707
        path names to programs,
            709-710
        removing empty, 708
    drive types, 299
    erasing, 765-766
    files, hidden, 765
    formatting, 79-80
        as system disks, 761
        low-level, 762-763
    interleave factors, 341-343
    maintaining, 23-24
    managing, 25-27, 704-705
    partitions, 303
    problems, physical and
        logical, 19-21
    recovering formatted, 189-190
        with IMAGE or MIRROR
            information, 191-194
        without IMAGE or MIRROR
            information, 194-196
    scanning with Norton Disk
        Doctor, 534
    tests, 443
    tree structures, 391
    volume labels, 391
hardware, 296-297, 436-437
Hardware Interrupts dialog box,
    296-315
Hayes-compatible modem, 602
Help, on-line, NDOS program,
    462-463
HELP command, NDOS, 491-492

Help menu, 32-38
    System Info program, 321
Help screens, commands, 41
Hewlett-Packard LaserJet
    printers, 50-51
hidden attributes, 165
hidden directories, 765
hidden files, 765
high-level formats, 77-79
highlighting commands, 30
HIMEM.SYS memory manager,
    306
HISTORY command, NDOS,
    492-493
hot keys, 33
HP LaserJet printers, *see*
    Hewlett-Packard LaserJet
    printers

I

I/O redirection, 467-469
IBM PC AT computer, 286
IBM PC XT computer, 286
IBM-compatible computers,
    video adapters, 294-295
IF command, NDOS, 493-494
IFF command, NDOS, 494-495
Image (IMAGE) command,
    655-656, 725-726
Image program, 55, 100-103
    recovering formatted hard
        disks, 191-196
In Box dialog box, 620
INC file extension, 542
Incorrect (or Invalid)
    Number of Parameters DOS
    error message, 772
Incorrect DOS Version DOS
    error message, 771
incremental backups, 524
Info menu, Disk Editor program,
    276-277
Information dialog box, 179

J-K

T